Teacher Edition

VISIONS

Language ✦ Literature ✦ Content

Mary Lou McCloskey

Lydia Stack

THOMSON
HEINLE

Australia ◇ Canada ◇ Mexico ◇ Singapore ◇ United Kingdom ◇ United States

VISIONS TEACHER EDITION BOOK C
Mary Lou McCloskey and Lydia Stack

Publisher: *Phyllis Dobbins*
Director of Development: *Anita Raducanu*
Director, ELL Training and Development: *Evelyn Nelson*
Developmental Editor: *Tania Maundrell-Brown*
Associate Developmental Editor: *Yeny Kim*
Associate Developmental Editor: *Kasia Zagorski*
Editorial Assistant: *Audra Longert*
Production Supervisor: *Mike Burggren*
Marketing Manager: *Jim McDonough*
Manufacturing Manager: *Marcia Locke*
Photography Manager: *Sheri Blaney*
Development: *Weston Editorial*
Design and Production: *Proof Positive/Farrowlyne Associates, Inc.*
Cover Designer: *Studio Montage*
Printer: *R.R. Donnelley and Sons Company, Willard*

Cover Image: © *George Grady Grossman/Index Stock Imagery, Inc.*

Printed in the United States of America.
4 5 6 7 8 9 10   08   07   06   05   04

For more information, contact Heinle, 25 Thomson Place, Boston, Massachusetts 02210 USA,
or you can visit our Internet site at http://www.heinle.com

For permission to use material from this text or product contact us:
Tel   1-800-730-2214
Fax   1-800-730-2215
Web www.thomsonrights.com

ISBN: 0-8384-5347-3

Contents

VISIONS

Language Acquisition through Literature and Content

Visions is a four-level language development program
that supports students from the pre-literacy level
through transition into mainstream classrooms.

By incorporating literature with content, students are
taught, and have ample practice with, the skills they need
to meet grade-level standards while being introduced to
the academic language needed for school success.

Visions has been student-tested and teacher-approved to ensure that learners have the best materials to guide them in their language acquisition.

Features:

- **4 levels:** Newcomer (Basic)
  Beginning (A)
  Intermediate (B)
  Advanced/Transition (C)

- **Basic Language and Literacy book for non-schooled and low-beginning students** provides systematic language development as well as literacy instruction.

- **Staff development handbook and video** is designed for easy program access.

- High-interest, low-level **literature and content-based readings** motivate students.

- **Scaffolding throughout all four books** uses a three-pronged approach to meeting the standards: Introduce, Practice, Assess.

- **Writing activities** reinforce and recycle strategic skills.

- **Quality assessment materials** and ExamView® test generating software are aligned with state standards.

- **Technology** reinforces listening/speaking, reading skills, and phonemic development.

- **Heinle Reading Library** gives students practice in independent reading with stories tied to Student Book themes.

THOMSON
HEINLE

Here's what teachers around the country have to say:

"All chapters were very relative to the themes. The vocabulary building activities are excellent!"

Minerva Anzaldua
Martin Middle School, Corpus Christi, TX

"Great ESL strategies for any level!"

"Clear directions for students!"

Gail Lulek
Safety Harbor Middle School, Safety Harbor, FL

"This is the type of literature and language series I've been looking for! I really like how each activity flows together and keeps the theme together."

Elia Corona
Liberty Middle School, Pharr, TX

"The readings were well-written. Students can relate and understand."

"The chapter goals and selections are clear and relevant to students' needs."

"The activities help students understand literary conventions."

James Harris
DeLeon Middle School, McAllen, TX

"The themes are well-developed. They provide conceptual frameworks within which students can understand the literature and learn language."

"The skills and information presented are important for students' academic success."

"The chapters are excellent because every activity has accessible vocabulary for ELL."

Donald Hoyt
Cooper Middle School, Fresno, CA

Components-At-A-Glance

Visions: Teacher Edition "Your guide to Standards-based instruction"

For Students		Basic Book	Book A	Book B	Book C
Student Book	offers accessible, authentic literature with a balance of fiction and nonfiction, including excerpts from novels, short stories, plays, poetry, narratives, biographies, and informational and content-based readings.	●	●	●	●
Activity Book	provides reinforcement of state standards and includes practice and expansion of skills and content presented in the Student Book.	●	●	●	●
Student Handbook	serves as a reference guide for students. It features listening, speaking, reading, writing, and viewing checklists, as well as grammar, vocabulary, and research reference information.	●	●	●	●
The Heinle Reading Library	offers 18 classic stories that are tied to every theme of Visions and designed for student independent reading. Examples include: *The Red Badge of Courage, Moby Dick, David Copperfield, Pride and Prejudice, 20,000 Leagues Under the Sea, Little Women.*		●	●	●
Student CD-ROM	provides an opportunity for practicing, reteaching, and reinforcing listening/speaking skills, reading skills, and phonemic awareness.	●	●	●	●
Audio CD*	features all reading selections recorded for building listening/speaking skills, fluency, and auditory learning.	●	●	●	●
Newbury House Dictionary with CD-ROM	helps students develop essential dictionary and vocabulary building skills. Features a pronunciation CD-ROM and a companion Web site.		●	●	●
More Grammar Practice	helps students learn and review essential grammar skills.		●	●	●
Web site (http://visions.heinle.com)	features additional skill-building activities and reference tools for students, including vocabulary activities, syllabication worksheets, and word lists.	●	●	●	●

*Also featured on Audio Tape.

For Teachers		Basic Book	Book A	Book B	Book C
Teacher Edition	contains point-of-use lesson suggestions, ongoing assessment, and multi-level activities developed specifically to state standard requirements.		•	•	•
Teacher Resource Book	provides easy-to-use and implement lesson plans aligned with state standards. Additional support includes graphic organizers to support lesson activities, CNN® video transcripts and Video Worksheets for students, and summaries of each reading in English and translated into Cambodian, Haitian Creole, Hmong, Chinese, Spanish, and Vietnamese. School-Home Newsletters, in English and the six languages, encourage family involvement. This component is also available on CD-ROM for teacher customization.	•	•	•	•
Assessment Program	features diagnostic tests and standards-based assessment items to ensure accountability, and tracking systems to monitor student progress. The Assessment Program is available on CD-ROM with the ExamView® test-generating software, designed to create customizable tests in minutes.	•	•	•	•
Transparencies	offers graphic organizers, reading summaries, and grammar charts for interactive teaching. The Basic Book Transparencies also include sentence builders, phonemic awareness, and syllabication.	•	•	•	•
Staff Development Handbook and Video	provide step-by-step training for all teachers. The video includes actual footage of classroom teaching.	•	•	•	•
CNN® Video	features thematic news segments from today's headlines to help build listening and content comprehension through meaningful viewing activities.	•	•	•	•
Web site (http://visions.heinle.com)	features additional teaching resources and an opportunity for teachers to share ideas and classroom management techniques with an online community.	•	•	•	•

Scope and Sequence

Unit 1: Mysteries

Chapter	Build Vocabulary	Text Structure	Reading Strategy	Spelling/ Punctuation/ Capitalization	Build Reading Fluency	Elements of Literature	Word Study	Grammar Focus	From Reading to Writing	Across Content Areas
1. "The Loch Ness Monster" by Malcolm Yorke p. 2	Use Language Structure to Find Meaning	Informational Text	Make Inferences Using Text Evidence	Capitalization: Titles Punctuation: Periods at the end of sentences	Repeated Reading	Use Visuals	Analyze Compound Words	Understand the Conjunction *But*	Write a Paragraph That Describes	Math: Understand Length
2. "Mystery of the Cliff Dwellers" p. 14	Learn Context Words by Grouping	Informational Text	Find the Main Idea and Supporting Details	Punctuation: Question marks Spelling: Irregular plurals	Read Silently and Aloud	Write Quotes	Root Words and Suffixes	Use Prepositional Phrases	Write an Informational Text	Social Studies: Read a Population Map
3. "Yawning" by Haleh V. Samiei p. 26	Identify Antonyms	Informational Text	Compare the Text to Your Own Experiences	Spelling: *You're* vs. *your* Capitalization: People's names	Rapid Word Recognition	Recognize Direct Address	Write Using Contractions	Write Dependent Clauses	Write a Paragraph Using Chronology	Math: Read a Bar Graph
4. "The Sneak Thief" by Falcon Travis p. 38	Learn Words Related to Train Travel	Mystery	Use Chronology to Locate and Recall Information	Punctuation: Apostrophes for singular possession Punctuation: Quotation marks for direct quotations	Adjust Your Reading Rate for Quotations	Recognize Problem and Resolution	Apply Knowledge of Letter-Sound Correspondences	Identify Simple, Compound, and Complex Sentences	Write Dialogue in a Mystery	Language Arts: Learn Words About the Law
5. "The Legend of Sleepy Hollow" by Washington Irving, Adapted by Jack Kelly p. 50	Spell Frequently Misspelled Words	Legend	Identify Imagery	Punctuation: Apostrophes for contractions Punctuation: Ellipses Spelling: Irregular plurals	Read Silently	Analyze Setting and Tone	Identify Root Words and the Suffix -less	Use Pronoun Referents	Write a Character Description	Social Studies: Read a Timeline

Apply and Expand

Listening and Speaking Workshop p. 64	Viewing Workshop p. 65	Writer's Workshop p. 66	Projects p. 68
Describe an Animal	View and Think: Analyze a Mystery Movie	Response to Literature: Compare Two Texts	1. Dramatize "The Legend of Sleepy Hollow"
			2. Make a Poster About a Mysterious Place

Unit 3: Journeys

Chapter	Build Vocabulary	Text Structure	Reading Strategy	Spelling/ Punctuation/ Capitalization	Build Reading Fluency	Elements of Literature	Word Study	Grammar Focus	From Reading to Writing	Across Content Areas
1. "I Have No Address" by Hamza El Din p. 152	Identify Multiple-Meaning Words	Poem	Recognize Figurative Language	Spelling: Ai/ay for long /a/ sound	Echo Read Aloud	Recognize Style, Tone, and Mood	Recognize the Suffix -ity	Use Apostrophes with Possessive Nouns	Write a Poem Using Figurative Language	Science: Learn About Migration of Birds
2. "The Voyage of the Lucky Dragon" by Jack Bennett p. 162	Learn Words Related to Emotions	Historical Fiction	Paraphrase to Recall Information	Punctuation: Hyphens with numbers Spelling: Nouns ending in -tion Spelling: Adverbs ending in -ly Capitalization: Nations and nationalities	Read Silently and Aloud	Recognize Mood	Analyze the Prefix un-	Identify Subject and Object Pronouns	Write to Solve a Problem	Social Studies: Describe Countries on a Map
3. "The Time Bike" by Jane Langton p. 178	Use Context to Understand New Words	Science Fiction	Predict	Punctuation: Commas Punctuation: Dashes Punctuation: Single quotes within a quotation	Repeated Reading	Recognize Foreshadowing	Study the Prefix bi-	Write Using Contractions	Write a Description	Social Studies: Learn About Time Zones
4. "Why We Can't Get There From Here" by Neil de Grasse Tyson p. 192	Apply Knowledge of Root Words	Informational Text	Reread and Record to Learn and Recall	Capitalization: Names of planets and stars Spelling: C for /s/ sound	Adjust Your Reading Rate to Scan	Analyze Organization and Presentation of Ideas	Identify the Suffixes -er and -est	Use Comparative and Superlative Adjectives	Use Multiple Resources to Write a Research Report	Math: Solve a Time Problem
5. "The California Gold Rush" by Pam Zollman, & "Dame Shirley and the Gold Rush" by Jim Rawls p. 204	Study Words Systematically	Nonfiction and Historical Fiction	Compare and Contrast	Spelling: Silent u Capitalization: Months Spelling: Silent gh	Read Silently	Analyze Character Traits and Motivation	Learn Words from Context and Experience	Use Adverbs	Compare and Contrast Two Reading Selections	Science: Learn About Natural Resources

Apply and Expand

Listening and Speaking Workshop p. 218	Viewing Workshop p. 219	Writer's Workshop p. 220	Projects p. 222
Exposition: Give a Presentation About a Place	View and Think: Compare and Contrast Cultures	Exposition: Write a Research Report	1. Research an Explorer
			2. Plan a Time Capsule

Unit 2: Survival

Chapter	Build Vocabulary	Text Structure	Reading Strategy	Spelling/ Punctuation/ Capitalization	Build Reading Fluency	Elements of Literature	Word Study	Grammar Focus	From Reading to Writing	Across Content Areas
1. "How I Survived My Summer Vacation" by Robin Friedman p. 72	Use Precise Wording	Realistic Fiction	Make Inferences Using Text Evidence and Experience	Punctuation: Exclamation point Punctuation: Hyphens for compound adjectives Capitalization: Days of the week	Audio Reading Practice	Analyze Plot	Identify Words with Latin Roots	Use Progressive Tenses	Write Realistic Fiction	Science: Identify Food Groups
2. "The Voyage of the *Frog*" by Gary Paulsen p. 86	Use Reference Sources	Adventure Story	Recognize Tone and Mood	Punctuation: Quotation marks for dialogue Punctuation: Semicolons Capitalization: Name of a type of transportation Spelling: Voiced vs. unvoiced /th/	Adjust Your Reading Rate for Quotations	Recognize and Analyze Problem Resolution	Understand the Suffix -ly	Use the Future Tense	Write a Story to Resolve a Problem	Social Studies: Find Compass Directions
3. "To Risk or Not to Risk" by David Ropeik p. 102	Learn Vocabulary Through Reading	Informational Text	Distinguish Fact from Opinion	Spelling: Plurals ending in -ies Punctuation: Periods for abbreviations Spelling: Plurals ending in -s vs. -es	Read Silently	Identify Transition Words	Identify Prefixes over- and under-	Use Present Tense and Subject-Verb Agreement	Write an Informational Text	Science: Learn About Psychology
4. "Island of the Blue Dolphins" by Scott O'Dell p. 116	Locate Pronunciations of Unfamiliar Words	Fiction Based on a True Story	Paraphrase to Recall Information	Spelling: *To/two/too* Spelling: Long and short sounds for /oo/ Spelling: *Ee/ea* for long /e/ sound	Read Aloud to Engage Listeners	Compare and Contrast Themes and Ideas Across Texts	Spell Frequently Misspelled Words	Identify the Past and the Past Perfect Tense	Write Instructions	The Arts: List Game Rules in Order
5. "The Next Great Dying" by Karin Vergoth and Christopher Lampton p. 130	Use a Word Wheel	Informational Text	Identify Cause and Effect	Spelling: *Au* for short /o/ sound Punctuation: Commas for large numbers Punctuation: Comma for series	Rapid Word Recognition	Analyze Deductive and Inductive Organization and Presentation	Identify the Suffix -ion	Recognize Dependent Clauses	Write an Informational Text	Social Studies: Read a Timeline

Apply and Expand

Listening and Speaking Workshop p. 144	Viewing Workshop p. 145	Writer's Workshop p. 146	Projects p. 148
Role-Play an Interview	View and Think: Describe How Pictures and Diagrams Show Text Meaning	Response to Literature: Write a Survival Manual	1. Research an Endangered Species
			2. Summarize a Real-Life Survival Story

Unit 4: Cycles

Chapter	Build Vocabulary	Text Structure	Reading Strategy	Spelling/ Punctuation/ Capitalization	Build Reading Fluency	Elements of Literature	Word Study	Grammar Focus	From Reading to Writing	Across Content Areas
1. "Water Dance" by Thomas Locker p. 226	Learn Vivid Verbs	Poem	Describe Mental Images	Spelling: Vowel-consonant-e long vowel sounds Spelling: Ou/ow for /ou/ sound	Read Aloud to Engage Listeners	Use Figurative Language	Distinguish Denotative and Connotative Meanings	Use Comparative Adjectives	Write a Poem	Math: Calculate Averages
2. "Persephone and the Seasons" by Heather Amery p. 238	Use a Dictionary to Find Definitions, Pronunciations, and Derivations	Myth	Use Chronology to Locate and Recall Information	Spelling: I before e Spelling: Silent b	Read Silently and Aloud	Recognize Foreshadowing	Recognize Contractions	Write Using Irregular Past Tense Verbs	Summarize and Paraphrase to Inform	Language Arts: Distinguish the Meanings of Myth
3. "The Circuit" by Francisco Jiménez p. 250	Study Word Origins and Guess Meaning	Autobiographical Short Story	Compare Text to Your Own Knowledge and Experience	Punctuation: Italics for words from other languages Punctuation: Apostrophes for time Capitalization: Languages	Rapid Word Recognition	Identify Language Use to Show Characterization	Apply Letter-Sound Correspondences	Identify Dependent Clauses	Write a Letter to an Author	Language Arts: Understand the Influence of Other Languages and Cultures on English
4. "The Elements of Life" by Paul Bennett p. 264	Learn Science Terms	Informational Text	Find the Main Idea and Supporting Details	Punctuation: Colon for lists Spelling: Irregular plurals	Adjust Your Reading Rate to Scan	Use a Diagram	Study Word Origins and Roots	Recognize the Active and Passive Voices	Write About a Process and Create a Diagram	Science: Understand Symbols for Elements

Apply and Expand

Listening and Speaking Workshop p. 276	Viewing Workshop p. 277	Writer's Workshop p. 278	Projects p. 280
Give an Oral Presentation	Interpret Events from Media	Compare and Contrast Ideas, Themes, and Issues	1. Explore Life Cycle Events
			2. Make a Poster About a Cycle

Unit 5: Freedom

Chapter	Build Vocabulary	Text Structure	Reading Strategy	Spelling/ Punctuation/ Capitalization	Build Reading Fluency	Elements of Literature	Word Study	Grammar Focus	From Reading to Writing	Across Content Areas
1. "Rosa Parks" by Andrea Davis Pinkney p. 284	Use Note Cards to Remember Meaning	Biography	Make Inferences Using Text Evidence	Capitalization: Institutions and organizations Punctuation: Parentheses Capitalization: Street names and public places Punctuation: Periods for initials	Read Silently and Aloud	Recognize Style	Recognize the Suffix -ment	Recognize Regular and Irregular Simple Past Tense Verbs	Write a Biography	Social Studies: Learn About Constitutional Amendments
2. "The Gettysburg Address" by Kenneth Richards, Including a Speech by Abraham Lincoln p. 300	Use Word Squares to Remember Meaning	Historical Narrative and Speech	Summarize and Paraphrase	Punctuation: Apostrophes for plural possession Punctuation: Using commas in dates Capitalization: Historical documents Spelling: Qu for the /kw/ sound	Adjust Your Reading Rate to Memorize	Analyze and Evaluate the Delivery of a Speech	Use the Suffix -or	Identify Clauses with Subject + Verb + Object + Infinitive	Write a News Article	Math: Use Vocabulary to Answer Math Problems
3. "So Far from the Bamboo Grove" by Yoko Kawashima Watkins p. 316	Use Text Features To Understand	Fiction Based on a True Story	Predict	Capitalization: Titles before names Spelling: Two-syllable words with -ed ending Spelling: Silent l	Repeated Reading	Analyze Character Motivation	Identify the Latin Root Word Grat	Use the Conjunction So That to Connect Ideas	Write a Historical Fiction Story	Language Arts: Use Punctuation and Intonation
4. "Alone" by Samantha Abeel, & "Samantha's Story" by Samantha Abeel p. 330	Spell Frequently Misspelled Words	Poem and Autobiography	Compare and Contrast Texts	Spelling: Silent w Spelling: Ch for /k/ sound	Read Aloud to Engage Listeners	Recognize Figurative Language	Learn Related Words	Use Superlative Adjectives	Write a Poem	Language Arts: Identify Genres

Apply and Expand

Listening and Speaking Workshop p. 342	Viewing Workshop p. 343	Writer's Workshop p. 344	Projects p. 346
Present an Autobiographical Narrative	View and Think: Compare and Contrast Visual Media with a Written Story	Response to Literature: Write a Biographical Narrative	1. Investigate Service Learning
			2. Start a Freedom Magazine

Unit 6: Visions

Chapter	Build Vocabulary	Text Structure	Reading Strategy	Spelling/ Punctuation/ Capitalization	Build Reading Fluency	Elements of Literature	Word Study	Grammar Focus	From Reading to Writing	Across Content Areas
1. "Mr. Scrooge Finds Christmas" by Aileen Fisher, Adapted from "A Christmas Carol" by Charles Dickens p. 350	Distinguish Denotative and Connotative Meanings	Play	Use Chronology to Locate and Recall Information	Punctuation: Colon to introduce dialogue Capitalization: Holidays Spelling: *Lie or lay*	Audio CD Reading Practice	Recognize Dialogue and Stage Directions	Analyze Contractions	Use the Present Perfect Tense	Write a Persuasive Letter	Math: Answer Math Questions About Currency
2. "The House on Mango Street" by Sandra Cisneros p. 364	Identify Antonyms	Fiction	Paraphrase to Recall Information	Spelling: *Their, there, they're* Punctuation: Italics for emphasis	Read Aloud to Engage Listeners	Recognize First-Person Narratives	Learn English Words from Other Languages	Spell Frequently Misspelled Words	Write a Description	Science: Learn About Animal Habitats
3. "The Pearl" by John Steinbeck p. 376	Locate Pronunciations and Derivations	Realistic Fiction	Make Inferences Using Text Evidence	Spelling: *Oy* vowel sound Spelling: *Ph* for /f/ sound Spelling: *Gh* for /f/ sound Spelling: Silent *k*	Repeated Reading	Analyze Plot and Problem Resolution	Learn Words from Latin	Use Conjunctions to Form Compound Sentences	Write a Fiction Story	Social Studies: Learn About Bodies of Water
4. "What Will Our Towns Look Like?" by Martha Pickerill p. 392	Put Words into Groups	Informational Text	Summarize Text to Recall Ideas	Capitalization: Headings Spelling: *Y* for long /i/ sound	Adjust Your Reading Rate to Scan	Identify Author's Purpose	Study the Latin Prefix *co-*	Use *Will* to Predict Future Events	Create a Form, Interview, and Summarize	Science: Learn About Acid Rain

Apply and Expand

Listening and Speaking Workshop p. 404	Viewing Workshop p. 405	Writer's Workshop p. 406	Projects p. 408
Write and Present a Persuasive Role Play	View and Think: Compare and Contrast a Play and a Movie	Response to Literature: Collaborate to Write a Persuasive Letter	1. Interpret Text Ideas in a Video
			2. Present "Vision for My Future"

Scientifically Based Research in the *Visions* Program

The *Visions* program was developed utilizing current, scientifically based research findings of the most effective methods to teach language mastery. The references for each section below identify specific areas within the *Visions* student materials where the research has been applied.

Vocabulary Development

Research shows students need to consistently work on vocabulary in three critical areas (Anderson, 1999) and to meet standards (California Dept. of Education, 1998).

Word Meaning: Students study vocabulary meanings and concepts, relate them to prior experience, and record them in their personal dictionary. See *Build Vocabulary* sections.

Word Identification Strategies: Students learn important skills such as context clues, roots, and affixes. See *Word Study* sections.

Vocabulary Across Content Areas: Students learn key words in science, math, and social studies in the *Content Connection* and *Across Content Areas* sections.

Reading Comprehension

Strategies: Reading strategies such as fact/opinion, cause/effect, prediction, summarization, and paraphrasing need to be directly taught before the reading, practiced during the reading, and then evaluated (Anderson, 1999). See *Reading Strategy* sections.

Types of Questions: Readings that are followed by literal, inferential, and evaluative comprehension questions develop higher order thinking skills (Fowler, 2003). See *Reading Comprehension* sections.

Reading Fluency

The ability to read rapidly, smoothly, and automatically while adjusting rate and reading with expression (Mather and Goldstein, 2001) defines reading fluency. English language learners and at-risk students need systematic scaffolding activities with repeated oral reading to become fluent readers (De la Colina, Parker, Hasbrouck, Lara-Alecia, 2001). See *Build Reading Fluency* sections.

Rapid Word Recognition: Practice of this skill can increase students' fluency (Cunningham and Stanovich, 1998; Torgesen et al., 2001).

Reading Chunks and Key Phrases: This helps ELL and at-risk students become more fluent and to understand what they read.

Adjusting Reading Rate: Students learn to vary reading rate according to the purpose and type of text.

Repeated Reading: Students reread words, phrases, and passages a specific number of times (Meyer and Felton, 1999) for consistent, positive support of effectiveness in increasing reading fluency (National Reading Panel, 2000). Six minutes a day of repeated oral reading practice (Mercer, et al., in press) was found to be highly effective in increasing fluency.

Reading Silently and Aloud: Practice and support using the teacher, a peer (Li and Nes, 2001), and the Audio CD (Blum, Koskinen, Tennant, and Parker, 1995) has been proven to increase reading fluency.

Sheltered Content Instruction

Using the strategies from Cognitive Academic Language Learning Approach (CALLA) and the Sheltered Instruction Observation Protocol (SIOP), students apply learning strategies to help them succeed academically in their content area classes. See *Use Prior Knowledge* and *Content Connection* sections.

Spelling Instruction

Students are taught orthographic patterns and frequently used words in conjunction with the readings. Students who receive direct instruction in word analysis and how to analyze speech sounds and spell words are more successful in reading and writing (Whittlesea, 1987). See *Visions Activity Book* and *Teacher Edition.*

Traits of Writing and Oral Presentations

Students can learn to write and give oral presentations with greater success when they are based on the model presented in their reading and when they are made cognitively aware of the traits that good writers and presenters use. In *Visions,* students write and present narrative, descriptive, technical, and persuasive writing, as well as research reports. Students analyze types of text structure used in various writing models. The writing process is used throughout. See *Text Structure, Writing Workshops,* and *Listening and Speaking Workshops.*

References

Anderson, Neil. *Exploring Second Language Reading.* Boston, MA: Heinle, 1999.

Becker, H. and Hamayan, E. *Teaching ESL K-12: Views from the Classroom.* Boston, MA: Heinle, 2001.

Blum, I.H.; Koskinen, P.S.; Tennant, N.; and Parker, E.M. "Using Audio Taped Books to Extend Classroom Literacy Instruction into the Homes of Second-language Learners." *Journal of Reading Behavior* 27 (1995): 535–563.

California Department of Education. *English-Language Arts Content Standards for California Public Schools Kindergarten Through Grade Twelve.* Sacramento, CA: 2001.

California Department of Education. *Strategic Thinking and Learning.* Sacramento, CA: 2001.

Chamot, A. and O'Malley, J. *The CALLA Handbook Addison-Wesley.* Reading, MA: 1995.

Cognitive Academic Language Learning Approach (CALLA) <http://www.writing.berkely.edu/TESL-EJ/ej07/r5.html>.

Cunningham, A.E. and Stanovich, K.E. "What Reading Does for the Mind." *American Educator* 22 (1998): 1–2, 8–15.

De la Colina, M.G.; Parker, R.I.; Hasbrouck, J.E.; Lara-Alecia, R. "Intensive Intervention in Reading Fluency For At-Risk Beginning Spanish Readers." *Bilingual Research Journal* 25 (2001): 503–38.

Fowler, B. *Critical Thinking Across the Curriculum Home Page* "Blooms Taxonomy and Critical Thinking (Questions)." Longview Community College, 1996. 22 January 2003 <http://www.kcmetro.cc.mo.us/longview/ctac/blooms.htm>.

Li, D., and Nes, S. "Using Paired Reading to Help ESL Students Become Fluent and Accurate Readers." *Reading Improvement* 38 (2001): 50–61.

Mercer, C.; Campbell, K.; Miller, M.; Mercer, K.; and Lane, H. in press. "Effects of a Reading Fluency Intervention for Middle Schoolers with Specific Learning Disabilities." *Learning Disabilities Research and Practice.*

Meyer, M.S., and Felton, R.H. "Repeated Reading to Enhance Fluency: Old Approaches and New Directions." *Annals of Dyslexia* 49 (1999): 283–306.

National Reading Panel. *Teaching Children to Read: An Evidence-based Assessment of the Scientific Research Literature on Reading and Its Implications for Reading Instruction* (National Institute of Health Publ. No 00-4769) Washington, DC: 2002 National Institute of Child Health and Human Development.

Nixon, Susan. *Six Traits Writing Assessment Home Page.* 22 January 2003 <http://6traits.cyberspaces.net>.

Short, Deborah J., and Echevarria, Jana. *ERIC Clearinghouse on Languages and Linguistics.* "Sheltered Instruction Observation Protocol: A Tool for Teacher-Researcher Collaboration and Professional Development." 1999. 22 January 2003 <http:// www.cal.org/ericcll/digest/sheltered.html>.

Torgesen, J.K.; Alexander, A.W.; Wagner, R.K.; Rashotte, C.A.; Voeller, K.; Conway, T.; and Rose, E. "Intensive Remedial Instruction for Children with Severe Reading Disabilities: Immediate and Long-term Outcomes from Two Instructional Approaches." *Journal of Learning Disabilities* 34 (2001): 33–58.

Visions Assessment Program At-A-Glance

The *Visions* Assessment Program was designed to ensure standards-based accountability for teachers and students alike. It begins with a Diagnostic Test to assess what students already know and to target students' needs in specific skill areas. The Assessment Program ensures ongoing as well as summative evaluation with the Chapter Quizzes, Unit Tests, and Mid-Book and End-of-Book Exams. Portfolio Assessment is also taken into account to measure the students' overall progress.

VISIONS Assessment Program		
	Name	**Purpose of Assessment**
Entry Level	**Diagnostic Test**	To enable teachers to ascertain their students' proficiency skills in vocabulary, reading, grammar, spelling, and writing, and to do a Needs Analysis in order to target specific instructional needs.
Monitor Progress	**Chapter Quizzes**	To monitor students' ongoing progress in vocabulary, grammar, reading, and writing. There are 27 Chapter Quizzes.
	Unit Tests	To monitor students' ongoing progress toward meeting strategies and standards in vocabulary, grammar, reading, and writing at the end of each unit. There are 6 Unit Tests.
	Mid-Book Exam	To monitor students' ongoing progress toward meeting strategies and standards in vocabulary, grammar, reading, and writing as taught throughout the first three units of the book.
	Student Resources Checklists	To promote student responsibility in meeting the standards. Students self-assess their strengths and weaknesses for purposes of reteaching if necessary.
Summative	**End-of-Book Exam**	To measure students' achievement and mastery in meeting the standards in vocabulary, reading, and writing as taught throughout the book.
Additional Tools to Monitor Progress	**Peer Editing Checklists**	To collaboratively involve classmates in giving and gaining feedback on their progress toward meeting the standards in writing.
	Active Listening Checklist	To collaboratively involve classmates in giving and gaining feedback on their progress in the area of listening and speaking during oral presentations.
	Teacher Resources Listening, Speaking, Reading, Writing, Viewing, and Content Area Checklists	To track ongoing progress of students in all domains of the standards, and to serve as a vehicle in planning instruction.
	Reading Fluency	To check students' progress in learning to read silently and aloud with expression, and to adjust their reading rates according to the purpose of their reading.
	Rubrics	To evaluate students' overall performance using a fixed measurement scale and a list of criteria taken from formal and informal outcomes. These rubrics should be part of each student's permanent record.
	Portfolio Assessment	To involve students in self-reflection on their progress in meeting their learning goals. This ongoing assessment is a collection of student work that exhibits the student's best efforts and progress.
	ExamView ® CD-ROM	To empower teachers to choose and customize test items to meet students' targeted needs; items chosen may be used to retest after intervention activities.

VISIONS

Language ◆ Literature ◆ Content

Mary Lou McCloskey

Lydia Stack

THOMSON

HEINLE

Australia ◆ Canada ◆ Mexico ◆ Singapore ◆ United Kingdom ◆ United States

VISIONS STUDENT BOOK C
Mary Lou McCloskey and Lydia Stack

Publisher: *Phyllis Dobbins*
Director of Development: *Anita Raducanu*
Director, ELL Training and Development: *Evelyn Nelson*
Developmental Editor: *Tania Maundrell-Brown*
Associate Developmental Editor: *Yeny Kim*
Associate Developmental Editor: *Kasia Zagorski*
Editorial Assistant: *Audra Longert*
Production Supervisor: *Mike Burggren*
Marketing Manager: *Jim McDonough*
Manufacturing Manager: *Marcia Locke*
Photography Manager: *Sheri Blaney*
Development: *Proof Positive/Farrowlyne Associates, Inc.; Quest Language Systems*
Design and Production: *Proof Positive/Farrowlyne Associates, Inc.*
Cover Designer: *Studio Montage*
Printer: *R.R. Donnelley and Sons Company, Willard*

Cover Image: © *George Grady Grossman/Index Stock Imagery, Inc.*

Printed in the United States of America.
4 5 6 7 8 9 10   08   07   06   05   04

For more information, contact Heinle, 25 Thomson Place, Boston, Massachusetts 02210 USA, or you can visit our Internet site at http://www.heinle.com

For permission to use material from this text or product contact us:
Tel   1-800-730-2214
Fax   1-800-730-2215
Web www.thomsonrights.com

ISBN: 0-8384-5249-3

Reviewers and Consultants

We gratefully acknowledge the contribution of the following educators, consultants, and librarians who reviewed materials at various stages of development. Their input and insight provided us with valuable perspective and ensured the integrity of the entire program.

Program Advisor
Evelyn Nelson

Consultants

Deborah Barker
Nimitz High School
Houston, Texas

Sharon Bippus
Labay Middle School
Houston, Texas

Sheralee Connors
Portland, Oregon

Kathleen Fischer
Norwalk LaMirada Unified
School District
Norwalk, California

Willa Jean Harner
Tiffin-Seneca Public Library
Tiffin, Ohio

Nancy King
Bleyl Middle School
Houston, Texas

Dell Perry
Woodland Middle School
East Point, Georgia

Julie Rines
The Thomas Crane Library
Quincy, Massachusetts

Lynn Silbernagel
The Catlin Gabel School
Portland, Oregon

Cherylyn Smith
Fresno Unified School District
Fresno, California

Jennifer Trujillo
Fort Lewis College
Teacher Education Department
Durango, Colorado

Teresa Walter
Chollas Elementary School
San Diego, California

Reviewers

Jennifer Alexander
Houston Independent School District
Houston, Texas

Susan Alexandre
Trimble Technical High School
Fort Worth, Texas

Deborah Almonte
Franklin Middle School
Tampa, Florida

Donna Altes
Silverado Middle School
Napa, California

Ruben Alvarado
Webb Middle School
Austin, Texas

Sheila Alvarez
Robinson Middle School
Plano, Texas

Cally Androtis-Williams
Newcomers High School
Long Island City, New York

Minerva Anzaldua
Martin Middle School
Corpus Christi, Texas

Alicia Arroyos
Eastwood Middle School
El Paso, Texas

Douglas Black
Montwood High School
El Paso, Texas

Jessica Briggeman
International Newcomer Academy
Fort Worth, Texas

Diane Buffett
East Side High School
Newark, New Jersey

Eva Chapman
San Jose Unified School
District Office
San Jose, California

Elia Corona
Memorial Middle School
Pharr, Texas

Alicia Cron
Alamo Middle School
Alamo, Texas

Florence Decker
El Paso Independent School District
(retired)
El Paso, Texas

Janeece Docal
Bell Multicultural Senior High School
Washington, DC

Addea Dontino
Miami-Dade County School District
Miami, Florida

Kathy Dwyer
Tomlin Middle School
Plant City, Florida

Olga Figol
Barringer High School
Newark, New Jersey

Claire Forrester
Molina High School
Dallas, Texas

Connie Guerra
Regional Service Center 1
Edinburg, Texas

James Harris
DeLeon Middle School
McAllen, Texas

Audrey Heining-Boynton
University of North Carolina-
Chapel Hill
School of Education
Chapel Hill, North Carolina

Carolyn Ho
North Harris Community College
Houston, Texas

Donald Hoyt
Cooper Middle School
Fresno, California

Nancy A. Humbach
Miami University
Department of Teacher Education
Oxford, Ohio

Marie Irwin
University of Texas at Arlington Libraries
Arlington, Texas

Mark Irwin
Cary Middle School
Dallas, Texas

Erik Johansen
Oxnard High School
Oxnard, California

Marguerite Joralemon
East Side High School
Newark, New Jersey

Karen Poling Kapeluck
Lacey Instructional Center
Annandale, Virginia

Lorraine Kleinschuster
Intermediate School 10 Q
Long Island City, New York

Fran Lacas
NYC Board of Education (retired)
New York, New York

Robert Lamont
Newcomer Center
Arlington, Texas

Mao-ju Catherine Lee
Alief Middle School
Houston, Texas

Leonila Luera
Pharr-San Juan-Alamo ISD
Pharr/San Juan, Texas

Gail Lulek
Safety Harbor Middle School
Safety Harbor, Florida

Natalie Mangini
Serrano International School
Lake Forest, California

Linda Martínez
Dallas Independent School District
Dallas, Texas

Berta Medrano
Pharr-San Juan-Alamo ISD
Pharr/San Juan, Texas

Graciela Morales
Austin Independent School District
Austin, Texas

Karen Morante
School District of Philadelphia
Philadelphia, Pennsylvania

Jacel Morgan
Houston ISD
Houston, Texas

Lorraine Morgan
Hanshaw Middle School
Modesto, California

Dianne Mortensen
Pershing Intermediate School 220
Brooklyn, New York

Denis O'Leary
Rio del Valle Junior High School
Oxnard, California

Jeanette Page
School District of Philadelphia (retired)
Philadelphia, Pennsylvania

Claudia Peréz
Hosler Middle School
Lynwood, California

Yvonne Perez
Alief Middle School
Houston, Texas

Penny Phariss
Plano Independent School District
Plano, Texas

Bari Ramírez
L.V. Stockard Middle School
Dallas, Texas

Jacqueline Ray
Samuel High School
Dallas, Texas

Howard Riddles
Oak Grove Middle School
Clearwater, Florida

R.C. Rodriguez
Northside Independent School District
San Antonio, Texas

Randy Soderman
Community School District Six
New York, New York

Rita LaNell Stahl
Sinagua High School
Flagstaff, Arizona

Dean Stecker
School District of Palm Beach County
West Palm Beach, Florida

Mary Sterling-Cruz
Jackson Middle School
Friendswood, Texas

Rosemary Tejada
Carlsbad High School
Carlsbad, California

Camille Sloan Telthorster
Bleye Middle School
Houston, Texas

Vickie Thomas
Robinson Middle School
Plano, Texas

Claudio Toledo
Lynwood Middle School
Lynwood, California

Christopher Tracy
Garnet-Patterson Middle School
Washington, DC

Lydia Villescas
Pharr-San Juan-Alamo ISD
Pharr/San Juan, Texas

Stephanie Vreeland
T.A. Howard Middle School
Arlington, Texas

Jennifer Zelenitz
Long Island City High School
Long Island City, New York

We wish to thank the students at the following schools who helped us select high-interest readings at an appropriate language level. Their feedback was invaluable.

Student reviewers

Cooper Middle School
Fresno, California

De Leon Middle School
McAllen, Texas

Garnet-Patterson Middle School
Washington, D.C.

Hanshaw Middle School
Modesto, California

Intermediate School 10 Q
Long Island City, New York

Jackson Middle School
Friendswood, Texas

L.V. Stockard Middle School
Dallas, Texas

Liberty Middle School
Pharr, Texas

Martin Middle School
Corpus Christi, Texas

Memorial Middle School
Pharr, Texas

Newcomer Center
Arlington, Texas

Nimitz High School
Houston, Texas

Oak Grove Middle School
Clearwater, Florida

Oxnard High School
Oxnard, California

Pershing Intermediate School 220
Brooklyn, New York

Samuel High School
Dallas, Texas

Serrano International School
Lake Forest, California

Silverado Middle School
Napa, California

T.A. Howard Middle School
Arlington, Texas

Trimble Technical High School
Fort Worth, Texas

Contents

Contents   **vii**

To the Student

We hope you like *Visions*
We wrote it for you
To learn speaking, reading, writing,
And listening, too.

You'll read all kinds of things —
Stories, poems, and plays,
And texts that will help you understand
What your content teacher says.

Mary Lou McCloskey

Use this book to "grow" your English,
To talk about what you write and read.
Use it to learn lots of new words
And new reading strategies you'll need.

Good authors, good activities,
And especially your good teachers,
Can also help you learn grammar and writing,
And lots of other language features.

Lydia Stack

So please open this book
And learn everything you can.
Then write and show us how far you've come
Since you first began.

M.L.M. and L.S.

http://visions.heinle.com

Unit Materials

Activity Book: *pp. 1–40*
Audio: *Unit 1; CD 1, Tracks 1–5*
Student Handbook
Student CD-ROM: *Unit 1*
CNN Video: *Unit 1*
Teacher Resource Book: *Lesson Plans, Teacher Resources, Reading Summaries, School-Home Connection, Video Script, Video Worksheet, Activity Book Answer Key*
Teacher Resource CD-ROM
Assessment Program: *Quizzes and Test, pp. 7–22; Teacher and Student Resources, pp. 115–144*
Assessment CD-ROM
Transparencies
The Heinle Newbury House Dictionary/CD-ROM
More Grammar Practice workbook
Heinle Reading Library: *The Adventures of Sherlock Holmes*
Web site: http://visions.heinle.com

Visions Staff Development Handbook

Refer to the Visions Staff Development Handbook for more teacher support.

Unit Theme: Mysteries

Use personal experience *Say: A mystery is something that is hard to explain or understand. Detectives and other people try to explain mysteries.* Have students talk about detectives and mysteries they know from TV or books.

Unit Preview: Table of Contents

1. **Use the table of contents to locate information** Read the titles and authors. *Ask: Which mysteries have you heard of?*
2. **Connect** *Ask: Which titles interest you?*

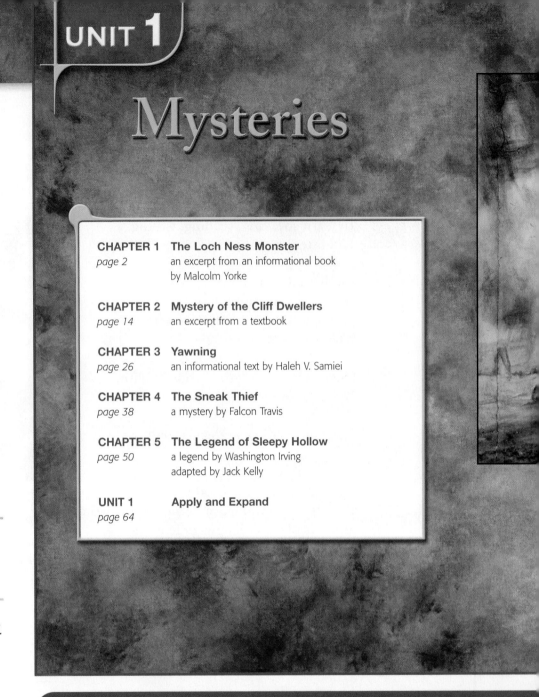

UNIT 1

Mysteries

UNIT OBJECTIVES

Reading
Make inferences using text evidence as you read an excerpt from an informational book • Find the main idea and supporting details as you read an excerpt from a textbook • Compare the text to your own experiences as you read an informational text • Use chronology to locate and recall information as you read a mystery • Identify imagery as you read a legend

Listening and Speaking
Present an interview • Distinguish fact and opinion • Give an informational presentation • Interpret text through dramatization • Talk about senses

Stonehenge, John Constable, oil on canvas, 1776–1837.

View the Picture

1. Who do you think put the stone posts here?

2. Why do you think they were put here?

3. What mysteries do you know about?

In this unit, you will read a mystery, a legend, and informational texts about mysteries. You will also practice writing these forms.

1

Grammar
Understand the conjunction *but* • Use prepositional phrases • Write dependent clauses • Identify simple, compound, and complex sentences • Use pronoun referents

Writing
Write a paragraph that describes • Write an informational text • Write a paragraph using chronology • Write dialogue in a mystery • Write a character description

Content
Math: Understand length • Social Studies: Read a population map • Math: Read a bar graph • Language Arts: Learn words about the law • Social Studies: Read a timeline

View the Picture

1. **Art background** This interpretation of Stonehenge in Salisbury, England, was a dramatic change for John Constable (1776–1837), a British landscape painter. Instead of his usual rustic English countryside, we see the ruins of an ancient civilization in a barren landscape under a dangerous-looking sky. Constable's subject here—a mysterious, circular arrangement of rough boulders weighing up to 50 tons each—was constructed by early nomads between 3500 and 1600 B.C.

2. **Art interpretation** *Ask: How are the arches of purple in the sky and the structures on land related?* (The arches seem to be piercing the stones.)

   a. **Explore and describe color** Ask students to contrast the purples, grays, and blacks in the sky with the neutral browns of the ground. (active, violent forces of nature contrasted with the flat, static structures of people)

   b. **Interpret the painting** Ask your students why the artist focused on the broken and scattered section of the ruin instead of the more orderly and upright circular structures in the background. (The ruins represent a lost civilization and the impermanence of man's largest and most impressive works.)

   c. **Connect to theme** *Say: The theme of this unit is* mysteries. *What mystery do you see in this painting?*

ASSESS

Have students name three geometric shapes they see in the painting. (triangles, rectangles, and squares)

CHAPTER
1

Into the Reading

The Loch Ness Monster

an excerpt from an informational book by Malcolm Yorke

Reading Make inferences using text evidence as you read an excerpt from an informational book.

Listening and Speaking Present an interview.

Grammar Understand the conjunction *but*.

Writing Write a paragraph that describes.

Content Math: Understand length.

Chapter Materials

Activity Book: *pp. 1–8*
Audio: *Unit 1, Chapter 1; CD 1, Track 1*
Student Handbook
Student CD-ROM: *Unit 1, Chapter 1*
Teacher Resource Book: *Lesson Plan, Teacher Resources, Reading Summary, Activity Book Answer Key*
Teacher Resource CD-ROM
Assessment Program: *Quiz, pp. 7–8; Teacher and Student Resources, pp. 115–144*
Assessment CD-ROM
Transparencies
The Heinle Newbury House Dictionary/CD-ROM
Web site: http://visions.heinle.com

Objectives

Prereading for vocabulary Read the objectives. *Ask: What is an interview? Can you describe your best friend?*

Use Prior Knowledge

Describe an Animal

1. **Gather and organize** Brainstorm a list of animals. In pairs, ask students to complete a web about an animal.
2. **Draw conclusions** Ask pairs to describe their animals. Have others in the class guess the identities of the animals.

Use Prior Knowledge

Describe an Animal

Prior knowledge is something that you already know. Use your prior knowledge to help you understand what you do not know.

There are many different animals. What animals do you know about?

1. Work with a partner. Think of animals that you know about. Choose one.
2. Make a web. List what you know about the animal. Answer these questions.
   a. What does the animal look like?
   b. Where does the animal live?
   c. What does the animal eat?
   d. Does the animal fly? Swim? Run fast? Climb trees?

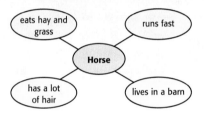

MULTI-LEVEL OPTIONS *Build Vocabulary*

Newcomer Write on the board: *search* and *look. Say: I will search for my book.* Act out searching for a book. Explain that when you *search* for something, you *look* for it. *Ask: What else can you search for? What else can you look for?* Hide items and have students search for them.

Beginning On the board, write: *big, large,* and *huge.* Hold up a picture of a small fish. *Ask: Is this a huge fish?* (no) Then hold up a picture of a very large fish. *Ask: Is this a huge fish?* (yes) Explain that *huge* means "very large." Have students list things that are huge.

Intermediate Write on the board: *enormous, snakelike, retreated, ferocious.* Divide students into pairs. Have each student choose 2 words and write sentences with the words that show their meanings. Have partners guess the meanings from the context.

Advanced Have students work independently. Ask them to write a sentence using language structure to define each of the following words: *legendary, enormous, swirled, reappeared, retreated.*

Build Background

Dinosaurs

Background is information that can help you understand what you hear or read.

Dinosaurs were animals that lived millions of years ago. Some were very large. Others were very small. Some ate meat. Others ate plants.

Content Connection

This is a picture of a *Tyrannosaurus rex*. It was a very large dinosaur that ate meat.

Build Vocabulary

Use Language Structure to Find Meaning

When you learn new words, you **build your vocabulary.**

You can use **language structure** to figure out what a word means. Language structure is the way language is organized. Authors often make statements in one sentence and give an example in the next sentence. The information in the second sentence will help you figure out the meaning of words.

Khalid adores carrots. He eats them every day.

The second sentence tells us that Khalid eats carrots every day. This probably means that he likes carrots a lot. You can guess that *adores* means "likes a lot."

Read these sentences. Use the second sentences to figure out the meanings of the underlined words.

1. The men searched for it. But they never saw it again.
   a. looked   **b.** caught
2. Some scans showed huge objects in the lake. The objects were bigger than sharks but smaller than whales.
   a. very large   **b.** very small

The Heinle Newbury House Dictionary   Activity Book p. 1   Student CD-ROM

Chapter 1 The Loch Ness Monster   **3**

UNIT 1 • CHAPTER 1
Into the Reading

Build Background

Dinosaurs

1. **Use books and pictures** Bring in books on dinosaurs. Have students describe various dinosaurs. *Ask: What animals today look like dinosaurs?*
2. **Content Connection** Explain that scientists learn about dinosaurs from their fossils, or bones that they have left behind. *Ask: Why do you think the Tyrannosaurus rex ate meat?* Point out teeth and claws in the illustration.

Build Vocabulary

Use Language Structure to Find Meaning

Teacher Resource Book: *Personal Dictionary, p. 63*

1. **Use experiences** Write the sample sentences on the board. *Ask: Do you think Khalid likes carrots?* (yes) *Why?* (He eats them every day.) *What do you think the word adore means?* (likes a lot)
2. **Use a dictionary** Introduce students to The Heinle Newbury House Dictionary. Walk them through the Introduction on pp. xiii–xxii. These notes instruct students on how to use a dictionary to clarify meaning, pronunciation, and usage.
3. **Use other sources** Tell students that dictionaries are also available online and as CD-ROMs. The CD-ROM version of The Heinle Newbury House Dictionary is found on the inside back cover. Students will find meanings, pronunciations, derivations, and usage notes in these other sources.
4. **Reading selection vocabulary** You may want to introduce the glossed words in the reading selection before students begin reading. Key words: *loch, creature, claim, mysterious, legends, prehistoric.* Instruct students to write the words with correct spelling and their definitions in their Personal Dictionaries. Have them pronounce each word and divide it into syllables.
5. **Multi-level options** See MULTI-LEVEL OPTIONS on p. 2.

Answers
1. a 2. a

 **ASSESS**

Write a sentence using both *search* and *huge*.

Chapter 1 / Into the Reading   **3**

 Content Connection
Math

Build Background Have students work in small groups. Ask each group to use an encyclopedia or other reference aids to find information about five or six different dinosaurs. Tell students to note the measurements of each dinosaur. Then have groups make simple scale drawings of each dinosaur across a piece of paper, from smallest to largest. Ask them to label each dinosaur's height and length.

Learning Styles
Linguistic

Build Vocabulary Have students work in pairs. Ask students to select five words from the dictionary. Tell them to use the dictionary to understand the meanings of the words they have chosen. Then have students give verbal clues to their partners that will help their partners figure out the meanings of the words.

Text Structure

Informational Text

1. **Recognize features** Copy the feature chart on the board. Review the features. Ask students to look through the reading selection for examples of the features.
2. **Multi-level options** See MULTI-LEVEL OPTIONS below.

Reading Strategy

Make Inferences Using Text Evidence

Teacher think aloud *Say: When I walk past the gym, I hear people cheering. I know that people cheer during games, so I can make an inference that there is a basketball game or some other game happening in the gym.*

ASSESS

Ask: What are three features of an informational text? (details and examples, experiences, visuals)

Text Structure

Informational Text

The **text structure** of a reading is its main parts and how they fit together.

"The Loch Ness Monster" is an **informational text.** An informational text gives facts about a topic. Look at the chart. It shows the features of an informational text. Look for these elements as you read or listen to "The Loch Ness Monster."

Informational Text	
Details and Examples	Details and examples explain the topic.
Experiences	Experiences are things that happened to real people.
Visuals	Visuals are pictures that help readers understand.

Student CD-ROM

Reading Strategy

Make Inferences Using Text Evidence

A **reading strategy** is a way to understand what you read. You can become a better reader if you learn good reading strategies.

Authors do not always tell you everything. Sometimes you have to **make inferences.** When you make inferences, you guess using information that you know. You also use **text evidence.** Text evidence is in what you read.

1. Read this sentence.

   A man comes into the room. He is wearing a wet raincoat.

2. Now read these sentences. Which one is an inference that you can make from the sentence in 1?
   a. It is raining.
   b. The man is cold.

Make inferences as you read "The Loch Ness Monster." Write your inferences in your Reading Log.

Reading Log

Student CD-ROM

4 Unit 1 Mysteries

MULTI-LEVEL OPTIONS *Text Structure*

Newcomer Write on the board: *details* and *experiences. Ask: Who can give me a detail about the first day of school? What kind of experiences did you have on the first day of school?* List responses on the board. Explain that students are sharing information.

Beginning Remind students that an informational text tells details, examples, and experiences about a topic. *Ask: What are some monsters you know about?* Brainstorm and list students' details, examples, and experiences.

Intermediate Have students list five important events in their lives. Ask them to include details and examples for each event. Ask student pairs to read their lists aloud to each other.

Advanced Ask students to practice writing an informational text. Have each student select a topic and write a paragraph that includes facts about that topic. Remind students to include details, examples, and experiences related to the topic.

THE LOCH NESS MONSTER

an excerpt from an informational book
by Malcolm Yorke

5

Reading Selection Materials

Audio: *Unit 1, Chapter 1; CD 1, Track 1*
Teacher Resource Book: *Reading Summary,*
  pp. 65–66
Transparencies: #31, *Reading Summary*

Suggestions for Using Reading Summary

- Introduce new vocabulary or cognates.
- Cut the summary into strips, or jumble the sentences on an overhead transparency. Students put the sentences in order.
- Practice the reading strategy.
- Students read aloud or with a partner.
- Students paraphrase the summary.
- Students do a cloze activity.
- Students create a visual or graphic organizer, such as a timeline or storyboard, to illustrate the summary.
- Students paraphrase the summary.

Preview the Selection

1. **Interpret the image** Tell students that the picture relates to the informational text that they will read. *Ask: What does this creature look like? Where does it live? What is it doing? Do you think it is real? Why or why not? What inference can you make about the selection from this picture?*
2. **Connect** Remind students that the unit theme is *mysteries.* Ask them what is mysterious about the picture. Remind students that in mysteries, people want to explain or understand something.

Content Connection
The Arts

Ask students to discuss the plots of mysteries they have seen in movies, in plays, or on television shows. *Ask: What is a mystery?* (something unknown or unsolved) Brainstorm elements of a mystery. (detectives, clues, crimes, puzzles, questions, answers, suspects, solution, etc.) Organize students' ideas on the board in a web.

▌ Teacher Resource Book: *Web, p. 37*

Learning Styles
Interpersonal

Tell students about other legendary creatures, such as Big Foot (yeti), the kraken, and mermaids. Explain that many people claim to have seen these creatures. Have students discuss why they think people make these claims. Ask them to provide their own ideas of what the people actually saw or what caused the visions. (*Example:* Some yeti "sightings" may be hallucinations from high-altitude oxygen deprivation.)

Read the Selection

1. **Use text features** Direct students to the numbers for each paragraph. Explain their purpose and use. Then direct students to glossed words. Explain that the information helps them understand the boldfaced words.

2. **Teacher read aloud** Read the selection aloud. Then have volunteers read aloud different paragraphs.

3. **Make inferences** *Ask: Why do you think Jim shouted?* (He was excited and scared.)

Sample Answer to Guide Question
The men rushed to Jim. They were excited and got into a boat to get a closer look.

See Teacher Edition pp. 434–436 for a list of English-Spanish cognates in the reading selection.

---

1 "Dad! Dad! What's that in the **loch?**" shouted Jim Ayton. It was a calm summer's evening in 1963. Jim was working on his father's farm on Loch Ness, a lake in **Scotland,** when he looked up to see a strange **creature** moving silently down the lake. It was huge! Jim had never seen anything like it before.

2 Two men nearby heard Jim's shouts and rushed to join him and his father. The excited group wanted a closer look. They ran to the lake, climbed into a boat, and headed straight toward the creature.

3 The creature's head looked a bit like a horse's head, only bigger. Its neck stretched nearly 6 feet (2 meters), as tall as a full-grown man. Its **snakelike** body was as long as a bus. Could it be the **legendary** Loch Ness **monster** that people had talked about for years?

4 Suddenly the creature rose out of the water. Then it dived. An **enormous** wave hit the small boat. It rocked and **swirled** around. Had the creature seen the men? Was it about to attack?

Make Inferences Using Text Evidence

You can make this inference: The two men and Jim's father have never seen a creature like this. What text evidence helps you make this inference?

Audio
CD 1. Tr. 1

---

loch a lake
Scotland one of the nations in the United Kingdom
creature a living thing
snakelike long; looking like a snake
legendary based on a story that is handed down over time

monster a scary creature
enormous very big
swirled turned

6 Unit 1 Mysteries

MULTI-LEVEL OPTIONS *Read the Selection*

Newcomer Play the audio. Read the pages aloud. *Ask: Was Jim working on his father's farm?* (yes) *Did Jim and the men get in a boat?* (yes) *Did Jim see a small animal in the lake?* (no) *Is Jim the only person who ever saw a monster in the lake?* (no) *Did many people try to take pictures of the monster?* (yes)

Beginning Read the Reading Summary aloud. *Ask: When did Jim see the monster?* (1963) *Where was it?* (in Loch Ness) *How did the men get closer?* (by boat) *Who saw it first?* (St. Columba) *When did it get famous?* (1933) *What did newspapers pay money for?* (photos of the monster)

Intermediate Have students do a paired reading. *Ask: Why did Jim and the men get in the boat?* (to get a closer look at the monster) *Why didn't they tell anyone what they saw?* (They didn't think people would believe them.) *What happened after the road was built?* (More tourists visited the area.)

Advanced Have students read silently. *Ask: Were Jim and the men scared of the monster? How can you tell?* (No, because they went closer.) *Why was the monster seen more after 1933?* (A road was built; more people could get there.) *Why did so many people try to see it?* (They wanted the money.)

5   A few seconds later the creature's head **reappeared.** It was farther away now. The monster seemed more **frightened** than **ferocious!** Then it was gone. The men searched and searched for it, but they never saw it again.

6   It was 20 years before anyone heard the story about what had happened that day. Jim and his father didn't think many people would believe them. But the Aytons and their friends are not the only people who **claim** to have seen this **mysterious** monster.

7   One of the earliest known **sightings** was made more than 1,400 years ago by Saint Columba, a traveling Irish holy man. **Legends** tell how, in 565 A.D.,

the saint saw a "water monster" attack a swimmer in Loch Ness. When the saint ordered it to leave the swimmer alone, the monster **retreated** immediately.

8   The Loch Ness monster first became famous in 1933, after a road was built around the steep sides of the Loch Ness valley. Tourists could now explore this **remote** area for the first time. It was not long before reports of monster sightings began appearing in newspapers all around the world.

9   **Spotting** the monster soon brought rewards. Newspapers would pay a lot of money for a photograph of the monster—even if it was **blurred!** Fortune seekers, scientists, and monster enthusiasts **swarmed** around the loch, all wanting to take the best monster picture ever.

Make Inferences Using Text Evidence

Were many people interested in seeing the Loch Ness monster? Make an inference. What text evidence did you use to make this inference?

---

reappeared appeared again, came back	**legends** stories from long ago
frightened scared	**retreated** moved away from
ferocious very fierce or cruel	**remote** far away from other places
claim say that something is true	**spotting** seeing
mysterious having no known cause	**blurred** not clear
sightings things that people see	**swarmed** moved together in a large group

Chapter 1   The Loch Ness Monster   **7**

Read the Selection

1. **Use graphic elements** Ask students to locate Loch Ness on the map.
2. **Reciprocal reading** Play the audio. Have students reread in small groups. Have each person take a turn reading a paragraph and asking questions about it to the others in the group.
3. **Locate derivations using dictionaries** Have students look at these glossed words and determine what words they are derived from: *legendary, swirled, reappeared, frightened, mysterious, sightings, spotting, blurred, swarmed.* Have students check the derivations in a print, an online, or a CD-ROM dictionary.
4. **Summarize** Ask questions to help students summarize the main points.
5. **Multi-level options** See MULTI-LEVEL OPTIONS on p. 6.

Sample Answer to Guide Question
Yes, many people were interested in the Loch Ness monster. The text says "fortune seekers, scientists, and monster enthusiasts swarmed around the loch."

 Capitalization

Titles

Tell students that the first letter of each main word in the title of a book, story, or poem should be capitalized. Explain that small words, such as *a, an, and, or,* and *the,* and prepositions, such as *at, of, in,* and *for,* are usually not capitalized. Point out that the first letter of a title is always capitalized. *Ask: Why are the words* Loch, Ness, *and* Monster *capitalized at the top of page 5?* (main words in the title of the story) *Why is* The *capitalized?* (first word of the title)

Have students copy these tips to refer to when they write:

CAPITALIZING TITLES

DO capitalize the first letters of main words.

DO capitalize the first letter of the first word.

DON'T capitalize the first letter of a small word. (a, an, and, or, the)

DON'T capitalize the first letter of short prepositions. (at, of, in, for)

Read the Selection

Paired reading Read the selection aloud. Then have students reread the selection in pairs.
Ask: What types of modern equipment have searchers and scientists used to look for the monster? (underwater cameras, sonar scanners)

Sample Answer to Guide Question
The text says that searchers and scientists used modern, high-tech equipment to check for the monster.

boats, each fitted with a **sonar** scanner, moved up the loch. What they discovered amazed them.

> **Make Inferences Using Text Evidence**
>
> You can make this inference: People want to know if the Loch Ness monster is real. What text evidence helps you make this inference?

10 Over the years, the searchers used more and more modern equipment. In 1972, an underwater camera produced a **close-up** of a strange object in the loch. When scientists used a special computer to **sharpen** up the image, this is what they saw. Could it be one of the monster's **flippers**?

11 The underwater photograph seems to show a flipper, but no one can be sure because the image is so **grainy.** It is hard to see or to take a photograph in the lake water because it is full of tiny pieces of peat, or dead plant material.

12 In 1987, a team of scientists searched the loch with high-tech equipment for a project called Operation Deepscan. A line of 19

13 Some scans showed huge objects moving deep in the lake. The objects were bigger than sharks but smaller than whales. Were they huge fish? Or was it a family of Loch Ness monsters? Again the **murky** water kept the scientists from knowing the answer.

14 Without clear pictures, scientists must rely on people's descriptions to know what the monster looks like. It seems that the creature has a long, thin neck, a **bulky** body with four flippers, and a long, powerful tail.

15 No animal living today fits this description. However, one **prehistoric** creature does.

---

close-up a picture of something up close
sharpen make better, make clearer
flippers wide parts of the body on certain sea animals, used for swimming
grainy unclear

sonar a tool used to find things under water
murky unclear and dark
bulky large
prehistoric the time before people wrote about history

8 Unit 1 Mysteries

MULTI-LEVEL OPTIONS *Read the Selection*

Newcomer *Ask: Did an underwater camera take a picture in 1972?* (yes) *Was the photo clear?* (no) *Did a team of scientists explore the lake in 1987?* (yes) *Did the scientists solve the mystery?* (no) *Does the monster look like a dinosaur?* (yes)

Beginning *Ask: When did an underwater camera take a picture?* (1972) *What did it look like?* (a flipper) *When was Operation Deepscan?* (1987) *What did they use to search the lake?* (sonar scanners) *What does the monster look like?* (a dinosaur) *What could the monster be?* (boats, logs, shadows, eels, jokes)

Intermediate *Ask: Why is it hard to take a picture in the lake's water?* (peat) *Why were scientists amazed in 1987?* (Scans showed huge objects moving in the lake.) *Why were the results of Operation Deepscan unclear?* (murky water) *Why must scientists rely on people's descriptions?* (They can't get clear pictures.)

Advanced *Ask: How has the search for the monster changed over the years?* (more modern equipment) *What evidence do you think would convince people of the existence of the Loch Ness monster?* (clear photographs or video; support from scientific community; its capture)

16 *Cryptocleidus* (krip-toe-KLIE-duss) was a **plesiosaur:** a huge fish-eating **reptile** that lived in the sea. Some people think it looked a lot like the Loch Ness monster. However, *Cryptocleidus* is thought to have disappeared from the Earth 70 million years ago! Could it have lived on unnoticed?

17 Is the Loch Ness monster a **survivor** from the dinosaur age? Or were the people who saw it simply fooled by boats, logs, shadows, or giant **eels**? Could some of the sightings be the result of **practical jokes**? No one knows the truth—yet.

> **Make Inferences Using Text Evidence**
>
> What inference can you make about what *Cryptocleidus* looked like?

plesiosaur a type of dinosaur
reptile an animal that is cold-blooded and lays eggs; snakes and lizards are reptiles
survivor something that still lives
eels fish that look like snakes
practical jokes tricks

About the Author

Malcolm Yorke (born 1938)

Malcolm Yorke has written more than 20 books. Many of these books are for young people. Yorke was once a college teacher. He taught people how to be teachers. Today, Yorke still writes books. He also paints and makes other kinds of art.

➤ What was Malcolm Yorke's purpose in writing about the Loch Ness monster? To entertain, to inform, or to persuade?

Chapter 1 The Loch Ness Monster **9**

❜ Punctuation

Periods at the end of sentences

Point out that all sentences must have end punctuation, such as a period or a question mark. Tell students that a sentence that makes a statement needs a period at the end.

Apply Have students correct sentences by adding periods. Write on the board:

Jim saw a strange creature in the lake

Reporters wrote stories about the monster

It looked like a giant snake with flippers

Evaluate Your Reading Strategy

Make Inferences Using Text Evidence
Say: You have practiced an important reading strategy. Now you can decide how well you have done. Does this statement describe how you read?

> I use text evidence and what I know to make inferences. Making inferences helps me better understand what I read.

Read the Selection

1. **Locate pronunciations using glossaries and other sources** Show students the pronunciation key for *Cryptocleidus* in paragraph 16. Point out that informational texts often give pronunciation keys within the reading and in glossaries at the back of the book. Show students the glossary at the back of a science and a social studies book. Have them locate words with pronunciation keys and practice pronouncing these words. Also show them other sources, such as a CD-ROM dictionary or an online dictionary, that show pronunciations of words.
2. **Reciprocal reading** Read the selection aloud as students follow along. Then have students reread in small groups, taking turns reading and asking questions.
3. **Multi-level options** See MULTI-LEVEL OPTIONS on p. 8.

Sample Answer to Guide Question
I can infer that *Cryptocleidus* had a long, thin neck; a bulky body with four flippers; and a long, powerful tail, just like the Loch Ness monster.

About the Author

1. **Explain author background** Malcolm Yorke enjoys painting and making carvings in wood and stone. *Ask: How do you think his paintings and carvings help him describe the Loch Ness monster?*
2. **Interpret the facts** *Ask: Do you think Malcolm Yorke believes there is a Loch Ness monster? Why do you think so?*

Across Selections

Discuss point of view Have students guess if the author has been to Loch Ness. *Ask: Does Malcolm Yorke think this mystery will be explained? If Malcolm Yorke saw the Loch Ness monster, how might his point of view in the text be different?* Have students discuss in groups.

Spelling, Punctuation, Capitalization

After the Reading Comprehension section, students will practice spelling, punctuation, and capitalization in the Activity Book.

Beyond the Reading

Reading Comprehension

Question-Answer Relationships

Sample Answers

1. Loch Ness is in Scotland.
2. The road was built in 1933.
3. The Loch Ness monster looks like *Cryptocleidus*.
4. It has a long neck, a large body, four flippers, and a long tail.
5. Operation Deepscan found large objects moving deep in the lake.
6. The newspapers wanted to be the first to prove there was a monster, so they offered a lot of money.
7. I think the author believes there is a monster because he ends the reading with *yet*. This means he expects they will find something in the future.
8. I think people will find the monster. They will just need more high-tech equipment.
9. What do the sightings have in common? What time of day were the sightings? What was the monster doing? What was the weather like?
10. This mystery is different from others I've read about. There is no crime to solve or detective to ask questions. It's more like a scientific mystery.

Build Reading Fluency

Repeated Reading

Assessment Program: *Reading Fluency Chart, p. 116*

As students read aloud, time the reading and count the number of incorrectly pronounced words. Record results in the Reading Fluency Chart.

Reading Comprehension

Question-Answer Relationships (QAR)

You can understand a selection better if you answer different kinds of questions.

"Right There" Questions

1. **Recall Facts** Where is Loch Ness?
2. **Recall Facts** When was the road built around Loch Ness valley?
3. **Recall Facts** What dinosaur does the Loch Ness monster look like?

"Think and Search" Questions

4. **Describe** Use your own words to describe what the Loch Ness monster looks like.
5. **Explain** What did Operation Deepscan discover?

"Author and You" Questions

6. **Draw Conclusions** Why do you think the newspapers paid a lot of money for pictures of the Loch Ness monster?

7. **Analyze Author's Perspective** Do you think the author believes there is a Loch Ness monster? Why do you think what you do?

"On Your Own" Questions

8. **Speculate** Do you think people will ever find the Loch Ness monster? Why or why not?
9. **Form Questions** What questions would you like to ask and research about this mystery? Write your questions. Then revise them.
10. **Connect Across Texts** Compare this reading with other mysteries that you have read about.

Activity Book Student
p. 2 CD-ROM

Build Reading Fluency

Repeated Reading

When you **build reading fluency,** you learn to read faster and to understand better.

Repeated reading helps increase your reading rate and builds confidence. Each time you reread you improve your reading fluency.

1. Turn to page 6.
2. Your teacher or partner will time you for six minutes.
3. With a partner, take turns reading each paragraph aloud.
4. Stop after six minutes.

10 Unit 1 Mysteries

MULTI-LEVEL OPTIONS *Elements of Literature*

Newcomer Help students understand that pictures give readers a better understanding of a topic. *Say: An elk is an animal with four legs.* Then hold up a picture of an elk. *Say: This is an elk. Did the picture help you better understand what an elk looks like?*

Beginning On the board, write: *elk. Say: An elk is an animal with four legs and antlers.* Have students draw an elk, based on your description. Then hold up a picture of an elk. *Say: This is an elk.* Have students compare their drawings to the picture. Discuss how a picture can help them understand a new idea.

Intermediate Ask students to find pictures of uncommon animals. Have students describe the animals to partners. Ask listeners to draw what they think the animal looks like based on the description. Then have students compare their drawings to the actual pictures.

Advanced Have students find pictures of exotic animals such as gazelles or platypuses. Have them write a two-sentence description of the animal. Have students exchange descriptions and draw what is described. Then have students compare their drawings to the actual pictures.

Listen, Speak, Interact

Present an Interview

When people listen and talk to each other, they **interact.**

During an interview, one person asks questions. Another person answers them.

1. Work with a partner. One student will be the interviewer. The other student will be Jim Ayton.
2. Work together to ask and answer questions.
   a. What were you doing when you saw the monster?
   b. What was the monster doing?
   c. How did you feel when you saw the monster?
3. Make up two more questions on your own. Share them with your partner. Then revise your questions.
4. Write each question on a note card. Write the answer on another card.

> *Question 1:*
> *Interviewer: What did the Loch Ness monster look like?*
>
> *Answer 1:*
> *Jim Ayton: The monster was very big! It . . .*

5. Use your note cards to present your interview to the class.

Elements of Literature

Use Visuals

Literature is something that you read. Writers use many different ways to express themselves. These ways are the **elements of literature.**

The **visuals** (pictures) in the selection show what the animals and places look like.

1. Work with a small group. Take turns reading paragraphs 3, 8, and 10 aloud. Look at the visuals.
2. Discuss the following questions:
   a. Did the visuals help you understand the text? Why or why not?
   b. Does it help to look at visuals before you read? Why or why not?

Activity Book p. 3   Student CD-ROM

Content Connection
Social Studies

Have students compare and contrast print media with written story. Ask students to research an article on the Loch Ness monster. They can look in encyclopedias, newspapers, and magazines. Have them compare and contrast the information included in this print article with what was included in the reading selection. *Ask: What does each article say that the other does not?*

Learning Styles
Natural

Ask students to work in pairs. Have pairs research the climate in northern Scotland, where Loch Ness is located. Ask students to imagine they are going to search for the Loch Ness monster. Have students create a list of clothing, equipment, and other supplies they think they will need for their mission.

Listen, Speak, Interact

Present an Interview

1. **Reread in pairs** Pair beginning and advanced students. Have them read alternate paragraphs.
2. **Compose, Organize, and Revise a News Story** Ask pairs of students to use the information they gathered in their interview to compose a newspaper aritcle about the Loch Ness monster. Tell students to organize the article by the questions and answers used in the interview. Have each pair exchange articles with another pair. Tell them to evaluate each other's articles for clarity and accuracy, and then revise the articles based on the feedback.
3. **Newcomers** Reread with this group. Have them answer the questions. Write key words and expressions on the board. Guide students to ask other questions about Jim's experience. Have students practice interviewing in pairs.

Elements of Literature

Use Visuals

1. **Identify visuals** Ask students to identify the types of visuals in this selection. (photos and maps) Have them read the paragraphs and answer the questions in small groups.
2. **Use personal experience** Ask students to share visuals in other textbooks.
3. **Multi-level options** See MULTI-LEVEL OPTIONS on p. 10.

Answers
Examples: **2. a.** The visuals helped me because they showed the things the text talks about and sometimes gave information that's not in the text. **2. b.** I think it helps to look at the visuals first and then read. It helps you get a general idea, and then the reading gives you more specific information.

ASSESS

Say: Describe how a visual in another textbook helped *you* better understand the text.

Word Study

Analyze Compound Words

Make a word map Write on the board and *say: playground.* Point out the component words. Help students explain the compound word.

Answers
2. under + water; news + paper
3. something that is under the water; a paper that gives the news

Grammar Focus

Understand the Conjunction *But*

Apply Ask students to write two sentences to contrast themselves and a friend. Have students exchange papers and combine the two sentences with *but.* Check for correct punctuation.

Answers
1. The men searched . . . for it, but they never saw it again.; . . . seems to show a flipper, but no one can . . . .
2. **a.** I saw the monster, but I couldn't take a picture.
   b. Some people don't believe in the monster, but I do.

ASSESS

Write on the board: *The man watched the lake for two days. He didn't see the monster.* Have students combine the two sentences using the conjunction *but.*

Word Study

Analyze Compound Words

Words can have several parts. In this section, you will learn what the different parts mean.

A **compound word** is two words joined together to make one word. Use the meaning of each word to find the meaning of the compound word.

Treetop has the words *tree* and *top. Treetop* means "the top part of a tree."

1. Copy the chart in your Personal Dictionary.
2. Write the words that make up each compound word in your chart.

First Word +	Second Word ⇒	Compound Word
tree +	top ⇒	treetop
		underwater
		newspaper

3. Guess the definitions. Check your answers with your teacher.

Personal Dictionary   The Heinle Newbury House Dictionary   Activity Book p. 4   Student CD-ROM

Grammar Focus

Understand the Conjunction *But*

Grammar is the way that a language is put together.

A conjunction is a part of speech. It can combine two sentences into one compound sentence. The word *but* is a conjunction.

Sentence 1	Sentence 2
Carlos wanted to play.	He had to finish his homework first.

Compound Sentence

Carlos wanted to play, **but** he had to finish his homework first.

The conjunction *but* shows **contrast**—how things are different. When you combine sentences with **but,** use a comma (**,**) after the first sentence. This helps make your meaning clear.

1. Find two sentences with the conjunction *but* in paragraphs 5 and 11. Write them on a piece of paper.
2. Combine these sentences with *but.* Be sure to use the comma correctly.
   a. I saw the monster. I couldn't take a picture.
   b. Some people don't believe in the monster. I do.

Activity Book pp. 5–6   Student Handbook   Student CD-ROM

12 Unit 1 Mysteries

MULTI-LEVEL OPTIONS *From Reading to Writing*

Newcomer Have students draw pictures of monsters. Ask them to say words that describe their monsters. Provide this frame: *This is _____. It has _____.*

Beginning Have students work in pairs to draw a picture of the Loch Ness monster. Help them add labels and descriptive captions to their pictures. Have pairs write a sentence that names and describes the creature.

Intermediate Provide a blank chart. Include these headings: *Size, Colors, Shape, Fur/Skin,* and *Other Features.* Ask students to complete their graphic organizers with information from the selection. Have students use the details in their charts to write their paragraphs.

Advanced Have students exchange their descriptive paragraphs with partners. Reviewers should check for mechanics and details. They may also suggest ideas for more descriptive writing. Remind students to be tactful. Also point out that final changes are up to the author.

From Reading to Writing

Write a Paragraph That Describes

In school, after you read literature, you often write about it. This section shows you how to do this.

Write a paragraph. Describe what the Loch Ness monster looks like.

1. Use the visuals to help you.
2. Review the selection to get ideas. Look at paragraphs 3, 11, and 13.
3. Draw a picture of the monster. Copy your paragraph below the picture.
4. Remember to indent your paragraph.

> The Loch Ness monster
> looks like _____
> _____.
> Its head looks like _____
> _____.
> Its body looks like _____
> _____.
> Its tail looks like _____
> _____.

Activity Book
p. 7

Student
Handbook

Across Content Areas

Understand Length

Content areas are the subjects you study in school. Math, science, social studies, language arts, and other arts such as music and drawing are content areas.

Length tells you how long something is. People in the United States use a system called the **U.S. Customary.** Most people in the world use the **metric** system.

Work with a partner. Use the chart to answer the following questions.

1. Are inches shorter than feet?
2. Which is longer, a yard or a meter?

3. Are miles longer or shorter than kilometers?

U.S. Customary	Metric
1 foot = 12 inches	30.5 centimeters
1 yard = 3 feet	.9 meters
1 mile = 1,760 yards	1.6 kilometers

Note: "foot" changes to "feet" for numbers larger than 1 (for example: 2 feet, 3 feet).

Activity Book
p. 8

Chapter 1   The Loch Ness Monster   **13**

Reteach and Reassess

Text Structure Ask students to name and describe the three features of an informational text. Then ask students to give examples from the selection for each feature.

Reading Strategy Ask students to write five facts about themselves. Tell them to write about things they like or activities they enjoy. Have students exchange their lists with partners. Tell students to write inferences about their partners based on the lists.

Elements of Literature Ask pairs of students to select a magazine article or an encyclopedia entry that includes visuals. Have pairs evaluate the benefits of the visuals. *Ask: How do the visuals help you understand the article?*

Reassess Have students use information from the selection to create a timeline that shows the history of people's search for and claimed sightings of the Loch Ness monster.

From Reading to Writing

Write a Paragraph That Describes

1. **Brainstorm** Have students brainstorm a list of descriptive phrases and expressions for the Loch Ness monster. Remind them to write down all their ideas and then pick the best ones.
2. **Draw-write-pair-share** Ask students to draw a picture of the Loch Ness monster and then write as much as they can about it. As students share with partners, they can help clarify ideas and add examples in their descriptions.
3. **Compose, Organize, and Revise a Record** Have pairs of students measure five items of varying lengths in the classroom. They should record the measurements in a chart that is organized with the heads: *Inches, Feet, Yards.* The items should be listed in the proper columns with their measurements. Then have two pairs of students measure each other's objects to check for accuracy. Students should revise their charts if necessary.
4. **Multi-level options** See MULTI-LEVEL OPTIONS on p. 12.

Across Content Areas: Math

Understand Length

Define and clarify Bring in rulers and metersticks to explain *length, U.S. Customary,* and *metric.* Have students practice measuring the objects in the room using both measurement systems. Have students compare the size of the different units for length in each system.

Answers
1. shorter 2. a meter 3. longer.

ASSESS

Say units of measurement and have students identify them as metric or U.S. Customary units.

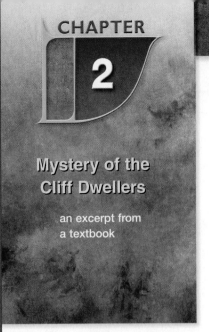

CHAPTER 2

Mystery of the Cliff Dwellers

an excerpt from a textbook

Into the Reading

Chapter Materials

Activity Book: *pp. 9–16*
Audio: *Unit 1, Chapter 2; CD 1, Track 2*
Student Handbook
Student CD-ROM: *Unit 1, Chapter 2*
Teacher Resource Book: *Lesson Plan, Teacher Resources, Reading Summary, Activity Book Answer Key*
Teacher Resource CD-ROM
Assessment Program: *Quiz, pp. 9–10; Teacher and Student Resources, pp. 115–144*
Assessment CD-ROM
Transparencies
The Heinle Newbury House Dictionary/CD-ROM
Web site: http://visions.heinle.com

Objectives

Paired reading Have students take turns reading the objectives section in pairs. *Ask: Is there an objective from the list that you can do already?*

Use Prior Knowledge

Talk About Your Community

Gather and organize Review the model web. Then arrange students in pairs to create a web about their community.

Objectives

Reading Find the main idea and supporting details as you read an excerpt from a textbook.

Listening and Speaking Distinguish fact and opinion.

Grammar Use prepositional phrases.

Writing Write an informational text.

Content Social Studies: Read a population map.

Use Prior Knowledge

Talk About Your Community

A community is a city, town, village, or neighborhood where people live. What is your community like?

1. Work with a partner. Describe your community.
   a. What is the name of your community?
   b. Is your community big, small, or medium-sized?
   c. What does your community look like? Are there many trees? Are there tall buildings?
   d. What do you like best about your community? What do you like least?

2. Use a web to brainstorm things about your community.

What It Looks Like: It has many trees and parks.

What I Like Least: There is no movie theater.

Name of Community: Smallwood

What I Like Best: It has an art museum.

Size: It is small.

14 Unit 1 Mysteries

MULTI-LEVEL OPTIONS *Build Vocabulary*

Newcomer Bring in samples of dirt and stones. Have students touch each and describe the differences. On the board, write: *farmland* and *cliffs.* Display pictures of both. Have students match the pictures to the materials in the bowls. Help them label the pictures.

Beginning Display pictures of cliffs, farmland, and a mesa. Hold up the pictures and point to each as you define them. *Say: A mesa is a high piece of land with a flat top. A cliff is a high piece of rock with a long drop. Farmland is land that is used to grow food.*

Intermediate Write on the board: *mesa, cliff, farmland,* and *mud.* Display pictures for each word. Have pairs look up each word in the dictionary. Then have the pairs match the pictures to the words. Have pairs write sentences for each word and share their sentences in groups.

Advanced On the board, write: *mesa, cliff, farmland,* and *mud.* Ask students to look up the words in the dictionary. Have them write a short story using all of the words. Challenge students to find and define other words that name landforms. Tell students to add the new words to their Personal Dictionaries.

Build Background

Archaeologists

Archaeologists are scientists who study the ways people lived long ago. They study what the people ate, how they got food, and where they lived. Archaeologists often dig into the earth where people lived long ago to find artifacts—parts of houses, tools, and even garbage. They study these things to learn about the culture—the ways of living—of the people of the past.

Content Connection

Today, some archaeologists study artifacts in Mesa Verde National Park in Colorado. This park has many Native American houses from long ago.

Build Vocabulary

Learn Context Words by Grouping

As you read or listen to the audio recording of "Mystery of the Cliff Dwellers," you will learn new words related to land.

Work with a partner. Read the words and definitions. Match each word with the correct definition. Use a dictionary if you need to, or ask your teacher. Write your answers in your Personal Dictionary.

Words	Definitions
1. mesa	**a.** land used to grow food
2. cliff	**b.** a high piece of land with a flat top (from the Spanish word for *table*)
3. farmland	**c.** a high piece of rock with a long drop
4. mud	**d.** a sticky mixture of water and dirt

Personal Dictionary · The Heinle Newbury House Dictionary · Activity Book p. 9 · Student CD-ROM

Content Connection
Social Studies

Build Vocabulary Have students work in small groups. Give each group a blank copy of a simple map of North America. Ask students to use a social studies text, an atlas, or another reference aid to locate different landforms in North America. Ask them to indicate the landforms on their maps with color-coded shading. Have them add a key that explains what each color represents.

Learning Styles
Intrapersonal

Build Background Ask students to do additional reading on archaeology. Tell them to find more information about being an archaeologist, including what kind of education and training is required and what kinds of tasks are involved. *Ask: Does this career interest you? Would you like to be an archaeologist? What would you like and dislike about being an archaeologist?* Have students record their answers in their Reading Logs.

Teacher Resource Book: *Reading Log, p. 64*

Build Background

Archaeologists

1. **Use pictures** Bring in pictures of archaeologists and archaeological sites. Have students guess what the archaeologists might find at the sites.
2. **Content Connection** Point out Spanish names on the map. Explain that the Spanish were the first Europeans to explore the area.

Build Vocabulary

Learn Context Words by Grouping

Teacher Resource Book: *Web, p. 37; Personal Dictionary, p. 63*

1. **Make a semantic word web** Write *land* on the board. *Say: High, pointed pieces of land are called mountains.* Have students suggest other terms about land. Add the words to make a semantic word web.
2. **Reading selection vocabulary** You may want to introduce the glossed words in the reading selection before students begin reading. Key words: *ancient, abandon, ancestors, dwellings, ruins, migrated, descendants.* Instruct students to write the words with correct spelling and their definitions in their Personal Dictionaries. Have them pronounce each word and divide it into syllables.
3. **Multi-level options** See MULTI-LEVEL OPTIONS on p. 14.

Answers
1. b **2.** c **3.** a **4.** d

 **ASSESS**

Have students write sentences using the new vocabulary words.

Text Structure

Informational Text

Define and explain Use questions to identify features: *What's it about?* (subject) *What did they say?* (quotes) *What's true?* (facts) *What does it mean?* (definitions) Ask each question and have students respond with the corresponding features.

Reading Strategy

Find the Main Idea and Supporting Details

1. **Teacher think aloud** Read the example. *Say: It says Atlanta is a great place. I see three reasons or details that tell me about the city.* Have students state the details.
2. **Multi-level options** See MULTI-LEVEL OPTIONS below.

ASSESS

Ask: What are the four features of an informational text? (subject, quotes, facts, definitions)

Text Structure

Informational Text

"Mystery of the Cliff Dwellers" is an **informational text.** It gives facts about a topic. This chart shows some features of this informational text.

"Mystery of the Cliff Dwellers" also includes **opinions.** Opinions are statements about what people think.

Informational Text	
Subject	what the text is about
Quotes	words that people have said; quotes usually have quotation marks (" . . . ") around them
Facts	information that is true
Definitions	the meanings of new words

Student CD-ROM

Reading Strategy

Find the Main Idea and Supporting Details

The **main idea** is the most important idea in a paragraph or text. Usually, you can find the main idea in the first sentence of a paragraph.

Supporting details give information about the main idea. Usually, you can find supporting details in the middle of a paragraph.

Look for main ideas and supporting details as you read or listen to "Mystery of the Cliff Dwellers." Write them in your Reading Log.

Main Idea —

> Atlanta is a great place to live. It has lovely sunny weather. The Atlanta Braves baseball team is there. It's a great team. Also, Atlanta has a good train system called MARTA.

Supporting Details

 Reading Log   Student CD-ROM

16 Unit 1 Mysteries

MULTI-LEVEL OPTIONS *Reading Strategy*

Newcomer *Say: The most important idea in a paragraph is the main idea. A main idea needs supporting details to make it interesting.* Hold up an empty box and *say: This is the main idea.* Add items to the box, such as pictures and pens. *Ask: What am I adding to make the box more interesting? These are supporting details.*

Beginning On the board, draw a box and write *sick* inside it. Add several outer boxes with: *doctor, fever,* and *medicine.* Explain that *sick* is the main idea and the other words are supporting details. Other main ideas that can be explored on this graphic organizer are: *homework, vacations, literature.*

Intermediate Ask pairs to choose objects. Have them discuss each object's main idea (*Example:* This is my notebook.) and supporting details. (*Example:* It's blue; I bring it to class; I write homework assignments in it.) Then have pairs create a graphic organizer to arrange their ideas.

Advanced Have students review paragraph 8 of "The Loch Ness Monster" (p. 7). Ask them to find the main ideas and supporting details. Suggest that they arrange their information in a graphic organizer and then compare their organizers in pairs.

The Mystery of the Cliff Dwellers

an excerpt from a textbook

17

Reading Selection Materials

Audio: *Unit 1, Chapter 2; CD 1, Track 2*
Teacher Resource Book: *Reading Summary, pp. 67–68*
Transparencies: #32, *Reading Summary*

Suggestions for Using Reading Summary

- Introduce new vocabulary or cognates.
- Cut the summary into strips, or jumble the sentences on an overhead transparency. Students put the sentences in order.
- Practice the reading strategy.
- Students read aloud or with a partner.
- Students paraphrase the summary.
- Students do a cloze activity.
- Students create a visual or graphic organizer, such as a timeline or storyboard, to illustrate the summary.
- Students paraphrase the summary.

Preview the Selection

Teacher Resource Book: *Know/Want to Know/Learned Chart (KWL), p. 42*

1. **Interpret the image** *Ask: Where is this place? What is near these buildings? How did people live there?*
2. **Make a KWL chart** Create a KWL chart. Have students brainstorm and list in column 1 what they know about Mesa Verde and the buildings in the picture. Then have students write questions about this place, such as who lived there, what they ate, when they lived there. List students' questions in column 2. Have students complete the KWL chart as they read the selection.
3. **Connect** Remind students that the unit theme is *mysteries*. Tell students they will read about the mysteries related to the people who lived there.

Content Connection
Technology

Have students work in pairs. Ask them to use the Internet or another electronic reference aid to find information about cliff dwellings. Suggest that students use the following key words: *cliff dwellings; Mesa Verde; Native American homes.* Suggest that students locate pictures of cliff dwellings and print out copies of any examples they find. Ask students to share their findings with the class.

Learning Styles
Musical

Use the Internet or a music store to find recordings of music performed by Native Americans of the Mesa Verde area. Play the recordings for the class. Ask students to write one paragraph that explains how they feel about the music they heard.

Read the Selection

1. **Use text features** Point out the illustration and have students compare it with the photo on p. 17. Direct students to the numbered paragraphs in the reading selection. Call attention to the glossed words. Remind students to use these features to help understanding.

2. **Teacher read aloud** Read the selection aloud. Pause to check understanding and to identify features: subject, facts, and definitions.

3. **Teacher think aloud** *Say: I see many questions about the Pueblo people in paragraph 2. So, I guess the questions are asking details about the main idea—the mystery of the Pueblo people.*

Sample Answer to Guide Question
There is a mystery about the ancient Pueblo people.

See Teacher Edition pp. 434–436 for a list of English-Spanish cognates in the reading selection.

1 An **ancient** people lived high in the cliffs . . . then **disappeared.** Or did they?

2 Mystery **surrounds** the ancestral Pueblo people. It **swirls** around them like the dry wind of the high country where they lived. Why did they build their homes in the cliffs? Why did they **abandon** those homes? And who were they, really? Even their name is a mystery. The Navajo called them the *Anasazi,* which means "ancient **enemies.**" Today Pueblo Indians call them their Pueblo **ancestors.** No one knows what they called themselves.

> **Find the Main Idea and Supporting Details**
>
> What is the main idea of this paragraph?

Audio
CD 1. Tr. 2

ancient very old	**abandon** leave something behind
disappeared went out of sight	**enemies** people who want to harm you
surrounds is all around something	**ancestors** people from whom you descend; for example, your grandparents, parents, and so on
swirls moves in a twisting and turning motion	

18 Unit 1 Mysteries

MULTI-LEVEL OPTIONS *Read the Selection*

Newcomer Play the audio. Read the pages aloud. *Ask: Did the ancient Pueblos live in cliffs?* (yes) *Do we know why they disappeared?* (no) *Do we know what they called themselves?* (no) *Did a group of them settle in Mesa Verde?* (yes) *Did they use ladders to get up the cliffs?* (yes)

Beginning Read the Reading Summary aloud. Then play the audio. *Ask: Where did the ancient Pueblo people build their homes?* (high in the cliffs) *Who called them the* Anasazi? (the Navajo) *When did they first settle in Mesa Verde?* (A.D. 550) *What did they use to get up to the dwellings?* (ladders)

Intermediate Have students do a paired reading. *Ask: Why is their name a mystery?* (No one knows what they called themselves.) *Why did they move to the higher dwellings?* (for protection; to cultivate more farmland)

Advanced Have students read independently. *Ask: Why are the ancient Pueblos a mystery?* (We don't know why they built homes in cliffs, why they left, or their real name.) *How do you think the cliff dwellings offered protection?* (good view of approaching enemies; hard for enemies to attack)

3   A group of these ancient people settled at what is now Mesa Verde, in Colorado, about A.D. 550. At first they dug **pit houses** in the mesa, or flat-topped hill. Around the year 1200, they began moving off the top of the mesa into **high-altitude dwellings** they built of stone and mud under the cliff **ledges.** No one knows why they made this move. It may have been to **cultivate** more farmland. Some archaeologists think they moved for **protection.**

"The cliff dwellings seem safe to me," says Kathrine Warren, ten, of Durango, Colorado. "People could climb up and pull the **ladders** behind them so their enemies couldn't get to them."   4

> **Find the Main Idea and Supporting Details**
>
> The main idea of this paragraph is that the cliff dwellings seem safe. What detail does Kathrine Warren give to support this idea?

---

pit houses   square houses that are dug into the ground
high-altitude   high above the ground
dwellings   places where people live
ledges   flat areas of rock that stick out

cultivate   prepare land to grow food, trees, and flowers
protection   something that keeps you from being hurt
ladders   sets of steps used for climbing

Chapter 2 Mystery of the Cliff Dwellers   **19**

Read the Selection

1. **Use the illustration** Ask students to describe the houses or dwellings in the illustration. Use the illustration to introduce new vocabulary: *dwellings, ledges, ladders.*
2. **Paired reading** Read the selection aloud. Then have students reread it in pairs.
3. **Identify facts and opinions** *Ask: When did the ancient people settle in Mesa Verde?* (about 550) *When did they move to the cliff houses?* (around 1200) *What does Kathrine say about the cliff dwellings?* (They seem safe.) *Does Kathrine give a fact or an opinion?* (an opinion) *How do you know?* (It is what she thinks about the houses. There is no proof.)
4. **Multi-level options** See MULTI-LEVEL OPTIONS on p. 18.

Sample Answer to Guide Question
People in the houses could pull up the ladders so enemies could not get into their houses.

❯ Punctuation

Question marks

Remind students that all sentences must have end punctuation. Tell them that a sentence that asks a question must have a question mark at the end. *Ask: Why is there a question mark at the end of paragraph 1?* (It shows that *Or did they* is a sentence that asks a question.) *Do you see other questions in paragraph 2?* (sentences 3–5) Demonstrate correct intonation for questions. Have students repeat after you.

Apply Tell students to correct these sentences by adding question marks. Write on the board:

Who would like to go first

Did you remember to do your homework

How many chairs will we need

Have you ever seen this movie

Where is the closest gas station

Am I in the right room

When was your birthday

Read the Selection

1. **Use the illustration** Ask students to describe the roles of women and men from the drawing.

2. **Locate pronunciations using glossaries and other sources** Have students locate the pronunciation key for *metates* in paragraph 5 and *kiva* and *sipapu* in paragraph 6. Remind students that informational texts often give pronunciation keys within the reading and in glossaries at the back of the book. Also remind them that other sources, such as CD-ROM dictionaries or online dictionaries, show pronunciations of words. Have students use one of these other sources to locate the pronunciations of *metates, kiva,* and *sipapu* and any other words from the reading that they are not familiar with.

3. **Paired reading** Read the selection aloud. Have students reread the selection with partners. *Say: Leighana thinks it would be great to live in the cliff dwellings. Do you agree with her? Why or why not?*

Sample Answer to Guide Question
The Pueblo people grew most of their food and used dams and reservoirs to store water.

---

5   Kathrine visited the **ruins** of Cliff Palace, one of the cliff dwellings, with Leighana Sisneros and Landon Wigton, both ten and from Durango. "It would have been **neat** to be an Anasazi kid," Leighana says. "But," Kathrine observes, "you wouldn't have had things like **lightbulbs,** and I would have missed reading books." Landon adds, "There weren't any grocery stores." But the ancestral Pueblo people didn't need grocery stores. They grew most of their own food. The men planted corn, squash, and beans on top of the mesa. They **conserved** water in the dry **climate** by building **dams** and **reservoirs.** The women ground the corn on metates (meh TAH tays), or **concave** stones, and cooked it in pottery they made with ridged surfaces. They often painted their serving bowls.

> **Find the Main Idea and Supporting Details**
>
> The ancestral Pueblo people did not need grocery stores. Which details support this idea?

ruins broken parts of old buildings	**dams** walls built across rivers to stop the water from flowing
neat slang for "great"	
lightbulbs round glass parts of electric lights	**reservoirs** bodies of water saved for use
conserved saved	**concave** curving inward
climate the type of weather that a place has	

20   Unit 1 Mysteries

MULTI-LEVEL OPTIONS *Read the Selection*

Newcomer *Ask: Did the Anasazi have lightbulbs, books, or grocery stores?* (no) *Did they grow their own food?* (yes) *Did they build dams?* (yes) *Did they grind and cook corn?* (yes) *Is a kiva an underground chamber?* (yes) *Were women allowed in the kiva?* (no) *Do scientists have ideas about why they left?* (yes)

Beginning *Ask: What modern things did the Anasazi not have?* (lightbulbs, books, grocery stores) *How did they get their food?* (They grew it.) *What foods did they grow?* (corn, squash, beans) *What is a kiva?* (an underground chamber) *Who was allowed in a kiva?* (men) *When were the cliffs abandoned?* (by 1300)

Intermediate *Ask: Why didn't the Anasazi need grocery stores?* (They grew their own food.) *What did they do with the corn they grew?* (They ground and cooked it.) *Why do scientists think they abandoned the area?* (drought, erosion, warfare, disease) *Who might be their descendants?* (Pueblo Indians of Arizona and New Mexico)

Advanced *Ask: Why do you think they painted their serving bowls?* (decoration; identification) *How does life for Anasazi women compare with life for women today?* (They had to work hard but weren't allowed in the kiva. Today, women can do anything.)

6 "We climbed down into a kiva (KEE vuh)," says Landon. A kiva is an **underground chamber.** In its floor is a sipapu (SEE pah poo), or hole, symbolizing an opening between the **physical** world and the place where the Pueblo ancestors believed that life began.

7 "Only the men were allowed in the kiva," Landon says. There they held religious ceremonies and gathered to talk, perhaps about the weather as people do today. By the late 1200s, the weather must have been on their minds a lot. Archaeologists know that for many years little rain fell in the region. By 1300 the cliff dwellings of Mesa Verde had been abandoned. "Maybe the people left because of the **drought,**" says Leighana. Some scientists agree. They think, too, that soil **erosion,** warfare, and disease may have driven them away. After so many years, the mysteries remain. But the ancient people probably did not **vanish.** Archaeologists and modern Pueblo people believe they **migrated** south. Today, through their **descendants**—the Pueblo Indians of Arizona and New Mexico—the ancient ones live on.

> ### Find the Main Idea and Supporting Details
>
> Archaeologists have many ideas about why the ancestral Pueblo people left Mesa Verde. This is a main idea of paragraph 7. What details support this main idea?

underground located below Earth's surface
chamber a room
physical related to objects in the real world
drought a time of little or no rainfall
erosion when soil washes away or blows away because of the weather

vanish disappear suddenly
migrated moved from one place to another
descendants your children, grandchildren, and so forth

Chapter 2 Mystery of the Cliff Dwellers **21**

 Spelling

Irregular plurals

Remind students that many words are made plural by adding -s or -es. Then explain that some words have irregular plural forms. Write on the board and *say: person, man, people, men.* **Ask:** *Which words are singular?* (person, man) *Which are plural?* (people, men) Direct students to paragraph 5. **Ask:** *Can you find another irregular plural?* (women) *What is the singular form?* (woman)

Evaluate Your Reading Strategy

Find the Main Idea and Supporting Details
Say: You have practiced an important reading strategy. Now you can decide how well you have done. Does this statement describe how you read?

> I look for the main idea and supporting details as I read a text. Finding the main ideas and supporting details helps me understand what the author is explaining.

Read the Selection

1. **Use the text features** Ask students to describe the person in the photo. Direct attention to the boldfaced words. Point out pronunciation of words in parentheses. Help students pronounce the new words.
2. **Teacher read aloud** Continue reading the story as students follow along. *Ask: Why was the weather important in the late 1200s?* (There had been very little rain.) *Would you have liked being an Anasazi? Why?*
3. **Locate derivations using dictionaries** Have students look at these glossed words and determine what words they are derived from: *conserved, reservoirs, erosion, migrated, descendants.* Have students check the derivations in a print, an online, or a CD-ROM dictionary.
4. **Multi-level options** See MULTI-LEVEL OPTIONS on p. 20.

Sample Answer to Guide Question
People may have left because of a drought, soil erosion, wars, or disease.

Across Selections

Teacher Resource Book: *Venn Diagram, p. 35*

Make comparisons and contrasts Compare the mystery of cliff dwellings with the mystery of the Loch Ness monster. *Ask: Who is trying to explain these mysteries?* (archeologists, scientists, reporters, ordinary people) *What clues are they finding?* (houses, pots, tools; photos and some people's reports) Record the ideas on a Venn diagram.

Spelling, Punctuation, Capitalization

After the Reading Comprehension section, students will practice spelling, punctuation, and capitalization in the Activity Book.

Beyond the Reading

Reading Comprehension

Question-Answer Relationships

Sample Answers

1. Anasazi or "ancient enemies"
2. around A.D. 550
3. A kiva is an underground room.
4. the Pueblo Indians of Arizona and New Mexico
5. The drought would mean there would not be enough water; it would be difficult to carry water up to the high cliffs.
6. drought, soil erosion, wars, or disease
7. The Pueblo people got their food by growing it and preparing it. We can grow some of our food and we usually prepare our food. It's different because we get most of our food from stores and we use many machines and appliances to help prepare our food.
8. Religious ceremonies are different; the men and women do not have to spend so much time growing their food.
9. Women usually prepare the food.

Build Reading Fluency

Read Silently and Aloud

Assessment Program: *Reading Fluency Chart, p. 116*

When students have completed the reading fluency activity, record their progress in the Reading Fluency Chart.

Reading Comprehension

Question-Answer Relationships (QAR)

"Right There" Questions

1. **Recall Facts** What did the Navajo call the ancestral Pueblo people?
2. **Recall Facts** About what year did a group of ancestral Pueblo people move to Mesa Verde?
3. **Identify** What is a kiva?
4. **Recall Facts** Who are the descendants of the ancestral Pueblo people?

"Think and Search" Questions

5. **Analyze Cause and Effect** Look at paragraphs 5–7. Why would a drought cause the ancestral Pueblo people to move?
6. **Analyze Cause and Effect** Name three reasons why the ancestral Pueblo people may have left the cliff dwellings.

"Author and You" Question

7. **Compare and Contrast** How did the ancestral Pueblo people get their food? How is this similar to how you get your food? How is it different?

"On Your Own" Questions

8. **Determine Distinctive Characteristics of Culture** In what ways is your culture different from the Anasazi culture?
9. **Determine Common Characteristics of Culture** In what ways is your culture similar to the Anasazi culture?

Activity Book
p. 10

Student
CD-ROM

Build Reading Fluency

Read Silently and Aloud

Reading silently for practice and reading aloud for expression are two important ways to become a fluent reader.

1. Listen to the audio recording of "Mystery of the Cliff Dwellers."
2. Follow along with the reading on page 18.
3. Read silently paragraphs 1–3 two times.
4. With a partner read aloud.
5. Your partner will time you reading aloud.

MULTI-LEVEL OPTIONS *Elements of Literature*

Newcomer Ask a student his/her name. Then write the exact words on the board: _____ *says, "My name is _____." Say: When we write, we put quotation marks around the words that people say.*

Beginning Have students work in groups of four. Instruct each pair to conduct a short conversation while the other pair records it on paper. Have them add quotation marks and commas as necessary.

Intermediate Ask pairs of students to write a paragraph about a conversation between an Anasazi boy and girl. Remind students to identify the speakers. Help them to use correct punctuation. Have students trade their paragraphs with another pair.

Advanced Ask students to write a narrative that includes dialogue. Remind them to use quotes and commas correctly. Have them exchange narratives for peer review. Ask students to revise as necessary. Then have them share their narratives with the class.

Listen, Speak, Interact

Distinguish Fact and Opinion

"Mystery of the Cliff Dwellers" includes quotes from people who are visiting Mesa Verde. Some of these quotes give facts, and some give opinions. Study the difference between facts and opinions.

Fact	You can show that a fact is true. Example: The moon comes up in the east.
Opinion	An opinion is what you believe or think. Example: The moon is beautiful tonight.

1. Work with a partner. One of you will read the quotes in paragraph 4 aloud. The other will read the quotes in paragraph 5 aloud.
2. As you read your quotes, your partner should not look at the reading.
3. Ask your partner to identify one fact and one opinion from the quotes.
4. Discuss your partner's answers.
5. Do the same thing with your partner's reading.

Elements of Literature

Write Quotes

"Mystery of the Cliff Dwellers" uses **quotes.** Writers use quotes to tell us the exact words that people say. Look at these quotes from paragraphs 5 and 6:

Landon adds**,** **"**There weren't any grocery stores.**"**

"We climbed down into a kiva**,"** says Landon.

The quotes can come before or after the name of the person who said the words.

How to Punctuate a Quote		
Quotation Marks	" . . . "	around the words the person says
Comma	,	• after the quote if the quote comes first • before the quote if the quote comes last

1. Ask a partner the following questions. Your partner should answer in complete sentences.
   a. What is your favorite food?
   b. What is your favorite color?
2. Write each answer as a quote.

Activity Book
p. 11

Student
CD-ROM

Chapter 2 Mystery of the Cliff Dwellers **23**

Listen, Speak, Interact

Distinguish Fact and Opinion

■ Teacher Resource Book: *Reading Log, p. 64*

1. **Reread in pairs** Pair beginning and advanced students. Have them read alternate paragraphs and identify the facts and opinions.
2. **Newcomers** Reread with this group. On the board, write key words for opinions: *I think, I feel, It seems.* Point out that facts can be proven or are true for everyone. Have students record the facts and opinions in their Reading Logs.

Answer
Sample answers: **3.** paragraph 4—fact: People could climb up and pull the ladders.; opinion: The cliff dwellings seem safe. **5.** paragraph 5—fact: You wouldn't have lightbulbs.; opinion: It would have been neat to be an Anasazi kid.

Elements of Literature

Write Quotes

1. **Write quotes** Write the quotation on the board. Call attention to the placement of quotation marks and commas. Have students practice punctuating other quotations.
2. **Provide examples** Discuss times when quotations are used, such as in newspaper articles, notes from meetings, and famous lines.
3. **Multi-level options** See MULTI-LEVEL OPTIONS on p. 22.

Answer
2. *Sample answers:* **a.** Ana said, "My favorite food is spaghetti." **b.** "Blue is my favorite color," said Martin.

 **ASSESS**

On the board, write: *Binh says It is a beautiful day.* Have students copy the sentence and add punctuation for the quotation.

Content Connection
Science

Explain that carbon dating is an important tool in archaeology. Tell students that carbon dating is a chemical procedure that helps archaeologists determine the age of an artifact. Have students work in groups to learn how carbon dating works. Ask students to create visual aids, such as flowcharts or labeled diagrams, to illustrate their findings.

Learning Styles
Kinesthetic

Make signs that show commas, quotation marks, periods, and question marks. Then write on index cards dialogue tags, such as *Carlos said* or *Miko asked,* and dialogue text, such as *I like pizza* and *Where is my hat.* Shuffle the cards and deal them to students. Have students take the appropriate punctuation signs and arrange themselves into properly punctuated sentences.

Word Study

Root Words and Suffixes

☐ Teacher Resource Book: *Web, p. 37*

Make a semantic word web Create a word map for roots and suffixes for *archae* ("very old"), *-logy* ("study of"), *-st* (designates a person). Have students create their own word maps for the other words on the chart.

Answers
1. geologist 2. biologist 3. entomologist

Grammar Focus

Use Prepositional Phrases

Apply Ask where students do different activities. Have them use prepositional phrases in their responses. Point out prepositions of location they use.

Answers
a. in the library b. in the pool c. in Mesa Verde
d. in the kiva

✓ ASSESS

Have students match a biologist, an archaeologist, and a geologist with the corresponding subjects: earth, life, very old things.

Word Study

Root Words and Suffixes

The word *archaeology* comes from two Greek words. The **root word** *archae* means "very old." The suffix (end of the word) *-logy* comes from a Greek word that means "word." In English, *-logy* usually means "study of."

The names of many sciences are formed from Greek words in this way. Guess what these sciences are about.

Root	Meaning	Suffix	Name of Science
bio	life		biology
geo	earth	+ logy	geology
entomo	insect		entomology

An **archaeologist** is a person who studies archaeology. Notice how this word is formed.

archaeolog~~y~~ + ist

You drop the *y* and add *ist*.
Copy and complete these sentences in your Personal Dictionary.

1. A _____ studies Earth.
2. A _____ studies life.
3. A _____ studies insects.

Personal Dictionary   Activity Book p. 12   Student CD-ROM

Grammar Focus

Use Prepositional Phrases

Prepositions are a part of speech. A preposition followed by a noun or pronoun is called a **prepositional phrase.**

One use of prepositional phrases is to say *where* something happens.

The people lived **in the cliffs.**

The prepositional phrase *in the cliffs* tells where the people lived.

Answer the following questions on a piece of paper. Use a prepositional phrase from the box in each of your answers.

in Mesa Verde	in the kiva
in the library	in the pool

a. Where are the students studying?
   They are studying _____ .
b. Where is Marta swimming?
   She is swimming _____ .
c. Where are the cliff dwellings?
   They are _____ .
d. Where did the men hold ceremonies?
   They held them _____ .

Activity Book pp. 13–14   Student Handbook   Student CD-ROM

24   Unit 1   Mysteries

MULTI-LEVEL OPTIONS *From Reading to Writing*

Newcomer Have students draw floor plans of their homes. Help them label the rooms and features. Ask students to add elements such as furniture and personal belongings that give clues about the people who live there and what they do in each room.

Beginning Ask students to tell partners about their homes. Provide these starters: *I live in a(n) _____. It has _____ rooms. I live there with _____.* Ask students to report what they learned about their partners in small groups.

Intermediate Have students create a pre-writing chart with the column headings *Dwelling Type, Interior, Exterior, People Who Live There.* Ask them to complete the chart with information that answers questions a–d. Have them use the charts to write their paragraphs.

Advanced Have pairs exchange paragraphs for peer review. Reviewers should check for a clear main idea that is supported with details. They should also check for prepositional phrases. Have students revise their paragraphs based on their partners' reviews.

From Reading to Writing

Write an Informational Text

Imagine that you are an archaeologist 500 years in the future. You are studying where you live today. Write an informational text that tells people about this home of the past. Write one paragraph.

1. Answer these questions:
   a. What is the place like? Is it an apartment or a house?
   b. What does it look like? How many rooms does it have?
   c. How many people lived there?
   d. How did the people live?
2. Use prepositional phrases that tell *where* something happened.
3. Exchange paragraphs with a partner. Proofread (look for errors in) your partner's paragraph.

Reading Log   Activity Book p. 15   Student Handbook

Across Content Areas

Read a Population Map

To find the population of Native Americans in a state, look at the state's color on the population map. Find the same color in the legend. The numbers next to the colored square tell the population of Native Americans in that state.

Complete these research notes on a piece of paper.

The states of ____ , ____ , ____ , and ____ have the most Native Americans. They all have between 134,355 and ____ Native Americans living there. The Native American population in ____ is between 36,355 and 85,698.

LEGEND
Native American State Populations
- 134,355–252,240
- 36,355–85,698
- 18,541–27,776

Activity Book p. 16

From Reading to Writing

Write an Informational Text

1. **Make a picture** Have students suggest rooms, activities, and other information to include in their texts. List ideas on the board. Students can make pictures to illustrate their informational texts.
2. **Think-pair-share** In pairs, have students explain their pictures or ideas before writing descriptions of the rooms and activities.
3. **Multi-level options** See MULTI-LEVEL OPTIONS on p. 24.

Across Content Areas: Social Studies

Read a Population Map

1. **Use a map** Direct attention to the map and legend key. Ask what the different colors on the map mean. Have students identify states with different ranges of population based on the colors of the state.
2. **Connect** Have students identify different ethnic or indigenous groups in other countries.

Answers

California, Arizona, New Mexico, Oklahoma; 252,240; Texas

ASSESS

Have students write a quiz question about the population map. Ask students to exchange papers and answer their classmate's question.

Reteach and Reassess

Text Structure Write on the board: *subject, quotes, facts,* and *definitions.* Ask students to give examples from the selection. Discuss the ways quotes, facts, and definitions add interest and help readers better understand an informational text.

Reading Strategy Draw a simple chair with four legs. *Say: A main idea is like the seat of the chair. Supporting details are like legs. A chair won't stand if it doesn't have enough legs.* Write a main idea on the seat. (*Example:* Winter is the best season.) Have

students provide "legs." (*Example:* fun holidays, sledding, skiing, no mosquitoes)

Elements of Literature Have students rewrite paragraph 2 (p. 18) as a conversation between Kathrine and Leighana. Remind them to add punctuation as needed.

Reassess Have students write one-paragraph summaries of the selection. Remind them to include a main idea and supporting details.

CHAPTER

3

Yawning

an informational text
by Haleh V. Samiei

Into the Reading

Chapter Materials

Activity Book: *pp. 17–24*
Audio: *Unit 1, Chapter 3; CD 1, Track 3*
Student Handbook
Student CD-ROM: *Unit 1, Chapter 3*
Teacher Resource Book: *Lesson Plan, Teacher Resources, Reading Summary, Activity Book Answer Key*
Teacher Resource CD-ROM
Assessment Program: *Quiz, pp. 11–12; Teacher and Student Resources, pp. 115–144*
Assessment CD-ROM
Transparencies
The Heinle Newbury House Dictionary/CD-ROM
Web site: http://visions.heinle.com

Objectives

Offer observations Read the objectives. *Say: We've read other informational texts. What other informational texts did we read?* ("The Loch Ness Monster" and "Mystery of the Cliff Dwellers")

Use Prior Knowledge

Discuss Yawning

Relate to personal experience Ask students to suggest words and experiences related to yawning. *Ask: When do you yawn?*

Answers
1. a. T b. T c. T d. T

Objectives

Reading Compare the text to your own experiences as you read an informational text.

Listening and Speaking Give an informational presentation.

Grammar Write dependent clauses.

Writing Write a paragraph using chronology.

Content Math: Read a bar graph.

Use Prior Knowledge

Discuss Yawning

You will read a selection about why people yawn. When people yawn, they open their mouth. They breathe in deeply. Then they breathe out. This picture shows a person yawning.

What do you know about yawning?

1. Read each statement below. Write *T* if the statement is true. Write *F* if the statement is false. Write your answers on a separate piece of paper.
   a. People yawn when they are tired.
   b. People yawn when they are bored.
   c. People yawn to stay awake.
   d. Some animals yawn.

2. Discuss your answers with another student.

MULTI-LEVEL OPTIONS *Build Vocabulary*

Newcomer Write on the board and *say: opposites: on/off.* Demonstrate how these words are opposites by turning the lights on and off. Then write: *hot/_____* and *high/_____.* Demonstrate and wait for a volunteer to call out the opposite. (cold, low) Provide answers if no one knows them.

Beginning Write on the board and *say: opposites: on/off.* Demonstrate how these words are opposites by turning the lights on and off. Write and *say: big/little, wet/dry.* Ask students to find pictures that show big and little items and wet and dry things.

Intermediate Divide students into small groups. Have each group select a short popular song, poem, jingle, or nursery rhyme. Ask groups to rewrite the text by replacing all the words they can with antonyms. Ask each team to recite their new text. Have other groups guess the original title.

Advanced Ask students to select antonym pairs from their completed charts. Have students write sentences using the selected pairs. Tell them that they can look up words in the dictionary if necessary. Ask students to share their sentences in small groups.

Build Background

Oxygen

People and animals need oxygen to live. Oxygen is part of the air that we breathe. We cannot smell, taste, or see oxygen. When we breathe in, oxygen from the air goes into our bodies. Our bodies use this oxygen to do many things. For example, oxygen helps us turn food into energy.

Content Connection
Fish also breathe oxygen. They get oxygen from the water that they live in.

Build Vocabulary

Identify Antonyms

An **antonym** is a word that has the opposite meaning of another word. For example, *little* and *big* are antonyms.

You can use the meaning of a word to find its antonym. You know that *little* means "not big." This helps you know that *big* is the antonym of *little*.

1. Copy the chart in your Personal Dictionary.
2. Write the correct antonym for each word. Choose one of these words:

   awake   calm   disagree

3. Ask your teacher or use a dictionary to find the meanings of any words that you do not know.

Word	Meaning	Antonym
little	not big	big
nervous	worried about something	
agree	have the same idea	
sleepy	tired	

Personal Dictionary

The Heinle Newbury House Dictionary

Activity Book p. 17

Student CD-ROM

Chapter 3 Yawning **27**

Community Connection

Build Vocabulary Have students find signs in the community that show words that have possible antonyms. Have them replace the words with antonyms. (*Examples:* Big Al's Used Cars / Little Al's New Cars; High Street / Low Street) Then have students draw simple maps labeled with their new signs. Ask them to add a title, such as *Antonym Town* or *Oppositeville.* You may wish to have students work in pairs or groups.

Learning Styles
Mathematical

Build Background Tell students that water is made up of oxygen and hydrogen; the ozone layer, which helps shield us from the sun, is a form of oxygen; and carbon dioxide, which plants need, is made up of carbon and oxygen. Have students find chemical equations for each of these compounds. *Ask: What if there were no oxygen?* Have students find other important oxygen compounds.

Build Background

Oxygen

1. **Use an illustration** Bring in illustrations of the respiratory system. Have students follow the flow of air from the nose or mouth to the lungs. *Ask: Why is it important to get oxygen?* (It's needed to live.)
2. **Content Connection** Fish have gills that get oxygen from water. People and animals use lungs to get oxygen. *Ask: Why can't people breathe under water?* (They don't have gills.) *Why can't fish breathe on land?* (They don't have lungs.)

Build Vocabulary

Identify Antonyms

Teacher Resource Book: *Personal Dictionary, p. 63*

1. **Contrast and analyze** Say adjectives and have students suggest their opposites. Explain antonyms. Have students guess or look up the antonyms.
2. **Reading selection vocabulary** You may want to introduce the glossed words in the reading selection before students begin reading. Key words: *pressure, ear drums, contagious, on purpose, purpose, habit.* Instruct students to write the words with correct spelling and their definitions in their Personal Dictionaries. Have them pronounce each word and divide it into syllables.
3. **Multi-level options** See MULTI-LEVEL OPTIONS on p. 26.

Answer
2. nervous: calm; agree: disagree; sleepy: awake

ASSESS

Have students draw pictures to illustrate two antonym pairs.

Text Structure

Informational Text

Define and explain Have students give examples or explain the features in the graphic organizer.

Reading Strategy

Compare the Text to Your Own Experiences

Teacher Resource Book: *Sunshine Organizer, p. 40*

1. **Sunshine interview** Draw a Sunshine Organizer with *yawning* in the center and with the question words *who, what, when, where, why* on each "ray." Have students work in pairs to write questions for a sunshine interview. Have pairs interview other pairs and record their responses.
2. **Multi-level options** SEE MULTI-LEVEL OPTIONS below.

ASSESS

Have students define: *purpose, facts, definitions.*

Text Structure

Informational Text

"Yawning" is an **informational text.** An informational text gives facts and details about a topic. The chart shows some features of an informational text.

When you read an informational text, you learn new things. Read this reading selection slowly. This will help you understand the facts in it.

Informational Text	
Purpose	to teach us about something
Facts	give us information and details about the subject
Definitions	explain the meanings of new words

Student CD-ROM

Reading Strategy

Compare the Text to Your Own Experiences

Everyone yawns sometimes. Try it right now. Open your mouth. Breathe in. Breathe out.

Can you remember times when you have yawned? Why do you think you did it? As you read the selection, compare what the author says about yawning to your own experiences. This strategy will help you better understand what you read.

As you read, ask yourself these questions:

1. What do I already know about what I am reading?
2. What is the new information that I am learning?

Student CD-ROM

MULTI-LEVEL OPTIONS *Reading Strategy*

Newcomer Display a world map. Ask students to name countries they or their families have lived in or visited. Have students raise their hands to show how many have been to the same countries. Have students share experiences. Help students to note common experiences.

Beginning Display a world map. *Ask: Where have you lived or visited?* Have students point out countries on the map. Tell them to write a paragraph that describes some of their experiences in other countries. Ask them to share their paragraphs and compare experiences.

Intermediate Display a world map. Have students point out what cities or countries they have lived in or visited. *Ask: What experiences did you have there?* Have them find a book, an article, or a story about somewhere they have lived or visited and compare the text to their own experiences.

Advanced *Ask: What kind of information can you learn from a book about a country?* (places, setting, geography, etc.) *How does this experience compare to the experience of living or visiting there?* Have students make a chart to compare the text to their own experiences.

Yawning

an informational text
by Haleh V. Samiei

29

Reading Selection Materials

Audio: *Unit 1, Chapter 3; CD 1, Track 3*
Teacher Resource Book: *Reading Summary,*
   pp. 69–70
Transparencies: *#31, Reading Summary*

Suggestions for Using Reading Summary

- Introduce new vocabulary or cognates.
- Cut the summary into strips, or jumble the sentences on an overhead transparency. Students put the sentences in order.
- Practice the reading strategy.
- Students read aloud or with a partner.
- Students paraphrase the summary.
- Students do a cloze activity.
- Students create a visual or graphic organizer, such as a timeline or storyboard, to illustrate the summary.
- Students paraphrase the summary.

Preview the Selection

1. **Teacher think aloud** Have students examine the photo and title. *Say: The title is "Yawning." I yawn. Everybody yawns. What is strange about yawning? This unit is about mysteries. Is there a mystery about yawning? This is an informational text. As I read, I want to look for facts and some mystery about yawning.* Allow students to make guesses about what the mystery about yawning is.
2. **Connect** Have students recall the meaning of *mystery.* Tell students they will read about a mystery related to a common, everyday act: yawning.

Cultural Connection

Tell students that yawning without covering your mouth or when someone is speaking to you is considered rude in the American culture. Ask students to suggest behaviors that are considered rude in other cultures they know about. For example, in many countries, pointing with one finger is considered rude, which is why flight attendants and many tour guides point using *two* fingers.

Learning Styles
Kinesthetic

Ask students to look at the picture on p. 29. *Ask: What is this person doing?* (yawning) Remind students that, like laughing or sneezing, many people have their own "personal" yawns. Ask students to demonstrate different types of yawns—from subtle, quiet yawns to loud, exaggerated, full-body yawns.

Read the Selection

1. **Use text features** Direct students to the illustration and labels. Explain their purpose and use. Then call attention to glossed words and have students find their meanings at the bottom of the page.

2. **Shared reading** Play the audio or read the selection to the students. Reread or have volunteers read different paragraphs.

3. **Compare the text to your own experiences** Ask volunteers to yawn. Have others watch and notice if the description in the first paragraph is the same as their experiences. Ask students if they yawn when they are bored, as described in paragraph 3.

Sample Answer to Guide Question
Yes. Why are yawns "contagious"?

See Teacher Edition pp. 434–436 for a list of English-Spanish cognates in the reading selection.

---

1 This article is going to **cast a spell** on you. As you read it, **pressure** will build behind your **ear drums,** and you'll lift your eyebrows and open your mouth wide. You'll hold this **position** for about six seconds as you take in a deep breath and then let a short one out.

2 Don't **panic.** It's just a **contagious** yawn. When you read about yawning, see someone yawning, or just think about yawning, you usually yawn yourself. But what's the purpose of yawning? Most people think that the answer is simple. You yawn when you're bored or sleepy. Some people think you yawn because you need **extra** oxygen. Is it true?

3 Robert Provine, a scientist at the University of Maryland-Baltimore County, set out to find out. The first thing he did was to test whether people yawn when they're bored. Provine had no problem boring an unlucky group of people by making them watch a video of color-bar **patterns.** A different, lucky group got to watch a music video. No need to say that the people in the first group won the yawning contest.

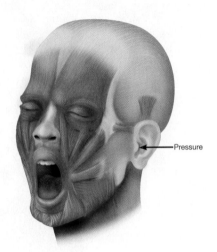
Pressure

> **Compare the Text to Your Own Experiences**
>
> Do you yawn when you see other people yawning? What questions do you have about this?

Audio
CD 1. Tr. 3

cast a spell cause a special effect	**panic** get very scared
pressure force, tension	**contagious** able to be given to others
ear drums parts inside the ear; they move so you can hear sound	**extra** more
position where something is	**patterns** designs of regular shapes and lines

30 Unit 1 Mysteries

MULTI-LEVEL OPTIONS *Read the Selection*

Newcomer Play the audio. Read the pages aloud. *Ask: Can a yawn be contagious?* (yes) *Is Robert Provine a scientist?* (yes) *Did he test people to see why they yawn?* (yes) *Do people only yawn at night?* (no) *Are yawning and stretching linked?* (yes) *Do sky divers, violinists, and athletes yawn?* (yes)

Beginning Read the Reading Summary aloud. *Ask: What did the people in the first test watch?* (music video, color patterns) *Who yawned more?* (color-pattern group) *When did the people in the second test yawn?* (night, morning) *Who else yawns?* (sky divers, athletes, nervous people)

Intermediate Have students do a paired reading. *Ask: What might you do when you think about yawning?* (yawn) *What did Provine want to find out?* (why people yawn) *What did his first test prove?* (People yawn when bored.) *Why might musicians and athletes yawn?* (to focus their attention when nervous)

Advanced Have students read independently. *Ask: What is being described in the first paragraph?* (yawning) *What did Provine's second test prove?* (People don't only yawn when they are sleepy.) *How do we know that yawning and stretching are linked?* (Paralyzed people's muscles jerk when they yawn.)

4 To see if people yawn more when they're sleepy, Provine had his students keep a yawn **diary** for a week. Whenever they yawned, they had to write down the time. As you might guess, they yawned at night when they were tired and sleepy. But Provine also found that they yawned when they woke up in the morning.

5 When he thought about it, he realized that when people **stretch,** there's a good chance they'll also yawn. In fact, other scientists have also noticed that yawning and stretching are **linked.** For example, the muscles of people **paralyzed** on one side of their body **jerk** as they yawn, even though they can't make the muscles move **on purpose.**

6 People also yawn when they can't possibly be bored or sleepy. Sky divers yawn just as they're about to jump out of an airplane. Concert **violinists** yawn just before going on stage. Olympic athletes yawn just before a big **competition.** Provine thinks these people may be yawning because they're nervous. He thinks that when you're nervous, sleepy, bored, or have just awakened, yawning can help focus your attention.

> **Compare the Text to Your Own Experiences**
>
> Have you ever yawned when you were nervous? Explain.

diary   a book where people describe what happened to them each day and how they felt
stretch   make a body part longer by pushing it out
linked   connected
paralyzed   not able to move your body
jerk   move suddenly

on purpose   meaning to do something
violinists   people who play the violin, a musical instrument
competition   an event in which people try to do something better than one another, such as a race

Chapter 3   Yawning   **31**

UNIT 1 • CHAPTER 3
Reading Selection

Read the Selection

1. **Use the photo** Direct students to the photo. Ask them to describe what the person is doing and to guess if the person is tired, bored, or saw another person yawn.
2. **Paired reading** Play the audio or read the selection aloud. Have students reread in pairs.
3. **Locale derivations using dictionaries** Have students look at these glossed words and determine what words they are derived from: *linked, paralyzed, violinists, competition.* Have students check the derivations in a print, an online, or a CD-ROM dictionary.
4. **Compare the text to your own experiences** Ask questions to help students compare what is in the text about stretching and nervousness with their own experiences.
5. **Multi-level options** See MULTI-LEVEL OPTIONS on p. 30.

Sample Answer to Guide Question
Yes, before a test, I am nervous and sometimes I yawn when the teacher starts passing out the exam.

---

th **Spelling**

You're vs. your

Write on the board and *say: you're* and *your.* Tell students that *you're* is a contraction of the words *you are.* Then tell students that *your* is a possessive adjective that means "belonging to you." *Ask: Which one of these words do you see in paragraph 1?* (your) *What does it mean?* (belonging to you) *Which one of these words do you see in paragraph 2?* (you're) *What does it mean?* (you are)

Apply Have students locate and copy the sentence on p. 31 with the words *your* and *you're.* (last sentence) *Say: Circle the contraction that means "you are."* (you're) *Underline the word that means "belonging to you."* (your)

Chapter 3 / Reading Selection   **31**

Read the Selection

1. **Use text features** Point out the illustration, labels, and glossed words. Remind students to use them as they read.
2. **Shared reading** Play the audio. Have students join in when they can. *Ask: What was the Baenningers' idea about why people yawn?* (Yawning helps you stay awake or become excited.) *How did they test the idea?* (They hooked people to some machines to measure changes in their bodies.) *What types of changes did they notice?* (People moved their wrists, sweated more, and their hearts beat faster.)

Sample Answer to Guide Question
Yes. This helps me think about all the facts and details that are described in the text and understand why I can stay awake and alert after I yawn.

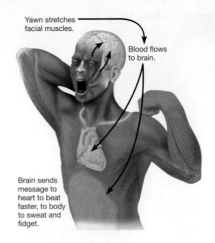

Yawn stretches facial muscles.

Blood flows to brain.

Brain sends message to heart to beat faster, to body to sweat and fidget.

7   Ronald Baenninger, a scientist at Temple University, agrees with Provine. He and his wife Mary Anne, a scientist at The College of New Jersey, guessed that yawning helps you stay awake or become excited. They tested their guess by hooking up people to machines that **measured** changes in their bodies as they yawned. They found that as people yawned, they moved their **wrists** more than usual, they began sweating, and their hearts beat faster. This shows that these people were trying to stay awake, not fall asleep.

So what does yawning do that helps keep you **alert**? Provine thinks that by yawning, you stretch the muscles in your face and bring more **blood** to the **brain.** "It stirs things up," he says. The brain can then wake up the body through the **fidgeting,** sweating, and the faster heartbeat. You can see how this might help you stay awake at night, wake up in the morning, or become alert when you're bored or nervous.   8

Compare the Text to Your Own Experiences

Do you yawn when you are tired? How does this experience help you understand paragraphs 7 and 8?

Provine also tested whether people yawn to breathe in more oxygen. He had people breathe in a special mix of air that had less oxygen than usual. To get the oxygen they needed, people had to breathe faster. "We had people **huffing and puffing,**" he says. "But they didn't yawn any more than they did before."   9

---

measured   figured out how much
wrists   the part of the body between the hand and the forearm
alert   paying attention
blood   the red liquid pumped by the heart through the body

brain   the part of the body used for thinking and feeling
fidgeting   moving the body in a nervous way
huffing and puffing   breathing quickly and a lot

32   Unit 1 Mysteries

MULTI-LEVEL OPTIONS *Read the Selection*

Newcomer *Ask: Is Robert Baenninger a scientist?* (yes) *Does he agree with Provine?* (yes) *Do people sweat when they yawn?* (yes) *Do people yawn to get more oxygen?* (no) *Do some scientists think that yawning has no purpose?* (yes)

Beginning *Ask: Do people yawn more or breathe faster when they get less oxygen?* (breathe faster) *What did they hook people up to?* (machines that test changes in the body) *What muscles are stretched when you yawn?* (facial muscles) *Why might animals yawn?* (to stay alert)

Intermediate *Ask: Why do the Baenningers think we yawn?* (to stay awake or become excited) *How does yawning keep you awake?* (It brings blood to the brain.) *Why did Provine have people breathe less oxygen?* (to see if people yawn to get more oxygen) *Why might unborn babies yawn?* (to get facial muscles working)

Advanced *Ask: What are some ways the brain can wake up the body?* (fidgeting, sweating, faster heartbeat) *What conclusion can you draw about scientists' opinions of why people yawn?* (They have many theories; they don't all agree; many of them wonder why we yawn.)

10　He didn't stop there. He also made people breathe in air that was *all* oxygen. They had more than enough oxygen in their blood, but they yawned just as much as before. So the idea that we yawn to get more oxygen can't be right.

11　But not everyone agrees with Provine and the Baenningers. Some scientists think that yawning has no **purpose.** They say that it's a **habit** left over from when you were **developing** as a baby in your mother's **womb** or one you **inherited** from our animal **ancestors.** Yawning might help get the face and jaw muscles of unborn babies working, and it might help animals stay alert.

> **Compare the Text to Your Own Experiences**
> Think about what you know about yawning. Do you think that yawning has no purpose? Explain.

12　It's **amazing** how difficult it is **get to the bottom of** something as simple as a yawn.

---

purpose reason
habit something that you do over and over
developing growing
womb the part of a woman's body where a baby can grow

inherited received from
ancestors people or animals from the past that you are related to
amazing surprising
get to the bottom of learn the truth about

About the Author

Haleh V. Samiei (born 1963)

Haleh V. Samiei lived in Iran as a child. She studied science in college. She also studied writing. Today, Samiei writes about science and health. She also writes articles for newspapers.

➤ How do you think Haleh V. Samiei learned about yawning? By talking to scientists? By reading books? Both? Why do you think she wrote this informational text?

A Capitalization

People's names

Tell students that a person's name is a proper noun, so the first letter is *always* capitalized. Direct students to p. 32. *Ask: Why does Ronald Baenninger's name start with capital letters?* (It's a proper noun.) *Can you find two more names that start with capital letters?* (Provine, Mary Anne)

Apply Have students correct the capitalization errors. Write on the board: *Give mateo this book. Is robert provine a famous scientist?*

Evaluate Your Reading Strategy

Compare the Text to Your Own Experiences *Say: You have practiced an important reading strategy. Now you can decide how well you have done. Does this statement describe how you read?*

> I ask myself this question when I do not understand something that I read: "What do I already know about this subject?" I use what I know to understand better what I read.

Read the Selection

1. **Teacher read aloud** Complete the reading of the selection aloud as students follow along. Ask questions to check comprehension. *Ask: How do you know that people don't yawn to get more oxygen?* (Baenninger had people breathe oxygen, but they yawned the same as people in normal air.)
2. **Summarize** Have pairs of students reread and summarize the facts about yawning.
3. **Multi-level options** See MULTI-LEVEL OPTIONS on p. 32.

Sample Answer to Guide Question
I think that yawning has a purpose because it happens when people feel a certain way and not all the time.

About the Author

1. **Explain author's background** Haleh V. Samiei has a Ph.D. in molecular biology. She is well respected for her science and health articles. In addition to Iran, she has also lived in Turkey, Singapore, and Canada.
2. **Interpret author's style** *Ask: Is this article like other science articles you have read? Why or why not?* (No. It's easier to understand.)

Answer
Sample answer: I think she learned from both talking to scientists and reading books. I think she wrote this informational text to inform and educate people about yawning.

Across Selections

Make comparisons and contrasts The first three chapters in this unit are informational texts. Have students compile a list of all the text features that were studied. (definitions, experiences, facts, main idea and supporting details/examples, purpose/subject, quotes, visuals) Then *ask: Do all features appear in all three informational texts?* (yes)

Spelling, Punctuation, Capitalization

After the Reading Comprehension section, students will practice spelling, punctuation, and capitalization in the Activity Book.

Reading Comprehension

Question-Answer Relationships

Sample Answers

1. a scientist at the University of Maryland-Baltimore County
2. He first tested whether people yawn when they are bored or not.
3. to stay awake or become excited
4. Sometimes, it makes you yawn, too.
5. First, there is pressure behind your ear drum. Then, you lift your eyebrows and open your mouth. Next, you take a deep breath. Last, you let a short breath out.
6. They move their wrists; they sweat; and their hearts beat faster.
7. I think they yawn because they are tired and to stay awake.
8. I learned that yawns can be contagious and that you don't yawn to get more oxygen.
9. I yawn when I am tired and sleepy. I also yawn when I am nervous, like before an oral presentation.

Build Reading Fluency

Rapid Word Recognition

Rapid word recognition is an excellent activity for students who struggle with irregular spelling patterns. Time students for 1 minute as they read the words in the squares aloud.

Reading Comprehension

Question-Answer Relationships (QAR)

"Right There" Questions

1. **Recall Facts** Who is Robert Provine?
2. **Recall Facts** Look at paragraph 3. What was the first thing that Robert Provine tested?
3. **Explain** Look at paragraph 7. What do Ronald and Mary Anne Baenninger think is the reason that people yawn?

"Think and Search" Questions

4. **Analyze Cause and Effect** What sometimes happens when you see another person yawn?
5. **Identify Steps in a Process** Look at paragraph 1. Identify the steps in yawning.

6. **Summarize** Look at paragraph 7. Name three things that people do when they yawn.

"Author and You" Question

7. **Evaluate Evidence** Why do you think people yawn?

"On Your Own" Questions

8. **Evaluate** Name two things that you learned from reading "Yawning."
9. **Compare Text Events with Experiences** Are your experiences with yawning similar to those discussed in the reading? Talk with a partner about his or her experiences.

Activity Book
p. 18

Student
CD-ROM

Build Reading Fluency

Rapid Word Recognition

Rapidly recognizing words helps increase your reading rate. It is an important characteristic of effective readers.

1. With a partner, review the words in the box.
2. Read the words aloud for one minute. Your teacher will time you.
3. Count how many words you read in one minute.

article	stretch	oxygen	bored	oxygen	article
breath	bored	stretch	oxygen	bored	oxygen
bored	diary	breath	article	diary	breath
oxygen	oxygen	bored	breath	article	diary
diary	breath	article	diary	stretch	bored

MULTI-LEVEL OPTIONS *Elements of Literature*

Newcomer On the board, write: *I, we, you.* Point to yourself and *say: I.* Indicate yourself and the students. *Say: we.* Indicate the students. *Say: you.* Have students look for these words paragraphs 1 and 2. *Ask: Which did you find?* (you) *To whom is the author speaking?* (me; the reader)

Beginning Hand a book to a student and *say: I am handing the book to* you. On the board, write: *you. Say: When a writer is talking to the reader, he or she uses the pronoun* you. Ask students to identify paragraphs where the author directly addresses the reader with *you.* (paragraphs 1, 2, 4, 7, 8, 11)

Intermediate Ask students to copy three sentences from the selection with the pronoun *you. Ask: Why does the writer use the pronoun* you *in this selection?* Explain that this is how an author speaks directly to a reader. Have pairs write sentences using *you* in direct address.

Advanced Direct students to one of the previous selections in the book. Have then work in pairs to rewrite one paragraph with direct address. Ask students to compare the difference between their paragraph and the original. *Ask: Which method was more effective?*

Listen, Speak, Interact

Give an Informational Presentation

Yawning is usually a reflex action—an action your body does that you can't really control. Two other reflex actions are sneezing and coughing.

Give an informational presentation about sneezing or coughing.

1. With a partner, decide which of you will present sneezing and which one will present coughing.
2. On your own, list facts about the reflex action that you chose. Answer these questions. Take notes on note cards.
   a. What happens in your body when you sneeze or cough?
   b. When do you sneeze or cough?
   c. Can you sneeze or cough whenever you want to, or is it always a reflex action?
3. Present your information to your partner.
   a. Use the information on your note cards. Clarify your information with examples.
   b. Act out what sneezing or coughing is.
4. Take notes as you listen to your partner's presentation. Ask yourself these questions.
   a. Did I understand my partner's nonverbal messages?
   b. Did my partner give facts, opinions, or both?

Elements of Literature

Recognize Direct Address

The author of "Yawning" uses **direct address.** This means that the author speaks directly to the reader. The author uses the pronoun *you.* Look at this example from paragraph 1.

> This article is going to cast a spell on <u>you</u>.

1. Reread paragraphs 1 and 2 of "Yawning."
2. Find three sentences that use the pronoun *you.* Write them in your Reading Log.

3. Why do you think the author uses direct address? Do you think that direct address makes the selection easier to understand?

Reading Log   Activity Book p. 19   Student CD-ROM

Chapter 3 Yawning   **35**

Home Connection

Have students conduct yawn research. Ask them to note each time their family members yawn. Have students collect information for one week and then analyze their data to answer the following questions: *Which family member yawns the most? The least? At what time of day do your family members yawn the most? The least? What other generalizations can you make about the yawning behavior of your family?*

Learning Styles
Visual

Students may better understand the concepts in the text by creating cause-and-effect graphic organizers. Have pairs create in-out graphics, flowcharts, or other organizers. Have them use data in the selection to complete their organizers. Remind students that: one cause can have multiple effects; one effect can have multiple causes; and an effect can lead to another effect (chain reaction).

Teacher Resource Book: *Timelines, p. 39*

Listen, Speak, Interact

Give an Informational Presentation

Teacher Resource Book: *Timelines, p. 39*

1. **Use a graphic organizer** Pair beginning and advanced students. Have them create a flowchart for sneezing and coughing. Help with vocabulary as needed. Have them use the flowchart as they prepare their informational talks.
2. **Newcomers** Guide this group to act out the two reflex actions and identify parts of the body affected and what happens. Help students use sequence expressions as they explain the actions.

Elements of Literature

Recognize Direct Address

1. **Explain terms** Point out and clarify the meaning of *direct address.* Have students find examples of the pronoun *you* in the selection.
2. **Personal reaction** Reread paragraph 1 (p. 30) first as it is written and then a second time substituting *people* for *you* and *their* for *your. Ask: Which way did you like better— with* you *or with* people? *Why? How does* you *make you feel? How does* people *make you feel?*
3. **Multi-level options** See MULTI-LEVEL OPTIONS on p. 34.

Answers
2. As you read it, . . . ; You'll hold this position . . . ; When you read about yawning, you usually yawn yourself; You yawn because. . . .
3. I think the author uses direct address to make the readers feel like they are part of a conversation. I think it makes it easier to understand.

ASSESS

Ask students to define *direct address.*

Word Study

Write Using Contractions

Apply Have students find examples of contractions in the reading. Make a chart of the contractions and component words.

Answers

1. **a.** you will **b.** they are
2. *Example:* I don't have a pencil. We can't go outside and play right now.

Grammar Focus

Write Dependent Clauses

Model combining sentences Write on the board: *The scientist discovered something. People yawn when they are tired.* Model combining the sentences using *that.* Point out the resulting dependent clause. Repeat with other examples as needed.

Answers

1. Provine made the discovery that they yawned when they woke up.
2. Some scientists have a theory that yawning has no purpose.

ASSESS

Say contractions and have students respond with the full forms.

Word Study

Write Using Contractions

Contractions are two words that are joined together. You drop one or more letter from the second word. An apostrophe (') replaces the letters.

It**'**s just a contagious yawn.

First Word +	Second Word ⇒	Contraction
it +	is ⇒	it's

Notice that you drop the *i* in *is* when you form the contraction *it's.*

It's is different from *its. Its* is a possessive form.

I have a fish. Its name is George.

1. Choose the words that the underlined contractions come from.
   a. You'll lift your eyebrows and open your mouth wide.

   you will   you are

   b. People yawn just as they're about to jump out of an airplane.

   they can   they are

2. Write two sentences with contractions.

Activity Book
p. 20

Student
CD-ROM

Grammar Focus

Write Dependent Clauses

Dependent clauses have a subject and a verb. They are part of a complex sentence. The word *that* often begins a dependent clause. Do not use a comma before dependent clauses starting with *that.*

I think **that** the answer is simple.

Here the dependent clause is *that the answer is simple.* The dependent clause tells what I think.

Look at the following pairs of sentences. Combine the two sentences into one sentence. Use a dependent clause with *that.* Underline the dependent clause. Be sure to start your sentences with a capital letter and end them with a period. Do not use a comma before dependent clauses starting with *that.*

1. Provine made the discovery. They yawned when they woke up.
2. Some scientists have a theory. Yawning has no purpose.

Activity Book
pp. 21–22

Student
Handbook

Student
CD-ROM

36 **Unit 1** Mysteries

MULTI-LEVEL OPTIONS *From Reading to Writing*

Newcomer Have students draw two or three pictures of their morning routines. Then have them place the pictures over a timeline. *Say: This shows the order that these events happened.* Display their timelines in the classroom.

Beginning Have students make timelines about a previous school year. Have them note at least four important events. Ask them to present their timelines in small groups. Direct them to tell about the events by using words like *first, next, then,* and *last.*

Intermediate Have students brainstorm and list words that show chronology for their paragraphs. (first, next, then, after that, finally) Tell them to refer to the list for ideas when writing. Remind students that these words will not only help show sequence, but will also help their sentences flow smoothly.

Advanced Have students review their paragraphs. Ask them to circle all the time words and any clauses that contain *that.* Have partners peer-edit to check that the time words were used correctly.

From Reading to Writing

Write a Paragraph Using Chronology

Chronology is the order in which events happen. Paragraph 1 of "Yawning" uses chronology. It describes the order in which things happen when you yawn.

1. Write a paragraph using chronology. Your paragraph will be about your morning routine.
2. Begin your paragraph with a sentence that tells what it is about.
3. Use time words such as *first, then, next,* and *last* to show chronology.
4. Write at least one sentence with a dependent clause with *that.*

This is the routine that I follow every morning before school.
First, ————————————————.
Then, ————————————————.
Next, ————————————————.
Finally, ——————————————.

Activity Book
p. 23

Student
Handbook

Across Content Areas

Read a Bar Graph

A **bar graph** uses bars to show amounts. This bar graph shows the number of people who believe each reason for yawning. Across the bottom are the different reasons. On the left side is the number of people who gave each reason.

To read the bar graph, look at the reason at the bottom of a bar. Then find the numbered line that the top of the bar hits.

1. How many people think that we yawn because we are bored?
2. Which bars show the same number of people?
3. Which reason do the fewest number of people believe?
4. How many people gave reasons?

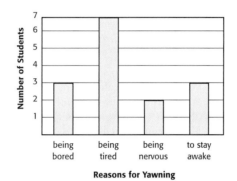

Reasons for Yawning

Activity Book
p. 24

UNIT 1 • CHAPTER 3
Beyond the Reading

From Reading to Writing

Write a Paragraph Using Chronology

Teacher Resource Book: *Storyboard, p. 43*

1. **Make a storyboard** Have students create storyboards for their morning routines and then add captions.
2. **Think-pair-share** As students share their storyboard morning routines in pairs, have them add time words and expressions and include a dependent clause.
3. **Language experience story** For less fluent students, have them dictate their routines as you write them. Then have students practice reading their routines in pairs and create timelines as illustrations.
4. **Multi-level options** See MULTI-LEVEL OPTIONS on p. 36.

Across Content Areas: Math

Read a Bar Graph

1. **Model organizing information** Have students line up by preferred drinks: milk, chocolate milk, orange juice, water. *Say: Let's make a picture of that.* Create a graph, listing drinks at the bottom and making a block for each student in the different rows.
2. **Apply** Help students determine the number of people represented in the bars on p. 37.

Answers
1. 7 people
2. "being bored" and "to stay awake"
3. being nervous
4. 15 people

ASSESS

Have students share the most important thing that they learned on the page.

Reteach and Reassess

Text Structure *Ask: What is the purpose of this selection?* (to teach us why people yawn) *What kinds of details does the selection give?* (information about scientists' theories and experiments)

Reading Strategy Ask students to share parts of the selection that they could relate to their own experiences. Provide a model. *Say: Paragraph 4 reminded me that I yawned when I woke up this morning.*

Elements of Literature Have students find an example of direct address in the selection. Ask students to tell partners whether they think direct address made the selection more interesting or easier to understand and why.

Reassess Provide two-column charts with the headings *Does Cause Yawning* and *Does NOT Cause Yawning*. Have students fill in the charts with details from the text.

CHAPTER 4

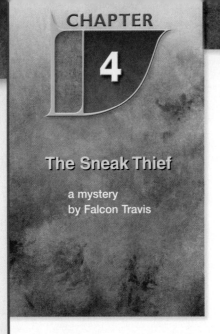

The Sneak Thief

a mystery
by Falcon Travis

Into the Reading

Chapter Materials

Activity Book: *pp. 25–32*
Audio: *Unit 1, Chapter 4; CD 1, Track 4*
Student Handbook
Student CD-ROM: *Unit 1, Chapter 4*
Teacher Resource Book: *Lesson Plan, Teacher Resources, Reading Summary, Activity Book Answer Key*
Teacher Resource CD-ROM
Assessment Program: *Quiz, pp. 13–14; Teacher and Student Resources, pp. 115–144*
Assessment CD-ROM
Transparencies
The Heinle Newbury House Dictionary/CD-ROM
Web site: http://visions.heinle.com

Objectives

Paired reading Have pairs take turns reading the objectives. Point out key words. *Ask: Is there an objective you can already do?*

Use Prior Knowledge

Discuss Rules

Teacher Resource Book: *Two-Column Chart, p. 44*

Gather and organize Have students list the rules at your school. Ask volunteers to explain the reasons for a few of the rules. Arrange students in pairs to create a two-column chart of school rules and explanations.

Objectives

Reading Use chronology to locate and recall information as you read a mystery.

Listening and Speaking Interpret text through dramatization.

Grammar Identify simple, compound, and complex sentences.

Writing Write dialogue in a mystery.

Content Language Arts: Learn words about the law.

Use Prior Knowledge

Discuss Rules

Rules are made to keep people safe. They tell us what we can and cannot do.

1. Work with a partner.
2. Copy this chart on a piece of paper.
3. Write the school rules that you know.
4. Write why each rule is needed.
5. Share your answers with the class.
6. Make a complete chart of rules to post in your classroom.

Rule	Why Rule Is Needed
No running in the halls.	So no one will fall down and get hurt

38 Unit 1 Mysteries

MULTI-LEVEL OPTIONS *Build Vocabulary*

Newcomer Write *train* on the board. Ask students to draw a picture of what they imagine when they think about trains. Help students add labels and captions to their drawings. Have them share their finished drawings in small groups.

Beginning Make a word web with a train in the center. Tell students to brainstorm all the words they know about trains for the web. Then have them discuss the meanings in small groups.

Intermediate Have students write one sentence using *passenger, ticket,* and *train station.* Ask them to share their sentences in groups.

Advanced On the board, write: *train station* and *airport.* Ask students to look up each word in the dictionary. *Ask: How are these words similar? How are they different?* Then have students write sentences using the words. Ask them to provide context clues in each sentence.

Build Background

Inspectors

Inspectors are types of police officers. They try to solve crimes. Crimes are actions that are against the law. Inspectors use clues to help them solve crimes. Clues are objects or facts that help answer a question.

Content Connection

Forensic doctors help solve crimes. They can get information by studying clues as small as a piece of hair.

Build Vocabulary

Learn Words Related to Train Travel

"The Sneak Thief" includes words related to train travel. Knowing the meanings of these words will help you understand the selection.

1. Copy the chart below in your Personal Dictionary.

2. Look at each word in the chart. Look at each word's meaning.
3. Write a sentence using each word.
4. Share your sentences with the class. Did you write similar sentences?
5. Look for these words as you read or listen to the audio recording of "The Sneak Thief."

Word	Meaning	Sentence
train station	a place where people go to get on the train	*I went to the train station.*
passenger	a person who rides in a train, car, boat, bus, or plane; it is not the driver	
ticket	a printed piece of paper that you buy; it lets you travel on a train, boat, bus, or plane	

Personal Dictionary

Activity Book p. 25

Student CD-ROM

Chapter 4 The Sneak Thief **39**

Community Connection

Build Background Arrange for a local law enforcement official to speak to the class. Ask the speaker to discuss different kinds of clues (evidence) his/her department has used to solve various crimes. Allow time for a question-and-answer session at the end. After the speech, have students write and send thank-you letters.

Learning Styles
Visual

Build Vocabulary Ask students to brainstorm a list of travel-related words. Have students cut out simple train, airplane, boat, and car shapes. Tell them to write the appropriate words from the list on each shape. Have students use their shapes to make collages or mobiles to display in the classroom.

Build Background

Inspectors

1. **Use a picture** Bring in pictures of police officers. Ask students to suggest different types of police and their duties. Remind them to think of officers and inspectors they have seen on TV or in movies for ideas.
2. **Content Connection** Forensic doctors look for medical information to prove a person committed a crime. The evidence is used in court. Ask students about forensic doctors and their jobs as seen on TV and in movies.

Build Vocabulary

Learn Words Related to Train Travel

Teacher Resource Book: *Personal Dictionary, p. 63*

1. **Explore information** Bring in train schedules, maps, and tickets for students to examine. Have students list words related to train travel.
2. **Reading selection vocabulary** You may want to introduce the glossed words in the reading selection before students begin reading. Key words: *briefcase, contents, suspect, arrested, charged.* Instruct students to write the words with correct spelling and their definitions in their Personal Dictionaries. Have them pronounce each word and divide it into syllables.
3. **Multi-level options** See MULTI-LEVEL OPTIONS on p. 38.

Answer

3. *Examples:* There is a train station near my house. The passengers talked and read during the train ride. I had to buy a ticket to get on the train.

 **ASSESS**

Have students use the vocabulary words in sentences.

Text Structure

Mystery

Clarify features Have students share mysteries they have read or seen. Ask them to give examples as you discuss the features of a mystery.

Reading Strategy

Use Chronology to Locate and Recall Information

1. **Use a calendar or schedule** Mark events on a calendar or schedule. Ask volunteers to tell the events in chronological order. Review time expressions used to order events.
2. **Multi-level options** See MULTI-LEVEL OPTIONS below.

Answer
2. b, d, a, c

ASSESS

Ask: What are five features of a mystery story?
(plot, problem, clues, suspense, resolution)

Text Structure

Mystery

"The Sneak Thief" is a **mystery** story. Reading a mystery is like solving a puzzle. The chart shows the special features of a mystery.

Mystery	
Plot	The plot is the series of events in the story.
Problem	The story is about a question that needs to be answered.
Clues	Clues are details in the story that help answer the question.
Suspense	Suspense is the feeling of not knowing what is going to happen next.
Resolution	Resolution is the answer at the end of the story.

Student CD-ROM

Reading Strategy

Use Chronology to Locate and Recall Information

Chronology is the order of events in a story. Notice chronology as you read. This will help you **locate** (find) and **recall** (remember) important information.

Authors often use words like *then, now, first, second, finally, before,* or *after* to show chronology.

1. Look at the timeline. The underlined words show chronology.

In 1998, we moved to San Diego.   Then we moved to Los Angeles.   Finally, we moved to Phoenix.

2. On a piece of paper, write these sentences in chronological order.
  a. Then my father hugged me.
  b. I woke up and went into the kitchen.
  c. Finally I remembered—it was my birthday!
  d. First my mother kissed me.
3. Look for words that show chronology as you read "The Sneak Thief."

Student CD-ROM

MULTI-LEVEL OPTIONS *Reading Strategy*

Newcomer Have students work in small groups to assemble simple jigsaw puzzles. *Ask: How did you solve the puzzle?* Explain that mystery writers give clues to solve their written puzzles. *Ask: What clues helped you put the puzzle together?* List students' ideas on the board.

Beginning Hide an object somewhere in the room. Provide and list simple clues, such as *It is higher than your knees* or *It is inside something else.* Have students search for the object. *Say: You solved the mystery by using clues. Reading a mystery story is like using clues to find a solution.*

Intermediate Hide an object somewhere in the room. Write on the board and *say: clues.* Provide and list simple clues, such as *It is higher than your knees* or *It is inside something else.* Direct students to the chart on p. 40. Have them provide examples for each feature based on the classroom mystery they just solved.

Advanced Hide an object somewhere in the room. Provide and list simple clues, such as *It is higher than your knees* or *It is inside something else.* Direct students to the chart on p. 40. Have them provide examples for each feature based on the classroom mystery they just solved.

The Sneak Thief

a mystery
by Falcon Travis

41

Reading Selection Materials

Audio: *Unit 1, Chapter 4; CD 1, Track 4*
Teacher Resource Book: *Reading Summary,*
pp. 71–72
Transparencies: *#32, Reading Summary*

Suggestions for Using Reading Summary

- Introduce new vocabulary or cognates.
- Cut the summary into strips, or jumble the sentences on an overhead transparency. Students put the sentences in order.
- Practice the reading strategy.
- Students read aloud or with a partner.
- Students paraphrase the summary.
- Students do a cloze activity.
- Students create a visual or graphic organizer, such as a timeline or storyboard, to illustrate the summary.
- Students paraphrase the summary.

Preview the Selection

1. **Teacher think aloud** Have students examine the illustration. *Say: The title of the story is "The Sneak Thief." I see one man carrying a briefcase. Another man is wearing a raincoat. He's watching the man with the briefcase. I wonder who the sneak thief is. I wonder what he stole. I wonder what clues the Inspector will find. I wonder if the Inspector will catch the thief.*
2. **Connect** Ask students to share their thoughts and questions about the title, the illustration, and the mystery. Ask what clues the Inspector might look for. Tell students they will need to read carefully and think about the details, or clues, to solve the mystery themselves.

Community Connection

Technology Tell students that criminologists are scientists who study evidence in order to figure out how a crime happened or who committed it. Explain that there are many areas of criminology, including fingerprint analysis, autopsy, DNA testing, hair and fiber testing, ballistics, and suspect and victim profiling. Ask groups to research the equipment and technology used by these scientists.

Learning Styles
Visual

Direct students to the picture on p. 41. *Ask: What do you think the people in this picture are doing? Who do you think they are? What kind of people do you think they are?* Have students write one-paragraph character analyses based on the picture.

Read the Selection

1. **Use text features** Call attention to the illustration and have students make guesses about the characters. Then direct students to glossed words and have them find their meanings at the bottom of the page. Remind students to think carefully about what the characters do and what their actions tell about them.

2. **Paired reading** Play the audio or read the selection aloud. Have students reread aloud in pairs.

Sample Answer to Guide Question
Inspector Will Ketchum notices a man with the restless eyes of a sneak thief.

See Teacher Edition pp. 434–436 for a list of English-Spanish cognates in the reading selection.

Use Chronology to Locate and Recall Information

What is the first thing that attracts Inspector Will Ketchum's attention?

Audio
CD 1. Tr. 4

1   Inspector Will Ketchum was **off duty.** He had just arrived at the train station to meet some friends, but their train was running an hour late. As he **strolled** across the main terminal, a man with the restless eyes of a **sneak thief** attracted his attention. Then he was lost in a sudden surge of passengers.

2   A few minutes later, the Inspector spotted the man, who was entering the station's coffee shop. Now he was carrying a leather **briefcase.** The man sat down at a **vacant** corner table, placing the briefcase between his chair and the wall.

3   The Inspector casually followed him in, sat at his table and, identifying himself as a police officer, asked if the man would mind stepping over to the **Station Master's** office to answer a few questions about the **ownership** of the briefcase that he had with him. The man claimed **indignantly** that the briefcase was his, but he agreed to go along.

4   In the Station Master's office the briefcase lay open on the desk, revealing a file of papers and an envelope containing about $200 in twenty-dollar bills.

---

off duty   not working
strolled   walked slowly
sneak thief   a person who steals, but tries to avoid being seen
briefcase   a small piece of luggage for holding books and papers

vacant   empty
Station Master   a person who watches over a train station
ownership   possession
indignantly   angrily

42   Unit 1   Mysteries

MULTI-LEVEL OPTIONS *Read the Selection*

Newcomer Play the audio. Read the pages aloud. *Ask: Was Inspector Ketchum on duty?* (no) *Was he at the train station?* (yes) *Did the man go into the coffee shop?* (yes) *Did Ketchum follow him?* (yes) *Did the man have a briefcase?* (yes) *Was the briefcase empty?* (no) *Did Mr. Fink say he wanted to buy books?* (yes)

Beginning Read the Reading Summary aloud. *Ask: Where is the Inspector?* (at the train station) *Where did the man go?* (into the coffee shop) *What was the man carrying?* (a briefcase) *What is in it?* (papers, $200) *What does the man say was in his case?* (magazines) *What did the man say he wanted to buy?* (books)

Intermediate Have students do a paired reading. *Ask: Why is the Inspector at the station?* (to meet friends) *Why did the man attract his attention?* (restless eyes) *Why does the man look puzzled?* (He says his case had magazines, not money.) *Why does the man say he took his briefcase?* (to carry books he planned to buy)

Advanced Have students read independently. *Ask: Why does the Inspector ask the man about the briefcase?* (He wasn't carrying it when the Inspector first saw him.) *Does Mr. Fink's explanation make sense so far? Explain.* (Yes, it's possible that his story is true.)

Use Chronology to Locate and Recall Information

What did Mr. Fink tell the Inspector *before* they opened the briefcase?

5   "Before we opened this briefcase, Mr. Fink," began the Inspector, "you told us it was definitely yours and that it contained only a couple of magazines. Now you **deny** that you are the owner. How do you explain that?"

6   Mr. Fink rubbed his chin and looked **puzzled.** "This definitely isn't the briefcase I handed in at the **checkroom** this morning," he said. "They must have given me someone else's. It looks exactly like mine, but I can see it isn't, now that it's open. My briefcase was locked and all it had in it were some magazines I was reading on the train. The owner of this briefcase shouldn't have left it open with all this money in it. If he got mine by mistake, he isn't going to be very happy about it."

7   "I'm sure he won't be," said the Inspector. "What is more, he's probably wondering, as I am, why anyone would **check** a briefcase that had only a couple of magazines in it."

8   "That's easy to explain," said Mr. Fink. "I got to town this morning just before noon on one of those one-day round-trip **excursion** tickets—and I'll be going back tonight—if you don't make me miss my train. I was reading the magazines on the train. I brought my briefcase because I was hoping to find some **secondhand** books, but I didn't get to the bookstores because I met an old friend who invited me over to his house."

deny   say something is not true
puzzled   confused
checkroom   a place where you sign in your luggage

check   give for safekeeping
excursion   a short trip
secondhand   used by someone else before

Chapter 4 The Sneak Thief   **43**

Read the Selection

1. **Understand terms** Have students find the meanings of the glossed words below the selection. Clarify meanings as needed.
2. **Student read aloud** Read the selection aloud. Then have volunteers reread different paragraphs aloud.
3. **Locate derivations using dictionaries** Have students look at these glossed words and determine what words they are derived from: *strolled, ownership, indignantly, puzzled.* Have students check the derivations in a print, an online, or a CD-ROM dictionary.
4. **Use chronology to recall information** Ask questions to help students summarize the sequence of events and developments in the story.
5. **Analyze character development** Ask students to describe Mr. Fink's attitude before they went to the Station Master's office and after. *Ask: How is Mr. Fink different from before going to the office?* (He's puzzled, not annoyed.)
6. **Make predictions** *Ask: What will the Inspector do now?*
7. **Multi-level options** See MULTI-LEVEL OPTIONS on p. 42.

Sample Answer to Guide Question
Before they opened the briefcase, Mr. Fink told the Inspector that it was his briefcase and that it only had a couple of magazines in it.

,   Punctuation

Apostrophes for singular possession

Tell students that apostrophes are often used to show possession. *Say: To show possession for a singular noun, add 's.* On the board, write: *The book belongs to Gus. It is Gus's book.* Review the pronunciation of singular possessive nouns, such as *Keomi's, school's, class's, Texas's,* and *girl's.* Direct students to paragraph 4. *Ask: Can you find a possessive noun?* (Station Master's) *To whom does the office belong?* (the Station Master)

Apply Have students correct errors to show possession. Write on the board:

We will meet at Marco house.

That is my mother secret recipe.

It was the boss decision.

What is Texas capital city?

Read the Selection

1. **Use the illustration** Have students identify the objects on the desk.
2. **Paired reading** Play the audio. Then have students reread the selection in pairs. Ask pairs to act out parts of the scene.
3. **Use chronology to recall information** Help students create a timeline to sequence the events of Mr. Fink's day. Remind students to use the timeline as they solve the mystery.

Sample Answer to Guide Question
Mr. Fink said he checked the briefcase before he visited his friend.

> **Use Chronology to Locate and Recall Information**
>
> What does Mr. Fink say he did before he visited his friend?

9   "So that's when you checked your briefcase?"

10   "That's right," continued Mr. Fink. "I didn't want to carry it around with me, so I left it here and went to visit with my friend. Got my **taxi fare** paid both ways, had a great time and all I had to spend since I got off the train this morning was what they charged me at the checkroom."

11   "Lucky you," said the Inspector. "Now would you mind emptying out all your pockets and placing their **contents** on this desk?"

12   "I don't mind at all," said Mr. Fink, "I've got nothing to hide. The sooner you're satisfied, the sooner I can get going. I have to take this briefcase back to the checkroom and see if mine is still there."

13   Mr. Fink's statement and the contents of his pockets (shown at the left) were enough to tell Will Ketchum whether or not the suspect was telling the truth. If you have decided, too, turn to the SOLUTION . . . and see if you reached the same conclusion as the Inspector, and for the same reasons.

14   If you haven't been able to decide yet, look at the CLUES . . . for some **pointers** to the clues that helped the Inspector make up his mind.

15   **CLUES**

There is a clue in each of the following statements:
1. "My briefcase was locked."
2. "I got to town this morning just before noon on one of those one-day round-trip excursion tickets—"
3. "I was hoping to find some secondhand books."
4. "All I had to spend since I got off the train this morning was what they charged me at the checkroom."

---

taxi fare   the cost to ride in a taxi
contents   things found inside of something

pointers   pieces of advice

44   **Unit 1**   Mysteries

MULTI-LEVEL OPTIONS *Read the Selection*

Newcomer *Ask: Did Mr. Fink take a taxi?* (yes) *Did he agree to empty his pockets?* (yes) *Did Mr. Fink have a key for the briefcase?* (no) *Did Mr. Fink have money to buy books?* (no) *Did Mr. Fink steal the briefcase?* (yes) *Was Mr. Fink arrested?* (yes)

Beginning *Ask: How did Mr. Fink get to and from his friend's house?* (a taxi) *Where does Mr. Fink say he will look for his own case?* (the checkroom) *What did Mr. Fink need that he didn't have?* (briefcase key, money, return ticket) *What happened to Mr. Fink?* (He was arrested and charged.)

Intermediate *Ask: Why did Mr. Fink check his case?* (He didn't want to carry it to his friend's house.) *Why does the Inspector ask him to empty his pockets?* (to look for clues) *Why are the missing key, return ticket, and money important clues?* (Mr. Fink couldn't open a locked case, return from his trip, or buy books.)

Advanced *Ask: What is interesting about the two main characters' names?* (Ketchum sounds like *"catch him,"* which is what the Inspector does. Fink is an unfavorable, derogatory word for a person.) *Can you think of a way Mr. Fink could explain the missing key, money, and return ticket?* (He lost them; he was robbed; etc.)

16 **SOLUTION**
The contents of the **suspect's** pockets
do not include:
A key to the briefcase
The "return" part of the ticket
Enough cash (and no other way of paying)
for buying books

17 Fink was **arrested** and **charged.** It was
easy to find the owner of the briefcase.
It turned out that he had put his case
down while buying a newspaper, and in
a matter of seconds it had **disappeared.**
The sneak thief had **rehearsed** this story
well, in case he was questioned, but he
hadn't allowed for the contents of his
pockets giving him away.

suspect a person who is thought to have committed
a crime
arrested brought into police holding

charged blamed someone for something
disappeared gone out of sight
rehearsed practiced

About the Author | **Falcon Travis**

➤ Why do you think Falcon Travis wrote exactly what the characters said to each other? Does this make the characters seem real? Does this allow readers to learn the characters' thoughts?

❥ Punctuation

Quotation marks for direct quotations

Remind students that writers show words that are spoken by writing them between quotation marks. *Say: I want you to sit down. How can I write a sentence that shows the words I just said?* Write on the board: *The teacher said, "I want you to sit down."* Circle the quotation marks. *Say: You know that the words between these marks are the words that I said. Can you find examples of words that were spoken on pp. 44–45?* (paragraphs 9, 10, 11, 12, 15)

Evaluate Your Reading Strategy

Use Chronology to Locate and Recall Information *Say: You have practiced an important reading strategy. Now you can decide how well you have done. Does this statement describe how you read?*

> I notice chronology as I read. This helps me find information and remember the order of events.

Read the Selection

1. **Use text features** Call attention to the clues and solution before the story's conclusion.
2. **Make predictions** Read the clues together and have students suggest solutions before checking to see if they were correct.
3. **Silent reading** Play the audio. Then have students reread silently.
4. **Multi-level options** See MULTI-LEVEL OPTIONS on p. 44.

About the Author

1. **Explain author's background** Falcon Travis has written other mystery books, including: *The Great Book of Whodunit Puzzles, The Spy's Guide Book,* and *The Knowhow Book of Spycraft.*
2. **Interpret the facts** *Ask: Where do you think Falcon Travis learned to tell mystery stories? Do you think he is good at mystery writing?*

Answer
Example: He wrote what people said so readers could learn their thoughts. This makes the characters seem real.

Across Selections

Contrast subject matter Discuss how the mystery in this story is different from "The Loch Ness Monster." *Ask: Are these mysteries real or made up? Who tries to solve these mysteries? Which type of mystery is easier to solve? Why do you think so?*

Spelling, Punctuation, Capitalization

After the Reading Comprehension section, students will practice spelling, punctuation, and capitalization in the Activity Book.

Beyond the Reading

Reading Comprehension

Question-Answer Relationships

Sample Answers

1. a briefcase
2. a file of papers and an envelope with about $200
3. a round-trip ticket
4. after Mr. Fink said what he had done that day
5. Mr. Fink looked suspicious.
6. Mr. Fink said he had some magazines. There were no magazines in the briefcase. The contents were a file of papers and an envelope with about $200.
7. No. Mr. Fink didn't expect to be asked to empty his pockets because he tries to act like he's in a hurry and wants to get out of there quickly.
8. Mr. Fink looked puzzled when the briefcase was opened because he was pretending to be surprised that it didn't have magazines in it.
9. I think Mr. Fink felt really angry after Inspector Ketchum found out the truth.

Build Reading Fluency

Adjust Your Reading Rate for Quotations

Demonstrate how to pause and read with expression when reading quotations. Explain that you change your rate of reading depending on the purpose and type of reading material.

Reading Comprehension

Question-Answer Relationships (QAR)

"Right There" Questions

1. **Recall Facts** What was Mr. Fink carrying when he entered the coffee shop?
2. **Recall Facts** What was in the briefcase?
3. **Recall Facts** What type of ticket did Mr. Fink say he bought?
4. **Use Chronology to Locate Information** Use your knowledge of chronology to find the place in the story when the inspector asked Mr. Fink to empty his pockets.

"Think and Search" Questions

5. **Make Inferences** Why did Inspector Ketchum follow Mr. Fink into the coffee shop?

6. **Contrast** What did Mr. Fink say was in the briefcase? How was it different from what Inspector Ketchum found in the briefcase?

"Author and You" Questions

7. **Evaluate Evidence** Did Mr. Fink expect to be asked to empty his pockets? What tells you this?
8. **Make Judgments** Why did Mr. Fink look puzzled when Inspector Ketchum opened the briefcase?

"On Your Own" Question

9. **Evaluate** How do you think Mr. Fink felt after Inspector Ketchum found out that he was not telling the truth?

Activity Book
p. 26

Student
CD-ROM

Build Reading Fluency

Adjust Your Reading Rate for Quotations

Reading quotations helps you learn to adjust your reading rate. You must pause and read with expression. Reading with expression makes others want to listen to you.

Reread the conversation between Inspector Will Ketchum and Mr. Fink. Look for the quotation marks ("...").

1. With a partner, take turns rereading paragraphs 5–6 on page 43 aloud.
2. Read the quotations with expression.
3. Pause after each quotation.
4. Choose the quotation you like best.
5. Read it aloud in front of the class.

MULTI-LEVEL OPTIONS *Elements of Literature*

Newcomer Hide an object you use every day. Act out being upset that you can't find it. Have the students help you locate it. *Ask: What problem did I have?* (lost item) *What was the solution?* (looked for the item and found it) *What other solutions can you think of?* (use something else, etc.) List solutions on the board.

Beginning Have students brainstorm school-related problems, such as *I forgot to bring home my science book, and I need to study.* Write one problem on the board. Have students list solutions and then vote on the best one. *Say: A mystery has a problem and a resolution. How did we solve our problem?*

Intermediate Have students work in pairs to write a short mystery with an unfinished resolution. Have them exchange stories with another pair. Ask the other pair to write the resolution. Then have students evaluate the finished stories. *Ask: Does the resolution solve the problem?*

Advanced *Ask: What problems have you had that you have had to resolve? Were they like a mystery to you?* Ask students to share their ideas. Explain that a resolution is reached through problem solving. List the steps to good problem solving on the board.

Listen, Speak, Interact

Interpret Text Through Dramatization

In "The Sneak Thief," the author uses dialogue, the actual words that characters say to each other. Read the story as a "Reader's Theater."

1. Work in groups of three.
2. Decide on roles. One person is the narrator. One person is the inspector. One person is Mr. Fink.
3. Dramatize the story by acting it out. As you read, show your understanding of the text and make your partners want to listen.
4. Show what the characters are thinking and feeling as you read their words.
5. Present your dramatization to the class.
6. Analyze your classmates' dramatizations. Are the characters believable?

Elements of Literature

Recognize Problem and Resolution

Most mysteries have a **problem** and a **resolution**. The **problem** is often a question that needs to be answered. The **resolution** is how a person solves the problem or answers the question.

Problem: Did Mr. Fink steal the briefcase?

Resolution: Inspector Ketchum uses clues. He figures out that Mr. Fink stole the briefcase. He arrests Mr. Fink.

1. Read these sentences. Decide whether they are problems or resolutions. Write your answers in your Reading Log.
   a. How can you learn more about outer space?
   b. You can read a book about outer space.
   c. You go to the movies first. Then you go to the park.
   d. Your friend wants to go to the movies. You want to go to the park. What should you do?
2. Write a sentence describing a problem that you have now or that you had in the past. Then write a possible resolution.

Reading Log   Activity Book *p. 27*   Student CD-ROM

Chapter 4   The Sneak Thief   **47**

Content Connection
Social Studies

Explain that some crimes go unsolved for a very long time. Tell students that scientists recently tried to figure out if King Tutankhamen was murdered over 3,000 years ago. Ask pairs to use the Internet or library to find information on this investigation and report their findings to the class. Have students evaluate the "evidence" they uncover and offer their own opinions.

Learning Styles
Musical

Tell students that suspense is an important part of a good mystery story. Explain that in movie or television mysteries, music helps establish or build suspense. View a video of a mystery. Ask students to pay attention to the ways music adds to the mood of suspense. View the video again without the sound. Ask students to discuss the difference, with emphasis on whether the music added to the feeling of suspense.

Listen, Speak, Interact

Interpret Text Through Dramatization

Teacher Resource Book: *Reading Log, p. 64*

1. **Reread in small groups** Arrange students into groups of three. Have them choose parts and reenact the story.
2. **Newcomers** Reread with this group. Have them practice reading aloud the dialogues using appropriate intonation and gestures.
3. **Evaluate** Have students write a critique of their own dramatic reading in their Reading Logs.

Elements of Literature

Recognize Problem and Resolution

1. **Explore solutions** *Say: There aren't enough seats and tables in the cafeteria for all the students to eat at the same time. What solutions can you suggest?* Have students work in groups to come up with resolutions. Share them with the class.
2. **Personal experience** Have students point out other school problems and have students suggest possible resolutions.
3. **Multi-level options** See MULTI-LEVEL OPTIONS on p. 46.

Answers
1. a. problem b. resolution c. resolution d. problem
2. *Example:* Problem: I don't have a pencil. Resolution: I'll borrow one from my friend.

 **ASSESS**

Ask: What is a problem? (a question to be answered) *What is a resolution?* (how a person solves a problem or answers the question)

Word Study

Apply Knowledge of Letter-Sound Correspondences

1. **Contrast *th* with *t*** Write on the board: *1. t; 2. th.* Model the sounds. *Say: thin, three, tree, tin.* Have students show one or two fingers for the sound they heard.

2. **Listen and imitate** Say the words and sentences and have students repeat. Help students pronounce properly *th.*

3. **Identify *th*** Play the audio or read aloud paragraphs 13–15 on p. 44. Have students raise their hands each time they hear the *th* sound.

Grammar Focus

Identify Simple, Compound, and Complex Sentences

Recognize clauses Write the samples on the board. Help students to pick out subjects and verbs in the clauses. Point out conjunctions between clauses in the compound sentence. Contrast the clauses in the compound and complex sentences. Have students identify the independent and dependent clauses.

Answers

1. compound 2. complex 3. simple

ASSESS

Have students write three sentences: a simple, a compound, and a complex sentence.

Word Study

Apply Knowledge of Letter-Sound Correspondences

Some English words contain the letters *th.* These letters usually stand for a sound that is different from the sounds of *t* and *h.*

1. Listen as your teacher pronounces the *th* sounds in these words. Then repeat after your teacher.

thief	thing
three	truth
thanks	tooth

2. Practice reading these sentences with a partner.
   a. A man with the eyes of a sneak thief attracted his attention.
   b. Were there three magazines?
   c. Was the suspect telling the truth?

Activity Book p. 28 — Student CD-ROM

Grammar Focus

Identify Simple, Compound, and Complex Sentences

All sentences have **clauses.** A clause has a subject and a verb. A **subject** is who or what the sentence is about. A **verb** tells something about the subject.

There are three main sentence types: **simple sentence, compound sentences,** and **complex sentences.**

A **simple sentence** has one **independent clause.** An independent clause is a clause that can stand alone as a sentence.

You want milk.

A **compound sentence** has two or more independent clauses. These independent clauses are joined by a comma and a conjunction like *or, but,* or *and.*

You want milk, but I want juice.

A **complex sentence** has one independent clause and one **dependent clause.** A dependent clause is a clause that cannot stand alone as a sentence. Dependent clauses begin with words like *because, when, that,* or *although.*

Although you want milk, I want juice.

Copy these sentences on a piece of paper. Write whether each sentence is a simple sentence, a compound sentence, or a complex sentence.

1. Mai plays the piano, and Luis plays the drums.
2. When Ali is at home, Anna is at work.
3. Alta ran home with her brother.

Activity Book pp. 29–30 — Student Handbook — Student CD-ROM

MULTI-LEVEL OPTIONS *From Reading to Writing*

Newcomer *Say: This is a good book.* Write on the board and *say: The teacher says, "This is a good book." Ask: Where is the ruler?* Write on the board and *say: "Where is the ruler?" she asks.* Indicate the words inside each set of quotation marks. *Say: I said these words.* Have volunteers dictate sentences to you. Add *he says* or *she says* and have students punctuate.

Beginning Ask pairs of students to create comic strips of the story. Help them to add important dialogue in speech bubbles. Remind students that their comic strips should use drawings or words to show the problem, clues, and resolution.

Intermediate Have pairs write dialogues between a police officer and a thief who has been caught stealing. *Ask: What words can you add to make this more exciting? What words can you use to show the order of the steps that the police officer took to solve the crime?* Ask students to revise the dialogues based on their responses. Have students act out their finished dialogues.

Advanced Have students exchange dialogues with partners. Ask partners to peer-edit for punctuation, sentence types, dependent clauses, and chronology words. Have pairs perform the dialogues.

From Reading to Writing

Write Dialogue in a Mystery

Many parts of "The Sneak Thief" have dialogue—what characters say to each other. However, the author does not use dialogue when he explains how Inspector Ketchum solves the crime. Write a dialogue between Inspector Ketchum and Mr. Fink for the solution of the crime.

1. Inspector Ketchum will explain what clues he used to solve the crime. Use the information in paragraph 16.
2. Mr. Fink will say why he is surprised that he was caught. Use information from paragraph 17.
3. Include how you think Mr. Fink feels after he is caught.
4. Reread paragraphs 6 to 8 of the selection. Use these as a model.

5. Use different sentence types— simple, compound, and complex.
6. Use correct punctuation for dependent clauses.
7. Use some chronology words such as *first, then, next,* and *after.*

> Inspector Ketchum said, "Mr. Fink, I know you stole the briefcase because you did not have _____, _____, and _____ in your pockets!"
>
> Mr. Fink said, "You caught me! I did not expect you to _____. I feel _____ because _____."

Activity Book
p. 31

Student Handbook

Across Content Areas

Learn Words About the Law

"The Sneak Thief" is about someone who broke the law (Fink) and someone who protects the law (Ketchum).

suspect: a person whom the police *think* committed a crime
criminal: a person who committed a crime
innocent: did not commit a crime
guilty: committed a crime

Copy these sentences. Complete each one with a law word.

1. The police aren't sure if the man stole the bicycle. He is still a ____ .
2. John Smith went to jail because he robbed a bank. He is a ____ .
3. Under U.S. law, you are ____ until you are proven ____ .

Activity Book
p. 32

Reteach and Reassess

Text Structure Draw a magnifying glass on the board. On the handle, write: *Mystery.* Inside the circle, write: *Problem, Clues, Suspense,* and *Resolution.* Have students identify each feature.

Reading Strategy Have pairs create timelines that show the order of the events in the story. Ask them to present their timelines using words such as *first, second, then,* and *finally.*

Elements of Literature Have students state a problem and a resolution that was described in "The Sneak Thief" (p. 41).

Reassess Ask students to write one-paragraph reviews of the story. Tell them to include what they liked or disliked about it and why. Also ask them to include whether they solved the mystery before reading the final page.

From Reading to Writing

Write Dialogue in a Mystery

1. **Use a role-play** Have students prepare dialogue for the characters. Arrange students in pairs to share ideas and develop a role-play. Ask pairs to perform their scenes.
2. **Language experience dialogue** For beginning students, have them dictate lines to you. Then have pairs practice the dialogues.
3. **Multi-level options** See MULTI-LEVEL OPTIONS on p. 48.

Across Content Areas: Language Arts

Learn Words About the Law

1. **Clarify meanings** Read the words and meanings. Have students work in small groups to discuss a movie or television mystery they know. Have them use all the vocabulary words.
2. **Locate pronunciations and derivations** Have students locate the pronunciations and derivations of these words using a large dictionary or a CD-ROM or an online dictionary.
3. **Recognize related words** Discuss related words. Discuss the forms and usage: *suspect* (n), *suspect* (v); *criminal* (n), *crime* (n), *criminal* (adj); *innocent* (adj), *innocently* (adv), *innocence* (n); *guilty* (adj), *guilt* (n).

Answers
1. suspect 2. criminal 3. innocent, guilty

 **ASSESS**

Have students write sentences using *suspect, innocent, criminal,* and *guilty.*

CHAPTER 5

Into the Reading

The Legend of Sleepy Hollow

a legend by
Washington Irving

adapted by
Jack Kelly

Chapter Materials

Activity Book: *pp. 33–40*
Audio: *Unit 1, Chapter 5; CD 1, Track 5*
Student Handbook
Student CD-ROM: *Unit 1, Chapter 5*
Teacher Resource Book: *Lesson Plan, Teacher Resources, Reading Summary, Activity Book Answer Key*
Teacher Resource CD-ROM
Assessment Program: *Quiz, pp. 15–16; Teacher and Student Resources, pp. 115–144*
Assessment CD-ROM
Transparencies
The Heinle Newbury House Dictionary/CD-ROM
Web site: http://visions.heinle.com

Objectives

Raise questions Read the objectives, explaining and raising questions. *Ask: What is a legend? What are the five senses?*

Use Prior Knowledge

Compare Oral Traditions

Share personal experience Have students discuss who tells stories in their families and the characters in the stories.

✔ ASSESS

Ask students to draw a picture of a story character and share it with a partner.

Objectives

Reading Identify imagery as you read a legend.

Listening and Speaking Talk about senses.

Grammar Use pronoun referents.

Writing Write a character description.

Content Social Studies: Read a timeline.

Use Prior Knowledge

Compare Oral Traditions

Most cultures and regions have stories that are very old. They are told from grandparent to parent to child. This is called the **oral tradition.** Examples are stories about La Llorona, Atlantis, Rip Van Winkle, and El Dorado.

1. With your class, talk about old stories that you know.
2. Make a chart of the oral traditions you and your classmates know. How are they the same? How are they different?

Oral Traditions	
Culture/Region of Origin	What the Story Is About

MULTI-LEVEL OPTIONS *Build Vocabulary*

Newcomer On the board, write: *hear/here. Ask: Do these words sounds alike?* Use each in a sentence. *Say: In English, there are many words that sound alike but are spelled differently. Read the whole sentence to understand the meaning of a word.*

Beginning Write on the board: *The boys put the boots over there. Where are their coats? They're in the closet.* Ask students to point to the words that sound the same. *Ask: Do they have different meanings?* (yes) *Do you know other words that sound the same but have different spellings and meanings?* (examples: your, you're; to, two, too) List responses on the board.

Intermediate Ask students to write one sentence with *your* and one with *you're.* Have students discuss the different meanings of the words. Help them write a rule for choosing the correct word. Have them list other words that sound the same but have different spellings and meanings. (*examples:* to, two, too; its, it's)

Advanced Ask students to write sentences for *there, their,* and *they're,* leaving blanks for those words. Have them exchange sentences with partners. Ask students to fill in the correct word for each sentence. Repeat the activity with *your/you're, here/hear,* and *whose/who's.*

Build Background

Sleepy Hollow

The selection you will read takes place in Sleepy Hollow. Sleepy Hollow is a real town in the state of New York. It is a quiet town near the Hudson River with many parks and forests. The people who live in Sleepy Hollow like the town because it is peaceful.

 Content Connection

The Dutch (people from The Netherlands) were the first Europeans to live along the Hudson River. They founded New York City and other cities and towns. One of them was Sleepy Hollow.

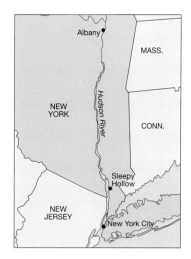

Build Vocabulary

Spell Frequently Misspelled Words

Some words are pronounced alike but have different spellings and meanings. Look at the example in the chart.

Copy these sentences in your Personal Dictionary. Fill in the blanks with *there, their,* or *they're.* Check your answers with a partner.

1. They didn't get up on time, so _____ late for school again.
2. I can't find my book. Oh! It's over _____ .
3. They have already finished _____ homework.

Word	Meaning	Example
there	a word used to start a statement or to indicate a place	**There** are many old stories in my culture. I'm going **there.**
their	possessive form of *they*	They told stories. **Their** stories were interesting.
they're	contraction of *they are*	My grandfather likes to tell stories. **They're** interesting.

 Personal Dictionary   Activity Book p. 33   Student CD-ROM

Chapter 5 The Legend of Sleepy Hollow **51**

Community Connection

Build Background Explain to students that many towns have names that describe them. *Say: Sleepy Hollow was probably named* Sleepy *because it was a quite, peaceful town. The word* Hollow *is an old-fashioned word that was used to name a small town in a valley.* Have students think about their city or town. Ask them to work in pairs to think of new names that describe the geography or "personality" of where they live. (*Examples:* Riverview, Desert's Edge)

Learning Styles
Interpersonal

Build Vocabulary Ask teams to list as many homophones as they can. Challenge them to find uncommon homophones such as *yore* for *you're* and *your* or *mete* for *meet* and *meat.* Encourage students to work cooperatively to succeed. The team with the longest list or the most uncommon or creative homophones wins. (new, knew, gnu)

Build Background

Sleepy Hollow

1. **Use a photo** Bring in books about the Hudson Valley region. Ask students to describe the area.
2. **Relate to personal experience** Have students talk about people they know or experiences they have had in this region of New York state.
3. **Content Connection** Henry Hudson, an Englishman, first explored the northeast area around the Hudson River. Later, Dutch settlers came. Have students find names of Dutch origin on a map of the area.

Build Vocabulary

Spell Frequently Misspelled Words

Teacher Resource Book: *Personal Dictionary,* p. 63

1. **Contrast and analyze** Write on the board: *there, their,* and *they're.* Point out differences in spelling and meaning. Say sentences and have students identify which word was used by spelling it.
2. **Reading selection vocabulary** You may want to introduce the glossed words in the reading selection before students begin reading. Key words: *apparition, stallion, haunted, terrors, fables, dread.* Instruct students to write the words with correct spelling and their definitions in their Personal Dictionaries. Have them pronounce each word and divide it into syllables.
3. **Multi-level options** See MULTI-LEVEL OPTIONS on p. 50.

Answers
1. they're 2. there 3. their

 **ASSESS**

Have students write a sentence for each of the words: *there, they're, their.*

Text Structure

Legend

1. **Clarify features** Direct attention to the chart. Have students give examples from legends they know.
2. **Multi-level options** See MULTI-LEVEL OPTIONS below.

Reading Strategy

Identify Imagery

Draw on experiences Have students close their eyes and listen as you open and drink a can of soda. On the board, write: *I opened the soda and drank it. I snapped open the can and swallowed the ice-cold drink.* **Ask:** *Which sentence gives a clearer image or sense of the action?* (second sentence)

Answer
2. small, perched, skinny; glow, heat, crackling

ASSESS

Have students name the three features of legends.

Text Structure

Legend

"The Legend of Sleepy Hollow" is a **legend**. A legend is a story that people have told for many years. Look for these features of a legend as you read the selection.

Legend	
Tradition	The story is told from generation to generation.
Setting	The story takes place a long time ago, in a real place.
Amazing Characters and Events	The story is based on truth, but some characters and events are exaggerated or made up.

Student
CD-ROM

Reading Strategy

Identify Imagery

Many writers use **imagery.** Imagery is writing that helps readers form **images** (pictures) in their minds. Imagery often refers to the senses: seeing, hearing, tasting, touching, or smelling.

He was a <u>tall</u>, <u>lanky</u> <u>young</u> man.

The words *tall, lanky,* and *young* help you picture the man in your mind.

Describing images can also help you learn and recall words.

1. Write these sentences from the reading in your Reading Log.

   His small head was perched on a skinny neck.

   The room would glow from the heat of a crackling wood fire.

2. Underline the words that help you form images in your mind.
3. Draw a picture for each sentence.
4. Share your pictures with a partner.

Reading Log

Student
CD-ROM

52 Unit 1 Mysteries

MULTI-LEVEL OPTIONS *Text Structure*

Newcomer Explain that a legend is a family story that is passed down through generations. Show a video or read a legend. (Johnny Appleseed, John Henry, Robin Hood, Paul Bunyan, etc.) Have students draw images of the characters, settings, and events.

Beginning Ask students to share family stories with the class. Remind them that when a story is passed down from generation to generation, it is called a *legend.* Explain that over time, these stories often change and become exaggerated. Demonstrate how these changes occur by playing the telephone game.

Intermediate On the board, write: *legend.* Ask students to work in pairs. Have them tell family stories. Have partners write down stories after hearing them and without asking any questions. Then have partners read back the stories. *Ask: Did the story change? How? Why do you think this happened?*

Advanced Have groups play the telephone game using family stories. Then have them compare the final story to the original. *Ask: How did it change? Were parts added to make it more interesting?* Explain that this is how a story becomes a legend. Have students find legends to share with the class.

THE LEGEND OF
Sleepy Hollow

by Washington Irving
adapted by Jack Kelly

53

Reading Selection Materials

Audio: *Unit 1, Chapter 5; CD 1, Track 5*
Teacher Resource Book: *Reading Summary,*
    pp. 73–74
Transparencies: *#33, Reading Summary*

Suggestions for Using Reading Summary

- Introduce new vocabulary or cognates.
- Cut the summary into strips, or jumble the sentences on an overhead transparency. Students put the sentences in order.
- Practice the reading strategy.
- Students read aloud or with a partner.
- Students paraphrase the summary.
- Students do a cloze activity.
- Students create a visual or graphic organizer, such as a timeline or storyboard, to illustrate the summary.
- Students paraphrase the summary.

Preview the Selection

Teacher Resource Book: *Know/Want to Know/Learned (KWL) Chart, p. 42*

1. **Use the illustration** Have students describe the picture. *Ask: Who is in the picture? What does he look like? What is he doing? Where do you think he is? How does the picture make you feel? Do you think this is a picture of something real or imaginary?*

2. **Use a KWL chart** Have students complete a chart with things they know about this legend (title, information from the illustration). Guide students to create questions for what they want to know about the legend and the headless man in the picture. Students can use the chart to guide their reading of the legend.

3. **Connect** Remind students that the unit theme is *mysteries. Ask: What is mysterious about this picture and about the man in the picture?*

Cultural Connection

Remind students that the Headless Horseman is a legendary American character. Have them provide examples of legendary characters from other cultures. Ask them to describe the characters. Discuss any similarities and differences among the legendary characters of different cultures.

Learning Styles
Musical

Introduce the idea that music can establish mood. Provide samples of instrumental music. Be sure to provide music that suggests an assortment of moods, such as funny, sad, or scary. Ask students to examine the picture on p. 53 and pick the piece of music they think would be most appropriate to accompany this selection. As students read the selection, play the music quietly in the background.

Read the Selection

1. **Use the illustration** Help students describe the people and setting and suggest what the people are talking about.
2. **Reciprocal reading** Play the audio. Then arrange students in groups for reciprocal reading. Assign each student a different portion of the selection. Each student should read aloud his/her part, ask questions to the group, and ask a member to summarize the part.
3. **Identify imagery** *Say: In paragraph 4, the farmers sometimes saw "this apparition go swooping past." The word* swooping *makes me hear the sound of something going fast. What other words make you see or hear something?* (paragraph 5, "go tearing through the Hollow")

Sample Answer to Guide Question
Together around the fire; dark, windy nights; mysterious being. I recall *dark, windy,* and *mysterious.*

See Teacher Edition pp. 434–436 for a list of English-Spanish cognates in the reading selection.

Identify Imagery

Which words in this paragraph help you form pictures in your mind? Think of your image of this paragraph. Which words do you recall in the image?

1 When the good folk of Sleepy Hollow got together around the fire on dark and windy nights, their talk often turned to a **mysterious** being who had been seen riding along nearby roads.

2 "He was a **Hessian cavalryman** who lost his head in the Revolutionary War," one said. "A **cannonball** took it clean off."

3 "He's a ghost, the commander of all the evil spirits in these parts," another claimed.

4 Nobody knew for sure. But many a farmer, out late at night, would see this **apparition** go swooping past—an enormous, terrible figure mounted on a powerful **stallion.** He was the Headless Horseman!

5 "His body's buried in the churchyard," said one man, who claimed to be an expert on the subject. "At night he rides out to the battlefield where he was killed to look for his missing head. Toward dawn you'll see him go tearing through the Hollow as fast as he can ride. He has to get back to his grave before **daybreak.**"

Audio
CD 1, Tr. 5

mysterious not known	**apparition** a ghostly figure
Hessian a soldier from the nation of Germany	**stallion** a horse
cavalryman a soldier trained to fight on horses	**daybreak** morning
cannonball a metal ball that is shot from a large gun	

54 Unit 1 Mysteries

MULTI-LEVEL OPTIONS *Read the Selection*

Newcomer Play the audio. Read the pages aloud. *Ask: Do the people of Sleepy Hollow talk around the fire?* (yes) *Do they talk about a mysterious rider?* (yes) *Do they know exactly who he is?* (no) *Is he the Headless Horseman?* (yes) *Is Ichabod Crane the schoolmaster?* (yes) *Is Ichabod fat?* (no)

Beginning Read the Reading Summary aloud. *Ask: What do the people of Sleepy Hollow talk about on dark, windy nights?* (the Headless Horseman) *Who is the schoolmaster?* (Ichabod Crane) *What does he look like?* (a scarecrow, a crane) *Where is the town?* (in a valley along the Hudson River)

Intermediate Have students do a paired reading. *Ask: Why does the Horseman go to the battlefield?* (to look for his head) *Why did Ichabod Crane listen so closely?* (He thought he knew about ghosts.) *What evidence does the farmer give to prove the spot is haunted?* (meteors, shooting stars, nightmares)

Advanced Have students read independently. *Ask: Why do you think the townspeople talk about the Headless Horseman so much?* (They wonder who he is and what his story is.) *Does Sleepy Hollow seem like a likely place for an evil spirit? Why?* (No, it's peaceful and quiet.)

6   One of those who listened most closely to these ghostly **tales** was Ichabod Crane. Ichabod was the town's schoolmaster, and a man who thought he knew a thing or two about ghosts himself.

7   Ichabod, indeed, looked something like a **crane.** He was a tall, **lanky** young man with long arms and legs, hands that **dangled** a mile out of his sleeves, and feet like shovels. His small head was perched on a skinny neck. He had huge ears and a long, pointed nose that made his head seem like a **weather vane** pointing the direction of the wind. Many said he looked like a scarecrow from some cornfield.

8   Now, Sleepy Hollow is one of the most peaceful spots in the world. It's a hidden valley along the Hudson River that's just as quiet and **drowsy** and dreamy as it can possibly be.

9   "This is a **haunted** spot," an old farmer whispered to Ichabod one night. "The sky is full of **meteors** and shooting stars. And there's nightmares that will slip into your dreams."

10   During the day, Ichabod didn't have time to think of ghosts and spirits. He was busy running his little one-room schoolhouse. If you went by on a warm drowsy day you might hear the **murmuring** voices of his pupils **reciting** their lessons.

> **Identify Imagery**
>
> Which words help you picture Ichabod Crane in your mind? Think of your image. Which words do you recall?

tales stories	**drowsy** sleepy
crane a tall, long-necked bird	**haunted** visited by someone or something as a ghost
lanky skinny	**meteors** large rocks or pieces of metal from outer space
dangled hung loosely	**murmuring** low and unclear sounding
weather vane an instrument that indicates wind direction	**reciting** repeating or saying aloud

Chapter 5   The Legend of Sleepy Hollow   **55**

Read the Selection

1. **Use the illustration** Have students describe Ichabod Crane. *Ask: What do you think he is like?*
2. **Reciprocal reading** Play the audio. Then arrange students in groups for reciprocal reading. Assign each student a different portion of the selection. Each student should read aloud his/her part, ask questions to the group, and ask a member to summarize the part.
3. **Analyze character and setting** Ask questions to help students describe Ichabod. Begin a story map to record important information from the legend.
4. **Multi-level options** See MULTI-LEVEL OPTIONS on p. 54.

Sample Answer to Guide Question
Like a crane; tall, lanky; hands that dangled a mile; feet like shovels; small head; skinny neck; huge ears; long, pointed nose; like a weather vane; like a scarecrow. I remember *crane, tall,* and *skinny.*

❜ Punctuation

Apostrophes for contractions

Tell students that sometimes two words can be combined and shortened into one word. Explain that this new word is called a contraction. On the board, write: *you will/you'll.* Explain that the apostrophe shows that letters have been removed. *Ask: What letters were removed in the word you'll?* (wi) Review common contractions such as *n't* for *not,* *'d* for *had* or *would,* *'ll* for *will,* *'s* for *is* or *has,* and *'ve* for *have. Ask: What contraction*

is in paragraph 3? (He's) What words were combined to make this contraction? (He is) What does the apostrophe show? (The letter i was removed.)

    Apply Have students locate other contractions on pp. 54–55. (body's, you'll, that's, It's, there's) Then have students write the words that were combined to form these contractions. (body is, you will, that is, It is, there is)

Read the Selection

1. **Use text features** Have students check the meanings of glossed words. Guide discussion of the illustration.

2. **Reciprocal reading** Play the audio. Then arrange students in groups for reciprocal reading. Assign each student a different portion of the selection. Each student should read aloud his/her part, ask questions to the group, and ask a member to summarize the part.

3. **Identify imagery** *Ask: What do you know about the school?* (It has one room. The students say their lessons out loud.) *What does it sound like?* (There are a lot of voices talking softly.) *What words in the story tell you that?* (busy, murmuring)

4. **Summarize** *Ask: What is Ichabod Crane's job?* (He's a teacher.) *Where does he live and where does he eat?* (He stays and eats with the families of his students.)

Sample Answer to Guide Question
He's like an anaconda, a large snake that swallows its food whole.

11　Ichabod liked his pupils. . . . He always tried hard to keep on good terms with [their] families. . . . He had no choice. His salary was very small, and his **appetite** was very large.

12　"What's for dinner?" were often the first words out of Ichabod's mouth. Though skinny, he could swallow a huge meal the way an **anaconda** snake does.

13　As part of his pay, he would room and take his meals with the farmers whose children went to his school. He lived with each family for a week, then moved on. Over the year, he made the rounds of the neighborhood, all his belongings tied up in a big cotton **handkerchief.**

14　Farmers in those days sometimes thought that schooling cost too much, or that schoolmasters were just lazy **drones.** To make the **burden** lighter, and to make himself useful, Ichabod would help his hosts with their chores whenever he could. He helped the farmers to make hay. He lent a hand when they **mended** their fences, took horses to water, drove cows to pasture, and cut wood for the winter fire.

> **Identify Imagery**
>
> What animal is Ichabod Crane compared to in this paragraph?

appetite   desire for food
anaconda   a very large snake
handkerchief   a cloth used for wiping the nose or mouth
drones   people who live off others
burden   a responsibility or duty
mended   fixed

56   Unit 1   Mysteries

MULTI-LEVEL OPTIONS   *Read the Selection*

Newcomer *Ask: Was Ichabod busy during the day?* (yes) *Did he like his pupils?* (yes) *Did he make a lot of money?* (no) *Did he eat a lot?* (yes) *Did he move from house to house?* (yes) *Did he help farmers with chores?* (yes) *Did he take care of the children?* (yes) *Did he like ghost stories?* (yes)

Beginning *Ask: Where did Ichabod live?* (with his pupils' families) *What else did he do besides teach?* (He helped with chores, took care of babies.) *Who did he share ghost stories with?* (the farmers' wives) *What kept the room warm?* (a fire)

Intermediate *Ask: Why did Ichabod have to get along with the families?* (He needed them to pay him to teach their children.) *Why did he do chores and take care of the babies?* (so they would think he was useful)

Advanced *Ask: Do you think Ichabod Crane liked children? Explain.* (Yes, he was a teacher and he took care of the farmers' babies. *or* No, he worked with children just to make money.) *Why does the author say ghosts wouldn't dare enter the room?* (The room was too warm, happy, and pleasant to invite ghosts.)

15　"Let me take care of the little lambs," he would say to the mothers. And he would sit for hours with one child on his knee, at the same time using his foot to rock another in its **cradle.**

16　One of Ichabod's great pleasures was to pass long winter evenings sitting by the fire with farmers' wives as they told tales of ghosts and **goblins.** They would talk while they spun wool and roasted apples in the fireplace.

17　"That field down **yonder** is haunted," someone would say.

18　"There's a goblin that lives under the bridge," another would claim. "I've seen him with my own eyes. . . ."

19　It was pleasant telling these tales while sitting **snug** in a chimney corner. The room would glow with the heat of the **crackling** wood fire. And of course no ghost dared to stick his head inside.

> **Identify Imagery**
>
> Which words in this paragraph help you form an image in your mind? Think of your image. Which words do you recall?

---

cradle　a small bed for a baby
goblins　make-believe creatures who do bad things
yonder　far away

snug　comfortable
crackling　making snapping or breaking noises

Chapter 5　The Legend of Sleepy Hollow　**57**

UNIT 1 • CHAPTER 5
Reading Selection

Read the Selection

1. **Use the illustration** Have students make predictions about the people and what they are talking about.
2. **Preview vocabulary** Have students check the meanings of the boldfaced words at the bottom of the page.
3. **Guided reading** Read aloud or ask volunteers to read. Pause to ask comprehension questions and to clarify vocabulary. *Ask: What did Ichabod like to do on winter evenings?* (sit by the fire and listen to stories)
4. **Use imagery** *Ask: How do you think it felt sitting by the fire?* (warm, nice, comfortable) *Do the stories sound very scary?* (no)
5. **Make predictions** Have students review the characters, setting, and situation. Guide them to make predictions about what might happen if Ichabod or someone went outside away from the fire.
6. **Multi-level options** See MULTI-LEVEL OPTIONS on p. 56.

Sample Answer to Guide Question
Pleasant, snug, glow, heat, crackling wood fire. I recall *pleasant* and *snug*.

❜ Punctuation

Ellipses

Write on the board: *I was just wondering about the test. . . .* Circle the last three dots. *Say: These are called ellipsis points. They show that the thought continues or that information has been left out.* Tell students that many writers use ellipses to leave a thought unfinished. *Ask: Where do you see ellipsis points on p.56?* (paragraph 11) *What does this ellipsis tell you?* (The thoughts are unfinished; the author wanted to leave the reader to fill in his/her own ideas.)

Reading Selection

Read the Selection

1. **Reciprocal reading** Play the audio. Then arrange students in groups for reciprocal reading. Assign each student a different portion of the selection. Each student should read aloud his/her part, ask questions to the group, and ask a member to summarize the part.

2. **Describe characters** Have students reread the selection with partners. *Ask: What shapes and noises does he see and hear when he walks home alone?* (He sees shadows and bushes. He hears footsteps.) *How does this make Ichabod feel?* (scared and frightened) *How is this different from what we learned about him before?* (He enjoyed listening to ghost stories. He thought he knew something about ghosts. He didn't seem scared of them before.)

Sample Answer to Guide Question
fearful shapes, shadows, snowy

Identify Imagery

Which words help you picture the snowy evening?

20   But walking home **afterwards** was another story. Then all the **terrors** of the **fables** took form around the **timid** schoolmaster. Fearful shapes and shadows **loomed** along his path in the snowy evening. Seeing the light of a distant window, he wished he were back safe inside.

21   "Oh, keep away from me!" he would **exclaim.** But it was only a bush covered with snow, not a ghost.

22   "What was that?" he whispered. But it was merely the sound of his own feet breaking through the snow.

23   It got so that he **dreaded** even to look over his shoulder, in case someone was following him. But there was one spirit that Ichabod Crane feared more than any other. It was the one the old farmers' wives called the Galloping Hessian of the Hollow.

afterwards at a later time	**loomed** waited
terrors intense fears	**exclaim** shout
fables stories that have a lesson	**dreaded** feared
timid shy, scared	

58   **Unit 1**   Mysteries

MULTI-LEVEL OPTIONS *Read the Selection*

Newcomer *Ask: Was Ichabod scared when he walked home?* (yes) *Did he imagine that he heard and saw soldiers?* (no) *Was Ichabod especially afraid of the Headless Horseman?* (yes)

Beginning *Ask: What sights scared Ichabod while he walked home?* (shapes and shadows) *What sounds scared him?* (his own footsteps, howling wind) *What ghost scared him the most?* (the Headless Horseman)

Intermediate *Ask: Why was Ichabod scared when he walked home?* (He was alone; it was dark; shapes and sounds seemed more frightening.) *What sound did Ichabod think was the Headless Horseman?* (a howling that came through the trees)

Advanced *Ask: Why was Ichabod afraid to look over his shoulder?* (He was afraid someone was following him.) *Do you think the story would be more or less scary if the author revealed more information about the Headless Horseman? Explain.* (less; leaving it open lets you imagine scarier things.)

Identify Imagery

What images are used to describe the glen? Think of your own images. Which words do you recall?

24   Sometimes, very late at night, walking through some dark, shadowy **glen,** Ichabod would suddenly hear a rushing blast come howling through the trees.

25   "It's only the wind," he would tell himself. But he could never completely convince himself that it wasn't—the Headless Horseman!

glen a low area of land between mountains or large hills

About the Author

Washington Irving (1783–1859)

Washington Irving was one of the first great writers in the United States. People all over the world know his stories. Washington Irving was born in New York City. He visited the Hudson Valley, and some of his greatest stories happen there. Washington Irving spent the last years of his life living near the town of Sleepy Hollow.

➤ Why do you think Washington Irving wrote "The Legend of Sleepy Hollow"? What questions would you ask Washington Irving?

Chapter 5 The Legend of Sleepy Hollow **59**

---

th **Spelling**

Irregular plurals

Remind students that they can form many plurals by adding -s or -es to singular nouns. *Say: When a noun ends with* -f *or* -fe, *however, the plural is usually formed differently. To form the plural for most words that end in* -f *or* -fe, *drop the* -f *or* -fe *and add* -ves. On the board, write: *wife/wives* and *elf/elves.*

Apply Have students write the plurals of *half, life, shelf, knife, self,* and *wolf.* (halves, lives, shelves, knives, selves, wolves)

Evaluate Your Reading Strategy

Identify Imagery *Say: You have practiced an important reading strategy. Now you can decide how well you have done. Does this statement describe how you read?*

> Imagery helps me picture what an author is describing. These pictures help me understand what is happening in a story.

Read the Selection

1. **Shared reading** Play the audio. Have students join in when they can. *Ask: Why do you think Ichabod Crane was scared at night?* (He had just heard scary stories. He is a silly, superstitious man.) Ask students to guess if there really is a Headless Horseman. Have them explain.
2. **Multi-level options** See MULTI-LEVEL OPTIONS on p. 58.

Sample Answer to Guide Question
Dark, shadowy; rushing blast, howling. I recall *dark* and *howling.*

About the Author

1. **Explain author's background** Washington Irving lived in Europe for many years and received literary awards in Spain and England.
2. **Interpret the facts** *Ask: How do you think Washington Irving learned about legends?* (He probably heard them from people in the area.)

Answer
Example: I think he wrote it because he enjoyed writing about a place he liked so much. I would ask if there is a real legend about the Headless Horseman.

Across Selections

Compare text structure Compare the text structure of this legend with the selection in Chapter 4. *Ask: What is the most important feature that this legend shares with the mystery story "The Sneak Thief"?* (suspense) *What important feature is missing from the legend?* (resolution)

Spelling, Punctuation, Capitalization

After the Reading Comprehension section, students will practice spelling, punctuation, and capitalization in the Activity Book.

Beyond the Reading

Reading Comprehension

Question-Answer Relationships

Sample Answers

1. a Hessian soldier who lost his head in the war
2. a schoolteacher
3. in a peaceful spot in a valley on the Hudson River
4. to look for his missing head
5. because he has to stay with them and depend on them for food
6. tall, lanky, and skinny
7. He's afraid because he just heard all the scary stories and it is dark and spooky outside at night.
8. Yes. The person telling the story made it sound like it really happened.
9. I think Sleepy Hollow is a good place for the story. One of the characters talks about dreams and nightmares that happen when you sleep. Also, Sleepy Hollow sounds so quiet that it makes the scary story seem even scarier.
10. I know a legend that has a scary person walking around late at night. It is different because the scary person does not ride a horse.

Build Reading Fluency

Read Silently

Assessment Program: *Reading Fluency Chart, p. 116*

When students have completed the reading fluency activity, record their progress in the Reading Fluency Chart.

Reading Comprehension

Question-Answer Relationships (QAR)

"Right There" Questions

1. **Recall Facts** Who do the townspeople think the Headless Horseman is?
2. **Recall Facts** What is Ichabod Crane's job?
3. **Recall Facts** Where is Sleepy Hollow located?

"Think and Search" Questions

4. **Give Reasons** Why does the Headless Horseman appear?
5. **Give Reasons** Why does Ichabod Crane like to stay on the good side of the townspeople?

"Author and You" Questions

6. **Describe** What are three words that the author uses to describe Ichabod Crane?

7. **Make Inferences** Why is Ichabod Crane afraid when he leaves the homes of the farmers' wives?

"On Your Own" Questions

8. **Compare Your Experiences** Have you ever been afraid because of a scary story? Explain.
9. **Understand Setting** Do you think that Sleepy Hollow was a good place for the story to happen? Why or why not?
10. **Compare Legends** Do you know a legend similar to this one? How is it the same? How is it different?

Activity Book
p. 34

Student
CD-ROM

Build Reading Fluency

Read Silently

Reading silently for long periods of time helps you become a better reader. It helps you learn to read faster.

1. Listen to the audio recording of "The Legend of Sleepy Hollow."
2. Listen to the chunks of words as you follow along on page 54.

3. Reread paragraphs 1–4 silently two times.
4. Your teacher will time your second reading.
5. Raise your hand when you are finished.

MULTI-LEVEL OPTIONS *Elements of Literature*

Newcomer Direct students to the illustration on p. 56. *Say: That is where Ichabod teaches school. That is the* setting *of his work. This classroom is* your setting. Have students draw pictures that compare and contrast the two classrooms. Display the drawings under two headings: *Sleepy Hollow School and (your) School.*

Beginning *Ask: What is special about this room?* Have students describe the classroom. Write their sentences on the board. *Say: This is our* setting. *This is how a writer tells the reader what a place looks like.* Help students write one or two sentences describing their favorite places.

Intermediate Have pairs write descriptions of the school cafeteria. Remind them to include details such as smells and sounds. Provide examples of descriptive writing for students to use as models. *Ask: What words did you use to help the reader "see" the cafeteria?*

Advanced Have students work independently to write a paragraph that summarizes the setting of "The Legend of Sleepy Hollow." *Ask: Have you included words that help the reader "see" the place you are describing?* Ask students to share their paragraphs.

Listen, Speak, Interact

Talk About Senses

"The Legend of Sleepy Hollow" uses imagery to help you form pictures in your mind. You use different senses to form these pictures. The five senses are touch, taste, smell, sight, and sound.

1. Work with a partner.
2. Read the sentences. For each sentence, decide which sense helps you form an image.
   a. The apples roasted in the fire.
   b. The room glowed with the heat of the crackling wood fire.
   c. The loud noise came howling through the trees.

Touch	Taste	Smell	Sight	Sound

   d. He had huge ears and a pointed nose.
   e. The bread was salty and sweet.
3. Copy the chart. Write the letters of the sentences in the columns.
4. Compare your answers to those of another pair of students. Use the names of the senses as you present. Are your answers the same as or different from the other pair's?

Elements of Literature

Analyze Setting and Tone

In "The Legend of Sleepy Hollow," Washington Irving tells us about the **setting** of the story—where it takes place.

We also learn about the main character, Ichabod Crane. Irving uses **tone** to tell us what he thinks about the character. His writing tells us what Ichabod is like.

1. With a partner, reread paragraphs 1 and 8. Then answer these questions.
   a. What kind of community is Sleepy Hollow? Describe the images of it that you have in your mind.
   b. This is a scary story. Why do you think the author describes Sleepy Hollow as he does?
2. What is Irving's tone in paragraph 7? Is it funny or serious?
3. Reread paragraphs 10 to 16.
   a. What do you learn about Ichabod?
   b. How would you describe him?
   c. What is Irving's attitude toward Ichabod? Does Irving suggest that Ichabod is a good teacher? Is he helpful?
4. Find other paragraphs in which Irving's tone tells you what he thinks about Ichabod Crane.

 Reading Log Activity Book p. 35 Student CD-ROM

Chapter 5 The Legend of Sleepy Hollow **61**

Content Connection
The Arts

Have students compare and contrast film with written story. Ask them to locate a film version of "The Legend of Sleepy Hollow" and compare and contrast it with the reading selection. They should talk about how the two versions are the same and how they are different, which version they preferred, and which media they feel is more effective.

Learning Styles
Linguistic

Have students form small groups. Ask groups to write and perform skits that summarize the story. Remind students that they can review the selection for ideas, but their dialogue and narration should restate the author's original text. Suggest that they use props, costumes, and background music to enhance their performances.

Listen, Speak, Interact

Talk About Senses

1. **Visualize** Ask students to describe the sights, sounds, smells, tastes, and feelings of a favorite meal.
2. **Newcomers** Read the sentences with this group. *Ask: Do you hear or smell the apples? The bread is salty—do you touch or taste it?* Mime actions of hearing, smelling, touching, and tasting.

Answer
2. touch (b), taste (e), smell (a), sight (d), sound (c)

Elements of Literature

Analyze Setting and Tone

1. **Clarify terms** Ask students to identify setting and main character of a story.
2. **Teacher think aloud** *Say: The author says Sleepy Hollow is hidden so I think there is something secret about this place.* Have pairs reread and discuss their answers.
3. **Personal experience** Have students suggest other settings or characters similar to those in the story.
4. **Multi-level options** See MULTI-LEVEL OPTIONS on p. 60.

Answers
1. a. Sleepy Hollow is a quiet and peaceful town. b. The author contrasts the quiet, sleepy town with the scary story.
2. Irving's tone is funny.
3. a. Ichabod liked his pupils; he was hungry; he tried to help his hosts with their chores. b. busy, hungry, helpful c. Irving suggests that Ichabod is not a good teacher, but he's helpful. He makes fun of Ichabod.
4. paragraphs 6, 7, and 20–23

✓ **ASSESS**

Have students identify the five senses and describe something they feel, taste, smell, see, or hear.

Word Study

Identify Root Words and the Suffix -less

Teacher Resource Book: *Personal Dictionary, p. 63*

Explain terms Write on the board: *help + -less = helpless.* Identify the root word and suffix. Explain the meaning of *helpless.*

Answers
2. careless; heartless; fearless
3. careless: without care; heartless: without a heart; fearless: without fear

Grammar Focus

Use Pronoun Referents

Review pronouns On the board, write the subject pronouns *she, he,* and *they.* Say sentences and have students choose the correct pronoun. ***Say:** Marie is a student. _____ is in this class.*

Answers
1. **a.** Sleepy Hollow **b.** Ichabod
2. *he:* a mysterious being; *it:* his head

ASSESS

Write on the board: *The story is scary. I like it. Ichabod is a teacher. He is funny.* Have students find the pronoun referents. (the story, Ichabod)

Word Study

Identify Root Words and the Suffix -less

Many English words have a root word and a suffix. A **root word** is the main part of a word. A **suffix** is a word part added to the end of a root word. Adding a suffix can change the meaning of the root word.

The suffix *-less* means "without." The word *headless* has the root word *head. Headless* means "without a head."

Words	Definitions
careless	without fear
heartless	without care
fearless	without a heart

1. Write the words in the box in your Personal Dictionary.
2. Circle the root word. Underline the suffix.

3. Match each word with the correct definition. Check your answers in a dictionary.

Personal Dictionary   The Heinle Newbury House Dictionary   Activity Book p. 36   Student CD-ROM

Grammar Focus

Use Pronoun Referents

A **pronoun** is a word that takes the place of a noun. *She, her, I, me, he,* and *him* are examples of pronouns.

A **pronoun referent** is the noun that the pronoun replaces. In writing it is important to keep your pronoun referents clear.

> <u>Marcos</u> is busy all day. <u>He</u> goes to school and then plays soccer.

The pronoun *He* takes the place of *Marcos.*

1. Copy these sentences on a piece of paper. Look at the underlined pronouns. Find the pronoun referent in the other sentence.

a. Sleepy Hollow is one of the most peaceful spots in the world. <u>It</u> is a hidden valley along the Hudson River.
b. Ichabod was the town's schoolmaster. <u>He</u> taught children all day.

2. Reread paragraph 2 of the reading. Find the referents for the pronouns *he* and *it.*

Activity Book pp. 37–38   Student Handbook   Student CD-ROM

MULTI-LEVEL OPTIONS *From Reading to Writing*

Newcomer Have students draw pictures of people they know. Help students label their drawings with descriptive adjectives. Invite students to share their drawings.

Beginning On the board, write: *bear.* Ask students to brainstorm words that describe it. (*examples:* big, furry, heavy) ***Say:** Writers use adjectives to describe a character.* Have students describe a celebrity they all know. List the adjectives. Help students use the list to write descriptive sentences. Provide this starter: *My person is _____. She/He is a _____ person.*

Intermediate Have students brainstorm a list of adjectives that describe a celebrity. Remind them that adjectives can describe a person's appearance as well as his/her personality or abilities. Have students refer to the list as they write their descriptive paragraphs.

Advanced Have students exchange paragraphs with partners. Ask partners to evaluate whether the descriptions are effective. Tell partners to circle all the adjectives. Have partners also check for proper spelling and punctuation.

From Reading to Writing

Write a Character Description

Washington Irving tells us what Ichabod Crane looks like. He uses adjectives such as *tall, lanky,* and *skinny.*

1. Choose a person that you know. This person can be a friend or family member. Or the person can be someone famous.
2. Write two adjectives that describe what this person looks like. Is the person very tall? Small? Beautiful?

> This person is named _____ . He/She is _____ as _____ . He/She is also _____ _____ . I think this person is very _____ .

3. Write a paragraph that describes this person. Remember to indent.
4. Use a dictionary or an online reference to check your spelling.
5. Be sure to use pronouns correctly and that the referents are clear.

Activity Book p. 39   Student Handbook

Across Content Areas

SOCIAL STUDIES

Read a Timeline

New York City, the largest city in the United States, had a different name when it was first settled. First study these facts.

a. In the 1500s and 1600s, Europeans explored North America.
b. The Netherlands sent explorers to North America.
c. The capital of The Netherlands is Amsterdam.
d. People from The Netherlands are called the Dutch.

Now look at the timeline and answer these questions.

1. What was New York City first called?
2. Why did they name it that?
3. How long did it take for the population to grow to 450 people?
4. When did the name change to New York?

Activity Book p. 40

1609	1624	1640	1664
Henry the Dutchman Hudson sailed up the Hudson River.	Dutch people settled a town called New Amsterdam.	There were about 450 people living in New Amsterdam.	The English took over New Amsterdam. They changed its name to New York.

Reteach and Reassess

Text Structure On the board, write: *Tradition, Setting, Amazing Characters/ Events.* Check each feature as students answer these questions: *Ask: How do you know the Headless Horseman story is a legend?* (retold from person to person) *When does the story take place?* (long ago) *Is it set in a real place?* (yes) *Do you think events or characters are exaggerated?* (yes)

Reading Strategy Ask students to draw pictures of the mental images of Ichabod Crane from descriptions in the reading.

Elements of Literature Have pairs discuss the setting and tone of the story. Ask one student to explain the setting. Have the other student explain the tone.

Reassess Ask groups to continue the story with an ending in which Ichabod meets the Horseman. Tell students to describe the Horseman and to use dialogue. Allow students to present their endings orally or in writing.

From Reading to Writing

Write a Character Description

Teacher Resource Book: *Web, p. 37*

1. **Use a web** Have students create a web about the person they want to describe. Have them add at least three adjectives. Model using the web to organize ideas.
2. **Use pronoun case** Before students begin writing, review subject nouns and object nouns. Provide model sentences with each. (Example: *The baseball landed between Julia and us.*) Then review subject pronouns and object pronouns. Have students replace the subject nouns and object nouns in the model sentences with pronouns. *(It landed between her and us.)*
3. **Think-quickwrite-pair-share** Ask students to use their webs and write as much as they can about their person. As students share with a partner, they can add other adjectives to describe their person.
4. **Multi-level options** See MULTI-LEVEL OPTIONS on p. 62.

Across Content Areas: Social Studies

Read a Timeline

Use a map Have students locate the following places on a world map: North America, Europe, The Netherlands, Amsterdam, New York City. Point out that *Holland* is another name for The Netherlands. Direct students' attention to the facts and timeline in their textbook.

Answers
1. New Amsterdam
2. It was settled by Dutch people, and they named it after the capital of their country, Amsterdam.
3. 16 years
4. in 1664

ASSESS

Have students write a quiz question about the timeline. Ask the questions and have students answer them.

Materials

Student Handbook
CNN Video: *Unit 1*
Teacher Resource Book: *Lesson Plan, p. 6;*
Teacher Resources, pp. 35–64; Video Script,
pp. 161–162; Video Worksheet, p. 173;
School-Home Connection, pp. 119–125
Teacher Resource CD-ROM
Assessment Program: *Unit 1 Test, pp. 17–22;*
Teacher and Student Resources, pp. 115–144
Assessment CD-ROM
Transparencies
The Heinle Newbury House Dictionary/CD-ROM
Heinle Reading Library: *The Adventures of*
Sherlock Holmes
Web site: http://visions.heinle.com

Listening and Speaking Workshop

Describe an Animal

Teacher Resource Book: *Sunshine Organizer,*
p. 40

Use adjectives Review descriptive adjectives
and expressions.

Step 1: Choose or create your animal.
Encourage students to add details in their
drawings.

Step 2: List details about your animal.
Model using a sunshine organizer to list
descriptive words and phrases that address
each of the senses.

Listening and Speaking Workshop

Describe an Animal

> **Topic**
>
> In this unit, you read about the
> Loch Ness monster. Some people
> believe that the monster is a real
> animal. Choose an animal. The
> animal can be real or made-up.
> Describe your animal to the class.

Step 1: Choose or create your animal.

1. Draw a picture of your animal.
   Include details.
2. Write the name of your animal.

Step 2: List details about your animal.

1. Write words that describe your
   animal.
2. Use your senses to describe your
   animal. How does your animal look?
   Sound? Smell? Feel?
3. Write your answers in a Sense Chart
   like the one shown.

Animal	See	Hear	Smell	Touch
Loch Ness monster	large teeth, big eyes	loud noises	like the lake	wet scales

Step 3: Write descriptive sentences.

1. Reread paragraphs 3 and 4 of "The
   Loch Ness Monster" on page 6. Use
   them as models for writing.
2. Write five short sentences that
   describe your animal. Use the details
   in the Sense Chart.

   The Loch Ness monster has large
   teeth and big eyes. It also has scales.

   Remember pronoun referents. Here,
   the word *it* means "the Loch Ness
   monster."
3. Write one or two sentences about
   where your animal lives and what
   it eats.
4. Use a variety of sentence types.
   a. Make sure each sentence has a
      subject and a verb.
   b. Make sure your pronoun
      referents are clear.

Step 4: Review your sentences.

1. Answer the following questions:
   a. Do I have enough facts?
   b. Are my details interesting?
   c. Do my descriptions make sense?
2. Review your sentences. Write your
   sentences on note cards.

MULTI-LEVEL OPTIONS *Listening and Speaking Workshop*

Newcomer Have students
create pictures of real or made-up
animals. Suggest that students
use original drawings, cut out and
glue pictures from magazines, or
use a computer to print clip art or
photographs. Help students to add
descriptive labels and captions.

Beginning Have students draw
pictures of animals. Encourage
them to use color and texture to
add details. Have them write three
sentences about their animals. Tell
them to describe what it eats,
where it lives, and the sounds it
makes. Invite students to share
their creatures.

Intermediate Have students
create fictional creatures by
combining real animals. Tell them
to choose distinct features from
several different animals. Have
students name their animals
based on the combination. (hippo-
moos-ephant, bumble-dolphi-
gator)

Advanced Have students
exchange note cards for peer
review. Tell reviewers to check for
descriptive words, pronoun
referents, and subject-verb
agreement. Ask students to revise
their presentations based on the
reviews.

Step 5: Practice your description.

1. Practice with a partner. Take turns.
2. Use your note cards and drawing.
3. Speak slowly and clearly. Listen carefully as your partner speaks.
4. Have your partner fill out the Active Listening Checklist on a piece of paper. You fill out the Speaking Checklist.
5. Use the checklists to revise your work.

Step 6: Present your animal.

1. Speak slowly and clearly.
2. Record your presentation. Use the Presentation Checklist in your Student Handbook to evaluate your presentation.

 Active Listening Checklist

1. The description was very detailed / not detailed.
2. There was enough / not enough information about the animal.
3. I want to know more about _____ .
4. I think this description could be more interesting if _____ .

 Speaking Checklist

1. Did I speak slowly and clearly?
2. Were my details interesting?
3. Did I show my drawing?

Student Handbook

Viewing Workshop

View and Think

Analyze a Mystery Movie

Not all mysteries are stories in books. Many movies also are mysteries.

1. Watch a mystery movie. Ask your school librarian to pick one out.
2. Take notes as you watch the movie.
   a. Write the problem that the characters are trying to solve.
   b. List clues that you notice.
   c. Write your ideas about how to solve the problem. Your ideas may change as you watch.
   d. Note how the characters solve the problem. Were your ideas right?
3. Write a summary of the movie.

Further Viewing

Watch the *Visions* CNN Video for Unit 1. Do the Video Worksheet.

CNN Video

UNIT 1
Apply and Expand

Step 3: Write descriptive sentences.
Help students create complete sentences using their organizers.

Step 4: Review your sentences.
Model the questions and encourage students to add and delete sentences as they consider their own work.

Step 5: Practice your description.
Go over the procedure and checklists before students practice in pairs.

Step 6: Present your animal.
Demonstrate effective presentation behavior. Remind students to listen carefully to one another's presentations.

 ASSESS

Have students write two sentences describing the advantages or disadvantages of having their animal as a pet.

Portfolio

Students may choose to record or videotape their speeches to place in their portfolios.

Viewing Workshop

View and Think

1. **Take notes** Help students create a chart to record the features of a mystery as they watch the movie.
2. **Write a summary** Remind students to include plot, characters, setting, problem, clues, and resolution in their summaries.

Content Connection
Science

Tell students that scientists who study animals are called zoologists. Explain that zoologists who study one specific kind or group of animals have special names, such as ornithologists (scientists who study birds) or entomologists (scientists who study insects). Challenge students to use the Internet or another resource to find, list, and define as many zoological specializations as they can.

Learning Styles
Kinesthetic

Have students work in groups. Ask them to use their summaries of the mystery movie they viewed to write short skits. Tell them that their skits can be summaries, parodies, or sequels. Have them present their skits to the class.

Writer's Workshop

Response to Literature: Compare Two Texts

Compare and contrast Review the features from the three informational texts, pointing out major similarities and differences between the three individual selections.

Step 1: Do research.
Have students use the chart to record specific similarities and differences between the texts.

Step 2: Choose your texts.
Help students decide which readings they are most interested in responding to.

Step 3: Make comparisons and contrasts.
Model examples. Review compound sentences with *and* and *but*.

Writer's Workshop

Response to Literature: Compare Two Texts

> **Writing Prompt**
>
> In this unit, you read three informational texts, "The Loch Ness Monster," "Mystery of the Cliff Dwellers," and "Yawning." Write a report in which you compare and contrast two of these.

Step 1: Do research.

Do your research with a partner.

1. Reread the three texts. Make a chart. Organize the chart into three columns. Write the name of each text at the top of the columns. Use the chart to write a summary of the kind of information each text gives and how the author presents information.

2. Discuss the questions in the chart. Write "yes" or "no" for each reading.

3. Form additional questions. Revise your questions and add them to the chart.

Step 2: Choose your texts.

Decide which two texts you want to write about.

Step 3: Make comparisons and contrasts.

1. Choose the two comparisons and two contrasts from the chart that you think are the most important.

2. Write a sentence for each comparison and contrast. Examples: "Both 'Yawning' and 'The Loch Ness Monster' tell about an experiment." "'Yawning' tells about an experiment, but 'The Mystery of the Cliff Dwellers' does not."

Does the text . . .	The Loch Ness Monster	Yawning	Mystery of the Cliff Dwellers
. . . include historical background?	yes	no	yes
. . . tell about the experiences or opinions of ordinary people?			
. . . include descriptions?			
. . . include scientific information?			
. . . ask questions?			
. . . talk about an experiment?			

MULTI-LEVEL OPTIONS *Writer's Workshop*

Newcomer Hold up a notebook and a textbook. Write on the board and *say: same. Say: These are both books.* Write and *say: different. Say: You can write in one, but not in the other. Can you tell me other things that are the same and different?* (apples and oranges, helicopters and jets)

Beginning Copy the chart on p. 66. Fill in the chart as a class. Then draw a two-column chart with the headings *Compare* and *Contrast*. **Ask:** *What things are alike in the texts? What things are different?* Use students' responses to fill in the chart. Have them refer to the charts as they write.

Intermediate Have students create Venn diagrams as pre-writing graphic organizers. Provide sample Venn diagrams as models. Tell students to organize their ideas in their own diagrams, then use the diagrams as they write their reports.

Advanced Have students work in groups. Tell groups to evaluate the comparisons and contrasts among the three texts. Have groups decide which two texts are *most* similar and which two are *most* different. Ask students to share their decisions. Remind them to support their claims with examples.

Step 4: Write your first draft.

1. Write your first paragraph.
   a. Name the two texts. Capitalize and punctuate the titles correctly to clarify meaning. Use capital letters for the first word and the important words, and put the title in quotation marks.
   b. Explain that informational texts use several ways of giving and explaining information.
   c. State that the two texts are both similar and different in the kind of information that they give and in how they do it. This is your **thesis statement**—the statement of your overall topic.

2. Write your second paragraph.
   a. State that the texts are similar in some ways. This is the **topic sentence** of this paragraph.
   b. Give examples to support this topic sentence. Use the two comparisons that you chose in Step 3.
   c. Use simple, compound, and complex sentences. Be sure to punctuate your independent and dependent clauses correctly.
   d. Use prepositional phrases, for example, "On page 8 of . . ."

3. Write your third paragraph.
   a. Write a topic sentence saying that the texts' features are different in some ways.
   b. Use the examples of contrast from Step 3.
   c. Make effective transitions between your sentences using words like *first, then,* and *finally.*

4. Write your conclusion.
   a. Say how these features can help the reader understand an informational text.
   b. Give your opinion. For example: Which text do you think has better features? Why? Use precise (exact) words in your answers.

Step 5: Revise.

1. Work with a partner. Listen as your partner reads your comparison to you.
   a. Is the right information in the paragraphs?
   b. Is the language precise?

2. Revise your text as necessary. You may want to:
   a. add or delete text
   b. elaborate unclear ideas
   c. combine sentences or ideas
   d. rearrange sentences

Step 6: Edit and proofread.

1. Proofread your story. Use a computer spell and grammar check, if possible.
2. Use the Editor's Checklist in your Student Handbook.

Step 7: Publish.

1. Type your final report on a computer or use your best handwriting.
2. Read your report to your class.

Student Handbook

Step 4: Write your first draft.
Explain the purpose of each of the paragraphs, clarifying terms and modeling sample sentences. Direct attention to punctuation and capitalization rules for titles and compound and complex sentences.

Step 5: Revise.
Arrange students in pairs to share their first drafts. Have students give each other suggestions.

Step 6: Edit and proofread.
Allow time for students to work on adding and refining as needed. Point out resources available for proofreading.

Step 7: Publish.
Allow time for students to make final copies of their essays.

 ASSESS

Have students generate their own individual checklist focusing on their own specific weaknesses.

Portfolio

Students may choose to include their writing in their portfolios.

 Content Connection
Math

Have students conduct a class survey to see which texts students chose to include in their compare-and-contrast reports. Have them record the statistics in a three-column chart. Ask them to use the totals to create word problems. Provide this example as a model: *There are 14 students in the class. Half of the students chose "Yawning" as one of their selections. How many students did NOT write about "Yawning"?* (7)

Teacher Resource Book: *Three-Column Chart, p. 45*

Learning Styles
Musical

Have students select two acceptable pieces of music. Suggest that they choose one instrumental piece and one piece with lyrics. Then have them write a report that compares and contrasts the two selections. Remind them to consider genre, style or mood, instruments, rhythm or beat, tempo or speed, lyrics, volume, length, and subject matter.

Projects

Project 1: Dramatize "The Legend of Sleepy Hollow"

1. **Brainstorm and list** As a group, brainstorm and list scary story ideas for sharing around the fireplace. Have students choose one.
2. **Role-play the scene** Model appropriate speaking tones and voices for scary stories. Remind students to use pauses for effect.

Project 2: Make a Poster About a Mysterious Place

1. **Brainstorm and list** Brainstorm a list of mysterious places. Ask what students already know about the places.
2. **Gather and organize** Allow time for students to use resources to answer questions and to prepare a poster of their findings.

Portfolio

Students may choose to include their projects in their portfolios.

Projects

These projects will help you learn more about real-life mysteries.

Project 1: Dramatize "The Legend of Sleepy Hollow"

In groups of three or four, act out part of "The Legend of Sleepy Hollow."

1. Reread paragraphs 1 to 5 of the story.
2. Study the main facts. Paraphrase them (tell them in your own words).
3. Each of you will be a person who lives in Sleepy Hollow. Imagine that you are sitting around a warm fire at night, telling scary stories.
4. As you speak, remember:
   a. Your purpose is to scare your friends. Speak in a way that does this.
   b. You are with family and friends. Speak in a way that shows this.
   c. Show that you are familiar with your audience and your topic.
5. As you listen, think about other speakers' purposes and perspectives—what they think or feel about the topic.

Project 2: Make a Poster About a Mysterious Place

Choose a mysterious place. Make a poster about it.

1. Choose one of these mysterious places or another one that you know about:
   a. Sleepy Hollow, New York
   b. Stonehenge, England
   c. Machu Picchu, Peru

2. Find pictures of your mysterious place. Use the name of your place to search on the Internet. Or make copies from books. Glue these pictures onto a poster.
3. Find facts about your mysterious place. Use reference books from the library or the Internet.
4. Organize and summarize the information you find in a chart.
5. Use your chart to write answers to these questions on your poster.
   a. What is the name of your mysterious place?
   b. Where is this place?
   c. Why is this place mysterious? What happened there?

Easter Island

Easter Island is an island in the South Pacific Ocean.

Easter Island has very large sculptures. People are not sure who made the sculptures.

MULTI-LEVEL OPTIONS *Projects*

Newcomer Pair newcomers with advanced students to create posters for Project 2. Have newcomers select a picture of the mysterious place and affix it to the top of the poster. At the bottom, have advanced students write the answers to the questions.

Beginning Have students review paragraphs 2–5, 9, 17, 18, 20–22, and 24 from "The Legend of Sleepy Hollow." Ask students to choose one paragraph and draw a picture of the image described in it. Have them describe their drawings using the style of a teller of ghost stories.

Intermediate Have students review paragraphs 2–5 of "The Legend of Sleepy Hollow." Ask students to create their own theories about the Headless Horseman and present them "around the fire" as residents of Sleepy Hollow.

Advanced Pair advanced students with newcomers. Have advanced students write answers to the questions on the newcomers' posters. Have pairs present their posters and read their sentences to the class.

Further Reading

These books discuss mysteries. Read one or more of them. Write your thoughts and feelings about what you read in your Reading Log. Answer these questions:

1. What is the most interesting mystery that you read about?
2. What are some explanations for the mysteries that you read about?

Great Book of Whodunit Puzzles: Mini Mysteries for You to Solve
by Falcon Travis, Sterling Publications, 1993. This book provides several short mysteries that you can try to solve yourself. There is a section with clues to help you. There is also a solutions section.

The Legend of Sleepy Hollow
by Washington Irving, William Morrow & Company, 1990. Ichabod Crane is the schoolmaster in Sleepy Hollow. First, Crane hears the story of the Headless Horseman. Then he actually sees him!

Seven Wonders of the Ancient World
by Lynn Curlee, Atheneum, 2002. Read about the Seven Wonders of the World that have puzzled people for centuries. This book describes the Hanging Gardens of Babylon and the Great Pyramid at Giza.

Great Mysteries of the West
by Ferenc Morton Szasz (editor), Fulcrum Publishing, 1993. There are many mysteries in the western United States. This book discusses the disappearance of the Anasazi Indians. It also looks at rock art in the Southwest and the sea serpents of the Pacific Northwest.

Strange Stuff: True Stories of Odd Places and Things
by Janet Nuzum Myers, Linnet Books, 1999. This book talks about real-life mysteries such as quicksand and black holes. It also discusses Bigfoot and the Bermuda Triangle.

Wolf Rider
by Avi, Bradbury Press, 1986. This psychological thriller shows Andy, 15, trying to convince skeptical adults that the crank call he received truly is a murderer's confession.

Time Stops for No Mouse
by Michael Hoeye, Putnum Publishing Group, 2002. Mouse watchmaker Hermux Tantamoq leads a simple life until he meets Linka Perflinger, adventuress. Her disappearance leads him overnight into a life of detection and danger. A cosmetics tycoon, a newspaper reporter, and assorted other citizens of Pinchester contribute to the action and mystery. Hoeye follows this easy-to-read mix of suspense, wit, and fantasy with another, *The Sands of Time*, about the same characters on a desert adventure that nearly costs them their lives.

The Ghost in the Tokaido Inn
by Dorothy and Thomas Hoobler, Philomel Press, 1999. A jewel theft, a wise judge, the theater world, and 18th century Japan combine to make a Sherlock Holmes style mystery that is much more than a ghost story. Seikei, 14, would like to be a Samurai. While on a business trip with his merchant father he has the most challenging, suspenseful adventure of his life. He discovers that merchants can also exhibit Samurai attitudes.

Companion Web site

Reading Log

Heinle Reading Library The Adventures of Sherlock Holmes

UNIT 1
Apply and Expand

Further Reading

1. **Locate resources** Arrange for students to tour the library to familiarize themselves with the different items available to them. Discuss proper behavior in the library.
2. **Check out books** Explain procedures for getting a library card and checking out books. Point out the usual amount of time that books can be borrowed. Encourage students to ask questions. Point out sections with books for their age group. Have students find sections for fiction and nonfiction mystery books.

▌ Assessment Program: *Unit 1 Test, pp. 17–22*

Heinle Reading Library

The Adventures of Sherlock Holmes
by A. Conan Doyle
In a specially adapted version
by Malvina G. Vogel

Match wits with the mastermind of mystery and suspense as the great Sherlock Holmes solves the most baffling crimes ever conceived! Here are three fantastic adventures in one book— *The Red-Headed League, The Speckled Band,* and *The Copper Beeches,* all guaranteed to keep you guessing and gasping for more!

Visions Companion Site

http://visions.heinle.com
For additional student activities and teacher resources, see the Visions Companion Web site.

Unit Materials

Activity Book: *pp. 41–80*
Audio: *Unit 2; CD 1, Tracks 6–10*
Student Handbook
Student CD-ROM: *Unit 2*
CNN Video: *Unit 2*
Teacher Resource Book: *Lesson Plans, Teacher Resources, Reading Summaries, School-Home Connection, Video Script, Video Worksheet, Activity Book Answer Key*
Teacher Resource CD-ROM
Assessment Program: *Quizzes and Test, pp. 23–38; Teacher and Student Resources, pp. 115–144*
Assessment CD-ROM
Transparencies
The Heinle Newbury House Dictionary/CD-ROM
More Grammar Practice workbook
Heinle Reading Library: *The Swiss Family Robinson*
Web site: http://visions.heinle.com

Visions Staff Development Handbook

Refer to the Visions Staff Development Handbook for more teacher support.

Unit Theme: Survival

Teacher think aloud *Say: The word* survival *makes me think of very difficult conditions, like a storm at sea. The waves can wash you overboard or sink the boat.*

Unit Preview: Table of Contents

1. **Use descriptions** *Ask: Which reading selections are based on real information?* ("To Risk or Not to Risk," "Island of the Blue Dolphins," and "The Next Great Dying") *Which are fiction or made-up stories?* ("How I Survived My Summer Vacation" and "The Voyage of the *Frog*")
2. **Connect** *Ask: Which chapter do you think is interesting?*

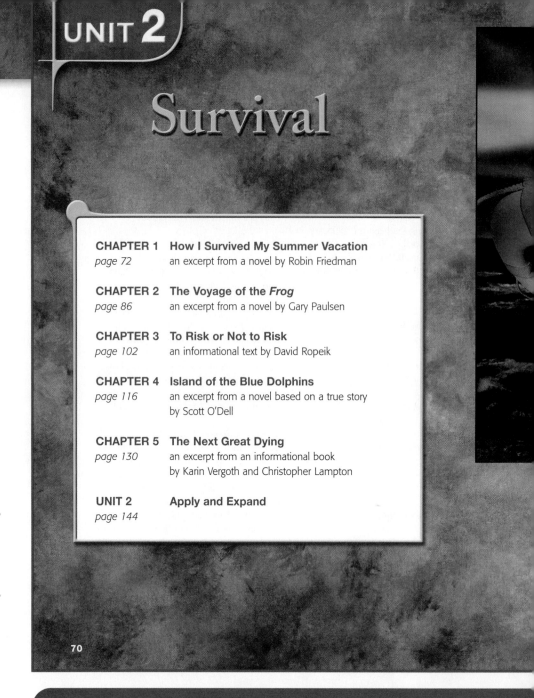

UNIT 2

Survival

70

UNIT OBJECTIVES

Reading

Make inferences using text evidence and experience as you read an excerpt from a novel • Recognize tone and mood as you read an excerpt from a novel • Distinguish fact from opinion as you read an informational text • Paraphrase to recall information as you read an excerpt from a novel based on a true story • Identify cause and effect as you read an excerpt from an informational book

Listening and Speaking

Predict a part of a story • Conduct an interview • Compare personal experiences • Compare ways of working • Talk about conserving natural resources

Ominous Coastline, photo by Sanford/Agliolo, 2000.

View the Picture

1. Describe what you see in this picture. How does it show survival?
2. Do you know any survival stories from current news or books you have read?

In this unit, you will read excerpts from three novels and two informational texts. You will learn about different survival problems that people can have. You will also learn to write these different forms.

71

View the Picture

1. **Art background** "The Ominous Coastline" is a color photograph by Sanford/Agliolo. This photo is full of contrasts: The crashing waves, the changing sky, and the swooping motion of the rope starkly contrast with the dark, forbidding cliffs and the piercing, stationary line of the lighthouse beam.

2. **Art interpretation** Have students discuss how both the vertical line of the lighthouse and the circular, flexible lifeline of the life preserver both aid in survival against dangers of the sea and the rocks.

   a. **Speculate** *Say: You can't see any people in this picture, but you sense they are there. How can you tell?* (The lighthouse beam is shining; someone is throwing a life preserver; and someone must need the life preserver.)

   b. **Interpret the painting** *Say: The dangerous rocks, the person overboard, and the rescuer are all unseen in this photograph. Why do you think the photographer focuses on the life preserver and the lighthouse instead?*

   c. **Connect to theme** *Say: The theme of this unit is* survival. *How do the lighthouse and life preserver in this photograph relate to the theme?*

ASSESS

Have students describe another kind of equipment that helps people survive in dangerous situations.

Grammar
Use progressive tenses • Use the future tense • Use present tense and subject-verb agreement • Identify the past and the past perfect tenses • Recognize dependent clauses

Writing
Write realistic fiction • Write a story to resolve a problem • Write an informational text • Write instructions • Write an informational text

Content
Science: Identify food groups • Social Studies: Find compass directions • Science: Learn about psychology • The Arts: List game rules in order • Social Studies: Read a timeline

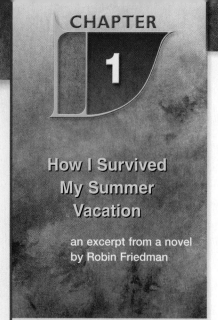

How I Survived My Summer Vacation

an excerpt from a novel
by Robin Friedman

Chapter Materials

Activity Book: *pp. 41–48*
Audio: *Unit 2, Chapter 1; CD 1, Track 6*
Student Handbook
Student CD-ROM: *Unit 2, Chapter 1*
Teacher Resource Book: *Lesson Plan, Teacher Resources, Reading Summary, Activity Book Answer Key*
Teacher Resource CD-ROM
Assessment Program: *Quiz, pp. 23–24; Teacher and Student Resources, pp. 115–144*
Assessment CD-ROM
Transparencies
The Heinle Newbury House Dictionary/CD-ROM
Web site: http://visions.heinle.com

Objectives

Preview Read aloud the objectives. *Say: These objectives are what we will learn in Chapter 1. Is there an objective you already know?*

Use Prior Knowledge

Discuss Summer Experiences

Gather and organize Model using a two-column chart as you talk about some of your own fun and difficult summer experiences. Have students create charts. Help with vocabulary as needed. After small groups share charts, ask the groups to tell the whole class about the most interesting summer experiences.

Objectives

Reading Make inferences using text evidence and experience as you read an excerpt from a novel.

Listening and Speaking Predict a part of a story.

Grammar Use progressive tenses.

Writing Write realistic fiction.

Content Science: Identify food groups.

Use Prior Knowledge

Discuss Summer Experiences

In this chapter, you will read about a boy's experience during his summer vacation. Tell a small group about your summer.

1. Recall some interesting experiences you had one summer. Include both fun and difficult experiences.
2. Write your ideas on a note card. Look at the example.
3. Meet with a small group. Use your notes to tell about your experiences. Listen to your classmates tell about their experiences.
4. If you do not understand something, ask a classmate to clarify (to explain).

My Summer
- *My best friend moved away.*
- *I went on a trip with my family.*
- *I took care of my little sister.*

MULTI-LEVEL OPTIONS *Build Vocabulary*

Newcomer Write each vocabulary word on the board. Say the words and demonstrate their meanings. Then have volunteers act out the situations in numbers 1–4.

Beginning Have students work in pairs. Ask them to take turns acting out the situations described in numbers 1–4. One student should act out a particular situation. The other should say the relevant vocabulary word for what his/her partner acts out.

Intermediate After students have completed writing their sentences, ask them to identify other situations in which they might yell, croak, enunciate, and interrupt.

Advanced Have students work in pairs to write a short dialogue based on one of the sentences. Then ask them to use the vocabulary words to describe how the characters are speaking. (*Example:* Chan yelled, "Sing the song louder!" "I can't," croaked Pablo. "I have already sung it ten times.")

Build Background

Tofu

The main characters in the reading eat a food called tofu. Tofu is made from soybeans. Tofu is usually white, and it looks like cheese. Some people eat tofu because it is healthy. Many people who do not eat meat eat tofu instead.

Content Connection

Farmers in the United States grow a lot of soybeans. The major growing areas are in the midwestern and southern states.

States that Grow the Most Soybeans

Build Vocabulary

Use Precise Wording

Good writers use precise (exact and accurate) words. Here are some words from the reading. They are all about speech. Learning and using these words will help you write well.

Word	Meaning
yell	to shout
croak	to make a deep sound like that of a frog
enunciate	to speak clearly and precisely
interrupt	to stop someone from doing something, such as talking

Write the words and their meanings in your Personal Dictionary. Then write a sentence using each one. Use these situations.

1. Your brother wakes up in the morning and has a sore throat.
2. Your teacher gives you advice about an oral presentation that you are going to give.
3. You are at a soccer game and your team makes a point.
4. Your friend is talking, but you hear your father calling you.

Personal Dictionary

The Heinle Newbury House Dictionary

Activity Book *p. 41*

Student CD-ROM

Cultural Connection

Build Background *Say: People in China have been eating tofu for 1,000 years. There are many recipes from Asia that use this food.* Have students who have visited or lived in Asian countries tell about any recipes using tofu that they know. Have other students find recipes that use tofu in cookbooks or on the Internet. Ask students to identify the country from which each recipe comes.

Learning Styles
Linguistic

Build Vocabulary Have students work in pairs. Ask them to use thesauruses to look up synonyms for the vocabulary words. Have them decide which of the synonyms they find apply to situations 1–4 in Build Vocabulary.

Build Background

Tofu

1. **Use resources** Bring in recipes or pictures of tofu dishes. Explain that it is commonly used in Asian cooking. Have students share experiences of cooking or eating tofu.
2. **Content Connection** Soybeans are native to Asia. They look more like peas than beans and are grown in the U.S. for food for people and animals, vegetable oil, soybean milk, and other products.

Build Vocabulary

Teacher Resource Book: *Personal Dictionary, p. 63*

Use Precise Wording

1. **Use experiences** Demonstrate the meanings of the words. Ask students to suggest situations or times when they did these precise actions.
2. **Reading selection vocabulary** You may want to introduce the glossed words in the reading selection before students begin reading. Key words: *inspiration, century, aroma, irritably, infamous, stormed.* Instruct students to write the words with correct spelling and their definitions in their Personal Dictionaries. Have them pronounce each word and divide it into syllables.
3. **Multi-level options** See MULTI-LEVEL OPTIONS on p. 72.

Answers

1. *Examples:* My brother croaked, "Good morning."
2. The teacher said to enunciate so others can understand.
3. We all yelled when the team got a goal.
4. I interrupted my friend in the middle of our conversation because my father called me.

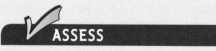
ASSESS

Say definitions and have students respond with the vocabulary words.

Text Structure

Realistic Fiction

1. **Understand terms** Point out key words on the chart. Have students work in groups to review "The Sneak Thief" (p. 42). Ask them to say the main characters, the setting, and the main events.
2. **Multi-level options** See MULTI-LEVEL OPTIONS below.

Reading Strategy

■ Teacher Resource Book: *Reading Log, p. 64*

Make Inferences Using Text Evidence and Experience

Relate to personal experiences *Say: When I see it snowing, I can make an inference that it is cold outside. I know that when it snows, it is cold.* Give other events or clues and have students make their own inferences.

Answer

1. a

ASSESS

Ask: What are three features of a realistic fiction? (characters, setting, events)

Text Structure

Realistic Fiction

This reading, "How I Survived My Summer Vacation," is from a **realistic fiction** novel. Realistic fiction is a made-up story. However, it could happen in real life.

As you read the selection, notice the characters, setting, and events. Think about how these features make the selection seem realistic. Use your own experience to help you.

Realistic Fiction	
Characters	The people in the story do and say things that people do and say in real life.
Setting	The story happens in a place that could be real.
Events	The things that happen in the story could happen in real life.

Student
CD-ROM

Reading Strategy

Make Inferences Using Text Evidence and Experience

Writers do not always tell us directly what is happening in a story. They may write clues (details). These clues are **text evidence.** You can also use your **experience** to help make inferences.

1. Read this sentence. What inference can you make?

   Yeny was yawning and stretching in class.

   a. Yeny was up until 2:00 A.M. this morning.
   b. Yeny is never tired.

2. Use text evidence and your knowledge to make inferences as you read and listen to "How I Survived My Summer Vacation." Organize your ideas in a chart like the one here in your Reading Log.

Clues in the Text	My Own Experience	Inference
yawning and stretching	I often yawn and stretch when I am tired.	**?**

Reading Log   Student
CD-ROM

MULTI-LEVEL OPTIONS *Text Structure*

Newcomer Show students visuals from a variety of pictures, books, or works of fiction. Point to characters, settings, and events. *Ask: Could this be real?*

Beginning Have students work in small groups. Give each a collection of a few realistic fiction and fantasy books. Ask them to write *real* on three slips of paper and *unreal* on three other slips. Have students use the slips to bookmark illustrations of realistic and unrealistic characters, places, and events in their books.

Intermediate Ask each student to write down the title of a realistic fiction book that they have read. Provide time for students to share their titles. *Ask: Who else has read this book? Do you agree or disagree that it is realistic fiction? Why?*

Advanced Have students look at the title and picture on p. 75. *Say: Describe a character, setting, and event you think you might find in this selection.* Have students share their ideas in pairs. Ask partners to comment on whether the ideas sound realistic.

How I Survived My Summer Vacation

an excerpt from a novel
by Robin Friedman

75

Reading Selection Materials

Audio: *Unit 2, Chapter 1; CD 1, Track 6*
Teacher Resource Book: *Reading Summary,*
    pp. 75–76
Transparencies: #34, *Reading Summary*

Suggestions for Using Reading Summary

- Introduce new vocabulary or cognates.
- Cut the summary into strips, or jumble the sentences on an overhead transparency. Students put the sentences in order.
- Practice the reading strategy.
- Students read aloud or with a partner.
- Students paraphrase the summary.
- Students do a cloze activity.
- Students create a visual or graphic organizer, such as a timeline or storyboard, to illustrate the summary.
- Students paraphrase the summary.

Preview the Selection

1. **Make inferences** Have students use the title of the reading selection and the illustration to make inferences about the main character, the setting, and the situation. *Ask: Who is in the picture? Where is he? What is he doing? Why do you think he is doing that? How is he feeling? How do you know? Do you think he's having a good summer or a difficult one?*

2. **Connect** Ask students how the picture relates to the unit theme, *survival. Say: The title is "How I Survived My Summer Vacation." Is the boy doing something that you do during the summer? What do you think is so difficult about the boy's summer vacation?* Point out that survival may be a "life and death" struggle or it may be used in a humorous way to refer to just getting through daily types of events. Tell students they will read about different types of survival situations in this unit.

Content Connection
Technology

Have students look at the picture on p. 75. *Ask: What is the boy trying to do?* (write something) *What device is he using?* (typewriter) Have students compare and contrast typewriters with computers. *Ask: How does the boy feel?* (frustrated, annoyed) *Why do you think he might feel that way?* (He is having trouble writing something. Since he is using a typewriter, he has to keep starting over.)

Learning Styles
Intrapersonal

Say: The boy is having trouble writing something. Through a journal entry or drawing, ask students to explore their own feelings about writing. *Ask: What do you like about writing? What do you find hard? What would make it easier for you to write? What is something you would like to write?*

Read the Selection

1. **Use text features** Direct students to the illustration and identify the book the boy is reading. Point out glossed words and have students find their meanings below.

2. **Paired reading** Play the audio. Have volunteers use gestures and facial expressions to show how the boy is feeling in the different paragraphs. Have students read the selection again in pairs.

3. **Make inferences** *Ask: How does the boy feel in paragraph 1? How do you know that?* (He's very happy because he feels "oh-so-pleased" with himself.)

Sample Answer to Guide Question
It is hard for the boy to write his novel; he says it will take a century to finish the book.

See Teacher Edition pp. 434–436 for a list of English-Spanish cognates in the reading selection.

Audio
CD 1. Tr. 6

1 I stared at my words until they began to **blur** into strange black shapes. A great opening line for a novel, I thought foolishly, grinning like an idiot and feeling oh-so-pleased with myself . . .

2 The next five minutes passed in slow motion while I struggled to think of another line. I stared out my window for **inspiration,** but our overgrown backyard offered up nothing. I looked at the roof, the fence, the driveway, the old oak tree, the herb garden.

3 Nothing. Absolutely nothing.

4 My eyes came to rest on the writing book next to me on the desk. GET RICH QUICK! the title screamed in bold, gold-stamped letters. *Write a Bestseller in Less Than a Year* it promised underneath the title in smaller type.

5 Less than a year? At this rate it would take a **century** . . .

6 I sighed.

7 If I was really going to write a novel this summer, then I had to write a second sentence. And a third, and a fourth, and a thousandth. But it was hopeless as usual, I thought in my **patented** grumpy way.

Make Inferences Using Text Evidence and Experience

Is the character finding it easy or hard to write his novel? What text evidence tells you?

blur make it harder to see clearly	**century** 100 years
inspiration something that makes a person work hard or be creative	**patented** individual, very own (humorous usage)

76 **Unit 2** Survival

MULTI-LEVEL OPTIONS *Read the Selection*

Newcomer Play the audio. *Ask: Does the boy want to write a book?* (yes) *Is he writing fast?* (no) *Does he keep starting over?* (yes) *Does his father want him to eat lunch?* (no)

Beginning Read the Reading Summary aloud. *Ask: What is the boy doing?* (writing) *What does he want to write?* (a book) *Is he at the beginning, middle, or end?* (beginning) *Who calls to the boy?* (father)

Intermediate Have students do a partner read aloud. *Ask: How does the boy want to spend his summer vacation?* (writing a book) *How is he doing?* (He is having trouble getting started.) *What is one way the author makes the boy seem real?* (*Example:* He doesn't like some things his parents do.)

Advanced Have students read silently. *Ask: Why do you think the boy is using a typewriter instead of a computer?* (The setting is before the time when a large number of people had home computers.) *How do you think the boy will act at breakfast?* (impatient because he is upset that his writing is not going well)

8 A few more minutes passed as I silently **groped** for inspiration. A bushy-tailed squirrel raced across the lawn under my window, momentarily giving me an idea, but as soon as it was gone, so was my idea.

9 "This isn't working," I said out loud. I pulled out the sheet of paper from my typewriter. I read the great opening line again, sighed again, and tore the paper into a million pieces. I fed another sheet of paper into the typewriter, trying to control my rapid breathing.

10 Stay calm, I told myself. It's going to be O.K. Panicking is for wimps.

11 The **aroma** of coffee began to drift into my room, which could only mean one thing. Dad was downstairs in the kitchen, preparing his signature breakfast dish: scrambled tofu with fig sauce.

12 Though all kids claim to have this problem, my parents are a *true* embarrassment to me.

13 "Jackie! **Grub**'s ready! Come on down!"

14 It was Dad, ready for breakfast at 9 A.M. on the dot, as usual. He always cooks precisely on the hour, whether it's lunch at 12 noon or dinner at 6 P.M. Mom says it's a **compulsion.** I say it's insanity.

> **Make Inferences Using Text Evidence and Experience**
>
> How do you think the character feels right now? How does your experience help you make this inference?

---

groped   searched for something with the hands as if in darkness
aroma   a pleasant smell, especially of cooking

grub   informal word for food
compulsion   a need to do something that cannot be stopped

Chapter 1   How I Survived My Summer Vacation   **77**

Read the Selection

1. **Use the illustration** Have students describe what the boy is doing and predict why he is doing that.
2. **Paired reading** Read the selection. Pause to ask comprehension questions. Then, have students reread it in pairs.
3. **Analyze character development** *Ask: What's the boy's name?* (Jackie) *Who is in his family?* (his parents) *What are some things that he doesn't like about his parents?* (His Dad makes tofu for breakfast.) Continue asking questions to help students identify and describe Jackie.
4. **Multi-level options** See MULTI-LEVEL OPTIONS on p. 76.

Sample Answer to Guide Question
I think he's feeling very frustrated. Sometimes I tear up paper when I'm not happy with what I am writing, too.

> ❜ **Punctuation**

Exclamation point

Direct students to paragraph 13. *Ask: Do you think Jackie's father wants him to come to breakfast right away or whenever he feels like coming?* (right away) *What in the sentences lets you know?* (exclamation points) *Yes, exclamation points let readers know that the character has a strong feeling. Jackie's father is trying to get the boy to act fast before his food gets cold.*

Apply   *Say: Jackie is feeling impatient and frustrated.* Ask pairs to create a sentence to show the strong feelings Jackie is having about his project. (*Examples:* This makes me mad! I can't believe that I don't have more written!)

Read the Selection

1. **Use the illustration** Call attention to the illustration and have students describe the father.

2. **Paired reading** Read aloud or play the audio as students read along in their books. *Ask: Why does Jackie yell?* (He's angry.) *Does the father get angry at Jackie?* (no) *Does the father notice when Jackie makes a face at the muffins?* (no) Have students reread the selection in pairs.

Sample Answer to Guide Question
Jackie doesn't like eating breakfast with his parents on Saturdays. It says Jackie is irritated and he gets angry as he goes downstairs.

15 "Just a second!" I yelled down **irritably** . . .

16 I glared in the direction of the stairs, as if Mom and Dad were standing on the landing with their wheat-germ muffins and scrambled tofu with fig sauce in hand. Their idea of eating breakfast together on Saturday mornings has always gotten on my nerves, but this summer it was bugging me extra good . . .

17 Sighing again, I **dragged** my body down the stairs and into the kitchen, getting angrier with each step.

18 "You know, I've been thinking," I said as I took a seat at the table. "I may be outgrowing Saturday morning breakfasts. After all, I'll be in high school next fall. I think we should reconsider its place in the family routine."

19 "Lighten up, Jackie," Dad replied, stirring his coffee. "Have a muffin." Though both my parents are committed to "healthful eating," Dad has a severe weakness for coffee, which he drinks black. I've never understood why he stirs it, since he never adds anything. Another compulsion, I guess.

20 I made a face as he passed me a plate of his **infamous, deformed**-looking, sawdust-tasting wheat-germ muffins. I might as well have been performing for my goldfish, though, because Dad didn't look at me. I passed the plate back to him, muffins intact.

> **Make Inferences Using Text Evidence and Experience**
>
> How do you think Jackie feels about eating breakfast with his parents? What text evidence can you use?

irritably   in an annoyed or bothered way
dragged   pulled with difficulty

infamous   famous because of something bad
deformed   not in its normal shape or appearance

78   **Unit 2**   Survival

MULTI-LEVEL OPTIONS *Read the Selection*

Newcomer *Ask: Is Jackie happy at breakfast?* (no) *Does he like his father's scrambled tofu and muffins?* (no) *Do his parents get upset with him?* (no) *Do Jackie's parents have some news for him?* (yes)

Beginning *Ask: What does Jackie's family have for breakfast?* (muffins, scrambled tofu) *How do Jackie's parents feel?* (good, cheerful) *How does Jackie feel?* (angry, annoyed) *What does his mom want to tell Jackie?* (some news)

Intermediate *Ask: How is Jackie acting?* (grouchy and unfriendly) *How are his parents acting?* (cheerful, as if they do not notice) *Compare how his mom feels about the news she is going to tell Jackie with how he feels.* (She is excited to tell him; he is worried about what it will be.)

Advanced *Ask: Why do you think Jackie wants to change his family's breakfast tradition?* (because he does not like the food; he wants to do something else during that time.) *What do you think his mom's news is?* (*Example:* Maybe she is going to tell him that the family is going to take a trip.)

Have a muffin, he says. That was Dad's answer to everything. Well, it wasn't going to do the trick this time. It might have worked when I was ten or eleven, but now . . . I knew better. And I knew what I wanted. I had sworn . . . that by the end of the summer I'd have written the great American novel. I had wanted to be a writer ever since I was five years old. Writing was what I loved. I was great at it, in fact.

22 As if reading my mind, Dad turned to me and said, "Are you thinking about your great American novel again?"

23 I involuntarily clenched my fists but told myself to be cool.

24 Mom didn't seem to hear me or Dad. Before I could respond, she interrupted cheerfully. "We have great news for you," she said, pouring Chinese green tea into a little white cup.

25 My stomach muscles tensed as I waited to hear this so-called great news. I was sure it would be another **diversion** from my writing. Mom and Dad don't take my writing seriously. You'd think that being **editors** themselves, they would support me. But no.

> **Make Inferences Using Text Evidence and Experience**
>
> Does Jackie expect to like the news? Why or why not?

---

diversion a break from normal activity

editors people who correct, clarify, and shape written and recorded works

Chapter 1 How I Survived My Summer Vacation **79**

UNIT 2 • CHAPTER 1
Reading Selection

Read the Selection

1. **Use the illustration** Help students to summarize the story. Then have them make predictions based on the expressions of the characters in the illustration.
2. **Shared reading** Read the text aloud. Have students follow along in their books and join in when they can. *Ask: What do you think the good news will be?* In pairs, students can reread the selection.
3. **Locate derivations using dictionaries** Have students look at these glossed words and determine what words they are derived from: *irritably, dragged, infamous, deformed, diversion, editors.* Have students check the derivations in a print, an online, or a CD-ROM dictionary.
4. **Analyze conflicts and relationships** Use guiding questions to help students describe the relationship between Jackie and his parents. *Ask: Do Jackie and his parents get along well?* (mostly) *Do the parents understand or believe that Jackie is going to write a novel?* (no)
5. **Multi-level options** See MULTI-LEVEL OPTIONS on p. 78.

Sample Answer to Guide Question
Jackie doesn't expect to like Mom's news. His stomach gets tense and he calls it "so-called" great news.

, Punctuation

Hyphens for compound adjectives

Direct students to the first sentence in paragraph 20. On the board, write: *deformed-looking, sawdust-tasting. Say: These words describe things. They are called compound adjectives. What do you notice about how the words are formed?* (They each have two parts; they are connected with a little line.) *Some compound adjectives with two parts are connected by a short line called a hyphen. Are these adjectives ones you have heard before, or do you think the*

author made them up? (made them up) *Yes, the author made them up to describe the muffins and make the story funny.*

Apply Ask students to think of a food they either love or hate. Have them make up two-part adjectives to describe the food. (*Example:* candy-tasting, juice-dripping peaches)

Chapter 1 / Reading Selection   **79**

Read the Selection

1. **Use the illustration** Call attention to the illustration, and have students describe the mother and what she is holding. Have students comment on Jackie's reactions to the mother.

2. **Shared reading** Read aloud or play the audio as students read along in their books. *Ask: Where is Jackie going this summer?* (computer camp) *Does Jackie often go to a camp in the summer?* (yes) *How do you know?* (He says "They always sprang camp on me at the last minute—I should've know this summer would be no different.")

Sample Answer to Guide Question

Jackie isn't happy about going to computer camp. He is quiet for a few seconds, and then his voice is like a frog's croak.

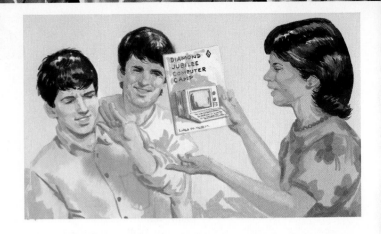

Make Inferences Using Text Evidence and Experience

How do you think Jackie feels about going to computer camp? What text evidence tells you this?

26   "You're going to love this, Jackie," Dad said in a **singsong** voice that reminded me of story time in kindergarten. "We're sending you to the best computer camp in the state this summer."

27   A few seconds of silence followed. "What?!" I finally said, in a voice that sounded like a frog croak.

28   "Diamond Jubilee Computer Camp," Mom said, enunciating each word carefully. "You'll love it. Guaranteed." She grinned at me. "If you do well, we'll even buy you a computer," she added in a playful tone.

29   I made a face. I didn't want a computer and I didn't want to go to Diamond Jubilee Computer Camp. I bet this camp started on Monday. They always sprang camp on me at the last minute—I should've known this summer would be no different.

30   Mom and Dad grinned at each other, then picked up their forks and started on the tofu. As far as they were concerned, the matter was closed. The only sound that followed was the **clink** of silverware against plates.

---

singsong   a way of speaking in which the voice rises and falls with little change

clink   a short, light, high sound

MULTI-LEVEL OPTIONS *Read the Selection*

Newcomer *Ask: Do Jackie's parents want him to go to computer camp?* (yes) *Does Jackie want to go?* (no) *Does Jackie say he will go to camp?* (no) *Does the writer tell whether Jackie goes?* (no)

Beginning *Ask: Where do Jackie's parents want him to go?* (computer camp) *How do his parents feel about the camp?* (excited) *What does Jackie want to do?* (write) *What does Jackie do at the end?* (leaves angry)

Intermediate *Ask: Was Jackie right to be worried about his mother's news? Explain.* (Yes, because he was afraid he wouldn't like it, and he didn't.) *How did Jackie's parents think he would feel about their news?* (happy and eager to go) *How do you think they felt when he stormed out?* (shocked and disappointed)

Advanced *Ask: How could Jackie's parents have avoided the problem in this part of the story?* (by talking with Jackie about their idea ahead of time) *How do you think Jackie's parents feel at the end?* (surprised and upset that he doesn't want to go to camp; upset about how he talked to them)

31   "Jackie, dear," Mom said, smiling gently, "your tofu's getting cold."

32   Well, as far as I was concerned, this summer I wasn't going to let them do it. "I am NOT going to computer camp," I said fiercely, rising from my chair in slow motion. "I'm not going to any kind of camp! Last year it was science camp, the year before it was tennis camp. No . . . more . . . camps! I'm staying in my room all summer and writing my novel!"

33   Both of them stared at me wordlessly, their forks frozen in midair.

34   "And I don't want any muffins—or tofu!"

35   With that, I **stormed** out.

> **Make Inferences Using Text Evidence and Experience**
>
> How does Jackie feel about his parents right now? What text evidence tells you?

---

stormed moved in an angry way

About the Author

Robin Friedman (born 1968)

Robin Friedman started writing when she was a little girl. Friedman got the idea for "How I Survived My Summer Vacation" from listening. She listened to her husband tell stories with his friends. The stories they told about growing up were funny and interesting. Friedman was glad to have an idea for a novel.

 What strategy did Friedman use to write this novel? What is Robin Friedman's point of view—how she thinks and feels—about Jackie? How does this affect the way she wrote the text?

A Capitalization

Days of the week

Direct students to paragraph 29. *Say: Find the word for a day of the week.* (Monday) *How does it start?* (with a capital letter) *Yes, days of the week are always written with a capital letter at the beginning.*

    Apply Ask students to create imaginary schedules for an ideal week of summer vacation. Remind them to start the days of the week with capital letters.

Evaluate Your Reading Strategy

Make Inferences Using Text Evidence and Experience *Say: You have practiced an important reading strategy. Now you can decide how well you have done. Does this statement describe how you read?*

> As I read, I look for how characters feel or what characters want. I understand the characters better when I make inferences using text evidence and experience.

Read the Selection

1. **Paired reading** Read the selection aloud. Then have students reread in pairs.
2. **Summarize** Help students to summarize the story.
3. **Multi-level options** See MULTI-LEVEL OPTIONS on p. 80.

Sample Answer to Guide Question
Jackie is angry. He speaks fiercely. His parents are surprised and don't say anything.

About the Author

1. **Explain author's background** Robin Friedman worked as an editorial assistant reading children's books.
2. **Interpret the facts** *Ask: How do you think Robin Friedman used her experiences in this story?* (She probably had trouble starting her book and getting inspiration.)

Answers
Example: Jackie is as determined as she was about being a writer. She wrote using first person and expressed her thoughts through Jackie telling his thoughts.

Across Selections

Compare text structure Discuss and compare the structure of this story with "The Legend of Sleepy Hollow." *Ask: What features do these selections share?* (Both have characters, settings, and events.) What features are different? (point of view; legends are oral traditions and fantasy; "How I Survived My Summer Vacation" is realistic fiction.)

Spelling, Punctuation, Capitalization

After the Reading Comprehension section, students will practice spelling, punctuation, and capitalization in the Activity Book.

Beyond the Reading

Reading Comprehension

Question-Answer Relationships

Sample Answers

1. He wants to write a novel.
2. They want him to go to computer camp.
3. Jackie can't find a good idea for his novel.
4. Jackie is angry with his parents for making him eat breakfast with them and for planning his summer.
5. I would be annoyed, too, because I would want my parents to listen to my ideas before making a decision.
6. I think Jackie should make plans with his parents, and his parents should listen to his ideas, too.
7. I think the author wrote the story to entertain.
8. I think Jackie's parents want him to go to computer camp to make sure he is busy and learning something rather than sitting around being bored.
9. Jackie wants to sit in his room and write all day. I'd rather go outside and play with my friends and go to computer camp.
10. In my culture, young people need to help more at home and sometimes work at a job when they are not in school.

Build Reading Fluency

Audio Reading Practice

Explain that reading silently while listening to the audio recording helps improve reading fluency. Remind them to keep their eyes on the words. Repeat the audio recording as needed.

Reading Comprehension

Question-Answer Relationships (QAR)

"Right There" Questions

1. **Recall Facts** What does Jackie want to do during his summer vacation?
2. **Recall Facts** What do Jackie's parents want him to do during his summer vacation?

"Think and Search" Questions

3. **Analyze Characters** Why is Jackie having trouble writing his novel?
4. **Make Inferences** Why is Jackie angry with his parents?

"Author and You" Questions

5. **Evaluate Ideas** Would you be annoyed if the adults in your family acted like Jackie's parents? Why?
6. **Make Judgments** Do you think Jackie should choose what he does during the summer, or do you think his parents should choose?

7. **Identify Author's Purpose** Why do you think the author wrote this story? To inform, to entertain, or to influence?

"On Your Own" Questions

8. **Speculate** Why do you think Jackie's parents want him to go to computer camp?
9. **Compare Your Experiences** How do Jackie's plans for the summer compare to yours?
10. **Compare Across Cultures** In your culture or region, how do young people usually spend their time when they are not in school? Compare and contrast your answer with the answers of students from other cultures or regions.

Activity Book
p. 42

Student
CD-ROM

Build Reading Fluency

Audio Reading Practice

Listening to the audio recording of "How I Survived My Summer Vacation" is good reading practice. It helps you to become a fluent reader.

1. Listen to the audio recording.
2. Follow along in your student book on page 76.

3. Listen to the phrases, pauses, and expression of the reader.

MULTI-LEVEL OPTIONS *Elements of Literature*

Newcomer Have students create a sequence chain to show the story events. Ask them to draw a series of boxes, connected with arrows. Tell them to draw one of the events (a–e) in each box. Have them outline the box showing the most exciting and important event with a colored pen or pencil.

Beginning Have students create a sequence chain, draw events a–e in the boxes, and mark the climax. Have them decide which boxes give a clue about a trait of the main character. Below those boxes, instruct them to write words or phrases to tell about Jackie.

Intermediate Have each student identify an event that he/she feels helps develop one of the story characters. Then have them explain to a group what he/she learned about the character through the event.

Advanced Remind students that authors develop characters through the character's thoughts, words, actions, and feelings about story events. Have students find places in the story related to events a–e. Ask them to note how the author developed the characters through each event. (Example: a. actions, thoughts)

Listen, Speak, Interact

Predict a Part of a Story

You can make inferences to guess how characters feel. You can also make inferences to predict (guess) what will happen next.

1. Work with a partner. Reread paragraphs 33–35.
2. Talk about how you think Jackie's parents felt when Jackie stormed out of the kitchen. Were they surprised? Angry? Sad?
3. Use your knowledge to help you predict the next part of the story.

One of you will be Jackie's mother. One of you will be Jackie's father. Use actions and words to show what the parents do next.

4. As you speak, use language that is right for these things:
   a. Your audience—your "husband" or your "wife."
   b. Your purpose—to explore why your son left.
   c. The occasion—a difficult event for a family.

Elements of Literature

Analyze Plot

Plot is an important element in fiction. It is the events that happen in the story. The plot includes the **climax**—the most exciting moment in the plot. Copy this chart in your Reading Log.

Plot	tells the main events
	develops character through events
Climax	the most exciting moment

1. These sentences describe events from the story. Decide if each of them *tells a main event, develops a character,* or both. Support your answers.

a. Jackie was working on his novel.
b. His father called him down to breakfast.
c. Jackie yelled irritably to his parents.
d. Jackie's parents said they were sending him to computer camp.
e. Jackie said that he wasn't going to computer camp, and he left the room.

2. Which of these sentences is the climax of the story?

Reading Log   Activity Book *p. 43*   Student CD-ROM

Content Connection
The Arts

Discuss with students how producers of television shows and movies use background music to signal the climax of a story. *Say: The music might get scary, tense, or exciting at the most important part of a show or movie.* Have students use drums or their hands to beat out a rhythm as you read aloud the events in Elements of Literature. Ask them to show with the beat when the most exciting part occurs.

Learning Styles
Intrapersonal

Say: What people say is important. How they say it is important, too. If you speak to someone calmly about a problem, they might calm down and work with you. If you speak angrily, they might get more upset. Ask students to think of the words and tone of voice Jackie's parents might use to help solve the problem without everyone getting more upset. Have them record their ideas in their Reading Logs.

Teacher Resource Book: *Reading Log, p. 64*

Listen, Speak, Interact

Predict a Part of a Story

1. **Reread in pairs** Pair beginning and advanced students. Have them read alternate paragraphs. Brainstorm questions, statements, and gestures the parents would make in response to Jackie's storming out of the kitchen. Have pairs present their role-plays.
2. **Newcomers** Reread with this group. List students' ideas for the reactions of the mother and father. Have volunteers demonstrate gestures and expressions as you read their ideas from the list.

Elements of Literature

Teacher Resource Book: *Reading Log, p. 64*

Analyze Plot

1. **Make a timeline** Have students work in groups to make a timeline of events in the story. Start with the events listed in item 1. Remind students that the father called Jackie at exactly 9 o'clock. Have them estimate the other times and a day and date for the story.
2. **Multi-level options** See MULTI-LEVEL OPTIONS on p. 82.

Answers
1. **a.** both; **b.** tells an event; **c.** develops a character; **d.** tells an event; **e.** both
2. e

ASSESS

Have students find sentences in the selection that tell a main event, develop a character, and do both.

Word Study

Teacher Resource Book: *Personal Dictionary,* p. 63

Identify Words with Latin Roots

1. **Use a dictionary** Have students look up the words in a large dictionary. Point out the word origin in the entries. Also point out any usage notes.
2. **Use reference aids** Point out that other reference aids, such as online or CD-ROM dictionaries, may also provide information on meaning, word origin, and usage. Have students use one of these references to locate the meaning, origin, and usage of three words of their choosing from the reading.

Answers
2. a. spirare; "to breathe"; b. "to drive"

Grammar Focus

Use Progressive Tenses

Demonstrate tenses Ask students to mime action verbs. Have other students describe the actions using the present progressive.

Answers
1. is 2. were 3. was

 **ASSESS**

Have students write two sentences using the present progressive and two with the past progressive.

Word Study

Identify Words with Latin Roots

Many English words come from Latin. Read these dictionary entries. Look for the Latin roots at the end of the entries.

> **in•spi•ra•tion** /ˌɪnspəˈreɪʃən/ *n.* someone or something that makes a person work hard or be creative [Latin *spirare,* to breathe]

> **com•pul•sion** /kəmˈpʌlʃən/ *n.* a need to do something that cannot be stopped [Latin *pellere,* to drive]

1. Copy the dictionary entries in your Personal Dictionary.
2. Write the answers to these questions.
   a. What is the Latin root for *inspiration?* What does it mean?
   b. What is the meaning of the Latin root *pellere?*

Personal Dictionary   The Heinle Newbury House Dictionary   Activity Book p. 44   Student CD-ROM

Grammar Focus

Use Progressive Tenses

Progressive tenses usually show that an action is going on at a point in time.

"This **isn't working,**" I said out loud.

Mom and Dad **were standing** on the landing.

Use the present progressive to talk about actions that are going on now.

Present Progressive Tense

Subject	Auxiliary	Verb + ing
I	am	
you/we/they	are	work**ing**
he/she/it	is	

Use the past progressive to talk about actions that were going on in the past.

Past Progressive Tense

Subject	Auxiliary	Verb + ing
I/he/she/it	was	
you/we/they	were	work**ing**

Copy and complete these sentences.

1. Jackie ____ working on his novel now.
2. My parents ____ making breakfast when I came in.
3. It ____ raining when I got up.

Activity Book pp. 45–46   Student Handbook   Student CD-ROM

84   Unit 2 Survival

MULTI-LEVEL OPTIONS *From Reading to Writing*

Newcomer Have students create a series of illustrations to show how the family resolves their problem. Help students write speech balloons for the drawings. Provide time for them to share their story endings.

Beginning Ask students to draw a series of pictures that show how the family resolves their problem. Have students write short captions for the drawings. Provide time for them to compare and contrast their story endings with those of classmates.

Intermediate If students do not have a resolution in mind, suggest that they continue the role-play they started in Listen, Speak, Interact to see what solution comes out.

Advanced Call attention to step 3c in the writing directions. Suggest that fiction writers often do not know how a story will end when they start writing. They say that the characters "tell them." Ask students to free-write their thoughts about what happens next and see what solution comes out.

From Reading to Writing

Write Realistic Fiction

In Listen, Speak, Interact you predicted a part of the selection. Now you will write what you predicted.

1. Recall the predictions you talked about with your partner.
2. Write this part of the story.
   a. Tell what Mom and Dad were doing when Jackie left the room. Use the progressive tense.
   b. Write dialogue that helps develop the characters of Mom and Dad.
   c. Write to discover a resolution to the conflict.

> *Mom and Dad were looking at each other. They were surprised. They didn't know what to say. Finally, Dad broke the silence. "What was that all about?" Dad asked.*
> *"I don't have a clue," Mom replied. "Maybe Jackie is having a bad day."*

Activity Book
p. 47

Student Handbook

Across Content Areas

Identify Food Groups

Healthy foods contain **nutrients**—substances in foods that help our bodies grow and work.

1. Match each food group with an example.
2. With a partner, list other examples for each food group.

3. With your partner, create a form that you can use to interview other students about the things they eat. Organize your form according to the food groups.
4. Interview a few students. Revise your form if necessary. Interview a few more students. What did you find out?

Food Groups	Examples
1. Breads, cereals, rice, and pasta	a. an apple
2. Meat, poultry, fish, beans, eggs, and nuts	b. a muffin
3. Dairy (foods made from milk)	c. tofu
4. Fruits and vegetables	d. cheese

Activity Book
p. 48

From Reading to Writing

Write Realistic Fiction

1. **Brainstorm** Help students recall their predictions. List ideas on the board. Include things the parents might say and do.
2. **Think-quickwrite-pair-share** Ask students to visualize the kitchen scene after Jackie leaves. Ask them to write as much as they can about it. Have students share with partners. Instruct them to check the use of progressive verbs.
3. **Multi-level options** See MULTI-LEVEL OPTIONS on p. 84.

Across Content Areas: Science

Identify Food Groups

1. **Define and clarify** Explain the meaning of *nutrients* and *food groups.* Bring in pictures of foods and have students categorize them.
2. **Use resource materials** Have students look up specific nutrients: *protein, carbohydrates, fats, fiber, vitamins, minerals.* Students can find nutritional content on foods containers.

Answers
1. b 2. c 3. d 4. a

 **ASSESS**

Have students name an example from each of the food groups.

Reteach and Reassess

Text Structure Remind students of the features of realistic fiction that they learned about. Ask them to test how realistic the story they read is by listing or drawing people, settings, and events in their lives that are similar to ones in the selection.

Reading Strategy Have students revisit the illustration on p. 76. *Ask: What can you guess about Jackie from this picture? What clues did you use?* (*Example:* He wants to sell his book; clue—title of the book he is holding)

Elements of Literature Read students a short tale. Ask them to create a sequence chain of events and mark the climax.

Reassess Have students list inferences about each character in the selection they read. Instruct them to draw or write predictions about how each would react if Jackie had a piece of his writing published in a magazine.

CHAPTER

2

The Voyage
of the *Frog*

an excerpt from a novel
by Gary Paulsen

Into the Reading

Chapter Materials

Activity Book: *pp. 49–56*
Audio: *Unit 2, Chapter 2; CD 1, Track 7*
Student Handbook
Student CD-ROM: *Unit 2, Chapter 2*
Teacher Resource Book: *Lesson Plan, Teacher Resources, Reading Summary, Activity Book Answer Key*
Teacher Resource CD-ROM
Assessment Program: *Quiz, pp. 25–26; Teacher and Student Resources, pp. 115–144*
Assessment CD-ROM
Transparencies
The Heinle Newbury House Dictionary/CD-ROM
Web site: http://visions.heinle.com

Objectives

Paired reading Have students work in pairs and take turns reading the objectives section.
Ask: Is there an objective from the list that you can do already?

Use Prior Knowledge

Talk About Dangerous Weather

Gather and organize Review the chart. Then arrange students in groups to complete it with weather conditions and problems they know.

<table>
<tr><td colspan="2">**Objectives**</td></tr>
<tr><td colspan="2">**Reading** Recognize tone and mood as you read an excerpt from a novel.</td></tr>
<tr><td colspan="2">**Listening and Speaking** Conduct an interview.</td></tr>
<tr><td colspan="2">**Grammar** Use the future tense.</td></tr>
<tr><td colspan="2">**Writing** Write a story to resolve a problem.</td></tr>
<tr><td colspan="2">**Content** Social Studies: Find compass directions.</td></tr>
</table>

Use Prior Knowledge

Talk About Dangerous Weather

Sometimes, bad weather can be dangerous. What are some types of dangerous weather? What problems can dangerous weather cause?

1. Work with a group. Make a chart like the one shown on a piece of paper.
2. List types of dangerous weather. Think about snow, rain, wind, and temperature.
3. List problems that dangerous weather can cause. Think about how it can hurt buildings, land, and animals.

4. Share your chart with the class. Work together to make one big chart on the board.

Dangerous Weather	Problems
a lot of rain	Land and houses can get covered with water.

MULTI-LEVEL OPTIONS *Build Vocabulary*

Newcomer Hold up a picture dictionary. Demonstrate how to match a word and picture and how to say the word. Point to a word and say it as students find the picture and repeat the word. Then point to pictures and have students find and try to say the word. Correct as necessary.

Beginning On the board, write: *sail.* Help students look up the word in a beginner's dictionary. Read aloud the simplest definition of the word as a verb. Have students use their hands to represent a boat and make a sailing motion. Then help students look up the word in a beginner's thesaurus. Write relevant synonyms on the board.

Intermediate *Ask: If you had no idea what a word in a book meant, what resource could you use?* (dictionary and/or glossary) *If you were writing a story and discovered you used a certain word too many times, what resource could you use?* (synonym finder) *If you don't know a word on a Web site, what resource could you use?* (reference software)

Advanced Provide students with several general dictionaries, specialized dictionaries such as rhyming dictionaries, and thesauruses. Have small groups discuss which resources would be most appropriate and helpful in their classroom and why.

Build Background

Sailboats

Sailboats are boats with sails—pieces of cloth that help boats move in the wind. Sailboats usually move in a zig-zag (like a *Z*). This means that sailboats turn in the water and change direction. Turning a sailboat helps the sails catch the wind.

Content Connection
A **sailor** is a person who knows how to use a sailboat. A sailor controls the direction in which the boat moves.

Build Vocabulary

Use Reference Sources

A **reference source** can help you find the meaning of a word. A reference source is something that gives you information.

Use any of these reference sources as you read. Write words and definitions you learn in your Personal Dictionary.

Reference Sources	
Dictionary	A dictionary gives the definitions of words. It tells how words are pronounced. Some dictionaries also give information about usage and word origin.
Thesaurus	A thesaurus shows **synonyms** for words. Synonyms are words with similar meanings. (*Mad* is a synonym for *angry*.) Some thesauruses also show word usage.
Synonym Finder	A synonym finder is a book that lists many synonyms. Like a thesaurus, it may show word usage.
Software	Software is a tool you use on a computer. Some dictionaries and thesauruses are available as software. They may give meanings, pronunciations, derivations, and usage information.

Personal Dictionary The Heinle Newbury House Dictionary Activity Book *p. 49* Student CD-ROM

Chapter 2 The Voyage of the *Frog* **87**

Content Connection
Social Studies

Build Background Have small groups of students use encyclopedias or other resources to find out about various kinds of boats. Ask each group to make a chart to show what they learned. Suggest the headings: *Type of boat, Invented by, Used for, Made of.* Some kinds of boats they may want to investigate are sailboats, canoes, and submarines.

Learning Styles
Kinesthetic

Build Vocabulary Introduce students to an American Sign Language dictionary. Show students the manual alphabet in the dictionary. *Say: There is a hand sign for each letter. You can use the signs to spell out words.* Demonstrate finger spelling a word. Have students finger spell their names or vocabulary words in the unit. You can also find animated ASL dictionaries online.

Build Background

Sailboats

1. **Use models** If possible, bring in small sailboats and have students experiment with moving the boat in a direction with the wind and against the wind.
2. **Relate to personal experiences** Ask students to talk about experiences they or others have had sailing.
3. **Content Connection** Explain that some sailboats are small, needing only one sailor. Others are larger and large teams of sailors are needed.

Build Vocabulary

Teacher Resource Book: *Personal Dictionary, p. 63*

Use Reference Sources

1. **Locate sources** Have students indicate where the different sources are located in the classroom or school. Ask volunteers to demonstrate using the resources.
2. **Internet resources** Explain that, in addition to print resources, there are electronic resources available on the Internet. Have students search for online dictionaries, thesauruses, and encyclopedias. Ask volunteers to demonstrate looking up definitions and synonyms.
3. **Reading selection vocabulary** You may want to introduce the glossed words in the reading selection before students begin reading. Key words: *freighter, cocky, gear, drift, current.* Instruct students to write the words with correct spelling and their definitions in their Personal Dictionaries. Have them pronounce each word and divide it into syllables.
4. **Multi-level options** See MULTI-LEVEL OPTIONS on p. 86.

ASSESS

Have students suggest resources for finding synonyms, definitions, and pronunciations of words.

Text Structure

Adventure Story

1. **Define and relate** Ask students to give examples of each feature from an earlier reading. (*Examples:* events: a plot summary of "The Legend of Sleepy Hollow"; description: Jackie's use of compound adjectives in "How I Survived . . ."; problem: how to prove Mr. Fink stole the briefcase in "The Sneak Thief")
2. **Multi-level options** See MULTI-LEVEL OPTIONS below.

Reading Strategy

Recognize Tone and Mood

Teacher think aloud Say: *Sometimes I sound angry! Sometimes I sound happy. Sometimes I sound worried. An author can tell us their feelings by using their tone and by making us feel a certain mood.*

Answers
1. a **2.** b

ASSESS

Ask: What are three features in an adventure story? (events, description, problem)

Text Structure

Adventure Story

"The Voyage of the *Frog*" is a type of fiction called an **adventure story.** An adventure story tells about exciting or dangerous events. Look for these features of an adventure story as you read the selection.

Adventure Story	
Events	Exciting things happen in the story. Characters can be in dangerous situations.
Description	The author uses words to describe people and things. These words help readers make pictures in their minds.
Problem	The characters must resolve a difficult problem.

Student
CD-ROM

Reading Strategy

Recognize Tone and Mood

Authors can make us feel emotions. Two ways that writers do this are through **tone** and **mood.**

Tone is the feeling the author shows toward a character or a situation. For example, the author may approve of or be angry with a character.

Mood is the feeling the reader gets from the story. For example, the author might want to make the reader feel worried or scared.

Read the following sentences. Then choose the description that fits each one.

1. He was used to sailing alone. He was always prepared for any emergency.
   a. The tone is admiring.
   b. The tone is disapproving.
2. The room was full of little kids running around and having a good time. In the middle of it all was Rosa, with a big smile on her face.
   a. The mood is sad.
   b. The mood is happy.

Pay attention to tone and mood as you read and listen to "The Voyage of the *Frog*."

Student
CD-ROM

MULTI-LEVEL OPTIONS *Text Structure*

Newcomer Show pictures of people in dangerous situations, such as mountain climbing during a blizzard, sailing a ship during a storm, or encountering a wild animal. Write on the board and *Say: danger, adventure.* Have students act out what the person in the picture might do to solve his/her problem.

Beginning Have students look at pictures in an adventure story from a children's magazine or heavily illustrated book. Point to parts of the illustrations that depict: *danger, problem, solution.* Ask students to repeat the words after you.

Intermediate Ask students to recall an adventure movie or television show they have seen. Tell them to identify examples of the features described in the chart on the top of p. 88.

Advanced Have small groups meet for book discussions. Ask each student to tell the other group members about the most adventurous book he/she has ever read and explain what features made it so exciting. Recommend that students note titles that they might like to read in the future.

The VOYAGE of the FROG

an excerpt from a novel
by Gary Paulsen

89

Reading Selection Materials

Audio: *Unit 2, Chapter 2; CD 1, Track 7*
Teacher Resource Book: *Reading Summary,*
  pp. 77–78
Transparencies: #34, *Reading Summary*

Suggestions for Using Reading Summary

- Introduce new vocabulary or cognates.
- Cut the summary into strips, or jumble the sentences on an overhead transparency. Students put the sentences in order.
- Practice the reading strategy.
- Students read aloud or with a partner.
- Students paraphrase the summary.
- Students do a cloze activity.
- Students create a visual or graphic organizer, such as a timeline or storyboard, to illustrate the summary.
- Students paraphrase the summary.

Preview the Selection

Teacher Resource Book: *Know/Want to Know/Learned Chart (KWL), p. 42*

1. **Interpret the image** *Ask: Where is this boat? Is it near land? Who do you think is on the boat? Why do you think the boat is here? What dangers might there be on the ocean or sea?*
2. **Make a KWL chart** Create a KWL chart and have students brainstorm what they know about the sailboat from the picture and the title. List their ideas in the first column of the chart. Then have students suggest questions they have about this boat, such as who is on it, where the boat is going, why it is going there. List students' questions in the second column. Refer students back to the KWL chart as they read the selection, noting answers to their questions and other information they learn about the story.
3. **Connect** Remind students that the unit theme is *survival*. Ask what survival situations a person might have sailing on the ocean.

 Home Connection

Invite students to draw or tell about any experiences they have had on boats of any type. *Ask: How big was the boat? What kind of weather was there on the day you were on the boat? Was the water calm or rough? How fast did the boat go? How did you feel? What did you like about being on a boat? Describe anything that was scary about being on a boat.* If some students have never been on a boat, they can describe what they think the experience would be like.

Learning Styles
Natural

Have students work in groups to plan a "voyage" in a sailboat. Have them decide what body of water they will sail, where they will leave from, what ports they will visit, and how long their trip will be. Have them figure out the supplies and equipment they will need and what safety gear they will take.

Read the Selection

1. **Use text features** Point out the illustration and have students compare it with the one on p. 89. Direct students to the prologue. Call attention to the glossed words. Remind students to use these features to help understanding.

2. **Teacher read aloud** Read the selection aloud. Pause to check understanding and to identify features: events, description, and problem. Clarify other vocabulary related to ships: *bow, deck, bridge, running with the wind.*

Sample Answer to Guide Question
David is feeling surprised and uncertain. Then he feels worried.

See Teacher Edition pp. 434–436 for a list of English-Spanish cognates in the reading selection.

Audio
CD 1, Tr. 7

Prologue
This selection is about a boy named David. He is 14 years old. He goes out on a boat in the Pacific Ocean. A storm comes and throws the boat off of its path. David is alone in the boat. He does not know how he will survive.

1   It was then that he saw the ship—a small, older ship, coming out of the dusk, **aiming** almost at him but slightly off his bow, running with the wind and sea. Right there. A ship. Right in front of him. She had been running without lights but as soon as the people on deck saw him—there were three of them—they yelled and the lights came on and they started to pass not a hundred yards away, the people waving and yelling and laughing.

2   For a moment he couldn't say anything. He just didn't think it would happen this way. He didn't know for certain how it would happen, but not this way. Not so sudden. Suddenly he was saved. She was an old, very small **coastal freighter** but had been fixed up and repainted and she carried an American flag above her bridge.

3   "Hey," he **croaked.** They were going to pass him and leave if he didn't wake up. "Hey, hey, hey, hey, *hey!*"

Recognize Tone and Mood

What is the mood of the story at this point? Ask yourself, "What is David feeling?"

---

aiming   pointing at, directing toward
coastal   along the coast, where the land and water meet

freighter   a ship designed to carry freight, goods, or cargo
croaked   made a deep sound like a frog

90   **Unit 2** Survival

MULTI-LEVEL OPTIONS *Read the Selection*

Newcomer Play the audio. *Ask: Is David on a boat alone?* (yes) *Does he know where he is going?* (no) *Does he see another boat?* (yes) *Did people on the other boat know David was lost?* (yes)

Beginning Read the Reading Summary aloud. *Ask: Where is David?* (on a boat) *What does he see?* (another boat) *What does the other boat do?* (stop) *Where had the people on the boat heard about David?* (newspaper)

Intermediate Have students do a paired reading. *Ask: Why is David yelling at the other boat?* (He wants the sailors on it to stop and help him.) *Why didn't people who were looking for David find him?* (They were looking too close to the place where he had started his trip.)

Advanced Have students read silently. *Ask: At first, why do the people on the other boat wave and keep going?* (They probably think David is just being friendly; they don't know he is in trouble.) *What do you think will happen next in the story?* (The people on the other boat will help David get home.)

4   He let go of the helm and waved with both arms, screamed, pointed at them and then at himself and at last they got the message and he heard the engines in the freighter **rumble** down to a stop west and slightly north of him.

5   He came about and let the *Frog* sail closer, came up into the wind and stopped about thirty yards away, rising and settling on the waves and swells. He looked up at the people on the rail.

6   "My name is David Alspeth," he yelled. "I was driven out to sea in a storm. . . ."

7   "It's him!" one of the young men yelled up at the **bridge** of the ship. "It's that kid they were searching for up off Ventura." He looked back down at David. "They had your picture in the paper and everything. Man, you are one heck of a distance from where they looked. They finally gave you up for dead, you know that?"

8   Well, I'm not, David thought. I'm not dead. Not even close. "Where am I?"

> **Recognize Tone and Mood**
>
> What is the tone of the story at this point? Ask yourself, "What is David's attitude toward the young man in paragraph 7?"

---

rumble   make a low rolling noise

bridge   the part of a ship where the officers stand to give orders

Chapter 2 The Voyage of the *Frog*   **91**

Read the Selection

1. **Use the illustration** Ask students to describe the people and situation. Use the illustration to have students suggest why the boy is jumping and yelling.
2. **Paired reading** Read the selection aloud. Then have students reread it in pairs.
3. **Summarize** *Ask: Where is David from?* (Ventura) *How far away is that?* (about 250 miles) *How did he get so far away?* (A storm blew him away.) *Why does the young man recognize David?* (He saw David's picture in a newspaper.) *Why are the people so surprised to see David?* (He has been missing a while. People believed David was dead.)
4. **Multi-level options** See MULTI-LEVEL OPTIONS on p. 90.

Sample Answer to Guide Question
The tone is approving and exciting. David is surprised and annoyed by the idea that rescuers assumed he was dead.

❝ Punctuation

Quotation marks for dialogue

Write on the board: *"My name is David Alspeth," he yelled.* Underline the portion in quotation marks. *Say: This part tells* exactly *what David said.* Circle the quotation marks. *Say: The marks around David's words are quotation marks. The part outside of the marks tells who said the words.* Direct students to paragraph 7. *Ask: What words did the character say?* (It's him!) *Who said these words?* (one of the young men)

Apply Write the following on the board and ask students to copy the sentences and insert quotation marks: *I need help, said David. What do you need? asked the man.*

Read the Selection

1. **Use a map** Have students find Ventura, San Diego, and Baja California on the map. Ask students to retell David's voyage using the map.

2. **Paired reading** Read the selection aloud. *Ask: Who is Henry Pierce?* (the captain) *How had people been looking for David?* (with planes and choppers) *Is David happy about the thought of going home soon?* (yes) *What does he miss?* (a hamburger, a malt, and his parents) Have students reread the selection in pairs.

Sample Answer to Guide Question
The mood is calm, relaxed, and relieved.

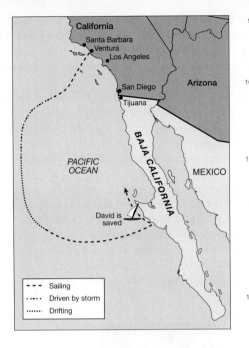

9   The man laughed. "About halfway down the coast of Baja. Maybe two hundred and fifty miles south of San Diego."

10   Another man came from the bridge, stepping down the ladder, to stand at the rail over the *Frog*. "I am Pierce. Henry Pierce. I am the captain."

11   David introduced himself— he almost added that he was the captain of the *Frog* but let it be. Captain Pierce was a heavy man, with round shoulders, gray hair, and pleasant eyes. It would sound **cocky**, smart-mouth to say that he, David, was captain of the *Frog*. But he felt like it.

12   "You gave everybody a rough time," the captain said. "They had planes and **choppers** looking for you."

13   "I was driven way south by the storm," David explained. "Way south. . . ."

14   "Well, you're all right now. We're down here to study whales but we're heading back tomorrow. We'll have you home in three to five days. . . ."

Recognize Tone and Mood

What is the mood of the story at this point?

15   David closed his eyes, sighed, leaned back against the **boom** with his shoulder. That was it, then. He was done. He was saved. In three to four days he'd be home and there'd be a malt and a hamburger and his mother and father. . . .

---

cocky   feeling sure of one's importance and abilities
choppers   helicopters

boom   a long, horizontal pole that holds the bottom of a sail on a boat

92   **Unit 2** Survival

MULTI-LEVEL OPTIONS *Read the Selection*

Newcomer *Ask: Is the captain worried about David?* (yes) *Is the captain going to take David home?* (yes) *Is the captain going to take David's boat?* (no) *Is David happy?* (no)

Beginning *Ask: Who is the captain of the other boat?* (Captain Pierce) *Where does the captain say he will take David?* (home) *What does the captain say David should do with the* Frog? (leave it) *How does David feel about that?* (upset)

Intermediate *Ask: How is Captain Pierce going to help David?* (by putting the boy on his ship and taking him home) *Why isn't David happy about this?* (because the captain says there is no way to take David's boat with them)

Advanced *Ask: What does paragraph 23 mean?* (David is not paying attention to the captain; he is remembering things that happened to him while he was lost at sea.) *What do you think David will do about his boat?* (*Example:* I think he will leave it but be very sad.)

16 "Get your **gear**," the captain interrupted his dreaming, "anything you want to bring and we'll lower a ladder for you."

17 David looked up at him. "What about the *Frog*—what about the boat?"

18 The captain hesitated. "Well . . . we'll have to leave it."

19 "No." It came out before he could think. Just the word. "No."

20 The captain of the **research vessel shrugged.** "We haven't any choice. I haven't got any way to lift it aboard or a place to put it if we did. It's too big."

21 "No." David shook his head. "We could tow her."

22 A small smile, a sad smile. "We couldn't pull it more than two or three knots and then it would probably tear the boat apart. Sailboats don't tow at all."

23 There was a pause; the *Frog* rolled in the swells. The captain stared down at him, the small smile still on his lips. David looked back up at him but wasn't seeing him, wasn't seeing anything; his mind rolled with memories, the shark, the killer whales, the storm, the moon pouring down the sails, the dolphin spinning up into the gold. . . .

> **Recognize Tone and Mood**
>
> What is the tone of this paragraph? Ask yourself, "Does the captain understand David's problem?"

gear   equipment
research vessel   a boat built for study

shrugged   lifted his shoulders upward as a sign of not caring or not knowing

Chapter 2   The Voyage of the *Frog*   **93**

Read the Selection

1. **Use the text features** Ask students to describe the scene. Direct attention to the boldfaced words. Help students pronounce the words and find their meanings.

2. **Shared reading** Play the audio. Then ask volunteers to join in as others follow along. *Ask: Why does the captain want to leave David's boat?* (They can't lift it up, and they can't pull it.)

3. **Explain meaning** Have students look up the meaning and speed of a *knot* in the dictionary. (1.85k/hr or 1.15m/hr) Guide students to explain the sentence in paragraph 22.

4. **Identify story features** Remind students of adventure story features. *Ask: What is David's problem now?* (He doesn't want to leave his boat.)

5. **Multi-level options** See MULTI-LEVEL OPTIONS on p. 92.

Sample Answer to Guide Question
The tone is sympathetic but realistic. Yes. You can tell the captain understands why David doesn't want to leave his boat when he gives him a small, sad smile.

, Punctuation

Semicolons

Tell students to look at the first sentence of paragraph 23. Copy the sentence on the board. Underline the part before the semicolon. *Ask: Is this a complete thought?* (yes) Circle the part after the semicolon. *Ask: Is this part a complete thought?* (yes) *Does a punctuation mark join the two complete thoughts?* (yes) *The mark is called a semicolon. Sometimes, writers use a semicolon to connect two thoughts that are closely related.*

Apply Write the following on the board. Ask students to use the model on the board to join the two thoughts with a semicolon. *David did not want to leave his boat. It was like a good friend to him.* (David did not want to leave his boat; it was like a good friend to him.)

Read the Selection

1. **Use the illustration** Ask students to describe what David is thinking about.
2. **Paired reading** Read the selection aloud to students. *Ask: Why doesn't David want to leave his boat?* (The *Frog* is special to him.) *How long will it take for David to sail back?* (two to three weeks) *Would you leave the boat or sail it back? Why?* Have students reread the selection in pairs.

Sample Answer to Guide Question
The tone is defiant and resolved. David is loyal and attached to the boat.

24   All of it in his mind. Then the sentence came. Leave the *Frog*.

25   Us. We. Leave her to float and die on the ocean. Alone. Leave her to **drift** and die alone on the ocean.

26   "No."

27   "What do you mean, 'no'?" the captain asked.

28   David shook his head. "I won't leave her. I won't leave the *Frog*."

29   "But there is no other way. . . ."

30   "I'll sail her." There, it was out. "I'll sail her home myself. I won't leave her to die . . . to sink. Alone. I'll go back with her."

31   "You know that it's three hundred and fifty miles back to Ventura? Against **prevailing** wind and **current**? You'll have to **tack** the whole way. It could take two, three weeks. More if you hit bad weather."

> **Recognize Tone and Mood**
>
> What is the tone of this paragraph? Ask yourself, "What does this paragraph tell me about David?"

---

drift   float, carried by wind or water currents
prevailing   usual, frequent

current   the flow
tack   change direction depending on the wind

94   Unit 2   Survival

MULTI-LEVEL OPTIONS *Read the Selection*

Newcomer *Ask: Will David leave his boat?* (no) *Does David want to sail the boat home?* (yes) *Will it be a short trip?* (no) *Does David ask the captain to call his parents?* (yes)

Beginning *Ask: What does David say he will do with his boat?* (sail it) *Does the captain think David will have a long or short trip?* (long) *Who offers to help David?* (Captain Pierce) *Who does David ask the captain to call?* (his parents)

Intermediate *Ask: How does David decide to get home?* (sail his boat) *What kind of trip do you think he will have? Why?* (long and hard because the captain said it is a 350-mile trip) *Why does David want the captain to call his parents?* (so they will know he is alive and safe)

Advanced *Ask: Why does David think he can get home now when he couldn't before?* (The captain probably helped him figure out where he had to go.) *How do you think David's parents will feel when the captain calls?* (very relieved and happy that he is all right, but worried about the rest of the trip)

32   David rubbed the wooden boom with one hand. The wood felt warm, smooth, alive. She was alive. The ship had blocked most of the wind but enough **flurried** around to make the *Frog's* sails slap a bit and they **jerked** the boom gently. There was no other way. "I got here with her and I'm going home with her. That's it."

33   Another long silence while the captain studied him, frowning. A gull which had been following the ship screeched and flew over, banking on a wind **eddy.**

34   "I'd do the same," the captain said at last, **abruptly,** nodding. "By God I'd do the same. Well, is there anything we can do for you, young sailor?"

35   David thought for a moment. "Two things. First, can you call my parents by radio or something and tell them that I'm all right and that I'll be home . . . well, whenever I get there. Explain everything to them." He gave the captain their phone number.

> **Recognize Tone and Mood**
>
> What is the tone of this paragraph? Ask yourself, "What is the author saying about the captain?"

flurried flowed lightly
jerked pulled quickly and sharply

eddy turning or swirling wind
abruptly in a sudden manner

Chapter 2   The Voyage of the *Frog*   **95**

Read the Selection

1. **Use the text features** Ask students to describe the scene. Have students suggest what the captain and David are talking about. Guide students to make predictions about whether or not David will leave the *Frog*.

2. **Break-in reading** Play the audio. Have students reread in groups. One student begins reading. When another student wants to take over, he/she "breaks in" by reading along with the first student. At the end of the sentence, the first student stops, and the second one continues until another student "breaks in." Read over until everyone has had a turn.

3. **Analyze character motivation** *Ask: Why does David choose to stay with his boat?* (He doesn't want the boat to sink all alone.) *How does he feel about his boat?* (He loves his boat and feels connected to it.) *Do you own anything that you would not give up?*

4. **Multi-level options** See MULTI-LEVEL OPTIONS on p. 94.

Sample Answer to Guide Question
The captain's tone is understanding and sympathetic. The captain loves his ships and takes care of them. He approves of David's decision.

A   Capitalization

Name of a type of transportation

Ask: What is the name of David's boat? (Frog) *Look at paragraph 32 to see what is special about the way* Frog *is written.* (different lettering) *Yes, special lettering called* italics *is sometimes used for the names of ships, trains, airplanes, or spacecraft. What else is special about the way the name of David's boat is written?* (starts with a capital letter)

   Apply *Say: The author doesn't tell us the name of Captain Pierce's ship.* Ask students to recall the purpose of his ship. (studying whales) Ask pairs of students to make up a name for the ship and write a sentence about it. (*Example:* The people on the *Whale Watcher* helped David.)

Read the Selection

1. **Break-in reading** Play the audio. Have students reread the selection aloud by taking turns "breaking-in" when they want to read.

2. **Identify features** Ask questions about the events and problem. *Ask: What is the second thing that David wants?* (food and fuel for his stove) *What types of things did the people on the research ship give David?* (water, canned chicken, and other supplies and food) *What problem does David have now?* (sailing back to Ventura by himself)

Sample Answer to Guide Question
The mood is optimistic and hopeful.

36   "Done."

37   "And the second thing is food and fuel for my stove. I don't have much food left. . . ."

> **Recognize Tone and Mood**
>
> What is the mood of the story at this point?

38   Before he could finish speaking, the other people on the boat, the whale researchers who had been standing silent all this time, started running in different directions and in ten or fifteen minutes had arranged a huge **bundle** of food and supplies on a blanket which they tied together and lowered to him into the **cockpit** of the *Frog*. David saw one can peeking through a corner as he put the heavy bundle below the cabin—the label said it contained a canned chicken. A whole chicken in one can.

39   "We put in a lot of extra goodies," a girl yelled down, laughing. "Be careful you don't get fat. There's also five gallons of water in a plastic jug."

---

bundle   things close together usually tied or fastened   **cockpit**   the area of a boat where the captain stands

96   **Unit 2** Survival

MULTI-LEVEL OPTIONS *Read the Selection*

Newcomer *Ask: Does David need food?* (yes) *Do the people on the ship give him some?* (yes) *Does the ship sail with David's boat?* (no) *Does David get ready to go home?* (yes)

Beginning *Ask: What does David ask the captain for?* (food) *What else does the captain give him?* (water) *What does the captain do then?* (leave) *Where is David going to go?* (home)

Intermediate *Ask: Why do the people on the other ship start gathering supplies so fast?* (They are eager to help David.) *Why didn't the captain stay and help David?* (He needed to continue his research and could not travel as slowly as David had to.)

Advanced *Ask: How can you tell that the other people on the boat are eager to help David?* (They get a huge amount of supplies and food together fast; they even give him "goodies.") *What do you think "stand well off from shore" means?* (stay away from the shore; you'll be safer and have better wind 100 miles off shore.)

Recognize Tone and Mood

What is the mood of the story in this paragraph?

40   David thanked them and they talked a little more—the captain told him to stand well off from shore, perhaps a hundred miles, to get good, steady wind—and then it was done. The captain went back up to the bridge, the engines changed their pitch, and the ship slid away into the dusk. As soon as it was clear, the wind hit the *Frog* and David was busy for a few moments **trimming** the sails and getting her going, and when he turned he could no longer see the ship except for the lights on her radar **mast**. . . .

41   He had some sailing to do.

---

trimming   placing the sails in the direction of the wind   **mast**   a pole on a boat to which the sails are connected

About the Author

Gary Paulsen (born 1939)

Gary Paulsen had an unhappy childhood. His family moved a lot because his father was in the army. He did not have many friends. A friendly librarian helped Paulsen find his love of reading. He once said that when this librarian gave him a library card, she gave him the world.

Gary Paulsen grew up to write many books for young adults. Most of his books are adventure stories. The main characters in his stories often must resolve problems.

➤ As you read or listened to "The Voyage of the *Frog*," did you determine Paulsen's purpose? Was it to inform, to entertain, to influence, or to express himself?

Chapter 2   The Voyage of the *Frog*   **97**

Read the Selection

1. **Paired reading**   Play the audio. Have pairs read the selection in pairs. *Ask: What advice does the captain give David?* (to stay away from the shore to get a good wind)
2. **Multi-level options**   See MULTI-LEVEL OPTIONS on p. 96.

Sample Answer to Guide Question
The mood is happy and encouraging.

About the Author

1. **Explain author's background**   Gary Paulsen was a sailor when he was young and now spends part of his year on a boat in the Pacific Ocean.
2. **Interpret the facts**   *Ask: How do you know that Gary Paulsen likes the ocean and boats?* (Both the captain and David loved boats. The ocean descriptions are very clear.)

Answer
Example: The purpose was to entertain and express ideas about working hard.

Across Selections

▌ Teacher Resource Book: *Venn Diagram, p. 35*

Make comparisons and contrasts   Use a Venn diagram to compare David's survival situation and Jackie's in "How I Survived My Summer Vacation." *Ask: What problems did the two boys have? What was similar and different? Which problem was more difficult?*

Spelling, Punctuation, Capitalization

After the Reading Comprehension section, students will practice spelling, punctuation, and capitalization in the Activity Book.

th **Spelling**

Voiced vs. unvoiced /th/

Write on the board and *say: them.* Exaggerate the /th/ sound and throat vibration. Have students put their hands on their throats and repeat *them* until they feel the vibration. Write and *say: thin.* Ask students to repeat and say if they felt the vibration. (no) Have students practice voiced *(those, this, that)* and unvoiced *(think, Thursday, math)* words by repeating them after you and then using them in sentences.

Evaluate Your Reading Strategy

Recognize Tone and Mood *Say: You have practiced an important reading strategy. Now you can decide how well you have done. Does this statement describe how you read?*

As I read, I try to identify the author's feelings toward a character or a situation and the feeling the reader gets from the story. Recognizing tone and mood helps me understand the text better.

Beyond the Reading

Reading Comprehension

Question-Answer Relationships

Sample Answers

1. The *Frog* is about 250 miles south of San Diego, in Baja California.
2. David Alepeth is sailing the *Frog*.
3. David was far away because a storm had blown him off course.
4. David feels connected to the boat, like it was a dog or other pet. When I spend a lot of time with someone or something, I don't want to lose that person or thing.
5. Gary Paulsen likes and admires David's courage and loyalty to his boat. He wants readers to feel the same way about David.
6. David was sailing by himself because he knows how to sail and maybe he got a new boat.
7. I think David will make it home safely because he is strong and brave.
8. I think it's a bad idea because it is very dangerous to sail by yourself in a little boat on the ocean.

Build Reading Fluency

Adjust Your Reading Rate for Quotations

Demonstrate how to pause and read with expression when reading quotations. Explain that you change your rate of reading depending on the purpose and type of reading material.

Reading Comprehension

Question-Answer Relationships (QAR)

"Right There" Questions

1. **Recall Facts** Where is the *Frog* when the story begins?
2. **Recall Facts** Who is sailing the *Frog*?

"Think and Search" Question

3. **Recognize Cause and Effect** Why was David so far away from where he was trying to go?

"Author and You" Questions

4. **Compare Your Experiences** Why do you think David wants to stay with the *Frog*? How do you feel about something or someone that you have spent a lot of time with?

5. **Understand Author's Perspective** How do you think Gary Paulsen feels about David? How does he want you to feel about David?

"On Your Own" Questions

6. **Speculate** Why was David sailing the *Frog* by himself?
7. **Predict** Do you think David will make it home safely? Why or why not?
8. **Make Judgments** David decides to sail the *Frog* home rather than leave her behind to sink. Do you think this is a good idea? Why or why not?

Activity Book
p. 50

Student
CD-ROM

Build Reading Fluency

Adjust Your Reading Rate for Quotations

Reading quotations helps you learn to adjust your reading rate. You must pause and read with expression.

Reread the conversation between David and the man. Look for the quotation marks (" . . . ") around each conversation.

1. With a partner, take turns rereading aloud paragraphs 6–9 on page 91.
2. Read the quotations with expression.
3. Pause after each quotation.
4. Choose the quotation you like best.
5. Read it aloud in front of the class.

MULTI-LEVEL OPTIONS *Elements of Literature*

Newcomer Have students draw a vertical and horizontal line on a page to form two columns and two rows. On the top left of the page, tell them to draw the first problem David has. On the top right, ask them to show how it is solved. In the bottom boxes, tell students to draw the other problem David has and its solution.

Beginning Have students create a problem-solution organizer. Ask them to make a box with a picture or a few words indicating David's problem in paragraphs 16–18. Below the "problem" box, have them make boxes showing possible solutions. Finally, have them make a solution box showing how David solves his problem.

Intermediate After students have answered questions 1–6, ask them to reread paragraph 23. *Ask: What other problems did David likely have on his trip?* Have students identify one problem and tell a possible solution. (*Example:* He saw whales in the distance. He changed his direction so he didn't get close to them.)

Advanced *Say: Make a sequence chain telling problems David may have on his way home.* Under each block on the chain, have students write a sentence or two about how David may solve that problem. Invite students to use these ideas to write an ending for the story.

Listen, Speak, Interact

Conduct an Interview

Suppose David has returned from his voyage. People want to know about his experience. Conduct an interview about his experience. In an interview, a person asks another person questions.

1. Work with a partner. One of you will be the interviewer (the person who asks questions). One of you will be David.
2. Write questions that the interviewer will ask David. Use the following list to help you.
   a. What happened when you were on the *Frog*?

   b. Why did you decide to stay on the *Frog*?
   c. How did you feel when you came home?
3. Guess how David might answer each question. Use text evidence and your personal knowledge. Take notes on the answers.
4. Perform your interview for the class.
5. Listen as your classmates perform their interviews. Did you understand the major ideas? If not, ask your classmates questions.

Elements of Literature

Recognize and Analyze Problem Resolution

In fiction, one or more of the characters usually has a problem. The story is mostly about how the problem is resolved (worked out).

1. With a partner, reread the prologue of "The Voyage of the *Frog*," on page 90. What is David's problem?
2. Now reread paragraphs 1 to 3. Is there a resolution to this problem? David thinks that his problem is resolved, but is it?

3. Reread paragraphs 16 to 18. What new problem does David have?
4. Reread paragraphs 19 to 30. What are David's choices?
5. Which choice does David take?
6. Do you agree with David's choice? Whether you agree or not, do you admire him?

Activity Book
p. 51

Student
CD-ROM

Content Connection
Science

Have students review the map on p. 92, which shows where David was sailing. Ask students to work in pairs to research what kinds of animals David may have seen and what kinds of weather he may have experienced in that part of the Pacific Ocean. Tell students that they should use what they learn to add realistic details to their interviews.

Learning Styles
Visual

Remind students about the purpose of flowcharts. Demonstrate how a flowchart includes branches indicating choices. *Say: Sometimes, a flowchart can help you think about a problem, different ways to solve it, and the outcome of each choice.* Have small groups construct flowcharts to identify problems or decisions related to class or school situations, possible solutions, and likely consequences of each.

Listen, Speak, Interact

Conduct an Interview

1. **Brainstorm** Have students suggest other interview questions for the list.
2. **Reread in pairs** Pair beginning and advanced students to reread and choose roles.
3. **Newcomers** Reread with this group. Help them write the answers to the interview questions in their Reading Logs. Help them with intonation as they practice.

Elements of Literature

Recognize and Analyze Problem Resolution

1. **Explain terms** Read together the explanation of problem and resolution.
2. **Personal experience** Have students share problems they resolved after considering the possible choices.
3. **Multi-level options** See MULTI-LEVEL OPTIONS on p. 98.

Answers
1. David is lost at sea.
2. Yes. A ship can rescue him, but they don't realize he needs help.
3. He doesn't want to leave the *Frog*.
4. He can leave the boat or sail it back himself.
5. He decides to continue sailing.
6. *Example:* I don't agree with his choice, but I admire his courage.

✓ ASSESS

Have students generate a checklist for interview presentations and complete it for their own presentations.

Word Study

Teacher Resource Book: *Personal Dictionary*, p. 63

Understand the Suffix *-ly*

Make a semantic word map Create a word map for adverbs showing adjectives + *-ly*. Have students create their own word maps for the other adverbs: *slowly, abruptly.*

Answers
3. abruptly, abrupt; slowly, slow

Grammar Focus

Use the Future Tense

Apply Ask students what they will do after school or on the weekend. Help them use *will* + verb. Point out contracted forms.

Answers
1. I'll sail her. I won't leave her . . . I'll go back . . .
2. I will sail her. I will not leave her . . . I will go back . . .

ASSESS

Write on the board: *The boat sailed _____.* Have students suggest adverbs to describe how the boat sailed.

Word Study

Understand the Suffix *-ly*

A **suffix** is a group of letters added to the end of a word. A suffix can change the meaning of a word. It can also change a word from one part of speech to another.

Adverbs describe verbs (words that show action). Adverbs tell how an action happens. Many adverbs have the suffix *-ly*. The root word is usually an adjective. The suffix *-ly* changes an adjective to an adverb.

Sudden**ly** he was saved.

Adverbs can help make your writing vivid (interesting) and precise (exact).

Adjective	Adverb
sudden	suddenly

1. Copy the chart above in your Personal Dictionary.
2. Read these sentences.
   a. The captain said it abruptly.
   b. They jerked the boom slowly.
3. Write the adverbs that end in *-ly*. Write the adjective root word.

Personal Dictionary   Activity Book p. 52   Student CD-ROM

Grammar Focus

Use the Future Tense

One way to talk about events in the future is with *will*. In speech, *will* is often contracted as *'ll*. *Will not* is contracted as *won't*.

Statements with the Future Tense		
Subject	**will/will not**	**Verb**
I You He/She/It We They	will **'ll** will not won't	leave it.

1. Find the sentences with the future tense in paragraph 30 of the reading. Copy them on a piece of paper.
2. The sentences are contracted forms. Rewrite them as full forms using *will* and *will not*.

Activity Book pp. 53–54   Student Handbook   Student CD-ROM

100   Unit 2   Survival

MULTI-LEVEL OPTIONS *From Reading to Writing*

Newcomer Help students construct a storyboard showing a problem, events, and a solution.

Beginning Show an example of an adventure comic book. Have small groups work together to create three-frame to six-frame comic strips that tell about the adventure of a character.

Intermediate Suggest that students look through newspapers to find feature stories about people who survived dangerous situations or overcame challenging obstacles. Suggest that these articles might spark ideas for their adventure stories.

Advanced Explain that adventure stories often take place in unusual or exciting places, such as caves, rain forests, or desert islands. Point out to students that if they decide to use this type of setting, they should take time to do a little research about the place so they can include realistic details.

From Reading to Writing

Write a Story to Resolve a Problem

Write an adventure story about a problem. The characters in your story will resolve the problem.

1. Use a Sunshine Organizer to help you plan your story:
   a. Who are the characters?
   b. What is the problem?
   c. When does the story happen?
   d. Where does the story happen?
   e. Why did it happen?
   f. How do the characters solve the problem?
2. Write a beginning, a middle, and an end. Indent each paragraph.

3. Use adverbs to make your writing vivid and precise.

Activity Book p. 55   Student Handbook

Across Content Areas

Find Compass Directions

A **compass** is a tool that shows direction. **Compass directions** tell people which way they are going. The four main compass directions are **north, east, south,** and **west.** These are called the **cardinal directions.** North and south are opposite directions. East and west are opposite directions.

You can also name the directions between each cardinal direction. Northwest is between north and west. These are called **intercardinal directions.**

1. Copy this compass on a piece of paper.

2. Label the directions with these words.
   a. northeast
   b. east
   c. south
   d. southwest
   e. southeast

Activity Book p. 56

From Reading to Writing

Write a Story to Resolve a Problem

1. **Brainstorm** Have students suggest situations or problems for adventure stories. List ideas on the board.
2. **Make a storyboard** Have students create storyboards for the main events in their stories.
3. **Think-pair-share** In pairs, have students explain their pictures and ideas. Then ask students to write their texts. Instruct them to identify the characters and setting. Tell them to include dialogue in their stories.
4. **Multi-level options** See MULTI-LEVEL OPTIONS on p. 100.

Across Content Areas: Social Studies

Find Compass Directions

1. **Use a map or compass** Direct attention to the compass rose on a map or a compass. Have students identify cardinal and intercardinal directions.
2. **Connect** Have students identify states, countries, and bodies of water in each of the directions from where they are right now.

Answers
2. clockwise: northeast, east, southeast, south, southwest

✓ ASSESS

Say a cardinal direction and have students give the opposite direction.

Reteach and Reassess

Text Structure Have students review the chart on p. 88. Then ask them to construct a story map showing the characters, problem, events, and solution for "The Voyage of the *Frog*."

Reading Strategy Ask pairs of students to share the adventure stories they drew or wrote. Have partners tell each other what the attitude toward the main character is and the mood concerning the story problem.

Elements of Literature Have students discuss a school or community problem that

has been solved. Ask them to identify the problem, the choices people had, and the solution they chose.

Reassess Read a short adventure story or chapter from an adventure novel to students. Ask them to identify the author's tone toward the character and the mood at the beginning, middle, and end of the selection.

To Risk or
Not to Risk

an informational text
by David Ropeik

Objectives

Reading Distinguish fact from opinion as you read an informational text.

Listening and Speaking Compare personal experiences.

Grammar Use present tense and subject-verb agreement.

Writing Write an informational text.

Content Science: Learn about psychology.

Chapter Materials

Activity Book: *pp. 57–64*
Audio: *Unit 2, Chapter 3; CD 1, Track 8*
Student Handbook
Student CD-ROM: *Unit 2, Chapter 3*
Teacher Resource Book: *Lesson Plan, Teacher Resources, Reading Summary, Activity Book Answer Key*
Teacher Resource CD-ROM
Assessment Program: *Quiz, pp. 27–28; Teacher and Student Resources, pp. 115–144*
Assessment CD-ROM
Transparencies
The Heinle Newbury House Dictionary/CD-ROM
Web site: http://visions.heinle.com

Objectives

Offer observations Read the objectives. *Ask: What other informational texts have we read?* ("The Loch Ness Monster," "Mystery of the Cliff Dwellers," "Yawning")

Use Prior Knowledge

Rate Risks

1. **Clarify** *Say: We take risks everyday. What are some everyday risks?* (*example:* carrying money with you because you might lose it or someone might steal it; riding a bike without a helmet because you might fall and injure your head)
2. **Relate to personal experience** *Ask: Do you like to take risks? Why or why not?*

Use Prior Knowledge

Rate Risks

To take a risk means that you take the chance of getting hurt or losing something. For example, when you travel in a car, you take a risk of getting in an accident.

Some risks are bigger than others. The risk of getting into an accident is bigger while traveling in a car than in an airplane. This means more accidents happen in cars than in airplanes.

1. Copy the chart. Think about each risk listed. Write 1, 2, 3, or 4 next to each risk.
2. Share your chart with a small group. Did everyone rate the risks the same?

1	2	3	4
Small Risk	Some Risk	Risky	Very Risky

Risk	How Big
falling while using a skateboard	
getting a cold after visiting a friend with a cold	
getting bitten by a dog while running in the park	
getting lost while walking home from school	

102   **Unit 2** Survival

MULTI-LEVEL OPTIONS *Build Vocabulary*

Newcomer Have students work with you to make a classroom resource chart. Draw actions students may take when they hear or see a word that is unfamiliar to them. Some of the techniques represented on the chart may include comparing the word to another word they know or asking someone else, such as a teacher.

Beginning Write a short sentence on the board. Include words that students know as well as ones that are unfamiliar. Write question marks on several small stick-on notes. Have volunteers place these notes above unfamiliar words in the sentence. Help students use the ideas on p. 103 to find the meaning of each.

Intermediate *Say: Cortex is probably a new word for you. You read a little about its meaning in Build Background. What can you do to learn more?* Have students work in pairs to find out more about the word. Provide time for students to share what they learn and tell how they found the information.

Advanced *Say: We use the term* user-friendly *to mean that something is easy to use. Books can also be user-friendly. Authors often give definitions, synonyms, antonyms, or other hints to the meaning of unusual words in their writing. As you read the selection, decide whether it is user-friendly. Be ready to defend your opinion.*

Build Background

The Brain

We use two parts of our brains to decide if something is a risk. We use the **limbic system** and the **cortex.** The limbic system is the part of the brain that controls feelings and learning. The cortex is the part of the brain that controls thinking. We use the cortex to write and solve puzzles.

Content Connection

The limbic system works faster than the cortex. You may feel scared before you have time to think about why.

Build Vocabulary

Learn Vocabulary Through Reading

When you see a new word when you are reading or listening to the selections, there are several things you can do. Here are some of them.

1. Reread and review text.
   a. Reread sentences that have words you do not know. Adjust your reading speed to a slower rate so that you can pay more attention to the important ideas.
   b. Reread using context clues (words that are around the new word).
2. Use glosses (definitions).
   a. The definitions of boldfaced words are at the bottom of the reading selection pages.
   b. Review the definitions of any boldfaced words you do not know.

3. Use reference sources.
   a. You learned about reference sources in Build Vocabulary for Chapter 2. These include dictionaries, thesauruses, synonym finders, and software.
   b. Use reference sources to help you learn new words and clarify their meanings, pronunciations, derivations, and usages.
4. Write new vocabulary in your Personal Dictionary to help you remember new words.

Personal Dictionary

The Heinle Newbury House Dictionary

Activity Book p. 57

Student CD-ROM

Content Connection
The Arts

Build Background *Say: When you think of art in books, you probably think of pictures in fiction books. Art is an important part of nonfiction books, too. Artists can help readers understand facts in an informational text.* Have students review what they learned about the function of the limbic system and cortex of the brain. Ask each of them to find a creative way to illustrate the purpose of these two parts of the brain.

Learning Styles
Linguistic

Build Vocabulary *Say: Some people love words. They collect them like other people collect stamps, autographs, or model cars.* Invite students to start a collection of interesting words and their meanings. Tell students that they can keep lists in the backs of their Reading Logs or get special notebooks for this purpose. Point out that collecting words will help them as speakers, readers, and writers.

Build Background

The Brain

1. **Use an illustration** Bring in illustrations of the brain. Have students find the cortex (outer layer of the brain) and the limbic system (a ring-shaped area in the center of the brain). *Ask: Which part controls fear?* (limbic) *Writing a letter?* (cortex)
2. **Content Connection** Explain that if you touch a hot iron, your brain tells you to move away quickly. You don't have to think about it, so it is the limbic system that helps keep you safe.

Build Vocabulary

Teacher Resource Book: *Personal Dictionary, p. 63*

Learn Vocabulary Through Reading

1. **Use experiences** Have students share how they find the meanings of new words. Make a list on the board and demonstrate if needed. Point out examples of glosses in the reading.
2. **Use glossaries** Help students locate the glossary in their science and social studies textbooks. Have them choose three words. *Ask: Does the glossary provide pronunciation of the words?* if so, have students pronounce them. *Ask: Does the glossary provide derivations of the words?* If so, have students provide them.
3. **Reading selection vocabulary** You may want to introduce the glossed words in the reading selection before students begin reading. Key words: *poisonous, risk, genes, tendency, psychologists, factor.* Instruct students to write the words with correct spelling and their definitions in their Personal Dictionaries. Have them pronounce each word and divide it into syllables.
4. **Multi-level options** See MULTI-LEVEL OPTIONS on p. 102.

ASSESS

Have students create their own checklists for learning vocabulary through reading.

Text Structure

Informational Text

Define and explain Have students give examples or explain the features in the graphic organizer. They can review "Yawning" (p. 30) for examples.

Reading Strategy

Distinguish Fact from Opinion

1. **Understand terms** Write key phrases for opinions: *I think, I feel, It seems.* Point out that facts can be proven or are true for everyone. Have students give opinions and facts about school.
2. **Multi-level options** See MULTI-LEVEL OPTIONS below.

Answers
1. **a.** opinion **b.** fact **c.** opinion

ASSESS

Have students write one fact and one opinion about this textbook.

Text Structure

Informational Text

"To Risk or Not to Risk" is an **informational text.** An informational text explains a topic. This selection explains how people respond to risk. Note the features of this informational text shown in the chart.

Look for questions and answers as you read "To Risk or Not to Risk."

Informational Text	
Facts	Facts are information that is true.
Questions	The text includes questions. The questions give clues about important ideas.
Answers	The text includes answers to the questions. The answers give details that support important ideas.

Student
CD-ROM

Reading Strategy

Distinguish Fact from Opinion

A **fact** is information that is true. A fact can be proven to be true. An **opinion** is a person's feelings about something. Opinions cannot be proven to be true. Read these sentences:

Jenny saw a movie. She thought the movie was very good.

Words like *think* and *feel* often express an opinion.

1. Are these sentences facts or opinions?
    a. That's a beautiful snake!
    b. Some snakes are poisonous.
    c. I think that snakes make great pets.

2. Look for facts and opinions as you read and listen to the selection. Write the facts and opinions in a chart.

Facts	Opinions
Jenny saw a movie.	She thought the movie was very good.

Student
CD-ROM

MULTI-LEVEL OPTIONS *Reading Strategy*

Newcomer Show a picture of a snake and use gestures and facial expressions to communicate the ideas in 1a–c. Tell students to point to their heads (to represent brains) if you express a fact and to their hearts (to represent feelings) if you express an opinion.

Beginning Have students draw a representation of a brain and a heart on their two-column charts to remind themselves of the meanings of the headings. Have them work in pairs to decide which of the sentences in 1a–c are facts and which are opinions.

Intermediate After students have completed 1a–c, ask them to look at the picture on p. 105. Tell them to list at least three facts and three opinions about what they see in the picture.

Advanced Ask students to read the title of the selection for this chapter. Have them list some facts and opinions they think the author might include in an article about risk taking.

To Risk or Not to Risk

an informational text
by David Ropeik

105

Reading Selection Materials

Audio: *Unit 2, Chapter 3; CD 1, Track 8*
Teacher Resource Book: *Reading Summary, pp. 79–80*
Transparencies: #35, *Reading Summary*

Suggestions for Using Reading Summary

- Introduce new vocabulary or cognates.
- Cut the summary into strips, or jumble the sentences on an overhead transparency. Students put the sentences in order.
- Practice the reading strategy.
- Students read aloud or with a partner.
- Students paraphrase the summary.
- Students do a cloze activity.
- Students create a visual or graphic organizer, such as a timeline or storyboard, to illustrate the summary.
- Students paraphrase the summary.

Preview the Selection

1. **Teacher think aloud** Have students examine the photo and title. *Say: The title is "To Risk or Not to Risk." The boy in the picture is skateboarding. That's risky. It is easy to fall down and get hurt. But he's wearing some safety equipment, so he knows the risks. And he still wants to do it! He's in the air and might get hurt! Why does he want to do this if it is dangerous? This unit is about survival. How are risks and survival connected? This is an informational text. As I read, I want to look for facts and answers to these and other questions about taking risks.*

2. **Connect** Have students recall the meaning of *survival*. Allow students to make guesses about the connection between risk taking and survival.

Content Connection *Social Studies*	**Learning Styles** *Intrapersonal*

Point out that the kinds of risks people take can depend on where they live and the time in which they are living. Ask students to identify a place or time they are studying in social studies. Have pairs work together to generate a list of at least three risks a person of that time or place might take. Tell students to underline any risks in their lists that could also be faced by people in their community today.

Ask students to reflect on their own opinions about risk taking. *Say: Write or draw a situation in which you think risk taking is good. (Example: introducing yourself to a new classmate) Write or draw a situation in which you think risk taking is foolish. (Example: riding a bike too fast)* Have students write about whether or not they like to take risks and why in their Reading Logs.

Teacher Resource Book: *Reading Log, p. 64*

Read the Selection

1. **Use text features** Direct students to the photograph and ask them to describe it. Then call attention to glossed words and have students find their meanings at the bottom of the page.
2. **Reciprocal reading** Play the audio. Then have small groups read together with a rotating "leader." The leader asks questions and helps others summarize the selection.
3. **Distinguish fact from opinion** *Say: It says that only 1 person out of every 40,000 gets bitten by a poisonous snake. Those numbers can be checked so I know it's not an opinion or what someone thinks. It's a fact.* Ask volunteers to decide if other statements from the selection are facts or opinions.

Sample Answer to Guide Question
It's a fact because you can check the numbers.

See Teacher Edition pp. 434–436 for a list of English-Spanish cognates in the reading selection.

---

1 The chances that you will be bitten by a **poisonous** snake are really low; about 1 out of every 40,000 people in this country is bitten each year. The chances of being bitten by a spider are pretty low, too. And the chances that anything bad will happen to you in the dark—except that you might trip and fall or bump into something—are far less than the chances that something bad will happen to you when the sun is out or the lights are on, which is when most of us are awake and active.

> ### Distinguish Fact from Opinion
> Is the statement "The chances of being bitten by a spider are pretty low" a fact or an opinion?

2 If the actual risk of these things isn't very big, why are we so afraid of them? Some scientists think our distant **ancestors** learned to be afraid of snakes, spiders and the dark millions of years ago. If you were living out in the savanna or in caves, snakes, spiders and the dark were bigger risks. So those who reacted fearfully to them survived and passed on their **genes**—and their fears—to us.

3 But why are many people also afraid of more modern risks that aren't that big? Like getting cancer from cell phones or dying from mad cow disease? Our distant ancestors didn't have cell phones or mad cows!

🎧 Audio
CD 1. Tr. 8

poisonous causing harm or death by poison
ancestors the people from whom one is descended (great-grandmother, father, and so on)

genes the basic part of a living cell that contains characteristics of one's parents

106 Unit 2 Survival

MULTI-LEVEL OPTIONS *Read the Selection*

Newcomer Play the audio. *Ask: Are the chances of bad things happening small?* (yes) *Are people scared anyway?* (yes) *Are people afraid of artificial things?* (yes) *Are people's fears usually based on facts?* (no)

Beginning Read aloud to students. *Ask: Are the chances of bad things happening to people low or high?* (low) *How do most people feel about things like snakes and spiders?* (scared) *Are people more afraid of "natural" or "artificial" things?* (artificial) *What can bottled water have in it?* (bacteria)

Intermediate Have students do a shared reading. *Ask: How do most people react to spiders and snakes?* (with fear) *Why do scientists think this is true?* (because we have learned to be afraid of them) *If people don't use facts in deciding what to fear, what do they probably use?* (feelings)

Advanced Have students read silently. *Say: Review the things the article mentions as fears. Which does the author probably think is the most likely to happen?* (getting hurt from not using seatbelts; getting sick from smoking) *What do some scientists think causes humans to be fearful?* (genetics)

And why don't people worry much about risks that *are* pretty big? Why do people refuse to wear seat belts in cars and continue to smoke?

4   It turns out that we react to most risks the same way we react to snakes, spiders and the dark: our fears are more important than the facts. But what makes us decide what to be afraid of and how afraid to be? To answer that question, scientists study the ways our fears seem to be at odds with reality. . . . And they've found some interesting patterns.

For example, suppose someone gives you two glasses, one filled with city tap water and the other with water bottled at a **rural** spring. Which would you drink? Surveys show that most people are less afraid of "natural" things than they are of **"artificial"** ones. Most people would pick the spring water, even though tests show bottled water often contains **bacteria** and other **impurities.**

5

> **Distinguish Fact from Opinion**
>
> Spring water is safer than water from a city tap. Is this a fact or an opinion? How can you tell?

---

rural   related to the countryside, not the city
artificial   made by humans, not made from natural things

bacteria   tiny living things; many cause diseases
impurities   dirty or bad things

Chapter 3 To Risk or Not to Risk   **107**

Read the Selection

1. **Understand terms** Have students find the meanings of the glossed words below the selection. Point out other words and expressions such as: *mad cow disease, react, at odds with, spring, tap water.* Clarify meanings as needed.
2. **Reciprocal reading** Play the audio. Have students continue to work in groups with a leader asking questions and other group members answering and summarizing.
3. **Compare the text to your own experiences** *Ask: Do you prefer things that are "natural" or things that are "artificial"? Do you feel safer drinking tap water or bottled water?*
4. **Multi-level options** See MULTI-LEVEL OPTIONS on p. 106.

Sample Answer to Guide Question
It's an opinion. The statement is not true because of the test results that are mentioned.

---

th Spelling

Plurals ending in *-ies*

Write on the board: *impurity/impurities*. *Say: Which word is singular (only one)?* (impurity) *Which one is plural (two or more)?* (impurities) Tell students there is a rule for making most nouns that end in *-y* plural. *Say: To make most nouns ending in -y plural, change the* y *to* i *and add -es.*

    Apply Write the following on the board. Ask students to write the plural for each: *baby, lady, country, city, family.* (babies, ladies, countries, cities, families)

Read the Selection

1. **Use text features** Point out the illustration and glossed words. Have students suggest if sky-diving is a risky activity or not.
2. **Paired reading** Read the selection aloud. Then have students reread the selection in pairs. *Ask: Are people more or less afraid of things they choose to do like sky-diving? (less afraid) What is an example of a new risk that people are not familiar with? (West Nile virus)*
3. **Teacher think aloud** *Say: In paragraph 7, I see* estimate *and* overestimate. *I know* estimate *means "to make a good guess about something."* Guide students to guess the meaning of *overestimate*.

Sample Answer to Guide Question
It's an opinion because it begins with "I think," which shows it's not a fact.

---

6   Here's another example. Some people like to go **sky-diving**. It's risky, but they are choosing to take the risk themselves. Nobody's forcing them to do it. Most of us are less afraid of risks that we choose for ourselves, such as scuba-diving or skateboarding, and more afraid of risks we're forced to take, such as eating food that has been **genetically modified** or treated with chemicals.

> ### Distinguish Fact from Opinion
>
> Is the statement "I think skateboarding is safer than eating tomatoes treated with chemicals" a fact or an opinion? How can you tell?

7   Another factor that shapes our opinion of a risk is trust. If we trust the people who are supposed to protect us from the risk, we're more **inclined** to estimate it correctly. But if someone has an **untrustworthy** past, such as tobacco companies do, for example, there's a **tendency** to overestimate the risk by way of compensation.

8   Another factor that affects our fear of risks is familiarity. Is the risk new, or is it something we're used to? When a new risk comes along, like the West Nile virus now spreading across the U.S., we tend to overestimate it. But when the risk has been around for a while—say, the risk of riding a bike on city streets—we tend to underestimate it.

---

sky-diving   jumping out of an airplane and floating to the ground with the help of a parachute

genetically modified   changed or altered in something's genes

inclined   likely to

untrustworthy   dishonest

tendency   an inclination or habit

108   Unit 2 Survival

Newcomer *Ask: Do some people choose to take risks? (yes) Are people more scared of new things? (yes) Are people less scared if something good could happen from the risk? (yes)*

Beginning *Ask: Are risks we choose more or less scary? (less) What kind of person is more likely to talk us into taking a risk? (one we trust) Are people more scared of things that are new or old? (new) What do we want to get out of taking a risk? (something good)*

Intermediate *Ask: How does the author say people react to taking risks they choose? (less scared) Are people likely to be less scared of a wild ride at an amusement park or of being robbed? Why? (amusement park ride, because there is a benefit)*

Advanced *Ask: Most people would be more willing to buy a new product that their best friend likes rather than one a salesperson is selling. This is an example of which idea on page 108? (being willing to take a risk because of someone we trust)*

9   It also matters whether the risk comes with a benefit. Skiing is risky, but it's fun. **Vaccines** cause harmful reactions in a few people, but they protect most people against disease. If we think the benefit is greater than the risk, we're less afraid. But if we think the risk is greater, we're more afraid.

10   **Psychologists** call the next factor **dread.** Death by shark attack scares most of us more than death by car crash, even though the outcome is the same. That might seem foolish, since the risk of being killed in a car crash is far higher than the risk of being killed by a shark. But the more awful the **outcome,** the more afraid of it we are, and the more we overestimate the chances of it happening.

Distinguish Fact from Opinion

Explain how the statement "Skiing is risky, but it's fun" is both a fact and an opinion.

---

vaccines   medication taken to prevent many diseases
psychologists   people who study human and animal behavior

dread   a strong fear of something happening in the future
outcome   the effect or result

Chapter 3   To Risk or Not to Risk   **109**

Read the Selection

1. **Use the photo** Call attention to the photo and ask students if this is a risky activity or not and explain why.
2. **Understand terms** Have students find the meanings of the glossed words below the selection. Point out other words and expressions, such as *benefit* and *outcome.* Clarify meanings as needed.
3. **Paired reading** After students listen to the audio or to you read the selection, have them read it again in pairs.
4. **Locate derivations using dictionaries** Have students look at these glossed words and determine what words they are derived from: *genetically, modified, untrustworthy, psychologists.* Have students check the derivations in a print, an online, or a CD-ROM dictionary.
5. **Compare the text to your own experiences** Ask students to consider and explain their own opinions about the risks and dangers mentioned in the selection.
6. **Multi-level options** See MULTI-LEVEL OPTIONS on p. 108.

Sample Answer to Guide Question
"Skiing is risky" is a fact that can be supported with numbers of accidents. "It's fun" is an opinion because not everyone likes skiing.

, Punctuation

Periods for abbreviations

Call attention to the abbreviation *U.S.* in paragraph 8. *Ask: What do the letters* U-S *stand for?* (United States) *What do you notice about the punctuation for this abbreviation or short way of writing* United States*?* (periods after *U* and *S*) *Yes, abbreviations sometimes have periods after the letters that stand for words.*

Apply Have pairs decide how to abbreviate the following: *Puerto Rico, Los Angeles, District of Columbia, New York.* (P.R., L.A., D.C., N.Y.)

Read the Selection

1. **Use text features** Point out the illustration and glossed words. Have students suggest if driving is a risky activity.
2. **Paired reading** Read the selection aloud. Then have students reread the selection in pairs. *Ask: Why aren't people more afraid of driving?* (They are in control of the car.) *What is a delayed risk?* (The risk or danger is not going to happen right away.)
3. **Summarize** Ask questions to help students summarize the main points of each of the paragraphs and identify factors that make people afraid of risks and factors that make them less afraid of risks.

Sample Answer to Guide Question
It contains opinions.

11   Here's a final **factor.** People are less afraid of risks when they feel in control. Most people aren't afraid of driving, even though the risk of an accident is **significant,** because they're holding the steering wheel and stepping on the gas pedal or the brakes, and so they have some control over what's happening.

12   Of course, these aren't the only factors that affect how we size up a risk. If the risk of harm is immediate, it seems bigger than if harm is **delayed.** Smoking is a good example of a delayed risk. If a great deal is known about the risk, we are less fearful than if there is little information. If the risk kills many at once, we fear it more than if it kills one at a time. If we've already been hurt, we're more afraid than if we have no painful memories.

13   You can probably come up with other **biases.** The more you think about it, the more interesting the psychology of fear becomes.

> **Distinguish Fact from Opinion**
>
> Does this paragraph contain facts or opinions?

14   Some people say that behaving this way is silly. They think we would make smarter decisions about risks if we just relied on the facts and not on our feelings. They say it shouldn't matter

---

factor a fact to be considered
significant large or meaningful

delayed moved to a later time
biases general tendencies

110 Unit 2 Survival

MULTI-LEVEL OPTIONS *Read the Selection*

Newcomer *Ask: Are people afraid of bad things that might happen right away?* (yes) *Are people afraid of things they know a lot about?* (no) *Do most people use facts to decide if something is dangerous?* (no)

Beginning *Ask: Are people more afraid of things that may happen now or in the future?* (now) *Are people more afraid when they know a little or a lot about something?* (a little) *Do most people use facts or feelings to decide whether something is dangerous?* (feelings)

Intermediate *Ask: How does the time when a bad effect would come from a risk affect people's fears?* (They are more scared of risks that would have a bad result right away.) *What is the smartest thing we could do if we have to decide whether to take a risk?* (gather facts about the situation, if there is time)

Advanced *Ask: If a person who is afraid of flying has to take a plane, what idea from the article might make him/her less fearful?* (*Example:* controlling when and where he/she flies) *What can people do to avoid deciding about risks based on feelings?* (notice the feeling they have, but take time to find out facts about the risk) whether a risk is natural or artificial, **voluntary** or not, whether the risk is new or familiar, has benefits that **outweigh** the possible harm, or has a really nasty outcome. They say the only things that should matter are the facts: the likelihood of death or injury.

Distinguish Fact from Opinion

Does this paragraph contain facts or opinions? What words help you tell?

But the way our brains evolved, we may not have much choice. . . . Long before our ancestors had the highly developed, reasoning brains we have now, they could still recognize and respond to danger. And those **ancient** ways of staying safe are still at work. Our brains are actually built, biologically, to fear first, and think second. So when it comes to protecting ourselves, what we feel often matters more than what we think.

15

voluntary   done without being forced or paid
outweigh   to be more important than something else

ancient   very old

About the Author

David Ropeik (born 1951)

David Ropeik studies the risks that people take. He works at the Harvard Center for Risk Analysis. Harvard is a university in Cambridge, Massachusetts (near Boston). You can sometimes hear David Ropeik on the radio, talking about risk. He has also written a book about this topic.

Ropeik studied journalism in college. (Journalism is the study of gathering and reporting news.) He worked as a television news reporter. He also wrote science articles for newspapers. Ropeik has won important awards and honors for his work in journalism.

➤ Why did David Ropeik write this article for young readers? What do you think he wants people to learn from this article?

Chapter 3   To Risk or Not to Risk   **111**

Spelling

_th_

Plurals ending in -s vs. -es

Write *bias* on the board. *Say: This word means "an unfair like or dislike of something." Look at paragraph 13 to see how we form the plural.* (biases) *When a word ends in* s, sh, ch, x, *or* z, *we add* -es *to make it plural.*

Apply   On the board, write: *class, dish, lunch, tax, whiz.* Ask students to form the plural. (classes, dishes, lunches, taxes, whizzes)

Evaluate Your Reading Strategy

Distinguish Fact from Opinion *Say: You have practiced an important reading strategy. Now you can decide how well you have done. Does this statement describe how you read?*

> When I read, I decide whether information is a fact or an opinion. Distinguishing facts and opinions helps me decide how I feel about the information in a text.

Read the Selection

1. **Silent reading** Have students read silently. *Ask: How do our brains help keep us from danger?* (They respond to danger first and then think.)
2. **Summarize** Have pairs of students reread and summarize.
3. **Multi-level options** See MULTI-LEVEL OPTIONS on p. 110.

Sample Answer to Guide Question
The words "say" and "think" tell me they are opinions.

About the Author

1. **Explain author's background** David Ropeik writes and speaks so people will keep risk in proper perspective.
2. **Interpret point of view** *Ask: Does David Ropeik want people to stop all risky sports? Why or why not?* (No. They need to choose for themselves and decide for themselves what is the proper risk.)

Answer
Example: He wants young readers to understand how to decide what is too risky or not.

Across Selections

Connect content Have students review the risk that David was willing to take in "The Voyage of the *Frog*." Have them explain why he chose to continue sailing his boat. Students can consider what their choice would be in David's situation and explain why they would make that choice.

Spelling, Punctuation, Capitalization

After the Reading Comprehension section, students will practice spelling, punctuation, and capitalization in the Activity Book.

Beyond the Reading

Reading Comprehension

Question-Answer Relationships

Sample Answers

1. A risk is a chance of danger or losing something important.
2. Most people measure risks through their fears.
3. This shows that people are afraid of artificial things. They are not afraid of natural things, which sound safer.
4. If you trust someone, then you are more likely to believe they will protect you from any danger. The risk seems smaller.
5. Yes. I don't like to try new foods.
6. When you choose something, you are in control of the choice. You can only blame yourself if it was not a good choice, and you can only blame yourself if you are in control.
7. No. The immediate risks may help you "survive" right now, but it may not be a good idea in all situations where harmful results may show up much later.
8. I think people should measure risk more by facts, but it's hard to not be affected by feelings.
9. How can people figure out what is a reasonable amount of risk?

Build Reading Fluency

Read Silently

Assessment Program: *Reading Fluency Chart, p. 116*

When students have completed the reading fluency activity, record their progress in the Reading Fluency Chart.

Reading Comprehension

Question-Answer Relationships (QAR)

"Right There" Questions

1. **Recall Facts** What is a risk?
2. **Recall Facts** Do most people measure risks through the facts or through their fears?

"Think and Search" Questions

3. **Find Supporting Arguments** The text says that most people choose spring water over city water. How does this example show that people make choices because of their fears?
4. **Identify Cause and Effect** According to the author, how does trust affect people's opinions about risk?

"Author and You" Questions

5. **Connect Your Experiences** The author says people fear new risks more than familiar risks. Is this true for you? Give some examples.

6. **Identify Theme** The author says people are less afraid of risks that they choose. He also says that people are less afraid of risks when they feel in control. What is the common theme in these two examples?

"On Your Own" Questions

7. **Make Judgments** The author says that people fear immediate risks more than delayed risks. Do you think this is a good idea? Why or why not?
8. **State an Opinion** Do you think people should measure risk by the facts or by their feelings? Explain.
9. **Raise Additional Questions** Based on your knowledge, form additional questions about risk that are *not* answered in the reading.

Activity Book Student
p. 58 CD-ROM

Build Reading Fluency

Read Silently

Reading silently is good practice. It helps you learn to read faster. An effective reader reads silently for greater periods of time.

1. Listen to the audio recording of paragraph 1 on page 106.

2. Listen to the chunks of words as you follow along.
3. Reread paragraph 1 silently two times.
4. Your teacher will time your second reading.
5. Raise your hand when you are done.

112 **Unit 2** Survival

Newcomer On the board, write: *but.* To the left of the word, draw a happy face and to the right draw a sad face. Write: *I like _____, but I don't like _____. Say: I like tuna sandwiches, but I don't like hamburgers.* Invite students to follow this model to show some things they do and don't like using *but.*

Beginning Write on the board: *I like _____, but I am afraid of _____.* Demonstrate completing the frames. *Say: I love cats, but I am afraid of tigers.* Circle the transition word, *but.* Ask students to complete the frame with their own likes and fears. Provide time for sharing.

Intermediate Have students make up sentences using each of the transition words. Ask them to tie their sentences to the theme of the selection they read. (*Example:* I walked across the bridge, even though I am afraid of high places.)

Advanced Have students use a thesaurus to find other transition words that are similar in meaning to the ones mentioned in Elements of Literature. (though, yet, in spite of, although, nevertheless) Challenge them to write three sentences about risks, using one of the transition words in each.

Listen, Speak, Interact

Compare Personal Experiences

"To Risk or Not to Risk" describes real risks that a person can take. Think about risks that you take every day.

1. List risks from the selection that you have taken, such as skateboarding.
2. List risks that you have taken that are not in the selection. For example, you may live in an area where there are many earthquakes.
3. Meet with a small group. Make a chart to compare your lists. Are many the same?
4. Talk about these risks. Which do you fear the most? Which do you fear the least? Why?
5. As you listen to your group members, distinguish between opinions and facts.

Elements of Literature

Identify Transition Words

Authors use **transition words** to connect ideas. These words help organize your sentences and paragraphs and blend them into larger units of text.

You can use transition words to contrast ideas. *But, however,* and *even though* are transition words. They show that you are about to read a different idea.

First Idea
Jo went to the party.

Second Idea
However, she did not have fun.

Usually, people have fun at parties. *However* shows that you will read a different idea: Jo did *not* have fun at the party.

1. Write these sentences in your Reading Log:
   a. Skiing is risky, but it's fun.
   b. Most people aren't afraid of driving, even though the risk of an accident is significant.
2. Circle the transition words. Then underline the ideas that are shown as different.

Reading Log   Activity Book   Student
                   p. 59   CD-ROM

Community Connection

Have students work in groups to list situations in their community that are risky or scary. (*Examples:* the dangerous intersection at Main and Second Street; people letting their dogs run loose) Have students select the situation that the group agrees is the riskiest. Tell them to brainstorm ways to lower or eliminate the risk.

Learning Styles
Mathematical

Remind students that transition words such as *but* let readers know that the ideas on either side of the transition are different. Point out that the mathematical symbol $\neq$ has a similar meaning in a number sentence or equation. It shows that the two things on either side of the symbol are not the same. Have students use $\neq$ to write some math sentences. (*Example:* $4 \times 3 + 10 \neq 14 - 6 \times 2$)

Listen, Speak, Interact

Compare Personal Experiences

1. **Use a graphic organizer** Pair beginning and advanced students and have them reread the selection for examples of risks. Have them add their own examples. Arrange students in groups to compare lists and to discuss facts and opinions about the risks.
2. **Newcomers** Guide discussion in this group. List ideas on the board, assisting with vocabulary as needed. Help students give facts and opinions about the items on their lists.

Elements of Literature

▌ Teacher Resource Book: *Reading Log, p. 64*

Identify Transition Words

1. **Explain terms** Explain the meaning and usage of transition words to show contrasts.
2. **Apply** Write simple sentences on the board and have students connect them with transition words. Write on the board: *The weather is cold. We want to go running in the park. / I'm tired. I want to go to the party.*
3. **Multi-level options** See MULTI-LEVEL OPTIONS on p. 112.

Answers

1. a. Skiing is risky, but it's fun.; b. Most people aren't afraid of driving, even though the risk of an accident is significant.

ASSESS

Ask students to write sentences using these transition words: *however, but, even though.*

Word Study

Teacher Resource Book: *Personal Dictionary,* p. 63

Identify Prefixes *over-* and *under-*

Use prefixes On the board, write: *charge, confident, do, fed, tired.* Ask students to make as many words as they can using these words and the prefixes *over-* or *under-*. Have them check the dictionary for any words they aren't sure of.

Answers
2. overcook (cook too much), undercook (not cook enough); overcharge (charge too much), undercharge (not charge enough)

Grammar Focus

Use Present Tense and Subject-Verb Agreement

Apply Point out the chart of forms. Ask questions to help students use the present tense. *Ask: What time does school start?* (It starts at _____.) *Do you like to draw?* (Yes, I like to draw.) Point out that *-s* is only added to the third-person singular.

Answers
1. gives 2. say

ASSESS

Have students write two sentences in the present tense to tell facts about school.

Word Study

Identify Prefixes *over-* and *under-*

A **prefix** is a group of letters that is added to the beginning of a root word. A prefix may change the meaning of a root word.

The prefix *over-* means "too much." The prefix *under-* means "not enough."

1. Read the example in the chart.
2. In your Personal Dictionary, complete a chart like the one shown for each word pair.

Root Word	Over + Root	Under + Root
estimate: guess the amount of	overestimate: guess too much	underestimate: guess not enough
cook: heat food until done		
charge: to put a price on		

Personal Dictionary　　The Heinle Newbury House Dictionary　　Activity Book p. 60　　Student CD-ROM

Grammar Focus

Use Present Tense and Subject-Verb Agreement

Use the present tense of verbs to talk about things that are generally true or that happen regularly.

> Some people **like** to go sky-diving.

> When a new risk **comes** along, we tend to overestimate it.

When the subject of a statement is *he, she,* or *it,* or a singular noun, you add an *s* to present tense verbs.

Choose the correct verb for each sentence.

1. He (give/gives) you two glasses.
2. Some people (say/says) that behaving this way is silly.
3. Psychologists (calls/call) the next factor dread.

Present Tense	
Subject	**Verb**
I you we they	work
he she it	work**s**

Activity Book pp. 61–62　　Student Handbook　　Student CD-ROM

114 Unit 2 Survival

MULTI-LEVEL OPTIONS *From Reading to Writing*

Newcomer Have the class select a topic. Divide the students into small groups. Help each student identify a question that can be answered by looking at pictures. Write the questions on chart paper, leaving space between each. Have students find answers and draw them under the questions.

Beginning Divide the class into groups. Have each student in the group decide on one question he/she has about a topic the group selects. Give students time to find answers to their questions. Help each group write its questions and answers. Display the results.

Intermediate After students have decided on topics, ask each to brainstorm a list of related questions. Then have them read their questions to partners. Tell students to ask their partners which questions sound most interesting. Suggest that students use these questions in their informational texts.

Advanced Point out that the author of "To Risk or Not to Risk" included some questions in the text. Explain that some authors use questions for chapter or paragraph headings. Others use an interview format. Have students find some examples and then make a decision about how they will include questions in their writing.

From Reading to Writing

Write an Informational Text

Write an informational text to explain something you like to do or a place you like to visit.

1. Make an outline to organize your ideas.
2. Use questions to get readers involved.
3. Write answers to your questions. The answers should include details.
4. Make sure subjects and verbs agree.
5. Write two or three paragraphs.
6. Use the present tense. Be sure your verbs agree with your subjects.
7. Use transition words to help organize your paragraphs and to blend your paragraphs together.

Outline for Working Out

I. Working out is important.
   A. You feel better.
   B. You feel stronger.
II. There are many ways to work out.
   A.
   B.

Activity Book
p. 63

Student Handbook

Across Content Areas

Learn About Psychology

Psychology is the study of how people act. People who study psychology believe these things affect how people act:

personality a person's qualities; what a person is like

environment where a person lives

habit a way of acting that a person often repeats without thinking

family background a person's family, including past generations

Match each sentence to the thing that affects how the person acts.

1. Alex keeps biting his fingernails.
2. Kasia is good at math. Her mother and aunt were also good at math.
3. Luis is a kind and creative person. However, he is not very patient.
4. Jim has lived in a large city his whole life.

Activity Book
p. 64

Chapter 3 To Risk or Not to Risk **115**

Reteach and Reassess

Text Structure Assign familiar topics to pairs of students. Ask each pair to review the chart on the top of p. 104. Have them identify one fact, one question, and one answer that could be included in an informational text about their assigned topic.

Reading Strategy Ask each student to identify one situation he/she feels is risky. Have them write one fact and one opinion about that situation.

Elements of Literature Write on the board: *I would like to try _____. I am not afraid of _____.* Have students complete sentence starters with words or pictures and a transition word.

Reassess Read a paragraph from an informational text to students. Ask them to tell one fact they learned from the piece and express one opinion they have about it.

From Reading to Writing

Write an Informational Text

1. **Brainstorm** Have students suggest topics. List the ideas on the board.
2. **Use an outline** Have students create outlines to organize their thoughts and ideas for their informational text.
3. **Think-pair-share** As students share outlines in pairs, have them add questions and details.
4. **Language experience writing** For less fluent students, have them dictate their ideas as you write them. Then have students practice reading in pairs.
5. **Multi-level options** See MULTI-LEVEL OPTIONS on p. 114.

Across Content Areas: Science

Learn About Psychology

Define vocabulary and concepts Read the information about psychology aloud. Point out the words and definitions. Have students suggest examples of the words.

Answers
1. habit
2. family background
3. personality
4. environment

ASSESS

Have students write two sentences that describe their own personality, environment, habits, or family background.

Island of the Blue Dolphins

an excerpt from a novel based on a true story
by Scott O'Dell

Chapter Materials

Activity Book: *pp. 65–72*
Audio: *Unit 2, Chapter 4; CD 1, Track 9*
Student Handbook
Student CD-ROM: *Unit 2, Chapter 4*
Teacher Resource Book: *Lesson Plan, Teacher Resources, Reading Summary, Activity Book Answer Key*
Teacher Resource CD-ROM
Assessment Program: *Quiz, pp. 29–30; Teacher and Student Resources, pp. 115–144*
Assessment CD-ROM
Transparencies
The Heinle Newbury House Dictionary/CD-ROM
Web site: http://visions.heinle.com

Objectives

Paired reading Have pairs take turns reading the objectives. Point out key words. *Ask: Is there an objective you can already do?*

Use Prior Knowledge

Distinguish Needs and Wants

Gather and organize Review the difference between wants and needs. Arrange students in pairs to create a two-column chart of their wants and needs.

Objectives

Reading Paraphrase to recall information as you read an excerpt from a novel based on a true story.

Listening and Speaking Compare ways of working.

Grammar Identify the past and the past perfect tenses.

Writing Write instructions.

Content The Arts: List game rules in order.

Use Prior Knowledge

Distinguish Needs and Wants

Needs are things that people must have in order to live. Food is a need. *Wants* are things that people would like to have. A new CD is a want. What are some other needs and wants?

1. Work with a partner. Make a chart like this one.
2. List the needs that you must have in order to live.
3. Talk about your wants. List them in your chart.

Needs	Wants
food	a new CD

116 Unit 2 Survival

MULTI-LEVEL OPTIONS *Build Vocabulary*

Newcomer Identify several key words from the selection. Point to relevant elements in the illustrations and say each word. Have students learn to say the words by imitating your pronunciations.

Beginning Write key words from the selection on the board. Compare the words to ones students have already learned. For example, *Karana* has the same beginning sound as *car.*

Intermediate Be sure that students are familiar with the pronunciation key in the dictionary. Have students use stick-on notes or bookmarks to mark this place in the dictionaries they use in your class. This strategy will allow students to return to the resource easily when they need reminders of certain sounds.

Advanced Have each student write a short sentence. Ask students to look up the words in dictionaries and then "translate" their messages into a "secret" code using phonetic spellings. Have everyone exchange sentences with a partner and see if the partner can use a pronunciation key to decode the "message."

Build Background

The Lost Woman of San Nicolas Island

"Island of the Blue Dolphins" tells about a young Native American girl named Karana. Karana lived on San Nicolas Island in the 1800s. At first, she lived with her people, but they decided to leave. They got on a ship to go to California, but the ship left without Karana and her brother. Karana's brother died, and she was left alone. She lived there by herself for eighteen years.

Content Connection
San Nicolas Island is about 60 miles (97 kilometers) from Los Angeles.

Build Vocabulary

Locate Pronunciations of Unfamiliar Words

When you learn the meaning of a new word, learn its pronunciation from a dictionary or software, or ask your teacher. Look at this dictionary entry.

> **gnaw** /nɔ/ *v.* to keep biting at something over a period of time: *Rats gnaw through the cartons to get the food inside.*

1. Discuss these questions.
  a. How is the /n/ symbol pronounced?
  b. Is the /ɔ/ symbol a letter in the alphabet? Ask your teacher to pronounce it for you.
  c. How is *gnaw* pronounced?
  d. We say that the letter *g* in *gnaw* is silent. Why do we say that?
2. As you learn new words in the reading selection, learn their pronunciations.

The Heinle Newbury House Dictionary

Activity Book *p. 65*

Student CD-ROM

Chapter 4 Island of the Blue Dolphins **117**

Content Connection
Technology

Build Vocabulary Familiarize students with online dictionaries that have pronunciation capabilities. Show them how they can enter a word and then select the icon to indicate they want to hear the word pronounced.

Learning Styles
Natural

Build Background Have students look up San Nicolas Island using the Internet. Ask them to find out what animals, plants, and landforms can be found on the island. Ask students to collaborate on drawing a mural to show some of these features. Display the mural while students work on the activities in this chapter.

Build Background

The Lost Woman of San Nicolas Island

1. **Use a map** On a map of California, have students find major cities and the Channel Islands. *Ask: Is San Nicolas west or east of Los Angeles?* (west) *In what ocean is San Nicolas Island?* (Pacific Ocean)
2. **Content Connection** Many different Native American groups lived in California. Based on the island's location, have students guess what food the people ate.

Build Vocabulary

Teacher Resource Book: *Personal Dictionary, p. 63*

Locate Pronunciations of Unfamiliar Words

1. **Use a dictionary** Talk about the pronunciation symbols used. Help students locate the Pronunciation Key in the front or back of the dictionary.
2. **Use a glossary or other sources** Have students look in the glossary of their science textbook. Ask them to choose a word and use the pronunciation symbols to pronounce the word. Also have them locate the pronunciation of a word using an online or a CD-ROM dictionary.
3. **Reading selection vocabulary** You may want to introduce the glossed words in the reading selection before students begin reading. Key words: *shelter, store, scarce, secure, utensils, ashes, prowling.* Instruct students to write the words with correct spelling and their definitions in their Personal Dictionaries. Have them pronounce each word and divide it into syllables.
4. **Multi-level options** See MULTI-LEVEL OPTIONS on p. 116.

Answers
a. like the /n/ sound in *not* **b.** no **c.** "naw"
d. You don't pronounce the *g.*

ASSESS

Ask: Where is San Nicolas Island?

Text Structure

Fiction Based on a True Story

Clarify features Have students share examples from other stories or movies they know as you discuss fiction based on a true story.

Reading Strategy

Paraphrase to Recall Information

1. **Understand terms** Model paraphrasing traffic signs or school rules. *Say: The sign says "No trespassing." It means "Don't go into that place without permission."*

2. **Multi-level options** See MULTI-LEVEL OPTIONS below.

Answers
island; lonely; shelter, food, protection

ASSESS

Say: Explain paraphrasing. (telling something in your own words)

Text Structure

Fiction Based on a True Story

"Island of the Blue Dolphins" is **fiction.** Fiction is a story that includes made-up events and people.

The selection is **based on a true story.** It has events that happened to a real person in history. The features of fiction based on a true story are shown in the chart.

As you read "Island of the Blue Dolphins," think about events in the selection. Which events could have really happened? Which events seem to be made up?

Fiction Based on a True Story	
Main Character	• who the story is about • may act or look like a real person in history
Plot	• what happens in the story • similar to events that happened to a real person in history
Setting	• where the story happens • usually a real place

Student
CD-ROM

Reading Strategy

Paraphrase to Recall Information

When you **paraphrase,** you tell a part of a text in your own words. Paraphrasing helps you recall what you have read.

1. Read this paragraph. Then complete the paraphrase on a piece of paper.

   The woman lived all alone on the island for 18 years. She had to build shelter, find food, and protect herself from wild animals.

   Paraphrase Life on the _____ was very _____ . The woman had to provide everything for herself— _____ , _____ , and _____ .

2. As you read and listen to "Island of the Blue Dolphins," stop often to paraphrase.

Student
CD-ROM

118 Unit 2 Survival

MULTI-LEVEL OPTIONS *Reading Strategy*

Newcomer Act out what you did in preparation for coming to school, such as waking up, getting dressed, eating breakfast, and driving to work. Have students paraphrase by creating a drawing of what you did.

Beginning Read and act out the paragraph at the bottom of p. 118. Have students draw pictures of the action. Then help them paraphrase by writing captions with words they know. (*Examples:* woman alone, home, food)

Intermediate Read one paragraph aloud from the selection. Then have students do a math problem. Have students write what they recall about the paragraph. Read a second paragraph. Have students paraphrase it. Have them do another math problem. Ask what they recall about the second paragraph. *Ask: Which time did you recall more? Why?*

Advanced Engage students in a discussion of when paraphrasing might be a useful skill. (*Examples:* studying for a test, telling a friend about something they learned from a book, checking whether they understand what someone has said or wrote)

Island of the Blue Dolphins

an excerpt from a novel based on a true story
by Scott O'Dell

119

Reading Selection Materials

Audio: *Unit 2, Chapter 4; CD 1, Track 9*
Teacher Resource Book: *Reading Summary,*
    pp. 81–82
Transparencies: *#35, Reading Summary*

Suggestions for Using Reading Summary

- Introduce new vocabulary or cognates.
- Cut the summary into strips, or jumble the sentences on an overhead transparency. Students put the sentences in order.
- Practice the reading strategy.
- Students read aloud or with a partner.
- Students paraphrase the summary.
- Students do a cloze activity.
- Students create a visual or graphic organizer, such as a timeline or storyboard, to illustrate the summary.
- Students paraphrase the summary.

Preview the Selection

1. **Teacher think aloud** Have students examine the photo. *Say: The title of the reading selection is "Island of the Blue Dolphins." I see that it's an excerpt from a novel based on a true story. There's a photo of the island. This photo makes me remember that this is a real place and that many parts of the story may be real events about a person's life. I imagine it would be hard for someone to live alone on an island. I know that people need food, shelter, and water to live. I wonder how this person managed to do all of this. I wonder if the person had any tools. It would take a lot of time and work to make a shelter and to get food. This person must be very strong and very smart.*

2. **Connect** Remind students the unit theme is *survival.* Help them share their thoughts and questions about the title and the photo. Ask what risks there might be living on the island. Tell students they will need to read carefully and think about what the main character needs to do to survive on this island.

Community Connection

Tell students to create a two-column chart. Have them head the left side *Our Community.* Ask students to list words that describe where they live. Have them head the right side *San Nicolas Island.* Tell them to look at the picture on p. 119 and list words that describe the island. Ask students to determine whether there is anything similar between the two locations.

Teacher Resource Book: *Two-Column Chart, p. 44*

Learning Styles
Intrapersonal

Tell students to look at the picture on p. 119. *Ask: Would you be able to survive on this island alone? What qualities do you have that would help you? What would you have to learn?* Have students record their answers in their Reading Logs.

Teacher Resource Book: *Reading Log, p. 64*

Read the Selection

1. **Use text features** Direct students to the illustration. Have them make guesses about the character. Then direct students to glossed words and have them find their meanings at the bottom of the page. Remind students that they read a prologue in "The Voyage of the *Frog*." Ask them to explain its purpose.

2. **Shared reading** Play the audio. Have students join in when they can.

3. **Analyze character** *Ask: What is Karana doing?* (building shelter) *Why is she building it? What does this tell you about her?*

Sample Answer to Guide Question
Karana made a fence from whale ribs and kelp to protect her from wild animals.

> See Teacher Edition pp. 434–436 for a list of English-Spanish cognates in the reading selection.

Audio
CD 1. Tr. 9

Prologue
At this point in the story, Karana's brother has been killed by wild dogs. Karana is all alone on the island. She has to build a **shelter** for herself.

1   Many years before, two **whales** had washed up on the **sandspit**. Most of the bones had been taken away to make **ornaments**, but ribs were still there, half-buried in the sand.

2   These I used in making the fence. One by one I dug them up and carried them to the headland. They were long and curved, and when I scooped out holes and set them in the earth they stood taller than I did.

> **Paraphrase to Recall Information**
>
> Paraphrase what Karana does in this paragraph.

3   I put the ribs together with their edges almost touching, and standing so that they curved outward, which made them impossible to climb. Between them I wove many **strands** of **bull kelp,** which shrinks as it dries and pulls very tight. I would have used seal **sinew** to bind the ribs together, for this is stronger than kelp, but wild animals like it and soon would have **gnawed** the fence down. Much time went into its building. It would have taken me longer except that the rock made one end of the fence and part of a side.

---

shelter   a building that protects people

whales   large animals that live in the ocean; they look like very big fish

sandspit   a thin piece of sandy land, sticking out into the water

ornaments   things that are pretty rather than useful

strands   long thin pieces of something

bull kelp   large brown plants that grow below the sea

sinew   in the body, strong material that connects muscle to bone

gnawed   kept biting something for a long time

120   **Unit 2** Survival

MULTI-LEVEL OPTIONS *Read the Selection*

Newcomer Play the audio. *Ask: Is Karana alone?* (yes) *Is she building a boat?* (no) *Is she building a safe place?* (yes) *Is she making it with bricks?* (no)

Beginning Read aloud the Reading Summary. *Ask: Who is the story about?* (Karana, a girl) *Where is she?* (island) *Who is with her?* (no one) *What is she building?* (home)

Intermediate Have students read silently. *Ask: How do you think Karana feels at the beginning of the story? Why?* (sad that she is alone; determined to survive) *What proof is there that Karana is smart?* (She is figuring out how to use things from nature to survive.)

Advanced Have students read silently. *Ask: Why is Karana building a fence when no one else is around?* (to protect herself from wild animals) *What will keep wild animals from crawling into the hole that Karana used to get under the fence?* (She probably uses the flat rock inside as a door.)

Paraphrase to Recall Information

Paraphrase this paragraph.

4   For a place to go in and out, I dug a hole under the fence just wide and deep enough to crawl through. The bottom and sides I **lined** with stones. On the outside I covered the hole with a **mat** woven of **brush** to shed the rain, and on the inside with a flat rock which I was strong enough to move.

5   I was able to take eight steps between the sides of the fence, which gave me all the room I would need to **store** the things I **gathered** and wished to protect.

6   I built the fence first because it was too cold to sleep on the rock and I did not like to sleep in the shelter I had made until I was safe from the wild dogs.

7   The house took longer to build than the fence because it rained many days and because the wood which I needed was **scarce**.

---

lined   put a border around
mat   a piece of material used on floors, in front of doors
brush   branches broken off from trees or plants

store   keep something to use later
gathered   collected, brought in
scarce   not a lot of

Chapter 4 Island of the Blue Dolphins   **121**

Read the Selection

1. **Use the illustration** Ask students to describe the fence and the girl. Have them guess the purpose of the hole under the fence.

2. **Understand terms** Have students find the meanings of the glossed words below the selection. Use the illustration to clarify meanings of some of the words.

3. **Paired reading** Play the audio or read the selection aloud. Have students read it again in pairs.

4. **Analyze character development** Ask students to describe Karana. *Ask: Do you think she is afraid? Is she lazy? How do you know she wants to survive?*

5. **Make predictions** *Ask: What do you think Karana will do after the house is finished?*

6. **Multi-level options** See MULTI-LEVEL OPTIONS on p. 120.

Sample Answer to Guide Question
Karana made a hole under the fence so she could go in and out. She put stones on the sides and bottom and covered it with a mat on the outside and a flat rock inside.

 Spelling

To/two/too

Write on the board: *To/two/too whales had washed up on the land.* **Say:** *T-O means "in the direction of."* T-W-O *is the number.* T-O-O *means "more of something than is necessary" or "also." Which word is correct for this sentence?* (two) Have students look at the second sentence in paragraph 2 and the first sentence in paragraph 6. Ask them to explain the spelling of *to* and *too* in these sentences.

Apply Have groups of three work together. Tell each student to choose one of the spellings of *two/to/too* and write or draw an example of its proper use. Provide time for groups to present their work. (Also see Word Study on p. 128.)

Read the Selection

1. **Shared reading** Read aloud or play the audio. Have students join in when they can. *Ask: What does the legend have to do with trees?* (In the beginning, there were many tall trees.) *Where did she look for poles?* (in some ravines)

2. **Analyze motivations** Ask questions to help students understand why Karana works so hard and patiently as she is looking for materials.

Sample Answer to Guide Question
Karana used a rock for the back wall. She cut poles for the sides and roof. She tied them together with sinew and covered the house with kelp leaves.

> **Paraphrase to Recall Information**
>
> Paraphrase what Karana does in this paragraph. Use your own words.

8   There was a **legend** among our people that the island had once been covered with tall trees. This was a long time ago, at the beginning of the world when Tumaiyowit and Mukat ruled. The two gods **quarreled** about many things. Tumaiyowit wished people to die. Mukat did not. Tumaiyowit angrily went down, down to another world under this world, taking his **belongings** with him, so people die because he did.

9   In that time there were tall trees, but now there were only a few in the **ravines** and these were small and **crooked.** It was very hard to find one that would make a good **pole.** I searched many days, going out early in the morning and coming back at night, before I found enough for the house.

10   I used the rock for the back of the house and the front I left open since the wind did not blow from this direction. The poles I made of equal length, using fire to cut them as well as a stone knife which caused me much **difficulty** because I had never made such a tool before. There were four poles on each side, set in the earth, and twice that many for the roof. These I bound together with sinew and covered with female kelp, which has broad leaves.

---

legend   a story from long ago
quarreled   argued
belongings   things you own
ravines   low areas in the earth with steep sides

crooked   bent, not straight
pole   a long rod, usually made of wood or metal
difficulty   trouble, problems

122   **Unit 2** Survival

MULTI-LEVEL OPTIONS *Read the Selection*

Newcomer *Ask: Are there lots of trees on the island?* (no) *Does Karana use a big rock for her house?* (yes) *Does she use rubber for its roof?* (no) *Is it summer when Karana finishes her house?* (no) *Does Karana make her own pots?* (yes)

Beginning *Ask: What does Karana have a hard time finding for her house?* (trees) *What does she use to make the back of the house?* (rock) *When does Karana finish her house?* (winter) *What does she use to cook in?* (stones)

Intermediate *Ask: What shows that Karana does not give up easily?* (She searches days for trees to use in making her house.) *How do you think Karana knows how to make a house?* (from watching her people before they left the island) *Does it take a long or short time for her to make pots? Explain.* (long, because she uses sand to rub away rock)

Advanced *Ask: Why do you think Karana has to make all of her own tools?* (Her people must have gathered up all their belongings when they left.) *Do you think Karana's diet will change now that she has a house? Explain.* (Yes. She will have a place to store different foods that she gathers, such as berries.)

11 The winter was half over before I finished the house, but I slept there every night and felt **secure** because of the strong fence. The **foxes** came when I was cooking my food and stood outside **gazing** through the cracks, and the wild dogs also came, gnawing at the whale ribs, **growling** because they could not get in.

12 I shot two of them, but not the leader.

13 While I was building the fence and the house, I ate shellfish and **perch** which I cooked on a flat rock. Afterwards I made two **utensils**. Along the shore there were stones that the sea had worn smooth. Most of them were round, but I found two with hollow places in the center which I **deepened** and **broadened** by rubbing them with sand. Using these to cook in, I saved the juices of the fish which are good and were wasted before.

secure safe	**perch** a small fish
foxes animals that look like small dogs with furry tails	**utensils** tools for eating food
gazing looking at something for a long time	**deepened** made deeper
growling making low, angry sounds	**broadened** made broader, or wider

Chapter 4 Island of the Blue Dolphins **123**

Read the Selection

1. **Use the illustration** Ask students to tell what the girl is doing and why the fence and house are important to her. Use the illustration to explain some of the glossed words. Have students find the meanings of the others words.

2. **Paired reading** Play the audio or read the selection. Then have students reread it aloud in pairs.

3. **Locate derivations using dictionaries** Have students look at these glossed words and determine what words they are derived from: *quarreled, belongings, difficulty, gazing, growling, deepened, broadened.* Have students check the derivations in a print, an online, or a CD-ROM dictionary.

4. **Make predictions** Say: *Karana has shelter—a house and strong fence. She also has food. What else do you think she needs? What do you think she wants?*

5. **Multi-level options** See MULTI-LEVEL OPTIONS on p. 122.

Sample Answer to Guide Question
It took a long time to finish the house and fence, but they were strong and Karana was safe. The foxes and dogs could not get inside.

---

th Spelling

Long and short sounds for oo

Have students review paragraph 9. *Ask: Which words have* oo *in the middle?* (crooked, good) Write these words on the board. Pronounce both and have students say them after you. *Ask: Does* oo *make the same sound in each?* (yes) *Find words that have* oo *in paragraph 10.* (tool, roof) Write these words on the board. Pronounce both and have students say them after you. *Does the* oo *in these words make the same sound as in* crooked *and* good? (no) *That is correct.*

The letters oo *can make a long sound, as in* tool, *or a short sound, as in* good.

   Apply Have volunteers find other *oo* words on p. 123. Ask them to write these on the board under *crooked/good* or under *tool/roof,* based on the sound that *oo* makes. (crooked/good: cooking, stood, cooked, cook; tool/roof: food, smooth)

Read the Selection

1. **Use text features** Have students check meanings of glossed words.
2. **Break-in reading** Play the audio. Have students reread in groups. Have one student begin reading. When another student wants to take over, he/she "breaks in" by reading along with the first student. At the end of the sentence, the first student stops and the second one continues until another student "breaks in." Read several times until everyone has had a turn.
3. **Analyze character development** *Ask: How do you think Karana feels being alone?* (She's lonely, but she keeps busy.)

Sample Answer to Guide Question
Karana made a small hole in the floor for a fire. She lined it with rocks. She made a fire that she kept covered with ashes so it didn't go out.

14. For cooking seeds and roots I wove a tight basket of fine **reeds,** which was easy because I learned how to do it from my sister Ulape. After the basket had dried in the sun, I gathered lumps of **pitch** on the shore, softened them over the fire, and rubbed them on the inside of the basket so that it would hold water. By heating small stones and dropping them into a mixture of water and seeds in the basket I could make **gruel.**

> **Paraphrase to Recall Information**
>
> Paraphrase this paragraph.

15. I made a place for fire in the floor of my house, **hollowing** it out and lining it with rocks. In the village of Ghalas-at we made new fires every night, but now I made one fire which I covered with **ashes** when I went to bed. The next night I would remove the ashes and blow on the **embers.** In this way I saved myself much work.

16. There were many gray **mice** on the island and now that I had food to keep from one meal to the other, I needed a safe place to put it. On the **face** of the rock, which was the back wall of my house, were several **cracks** as high as my shoulder. These I cut out and smoothed to make **shelves** where I could store my food and the mice could not reach it.

---

reeds long stems of certain plants
pitch a dark, sticky material; used to cover things so water does not go through them
gruel hot cereal that is watery and not tasty
hollowing taking out what is inside of something
ashes powder left after something has burned

embers a very hot piece of wood left after a fire
mice very small animals; they often eat food that is left out
face the front part of something
cracks splits; breaks in a surface
shelves flat pieces that are attached to a wall; used to hold objects

124 Unit 2 Survival

MULTI-LEVEL OPTIONS *Read the Selection*

Newcomer *Ask: Does Karana put food in a basket?* (yes) *Does she cook inside her house?* (yes) *Do mice eat all her food?* (no) *Does Karana have everything she needs?* (yes)

Beginning *Ask: Where does Karana put seeds and roots?* (basket) *What does she use to cook her food?* (hot stones) *What does she build to keep mice away from her food?* (shelves) *How long does Karana live on the island?* (18 years)

Intermediate *Ask: What is pitch probably like?* (tar, gum) *What do you think Karana uses to hollow out her fireplace in her floor?* (a stone tool she made or a stick) *How does Karana probably feel when winter is over?* (proud that she has survived)

Advanced *What is another way Karana might have saved her food from the mice?* (putting it in one of her baskets and covering the basket with a flat rock) *How do you think Karana probably felt about leaving the island?* (sad to leave her home; curious about what another place would be like; happy that she won't be alone anymore)

Paraphrase to Recall Information

Paraphrase this paragraph.

17   By the time winter was over and grass began to show green on the hills my house was **comfortable.** I was sheltered from the wind and rain and **prowling** animals. I could cook anything I wished to eat. Everything I wanted was there at hand.

Epilogue

Karana lived alone on the island for about 18 years. Someone finally found her. She was taken to California.

---

comfortable   something that is nice to be in or around   **prowling**   hunting quietly

About the Author

Scott O'Dell (1898–1989)

Scott O'Dell grew up in Los Angeles, California. O'Dell wrote more than 20 books for young people. Many of them tell stories about brave young people who face challenges and survive. O'Dell has said, "The only reason I write is to say something. I've forsaken [given up on] adults because they're not going to change, although they may try awfully hard. But children can and do change."

➤ What challenges do you think Scott O'Dell faced when he wrote "Island of the Blue Dolphins"? Why did he write the story?

Chapter 4   Island of the Blue Dolphins   **125**

 Spelling

Ee/ea for long /e/ sound

Say: What words in the first sentence on p. 124 have the long /e/ sound? (seeds, reeds, easy) *What do you notice about how the sound is spelled?* (ee and ea) *Yes, both of these are ways of spelling the sound.* Put the three words on a two-column chart headed ee and ea.

    Apply *Say: Find the ee and ea words in paragraphs 16–17. Place them on our chart.* (keep, meal, needed, reach, green, eat)

Evaluate Your Reading Strategy

Paraphrase to Recall Information *Say: You have practiced an important reading strategy. Now you can decide how well you have done. Does this statement describe how you read?*

> When I read, I stop often to tell the text in my own words so I can remember what I read. Paraphrasing helps me to recall what happened.

Read the Selection

1. **Use text features** *Ask: What is an epilogue?* (the concluding section at the end of a story or play that tells what happened or will happen) *How is this different from a prologue?* (A prologue is an introduction that comes at the beginning and tells what happened before or will happen.)
2. **Silent reading** Play the audio. Then have students finish the story by reading silently.
3. **Compare and contrast print media with written story** Have students research the real story of Karana and compare and contrast it with "Island of the Blue Dolphins." They may want to do an Internet search using the key words "Karana San Nicolas Island."
4. **Multi-level options** See MULTI-LEVEL OPTIONS on p. 124.

Sample Answer to Guide Question
When spring came, she was safe, dry, and comfortable in the house. She also had plenty of food.

About the Author

1. **Explain author's background** Scott O'Dell spent most of his life in California, especially by the ocean.
2. **Interpret the facts** *Ask: What details in the story show that Scott O'Dell knew this area well?* (He knew what kind of plants and trees were on the island and what kind of fish would be caught. He knew the legend that was told about the island.)

Answers
Example: It was probably difficult to make the story interesting and keep it realistic at the same time. It might have been hard to imagine what life was like for Karana. He wrote to show readers that it is possible for people to survive on their own and to help themselves.

Across Selections

Contrast point of view Contrast the first-person point of view in this story and in "How I Survived My Summer Vacation" (p. 76). *Ask: What is the difference in the narrators' tones?* (". . . Blue Dolphins": calm, serious; ". . . My Summer Vacation": tense, funny)

Beyond the Reading

Reading Comprehension

Question-Answer Relationships

Sample Answers

1. on San Nicolas Island, off the coast of California
2. Karana, a Native American girl
3. The other people on the island left; they forgot about Karana and her brother. Her brother died, so now she is all alone.
4. whale rib bones and bull kelp
5. First, she builds the fence so she has a safe area and can sleep. Then she builds a house.
6. to protect herself from the rain, the wind, and wild animals
7. Karana is a very resourceful person. She is very patient and works carefully.
8. I think Karana knew what materials to use from watching other people in her group when they were on the island.
9. I think it would be hard to live on an island by myself. I would like not having anyone tell me what to do, but I would be lonely and want someone to talk to.
10. I would take a hatchet, a cup, and some matches.

Build Reading Fluency

Read Aloud to Engage Listeners

Model reading aloud with expression. Remind students to keep their eyes on the words as they read. This will help them with phrasing, intonation, and pronunciation.

Reading Comprehension

Question-Answer Relationships (QAR)

"Right There" Questions

1. **Recall Facts** Where does the story take place?
2. **Recall Facts** Who is the main character in this story?
3. **Recall Facts** Why is she the only person on the island?
4. **Recall Facts** What does Karana use to make the fence?

"Think and Search" Questions

5. **Determine Sequence of Events** What is the first thing that Karana builds? Why does she build this first? What does she build next?
6. **Identify Cause and Effect** Why does Karana build the shelter?

"Author and You" Questions

7. **Analyze Character Traits** What kind of person is Karana? Describe her character traits.
8. **Make Inferences** How do you think Karana knew what materials to use for her projects?

"On Your Own" Questions

9. **Support Your Opinion** Do you think it would be hard to live on an island by yourself? What would you like about it? What would you not like? Explain.
10. **Connect Your Experiences** If you could take three things with you on an island, what would you take?

Activity Book p. 66   Student CD-ROM

Build Reading Fluency

Read Aloud to Engage Listeners

Reading aloud helps increase your fluency and expression. Learning to read with expression makes others want to listen to you.

1. Listen to the audio recording of "Island of the Blue Dolphins."
2. Turn to page 120 and follow along.
3. Pay attention to phrasing and expression.
4. With a partner, read aloud paragraphs 1–7 three times.
5. Select your favorite two paragraphs.
6. Read them in front of the class with expression.

MULTI-LEVEL OPTIONS *Elements of Literature*

Newcomer Have students fold a paper in half vertically. Ask them to draw side-by-side pictures representing both stories. Tell students to draw arrows connecting similar ideas between the two selections.

Beginning Have students work in pairs to compose phrases that complete the Venn Diagram.

Intermediate Have students use the information on their completed charts to complete the sentence: *If you enjoyed "The Voyage of the Frog," you will like "Island of the Blue Dolphins" because . . .*

Advanced Ask small groups to identify other titles students have read that have a theme similar to "Island of the Blue Dolphins." Ask students to compose short paragraphs about the books and how they are similar to the selection in this chapter. Bind the pages together to form a resource for your classroom library.

Listen, Speak, Interact

Compare Ways of Working

In "Island of the Blue Dolphins," Karana must work alone to build her shelter. Do you think it is better to work alone or with other people?

1. Work alone. List as many states in the United States as you can.
2. Work with a small group. Again, list as many states as you can.

3. Talk about these questions:
   a. Did you list more states working alone or with the group?
   b. Did you have any problems working alone? Working with the group? Explain.
   c. Which did you like better: working alone or with the group? Why?

Elements of Literature

Compare and Contrast Themes and Ideas Across Texts

"Island of the Blue Dolphins" and "The Voyage of the *Frog*" have the same theme—survival. Both characters, Karana and David, have problems. Compare and contrast the theme and the idea of problem resolution in these two stories.

1. Read the following questions. Then reread both selections. As you read, take notes on these questions. You can add additional questions.
   a. What problems do the characters have?
   b. What is their most important problem?
   c. What help can they get from other people?
   d. What choices do they have?
   e. How do they resolve their problems?

2. Use your notes to complete a Venn Diagram.

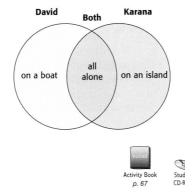

Activity Book p. 67 Student CD-ROM

Content Connection
The Arts

After students have completed the task in Listen, Speak, Interact, give each small group a collection of random craft materials and ask them to create a piece of art related to the story. Give no further directions. After students have completed their work, discuss with them how doing a creative task as a group differed from working alone on the activity related to states.

Learning Styles
Visual

Remind students that they identified the tone and mood in "The Voyage of the *Frog*" (p. 88). Ask them to draw pictures of David and Karana in their settings that express similarities and differences concerning tone and mood between the two stories. (*Example:* Students might show both as strong and confident. They might show David's setting as dangerous and dark but Karana's as warm and bright.)

Listen, Speak, Interact

Teacher Resource Book: *Reading Log, p. 64*

Compare Ways of Working

1. **Work alone and in groups** Have students work alone to complete number 1. Then arrange them into groups of four to repeat the activity. Discuss the answers to the questions.
2. **Newcomers** Have a discussion with this group. Help them express their preferences.
3. **Evaluate** Have students write in their Reading Logs a short paragraph describing their own working styles and preferences.

Elements of Literature

Compare and Contrast Themes and Ideas Across Texts

1. **Pair work** Pair advanced with beginning students. Have pairs reread and answer the questions.
2. **Multi-level options** See MULTI-LEVEL OPTIONS on p. 126.

Answers

1. *Examples:* **a.** They are both alone, in dangerous situations, and have the challenge of surviving. **b.** David doesn't know where he is. Karana needs shelter and food. **c.** The ship can take David back and give him food. No one can help Karana. **d.** David can leave his boat or sail alone. Karana can sit and wait for people to rescue her or make a house for herself. **e.** David sails home alone. Karana makes herself as comfortable as possible.

✓ ASSESS

List two similarities and two differences between David's and Karana's problems.

Word Study

Teacher Resource Book: *Personal Dictionary, p. 63*

Spell Frequently Misspelled Words
Use a graphic organizer Clarify the meanings of the three words in the chart. Have students use the words in sentences.

Answers
1. two **2.** to **3.** too, two

Grammar Focus

Identify the Past and Past Perfect Tense
Recognize tenses Write the samples on the board. Help pick out verbs and the verb tenses. Contrast the time of past and past perfect actions.

Answers
1. a. had dried; gathered; **b.** did not like; had made; was

ASSESS

Write on the board: *We had finished the story before we ate lunch.* Have students identify past and past perfect verbs.

Word Study

Spell Frequently Misspelled Words

Some words are pronounced alike but have different spellings and meanings. Notice the differences between these words.

Word	Meaning	Example
two	the number 2	I needed **two** things—food and water.
too	more than enough; also	It was **too** cold to sleep on the rock. There were mice, **too**.
to	a preposition or a word used to introduce a verb	He sailed **to** the ship. It was too cold **to** sleep on the rock.

Copy these sentences in your Personal Dictionary. Fill in the blanks with *two, too,* or *to.* Check your answers with a partner.

1. May I please have _____ apples from the refrigerator?
2. Why? Because I want _____ eat them. I'm hungry.
3. No, not three. That's _____ many apples! I only want _____ !

Personal Dictionary   Activity Book p. 68   Student CD-ROM

Grammar Focus

Identify the Past and the Past Perfect Tense

All verbs have a **tense.** The tense tells you when an action happened.

The **past tense** describes an action that happened at a specific time in the past. The **past perfect tense** describes an action that happened before another action. *Both* of these actions have already happened.

happened first

Miguel <u>had finished</u> the book before I <u>started</u> it.

happened after

Most past tense verbs have *-d* or *-ed* at the end, such as *finished.* Past perfect tense verbs include *had* + a past participle.

1. Write the sentences below on a piece of paper. Underline the past tense verbs. Circle the past perfect tense verbs.
   a. After the basket had dried in the sun, I gathered lumps of pitch.
   b. I did not like to sleep in the shelter I had made until I was safe from the wild dogs.
2. Write two sentences, each one using the past tense and the past perfect tense.

Activity Book pp. 69–70   Student Handbook   Student CD-ROM

128 Unit 2 Survival

MULTI-LEVEL OPTIONS *From Reading to Writing*

Newcomer Have students draw series of detailed pictures to show the steps for their activities. Help them label the materials that are needed in each step.

Beginning Ask students to draw detailed illustrations showing the steps for their activities. Tell them to label the materials needed and write a caption for each picture.

Intermediate During the peer-response stage, have students meet with a partner. Tell each student to read his/her writing aloud. Ask the other student to act out the steps being described. Have the reader notice anything his/her partner misunderstands and plan to revise these problem areas.

Advanced Provide a variety of instructions for students to examine, such as how to operate a machine, install a smoke detector, or how to use a phone card. Have them note what makes these easy or hard to understand. Ask students to comment on whether visuals that the writer included are helpful.

From Reading to Writing

Write Instructions

Write a short list of instructions explaining how to do something. Each step in the list tells the reader what to do. Use this as a guide.

1. Choose an activity to explain.
2. Think about how to do the activity. What steps must you take?
3. List the steps in chronological order (the order in which they happen).

How to Build a Fence on San Nicolas Island

○ **Step 1:** Gather whale ribs. You can find whale ribs buried in the sand.

○ **Step 2:** Gather some bull kelp. It is a plant that grows in the ocean.

○ **Step 3:** Put whale ribs in the ground next to each other.

○ **Step 4:** Tie the whale ribs together with bull kelp.

Activity Book
p. 71

Student
Handbook

Across Content Areas

List Game Rules in Order

The Chumash were Native Americans who lived and worked together in villages. They also played games together.

The Game of *Payas*

Chumash boys and men played a game called *payas*. Two or more people could play *payas*. They used a large ring. Someone rolled the ring on the ground in a straight line. The players tried to throw a long stick into the middle of the ring. This was hard because the ring was moving. Players got 1 point if they got the stick into the middle of the ring. The player who got 12 points won the game.

Put the statements below in the correct order.

a. A player tries to throw a stick into the middle of the ring.

b. A player gets 1 point.

c. Someone rolls a ring on the ground in a straight line.

d. A player gets 12 points.

Activity Book
p. 72

From Reading to Writing

■ Teacher Resource Book: *Storyboard, p. 43*

Write Instructions

1. **Make a storyboard** Have students prepare a storyboard or illustrations for the instructions. Arrange students in pairs to share their instructions.
2. **Language experience activity** For less fluent students, have them dictate as you write the instructions. Have pairs practice explaining the instructions.
3. **Multi-level options** See MULTI-LEVEL OPTIONS on p. 128.

Across Content Areas: The Arts

List Game Rules in Order

1. **Clarify meanings** Read the explanation of the game. Clarify meanings of key words. Have students paraphrase the rules.
2. **Sequence events** Have students arrange the statements in order. In pairs, have them compare their answers and discuss differences.

Answer
correct order: c, a, b, d

 **ASSESS**

Have students summarize how to play *Payas*.

Reteach and Reassess

Text Structure Have students work in pairs to create two-column charts with the headings *Real* and *Made Up.* Have students revisit the selection and find at least three examples of details to place in each column.

Reading Strategy Ask students to work in small groups to paraphrase, through drawing or writing, the information in About the Author.

Elements of Literature Have students revisit "How I Survived My Summer Vacation" and "The Voyage of the *Frog*" to see if they can find any ideas that the two selections have in common. (*Example:* Both children persisted in doing something that was important to them.)

Reassess Have students read the instructions that they wrote to a partner. Ask the partners to paraphrase the steps involved.

The Next
Great Dying

an excerpt from an
informational book
by Karin Vergoth and
Christopher Lampton

Chapter Materials

Activity Book: *pp. 73–80*
Audio: *Unit 2, Chapter 5; CD 1, Track 10*
Student Handbook
Student CD-ROM: *Unit 2, Chapter 5*
Teacher Resource Book: *Lesson Plan, Teacher Resources, Reading Summary, Activity Book Answer Key*
Teacher Resource CD-ROM
Assessment Program: *Quiz, pp. 31–32; Teacher and Student Resources, pp. 115–144*
Assessment CD-ROM
Transparencies
The Heinle Newbury House Dictionary/CD-ROM
Web site: http://visions.heinle.com

Objectives

Raise questions Read the objectives, explaining and raising questions. *Ask: What is an informational book? What are resources?*

Use Prior Knowledge

Think About Plants and Animals

Gather and organize Model using a two-column chart as you talk about some plants and animals. Have students create charts. Help with vocabulary as needed. Draw pictures or have volunteers draw pictures on the board for clarification.

Objectives

Reading Identify cause and effect as you read an excerpt from an informational book.

Listening and Speaking Talk about conserving natural resources.

Grammar Recognize dependent clauses.

Writing Write an informational text.

Content Social Studies: Read a timeline.

Use Prior Knowledge

Think About Plants and Animals

No matter where you live, you see plants and animals. What plants and animals have you seen today? Which of these plants and animals do you see often? Which have you seen only a few times?

1. Work with a partner. Complete a chart like the one below.

See Often	Have Seen Only a Few Times
dogs	elephant
cactus	palm tree

2. List plants and animals that you have seen—around your school, in your community, in a movie, etc.
3. Which animal or plant do you think is special? Why?
4. Compare your chart with those of your classmates. Are there any unusual animals or plants listed?

130 Unit 2 Survival

MULTI-LEVEL OPTIONS *Build Vocabulary*

Newcomer Find a book that has illustrations of extinct animals and plants. Introduce the concept of *extinction* by showing a picture of one of the animals. Place your hand over the animal. *Say: gone.* Have students sketch pictures of extinct animals or plants in their Word Wheels and draw lines over each to show that it is extinct.

Beginning Have students work in pairs. Provide them with books showing extinct animals and plants. Tell students to draw some of these animals in their Word Wheels. Help students write synonyms for *extinct*, such as *gone, lost*, and *dead*, under the pictures.

Intermediate Have students complete Word Wheels for *extinction*. Then ask them to create Word Wheels for the word *endangered*. Discuss with students how these terms are similar and different.

Advanced Have students look at their completed Word Wheels. Tell them that the title for the selection in this chapter is "The Next Great Dying." *Ask: How do you think the ideas on your Word Wheel may relate to the title of the selection?*

Build Background

Endangered Species

An **endangered species** is a plant or an animal that is rare. There are very few of them. An endangered species is so rare that it may disappear from Earth within 20 years. There are thousands of endangered species in the world, for example, the Mexican grizzly bear, the giant panda, and the California condor.

 Content Connection

The ocelot is an endangered species. There are between 80 and 120 ocelots left in Texas.

Ocelot

Build Vocabulary

Use a Word Wheel

"The Next Great Dying" has words that may be new to you. A Word Wheel can help you remember these new words.

1. Work with a partner. Look up *extinction* in a dictionary. Write the word and its definition in your Personal Dictionary.
2. Make a Word Wheel like the one here. Write the word *extinction* in one part of the Word Wheel.
3. List words related to *extinction* on a piece of paper.
4. Choose three words from your list to help you remember the meaning of *extinction*. Write these three words in your Word Wheel.

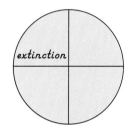

 Personal Dictionary

 The Heinle Newbury House Dictionary

 Activity Book p. 73

 Student CD-ROM

Chapter 5 The Next Great Dying **131**

 Content Connection
Science

Build Background Have students use books or online resources to find lists of endangered animals and plants. Ask them to identify any of these animals that inhabit their area of the country. Have each student make a poster to encourage people to protect this plant or animal. Hang the posters in an area of the school where other students and visitors may see them.

Learning Styles
Linguistic

Build Vocabulary Tell students that *extinct* is related to the Latin word *extinguere*, which means "to extinguish." Have them look up *extinguish* and discuss the relationship between the two words.

Build Background

Endangered Species

1. **Use illustrations** Bring in books on endangered species. Ask students to describe animals they know that are endangered.
2. **Relate to personal experience** Have students talk about animals they have seen at a zoo or in the wild.
3. **Content Connection** The ocelot is a large, yellow cat, native to North and South America. *Ask: What other large cats does this ocelot look like?* (mountain lion, puma)

Build Vocabulary

Teacher Resource Book: *Personal Dictionary, p. 63*

Use a Word Wheel

1. **Use a dictionary** Have students find *extinction* and choose words they associate with it for their Word Wheel.
2. **Reading selection vocabulary** You may want to introduce the glossed words in the reading selection before students begin reading. Key words: *extinct, catastrophe, species, climate, alarming, exploitation, neglect.* Instruct students to write the words with correct spelling and their definitions in their Personal Dictionaries. Have them pronounce each word and divide it into syllables.
3. **Multi-level options** See MULTI-LEVEL OPTIONS on p. 130.

 **ASSESS**

Have students write a sentence using the word *extinction*.

Text Structure

Informational Text

Clarify features Direct attention to the chart. Explain *scientific process* and relate to what students know about scientists and their work. Remind students of scientific processes they read about in "The Loch Ness Monster" and "Yawning." (scientists' search for the monster, scientific studies conducted on yawning)

Reading Strategy

▌ Teacher Resource Book: *Reading Log, p. 64*

Identify Cause and Effect

1. **Draw on experiences** Write on the board: *I got a drink of water because I was thirsty.* Have students explain what you did and why. Use arrows to show the cause leading to the effect.
2. **Multi-level options** See MULTI-LEVEL OPTIONS below.

Answers
1. **a.** effect **b.** cause

ASSESS

Have students name four features of informational texts.

Text Structure

Informational Text

"The Next Great Dying" is an **informational text.** An informational text explains about a topic. The chart shows features of some informational texts.

Look for how the authors describe scientific processes. Does knowing about the scientific processes help you understand what you read?

Informational Text	
Topic	Many informational texts are about science topics.
Scientific Process	A scientific process is how scientists figure out something.
Facts and Examples	Facts and examples help to explain new ideas.
Definitions	The meanings of new words are given.

Student CD-ROM

Reading Strategy

Identify Cause and Effect

A **cause** is the reason something happens. An **effect** is what happens because of the cause.

1. Read these two sentences. Which one is the cause, and which is the effect?
   a. The cat ran away.
   b. You teased the cat.
2. Notice causes and effects as you read and listen to the selection.
3. Use your Reading Log. Write causes and effects in a chart like the one here.

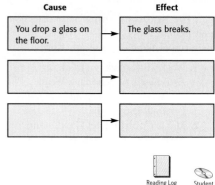

Reading Log

Student CD-ROM

MULTI-LEVEL OPTIONS *Reading Strategy*

Newcomer Act out dropping a glass. *Say: cause* and have students repeat the word. Act out picking up the pieces of a broken glass. *Say: effect* and have students repeat the word. Use this process with other cause-and-effect situations, such as jogging in place resulting in getting tired. Have students act out 1a–b and say *cause* or *effect*.

Beginning When students create their charts to record story causes and effects, have them write *why* by the heading *Cause* and *what* by the heading *Effect* to remind themselves of the meanings of these words.

Intermediate Tell students to predict what cause-and-effect relationship might be discussed in "The Next Great Dying." Ask them to base their predictions on the activities they have done so far in this chapter and on the selection title.

Advanced Point out that a result may have several causes and a cause may have several results. *Ask: What else might happen as a result of teasing the cat? (Example:* It may hiss.) Tell students to be on the look for multiple causes and effects as they read "The Next Great Dying."

The Next Great Dying

an excerpt from an informational book
by Karin Vergoth and Christopher Lampton

133

Reading Selection Materials

Audio: *Unit 2, Chapter 5; CD 1, Track 10*
Teacher Resource Book: *Reading Summary,*
pp. 83–84
Transparencies: *#36, Reading Summary*

Suggestions for Using
Reading Summary

- Introduce new vocabulary or cognates.
- Cut the summary into strips, or jumble the sentences on an overhead transparency. Students put the sentences in order.
- Practice the reading strategy.
- Students read aloud or with a partner.
- Students paraphrase the summary.
- Students do a cloze activity.
- Students create a visual or graphic organizer, such as a timeline or storyboard, to illustrate the summary.
- Students paraphrase the summary.

Preview the Selection

Teacher Resource Book: *Know, Want to Know, Learned Chart (KWL), p. 42*

1. **Make a KWL chart** Have students complete a chart with things they know about the title and information from the illustration. Have them create questions about what they want to know about the title and the reading selection. Students can use the chart to guide their reading of the text.
2. **Connect** Remind students that the unit theme is *survival*. **Ask:** *Why is it hard for some animals to survive?*

Content Connection
Science

Learning Styles
Visual

Use the KWL chart to record any facts students think they know about why dinosaurs no longer live on Earth. List what students want to know about why dinosaurs disappeared. Leave space to fill in facts students learn from reading.

Say: People who decide on illustrations for books make careful decisions about the topic of the pictures they select. They also must think about how they put the pictures on the page. Why do you think the designer of this cover chose these photos? Why do you think the photos are placed as they are?

Read the Selection

1. **Use the illustration** Help students describe the event and suggest what effect the explosion would have on the animals.

2. **Jigsaw reading** Play the audio. Assign small groups to prepare different sections of the selection for a jigsaw reading. Then have the groups teach the class their sections and "put the pieces together" by reading aloud in sequence.

3. **Analyze cause and effect** *Say: In paragraph 1, I read about the dinosaurs. I know they are all dead. That's the effect. In paragraph 2, the author explains an idea of why they died. That's the cause.* Have students suggest the cause as stated in paragraph 2.

Sample Answer to Guide Question
Scientists think a comet or an asteroid crashed into Earth and destroyed the dinosaurs.

See Teacher Edition pp. 434–436 for a list of English-Spanish cognates in the reading selection.

1 There are some things money can't buy. One of them is a live dinosaur. Try though you might, you'll never find a living dinosaur for sale. If you're lucky, you may find enough pieces of a dinosaur to put a **skeleton** together. If you have enough money, you may even be able to buy a dinosaur skeleton. Not long ago, the largest and most complete *Tyrannosaurus rex* skeleton ever found was bought at an **auction** by the Field Museum in Chicago for $7.6 million. But a **fossilized** skeleton, or a fossilized dinosaur egg, is as close as you'll ever get to owning the real thing.

2 Of course, everybody knows that you can't buy a live dinosaur, or even find one. Dinosaurs lived on Earth a long time ago, but now they're gone. Nothing can bring them back. Dinosaurs became **extinct** 65 million years ago. They were wiped out by a deadly **catastrophe** that many scientists believe was **triggered** by a huge **comet** or **asteroid** crashing into Earth.

> **Identify Cause and Effect**
>
> What do many scientists think caused dinosaurs to become extinct?

Audio
CD 1. Tr. 10

skeleton a body's bones
auction a sale in which items are sold to the person who offers the most money
fossilized when a dead animal or plant was buried and became hard like a rock
extinct no longer in existence

catastrophe a great disaster
triggered caused
comet an object made of dust, gas, or ice that travels in outer space
asteroid a large rock in outer space

134 Unit 2 Survival

MULTI-LEVEL OPTIONS *Read the Selection*

Newcomer Play the audio. *Ask: Were dinosaurs probably killed by something big crashing into Earth?* (yes) *Did other animals die out then, too?* (yes) *Did ice also cause animals to die long ago?* (yes) *Are many animals dying out right now?* (yes)

Beginning Read aloud the Reading Summary. *Ask: What may have crashed into Earth long ago?* (comet) *What did the crash kill?* (dinosaurs and other animals) *What else caused animals to die out long ago?* (ice) *What is making many animals die out now?* (what humans are doing)

Intermediate Have students do a reciprocal reading. *Ask: How do scientists find out about dinosaurs since the animals are gone?* (by studying bones, fossils) *How were past extinctions similar or different from now?* (In both, many animals were lost; past losses were caused by nature, but today's are caused by humans.)

Advanced Have students do a reciprocal reading. *Ask: Why do scientists want to know why dinosaurs became extinct?* (Knowing how they became extinct may help us prevent other animals from dying out.) *Why is it more likely that people can stop the Sixth Extinction than past ones?* (because humans, not nature, are causing this one)

3　It wasn't only the dinosaurs that became extinct in this "great dying"; scientists estimate that up to 90 percent of all other **species** living at that time disappeared as well. Because so many species **died off** in a fairly short period of time, we refer to this great dying as a **mass extinction.** Scientists who study the **remains** of ancient life tell us that there have been five major mass extinctions in our planet's long history. Each one was caused by natural events, such as the changes in Earth's **climate** that caused the **ice ages** or the **impact** of comets and asteroids.

> **Identify Cause and Effect**
>
> What caused the five major mass extinctions in Earth's history?

4　We're in the middle of another mass extinction right now. Many people are calling it the "Sixth Extinction." But unlike past extinctions, this one isn't being caused by icy rocks from space or sudden changes in the climate. It is being caused by humans.

And it's happening much faster 　5 than the natural rate of extinction— the rate at which living things have disappeared over millions of years of Earth's history. It's difficult to say how much faster the present extinction is **progressing** because most of the species going extinct are unknown to science. Plus, scientists aren't really sure how many species there are on Earth.

species　groups of living things
died off　died one after another
mass extinction　the death of all animals or plants in many species
remains　parts or things that are left

climate　the type of weather that a place has
ice ages　periods of time when Earth was very cold and much of Earth's water turned to ice
impact　a hard hit
progressing　advancing, moving forward

Chapter 5　The Next Great Dying　**135**

Read the Selection

1. **Use text features**　Have students check the meanings of the boldfaced words.
2. **Reciprocal reading**　Read the selection aloud. Arrange students in groups for reciprocal reading. Assign each student a different portion of the selection. One student should read aloud his/her part, ask questions to group members, and ask them to summarize it.
3. **Use the illustration**　Ask questions to help students restate the reasons for extinction of species. Have them explain the significance of the illustration.
4. **Multi-level options**　See MULTI-LEVEL OPTIONS on p. 134.

Sample Answer to Guide Question
The five major mass extinctions were caused by natural events like changes in climate and comets and asteroids hitting Earth.

 Spelling

Au for short /o/ sound

Ask: What vowel sound do you hear at the beginning of the word auction? (short *o*) Have students return to paragraph 1 to find the word. *Ask: What letters make that sound?* (au) *Yes,* au *can make the short /o/ sound. Find another example of* au *making this sound in paragraph 3.* (caused)

　Apply　Write on the board: *launch, haunt, August.* Tell students to work in pairs to pronounce the words. Monitor their pronunciations. Have volunteers say the words aloud.

Read the Selection

1. **Shared reading** Read or play the audio. Have students join in when they can.

2. **Identify main idea** *Ask: Why are scientists worried in paragraph 7?* (Animal species are becoming extinct more quickly than in the past.) *At the present rate of extinction, how many species of birds will become extinct in 100 years?* (100)

3. **Give personal response** *Ask: Do you think this is alarming or something to worry about? Why or why not?*

Sample Answer to Guide Question
Humans are making about one or more species of birds become extinct every year.

Bald eagle

6   They've **identified** about 1 million different plants, animals, and other life forms, but that's just a drop in the bucket. Most scientists believe there are probably about 10 million species on Earth, and some think there may be as many as 100 million species.

7   So how many species are becoming extinct? Let's first consider the natural rate of extinction. If there were just 1 million species on Earth, and scientists could check up on each species every year to see if it was still surviving, they would **expect** that about one species would become extinct each year. Of course scientists can't **track** all species that closely—but they do **keep close tabs on** birds. There are about 10,000 species of birds. If birds were going extinct at the natural rate, one bird should be lost to extinction about every 100 years. What scientists are actually seeing is that one or more birds are going extinct each year. This means that the actual rate of extinction today is 100 times **greater** than the natural rate of extinction. That's **alarming!**

> **Identify Cause and Effect**
>
> Paragraph 4 says that humans are causing the "Sixth Extinction." Look at paragraph 7. What effect are humans having on birds?

---

identified   named
expect   think something will happen
track   follow the movement of something

keep close tabs on   notice what something is doing
greater   larger
alarming   shocking, scary

136   Unit 2   Survival

MULTI-LEVEL OPTIONS *Read the Selection*

Newcomer *Ask: Are there more than 1 million kinds of plants and animals on Earth?* (yes) *Are animals dying out slower than in the past?* (no) *Will animals most likely die out faster in the future?* (yes) *Are animals dying out because of what humans do?* (yes)

Beginning *Ask: How many kinds of plants and animals do we know about?* (more than a million) *Are animals dying out faster or slower than in the past?* (faster) *What is one thing that is making animals die out faster?* (humans using too many resources)

Intermediate *Ask: Why do scientists disagree about how many animals are on Earth?* (Wild animals are hard to count.) *Based on paragraph 7, how many birds will become extinct between now and your 20th birthday?* (20 minus current age) *Name one thing people in your city do that may affect extinction?* (*Example:* waste resources by wasting paper)

Advanced *Ask: Compare how many plants and animals may be extinct by 2050 to the percent that died out during the time of the dinosaurs.* (50% vs. 90%) *Give an example of how human actions could cause a plant or animal to become extinct.* (*Example:* People throwing garbage in a river could cause fish to die.)

8 Taking all species of animals and plants together, scientists **estimate** that during the past century, the actual rate of extinction has been 100 to 1,000 times greater than expected. If there are indeed 10 million species on the planet, then 30 species are going extinct each day. In the next century, scientists predict the actual rate of extinction may be as much as 10,000 times greater than the natural extinction rate. In fact, some scientists warn that by the middle of the next century—about 50 years from now— half of all the species now living on Earth may be extinct. Another great dying is in progress—and very little is being done to stop it.

9 How did this mass extinction come about? Scientists do not need to **devise elaborate** theories to explain this twentieth-century disaster. The causes are all around them. Human beings— through **exploitation, neglect,** and overuse of Earth's resources—are engaged in **wholesale destruction** of the other living **organisms** on this planet. We are killing off our fellow species at an **appalling** rate.

> **Identify Cause and Effect**
>
> How are humans causing a mass extinction?

---

estimate   make a judgment about

devise   create, invent, think of

elaborate   complex, detailed

exploitation   using too much of something, usually in a greedy way

neglect   a state of not giving enough attention to something

wholesale destruction   very bad damage that affects many things

organisms   living things

appalling   shocking, very upsetting

Chapter 5   The Next Great Dying   **137**

Read the Selection

1. **Use the photos** Have students make predictions about human activities and their effects on animal life.
2. **Preview vocabulary** Have students check the meanings of the boldfaced words at the bottom of the page.
3. **Guided reading** Read aloud or ask volunteers to read. Pause to ask comprehension questions and to clarify vocabulary. *Ask: Who is causing so many animals species to become extinct?* (people)
4. **Locate derivations using dictionaries** Have students look at these glossed words and determine what words they are derived from: *identified, greater, alarming, exploitation, destruction, appalling.* Have students check the derivations in a print, an online, or a CD-ROM dictionary.
5. **Give examples** *Ask: How do people "exploit" animals and plants?* (cutting trees, fishing) *How do people "neglect" plants and animals?* (by not taking care of them, by dumping garbage in the ocean)
6. **Analyze relationships** Have students review the problem and causes. Guide them to explain the relationship between people and plants and animals.
7. **Multi-level options** See MULTI-LEVEL OPTIONS on p. 136.

Sample Answer to Guide Question
Humans are using too much of Earth's resources and not taking good care of Earth. They kill plants and animals with their activities.

---

9 Punctuation

Commas for large numbers

Say: Commas are used to divide the digits of long numbers. We start at the right and count off groups of three. Look at paragraph 8 to see how the writer used commas for long numbers.

Apply Write on the board: *There are ten thousand kinds of birds. If half of them died out, only five thousand kinds would be left.* Have students rewrite the sentences using numbers. (There are 10,000 kinds of birds. If half of them died out, only 5,000 kinds would be left.)

Read the Selection

1. **Reciprocal reading** Play the audio. Then arrange students in groups for reciprocal reading. Students should read aloud their portions, ask questions to others in the group, and ask them to summarize the selection.

2. **Compare and contrast** Have students reread paragraph 10. *Ask: What is the difference between when one individual animal dies and when a whole species dies?* (When one individual dies, others of their species can continue to live and reproduce. But when a species dies, they can never be reproduced.)

Sample Answer to Guide Question
The grasslands of the cheetah are being used for farmlands and pasture, so the cheetahs are losing their homes.

Woolly mammoth

Passenger pigeon

Dodo bird

10   When a species becomes extinct, no power on Earth can bring it back. Nothing can bring back the dinosaurs. If a particular species of bird, plant, or insect **ceases** to exist, no amount of money can bring it back. Extinction is forever. It's far worse than the death of an **individual** organism. When an individual dies, the children of that individual survive to carry on the species. But when a species becomes extinct, there are no children. The last dinosaurs left behind no **descendants**— neither did the woolly mammoth, or the dodo bird, or the passenger pigeon. Each of these creatures is now **absent** from Earth. If nothing is done, they will be followed into **oblivion** by the Bengal tiger, the California condor, and hundreds of other *endangered species*—species that are **teetering** on the **brink** of extinction at this very moment.

11   Dozens of species are nearing extinction right now. The African cheetah has been **displaced** from its natural home as humans **convert** its grasslands to pasture and farmland. The black rhinoceros is illegally hunted for its horns, which are used for medicines and dagger handles. The black-footed ferret was nearly starved out of existence when its food supply—prairie dogs—was **eliminated** by human hunting and disease. The cichlid, a small fish native to Lake Victoria in East Africa, was nearly wiped out when **non-native** Nile perch were introduced into the lake.

> **Identify Cause and Effect**
>
> The African cheetah is almost extinct. What is causing this?

ceases stops an action	**teetering** rocking back and forth in a dangerous way
individual one of a group	**brink** the top edge of a steep incline
descendants people or animals born into a certain family or group	**displaced** removed
absent not present, missing	**convert** change
oblivion nothingness	**eliminated** removed or gotten rid of
	non-native from somewhere else

138   Unit 2 Survival

MULTI-LEVEL OPTIONS *Read the Selection*

Newcomer *Ask: Can we bring back animals that die out?* (no) *Are some kinds of tigers in danger of dying out?* (yes) *Are lots of animals in danger of dying out?* (yes)

Beginning *Ask: When can we bring back animals that have died out?* (never) *Are there few or many animals in danger of dying out now?* (many) *What is one animal in danger of dying out?* (Bengal tiger) *What is one reason animals die out today?* (sickness)

Intermediate *Ask: Why is the authors' tone so serious?* (Once living things die out, we can't get them back.) *Explain how putting Nile perch in with cichlid could cause harm.* (Maybe the perch ate the little fish or ate all their food.) *Can humans solve the problem of endangered animals? Explain.* (Yes. Humans caused the problems, so they can change or reverse certain behaviors to undo the damage.)

Advanced *Ask: Tell a way humans could protect the black rhinoceros.* (Find another way to make medicines.) *Explain why the last sentence of paragraph 12 is true.* (Even unknown insects or plants might be an important part of the food chain for another animal.)

12 These are only a few of the species now on the road to extinction. And though you have probably heard about some of the most **glamorous** species in danger of extinction, many others are unknown to all of us. These unidentified plants, insects, and **fungi** represent a valuable part of life on Earth.

> **Identify Cause and Effect**
>
> Many plants and animals are becoming extinct. What will be the effect of this?

---

glamorous   seen as interesting and exciting

fungi   living things that eat dead plants or animals and cannot survive apart from them

About the Authors

Karin Vergoth

Karin Vergoth helps adults and young people learn about science. She writes about science for magazines. Vergoth also works on a radio show about science. Today, Vergoth lives in Jersey City, New Jersey.

Christopher Lampton

Christopher Lampton has written more than 75 books about science. He has written about computers, the environment, and outer space. He also writes novels for young readers and adults. Lampton lives in Gaithersburg, Maryland.

➤ Why do you think Karin Vergoth and Christopher Lampton wrote "The Next Great Dying"? Did they want to entertain, inform, influence, or express themselves? Did they want to get readers to think about how humans are hurting the planet? Explain.

Chapter 5   The Next Great Dying   **139**

9 Punctuation

Comma for series

Write on the board: *We cannot bring back a bird plant or insect that has died out.* **Ask:** *Is a bird plant a type of plant or are bird and plant two different things? We can't tell.* Look at sentence 3 in paragraph 10 to see how the writers solved this problem. Yes, they used commas between the words to show they are different things.

Apply   Have students write sentences using commas to tell about three animals that are endangered.

Evaluate Your Reading Strategy

Identify Cause and Effect   *Say: You have practiced an important reading strategy. Now you can decide how well you have done. Does this statement describe how you read?*

> As I read, I notice whether one event causes another event. Identifying causes and effects helps me understand why events happen.

Read the Selection

1. **Read aloud**   Ask a volunteer to reread paragraph 12. *Ask: Why are the authors concerned?* (There are many species that are in danger of disappearing.)
2. **Paired reading**   After pairs reread, ask them to summarize the main points of the selection.
3. **Multi-level options**   See MULTI-LEVEL OPTIONS on p. 138.

Sample Answer to Guide Question
A valuable part of life will disappear and it will affect all life on Earth.

About the Authors

Interpret the facts   *Ask: How do you think Karin Vergoth and Christopher Lampton learned about these scientific processes?* (They studied and asked scientists.)

Answer
Example: They wrote to inform people about a problem and to influence them to think about the problem and change any harmful behaviors.

Across Selections

Compare text structure   Compare the structure of this informational text with "To Risk or Not to Risk." *Ask: What is similar about these texts?* (Both have facts, give opinions, and talk directly to the reader.) *How are they different?* ("To Risk or Not to Risk" asks a lot of questions. "The Next Great Dying" doesn't. "To Risk or Not to Risk" examines a psychological phenomenon; "The Next Great Dying" examines a physical one.)

Spelling, Punctuation, Capitalization

After the Reading Comprehension section, students will practice spelling, punctuation, and capitalization in the Activity Book.

Beyond the Reading

Reading Comprehension

Question-Answer Relationships

Sample Answers

1. about 65 million years ago
2. more than 1 million plants and animals
3. African cheetah, the black rhinoceros, and the black-footed ferret
4. This one is caused by humans. The others were caused by natural disasters.
5. humans' exploitation, neglect, and overuse of Earth's resources; I agree because we don't consider the results of what we are doing.
6. The authors feel concerned about the species and think all species are important. In paragraph 10; the authors describe how final it is when a species dies.
7. I think it is important to save endangered species. It's not right for people to destroy everything for themselves.
8. I can learn more about endangered species and try to make sure I don't pollute land and water.
9. How did you find this scientific information? What is the most important thing I can do to stop the latest mass extinction?

Build Reading Fluency

Rapid Word Recognition

Rapid word recognition is an excellent activity for students who struggle with irregular spelling patterns. Time students for 1 minute as they read the words in the squares aloud.

Reading Comprehension

Question-Answer Relationships (QAR)

"Right There" Questions

1. **Recall Facts** When did dinosaurs become extinct?
2. **Recall Details** How many species have scientists identified so far?

"Think and Search" Questions

3. **Identify** List three species that the text says are nearing extinction.
4. **Contrast** How is the latest mass extinction different from the five other mass extinctions in Earth's history?

"Author and You" Questions

5. **Evaluate Evidence** Reread paragraph 9. What do scientists say are the causes of the latest mass extinction? Do you think the scientists are right? Why or why not?

6. **Understand Authors' Perspective** How do you think the authors feel about endangered species? What evidence can you find to support your answer?

"On Your Own" Questions

7. **Support Your Opinion** Do you think it is important to save endangered species? Why or why not?
8. **Connect Your Experiences** What are some things that you could do to protect endangered species?
9. **Ask Questions** What questions would you like to ask the authors of "The Next Great Dying"?

Activity Book p. 74   Student CD-ROM

Build Reading Fluency

Rapid Word Recognition

Rapidly recognizing words helps increase your reading rate. It is an important characteristic of effective readers.

1. With a partner, review the words in the box.
2. Read the words aloud for one minute. Your teacher will time you.

3. Count how many words you read in one minute.

pieces	caused	wiped	extinct	wiped	pieces
action	extinct	caused	wiped	extinct	wiped
extinct	estimate	action	pieces	estimate	action
wiped	wiped	extinct	action	pieces	estimate
estimate	action	pieces	estimate	caused	extinct

MULTI-LEVEL OPTIONS *Elements of Literature*

Newcomer Draw on the board a large, empty circle surrounded by small circles containing pictures of endangered animals. Draw arrows from the pictures to the central circle. Point to the pictures and then write *dying out* in the central circle to show inductive thinking. Reverse the process to show deductive.

Beginning Present the diagrams explained for the Newcomer level. Then ask students to work in pairs. Have one student draw a diagram to show inductive thinking for the example related to a cold in Elements of Literature. Have the other make a diagram to show deductive thinking.

Intermediate Draw a lightbulb followed by a space, then the letters *EX.* Explain that the bulb stands for an idea and *EX* for examples. Draw an arrow from the bulb to *EX.* **Say:** *This is another way to think about deductive thinking. The writer goes from the big idea to examples. How can we show inductive thinking?*

Advanced Ask students to look in their science or social studies texts to find examples of inductive and deductive organization.

Listen, Speak, Interact

Talk About Conserving Natural Resources

Natural resources are things from nature that people use. We should try to conserve our natural resources—use less of them. How can we do this?

1. Work with a small group. Think of ways to conserve natural resources. For example, you could turn off the water while you are brushing your teeth.
2. List your ideas on a piece of paper. Does everyone in the group agree with all of the ideas?

3. Choose an idea you like. Present it to the class. Persuade your audience to do what you suggest.
4. As you listen to your classmates' presentations, take notes on these questions:
   a. What is the presenter trying to persuade me to do?
   b. Is the presenter giving examples and reasons?
   c. Did the presenter persuade me? Why or why not?

Elements of Literature

Analyze Deductive and Inductive Organization and Presentation

Sometimes authors tell you the point they want to make, and then they give you facts and examples to support it. This is **deductive** presentation and organization. Read this deductive example.

"The doctor could tell that the man had a cold. He was sneezing and coughing."

Authors can also give you examples and facts first. This is **inductive** presentation and organization.

Here is the same information as before as an inductive example.

"The man was sneezing and coughing. The doctor could tell that he had a cold."

1. With a partner, read paragraphs 3 and 7 of the selection.
2. Is the presentation and organization of each paragraph inductive or deductive?
3. Talk about the choice of inductive and deductive presentation and organization. Would it make a difference if the author had switched them? Why?

Activity Book
p. 75

Student
CD-ROM

Cultural Connection

Have students find out what animals and plants are endangered in another country. Ask students to show pictures of these animals and plants from a book or Web site. Ask students to draw or explain why these species are endangered and to share anything they are able to discover about efforts to save them.

Learning Styles
Musical

Ask students to think of examples of jingles or songs written to convince people to buy or do certain things. Challenge small groups to create jingles or rap songs to persuade people to take a particular action to protect endangered animals or plants.

Listen, Speak, Interact

Talk About Conserving Natural Resources

1. **Brainstorm ideas** Provide students with categories of natural resources, such as water, air, land, and oil. List their ideas on the board.
2. **Gather and organize** In small groups, have students choose conservation ideas and prepare a persuasive presentation.
3. **Newcomers** Work with this group. Help them with expressions for presenting ideas persuasively.

Elements of Literature

Analyze Deductive and Inductive Organization and Presentation

1. **Teacher think aloud** Direct attention to the first example. *Say: The man was sneezing and coughing. Sneezing and coughing are facts. They are first, so the author is using inductive organization.* Guide students to explain the other example. Then have pairs reread individual paragraphs and decide which type of presentation and organization the authors used.
2. **Personal experience** Have students identify the type of organization they prefer to use.
3. **Multi-level options** See MULTI-LEVEL OPTIONS on p. 140.

Answers
2. paragraph 3: deductive; paragraph 7: inductive

✓ ASSESS

Have students rewrite paragraph 4 in an inductive form.

Word Study

Teacher Resource Book: *Personal Dictionary,*
p. 63

Identify the Suffix *-ion*

Explain spelling rules Point out that for some verbs that end in -*ate,* students must drop the -*e* before adding the suffix. (*Example:* estimate/estimation)

Answers
1. distraction 2. construction

Grammar Focus

Recognize Dependent Clauses

Review clauses Point out the subjects and verbs in each clause. Point out the use of *that* at the beginning of the dependent clause.

Answers
1. **a.** Everybody knows *that you can't buy a live dinosaur.* **b.** This means *that the actual rate of extinction today is 100 times greater.* **c.** They would expect *that about one species would become extinct each year.*

ASSESS

Have students add -*ion* to *predict.* Then have them write a sentence using *predict* and one using the new word.

Word Study

Identify the Suffix *-ion*

A **suffix** is a word part added to the end of a word. A suffix sometimes changes the part of speech of a word. The suffix -*ion* changes a word into a noun (a person, a place, or a thing).

Extinct**ion** is forever.

Word	Suffix	Noun
extinct	+ -ion →	extinction

Write these sentences in your Personal Dictionary. Complete the sentences. Use the underlined words to form a noun by adding the suffix -*ion.*

1. You always distract me from my work! You are a _____ .
2. Those men construct buildings. _____ is hard work.

Personal Dictionary • Activity Book p. 76 • Student CD-ROM

Grammar Focus

Recognize Dependent Clauses

A **dependent clause** has a subject and a verb, but it cannot be a sentence on its own. It must be used with an independent clause. Many dependent clauses begin with the word *that.*

independent clause **dependent clause**

Scientists say **that** there have been five major mass extinctions.

1. Write these sentences on a piece of paper.
   a. Everybody knows that you can't buy a live dinosaur.

b. This means that the actual rate of extinction today is 100 times greater.
c. They would expect that about one species would become extinct each year.
2. Underline the dependent clause.
3. Write your own sentence using a dependent clause with *that.* Do not use a comma to separate dependent clauses with *that* from the independent clause.

Activity Book pp. 77–78 • Student Handbook • Student CD-ROM

MULTI-LEVEL OPTIONS *From Reading to Writing*

Newcomer Have students use the kind of diagram described in Elements of Literature to share their ideas. (*Example:* A student may draw resources, such as trees, water, and birds, surrounded by sketches showing how to save these resources.) Remind students that they may start from the main point or examples.

Beginning Have students complete the following frame: _____ is an important resource. We can save it by _____. We can also save it by _____. Another way we can save _____ is by _____. It is important to save this resource because _____.

Intermediate Remind students that the authors of "The Next Great Dying" use some statistics, or number facts, to make readers see how important the problem of extinction is. Ask students to find at least one statistic that they can include in their writing.

Advanced Point out that people are more likely to be convinced that there is a problem if an author talks about how an action will affect the reader. Ask students to identify the audience they are writing for, such as students or government leaders. Tell them to focus on ideas, examples, and reasons that are important to their audience.

From Reading to Writing

Write an Informational Text

Write an informational text that explains how people can consume fewer natural resources. Use what you learned in Listen, Speak, Interact.

1. Write an introduction, a body, and a conclusion.
2. Choose an inductive or deductive organization and presentation for each paragraph.
3. Use some dependent clauses with *that*. Punctuate them correctly.
4. Use the present and future tenses in some of your sentences.

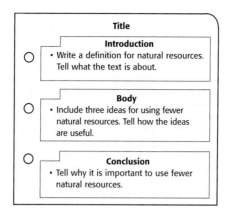

Title

Introduction
• Write a definition for natural resources. Tell what the text is about.

Body
• Include three ideas for using fewer natural resources. Tell how the ideas are useful.

Conclusion
• Tell why it is important to use fewer natural resources.

Activity Book
p. 79

Student Handbook

Across Content Areas

Read a Timeline

A **timeline** lists events in the order in which they happened. The earliest event is usually on the left. The latest event is usually on the right.

Look at the timeline. It lists the dates when certain animals became extinct.

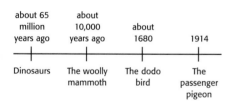

about 65 million years ago — Dinosaurs
about 10,000 years ago — The woolly mammoth
about 1680 — The dodo bird
1914 — The passenger pigeon

Answer these questions:

1. In what year did the passenger pigeon become extinct?
2. Which animal was the first to become extinct?
3. Did the dodo bird become extinct before or after the woolly mammoth?

Activity Book
p. 80

Chapter 5 The Next Great Dying **143**

Materials

Student Handbook

CNN Video: *Unit 2*

Teacher Resource Book: *Lesson Plan, p. 12;*
Teacher Resources, pp. 35–64; Video Script,
pp. 163–164; Video Worksheet, p. 174;
School-Home Connection, pp. 126–132

Teacher Resource CD-ROM

Assessment Program: *Unit 2 Test, pp. 33–38;*
Teacher and Student Resources,
pp. 115–144

Assessment CD-ROM

Transparencies

The Heinle Newbury House Dictionary/CD-ROM

Heinle Reading Library: *The Swiss Family*
Robinson

Web site: http://visions.heinle.com

Listening and Speaking Workshop

Role-Play an Interview

Ask questions Review question formation and
information question words for interviews.

**Step 1: Take notes on what you
know.**

Brainstorm facts about endangered species.
Have students record their questions on a two-
column chart.

**Step 2: Write your interview
questions.**

Model information questions. Guide students as
they prepare their questions.

Listening and Speaking Workshop

Role-Play an Interview

> **Topic**
>
> In this unit, you read about
> scientists who study the survival of
> endangered species. Work with a
> partner. Role-play an interview with a
> scientist. Your interview will be about
> endangered species.

Assign roles. The interviewer asks
questions. The interviewee is the scientist.

Step 1: Take notes on what you know.

1. Think about what you know about
   endangered species and extinction.
2. Ask your parents or a science
   teacher about endangered species.
3. Use resources in your library or on
   the Internet to find more
   information to add to your chart.
4. Organize your information in a
   chart.
5. Take notes on these topics:
   a. which animals are endangered
      today
   b. what people can do to save
      endangered species

Facts About Endangered Species	Causes of Extinction
About one bird species goes extinct each year.	Changes in climate

Step 2: Write your interview questions.

Use the chart and notes from Step 1
to write interview questions. Write each
interview question on its own note card.
Number each question.

**Step 3: Answer the questions before
role-playing the interview.**

1. Work with your partner. Answer the
   interview questions. Use your notes
   from Step 1 to help you.
2. Write each answer on its own note
   card. Each answer note card should
   have the same number as the
   question it answers.

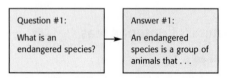

Question #1:		Answer #1:
What is an endangered species?	→	An endangered species is a group of animals that . . .

Step 4: Practice your interview.

The interviewer should:

1. Introduce the interviewee.
2. Use vocabulary about extinction in
   your questions.
3. Thank the interviewee at the
   beginning and end of the interview.

MULTI-LEVEL OPTIONS *Listening and Speaking Workshop*

Newcomer Have each student
prepare sketches showing an
endangered animal, the reason it
is endangered, and one thing
people can do to protect the
animal. Interview each student.
*Ask: What animal? Why? What to
do?* Have him/her hold up the
appropriate picture to answer
each question.

Beginning Have each student
draw an endangered animal, a
reason it is endangered, and an
action people can take to help.
Assist students in writing short
captions for their pictures.

Intermediate Remind students
that television interviews are often
conducted in places related to the
topics of the interviews. Ask each
pair to draw a backdrop on a
large piece of paper to simulate a
setting appropriate for their
interview. Have students use their
backdrops when they role-play
their interviews.

Advanced Point out that a
good interview depends partly on
good questions. Instruct students
to avoid questions that can be
answered *yes* or *no.* Tell them to
think of questions that will provide
opportunities to share interesting
information that their audience
will not already know, such as
ones beginning with *how* or *why.*

The interviewee should:

1. Answer the questions slowly and clearly.
2. Try not to read from the note card.

Step 5: Present your interview.

1. Speak slowly and clearly.
2. Look at your partner when you are speaking.

Step 6: Ask your classmates to evaluate your interview.

1. Ask your classmates to evaluate your interview by using the Active Listening Checklist. Then talk about how you could improve.

2. Ask your classmates to identify your purpose in speaking and major idea.
3. Ask your classmates, "What was the interviewee's perspective?"

Active Listening Checklist

1. Did the presenters speak too slowly, too quickly, or just right?
2. Did the presenters speak loudly enough?
3. Were the presenters' questions and answers interesting and correct?

Student Handbook

Viewing Workshop

View and Think

Describe How Pictures and Diagrams Show Text Meaning

1. View the pictures or diagrams that appear with one of the selections in this unit. Choose your favorite one.
2. Answer the following questions.
   a. What does the picture or diagram show?
   b. How does the picture or diagram help you understand the text?

3. Think about other pictures or diagrams that could help readers. Draw one of these.
4. Describe your drawing to the class. Explain how it helps understanding.

Further Viewing

Watch the *Visions* CNN Video for Unit 2. Do the Video Worksheet.

CNN Video

Content Connection
Math

Have students return to the selection "The Next Great Dying." Ask them to notice how the authors used statistics to make their points. Tell students to find statistics related to their topics. Ask them to use a percentage to compare two facts. (*Example:* Facts found: There are 65 endangered mammals in U.S and 251 in other countries; Fact to include in interview: 26% of endangered mammals are in the United States.)

Learning Styles
Natural

Divide the class into small groups. Provide each with several fiction and nonfiction books about nature. Have groups work together to look at and discuss the illustrations or photographs in each book. *Ask: Does the book show nature in a real or fanciful way? How do the pictures fit with the topic of the book? What do you think the illustrator or photographer is trying to say with these pictures?*

Step 3: Answer the questions before role-playing the interview.
Have student pairs prepare the responses for the interview. Point out that scientists base their opinions on scientific facts. Suggest that they include some interesting facts to support their answers.

Step 4: Practice your interview.
Help students with question intonation. Model how to use gestures and expressions as they speak.

Step 5: Present your interview.
Demonstrate effective presentation behavior. Remind students to listen carefully to their classmates' presentations.

Step 6: Ask your classmates to evaluate your interview.
Go over the checklists with students. Point out that it is important to give a balanced evaluation. Instruct students to first say what was good and then suggest areas of improvement.

ASSESS

Have students write a sentence evaluating their own role and identifying something they would like to do better the next time.

Portfolio

Students may choose to record or videotape their speeches to place in their portfolios.

Viewing Workshop

View and Think

1. **Take notes** Create a chart to record ideas as students examine a picture or diagram.
2. **Create a visual** Remind students to focus on the main idea they want to communicate in their visual.

Writer's Workshop

Response to Literature: Write a Survival Manual

Brainstorm and list Have students suggest topics for their survival manuals. List ideas on the board. Remind students that the point is to explain how to "survive" a situation.

Step 1: Ask questions.
Have students imagine they are in the situation and think about what questions they would have.

Step 2: Find answers to your questions.
Help students as they look for resources to answer their specific questions. Point out that answers may lead to new questions. Have students add new questions to their list.

Step 3: Organize your survival manual.
Tell students to arrange the information in logical order. Point out that *Frequently Asked Questions* are abbreviated as *FAQ's.*

Step 4: Write a first draft.
Model sample sentences. Direct attention to punctuation and capitalization. Have students check for correct usage of dependent clauses.

Writer's Workshop

Response to Literature: Write a Survival Manual

> **Writing Prompt**
>
> Write part of a survival manual for new students at your school. A survival manual tells people how to survive or deal with a new or difficult situation. Here are some topics.
>
> 1. how to find the way around school
> 2. the most important rules
> 3. what to do if you need help
> 4. some things to do for fun

Step 1: Ask questions.
1. Think about these questions:
   a. What does a new student need to know to survive at your school?
   b. What problems would a new student face?
   c. How could a new student solve these problems?
2. Choose the most important problems.

Step 2: Find answers to your questions.
1. These resources can help you answer the questions in Step 1:
   a. teachers
   b. other students
   c. guidance counselor
   d. your school's student handbook
2. You might discover new questions as you answer other questions. Try to find answers to these new questions as well. For example:

Question: What do you do if you are sick and can't come to school?
Answer: An adult at home should call the office.
This leads to:
Question: What if you miss a test?
Answer: Talk to your teacher about making it up.
3. Write your answers in a chart.

How to Survive as a New Student at Sierra School	
Survival Problems	How to Solve These Problems
sick—can't come to school	adult at home—call the office
miss a test	talk to teacher—make up test

Step 3: Organize your survival manual.
1. You can use chronological order. What does a new student need to know first? Second? Next?
2. You may want to create a chart of Frequently Asked Questions.

Step 4: Write a first draft.
If possible, type your first draft on a computer.
1. Write a title for your survival manual.
2. Write an introductory paragraph to explain your purpose.

MULTI-LEVEL OPTIONS *Writer's Workshop*

Newcomer Have students work with you to create a class survival manual. Make a web on chart paper. Label branches with words such as *Lost? Sick? Rules?* Have each student draw what to do in one of the situations. Attach the drawings to the web and display the finished product.

Beginning Brainstorm with students questions newcomers to your class might have. Write each question on a piece of unlined paper and give one to each student. Have students draw captioned pictures to answer their questions. Bind the pages to form a book. Save the manual to use as a resource for new students.

Intermediate Divide students into small groups. Give each group a different handbook or manual. Have groups look at their manuals and make Plus/Minus Charts showing what they think is effective and not effective. Provide time for group sharing. Ask students to add some of the pluses to their own manuals and to avoid the minuses.

Advanced *Say: People often use a manual to get an answer to a specific question rather than read the whole book.* Demonstrate using an index to find specific information in a manual from the school library. Ask students to revisit the manuals they wrote to find key words. Have them use these to create indexes.

3. Include your chart of Frequently Asked Questions.

4. Write a conclusion. Explain why following your recommendations is important.

5. Use correct grammar.
  a. Begin sentences with words such as *another problem, also,* or *finally* to show new ideas.
  b. Be sure that your present tense verbs agree with their subjects.
  c. Vary your sentences by using dependent clauses.

```
How to _____

        Introduction
○  This manual will help you _____
   _____

    Frequently Asked Questions
○  QUESTION: _____
   ANSWER: _____
   QUESTION: _____
   ANSWER: _____

        Conclusion
○  These points are important because
   _____
```

Step 5: Add pictures.

Also include visuals (photographs, drawings, or diagrams). These visuals should help readers understand. For example, you might show a map of your school.

Step 6: Revise and edit your draft.

1. Exchange drafts with two classmates. Ask your classmates these questions:
  a. Is my manual useful and correct?
  b. Have I used simple language?
  c. Is there anything that you do not understand?
  d. Did I make spelling, punctuation, or grammar mistakes?
  e. Is my manual organized clearly?

2. Make any changes that are necessary. You may want to:
  a. add or delete text
  b. elaborate ideas
  c. combine text
  d. rearrange text

3. Use resource materials (dictionary, thesaurus, your Student Handbook) to help you revise and edit.

Step 7: Publish your survival manual.

1. Make a final draft. Use your best handwriting if you are writing your report by hand. Check for spelling and grammar mistakes if you are using a computer.

2. Make a cover page for your survival manual. The cover page should have the title and your name.

3. Invite the principal and the guidance counselor to read your survival manual. Ask if you can give them to new students.

The Heinle Newbury House Dictionary

Student Handbook

UNIT 2
Apply and Expand

Step 5: Add pictures.
Have pairs work together to decide on visuals that will clarify the information in their manuals. Tell students to prepare drafts and then final versions.

Step 6: Revise and edit your draft.
Arrange students in pairs to share their first drafts. Have students give each other suggestions. Students can use the questions to guide their discussion. Allow time for students to work on adding and refining as needed. Point out resources available for proofreading.

Step 7: Publish your survival manual.
Allow time for students to make final copies of their manuals. Display the manuals for others to read and use.

 ASSESS

Have students generate their own individual checklists focusing on their own specific weaknesses.

Portfolio

Students may choose to include their writing in their portfolios.

Home Connection

Suggest that students may use the skills they learned to make a manual for their family to use. Help them identify topics, such as what to do if someone gets hurt playing in their yard. Ask students to interview their parents about what they want their children to do in the situations. Tell students to make manuals sharing information through drawings or writing.

Learning Styles
Kinesthetic

Have small groups share their manuals. Ask each group to select one manual and rehearse having a group member read its content aloud while others act out the instructions. If possible, videotape students' performances and keep the videotape recordings as another resource for students new to the school.

Projects

Project 1: Research an Endangered Species

1. **Brainstorm and list** Brainstorm and list endangered species. Have students choose one.

2. **Gather and organize** Have students use charts and organizers as they research the species. Remind students of the importance of visuals. Tell them to plan and use visuals effectively.

Project 2: Summarize a Real-Life Survival Story

1. **Use resources** Brainstorm possible topics. Remind students that friends and family members are good sources. Allow time for students to research and take notes.

2. **Summarize** Remind students to identify the setting and problem. Have them include details that add to the story.

Portfolio

Students may choose to include their projects in their portfolios.

Projects

These projects will help you learn more about survival. Work alone, with a partner, or with a small group. If you need help, ask a teacher, a parent, or your school librarian.

Project 1: Research an Endangered Species

Learn about an endangered species. Choose one listed in "The Next Great Dying," or you may choose another one.

1. Find information in several sources in your school library. You can also search the Internet to find information. These search words are helpful: *endangered species, extinction.*

2. Gather information on these topics:
   a. the name of the animal or plant
   b. places where it lives today
   c. where it used to live
   d. interesting information
   e. why it is endangered

3. Make a poster about your animal or plant. Include the information you learned and pictures.

4. Use punctuation and capitalization to enhance your message.

AFRICAN CHEETAH

It lives in sub-Saharan Africa today. It used to live in most of Africa, in southern Asia, the Middle East, and India.

It eats small antelopes.

It can run 70 miles per hour!

Project 2: Summarize a Real-Life Survival Story

In Chapter 4, you read about the Lost Woman of San Nicolas Island. Find another story about a real person who survived a hard situation. Then summarize this real-life survival story.

1. Find a true survival story. Try these resources:
   a. Find a book in your school library. Ask the librarian for help.
   b. Look in current newspapers or magazines.
   c. Ask family members or friends.

2. Summarize the person's story. Write one or two paragraphs. Be sure to cite your sources.

3. Include pictures to help tell the story.

4. Present your summary and pictures to the class. You might record the summary on audio or video. You might also use presentation software. Add music to create an exciting mood.

MULTI-LEVEL OPTIONS *Projects*

Newcomer Have students use illustrated story maps to summarize their survival stories. Ask them to draw their main characters in the appropriate settings. Tell them to show their characters' survival problems, the steps used in overcoming them, and the final outcomes.

Beginning Have students use a summary frame in sharing their stories. Tell them to complete the following: _____ (character) was in _____ (setting). His/Her problem was _____. He/She solved it by _____. In the end, _____ (character) felt _____.

Intermediate In sharing their stories, ask students to tell what qualities and skills the person used to survive.

Advanced Have students use Venn diagrams to compare and contrast the stories they summarize with either "The Voyage of the *Frog*" or "Island of the Blue Dolphins."

Further Reading

The following books discuss the theme of survival. Choose one or more of them. Write your thoughts and feelings about what you read in your Reading Log. Take notes about your answers to these questions:

1. Think about the situations that the people faced. How would you feel if you faced these situations?
2. Have you ever been in situations like the ones you read about? Explain.

How I Survived My Summer Vacation: And Lived to Write the Story
by Robin Friedman, Cricket Books, 2000. Jackie wants to write a novel during the summer before he starts high school. But he cannot get past the first sentence! He asks his friends for help and ideas.

Voyage of the Frog
by Gary Paulsen, Yearling Books, 1990. David gets caught in a storm as he is trying to sail his boat, the *Frog*. After the storm ends, David must figure out how to get back home on his own.

Island of the Blue Dolphins
by Scott O'Dell, Scott Foresman, 1987. Karana, an American Indian girl, is left behind on her tribe's island. This story tells how Karana survives alone on the island for 18 years!

Backwater
by Joan Bauer, G.P. Putnam, 1999. Ivy, at age 16, finds great fascination in tracking and recording her family's history, especially after she discovers an eccentric aunt she's never met. Her attempt to interview Aunt Jo involves mountaineering, storms, shifting lake ice, and other adventures.

Climb or Die
by Edward Myers, Hyperion Press, 1996. This book tells the story of Danielle and her brother, Jake. Their family's car crashes in the Rocky Mountains during a snowstorm. Danielle and Jake must climb a mountain to find help for their parents.

Far North
by Will Hobbs, Morrow, 1996. Fifteen-year-old Gabe enrolled in a school in Canada's Northwest Territories so that he could be closer to his dad, an oil-field worker. Instead, he got an airplane accident, the friendship of two Dene Indians, a grizzly bear, starvation, extreme cold, and a blizzard. Breathless action and the Canadian landscape pervade Gabe's struggle to survive.

Memory Boy
by Will Weaver, HarperCollins, 2001. It's 2008, two years after a massive volcano completely changes life in the United States as we know it. Miles, sixteen, and his family leave the city to find refuge in their country cottage, only to find it inhabited by other desperate people who refuse to leave. Miles remembers enough from a school project to work out another refuge for his family.

The Extreme Survival Guide
by Rory Storm, Element Books, 1999. This compilation of tips and accounts about surviving disasters and emergencies draws from situations that actually happened around the globe.

Companion Web site

Reading Log

Heinle Reading Library
The Swiss Family Robinson

Further Reading

▪ Teacher Resource Book: *Reading Log, p. 64*

Write a review Have students select a book about people surviving difficult situations and experiences and write a review of it. Students can organize their review into three paragraphs. In the first paragraph, students can tell about the title and main idea with a brief summary of the problem and resolution. In the second paragraph, students can explain their reaction to the story and main character by telling how they feel and why they feel that way. In the last paragraph, direct students to tell what they learned from the story and from the character's responses to the survival situation.

▪ Assessment Program: *Unit 2 Test, pp. 33–38*

Heinle Reading Library

The Swiss Family Robinson by Johann Wyss In a specially adapted version by Eliza Gatewood Warren

When a violent storm at sea destroys their ship, the parents and four young sons of the Robinson family make their way to a deserted island. Far from civilization in the endless South Pacific, the family must learn to do everything—from finding food to building shelter to protecting themselves from the unknown dangers that constantly beset them. Mostly they learn about loving their new wilderness home and the strength and closeness they find in each other.

Visions Companion Site

http://visions.heinle.com
For additional student activities and teacher resources, see the Visions Companion Web site.

Unit Materials

Activity Book: *pp. 81–120*
Audio: *Unit 3; CD 2, Tracks 1–6*
Student Handbook
Student CD-ROM: *Unit 3*
CNN Video: *Unit 3*
Teacher Resource Book: *Lesson Plans, Teacher Resources, Reading Summaries, School-Home Connection, Video Script, Video Worksheet, Activity Book Answer Key*
Teacher Resource CD-ROM
Assessment Program: *Quizzes, Test, and Exam, pp. 39–60; Teacher and Student Resources, pp. 115–144*
Assessment CD-ROM
Transparencies
The Heinle Newbury House Dictionary/CD-ROM
More Grammar Practice workbook
Heinle Reading Library: *20,000 Leagues Under the Sea*
Web site: http://visions.heinle.com

Visions Staff Development Handbook

Refer to the Visions Staff Development Handbook for more teacher support.

Unit Theme: Journeys

▌ Teacher Resource Book: *Web, p. 37*

Create a word web In the center of a web, write: *journeys.* Have students dictate words and ideas related to *journeys.*

Unit Preview: Table of Contents

Use the table of contents Read the chapter titles and authors. *Ask: What are the different genres of the reading selections in this unit?* (poem, novel, science fiction novel, informational text, informational book, historical novel)

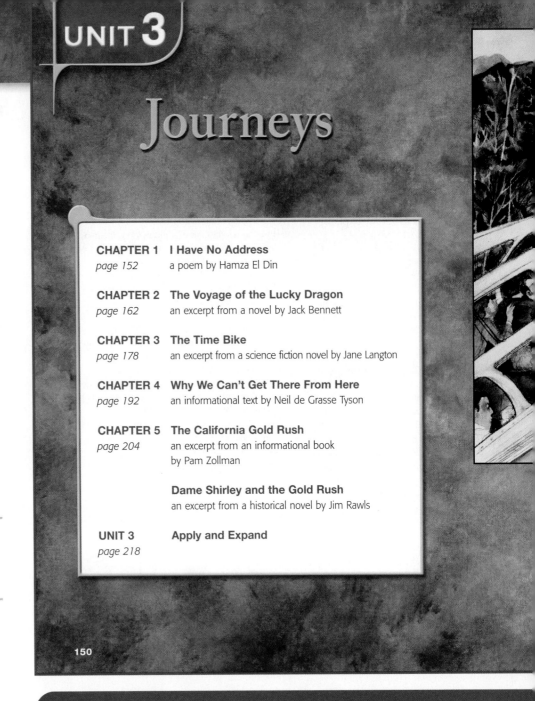

UNIT 3

Journeys

150

UNIT OBJECTIVES

Reading

Recognize figurative language as you read a poem • Paraphrase to recall information as you read an excerpt from a novel • Predict as you read an excerpt from a science fiction novel • Reread and record to learn and recall as you read an informational text • Compare and contrast as you read an excerpt from an informational book and a historical novel

Listening and Speaking

Draw and present images based on text • Have a debate • Give a presentation • Listen to an informational text • Present the story of a journey

Railroad Observation Car Heading West, photo, Franklin McMahon, 20th century.

View the Picture

1. A journey is a long trip. What kind of journey do you think these people are taking?

2. Why do you think these people are on this journey?

In this unit, you will read several selections about journeys. You will read a poem, a story, a science fiction story, informational texts, and a historical story. You will also learn the elements of these writing forms and how to write them yourself.

151

Grammar
Use apostrophes with possessive nouns • Identify subject and object pronouns • Write using contractions • Use comparative and superlative adjectives • Use adverbs

Writing
Write a poem using figurative language • Write to solve a problem • Write a description • Use multiple resources to write a research report • Compare and contrast two reading selections

Content
Science: Learn about migration of birds • Social Studies: Describe countries on a map • Social Studies: Learn about time zones • Math: Solve a time problem • Science: Learn about natural resources

View the Picture

1. **Art background** Franklin McMahon (1921–) is called an artist/reporter because his art is a record of contemporary world events. His illustrations bring history alive with subjects ranging from civil rights to AIDS to *Apollo XI.* His book of political art, *The Constitution,* is used in many middle and high schools throughout the United States.

2. **Art interpretation** *Ask: Where do you think these people are going?* (on a sightseeing trip; visiting someone in another part of the country) *This is an observation car. What the passengers are doing?* (drinking tea, reading, listening to headphones) *Why aren't they "observing"? Would you like to go on a trip like this? What part of the United States would you like to see?*

   a. **Explore and describe line and color** In "Railroad Observation Car Heading West," McMahon contrasts the blue and white diagonal of the speeding train with the dark, wild, vertical landscape. *Ask: Why do you think the artist did that?* (to show that human "progress" can encroach on the wilderness, despite the wilderness's strength and endurance)

   b. **Connect to theme** *Say: The theme of this unit is* journeys. *What kind of journeys have you taken?*

ASSESS

Have students write two sentences about a journey they want to take.

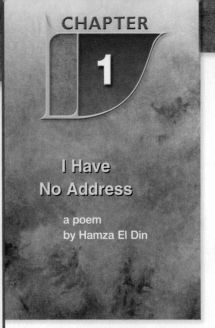

CHAPTER
1

Into the Reading

Chapter Materials

Activity Book: *pp. 81–88*
Audio: *Unit 3, Chapter 1; CD 2, Track 1*
Student Handbook
Student CD-ROM: *Unit 3, Chapter 1*
Teacher Resource Book: *Lesson Plan, Teacher Resources, Reading Summary, Activity Book Answer Key*
Teacher Resource CD-ROM
Assessment Program: *Quiz, pp. 39–40; Teacher and Student Resources, pp. 115–144*
Assessment CD-ROM
Transparencies
The Heinle Newbury House Dictionary/CD-ROM
Web site: http://visions.heinle.com

Objectives

Preview Have students read the objectives in pairs. *Ask: What do you know about migration?*

Use Prior Knowledge

Talk About Journeys

Give details in an interview Draw the Sunshine Organizer on the board. Have students ask you the questions, and fill in the triangles. At first, just give short answers with no details. *Ask: Would it be more interesting if I gave more details?* Then continue answering questions, giving more details.

I Have No Address

a poem
by Hamza El Din

Use Prior Knowledge

Talk About Journeys

When you make a journey, you travel to different places. You may travel to a different country or another city. You may travel to the beach or the grocery store.

1. Work with a partner. Talk about a place where you have traveled.
2. Use a Sunshine Organizer to answer these questions. Write the answers next to the triangles.
   a. Where did you go?
   b. Who went with you?
   c. When did you go there?
   d. Why did you go there?
   e. What did you do there?
   f. How did your journey change you?

MULTI-LEVEL OPTIONS *Build Vocabulary*

Newcomer On the board, write: *beat.* Draw a picture of a heart. Point to the picture. Mime *fast.* **Say:** *My heart is* beating *fast.* Then mime *slow.* **Say:** *My heart is* beating *slowly. Show me how your heart beats when you run/when you're sleeping.* Have students draw their answers.

Beginning Have students work in groups of mixed language abilities. Have them take turns acting out the word *beat* in a different context from the picture. (The bird's wings are beating fast; Our team beat the other team, etc.)

Intermediate Have students work in small groups. Have them use words from the poem to create new sentences incorporating two meanings of *beat.* (I am a sparrow with beating wings; My boat beat the other boat, etc.) Have students take turns restating the new sentences.

Advanced Have students work in groups. Tell them to look up in a dictionary all the different meanings of *beat* as both a verb and noun. Ask them to write one sentence for each. Then have them read and act out those sentences.

Build Background

Song Sparrows

Sparrows are small birds. They live in many places around the world. There are many different types of sparrows. The song sparrow is one type. They are called song sparrows because they sing songs. In some places, these songs tell us that spring has arrived. Song sparrows live in North America. You may even see them in your own backyard.

Content Connection

Many sparrows **migrate**—move from one place to another. They move to warmer, southern areas in the fall, when the weather gets cool. They move back to northern areas in the spring, when the weather gets warm.

Build Vocabulary

Identify Multiple-Meaning Words

Some words can mean more than one thing. These words are called **multiple-meaning words.** You can figure out what these words mean by reading the words around them (the context).

Read each sentence. The underlined words are multiple-meaning words. Choose the correct definition.

1. Anna lived in different countries and learned different <u>tongues</u>.
   a. parts of your mouth that help you talk and taste food
   b. spoken languages

2. We cannot go swimming. The <u>waves</u> are too high.
   a. raised areas of water that move across the surface of the sea
   b. hand signals

3. The fishermen <u>cast</u> their nets into the water.
   a. assigned a part in a play or movie
   b. threw

The Heinle Newbury House Dictionary

Activity Book p. 81

Student CD-ROM

Chapter 1 I Have No Address **153**

Community Connection

Build Background Invite a local ornithologist to talk with students about local birds and migration patterns. Have students generate lists of questions. (*Examples:* Which birds migrate? Why? Where do they go? How long do they stay?) Have volunteers do Q&A with the speaker.

Learning Styles
Visual

Build Vocabulary Write on the board: *note, keyboard, compose, sheet, key, tune.* Tell students to make a three-column homonym chart with the words down the middle column. Have small groups create pictures of the two contexts the words fit into (piano keyboard/computer keyboard) with sentence captions for each. Have groups share their work.

> Teacher Resource Book: *Three-Column Chart, p. 45*

Build Background

Song Sparrows

1. **Use prior knowledge** *Ask: What kinds of birds do you see in your neighborhood? Can you describe them, or identify them?* (*Possible answers:* pigeons, crows, seagulls, jays, sparrows, mockingbirds) *Can you make any bird sounds?*

2. **Content Connection** Other animals and species that migrate include butterflies, geese, turtles, and whales.

Build Vocabulary

Identify Multiple-Meaning Words

Teacher Resource Book: *Personal Dictionary, p. 63*

1. **Use multiple-meaning words** To help reinforce new words, ask students various questions. *Ask: How many different tongues are spoken in your home or neighborhood? What tongues do you know? Do you know what it means to be tongue-tied?* (You don't know what to say; you can't speak.) *How do you usually wave goodbye? How do very young children wave goodbye? Do you like to swim in the waves at the beach or surf the waves? Have you ever been part of a play cast? Have you ever seen people casting a fishing rod or net?*

2. **Reading selection vocabulary** You may want to introduce the glossed words in the reading selection before students begin reading. Key words: *globe, humanity, tranquil, universe.* Instruct students to write the words with correct spelling and their definitions in their Personal Dictionaries. Have them pronounce each word and divide it into syllables.

3. **Multi-level options** See MULTI-LEVEL OPTIONS on p. 152.

Answers
1. b 2. a 3. b

ASSESS

Have students work in pairs to write sentences with the vocabulary words.

Text Structure

Poem

Review features of poems Before students look at the chart, have them tell you what they already know about poetry. *Ask: What do you call the sections of a poem?* (stanzas) *Do poems always rhyme?* (no) *What other features do you remember about poems?* (They use images and repetition.) *Are poems and songs similar?* (yes)

Reading Strategy

Recognize Figurative Language

1. **Use figurative language to describe people** *Say: We can use figurative language to describe people in imaginative ways. For example, I could say, "My sister is a cat. She loves to sleep."* Have students use figurative language to describe people they know. Point out that similes ("My sister is like a cat.") are another kind of figurative language.
2. **Locate pronunciation** Have students locate the pronunciation of *metaphor* in the glossary of their Student Handbook and record it in their Reading Logs.
3. **Multi-level options** See MULTI-LEVEL OPTIONS below.

ASSESS

Have students write down four features of a poem.

Text Structure

Poem

"I Have No Address" is a **poem.** A poem is a type of writing that expresses feelings or ideas. The chart shows the features of this poem.

Think about how these features help the author show feelings and ideas.

Poem	
Stanzas	The poem is organized in groups of lines.
Images	The author describes people, places, and things.
Free Verse	The words at the end of lines do not rhyme (do not have the same ending sounds).
Repetition	Words and ideas are repeated (said more than once). This shows strong feelings or important ideas.

Reading Log   Student CD-ROM

Reading Strategy

Recognize Figurative Language

Authors often use **figurative language** to describe people, places, and things. Figurative language is not literal. That is, it does not mean exactly what the individual words mean. Look at this example:

The idea was a <u>flash of light</u> in my brain.

This does not mean that there was a real "flash of light." It means that the idea came quickly, like a flash of light.

This kind of figurative language is called a **metaphor.** A metaphor describes one thing as if it is another thing.

Metaphors are often used in literary writings, especially in poems. You will understand poems better if you look for them as you read or listen.

In your Reading Log, write the metaphors that you find as you read or listen to the audio recording of "I Have No Address."

Reading Log   Student CD-ROM

MULTI-LEVEL OPTIONS *Reading Strategy*

Newcomer Have students draw pictures that show their ideas of the sentence, *The idea was a flash of light in my brain.* Then arrange their drawings around the sentence on a class bulletin board.

Beginning Help students to understand some examples of figurative language. Write on the board: *Tears wash my face like water.* **Ask:** *Do tears really wash your face?* (no) *Do you wash your face with water?* (yes) *When you cry, do your tears run down your face like water?* (yes) Point out that the word *like* is often a clue to figurative language.

Intermediate Have students work in small groups. Provide them with four sentence starters: *The ocean was like a _____. The snake moved as if _____. The painting seemed like _____. The light in the sky was like _____.* Ask students to create examples of figurative language with them. Have students share their work.

Advanced Have students work in pairs. Provide them with several pictures that lend themselves to figurative constructions. Have students create some metaphors based on the pictures and, if possible, create a short poem with them. Have them share their work with the class.

I Have No Address

a poem
by Hamza El Din

155

Reading Selection Materials

Audio: *Unit 3, Chapter 1; CD 2, Track 1*
Teacher Resource Book: *Reading Summary,*
   pp. 85–86
Transparencies: #37, *Reading Summary*

Suggestions for Using Reading Summary

- Introduce new vocabulary or cognates.
- Cut the summary into strips, or jumble the sentences on an overhead transparency. Students put the sentences in order.
- Practice the reading strategy.
- Students read aloud or with a partner.
- Students paraphrase the summary.
- Students do a cloze activity.
- Students create a visual or graphic organizer, such as a timeline or storyboard, to illustrate the summary.
- Students paraphrase the summary.

Preview the Selection

1. **Interpret the image** Have students look at the illustration. *Ask: What is the bird doing? How do the colors make you feel? What do you think the bird may symbolize?*
2. **Connect to theme** *Ask: What kind of journey do you think this poem may be about? Do you think it is a real journey or an imaginative, figurative journey?*

Content Connection
The Arts

Have students work in groups to interview friends and neighbors about their favorite poems. Have groups brainstorm the types of questions they will ask (what type of poem, why they liked it, how they felt, and so on). Then have groups put the information in chart form and present it.

Learning Styles
Mathematical

Ask: Do all birds stay in the same place all year long? (no) Explain that certain birds fly south in fall as the weather turns cold, and then they come back north in spring. Have each group compile a chart of which birds migrate in fall, where they go, and how many miles they must travel in each direction. Then have the groups compare and revise their charts.

Read the Selection

1. **Listen to poetry for tone** Have students close their books and listen to the audio for the poem. *Ask: What is the feeling, or tone, of the poem?*

2. **Choral reading** Lead students in a choral reading.

3. **Multiple-meaning words** Have students find the multiple-meaning words in stanzas 1 and 3—*tongues, waves, cast, dock*—and tell the meaning that is used in the poem.

4. **Identify words that create tone** Have students find words in stanzas 1–3 that help create the tone of peace and hope in the poem. They may identify the following words: *peace, love, humanity, dreams, united, smiling hope, wish good, tranquil, tranquility.*

Sample Answer to Guide Question
The metaphor is that the author is a sparrow flying around the globe.

See Teacher Edition pp. 434–436 for a list of English-Spanish cognates in the reading selection.

Audio
CD 2, Tr. 1

Recognize Figurative Language

What is the metaphor in this stanza?

1   I am a sparrow with a white heart and a thousand tongues.
    I fly around the **globe**
    Singing for peace, love and **humanity**
    In every place.
    I have no address.

2   My address is lines **ornamented** by dreams, beating hearts
        united by smiling hope
    For people who wish good for other people all the time.
    I sing, smile and cry.
    My tears wash away pain
    In every place.

3   Our paths are boats of longing, turning round and round
        with us—
    One day to the east, another to the west, to **tranquil**
        moorings.
    And when the waves go against us and cast us away,
    Then the echo of my sounds at midnight will be a dock at the
        shore of tranquility,
    In every place.

---

globe the world
humanity the state or condition of being human
ornamented decorated

tranquil calm, peaceful
moorings places where something, especially a boat, can be tied and made secure

156 **Unit 3** Journeys

MULTI-LEVEL OPTIONS *Read the Selection*

Newcomer Play the audio. Then read aloud and have students join in when they can. *Ask: Is the sparrow talking to the reader?* (yes) *Does the bird stay in the same place all the time?* (no) *Does the sparrow make people happy?* (yes)

Beginning Read the Reading Summary aloud. Then do a paired reading of the poem. *Ask: Where does the sparrow fly?* (around the globe) *What does* tranquility *mean?* (calm) *What does the writer compare our universe to?* (a rose garden)

Intermediate Have students do a paired reading. *Ask: What does the author want us to think when he says the sparrow has a "white heart"?* (that the sparrow is pure and represents goodness) *Why does the sparrow fly "around the globe"?* (to tell the world about peace, love, and humanity)

Advanced Have students do a partner read aloud. *Ask: Why do you think the author chose a sparrow as the narrator?* (because it is free to fly anywhere) *What is the poet saying about life in stanza 3?* (It can be calm or troubled.) *What do you think the author is urging us to do?* (to love and care for others)

Recognize Figurative Language

What is the metaphor in this stanza?

4 The day we join hands with others' hands, our **universe** is
A rose garden blooming in the holy night.
It contains us, with hope, love and **alleluias.**

5 And I am the sparrow on the branch.
I sleep, dream and fly happily
In every place.
I have no address.

universe the stars, planets, other heavenly bodies, and all of space

alleluias expressions of joy

About the Author

Hamza El Din (born 1929)

Hamza El Din was born in Sudan, a country in Africa. When El Din was a young boy, his village was flooded (covered with water). He and his family were forced to leave their home. When El Din was in college, he began singing. He also learned to play the oud, a stringed instrument from Africa and the Middle East. Today El Din travels all over the world, playing and singing his music for others.

➤ Hamza El Din moved as a young boy. Do you think this event affected his poetry? How do the main ideas and details in his poem support your ideas?

Chapter 1 I Have No Address **157**

Read the Selection

1. **Choral reading** Play the audio. Then assign a few students to lead a choral reading.
2. **Identify metaphors** Have students identify the metaphors used in the poem: *I am a sparrow; my address is lines ornamented by dreams; our paths are boats of longing; our universe is a rose garden.*
3. **Multi-level options** See MULTI-LEVEL OPTIONS on p. 156.

Sample Answer to Guide Question
The metaphor is "our universe is a rose garden."

About the Author

❚ Teacher Resource Book: *Timelines, p. 39*

1. **Explain author's background** Hamza El Din is considered the father of modern Nubian music, fusing traditional Nubian and Arabic musical forms with influence from his Western conservatory training.
2. **Use chronology to organize facts** Have students create a timeline with facts from the author's life. Have students paraphrase the information.

Answer
Sample answer: Perhaps moving as a young boy gave the author an appreciation of other cultures and a connection with people around the world.

Across Selections

Say: Not all figurative language creates positive, beautiful images. Have students work in pairs to contrast the figurative language in this poem with that used to describe Ichabod Crane in paragraphs 7 and 12 of "The Legend of Sleepy Hollow" (pp. 55–56).

Spelling, Punctuation, Capitalization

After the Reading Comprehension section, students will practice spelling, punctuation, and capitalization in the Activity Book.

 Spelling

Ai/ay for long /a/ sound

On the board, write: *pain/away.* Underline the long *a* in both words. Tell students that *ai* and *ay* are two ways to spell the long /a/ sound. Have them find another word in paragraph 4 that has a long *a* (contains).

Apply On the board, write: *am, main, address, around, rain, today.* Underline and pronounce each word. *Ask: Which words have the long /a/ sound?* (main, rain, today)

Evaluate Your Reading Strategy

Recognize Figurative Language *Say: You have practiced an important reading strategy. Now you can decide how well you have done. Does this statement describe how you read?*

As I read, I look for figurative language that describes people, places, and things. Recognizing figurative language helps me understand the text better.

Beyond the Reading

Reading Comprehension

Question-Answer Relationships

Sample Answers

1. a sparrow
2. It flies around the world, singing for peace.
3. The garden contains "us," the people.
4. The dock is a safe place, a destination, a place to rest.
5. The sparrow's song is a reminder that there is a safe place to dock.
6. in every place
7. A bird represents freedom.
8. The address has a beating heart; it's alive.
9. I like stanza 1; the image of a brown sparrow with a white heart singing to everyone everywhere makes me feel good.
10. Our lives are like boats that turn around in circles. The boats keep leading us back to ourselves.
11. The author wants to wash away pain and bring peace and love to the world.

Build Reading Fluency

Echo Read Aloud

Model reading aloud with expression. Read one line at a time. Ask the class to read (echo) the same line you just read before going on to the next line or sentence.

Reading Comprehension

Question-Answer Relationships (QAR)

"Right There" Questions

1. **Recall Facts** What type of bird does the author describe himself as?
2. **Recall Facts** What does this bird do?
3. **Recall Facts** What does the rose garden contain?

"Think and Search" Questions

4. **Understand Figurative Language** What does the author mean by the metaphor "a dock at the shore of tranquility"?
5. **Understand Figurative Language** What does "a dock at the shore of tranquility" have to do with the bird's song?

"Author and You" Questions

6. **Identify a Recurrent Theme** Where does the sparrow sing?

7. **Understand Characterization** Why do you think the author chose a bird to represent himself?
8. **Describe Mental Images** What image do you have of the address in stanza 2?
9. **Appreciate Writer's Craft** Choose a stanza that you like. Explain how the way it is written helps you enjoy it.

"On Your Own" Questions

10. **Understand Figurative Language** What do you think the author means by "Our paths are boats of longing, turning round and round with us—"?
11. **Understand Author's Perspective** What do you think the author wants for everybody?

Activity Book
p. 82

Student
CD-ROM

Build Reading Fluency

Echo Read Aloud

Effective readers learn to read with feeling. Echo reading helps you read with feeling and expression. Your teacher reads a line. Then the class reads (echoes) the same line aloud. Turn to page 156.

1. Listen to your teacher read.
2. Read the same line aloud with expression.
3. Continue listening and reading.

MULTI-LEVEL OPTIONS *Elements of Literature*

Newcomer Have students illustrate different stanzas of the poem. Have them work in groups to find key words that express the mood of each illustration.

Beginning Have students illustrate different stanzas of the poem. Tell them to work in small groups to write captions for the pictures.

Intermediate Ask students to rewrite the poem, substituting third-person singular *it* for first-person *I*. Have them read the revised poem aloud. *Ask: Does the change in style make the poem feel different? Does it bring the reader closer or keep the reader at a distance?* (distance)

Advanced Provide students with another poem where the style, tone, and mood are different from "I Have No Address." Have pairs create a chart comparing and identifying the differences between the two. Ask them to identify which lines in each poem show those elements.

Listen, Speak, Interact

Draw and Present Images Based on Text

The poet (author of the poem) writes descriptions of people, places, and things. He writes about a bird flying around the world. He also writes about people holding hands.

Descriptions help you draw **images** (pictures) in your mind. When you read or listen to the poem, what pictures do you make in your mind?

1. Listen to the audio recording of the poem.
   a. What effect did the reader's interpretation have on you?
   b. How did the words affect you?
2. Reread the poem. Pay attention to the images you make in your mind.
3. Draw one of these images on a piece of paper.
4. Read the poem aloud to the class. Ask your classmates, "Which words from the poem does my drawing show?"

Elements of Literature

Recognize Style, Tone, and Mood

Authors use several elements of literature to create an effect on the reader. Three of these are **style, tone,** and **mood.** Read the meanings in the chart.

Reread "I Have No Address" and answer these questions in your Reading Log.

1. The author uses first-person narration as an element of style.
   a. What effect does this have on you?
   b. Explain how the effect would be different if the poem was in third-person narration.
2. What is the author's tone? Is it negative or positive?
3. What is the mood? Do you feel sad? Hopeful? Disappointed? Happy?

Element	Meaning
Style	how authors use language to express themselves
Tone	the author's attitude (how the author feels) toward the topic
Mood	the feeling that you get from reading a text

Reading Log   Activity Book   Student
                  p. 83   CD-ROM

Chapter 1   I Have No Address   **159**

Listen, Speak, Interact

Draw and Present Images Based on Text

1. **Caption images** After students have drawn their images and discussed them, have them write the lines from the poem that the drawing illustrates. Display the drawings together in the classroom.
2. **Newcomers** Have newcomers pair up with other students to discuss ideas for their drawings before doing the art.

Elements of Literature

Recognize Style, Tone, and Mood

1. **Discuss style, tone, and mood** Have students work in groups. Ask them to choose "The Legend of Sleepy Hollow" (p. 54) or "The Voyage of the *Frog*" (p. 90) and compare its style, tone, or mood with "I Have No Address." Have students present their findings to the class.
2. **Multi-level options** See MULTI-LEVEL OPTIONS on p. 158.

Answers
Possible answers: **1. a.** It makes it seem more personal. **b.** In third person, the author would seem like an objective observer. **2.** positive **3.** hopeful, happy, calm

 **ASSESS**

Have students write a sentence describing the tone and mood of the poem.

Content Connection
Technology

Provide students with some suitable poetry sites on the Internet. Have students work in groups to choose one poem and identify its stylistic elements. Then have them write a group poem, using the same style, tone, or mood, but changing the subject matter. Provide help as needed.

Learning Styles
Kinesthetic

Have students create a mime of their group poem. Have volunteers read different stanzas as others act them out for the class.

Word Study

Recognize the Suffix -ity

Add -ity to new words Write on the board: *national, real, popular.* Have students explain what the adjectives mean. Then have volunteers come to the board and add *-ity* to each one to form a noun. Ask students to make sentences with the new words.

Answers
2. tranquility: being tranquil or calm; maturity: being adult or grown up

Grammar Focus

Use Apostrophes with Possessive Nouns

1. **Clarify for accuracy** Point out that when a singular noun ends in an *-s, 's* must be added to the end to form a possessive noun. (*Example:* Texas's state bird is the mockingbird.) Remind students that when a *plural* noun ends in an *-s,* an apostrophe is added. (*Example:* birds' nest, *not* birds's nest)
2. **Use apostrophes** Have students add apostrophes. Write on the board: *Where is the mens room? The two boys grades were excellent. The childrens teacher is Carlos aunt.* (men's, boys', children's, Carlos's)

Answers
1. The two brothers' room is messy. 2. The women's coats are in the closet.

ASSESS

Have students write two sentences using *maturity* and *tranquility.*

Word Study

Recognize the Suffix -ity

A **suffix** is a group of letters added to the end of a word. A suffix changes the meaning of a root word.

Singing for peace, love, and human**ity**

The root word of *humanity* is *human* (a person). When the suffix *-ity* is added, the meaning of the word becomes "condition or state of" being human.

If the root word ends in *e,* drop the *e* before adding *-ity.*

1. Copy the chart in your Personal Dictionary.

Root Word + -ity ⇒ New Word	=	Meaning
tranquil + -ity ⇒ tranquility	=	
mature + -ity ⇒ maturity	=	

2. Write the meaning of each word with the suffix *-ity* in the boxes.
3. Use a dictionary to check if your ideas are correct.

Personal Dictionary · The Heinle Newbury House Dictionary · Activity Book p. 84 · Student CD-ROM

Grammar Focus

Use Apostrophes with Possessive Nouns

Possession means belonging to someone. An apostrophe (') shows possession when used with a noun and sometimes the letter *s.*

The poet**'s** tears wash away the pain.

Use the chart to learn when to use *'s* with a noun, and when to just use *'.*

Add apostrophes to the underlined words.

1. The two <u>brothers</u> room is messy.
2. The <u>womens</u> coats are in the closet.

Most Nouns

Singular Noun	Add 's	Possessive Singular Noun
poet	's	poet's
Plural Noun	**Add '**	**Possessive Plural Noun**
poets	'	poets'

Plural Nouns that Do Not End in s

Plural Noun	Add 's	Possessive Plural Noun
children	's	children's

Activity Book pp. 85–86 · Student Handbook · Student CD-ROM

MULTI-LEVEL OPTIONS *From Reading to Writing*

Newcomer Draw the poem model from p. 161 on the board. Divide the class into groups of four, each group containing an even mix of language abilities. Have the newcomer students in each group create a storyboard to illustrate their group's poem.

Beginning Have beginning students choose a subject for the poem. Tell them it must be someone recognizable to the class. It can be a class member or a public or historical figure. Have them also be responsible for writing out the finished poem.

Intermediate Have intermediate students work with advanced students to brainstorm the type of figurative language needed for their poem. Have them also work together to decide on what style and tone should be used.

Advanced Have students write the stanzas of the poem with input from the others in the group. Remind them to include possessive forms and *-ity* nouns if possible. Have the groups revise their poems and then present them to the class.

From Reading to Writing

Write a Poem Using Figurative Language

Write a poem about a person you know. The poem can be serious or funny.

1. Separate your poem into stanzas.
2. Use figurative language to describe the person. Reread stanza 1 on page 156 as a model.
3. Use free verse. The words at the end of lines do not need to rhyme (have the same ending sounds).
4. Repeat words to show strong feelings or important ideas.
5. Use some possessive noun forms.

6. Choose how to present your poem in writing. Use handwriting, printing, or a special font on a computer.

(Title of Poem)

(Name) is a _____ .
(He or She) does ____ *and* ____ .

(He or She) has ____ *of* ____ .
(Name) is a _____

Activity Book
p. 87

Student
Handbook

Across Content Areas

Learn About Migration of Birds

When birds **migrate,** they travel from one area to another. This is called **migration.** Some birds travel thousands of miles during their migration. They do this in order to find warmer temperatures, more food, and more water. For example, some North American birds migrate south to Central and South America. The birds' migrations give them warmer temperatures, more food, and more water.

Most migrating birds follow the same **migration route.** A route is a path of travel. The same routes are used every year.

Complete each sentence with a word from the box.

---

migrate   south   route

---

1. In the spring, some birds ____ from Mexico to parts of Canada.
2. Groups of sparrows fly through our town every April. Our town must be on the birds' migration ____ .
3. The birds began migrating in October. They traveled ____ to Central America.

Activity Book
p. 88

Chapter 1 I Have No Address   **161**

From Reading to Writing

Write a Poem Using Figurative Language

1. **Collaborative writing** Write the model on the board. Have students help select a person to write a poem about. Fill in the model as students come up with language and ideas. They may come up with enough for two different poems.
2. **Multi-level options** See MULTI-LEVEL OPTIONS on p. 160.

Across Content Areas: Science

Learn About Migration of Birds

Use prior knowledge *Ask: What animals do you know that migrate? When do they usually migrate? What else do you know about migration?*

Answers
1. migrate 2. route 3. south

 **ASSESS**

Have students write two sentences about migration in their local environment.

Reteach and Reassess

Text Structure Have students review "I Have No Address," the group poem, and their From Reading to Writing poem. Instruct them to chart the number of lines in each stanza and their length, the imagery, whether each poem is free verse or rhyme, and what degree of repetition is found in each.

Reading Strategy Have small groups add to the chart the figurative language in their poems and explain what they represent.

Elements of Literature Have students work in pairs to chart the style, tone, and mood of each poem.

Reassess Provide students with a new poem. Have pairs read alternate stanzas. Ask students to identify the author's style, tone, and mood.

CHAPTER
2

Into the Reading

Chapter Materials

Activity Book: *pp. 89–96*
Audio: *Unit 3, Chapter 2; CD 2, Track 2*
Student Handbook
Student CD-ROM: *Unit 3, Chapter 2*
Teacher Resource Book: *Lesson Plan, Teacher Resources, Reading Summary, Activity Book Answer Key*
Teacher Resource CD-ROM
Assessment Program: *Quiz, pp. 41–42; Teacher and Student Resources, pp. 115–144*
Assessment CD-ROM
Transparencies
The Heinle Newbury House Dictionary/CD-ROM
Web site: http://visions.heinle.com

The Voyage of the Lucky Dragon

an excerpt from a novel
by Jack Bennett

Objectives

Reading Paraphrase to recall information as you read an excerpt from a novel.

Listening and Speaking Have a debate.

Grammar Identify subject and object pronouns.

Writing Write to solve a problem.

Content Social Studies: Describe countries on a map.

Objectives

Preview Have a student read the objectives.
Ask: What is a debate?

Use Prior Knowledge

Talk About Problems

Teacher Resource Book: *Cluster Map, p. 38*

Teacher think aloud Give examples from your own life. *Say: I once had a problem getting along with a good friend in college. She always wanted to borrow things, but she didn't return them. We resolved it by making an agreement. We agreed that I would only lend her one item at a time. She couldn't borrow another item until she returned the last one she had borrowed from me.*

Use Prior Knowledge

Talk About Problems

We must often face problems in our lives. Sometimes we can resolve our problems. Sometimes we cannot. Trying to resolve problems helps us learn and grow.

1. Think about a problem in your life that you had to resolve. Use these questions to help you brainstorm:
   a. Did you ever have problems getting used to a new place?
   b. Did you ever have problems getting along with a friend?
   c. Did you ever have problems understanding schoolwork?
2. Use a Cluster Map to organize your notes.

3. Work with a partner to compare and contrast your problems. Interpret your partner's verbal and non-verbal messages (what he or she says and does).

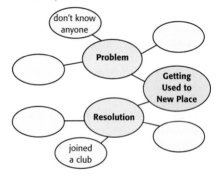

MULTI-LEVEL OPTIONS *Build Vocabulary*

Newcomer Write on the board: *sad, puzzled,* and *cheerful.* Model a facial expression for each. Point and *ask: How do you look when you're sad? How do you look when you feel happy or cheerful?* Have students draw pictures of themselves with facial expressions for each word.

Beginning Have students draw pictures of themselves with facial expressions for each word. Then ask them to work in pairs to create captions for the pictures and take turns acting out each word.

Intermediate Have students work in groups with a dictionary to create a chart of emotion words. Tell them to list any synonyms or antonyms in separate columns. Have students alternate turns presenting their work to the class.

Advanced Assign new vocabulary words and have students create a sentence for their word and sentences for any synonyms or antonyms as well. Have each present their sentences to the class.

Build Background

Vietnam

Vietnam is a country in Southeast Asia. For many years Vietnam was divided into North Vietnam and South Vietnam. North Vietnam had a communist government. South Vietnam did not have a communist government.

The communists wanted to control both parts of Vietnam. This led to a war between North Vietnam and South Vietnam. A war within a country is called a **civil war.** The war ended in the 1970s. North Vietnam and South Vietnam became one country with a communist government.

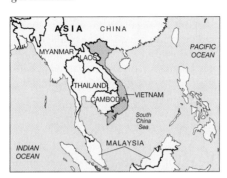

Content Connection
In a **communist** country, the government usually owns all of the land and businesses.

Build Vocabulary

Learn Words Related to Emotions

The words below relate to **emotions** (feelings). Read the words and their definitions. Then complete each sentence with the correct word. Write in your Personal Dictionary.

shocked felt a lot of surprise

anxiously in a worried way

delighted very happy, pleased

mournfully in a very sad way

guilty a feeling of having done something wrong

1. "My dog ran away," he said _____ .
2. Sasha was _____ to get a new bike.
3. I wish I had never said those hurtful words. I felt _____ .
4. He never thought this would happen. He was _____ .
5. Juan did not study yesterday. He took the test _____ .

Personal Dictionary

Activity Book p. 89

Student CD-ROM

Chapter 2   The Voyage of the Lucky Dragon   **163**

Content Connection
The Arts

Build Vocabulary Have students of mixed language abilities work in groups to each choose a piece of music. Tell them to brainstorm a short description of how the music makes them feel. Instruct them to use as many emotion words as necessary. Have the groups present both the music and their descriptions.

Learning Styles
Mathematical

Build Background Have students research and chart the populations of the following countries in 1970 and now: Vietnam, Thailand, Cambodia, Laos, and Myanmar. Then ask them to calculate the change in population numbers.

Build Background

Vietnam

Teacher Resource Book: *Know/Want to Know/Learned Chart (KWL), p. 42*

1. **Use a map** Have students locate Vietnam and identify the nearby countries on the map.
2. **Do a KWL chart** Have students help you fill in the first two columns of a KWL chart on the board. Complete the chart as you do the chapter.
3. **Content Connection** The South Vietnamese government collapsed in 1975. In 1976, the two Vietnams became the Socialist Republic of Vietnam.

Build Vocabulary

Learn Words About Emotions

Teacher Resource Book: *Personal Dictionary, p. 63*

1. **Locate derivations of words** Point out to students that these words are derivations of other words; for example, **shocked** is a derivative of **shock.** Many dictionaries (and other sources such as online dictionaries, CD-ROMS, and glossaries) list the derivations, not the derivatives.
2. **Use words related to emotions** Have students finish sentences with their own words. On the board, write: *I was shocked/delighted when _____. I felt guilty when _____. I waited anxiously because _____. I walked mournfully because _____.*
3. **Reading selection vocabulary** You may want to introduce the glossed words in the reading selection before students begin reading. Key words: *authority, abolished, hush, traitors, declared, communists.* Instruct students to write the words with correct spelling and their definitions in their Personal Dictionaries. Have them pronounce each word and divide it into syllables.
4. **Multi-level options** See MULTI-LEVEL OPTIONS on p. 162.

Answers
1. mournfully 2. delighted 3. guilty 4. shocked
5. anxiously

ASSESS

Say: Write two sentences about Vietnam.

Text Structure

Historical Fiction

1. **Compare genres** *Ask: What are some of the features of historical fiction?* (setting: place and time are real; characters: real or made up; plot: made-up events and real historical events) *Can historical fiction stories include imaginary events?* (yes) *Do they sometimes include fictional characters?* (yes)

2. **Multi-level options** See MULTI-LEVEL OPTIONS below.

Reading Strategy

Paraphrase to Recall Information

Paraphrase Have groups read the text from the Reading Selection example and close their books. Ask them to record their paraphrases on the board. Compare their versions with the text. Point out that there are different ways to paraphrase something, but the important thing is to recall the facts. Underline the facts on the board.

✓ ASSESS

Ask: When is it helpful to use paraphrasing? In which classes could this strategy be useful?

Text Structure

Historical Fiction

"The Voyage of the Lucky Dragon" is **historical fiction.** Historical fiction is a made-up story that is set during a real time in history. Look at the features of historical fiction in the chart.

Look for details that tell you about the setting of the story. Use the **prologue** (introduction) to help you learn about background events in history. Analyze the story plot to see the characters' problems and how they resolve them.

Historical Fiction	
Setting	The story is set in a real place and time.
Characters	The characters may be made-up. Some characters may also be real people.
Plot (Series of Events)	Historical fiction stories combine made-up events with events that really happened.

Student CD-ROM

Reading Strategy

Paraphrase to Recall Information

When you tell a part of a reading selection in your own words, you **paraphrase.** This can help you recall what you have read. Read this example:

Text from the Reading Selection:
She came back in a few seconds, her face pale. "Father," she said. "Please come. There's a—a young man to see you. He's strange—"

Paraphrase:
She came back right away. She looked scared. She asked her father to come because there was a young man who wanted to see him. She thought he looked odd.

When you paraphrase, follow these steps:

1. Read the text several times until you understand it.
2. Close your book.
3. Write your paraphrase.
4. Check your paraphrase against the text. Revise your paraphrase to include all of the important information.

As you read or listen to "The Voyage of the Lucky Dragon," paraphrase some of the paragraphs.

Student CD-ROM

164 Unit 3 Journeys

MULTI-LEVEL OPTIONS *Text Structure*

Newcomer Choose a work of historical fiction that students know, such as *Sarah, Plain and Tall*. Write the title on the board. *Ask: Was Sarah a real person?* (no) *Is the Kansas prairie a real place?* (yes) Have students draw a character from another such book.

Beginning Have students create a two-column chart with the headings *real* and *fictional*. Have them enter the real things (places and events) and the fictional elements (characters) in the correct columns.

Intermediate Have students work in groups to choose two works of historical fiction and one of nonfiction. Instruct them to write a sentence or two about each, describing the fictional and nonfictional elements. Have each group present their work.

Advanced Tell student pairs to create a brief story with fictional characters in a historical setting. Have pairs take turns presenting their stories to the class.

The Voyage of the Lucky Dragon

an excerpt from a novel
by Jack Bennett

165

Reading Selection Materials
Audio: *Unit 3, Chapter 2; CD 2, Track 2*
Teacher Resource Book: *Reading Summary, pp. 87–88*
Transparencies: *#37, Reading Summary*

Suggestions for Using Reading Summary

- Introduce new vocabulary or cognates.
- Cut the summary into strips, or jumble the sentences on an overhead transparency. Students put the sentences in order.
- Practice the reading strategy.
- Students read aloud or with a partner.
- Students paraphrase the summary.
- Students do a cloze activity.
- Students create a visual or graphic organizer, such as a timeline or storyboard, to illustrate the summary.
- Students paraphrase the summary.

Preview the Selection

1. **Interpret the image** Have students describe the photo. *Say: This is a photo of Ho Chi Minh City in the 1970s. It used to be called Saigon.*
2. **Connect to theme** Remind students that the unit theme is *journeys.* *Ask: Imagine that you took a journey to Vietnam. How would you go there? How long do you think it would take? What would you like to see?*

Cultural Connection

Ask students to research some cultural facts about Vietnam, such as holidays, climate, typical foods, and how to say a few common words such as *mother, father, sun, water,* or *summer.* If there is a local Vietnamese community, tell students to get the information locally. Have them put it in chart form and present their work.

Learning Styles
Intrapersonal

Ask: How would you prepare yourself for life in another country? What would the three hardest and easiest things be? Have students write or draw their answers in their Reading Logs.

Teacher Resource Book: *Reading Log, p. 64*

Read the Selection

1. **Use illustrations to predict** Have students look at the young man shown on pp. 166–167. *Ask: How would you describe this man? Is he friendly?* (no) *What do you think he might be telling the family?* (bad news about their shop)

2. **Read the prologue** Have a volunteer read the prologue. *Ask: Who is the young man?* (He works for the new government of Vietnam.)

3. **Read aloud** Play the audio. Then have students take turns reading the text aloud.

4. **Check comprehension** *Ask: What was the family doing when the man arrived?* (having supper) *Who went out to serve him?* (Ly)

Sample Answer to Guide Question
Phan Thi Chi's family was having supper in the back room of their store when a young man interrupted them.

See Teacher Edition pp. 434–436 for a list of English-Spanish cognates in the reading selection.

Audio
CD 2, Tr. 2

Prologue

This story is about a family in Vietnam. The time of the story is the late 1970s. The Vietnam War has ended. The communists have taken control of the government. They have also taken control of all the businesses in Vietnam.

When this reading begins, the family receives a visitor. This visitor is a young man who works for the new government in Vietnam.

> **Paraphrase to Recall Information**
>
> Paraphrase this paragraph.

1 There was no letter from Phan Thi Chi's father the next day. But that evening, while the whole family was having supper around the big table in the back room, a young man came into the shop. He **rapped rudely** on the counter and Ly ran out to serve him.

2 She came back in a few seconds, her face **pale.** "Father," she said. "Please come. There's a—a young man to see you. He's strange—"

3 Phan Thi Chi and his wife got up **hastily,** their food unfinished. Ah Soong, Uncle Tan and Quan and Ly exchanged uneasy glances. Then, with one accord, they crowded into the narrow, short passage between the back room and the shop.

rapped struck or hit	**pale** lacking color
rudely without manners	**hastily** quickly

MULTI-LEVEL OPTIONS *Read the Selection*

Newcomer Play the audio, pausing between paragraphs. Show students the illustrations as you play the audio. *Ask: Is the girl's name Ly?* (yes) *Is Ly's father a soldier?* (no) *Is he a shopkeeper?* (yes)

Beginning Read the Reading Summary aloud. Do a paired reading of the story. *Ask: Where does this story take place?* (in Vietnam) *Does it take place now or in the 1970s?* (the 1970s) *Who is the young man?* (a government official) *Is he a friend of the family or not?* (He isn't a friend.)

Intermediate Have students do a paired reading. *Ask: What time of day did the young man arrive?* (in the evening) *Who does the young man work for?* (the government) *When was the government decree issued?* (March 23)

Advanced Have students do a partner read aloud. Have pairs read alternate paragraphs. *Ask: What are the young man's feelings about the family?* (He feels contempt.) *Why do you think he feels that way?* (because having a shop is "bourgeois")

Paraphrase to Recall Information

Paraphrase this paragraph.

4   The strange young man was quietly dressed in a white short-sleeved shirt, black trousers and black shoes. He was about twenty-two or twenty-three; no older. His young face held **authority** and, as he glanced around the little shop, a cold **contempt.** He put back in his pocket a card he had just showed Phan Thi Chi and glanced at the expectant faces crowding the passage.

5   "Family?" he asked.

6   "Yes," said Phan Thi Chi. After all, he thought, **defensively,** Ah Soong is family.

7   The young man unfolded a sheet of typewritten paper.

8   "You are Phan Thi Chi, shopkeeper, of thirteen Bach Dang, Gia Dinh?"

9   "Yes."

10   "You have heard of the government **decree** of March twenty-three?"

11   "It is only March twenty-four today and I have heard no news all day."

12   "From March twenty-three—that is yesterday—all trading and business operations by **bourgeois** elements of the population are **abolished.** Do you know what that means?"

---

authority   power to command
contempt   disfavor
defensively   protectively

decree   an official order
bourgeois   middle class
abolished   stopped

Chapter 2   The Voyage of the Lucky Dragon   **167**

Read the Selection

1. **Reciprocal reading**   Play the audio. On the board, write: *Who, What, Where, When, How, Why.* Have volunteers ask the class questions about page 167.

2. **Discuss connotative meaning**   Have students look up *bourgeois* in the dictionary and read the definitions and examples aloud. Point out that the meaning in the dictionary is the denotative meaning. *Ask: Does this sound like a positive or negative word?* (negative) *Do you think the young man said this to insult the family?* (yes) Point out that the negative meaning is the word's connotative meaning.

3. **Locate derivations using dictionaries**   Have students look at these glossed words and determine what words they are derived from: *rapped, rudely, hastily, defensively, abolished.* Have students check the derivations in a print, online, or CD-ROM dictionary.

4. **Multi-level options**   See MULTI-LEVEL OPTIONS on p. 166.

Sample Answer to Guide Question
The young man wore simple clothes and seemed to look down on the store. He showed Phan Thi Chi a card and looked at his family in the passage.

---

9 Punctuation

Hyphens with numbers

Tell students that when two-word numbers are spelled out, the words are always connected with a hyphen. On the board, write: *thirty-three.* Underline the two number words. Circle the hyphen. Have students look over the reading selection to find other examples. (paragraph 4: twenty-two, twenty-three; paragraph 11: twenty-four; paragraphs 10, 12: twenty-three)

Apply   Write these numerals on the board: 3, 12, 27, 49 and have students pronounce each one. *Ask: Which are the two-word numbers?* (27, 49) Write them out without the hyphens and have students correct the errors.

Read the Selection

1. **Use art to understand a story** Have students look at the art and discuss the ages and relationships between the family members. *Ask: How do you think the family feels to receive the news?*

2. **Paired reading** Read the selection aloud. Then have students read in pairs.

3. **Make inferences** Ask students to make inferences about the story and support their inferences with details. Model an example. *Say: I can infer that the family is poor because they are dressed in simple clothes and live together in a small area. What do you think the man's opinion of the family is? Do you think the family understood how serious the situation was? Why?*

Sample Answer to Guide Question
When the father asked about the family, everything was very quiet, deadly quiet. They were all waiting for an answer from the young man.

13   "Yes," said Phan Thi Chi quietly. "It means you take my shop away from me."

14   "That is right. This shop is now owned by the state. You will remain in control of it until the state sends a manager to take over."

15   "How do I and my family live?"

16   There was suddenly a deadly **hush** in the room: it was as though everyone had stopped breathing. Out in the street a dog barked suddenly. It seemed very loud. The young man read from his piece of paper:

Paraphrase to Recall Information

Paraphrase this paragraph.

17   "Phan Thi Chi will be sent to a re-education camp in Ho Chi Minh City. After showing progress, he will be sent to a New Economic Zone in An Gian Province—"

18   "I know nothing about farming," said Phan Thi Chi.

19   The young man **shrugged.** "You'll learn. It will be part of your re-education."

20   "And my family?"

21   "Your wife will go to a re-education centre at Long Tanh. Your children will be sent to a New Economic Zone at Le Minh Xuan."

22   "Will we be allowed to visit each other? To write?"

---

hush   silence   **shrugged**   raised one's shoulders to express doubt

168   Unit 3   Journeys

MULTI-LEVEL OPTIONS *Read the Selection*

Newcomer *Ask: Is the government going to take the father's shop away?* (yes) *Is the government going to pay for the shop?* (no) *Is Phan Thi Chi going to be sent away from his family?* (yes)

Beginning *Ask: Where is the father going?* (to a re-education camp) *What will they teach him there?* (to be a farmer) *Can his family go with him?* (No, they can't go with him.)

Intermediate *Ask: Why do they want to send the father to a re-education camp?* (to teach him to be a farmer) *Why has the government taken away the father's shop?* (because the government owns everything) *Where will Ly's mother be sent?* (to a different re-education camp)

Advanced *Ask: How do you think Uncle Tan lost his leg?* (fighting against the communist soldiers) *What shows you how the young man feels about Uncle Tan?* (He compares him to traitors.)

23   The young man shrugged again.

24   "I don't know. That depends on the **authorities,** I suppose."

25   Phan Thi Chi felt himself growing angry despite the cold fear that gripped him.

Paraphrase to Recall Information

Paraphrase this paragraph.

26   "What about the rest of my family?" He pointed to Ah Soong, her face **inscrutable,** to Aunt Binh and Uncle Tan. Uncle Tan balanced on his **crutch,** his eyes on the young man.

27   The young man consulted his paper again.

28   "I have no instructions about these people," he said. He looked at Uncle Tan.

29   "Where did you lose your leg?"

30   "It's buried at Hue."

31   "With a lot of Americans and **traitors,**" said the young man.

32   Uncle Tan just stared at him. The young man folded his paper and put it in his pocket.

33   "Well, I have no instructions about you, one-leg. Nor about these two ladies—" he nodded at Ah Soong and Aunt Binh.

authorities those in control	**crutch** a tool to help someone walk
inscrutable difficult to understand	**traitors** people who betray their country

Chapter 2   The Voyage of the Lucky Dragon   **169**

Read the Selection

1. **Understand historical context**   *Say: During the Vietnam War, the North Vietnamese fought the South Vietnamese for control over the country. The South Vietnamese were helped by the United States. In 1973, the Americans left. But the war between north and south continued. Eventually, the North Vietnamese took over the country, and the South Vietnamese lost power. The North Vietnamese often made life difficult for people who had fought with the South Vietnamese and the Americans. Do you think this family was with the South Vietnamese?* (yes) *Why?*

2. **Read dramatically**   Play the audio. Ask volunteers to read the spoken parts of the young man and Phan Thi Chi. Direct them to reflect the characters and tone when they read and to include pauses and silences.

3. **Multi-level options**   See MULTI-LEVEL OPTIONS on p. 168.

Sample Answer to Guide Question
Phan Thi Chi asked about the fate of his other family members.

   ## Spelling

Nouns ending in *-tion*

On the board, write: *preparation.* Underline the *-tion* ending. Explain that many nouns that began as verbs end in *-tion* (e.g., *prepare/preparation; educate/education*). Have student pairs look through the reading selection to find nouns ending in *-tion.* (paragraphs 17, 19, 21: *re-education;* paragraphs 28, 33: *instructions*)

Apply   Have student groups generate as many nouns as possible with *-tion* endings. Have the groups exchange lists and then present them to the class.

Read the Selection

Reciprocal reading Have students read silently. Then have volunteers take turns reading aloud and asking the class questions about the content.

Sample Answer to Guide Question
The young man told Phan Thi Chi that someone from the government would probably contact him about his other family members. He also said he could continue to sell merchandise in his store until the government takes control of it, except items the government won't allow.

> **Paraphrase to Recall Information**
>
> Paraphrase this paragraph.

34   "No doubt you will hear from the authorities soon enough." He turned to the **ashen-faced** Phan Thi Chi. "You may operate your shop until the state official arrives. That may take a few days or a week. You must not sell any goods which have been **declared** subject to state control—"

35   "How do I know what they are?"

36   "You must find out. Don't ask me how. But you must find out. Go to the Public Security Bureau. It is a serious offense to trade in state-controlled goods, you know."

37   And then he was gone, leaving a shocked silence which Phan Thi Chi was the first to break.

38   "Shut the door," he said to his wife. "Quan, shut the back door. Lock it. Then all come upstairs, to the roof. Nobody can hear us there."

39   When they were all on the roof, **dodging** Ah Soong's washing, he told them of his plan to escape to Rach Gia, and start a new life on his old father's boat. When he had finished talking, he watched their faces anxiously.

40   Quan was the first to speak. To his father's **relief,** he was delighted. Quan was a strange boy sometimes, with his own ideas.

ashen-faced   gray, gloomy
declared   said out loud

dodging   avoiding
relief   ease from discomfort

MULTI-LEVEL OPTIONS *Read the Selection*

Newcomer *Ask: Is the family happy about the young man's visit?* (no) *Can the father sell everything in his shop?* (no) *Can he sell some things?* (yes)

Beginning *Ask: What is the son's name?* (Quan) *Where does the family go to talk?* (to the roof) *Who has an escape plan?* (the father)

Intermediate *Ask: How does the family react to the news?* (They are shocked.) *Where are they going to escape to?* (to a small village) *What's the name of the village?* (Rach Gia)

Advanced *Ask: How will the family be able to stay together?* (by escaping to Rach Gia) *Why do you think they choose Rach Gia?* (because it's the father's hometown) *How do the different family members feel about moving?* (Quan is happy; Ly is suspicious; Aunt Binh is sad.)

41   "When do we go?" was all he said. "I'd love to be a fisherman—"

42   "You mustn't forget your schoolwork," said his mother. "There'll be a school at Rach Gia, you know—"

43   "Not like the one here, I hope," said Ly, **wrinkling** her nose.

44   "Things will be different in Rach Gia," their father promised them. "It's a little village. People are different down there."

45   "If I like working on the boat, I might become a marine engineer," said Quan. "Eh, mother? I could see the world!"

46   "I don't like the sea," said Aunt Binh **mournfully.** "I went out on a junk at Da Nang. I got sick. And boat people aren't like us. But don't worry about me, please. I know I have to do as I'm told."

47   "No you don't," said Phan Thi Chi rather **cruelly.** "You can always go to one of their New Economic Zones, and learn to be a rice-farmer."

48   Aunt Binh turned her head away, sniffling quietly, and Phan Thi Chi felt guilty.

> **Paraphrase to Recall Information**
>
> Paraphrase this paragraph.

---

wrinkling   folding or shrinking
mournfully   sadly

cruelly   in a mean way

Chapter 2   The Voyage of the Lucky Dragon   **171**

Read the Selection

1. **Reciprocal reading**   Have students read silently. Then have volunteers take turns reading aloud and asking the class questions about the content.
2. **Discuss characters' reactions**   Have students work in small groups. Ask them to make a list of the family members and note how each one probably feels about leaving their home for a small village.
3. **Multi-level options**   See MULTI-LEVEL OPTIONS on p. 170.

Sample Answer to Guide Question
Aunt Binh doesn't like the sea because she got seasick once, and she thinks people who live on boats are different. But she knows that she doesn't have a choice.

 Spelling

Adverbs ending in -ly

Write on the board: _How does Ramon speak? He speaks _____. **Say:** Many adverbs answer the question about_ how _something is done._ Write _slowly,_ underlining the _-ly_ part of the adverb. **Say:** Many adverbs that tell how end in -ly. Have student groups review the reading selection to find all the _-ly_ adverbs. (paragraph 39: anxiously; paragraph 46: mournfully; paragraph 48: quietly)

Apply   Write on the board: _quickly, slowly, shyly, loudly, carefully, quietly._ Have groups use these adverbs to create several sentences describing how someone does something.

Read the Selection

1. **Shared reading** Play the audio. Have students join in for dialogue.
2. **Identify conflict** Ask students to define *conflict* in their own words. *Ask: Who is the conflict between?* (Phan Thi Chi and Ah Soong) *Does Phan Thi Chi want Ah Soong to come with them to Rach Gia?* (no) *Why not?* (He says that it could be a rough life and that they aren't sure if there will be room for all of them.) *Where does Phan Thi Chi think Ah Soong will go?* (to China) *Why doesn't she want to go to China?* (She hasn't been there in 50 years, she hasn't written to her family, and she doesn't like the communists.)

Sample Answer to Guide Question
Ah Soong doesn't want to return to China because she has lost touch with her family there and the communists now control China.

49   "Well, if that is decided then, I'd better go and get some food ready for the trip," said Ah Soong, as though Phan Thi Chi had announced that a bus was waiting to **whisk** them to Rach Gia on the instant.

50   Phan Thi Chi cleared his throat **nervously** and his wife glanced at him with a sly smile.

51   "Ah, well," said Phan Thi Chi, and the old woman looked at him sharply.

52   "We—ah, I, had thought, Ah Soong, that, ah, you—well, it could be a rough life down at Rach Gia and ah, well, we don't know what sort of house we will find, you know, and so—"

53   "And so you thought I'd go back to China! At my age! After nearly half a **century** in Vietnam! What nonsense!"

54   "Now just listen, Ah Soong," said Phan Thi Chi nervously, rolling a desperate eye at his wife, who was **gazing steadfastly** over the rooftops as though entranced by some sight in the general direction of the National Assembly Building.

Paraphrase to Recall Information

Paraphrase this paragraph.

55   "Besides," said Ah Soong, "besides the fact that I haven't written to my family in China for years, have you forgotten who runs the country now? When I left it was the Kuomintang, and now it is the **communists.** Well, I didn't like the Kuomintang when I was a girl in China, and I don't like what I've seen of the Vietnamese communists. Why should the Chinese communists be different? Or better? No, I'm coming with you. I have some money of my own.

---

whisk   take away
nervously   uneasily, uncomfortably
century   a time period of 100 years
gazing   staring

steadfastly   steadily
communists   members of the Communist Party; a social system marked by the common ownership of goods and services

172   Unit 3   Journeys

MULTI-LEVEL OPTIONS *Read the Selection*

Newcomer *Ask: Is Ah Soong Vietnamese?* (no) *Is she Chinese?* (yes) *Is Ah Soong going with the family to Rach Gia?* (yes)

Beginning *Ask: What country does Ah Soong come from?* (China) *About how long has she been in Vietnam?* (half a century) *Does the father expect her to come with them or go back to China?* (go back to China)

Intermediate *Ask: Why doesn't Ah Soong want to go back to China?* (because she has been in Vietnam a long time) *Are the Kuomintang the same as the communists?* (no) *Why does Ah Soong want to go with the family?* (because they are her family)

Advanced *Ask: Why do you think the father doesn't want Ah Soong to come along?* (because she may be too old for the rough life in the village) *About how old do you think Ah Soong is?* (about 60) *Why do you think so?* (She was a girl when she left China and has been in Vietnam almost 50 years.)

Besides—" and the old woman drew herself up and glanced **scathingly** at the rest of the family, "you couldn't get on without me! Now I have things to do." And she shuffled off downstairs, leaving Phan Thi Chi embarrassed behind a flapping wet sheet.

Paraphrase to Recall Information

Paraphrase paragraphs 57–60.

56   "I told you," said Ly's mother after a short silence.

57   "Are you coming, Uncle Tan?" asked Quan.

58   Uncle Tan twirled his crutch.

59   "I saw a movie about a one-legged **pirate** once," he said with a grin. "And he had only one eye, too. Yes I'm coming."

60   So it was decided.

---

scathingly extremely harshly   **pirate** one who robs at sea

About the Author

Jack Bennett

Jack Bennett has traveled all over the world writing for magazines and newspapers. He has also written books for adults and children. He wrote a novel for young adults called *The Lieutenant.*

➤ How do you think Jack Bennett got the information he needed to write this story? Why do you think he wrote it?

Chapter 2 The Voyage of the Lucky Dragon   **173**

A   Capitalization

Nations and nationalities

Write on the board: *mexico* and *Mexico.* *Ask: Which is correct?* (Mexico) *Names of countries and nationalities also start with capitals.* Write: *America/American.* Have students find the country and nationality names in paragraph 53 (China, Vietnam) and paragraph 55 (Chinese, Vietnamese).

Apply Have students brainstorm a list of countries and nationalities. Go over correct capitalization as a group.

Evaluate Your Reading Strategy

Paraphrase to Recall Information *Say: You have practiced an important reading strategy. Now you can decide how well you have done. Does this statement describe how you read?*

When I read, I stop often to tell parts of the reading selection in my own words so I can remember the text. Paraphrasing helps me to recall what I read.

Read the Selection

1. **Paired reading** Play the audio. Then have students practice reading aloud in pairs.
2. **Locate derivations using dictionaries** Have students look at these glossed words and determine what words they are derived from: *nervously, gazing, steadfastly, scathingly.* Have students check the derivations in a print, online, or CD-ROM dictionary.
3. **Multi-level options** See MULTI-LEVEL OPTIONS on p. 172.

Sample Answer to Guide Question
When asked if he was going to Rach Gia, Uncle Tan mentioned a movie that had a pirate with one leg and said he would join them.

About the Author

Analyze facts about the author

Ask: Do you think the Vietnam War affected his life? (Yes. He is still writing about it.)

Answers
Sample answers: He probably got his information from historical accounts and from talking with people who lived in Vietnam during this time. He wrote the story to inform people about what it was like in Vietnam.

Across Selections

Say: "Island of the Blue Dolphins" is based on a true story, and "The Voyage of the Lucky Dragon" is historical fiction. Ask students to work in pairs to find similarities between these two stories. (Settings are in real places and times; events are based on real incidents, but details were made up or changed for the sake of the story.)

Spelling, Punctuation, Capitalization

After the Reading Comprehension section, students will practice spelling, punctuation, and capitalization in the Activity Book.

Beyond the Reading

Reading Comprehension

Question-Answer Relationships

Sample Answers

1. in Vietnam, in Gia Dinh
2. March 23
3. Rach Gia, so the family can stay together
4. a few days or a week
5. They wanted to have control over stores and merchandise.
6. They decide to flee to Rach Gia. I think this is the best resolution since they can be together and still stay in their country.
7. The young man doesn't care that he is disrupting Phan Thi Chi's life and doesn't have any respect for him or his concerns. When Phan Thi Chi asks him questions, he shrugs.
8. He seems interested in the adventure and in a different future.
9. He might be put in jail or be sent away to a camp.
10. I don't think it will be easy because it sounds like a small village, and they will have nothing. They will have to leave everything behind.

Build Reading Fluency

Read Silently and Aloud

| Assessment Program: *Reading Fluency Chart, p. 116*

When students have completed the reading fluency activity, record their progress in the Reading Fluency Chart.

Reading Comprehension

Question-Answer Relationships (QAR)

"Right There" Questions

1. **Recall Facts** Where does the story take place?
2. **Recall Facts** On what day is Phan Thi Chi supposed to hand over his shop?
3. **Recall Facts** What city does Phan Thi Chi plan to take his family to? Why?

"Think and Search" Questions

4. **Explain** How long will it be before the government manager will take over?
5. **Analyze Plot** Why would the government want to take Phan Thi Chi's shop?
6. **Recognize and Analyze Problem Resolution** How does the family resolve their problem? Do you think this is the best resolution? Explain.

"Author and You" Questions

7. **Recognize Character Traits** How do you think the young man feels about telling Phan Thi Chi his shop will be taken from him? What text evidence do you find?
8. **Recognize Character Traits** Why is Quan excited about leaving?

"On Your Own" Questions

9. **Predict** What do you think might happen to Phan Thi Chi if he does not turn over his shop?
10. **Predict** Do you think life will be easy for the family in Rach Gia? Why?

Activity Book
p. 90

Student
CD-ROM

Build Reading Fluency

Read Silently and Aloud

Reading silently for practice then reading aloud helps you read with expression and understanding.

1. Listen to the audio recording of "The Voyage of the Lucky Dragon."
2. Follow along with the reading on page 166.
3. Read silently paragraphs 1–3 two times.
4. With a partner read aloud.
5. Your partner will time you reading aloud.

MULTI-LEVEL OPTIONS *Elements of Literature*

Newcomer On the board, write: *Mood: excited, sad, angry, afraid.* Clarify meaning by miming each mood. Replay the audio. Ask newcomers to work in groups and choose a mood word. Have them act out a scene in the story or the character that shows that mood.

Beginning Write on the board: *Mood: annoyed, sad, angry, afraid.* Replay the audio. Have students draw pictures of scenes or the character that show each mood. Have students work in groups to write captions for the pictures. (*Examples:* The young man is annoyed. The father is angry.)

Intermediate Have students work in pairs to create a chart of mood words. Instruct them to put the name of the character who demonstrates this mood and/or the paragraph number that has that mood under the correct heading.

Advanced Have pairs isolate the words in each paragraph that reveal its mood. Then tell them to create their own sentences with those words. Have pairs exchange and then revise the sentences.

Listen, Speak, Interact

Have a Debate

When people have a **debate,** they give arguments to support different opinions. When you debate, you do not always agree with the opinions you are arguing for.

1. Work in a group of four. Divide into two sides:

   Side 1: Argue that Phan Thi Chi and his family should leave their home.
   Side 2: Argue that Phan Thi Chi and his family should stay at their home.

2. Each side lists reasons—with evidence, elaborations, and examples—to support their argument on note cards.
3. Present your debate to the class. One debater from Side 1 presents one or two arguments. Then one debater from Side 2 speaks. Then the other debater from Side 1 gives more arguments. Finally the other debater from Side 2 speaks.
4. As a class, analyze the debates. How believable and persuasive were the debaters?

Elements of Literature

Recognize Mood

Authors use words to create a **mood.** A mood is a feeling that the reader gets from the text. Happiness, sadness, and anger are examples of mood.

> There was suddenly a deadly hush in the room: it was as though everyone had stopped breathing.

These sentences create a mood of **suspense.** Suspense is a feeling of fear and nervousness from not knowing what will happen next. The words *suddenly* and *deadly hush* create this mood.

1. Match each sentence with the mood it creates.

   | happiness   anger   sadness |

   a. Phan Thi Chi felt himself growing angry.
   b. Quan was the first to speak. To his father's relief, he was delighted.
   c. Aunt Binh turned her head away, sniffling quietly, and Phan Thi Chi felt guilty.

2. With a partner, discuss how these moods add to the effect of the text. Do you understand the characters and the story better because of the moods?

Activity Book
p. 91

Student
CD-ROM

Chapter 2   The Voyage of the Lucky Dragon   **175**

Listen, Speak, Interact

Have a Debate

1. **Discuss reasons to support arguments** Before students work in groups, have a general discussion about some of the reasons for each position. List key words on the board.
2. **Newcomers** Work with these students separately, helping them list reasons to stay or leave.

Elements of Literature

Recognize Mood

1. **Discuss mood** Discuss with students how the mood in the story could be different. *Ask: When the family went up to the roof, how would the mood be different if Quan started crying? When the young man spoke to Phan Thi Chi, how would the mood be different if the father had spoken very angrily to the young man? Or if the young man had been very polite?*
2. **Multi-level options** See MULTI-LEVEL OPTIONS on p. 174.

Answers
1. a. anger b. happiness c. sadness

 **ASSESS**

Have pairs work together to write a description of the mood of the story.

Content Connection
Social Studies

Have students work in groups to use encyclopedias, atlases, and the Internet to find out facts about these Asian countries: Vietnam, China, Thailand, Myanmar, Cambodia, and Laos. Have each group make a chart showing the language, country size, major bodies of water, export items, and other facts. Then have the groups compare and revise their charts.

Learning Styles
Interpersonal

Have students interview one another about how they would react if they were in the same situation as the family in the story. Students of limited language proficiency can draw their responses. Help the groups organize their material into chart form.

Word Study

Analyze the Prefix *un-*

Use words with the prefix *un-* Have students find words in the dictionary beginning with the prefix. Have them write common ones on the board and then make up sentences with the new words.

Answers

Chart top to bottom: unhappy, sad; untrue, false; uncommon, different

Grammar Focus

Identify Subject and Object Pronouns

Review parts of speech Write on the board: *Maria gave it to Will. Sarah called her brothers. The boy called his mother.* Have students come to the board and substitute subject and object pronouns. (She gave it to him. She called them. He called her.)

Answers

2. **a.** He just stared at her. **b.** I got sick. **c.** You will remain in control of it.

ASSESS

Have students work in small groups to list as many words beginning with *un-* as they can in three minutes.

Word Study

Analyze the Prefix *un-*

A **prefix** is a group of letters added to the beginning of a word. A prefix often changes the meaning of a root word. You can learn the meaning of a word if you know the meaning of a prefix.

The word **un**finished has the prefix *un-*. This prefix means "not." The root word is *finished*. When the prefix *un-* is added to *finished*, the meaning becomes "not finished" (not done).

Copy and complete the chart in your Personal Dictionary. For the meaning, choose a word from the box above the chart.

false	sad	different

un- +	Word ⇒	New Word	Meaning
un- +	finished ⇒	unfinished	not finished, not done
un- +	happy ⇒		
un- +	true ⇒		
un- +	common ⇒		

Personal Dictionary   The Heinle Newbury House Dictionary   Activity Book p. 92   Student CD-ROM

Grammar Focus

Identify Subject and Object Pronouns

A **pronoun** is a word that is used in place of a noun. *I, you, it,* and *them* are examples of pronouns.

A **subject pronoun** can be used as the subject of a sentence.

An **object pronoun** is used after some verbs or after a preposition.

1. Copy the sentences below on a piece of paper.
2. Underline the subject pronouns and circle the object pronouns.
   a. He just stared at her.
   b. I got sick.
   c. You will remain in control of it.

Subject Pronoun	Object Pronoun
I	me
you	you
he/she/it	him/her/it
we	us
they	them
Examples:	**Examples:**
He lives with Aunt Binh.	Phan Thi Chi lives with *her*.
She walked between Tan and Quan and us.	She walked between *them* and us.

Activity Book pp. 93–94   Student Handbook   Student CD-ROM

MULTI-LEVEL OPTIONS *From Reading to Writing*

Newcomer Tell students to decide if the story will have a happy or sad ending. Have students illustrate their ending and provide key words.

Beginning Write on the board: *Problem: dangerous to stay and to leave.* Have students work in groups and decide whether the story has a happy or sad ending. Have the groups draw a series of events resulting in the ending they have chosen.

Intermediate Have this level work in groups with advanced students. They will select an ending and create sentences to describe the events leading up to the ending.

Advanced Have these students work in groups with intermediate students. Remind them to capitalize words carefully and to use *-ly* adverbs. Have the groups revise their work and explain their reasoning to the class.

From Reading to Writing

Write to Solve a Problem

The family of Phan Thi Chi has a problem. Write how they will solve their problem.

1. Work with a partner. Decide how the story will end.
2. Answer these questions to help you brainstorm:
   a. What happened while the family traveled to Rach Gia?
   b. What happened when the family arrived in Rach Gia?
   c. Was the family happy living in Rach Gia? Why or why not?
3. Write three paragraphs. Make sure your story has a beginning, a middle, and an end.
4. Give your story a title.
5. Be sure that you use subject and object pronouns correctly.
6. Use possessive nouns. Be sure to use the apostrophe correctly.

Activity Book
p. 95

Student
Handbook

Across Content Areas

Describe Countries on a Map

First, look at the map on page 163. Then read this paragraph. Pay attention to the words in bold type.

Thailand is a country in Southeast Asia. It **borders** four other countries, Laos, Cambodia, Myanmar, and Malaysia. Thailand **lies between** Laos **to the north and east,** Cambodia and Malaysia **to the south,** and Myanmar **to the west.** Thailand has a **coast** on the South China Sea.

Now use the map on this page to write a similar paragraph about the state of Georgia.

Activity Book
p. 96

From Reading to Writing

Write to Solve a Problem

1. **Use resources** Bring in library books or find Web sites that show what the land and way of life is like in Vietnam or was like during the 1970s. Discuss with students how the family might have traveled to Rach Gia, what a small village might have looked like, and how people made a living. Write useful vocabulary on the board.
2. **Write collaboratively** Students may wish to write in small groups or pairs. Tell students to illustrate their paragraphs and display their work in the classroom.
3. **Multi-level options** See MULTI-LEVEL OPTIONS on p. 176.

Across Content Areas: Social Studies

Describe Countries on a Map

Review geographical terms Review the following geographical terms by asking students about local geography: *north, south, east, west, coast, ocean, border.* **Ask:** *What state is north of us? Where is the nearest coast? What direction is it from here?*

✔ ASSESS

Have pairs use the new terms to describe the location of their state.

Reteach and Reassess

Text Structure Have students review the reading selection and the definition of historical fiction. Ask them to find and record at least two examples each of real and fictional elements.

Reading Strategy Ask students to paraphrase the information in Build Background.

Elements of Literature Ask students to choose three scenes from the reading selection. Have them describe the mood of each and list the specific words that set that mood.

Reassess Have a student pair alternate reading a scene from the selection aloud. Then have the class identify that scene's mood and describe at least one element that supports their conclusion.

CHAPTER

3

The Time Bike

an excerpt from a
science fiction novel
by Jane Langton

Into the Reading

Chapter Materials

Activity Book: *pp. 97–104*
Audio: *Unit 3, Chapter 3; CD 2, Track 3*
Student Handbook
Student CD-ROM: *Unit 3, Chapter 3*
Teacher Resource Book: *Lesson Plan, Teacher
    Resources, Reading Summary, Activity Book
    Answer Key*
Teacher Resource CD-ROM
Assessment Program: *Quiz, pp. 43–44; Teacher
    and Student Resources, pp. 115–144*
Assessment CD-ROM
Transparencies
The Heinle Newbury House Dictionary/CD-ROM
Web site: http://visions.heinle.com

Objectives

Preview Read the objectives. *Ask: What do you
already know about science fiction? What time
zone are we in?*

Use Prior Knowledge

Think About Gifts

Brainstorm Talk with students about different
occasions for gift giving. *Ask: When do we give
and receive gifts?* (birthday, holiday, graduation,
retirement, anniversary, going away, and so on)

Objectives

Reading Predict as you read an excerpt
from a science fiction novel.

Listening and Speaking Give a
presentation.

Grammar Write using contractions.

Writing Write a description.

Content Social Studies: Learn about time
zones.

Use Prior Knowledge

Think About Gifts

Most of us enjoy getting gifts—things
given to us for a birthday or a special
occasion.

1. Think of gifts that you have received
   or would like to receive. Which
   gifts do you like? Which gifts don't
   you like?
2. Write your answers in a Cluster Map
   like the one here on a piece
   of paper.
3. Share your ideas with a small group.
4. Tell why you like and do not like
   different gifts.

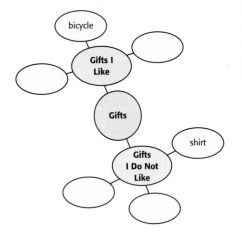

MULTI-LEVEL OPTIONS *Build Vocabulary*

Newcomer Write on the board
and *say: The light flickered and
went out.* Then flick the light
switch on and off several times.
Leave it off for a few seconds.
*Say: Guess the new word's
meaning from the rest of the
sentence and what I did.*

Beginning Write on the board
and *say: The light flickered and
went out. Say: Guess the new
word's meaning from the rest of
the sentence. What words helped
you figure out what* flickered
means? (went out)

Intermediate Have students
work in pairs and use a dictionary
to confirm their ideas once they
have guessed the meaning
through context. Ask pairs to
present their conclusions.

Advanced Have students work
in pairs to choose their own
sentences from a passage. Tell
them to confirm their conclusions
with a dictionary. Then have pairs
exchange papers with others and
work with a thesaurus to find
synonyms for the new words.

Build Background

Time

People use time to tell when things happen. Time tells us when things happened in the past, are happening in the present, and will happen in the future. Clocks and watches help us measure time within a day. They tell us seconds, minutes, and hours. We use calendars to measure days, months, and years.

Sundial

 Content Connection

Long ago, some people used **sundials** to tell time. Sundials were placed outdoors. People told time by looking at the sun's shadow on the sundial.

Build Vocabulary

Use Context to Understand New Words

You can learn the meaning of a word by finding clues in its **context.** The words and sentences that surround a word are its context.

> There was a sound, a kind of whispering murmur.

The words *sound* and *whispering* can help you figure out the meaning of *murmur. Murmur* means a "a low sound."

1. Use context to guess the meaning of the underlined words.

a. In the dark it gleamed a little, the way his old rocket model had glowed in the dark.
b. It sparkles like a diamond.
c. The bike was a failure. It didn't work.
2. Use a dictionary to check if your ideas are correct.
3. Write the words and their meanings in your Personal Dictionary.

Personal Dictionary

The Heinle Newbury House Dictionary

Activity Book p. 97

Student CD-ROM

Chapter 3 The Time Bike **179**

 Community Connection

Build Vocabulary Have students visit places within the community that display information or notices, such as the post office or city hall. Have them keep a log of sentences whose meaning they have figured out through the use of context clues.

Learning Styles
Natural

Build Background Have groups chart the hours of one day *only* by observing the sun's movement. Ask them to start by noting the official times for sunrise and sunset on that date. Then instruct them to divide the day into sections based on the direction of the light. Assign one student to act as timekeeper, checking a watch and noting the exact time. Have the groups compare their chart with the timekeeper's notes.

Build Background

Time

1. **Use prior knowledge** *Ask: What are all of the different ways we measure time? How do we measure very long periods of time?* Discuss with students how many seconds there are in a minute, minutes in an hour, hours in a day, and so on.
2. **Content Connection** The first clocks were probably used in monasteries. The first public clock in Europe was erected in Milan in 1335.

Build Vocabulary

Use Context to Understand New Words

Teacher Resource Book: *Personal Dictionary, p. 63*

1. **Use new vocabulary in sentences** Have volunteers come to the board and write sentences using the new vocabulary. Discuss word choice.
2. **Reading selection vocabulary** You may want to introduce the glossed words in the reading selection before students begin reading. Key words: *crimson, shameful, phosphorescent, speedometer, majestic, dignified.* Instruct students to write the words with correct spelling and their definitions in their Personal Dictionaries. Have them pronounce each word and divide it into syllables.
3. **Multi-level options** See MULTI-LEVEL OPTIONS on p. 178.

Answers
1. **a.** gleamed: glowed **b.** sparkles: shines **c.** failure: doesn't work

 **ASSESS**

Have students list as many words as they can that are associated with time, divisions of time, or ways to measure time. Give them three minutes.

Text Structure

Science Fiction

Identify science fiction shows *Ask: Have you seen any science fiction movies or TV shows? What was the title? What was it about? Do you enjoy science fiction?*

Reading Strategy

Predict

1. **Predict content** Have students review pp. 178–180. *Ask: What topics and ideas are introduced on these pages?* (gifts, time, science fiction) *What can you predict about the reading selection?*
2. **Multi-level options** See MULTI-LEVEL OPTIONS below.

ASSESS

Have students work in pairs to write three features of science fiction.

Text Structure

Science Fiction

In this chapter, you will read **science fiction.** A science fiction story is not a true story. It uses ideas from science and technology to show how life, usually in the future, could be different. Look for these features of science fiction as you read the selection.

Science Fiction	
Characters	the people in the story
Scientific Ideas	imaginary scientific inventions or discoveries that affect the characters
Plot	events that might happen in the future, usually based on scientific ideas

Student
CD-ROM

Reading Strategy

Predict

When you **predict** something, you guess what will happen next. You can use clues in the text to predict what will happen in a story. Read this paragraph:

> It was a hot summer day. Alex had been running. He was tired and thirsty. He saw a water fountain in the park ahead. He slowed down and turned.

What do you think Alex will do next? This is predicting.

Clues	Alex is thirsty. He sees a water fountain in the park.
You Can Predict	Alex will walk to the park. He will drink water from the water fountain.

1. Study the title page of the reading selection on page 181. What does the title tell you? What does the picture tell you?
2. Predict what will happen in the story. Record your answers in your Reading Log.
3. Review what you predicted when you finish the selection. Were you right?

Reading Log

Student
CD-ROM

180 Unit 3 Journeys

MULTI-LEVEL OPTIONS *Reading Strategy*

Newcomer Look at your watch. Erase the board, sit at your desk, close your books, and put away your pencils. *Say: It's three o'clock. Can you predict what will happen?* (The bell will ring. School will be over.)

Beginning Have students draw their story predictions. Then have students work in pairs to explain their reasoning or write a short caption about the drawing.

Intermediate Have students work in pairs to write a prediction and list three reasons for their conclusions.

Advanced Have pairs come up with two likely predictions for the title and picture on p. 181. Have them explain why each prediction is possible and which of the two is more likely.

The Time Bike

an excerpt from a science fiction novel

by Jane Langton

Reading Selection Materials

Audio: *Unit 3, Chapter 3; CD 2, Track 3*
Teacher Resource Book: *Reading Summary, pp. 89–90*
Transparencies: *#38, Reading Summary*

Suggestions for Using Reading Summary

- Introduce new vocabulary or cognates.
- Cut the summary into strips, or jumble the sentences on an overhead transparency. Students put the sentences in order.
- Practice the reading strategy.
- Students read aloud or with a partner.
- Students paraphrase the summary.
- Students do a cloze activity.
- Students create a visual or graphic organizer, such as a timeline or storyboard, to illustrate the summary.
- Students paraphrase the summary.

Preview the Selection

1. **Interpret art** Have students look at the illustration. *Ask: What does this bike look like? What is unusual about it? How is it different from bikes you use? The title of the reading is "The Time Bike." How do you think this might be a "time bike"?*
2. **Connect** *Ask: Do you have a bike? What does it look like? If you had a bike, where would you ride it?* Remind students that the theme of this unit is *journeys. Ask: What kinds of journeys could you take on a bike?*

 Home Connection

Point out that the story is about a special bicycle. Have students tell about or draw their own experiences with bicycles or the experiences of someone they know. Have students mention the size, speed, and color of the bike, how the ride felt, how they liked it, and so on.

Learning Styles
Linguistic

Have students work in small groups. Ask them to use dictionaries to look up the vocabulary words from the selection. Have them note the part of speech of each word and create a chart with categories for each type. Have one member from each group present the chart to the class and, if possible, explain the function of each part of speech.

Read the Selection

1. **Paired reading** Have students read aloud in pairs.
2. **Discuss character's motives** *Ask: Why was Eddy disappointed in the bike from his uncle?* (It was old and out of style.) *Why do you think he hid it under the front hall stairs?* (so no one else would see it) *Did he hide it there so it wouldn't get stolen?* (No, he didn't think anyone would want it.)

Sample Answer to Guide Question
I think he will change his mind because the title of the story suggests that it has some sort of magic.

See Teacher Edition pp. 434–436 for a list of English-Spanish cognates in the reading selection.

Audio
CD 2, Tr. 3

Prologue

This story takes place in Concord, Massachusetts. The main character is an eighth grader named Eddy Hall. The expensive new bike that Eddy gets for his birthday is stolen. He receives another bike from his mysterious uncle, Prince Krishna from India. Eddy is disappointed with this bike. He thinks that it looks old and out of style. However, he soon learns that you cannot always judge something by how it looks.

1   Three days went by, and the bicycle from India was still in the front hall beside the stairs, in the way.

2   "Eddy," said Uncle Freddy, "would you move it? Why not put it on the front porch where you kept the other one? But lock it to the railing this time."

3   So it won't be stolen? Eddy smiled grimly. Who would steal such a dumb old bike? But even so, he didn't put it on the front porch where anybody could see it. He found a perfect hiding place for it, a shadowy **triangular nook** next to the coat closet under the front hall stairs.

4   It was just the right size, and it had a **crimson** velvet curtain on a **drawstring** that hid his skateboard and Uncle Freddy's old golf bag and a croquet set with a couple of broken mallets.

> **Predict**
>
> Eddy doesn't like this bike. Do you think he will change his mind?

triangular like a triangle
nook a small room

crimson red
drawstring a string that moves a curtain

182   Unit 3 Journeys

MULTI-LEVEL OPTIONS *Read the Selection*

Newcomer Play the audio, repeating the prologue at least once. *Ask: Is this Eddy's first bicycle?* (no) *Does he like this one?* (no) *Is the bicycle from India?* (yes)

Beginning Read the Reading Summary aloud. Then do a paired reading. *Ask: Did Eddy like the first bike better than this one?* (yes) *Where does this bike come from?* (India) *Did Uncle Krishna or Uncle Freddy give him this bike?* (Uncle Krishna)

Intermediate Have students do a paired reading. *Ask: What happened to Eddy's first bicycle?* (It was stolen.) *Where does Eddy keep the second bike?* (in a hiding place under the stairs) *Where did he keep the first bike?* (on the front porch)

Advanced Have students do a partner read aloud. *Ask: Whose fault was it that Eddy's first bike was stolen?* (It was Eddy's fault.) *What should he have done to protect that bike?* (He should have chained it.) *Why is he disappointed in the second bike?* (because it looks old)

5 **Laboriously,** Eddy carried the old stuff up to the attic. Then he wheeled his **shameful** new bicycle into the space behind the curtain.

6 In the dark it gleamed a little, the way his old rocket model had glowed in the dark because **phosphorescent** stuff was mixed with the plastic. His embarrassing new bicycle must be coated with phosphorescent paint.

Predict

Predict what Eddy will find out about this bike.

7 It trembled slightly under his hands as he propped it upright, almost as if it were alive. Little sparkles flickered around the rims of the wheels. And there was a sound, a kind of whispering **murmur.**

8 Eddy pulled the curtain aside to let in light and peered at the dial mounted on the handlebars. It wasn't a **speedometer**—it was a clock. And there was a dome-shaped bell on top, just like the one on an old-fashioned alarm clock. The whole thing looked just like a clock in a cartoon, the kind that bounces up and down when the alarm goes off.

9 He looked more closely at the dial. How weird! It didn't say 1, 2, 3, 4, all the way to 12. In fact, there were two dials. The words printed on them were very small. One said:

Days

and the other:

Years

---

laboriously requiring hard work
shameful embarrassing
phosphorescent a quality that makes something glow

murmur a low, unclear sound
speedometer an instrument that measures how fast something is going

Chapter 3 The Time Bike **183**

Read the Selection

1. **Paired reading** Play the audio. Then have students practice reading in pairs.
2. **Ask questions about the story** Have students work in small groups to write four questions about the story so far. Then have groups exchange and answer the questions.
3. **Locate derivations using dictionaries** Have students look at these glossed words and determine what words they are derived from: *triangular, laboriously, shameful, phosphorescent.* Have students check the derivations in a print, online, or CD-ROM dictionary.
4. **Relate to personal experience** *Ask: Have you ever received a gift from a relative that you didn't really like at first, but then you liked it later? What was the gift? Why did you change your mind about the gift?*
5. **Multi-level options** See MULTI-LEVEL OPTIONS on p. 182.

Sample Answer to Guide Question
I predict that Eddy will find out that his bike has special powers.

❚ Punctuation

Commas

Have students look at the prologue of the reading. *Ask: What city does Eddy live in?* (Concord) *What state does he live in?* (Massachusetts) Write them on the board. Remind students that the first letter in names of towns, cities, and states is always capitalized, just like in the names of countries or people. Then add a comma between the city and state. Explain that we always insert a comma between a city and the state to show that they are two separate names. Also note that the city is placed before the state.

Apply Have the class generate the names of cities and the states they are in. Write them on the board without any capitals or commas. Have students rewrite the names, correcting the capitalization and punctuation errors.

Read the Selection

1. **Reciprocal reading** Play the audio. Have volunteers read paragraphs and ask the class questions. Then have them ask students to summarize.

2. **Analyze character changes** *Ask: What did Eddy think about the bike at first?* (He thought it was embarrassing and out of style.) *What evidence supports this?* (He hid it in a closet.) *How do you think he feels about the bike now?* (He's more interested and curious about it.) *What evidence supports this?* (He is wondering about the plus-and-minus switch; he tries sitting in it; he wonders about the tag.)

Sample Answer to Guide Question
Perhaps the tab switch turns on the time machine, and the bike can go back or forward in time.

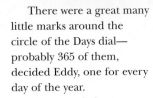

10   There were a great many little marks around the circle of the Days dial— probably 365 of them, decided Eddy, one for every day of the year.

11   The Years dial was different. It went from 0 to 10 to 100 to 1,000 to 10,000 to 100,000. A hundred thousand years! What did it mean, a clock that told the time in thousands of years?

Predict

Predict what the tab switch will do.

12   And there was a **tab** at the side, some sort of on-off switch. No, it wasn't an on-off switch, it was a plus-and-minus switch. What did that mean, plus and minus?

13   "Why, Eddy," said Aunt Alex, suddenly appearing in the front hall with Eleanor, "what a lovely headlight. It sparkles like a diamond."

14   "It does?" Eddy looked. The rocket-shaped headlight on the front **fender** was just one more thing that was out of style. He tried to turn it off, but there was no switch.

15   "It reminds me of something," said Eleanor, narrowing her eyes, staring at it through her big glasses.

16   Eddy knew what she was thinking of—the big jewel that had once been part of the stained-glass window in the attic, that huge chunk of glass that had turned out in the end to be a diamond, a real diamond, so valuable that it was beyond price. "It's not much good without a switch," he said. "The battery will run down any minute."

---

tab   a projection or flap attached to something else   **fender**   a part of a bike that protects the wheel

---

MULTI-LEVEL OPTIONS *Read the Selection*

Newcomer Have students look at the art on pp. 184–185. *Ask: Is Eddy's bike just like an ordinary bike?* (no) *Are there two dials on the bike?* (yes) *Do the dials show days and years?* (yes)

Beginning *Ask: Does the bike have a headlight?* (yes) *How many dials does it have?* (two) *Who thinks the headlight is lovely?* (Aunt Alex)

Intermediate *Ask: What does Aunt Alex compare the headlight and rear reflector to?* (a diamond and a ruby) *Where are they mounted?* (on the front and back fenders) *Where had Eddy seen a real diamond?* (in the stained-glass window in the attic)

Advanced *Ask: What sort of mood does this part of the story create?* (a suspenseful one) *When does that mood begin?* (when Eddy discovers the strange dials) *Why does Eddy think the headlight is impractical?* (because he thinks the battery will run down)

17 "The one in back is pretty too," said Aunt Alex, bending low over the rear fender, where the red reflector shone in the light of the desk lamp. "It's like a ruby, a real ruby." She stood up and smiled at Eddy. "It's like a bicycle from fairyland."

18 Then she went into the kitchen with Eleanor, and Eddy went back to studying his new bicycle with more interest than before.

19 He climbed on the seat to see what it felt like and dropped the curtain again. Now he was alone in the dark with the bike. In front of him the headlight shone on the wall of the coat closet, making a bright pattern like a star.

20 To his surprise it felt good to **perch** erect, high above the floor. It was sort of **majestic** and **dignified,** like riding an elephant.

21 Something white twirled in front of him—the tag on the handlebars. Eddy reached for it, but it kept fluttering and twisting. Finally he got it between his fingers. Pulling open the curtain he looked at the tag. One side still said *Srinagar, Kashmir.* The other said:

> TIME BIKE

22 *Time Bike!* What did that mean?

23 He could hear Aunt Alex talking quietly from the kitchen with Eleanor, who was complaining loudly about Amanda Upshaw's party.

perch sit, usually on a high place
majestic showing greatness

dignified noble, honorable

Chapter 3 The Time Bike **185**

Predict

What do you think Eddy will do next?

Read the Selection

1. **Reciprocal reading** Play the audio. Have volunteers read paragraphs and ask the class questions. Then have them ask students to summarize.

2. **Discuss how an author creates interest** *Say: Are you more interested in the story now than at the beginning? I am. The author is making the story more and more interesting. She does this by including hints or clues about what might happen and including questions or strange details. Can you find the questions in paragraphs 11 and 12?* (What did it mean . . . years? What did that mean . . . minus?) *What is strange about the headlight in paragraph 14?* (There is no switch.) *What clue does the Aunt give about the bike in paragraph 17?* (She says it's like a bicycle from fairyland.) *What hint is there in paragraph 22?* (The tag says *Time Bike.*)

3. **Make predictions** Discuss with students what they think might happen if Eddy can "turn on" the time bike.

4. **Multi-level options** See MULTI-LEVEL OPTIONS on p. 184.

Sample Answer to Guide Question
Eddy might try to figure out how the bike works, or he might try to "start" it.

---

9 Punctuation

Dashes

Write on the board: *Luis plays baseball and soccer—Oh, and he's a good swimmer, too.* Tell students that dashes are often used in writing to add information we forgot to include or to show a break in the thought. Point out that these dashes are not the same as hyphens; dashes are longer in length and are used for a different purpose. Have students go back through the story to see how the dash was used in paragraphs 10, 16, and 21.

Apply Ask students to write some sentences and then some additional information as an afterthought. Have them put those sentences into written form with dashes in the appropriate places. Then have them share and revise their work.

Read the Selection

1. **Choral reading** Play the audio. Then have the class read the narration with you chorally. Have volunteers take the roles of Aunt Alex and Eleanor. Instruct them to read their parts dramatically.

2. **Make predictions** Have volunteers read paragraphs 28 and 29 aloud. Then discuss the guide question as a class before reading any further.

3. **Analyze character's actions** *Ask: What evidence is there that Eddy is starting to believe that the bike is magic?* (He thinks that maybe it really is a time bike.) *Why does he think going back to December might be a bad idea?* (He thinks it might be scary because in fairy stories people make wishes without thinking and get into trouble.) *Is he being reckless or careful?* (careful)

Sample Answer to Guide Question
Maybe the bike will take him back to December.

Predict

What do you predict will happen next? Do you predict the bike will take Eddy to the past?

24 "I still don't have an **invitation!** Becky's got one. Lisa's got one. It's only me, I'm the only one that hasn't got one. I mean, they've all got invitations already, all the best kids!"

25 There was a pause and then Aunt Alex said, "What do you mean by 'best kids'?"

26 "Oh, you know, Aunt Alex. They're— oh, I don't know. If you could see them, you'd know what I mean."

27 "I see," said Aunt Alex.

28 Eddy stopped listening. What if he set the dial of the clock for some time in the past, like six months ago? Maybe it really was a time bike. Maybe it would really take him back to last December. Dreamily, he put his fingers on the setscrew that moved the hand of the dial that counted days.

29 Then he came to his senses. The idea was too scary. He should think it over first and then try it very carefully. Those people in fairy stories who were given three wishes always got in trouble. They wasted all three because they didn't think. He would be more careful.

30 But at that instant the little **rooster** in the backyard crowed noisily, and the silly cuckoo popped out of the clock and squawked.

31 Eddy's hand jerked. The bicycle jiggled, and the bell went *ding*. There was a flash of lightning in the little round mirror on the handlebars, and a humming noise from the wheels as if they were going around.

invitation a card or letter that asks someone to come to an event

rooster a male chicken

186 Unit 3 Journeys

MULTI-LEVEL OPTIONS *Read the Selection*

Newcomer *Ask: Does Eleanor want to go to a party?* (yes) *Does Eddy want to go back to December?* (yes) *Does he want to go to back to May?* (no) *Does Eddy think the time bike is a failure?* (yes)

Beginning *Ask: Who is talking to Aunt Alex?* (Eleanor) *What month is it?* (June) *What does Eleanor want?* (a party invitation)

Intermediate *Ask: What does Eddy want the time bike to do?* (He wants it to take him back in time.) *How does Eddy feel about using the time bike?* (He's afraid.) *What is he afraid of?* (getting into trouble)

Advanced *Ask: What made Eddy accidentally start the time bike?* (the sound of the rooster) *Does the time bike work, or is it a failure?* (It works.) *What makes you think so?* (Eddy hears the same conversation repeated when the bike stops moving.)

32 It was only for a moment. Then the vibration stopped. The **dinging** stopped. Eddy got off the bike and opened the curtain.

33 Through the **oval** window in the front door he could see the trees across the road, and the grass in the front yard. Everything was green. It was still June, not last December.

34 The bike was a failure. It didn't work. It wasn't a time bike. The strange dials didn't mean anything at all.

35 Aunt Alex and Eleanor were still talking in the kitchen.

36 "What do you mean by 'best kids'?" said Aunt Alex.

37 "Oh, you know, Aunt Alex. They're—oh, I don't know. If you could see them, you'd know what I mean."

38 "I see," said Aunt Alex.

Predict

What do you predict will happen after this part of the story?

---

dinging   light ringing

oval   shaped like an egg

About the Author

Jane Langton (born 1922)

Jane Langton has been writing for more than 40 years. She is best known for writing adult mysteries. She also writes fiction for young adults. Langton lives in Massachusetts, and many of her stories take place there. Langton says she enjoys putting realistic characters into this setting.

➤ Why do you think Jane Langton wrote this story? Was it to entertain, inform, or persuade?

Chapter 3 The Time Bike   **187**

🖋 Punctuation

Single quotes within a quotation

Write on the board: *"Dad said, 'Don't make noise.' "* **Ask:** *Is Dad really talking?* (no) *Is someone telling us what Dad said?* (yes) *When we write someone's words, we use* double *quotes, but if part of those words are somebody else's, we must use* single *quotes around those.*

Apply Dictate paragraph 25 without punctuation. Then have students insert the correct quote marks and read the paragraph to check.

Evaluate Your Reading Strategy

Predict *Say: You have practiced an important reading strategy. Now you can decide how well you have done. Does this statement describe how you read?*

> I ask, "Why is the author telling me this information? Can I use this information to predict what will happen next?" Predicting helps me understand why the author includes certain details.

Read the Selection

1. **Choral reading** Play the audio. Do a choral reading as volunteers take the roles of Aunt Alex and Eleanor. Instruct them to read their parts dramatically.

2. **Draw conclusions** Give students a chance to reread the selection silently. *Ask: Why do you think the time bike only went back in time a few minutes?* (Eddy only moved the clock slightly.)

3. **Multi-level options** See MULTI-LEVEL OPTIONS on p. 186.

Sample Answer to Guide Question
Eddy will try again in a few days.

About the Author

Explain author background Jane Langton's popular mysteries are usually accompanied by her own appealing line drawings. "The Time Bike" is one of several books she wrote about the eccentric Hall family who live in Concord, Massachusetts. *Ask: How is this story like a mystery?* (There are unusual events and mysterious clues.) *The author's biography says that she likes to put realistic characters in her stories. Which characters seemed realistic or believable?*

Answer
Example: She wrote the story to entertain.

Across Selections

Have students think about the story "The Voyage of the Lucky Dragon." *Say: Both stories are about journeys, but they are very different types of stories. One is historical fiction, and one is science fiction. Which story did you enjoy more, and why?*

Spelling, Punctuation, Capitalization

After the Reading Comprehension section, students will practice spelling, punctuation, and capitalization in the Activity Book.

Beyond the Reading

Reading Comprehension

Question-Answer Relationships

Sample Answers

1. from India, from his uncle, Prince Krishna
2. days, years
3. Srinagar, Kashmir; Time Bike
4. It looked old and is out of style.
5. It was stolen.
6. Eddy becomes interested and curious about the bike.
7. The bike was mysterious, and he wasn't sure if something bad might happen.
8. The bike had phosphorescent paint, the wheels sparkled, there were jewels in the fenders, and the clock had dials.
9. Eddy goes back in time only a few moments.
10. to visit his uncle in India to find out more about the bike
11. No, I don't think time travel will be possible. Once time has passed, it doesn't exist anymore. Time that hasn't passed doesn't exist yet, so there's nothing to "travel" to.

Build Reading Fluency

Repeated Reading

Assessment Program: *Reading Fluency Chart, p. 116*

As students read aloud, time the reading and count the number of incorrectly pronounced words. Record results in the Reading Fluency Chart.

Reading Comprehension

Question-Answer Relationships (QAR)

"Right There" Questions

1. **Recall Facts** Where did the mysterious bike come from?
2. **Recall Facts** How were the two dials labeled?
3. **Recall Facts** What did the two sides of the bike's tag say?

"Think and Search" Questions

4. **Draw Conclusions** Why was Eddy embarrassed by the bike?
5. **Explain** What happened to his last bike?
6. **Analyze Character Changes** How does Eddy's point of view change during the story?

"Author and You" Questions

7. **Draw Conclusions** Why do you think Eddy hesitated to use the bike?
8. **Identify Elements** What makes the bike different?
9. **Draw Conclusions** What happens at the end of the story?

"On Your Own" Questions

10. **Predict** What do you predict Eddy will use the bike for?
11. **Predict** Do you think time travel will be possible in the future? Explain.

Activity Book
p. 98

Student
CD-ROM

Build Reading Fluency

Repeated Reading

Repeated reading helps increase your reading rate and builds confidence. Each time you reread, you improve your reading fluency.

1. Turn to page 182.
2. With a partner, take turns reading each paragraph aloud.
3. Your teacher or partner will time six minutes for you.
4. Stop after six minutes.

MULTI-LEVEL OPTIONS *Elements of Literature*

Newcomer Tell students to listen for things that aren't ordinary. Then replay the audio. *Ask: Do most bikes have headlights that look like diamonds?* (no) Explain that these are the author's clues about what will happen later. Have groups draw pictures of the scenes with these clues.

Beginning Ask students to select a part of the story that gives them clues to the magic of the bike. Tell them clues can be in the setting or the action. Then have them draw a picture that shows their clues. Have students work in pairs to add one-word or one-sentence captions.

Intermediate Have students work in groups to explain how parts of the setting (the nook and the crimson, velvet curtain) and at least one character (Uncle Krishna) provide foreshadowing clues of the magic in the bike. Have them present their conclusions to the class.

Advanced Have students work with a partner to identify foreshadowing clues across the whole reading selection. Remind them that characters, setting, and events contribute to foreshadowing clues.

Listen, Speak, Interact

Give a Presentation

In the selection, Eddy learns that his bike can travel in time. Suppose you had a Time Bike.

1. Decide where you would go if you had a Time Bike. Would you go to a certain time and place in history? A certain time and place in your life?
2. Answer these questions on a piece of paper:
   a. Where would you like to go? What is the time and place?
   b. Why do you want to go to this time and place?
   c. What is life like in this time and place?
   d. What do you want to do when you are there?
3. Present your answers to the class.
4. As you listen to your classmates' presentations, take notes.
5. With a partner, compare your notes on one classmates' presentation. Are your perceptions of the presentation the same or different?

Elements of Literature

Recognize Foreshadowing

In fiction, authors often give the reader clues about what will happen later in the story. This is called **foreshadowing.**

You know that Eddy didn't think that his bike was special at the beginning of the story. Read this sentence about the bicycle in paragraph 7:

> It trembled slightly under his hands as he propped it upright, almost as if it were alive.

Ordinary bicycles don't tremble, and they don't seem to be alive. This tells us that this might be a special bicycle after all.

Write answers to these questions in your Reading Log.

1. What other examples of foreshadowing about the bicycle do you find in paragraphs 7 and 8?
2. Reread paragraphs 31 and 32. What do these paragraphs foreshadow?

Reading Log   Activity Book p. 99   Student CD-ROM

Chapter 3 The Time Bike   **189**

Word Study

Study the Prefix *bi-*

Extend vocabulary Write on the board: *bicentennial, biped, biathlon, bifocals.* Have students work in pairs to discuss or use the dictionary to find out meanings.

Answers
1. b 2. c 3. a

Grammar Focus

Write Using Contractions

Use contractions Say sentences and have students repeat the sentence with contractions. *Say: I am going home. My sister has not called me. They have not finished the test. You will have to stay here. He had already spent the money.*

Answers
1. I still do not have an invitation! Becky has got one. Lisa has got one. It is only me, I am the only one that has not got one. I mean, they have all got invitations already, all the best kids!

ASSESS

Have students write two sentences using different words beginning with the prefix *bi-*.

Word Study

Study the Prefix *bi-*

A **prefix** is a group of letters added to the beginning of a word. A prefix may change the meaning of a word.

The word **bi**cycle has the prefix *bi-*. *Bi-* means "two." *Cycle* is the root word of *bicycle*. The word *cycle* means "wheel." When *bi-* is added to *cycle*, the word *bicycle* is formed. A bicycle is a vehicle with two wheels.

Match each of the following words with the correct definition. Use a dictionary if you need help.

1. *bicultural*
2. *biweekly*
3. *bilingual*

a. able to speak two languages
b. made up of two cultures
c. happening every two weeks

The Heinle
Newbury House
Dictionary

Activity Book
p. 100

Student
CD-ROM

Grammar Focus

Write Using Contractions

Some auxiliary verbs can be made into a **contraction.** An apostrophe (') replaces the letters that are taken out. Look at the chart.

The word *not* can be contracted with any auxiliary verb:

Did you do your homework? No, I <u>didn't</u>.

Would you travel in time? No, I <u>wouldn't</u>.

The contraction of *will* + *not* is *won't*.

1. Copy paragraph 24 on a piece of paper, but change all of the contracted forms to full forms.
2. Write a sentence for each contracted form in the chart.

Auxiliary Verb	Contracted Form	Example
am	'm	I'm a student.
is	's	She's a student.
are	're	We're students.
have	've	I've eaten sushi.
has	's	He's eaten sushi.
had	'd	I'd already done my homework.
will	'll	They'll be there.
would	'd	I said I'd be there.

Activity Book
pp. 101–102

Student
Handbook

Student
CD-ROM

MULTI-LEVEL OPTIONS *From Reading to Writing*

Newcomer Write a Language Experience story with this group. Have them brainstorm ideas for you to list. Have them sequence the ideas, draw pictures that depict the ideas, and then write key words on each drawing.

Beginning Have students work in groups. Brainstorm and list plot events. Have groups sequence their stories and draw pictures to illustrate them. Help students to write captions for each picture.

Intermediate Have these students work with advanced students to research the details of a period of history the group wants to set their story in. They can use a library or the Internet. Remind them that the details should be as accurate as possible.

Advanced (See Intermediate.) Tell advanced students that they must note the sources used for background information. Have the group members take turns presenting their finished work to the class.

From Reading to Writing

Write a Description

Write a paragraph that describes a place in the past. You may write about the place you presented in Listen, Speak, Interact, or you may write about another place. This paragraph will be a part of a larger piece of writing. It can be a letter, journal entry, narrative, memoir, or other form of writing. Decide which form you want to use.

1. Include information that answers these questions:
   a. What is the name of the place?
   b. Where is the place?
   c. What is the time and date?
   d. What people and things would you see in this place?
   e. What do people do there?

2. Use figurative language to help readers picture the place in their minds.
3. Find information in your school library or on the Internet. Use the name of the place as a keyword (for example, "Ancient Rome").
4. List the sources you use to write your paragraph. Check your Student Handbook for the correct form.
5. Place a drawing or a photograph below your paragraph. The picture should help readers understand your description.

 Activity Book p. 103

 Student Handbook

Across Content Areas

Learn About Time Zones

A **time zone** is an area that has the same time. Most of the United States is in four time zones. These time zones are called Eastern, Central, Mountain, and Pacific.

Suppose it is 11:00 P.M. in New York City. Then it is 10:00 P.M. in Chicago.

Use the map to answer the questions:

1. It is 3 P.M. in New York City. What time is it in Denver?
2. It is 10 P.M. in Los Angeles. What time is it in Chicago?

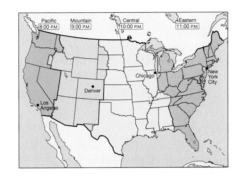

 Activity Book p. 104

Chapter 3 The Time Bike **191**

From Reading to Writing

Write a Description

Teacher Resource Book: *Web, p. 37*

1. **Brainstorm** Before students write, have them think of a place to describe and do a quick word web about the place. Then have them describe their places to one another in small groups. Have them explain why the place is important to them.
2. **Provide definitions** Give the definitions of *memoir* and *journal*.
   A *memoir* tells about people and events that the writer remembers. Some of the features of a memoir are:
   a. the use of personal pronouns *I, me, we, us*
   b. interesting facts and memories
   c. a beginning, a middle, and an end
   d. the writer's feelings and perspectives about the events and people
   e. a setting that is usually a long time ago
   A *journal* is a place where you record daily experiences and special events. Some of the features of a journal are:
   a. dates
   b. events
   c. thoughts, feelings, and reflections
3. **Multi-level options** See MULTI-LEVEL OPTIONS on p. 190.

Across Content Areas: Social Studies

Learn About Time Zones

Talk about time zones Have volunteers ask the class questions about time zones. Model a question first. *Say: It's 9:00 A.M. here. What time is it in Miami?*

Answers
1. 1:00 P.M. **2.** 12:00 midnight

 **ASSESS**

Have students state what time zone they are in and what time it is in two cities in other time zones.

Reteach and Reassess

Text Structure Have students list the features of science fiction. Then have them give one example of each feature from "The Time Bike" and their own Reading to Writing paragraph.

Reading Strategy Have students review their predictions about the selection for accuracy.

Elements of Literature Have students review "The Voyage of the Lucky Dragon" (p. 166). Ask them to find two examples of foreshadowing in paragraphs 1–3.

Reassess Have students read their Reading to Writing paragraph to a partner. Have partners identify instances of foreshadowing and predict what the ending will be.

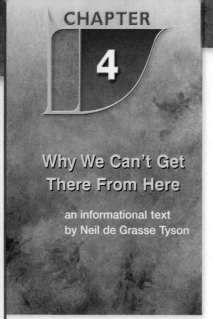

CHAPTER

4

Why We Can't Get
There From Here

an informational text
by Neil de Grasse Tyson

Into the Reading

Chapter Materials

Activity Book: *pp. 105–112*
Audio: *Unit 3, Chapter 4; CD 2, Track 4*
Student Handbook
Student CD-ROM: *Unit 3, Chapter 4*
Teacher Resource Book: *Lesson Plan, Teacher
    Resources, Reading Summary, Activity Book
    Answer Key*
Teacher Resource CD-ROM
Assessment Program: *Quiz, pp. 45–46; Teacher
    and Student Resources, pp. 115–144*
Assessment CD-ROM
Transparencies
The Heinle Newbury House Dictionary/CD-ROM
Web site: http://visions.heinle.com

Objectives

Preview Read the objectives. *Ask: What do you
know about doing a research report? In which
classes would you do a research report?*

Use Prior Knowledge

Talk About Ways to Travel

Use a bar graph to present information
Brainstorm and list ways to travel. Have
volunteers ask and record how many students
have used each means of travel. Then have
students make a bar graph of the information,
with number of students on the vertical axis and
type of transportation on the horizontal axis.

Objectives

Reading Reread and record to learn and
recall as you read an informational text.

Listening and Speaking Listen to an
informational text.

Grammar Use comparative and
superlative adjectives.

Writing Use multiple resources to write a
research report.

Content Math: Solve a time problem.

Use Prior Knowledge

Talk About Ways to Travel

There are many ways to travel. For
example, you can travel by car or bicycle.

1. Brainstorm a list of ways to travel.
2. Choose your two favorite ways. Use a
   Venn Diagram to show how they are
   the same and how they are different.

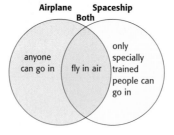

Airplane   Spaceship
Both

anyone
can go in
fly in air
only
specially
trained
people can
go in

3. Tell your partner about these ways
   to travel, and listen to your partner's
   response. After your partner speaks,
   summarize what he or she said.
4. With your class, organize a chart of
   all the ways to travel.
5. Take a survey. Organize a record of
   how many students have traveled
   each way.
6. Ask and answer questions like these
   to compare ways of travel.
   a. Which way of travel is the most
      popular? Why?
   b. Which is the least popular? Why?

192   Unit 3 Journeys

MULTI-LEVEL OPTIONS *Build Vocabulary*

Newcomer Make a web with
earth in the middle. List these
affixes in a column: *-ly, -ling,
-quake.* **Say:** Earth *is a root word.
You can make new words by
adding letters to the beginning or
end of* earth. Show students how
to combine the affix and root.
Have them draw pictures that
show the meaning of new words.

Beginning Make a web with
earth in the middle. **Say:** Earth *is
a root word. You can make new
words by adding letters to the
beginning and end of a word.* Ask
students for any words they know
to write on their web, or suggest:
-ling, -ly, -quake, un-.

Intermediate Have these
students work in pairs with
advanced students to find
additional words with the roots
earth, typical, and *rough.*

Advanced Have students
create sentences with the new
words. Instruct one pair of
advanced and intermediate
students to take turns presenting
definitions of the words and the
sentences they have written.

Build Background

Space

Space is the area outside the atmosphere of Earth. (The atmosphere is the air that is around Earth.) In space there are stars, moons, and planets. Planets, like Earth, move around a star such as the sun. Some planets are very hot. They are close to the sun. Some planets are cold. They are far away from the sun.

Content Connection
Neil Armstrong was the first person to walk on the moon. This was in 1969.

Build Vocabulary

Apply Knowledge of Root Words

You can expand your vocabulary by looking for words made from root words that you already know. Read this example:

The spaceship was **un**man**ned**.

In the word *unmanned,* **man** is the root word. Remember that the prefix *un-* means *not,* so an *unmanned* spaceship is one with no people on it.

1. In your Personal Dictionary, copy these words. Underline the root words. Guess the definitions.
   a. earthly
   b. typically
   c. roughly

2. As you read or listen to the selection, look for root words to help you understand and to expand your vocabulary.

Personal Dictionary

The Heinle Newbury House Dictionary

Activity Book *p. 105*

Student CD-ROM

Chapter 4 Why We Can't Get There From Here **193**

Cultural Connection

Build Vocabulary Have students use dictionaries, the Internet, or native-speaker classmates to look up the words for *Earth, moon, star, sun, planet* in other languages. Tell them to put their findings into chart form. If possible, have them add the word symbols for languages using pictographs or phonetic scripts.

Learning Styles
Linguistic

Build Background Have students present the previous chart to the class along with short explanations about differences among the languages. They should research and include linguistic facts. *Examples:* In Spanish and French, the nouns have genders (*la* luna, *le* soleil); Chinese has no plurals (1 star, 100 star) and uses no articles at all.

Build Background

Space

1. **Activate prior knowledge** Bring in library books or bookmark Internet sites with pictures of outer space and the solar system. As you look at the pictures with students, ask them what they already now about space.
2. **Content Connection** After the first manned lunar landing in 1969, both the United States and the former Soviet Union launched unmanned lunar explorations. Since the 1970s, the United States has focused on the space shuttle and on developing the International Space Station.

Build Vocabulary

Apply Knowledge of Root Words

Teacher Resource Book: *Personal Dictionary, p. 63*

1. **Use prior knowledge** On the board, write: *unmanned; un-* + _____. Help students think of words that begin with the prefix *un-* and write them on the board. Some words they might think of are: *unusual, uncover, uncomfortable, unhappy, unlikely, unlucky.*
2. **Reading selection vocabulary** You may want to introduce the glossed words in the reading selection before students begin reading. Key words: *measure, galaxy, speed of light, universe, astronauts, calculation, breakthrough.* Instruct students to write the words with correct spelling and their definitions in their Personal Dictionaries. Have them pronounce each word and divide it into syllables.
3. **Multi-level options** See MULTI-LEVEL OPTIONS on p. 192.

Answers
1. **a.** earth (related to earth); **b.** typical (in a typical manner); **c.** rough (with roughness or approximately)

 ASSESS

Have students write sentences with each of these words: *earthly, typically, roughly.*

Text Structure

Informational Text

1. **Review text features** Remind students that some informational texts use features such as headings and boldface type. Point out that this selection does not show headings. Have students suggest headings as they read.
2. **Multi-level options** See MULTI-LEVEL OPTIONS below.

Reading Strategy

Reread and Record to Learn and Recall

Use preview questions Have students look at the illustrations and photos in the selection. *Ask: What questions do you think of when you look at the photos? For example, when I look at the photo on p. 197, my question is: How fast does this spaceship travel?* Write questions students think of on the board.

ASSESS

Have students write three features of an informational text.

Text Structure

Informational Text

"Why We Can't Get There From Here" is an **informational text.** An informational text explains a topic. Look at the chart. It shows some features of an informational text that are in the selection.

Informational Text	
Facts	true information about the topic
Examples	details that show how information is true
Pictures	visuals that help readers see examples of important ideas

Student CD-ROM

Reading Strategy

Reread and Record to Learn and Recall

As you read an informational text, you can take special steps to learn and recall new information. These steps will help you in your other courses, especially science and social studies.

As you read "Why We Can't Get There From Here," follow the steps in the chart.

Step	What to Do
1. Preview questions	Look over the text. Ask yourself: What do the title and headings tell me? What do I know about this topic?
2. Read	Read to find answers to your questions.
3. Reread	Go back and read again, slowly and carefully. Reread aloud if you do not understand.
4. Record	Take notes on important facts.

Student CD-ROM

MULTI-LEVEL OPTIONS *Text Structure*

Newcomer Provide examples of several types of informational texts, such as manuals, cookbooks, or how-to books. Have students work in small groups to point out the different features.

Beginning Provide examples of several types of informational texts, such as manuals, cookbooks, or how-to books. Give groups adhesive notes with the words *facts, examples,* and *visuals* written on them. Have groups identify and share examples of the different features.

Intermediate Have students work in groups to examine informational texts from their content courses. Have them use adhesive notes to bookmark features to share with other groups.

Advanced Have students find library books or texts from their content courses that show features of informational texts. Have them bookmark their findings and share them with the class.

Why We Can't Get There From Here

an informational text by Neil de Grasse Tyson

195

Reading Selection Materials

Audio: *Unit 3, Chapter 4; CD 2, Track 4*
Teacher Resource Book: *Reading Summary,
    pp. 91–92*
Transparencies: #38, *Reading Summary*

Suggestions for Using Reading Summary

- Introduce new vocabulary or cognates.
- Cut the summary into strips, or jumble the sentences on an overhead transparency. Students put the sentences in order.
- Practice the reading strategy.
- Students read aloud or with a partner.
- Students paraphrase the summary.
- Students do a cloze activity.
- Students create a visual or graphic organizer, such as a timeline or storyboard, to illustrate the summary.
- Students paraphrase the summary.

Preview the Selection

1. **Interpret art** Have students look at the photo. *Ask: What is this instrument called?* (telescope) *What do you think you can see through this telescope? Have you ever looked through a telescope? What did you see?*
2. **Connect** Remind students that the theme of this unit is *journeys.* Ask them to speculate about the kind of journey that they will read about in this chapter.

Content Connection
Math

Learning Styles
Visual

Tell students that because there is no gravity on the Moon, items weigh only 1/6 of their weight on Earth. Have them calculate the relative weights of various items (including some classmates) on Earth and on the Moon. Then instruct them to create a chart showing the results. They can either weigh the items or get the information from a list of weights.

Have students draw a cartoon-style storyboard contrasting the effects of gravity on Earth vs. the lack of gravity on the Moon. Have volunteers take turns narrating the events shown in each panel.

Read the Selection

1. **Paired reading** Read the selection aloud. Then have pairs read aloud. Have them write answers to the guide question.

2. **Identify main idea** Have a student read paragraph 1 aloud. *Ask: What is the main idea of this paragraph? Sometimes it helps to read the first and last sentences of the paragraph.* Help students formulate a main idea. (*Example:* The distances in space are so great that it makes it impossible to travel to them.)

3. **Understand analogies** *Say: In paragraph 2, the author uses an analogy, or an example, to explain a concept.* Reread the paragraph aloud. Have a student pace out ten strides, and pretend to hold a softball. *Ask: Can you imagine a distance of 100 miles from here? What town or city would that be? That is how far away Pluto would be in this example.*

Sample Answer to Guide Question
Why can't we get to stars from Earth?

See Teacher Edition pp. 434–436 for a list of English-Spanish cognates in the reading selection.

---

1   Space. Why can't we get there from here? Well, one problem is the distance to the nearest star. Space is **vast** and empty beyond all earthly **measure.** When **Hollywood** movies show a starship cruising through the **galaxy,** they typically show points of light (stars) drifting past like **fireflies** at a rate of one or two per second. But the distances between stars in the galaxy are so great that a spaceship would have to be traveling roughly 500 million times faster than the **speed of light** for the stars to rush by like that.

2   The Moon is far away compared with where you might go in a jet airplane, but it sits at the tip of your nose compared with anything else in the **universe.** If Earth were the size of a basketball, the Moon would be the size of a softball some ten **paces** away—the farthest we have ever sent people into space. On this scale, Mars (at its closest) is a mile away. Pluto is 100 miles away. And Proxima Centauri, the star nearest to the Sun, is a *half-million miles* away!

> **Reread and Record to Learn and Recall**
>
> Reread paragraph 1. What question is the author going to answer?

🎧
Audio
CD 2, Tr. 4

---

vast   large
measure   an amount of something
Hollywood   a city in the state of California where lots of movies are made
galaxy   a large group of stars and planets

fireflies   insects that light up
speed of light   the rate at which light moves
universe   all of space including galaxies, stars, and planets
paces   steps

196   **Unit 3**   Journeys

MULTI-LEVEL OPTIONS   *Read the Selection*

Newcomer Play the audio. *Ask: Is the Moon closer to the Earth than Mars?* (yes) *Is Proxima Centauri a planet?* (no) *Is Proxima Centauri a star?* (yes)

Beginning Read the Reading Summary aloud. Then do a paired reading. *Ask: Which planet is farther away from Earth, Mars or Pluto?* (Pluto) *When was the Helios B launched?* (1976) *What is Proxima Centauri near?* (the Sun)

Intermediate Have students do a paired reading. *Ask: What word does the author use to describe space?* (vast) *How far away is Proxima Centauri from the Sun?* (a half-million miles) *How fast did the Helios B travel?* (42 miles per second)

Advanced Have students do a partner read aloud. *Ask: How long would it take for a spaceship to reach the nearest star?* (100,000 years) *If the spaceship traveled at the speed of the Helios B, how long would the same trip take?* (15,000 years) *How long is that compared to recorded human history?* (three times longer)

3 Let's **assume** money is **no object.** If a spaceship **sustained** the speed needed to escape Earth—seven miles per second—the trip to the nearest star would last a long and boring *100,000 years!* Too long, you say?

4 How about a spaceship that travels as fast as *Helios B,* the U.S.-German **solar probe** that was the fastest-ever **unmanned** space probe? Launched in 1976, it was clocked rising through 42 miles per second (150,000 miles per hour) as it accelerated toward the Sun. This craft would cut the travel time to the nearest star down to a **mere** 15,000 years—*three times the length of recorded human history.*

> **Reread and Record to Learn and Recall**
>
> Reread this paragraph aloud. What is the most important thing you learned?

5 What we really want is a spaceship that can travel near the speed of light. (*Helios B* was traveling at only one-fiftieth of one percent of the speed of light.) How about 99 percent the speed of light? All you would need is *700 million times* the energy that **thrust** Apollo **astronauts** toward the Moon!

> **Reread and Record to Learn and Recall**
>
> Take notes on the important facts in paragraphs 4 and 5.

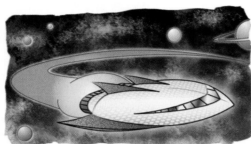

---

assume believe something is true
no object not a problem; not worth anything
sustained kept up or maintained
solar probe a small spacecraft sent to study the Sun

unmanned having no crew or passengers
mere small, only
thrust forced
astronauts people trained to fly a spacecraft

Chapter 4 Why We Can't Get There From Here **197**

Read the Selection

1. **Choral reading** Play the audio. Then divide the class into two groups and have each group read every other paragraph with you.
2. **Find details** Write on the board: *How long would it take to travel to the nearest star?* (100,000 years; 15,000 years by *Helios B*) *Where was the Helios B traveling to?* (the Sun) Have students work in pairs or small groups to write answers to these questions and the guide questions.
3. **Multi-level options** See MULTI-LEVEL OPTIONS on p. 196.

Sample Answer to Guide Question
It would take 15,000 years to reach the nearest star.

A Capitalization

Names of planets and stars

Tell students that the first letter in names of planets and stars is always capitalized. *Ask: What other things always start with a capital letter?* (names of people, countries, nationalities, cities, and states) Have students read paragraph 2 of the selection and find the names of planets and stars. Have volunteers take turns writing the names on the board. Correct any mistakes in capitalization (for example, *the* is lowercase in *the Moon*).

Apply Have the class name other planets in the solar system. Then have students write a list of them all and exchange papers, correcting any capitalization errors.

Read the Selection

1. **Reciprocal reading** Play the audio. Have volunteers read paragraphs and ask the class questions. Then have them ask students to summarize.

2. **Clarify meaning** Some concepts in this selection may be difficult for students to understand, so you may need to spend additional time discussing the content. For example, in paragraph 6, when mass increases it means it becomes heavier, which is why you would need more energy to accelerate.

3. **Provide background** Albert Einstein (1879–1955) was an American physicist best known for developing the theory of relativity. He was awarded the Nobel Prize in Physics in 1921 for his work on the photoelectric effect. Born in Germany, he moved to the United States in 1933 and assumed a professorship at Princeton University. With his brilliant mind and ground-breaking work in physics, Einstein is considered by many to be the greatest physicist of modern time.

4. **Relate to experience** *Ask: Have you seen any science fiction movies about traveling through time? Can you explain what happened? Did people age more slowly?*

Sample Answer to Guide Question
Time slows down as you approach the speed of light, so you age more slowly than on Earth.

---

6 But, wait, that's not quite right. As **Einstein** correctly **predicted,** when your speed increases, so does your **mass,** forcing you to spend even more energy to **accelerate** your spaceship to near the speed of light. A back-of-the-envelope **calculation** shows that you would need at least *ten billion times the energy used for our Moon voyages!*

7 No problem. These are very **clever engineers** we've hired. But now we learn that the closest star known to have planets is not Proxima Centauri, but one that is much farther, about 15 light-years away. Einstein showed that, while traveling at 99 percent of the speed of light, you will age at only 14 percent the pace of everybody back on Earth, so the round trip for you will last not 30 years but about four. On Earth, however, 30 years actually do **pass by,** and *everybody has forgotten about you! . . .*

Reread and Record to Learn and Recall

Record what this paragraph means. Use your own words.

Proxima Centauri

Einstein a great scientist
predicted guessed, based on knowledge
mass the measure of a solid body
accelerate increase speed

calculation math
clever smart
engineers people who design or construct structures
pass by go on

198 Unit 3 Journeys

MULTI-LEVEL OPTIONS *Read the Selection*

Newcomer *Ask: Is Proxima Centauri the only star that has planets?* (no) *Is the other star farther away?* (yes) *Would a round trip to that star last the same amount of time in space as on Earth?* (no)

Beginning *Ask: If you are traveling at 99 percent the speed of light, will you age the same way as people on Earth?* (no) *At what pace would you age compared to people back on Earth?* (14 percent) *How do they measure time in space?* (in light-years)

Intermediate *Ask: How far away is the closest star known to have planets?* (15 light-years away) *How long would a round-trip space voyage last at 99 percent the speed of light?* (four years) *Why is it unlikely we'll be able to travel to the stars?* (because of the great distances)

Advanced *Ask: How much more energy would be needed to near the speed of light than is used for a Moon voyage?* (ten billion times) *How could we make a breakthrough in space travel?* (by exploiting shortcuts in the space-time continuum)

8   Given . . . the great distances involved, it is unlikely we will travel to the stars. What we need, but may never have, is a **breakthrough** in our scientific understanding of the **structure** of the universe, so that we might **exploit** shortcuts through the **space-time continuum**—perhaps through **wormholes** that connect one part of the **cosmos** to another. Then, once again, reality will become stranger than fiction.

> **Reread and Record to Learn and Recall**
>
> Reread the author's preview question in paragraph 1. Can you answer it now? If not, reread the selection. Read slowly and carefully. Record your answer.

breakthrough   an advance or discovery
structure   the way parts are put together
exploit   use or develop
space-time continuum   how space and time work together

wormholes   holes that lead somewhere else in space
cosmos   everything that is in space

About the Author

Neil de Grasse Tyson (born 1958)

As a young boy Neil de Grasse Tyson was interested in space. He got a telescope so that he could look at the planets and stars.

Tyson wrote his first book about space in 1989. He makes his books about space easy to understand. He wants his books to be fun for people to read.

➤ How did Tyson organize "Why We Can't Get There From Here"? Did he use cause and effect? Did he use inductive or deductive presentations? (See page 141.) Give examples.

Chapter 4   Why We Can't Get There From Here   **199**

---

th   Spelling

C for /s/ sound

On the board, write: *pace, forcing, cent.* Have students read them aloud as a group. *Ask: What is the underlined letter? (c) What is its sound? ("sss")* Explain that when the letter *c* is followed by *e* or *i,* it makes an /s/ sound, not a /k/ sound. Have students reread the story to find words with this sound. (paragraph 4: spaceship, space, accelerated; paragraph 5: percent; paragraph 6: forcing)

Evaluate Your Reading Strategy

Reread and Record to Learn and Recall
Say: You have practiced an important reading strategy. Now you can decide how well you have done. Does this statement describe how you read?

> As I read, I take special steps to preview questions, read, reread, and record new information. Rereading and recording help me to learn and recall the text.

Read the Selection

1. **Silent reading**   Play the audio. Then give students time to read silently.
2. **Draw conclusions**   *Ask: What conclusion can you draw from paragraph 8? Does the author think that we will ever travel to the stars?* (It's a very remote possibility.)
3. **Multi-level options**   See MULTI-LEVEL OPTIONS on p. 198.

Sample Answer to Guide Question
Most likely, we will never travel to the stars because we can't go fast enough; the stars are too far away.

About the Author

1. **Explain author's background**   Tell pairs of students to write two questions about the author. Then have them exchange questions with another pair to answer.
2. **Use a dictionary**   Have students look up *induction* and *deduction.* Discuss and clarify the terms. Also refer students to p. 141.

Answer
Sample answer: The author uses deductive and inductive presentations. For example, in paragraph 2 he uses a deductive presentation. He says the Moon is close compared to anything else in the universe. Then he gives an example of the Moon's distance from Earth using sizes of balls and paces. In paragraph 4 he uses an inductive presentation. He gives facts first, such as *Helios B* traveling 42 miles per second. Then he concludes that it would take 15,000 years to travel to the nearest star.

Across Selections

Ask: What concept about space travel was used in the science fiction story "The Time Bike"? (The bike was going to enable the boy to travel back or forward in time and be able to return to the present.)

Spelling, Punctuation, Capitalization

After the Reading Comprehension section, students will practice spelling, punctuation, and capitalization in the Activity Book.

Beyond the Reading

Reading Comprehension

Question-Answer Relationships

Sample Answers
1. Proxima Centauri
2. *Helios B*
3. the Moon
4. near the speed of light
5. the great distances
6. We can't travel to the nearest star because the distance is too great.
7. He needed to do research to check his information, make calculations to compare and contrast statistics, and write about science facts in an interesting way.
8. I don't think it's possible. The distances are too great.
9. I look forward to space travel. I think it would be amazing to see Earth from another perspective.
10. Similarities: Both stories deal with traveling through time. Differences: In "The Time Bike," the boy travels through time, not through space; he uses a bike, not a spaceship; it is not based on facts.

Build Reading Fluency

Adjust Your Reading Rate to Scan

Explain that students need to adjust their reading to quickly scan the text to locate key words. Have them read the question then quickly scan to find the answer and identify key words.

Answers
1. 100 miles 2. 150,000 3. When your speed increases, so does your mass. 4. Proxima Centauri

---

Reading Comprehension

Question-Answer Relationships (QAR)

"Right There" Questions

1. **Recall Facts** What star is nearest the Sun?
2. **Recall Facts** What is the name of the fastest-ever unmanned space probe?
3. **Recall Facts** Where is the farthest distance a person has been in space?

"Think and Search" Questions

4. **Identify** What speed would be best for a spaceship to reach another planet?
5. **Evaluate Evidence** What is stopping us from reaching other planets?

"Author and You" Questions

6. **Summarize** What is the author's main point in this selection?

7. **Identify Author Challenges** What challenges did the author face in writing this selection?

"On Your Own" Questions

8. **Present Opinions** Do you think humans will ever travel to the other planets? Support your opinion.
9. **Present Opinions** Would you like to travel to another planet? Why or why not? Record your thoughts as a journal entry.
10. **Find Similarities and Differences Across Texts** Compare and contrast this reading with "The Time Bike." How is it similar? How is it different?

Activity Book
p. 106

Student
CD-ROM

Build Reading Fluency

Adjust Your Reading Rate to Scan

When you scan you adjust your reading rate to read fast. Scanning means looking at the text for key words to help you answer questions. Work with a partner. Read aloud key words as you look for information. Write your answers on a piece of paper.

1. If Earth were the size of a basketball, how far away would Pluto be from Earth?
2. How many miles per hour does the spaceship *Helios B* travel?
3. What did Einstein predict?
4. What is the closest known star to the sun?

MULTI-LEVEL OPTIONS *Elements of Literature*

Newcomer Have students look at the chart on page 201. Have them create a similar chart with the same heads. Guide them through the reading selection to find examples of each way of presenting information.

Beginning Have these students work with other levels to review this reading selection and a fictional one such as "The Time Bike" in Chapter 3. Have them compare and contrast ways of organizing and presenting ideas from the two selections.

Intermediate Have these students work with other levels to review this reading selection and a fictional one such as "The Time Bike" in Chapter 3. Have them compare and contrast ways of organizing and presenting ideas from the two selections.

Advanced Have these students work with other levels to review this reading selection and a fictional one such as "The Time Bike" in Chapter 3. Have them compare and contrast ways of organizing and presenting ideas from the two selections.

Listen, Speak, Interact

Listen to an Informational Text

Listen to the audio recording of "Why We Can't Get There From Here" and do the following:

1. First determine what you want to listen for. Do you want to gain information, solve a problem, or enjoy?
2. As you listen, take notes on the major ideas.
3. Listen for the way the speaker uses sounds and intonation to give meaning.
4. Write down two new vocabulary words that you learned.

5. With a partner, discuss how well you understood the recording. Ask your partner to help you with things you did not understand. Listen again and try to understand more.
6. Write a summary of the selection in one paragraph.
7. Compare your summary with your partner's.
8. Think about your experiences and knowledge. How do these relate to the selection? Discuss this with your partner.

Elements of Literature

Analyze Organization and Presentation of Ideas

In "Why We Can't Get There From Here," the author presents information in several ways.

Record answers to these items in your Reading Log.

1. Find an example of a question that the author asks the reader. What effect does this question have on you?
2. Find an example of comparing and contrasting. How does this help you understand?
3. The author uses a deductive presentation: He says that people can't go to faraway stars. Then he gives the reasons. Work with your teacher and the class to list the reasons.

Ways to Organize and Present Ideas

Questions	The author asks questions to the reader.
Compare and Contrast	The author shows how things are the same or different.
Deductive Presentation	The author makes a general statement and then gives reasons or details to show why the statement is true.
Inductive Presentation	The author gives examples and then states a conclusion based on the examples.

Reading Log   Activity Book   Student
                  p. 107   CD-ROM

Content Connection
Technology

Explain that using a computer and connecting to the Internet require a precise combination of steps that are executed in a particular sequence. Have students research these procedures and steps through instructional/procedural texts and by asking for information from computer-literate peers or adults. Have them draw up and organize their information according to the chart on page 201.

Learning Styles
Interpersonal

Help students arrange an interview with a local Internet service provider engineer or other computer expert. Have students prepare their interview questions and organize the ideas in a logical sequence. During the interview, have them show their chart and confirm/disprove their conclusions. Have them revise the chart as needed, and present it along with the details of the interview.

Listen, Speak, Interact

Listen to an Informational Text

1. **Model taking notes** Model taking notes by writing notes on the board as you play the audio.
2. **Newcomers** Work with these students to go over their notes and give suggestions. Write a group summary with these students.

Answers

6. *Example:* The author examines the reasons why we can't get to the stars from Earth. He gives reasons and examples based on what we know about the universe and actual space travel. The main obstacle to space travel is the great distances between planets and stars.

Elements of Literature

Analyze Organization and Presentation of Ideas

1. **Discuss effectiveness of author's presentation** *Ask: Did you find this information hard to understand? What ways of presenting ideas were the most helpful to you? Give an example.*
2. **Multi-level options** See MULTI-LEVEL OPTIONS on p. 200.

Answers

Example: **1.** "How about 99 percent the speed of light?" This question made me wonder what the speed of light is. **2.** The author compared Hollywood movies of space travel with what it might really look like. This made me realize how fast it would really be to travel in space.

 **ASSESS**

Have small groups write up tips for good note taking.

Word Study

Identify the Suffixes *-er* and *-est*

Clarify usage Point out that the comparative is used when comparing two items and the superlative is used when comparing three or more items.

Answers
1. faster 2. nearest

Grammar Focus

Use Comparative and Superlative Adjectives

Use superlative adjectives For additional practice, ask students questions about their community. *Ask: Where is the quietest place in your community? At which restaurant can you find the healthiest food? Which store sells the most interesting things?*

Answers
Examples: **1.** Ana is a faster runner than John. I think my little brother is the strangest person in my family. **2.** Foxes are more clever than turtles. Being a teacher is the most important job in the world.

 **ASSESS**

Have students write three sentences using superlative adjectives.

Word Study

Identify the Suffixes *-er* and *-est*

To compare one thing to another, you add the suffix *-er* to an adjective. This is the **comparative** form of the adjective.

> This risk is great**er** than that one.

To show that something is the most of its kind, you add the suffix *-est* to an adjective. This is the **superlative** form.

> Proxima Centauri, the star near**est** to the Sun . . .

This means that no other star is nearer.

1. Reread paragraph 1 on page 196. Find one example of a comparative adjective with the suffix *-er.*
2. In the same paragraph, find one example of a superlative adjective with the suffix *-est.*

Personal Dictionary | The Heinle Newbury House Dictionary | Activity Book p. 108 | Student CD-ROM

Grammar Focus

Use Comparative and Superlative Adjectives

In Word Study, above, you learned that adding the suffixes *-er* and *-est* to an adjective allows you to compare two or more things. They make your writing more precise.

Most Short Adjectives:
Add *-er* or *-est* to the adjective

Adjective	Suffix	Comparative Superlative	Changes
great	-er -est	greater greatest	
close	-er -est	closer closest	drop the e
noisy	-er -est	nois**i**er nois**i**est	change y to i

Long Adjectives:
Use *more* or *most* in front of the adjective

Adjective	Superlative
interesting	more interesting most interesting
beautiful	more beautiful most beautiful
difficult	more difficult most difficult

1. Write one comparative sentence and one superlative sentence with the adjectives *fast* and *strange.*
2. Write one comparative sentence and one superlative sentence with the adjectives *clever* and *important.*

Activity Book pp. 109–110 | Student Handbook | Student CD-ROM

202 Unit 3 Journeys

MULTI-LEVEL OPTIONS *From Reading to Writing*

Newcomer Have students work in groups. Give them key words to look up on the Internet, such as *solar system* or the names of individual planets. Have them draw or make dimensional models of the solar system with the Sun and planets labeled.

Beginning Have students work in groups to find out about individual planets. Have them draw information they find and write captions for each picture.

Intermediate Have students brainstorm a list of positives and negatives of each resource.

Advanced Have students discuss which resources would be most helpful for a research report on a scientific subject. Have them discuss research problems with using the Internet. (questions about the validity of information or finding out who an "expert" might be)

From Reading to Writing

Use Multiple Resources to Write a Research Report

You should do research on a topic before you write about it. There are many research resources that you can use.

1. Brainstorm science topics you would like to know more about.
2. Think of at least three keywords that you can look up. For example, if your topic is the planet Mars, your keywords might be *Mars, planets,* and *solar system.*
3. Do your research. Use your keywords to find information about your topics. Use at least two of the resources listed in the chart. Take notes on what you find.
4. Be sure to cite your sources using the correct format shown in your Student Handbook.
5. Write your report in three paragraphs.
6. Use comparative and superlative adjectives to make your writing more vivid and precise.

Research Resources	
Type of Resource	**Description**
Encyclopedia	general information in alphabetical order; often available on CD-ROM
Atlas	a book of maps
Thesaurus	lists of words with similar meanings (synonyms)
Dictionary	alphabetical list of words with meanings, pronunciations, and origins
Newspapers and Magazines	current and recent events
Internet	many kinds of information
Experts	anyone who knows about the topic, such as a teacher or a librarian

Student Handbook

Activity Book p. 111

Across Content Areas

Solve a Time Problem

Work with a small group to solve this time problem.

> Juan has to be at his grandmother's house in Los Angeles at 3:00 P.M. He lives 240 miles away. He can travel there at 60 miles per hour. What time should he leave home to get there on time?

Make up another time travel problem. Have a classmate solve it.

Activity Book p. 112

Reteach and Reassess

Text Structure Have students make a two-column chart with the headings *Informational* and *Fictional.* Have students compare this selection with "The Time Bike." Ask them to find examples of details from each reading.

Reading Strategy Have students work in small groups to apply previewing, rereading, and note-taking strategies to a new text. Ask groups to compare their conclusions.

Elements of Literature Have students review "The Next Great Dying" (p. 134). Ask

them to find an example of deductive presentation.

Reassess Have students list all the items that distinguish an informational text and which resources would be most useful if they were preparing an informational text of their own.

From Reading to Writing

Use Multiple Resources to Write a Research Report

1. **Plan a group research project** After students have thought of topics, have them form groups according to the topics. Tell them to discuss keywords and resources and assign research tasks to each person.
2. **Write collaboratively** Have students write up their information collaboratively. Suggest that they do an outline of the report before writing it. Have them check the report for correct capitalization and spelling.
3. **Multi-level options** See MULTI-LEVEL OPTIONS on p. 202.

Across Content Areas: Math

Solve a Time Problem

Discuss math strategies Work in groups. Have students discuss the best way to solve the problem. Ask a volunteer in each group to record the ideas and allow the group to come to a consensus. Then tell them to share the method with another group. For additional practice, have students make up a similar math problem about their local area and exchange their word problem with another group.

Answer
11:00 A.M.

ASSESS

Have students list 5 types of resources and give their descriptions.

CHAPTER 5

Into the Reading

The California Gold Rush
an excerpt from an informational book
by Pam Zollman

Dame Shirley and the Gold Rush
an excerpt from a historical novel
by Jim Rawls

Objectives

Reading Compare and contrast as you read an excerpt from an informational book and a historical novel.

Listening and Speaking Present the story of a journey.

Grammar Use adverbs.

Writing Compare and contrast two reading selections.

Content Science: Learn about natural resources.

Chapter Materials

Activity Book: *pp. 113–120*
Audio: *Unit 3, Chapter 5; CD 2, Tracks 5–6*
Student Handbook
Student CD-ROM: *Unit 3, Chapter 5*
Teacher Resource Book: *Lesson Plan, Teacher Resources, Reading Summary, Activity Book Answer Key*
Teacher Resource CD-ROM
Assessment Program: *Quiz, pp. 47–48; Teacher and Student Resources, pp. 115–144*
Assessment CD-ROM
Transparencies
The Heinle Newbury House Dictionary/CD-ROM
Web site: http://visions.heinle.com

Objectives

Preview Read the objectives. *Ask: What do you already know about historical fiction?*

Use Prior Knowledge

Talk About Challenges

Teacher think aloud *Say: Some challenges are physical. For example, learning to ski is a big challenge. But other challenges are mental. Speaking in front of a very large group is a big challenge for me.* Choose one example from your own life to discuss, filling in an organizer on the board.

Use Prior Knowledge

Talk About Challenges

A challenge is something difficult that you must do. Climbing a mountain is a big challenge. Learning to skate is a smaller challenge.

Draw a web to organize your ideas about a challenge.

1. Think about a challenge you have met. Write this in the center.
2. Read these questions and write the answers in the web.
   a. Where did the challenge happen?
   b. When did it happen?
   c. Why did you accept the challenge?
   d. How did you get ready?
   e. How did you feel afterward?

3. Share your challenge with the class.

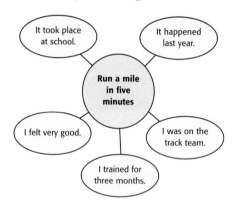

- It took place at school.
- It happened last year.
- **Run a mile in five minutes**
- I felt very good.
- I was on the track team.
- I trained for three months.

204 Unit 3 Journeys

MULTI-LEVEL OPTIONS *Build Vocabulary*

Newcomer Match groups of newcomers with beginners to make charts with the headings *Math, Science,* and *Social Studies.* Say that each subject uses certain words. Show examples in pictures or symbols, such as *minus (−), telescope, map, equals (=), test tube, newspapers.* Have students affix art or write words under the correct subject. Help them add words as they go through the chapter.

Beginning See Newcomer.

Intermediate Have pairs look up the definitions of the content words and enter them on the chart. Have them add words as they go through the chapter.

Advanced Have students work in pairs to write sentences with the new vocabulary. Ask them to add words as they go through the chapter.

Build Background

The Frontier

Before the 1800s, land west of the Mississippi River was called the frontier. Mainly Native Americans lived on this land. Settlers began to move to the frontier in the early 1800s. These settlers were called pioneers.

The land of the frontier had many natural resources. Natural resources are things from nature that people use. Some natural resources are trees, water, and metals, such as gold. Gold was a very important natural resource in California.

Content Connection
The Mississippi River is located in the center of the United States. It is one of the longest rivers in the world. It runs 2,350 miles.

Build Vocabulary

Study Words Systematically

One way to study the meanings of words is to make a word list.

1. Study these words that are useful in your social studies classes.
   a. Make a section in your Personal Dictionary. Copy the chart.
   b. As you read, fill in the meanings of the words. Use a dictionary or ask your teacher.
2. Look through a newspaper or a magazine. Find current articles on natural resources. Read the articles and add new words to your list.

Social Studies Vocabulary	
Word	**Meaning**
covered wagon	a large wagon covered with cloth
mining	
ranch	
stagecoach	
mule	

Personal Dictionary

The Heinle Newbury House Dictionary

Activity Book p. 113

Student CD-ROM

Chapter 5   The California Gold Rush *and* Dame Shirley and the Gold Rush   **205**

Content Connection
Social Studies

Build Vocabulary Have students work in small groups. Help them to use encyclopedias and the Internet to research vocabulary that described life in mining camps during the California Gold Rush. Instruct them to create a Venn diagram to compare and contrast items used during the Gold Rush with the present day. Have them download pictures from the Internet to illustrate their work.

Learning Styles
Kinesthetic

Build Background Have the class create and act out a short mime play about frontier life at the time of the Gold Rush. Have them research the necessary elements of a mime, the need for a conflict and climax, and so on. Then have them present their work.

Build Background

The Frontier

1. **Use prior knowledge** *Ask: What do you already know about pioneers in the western frontier?* Write useful vocabulary on the board.
2. **Content Connection** The first gold nuggets were found in 1849 near Sacramento, California. This began one of the largest human migrations in history. A total of about 300,000 people moved to California in search of instant wealth. This resulted in a dramatic increase in the population of California. The Gold Rush continued until 1864.

Build Vocabulary

Study Words Systematically

Teacher Resource Book: *Personal Dictionary, p. 63*

1. **Locate pronunciations using glossaries** Have students look at their social studies textbooks and locate the glossary. Ask them to scan the glossary to see how it is organized and how they can use it. Point out that pronunciations are provided for some words. Have them locate a word and its pronunciation and practice saying it.
2. **Reading selection vocabulary** You may want to introduce the glossed words in the reading selections before students begin reading. Key words: *prospectors, miner, nugget, lured, restlessness, nomad, saddle.* Instruct students to write the words with correct spelling and their definitions in their Personal Dictionaries. Have them pronounce each word and divide it into syllables.
3. **Multi-level options** See MULTI-LEVEL OPTIONS on p. 204.

Answers
1. mining: taking minerals from the earth; ranch: a large farm where animals are kept; stagecoach: a closed vehicle pulled by horses; mule: an animal whose mother is a horse and whose father is a donkey

ASSESS

Have pairs of students write three sentences with new vocabulary.

Text Structure

Nonfiction and Historical Fiction Text

1. **Review features of historical fiction** *Ask: What other historical fiction did we read?* ("The Voyage of the Lucky Dragon") *Did that story use the same features for historical fiction?* (yes)

2. **Multi-level options** See MULTI-LEVEL OPTIONS below.

Reading Strategy

Compare and Contrast

Apply strategy to content classes *Ask: Do you ever compare and contrast in your other classes? In which classes would it be especially useful?* (science, social studies, art, music) *Do you ever use a Venn diagram to chart those comparisons?*

 **ASSESS**

Have students write three features of historical fiction.

Text Structure

Nonfiction and Historical Fiction

"The California Gold Rush" is **nonfiction.** Nonfiction tells about real people and events. It also includes facts.

"Dame Shirley and the Gold Rush" is **historical fiction.** Historical fiction is a made-up story that happens during a real time in the past.

Look for features of nonfiction and historical fiction as you read.

	Nonfiction	Historical Fiction
Characters	real people	real people and/ or made-up people
Setting	real time and place	real time and place
Events	real events to tell the story	real events and made-up events to tell the story

Student CD-ROM

Reading Strategy

Compare and Contrast

When you **compare,** you notice how two or more things are similar. When you **contrast,** you notice how two or more things are different.

You can use a Venn Diagram to compare and contrast bananas and apples. Bananas and apples are similar because they are types of fruit. However, they are different colors.

1. Make a diagram like this one in your Reading Log. In place of "Bananas" and "Apples" write the titles of the selections.
2. Compare and contrast the events of each selection.

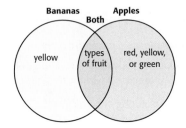

Reading Log

Student CD-ROM

206 Unit 3 Journeys

MULTI-LEVEL OPTIONS *Text Structure*

Newcomer Make a three-column chart headed: *Title, Real,* and *Made-up.* Have students write their three favorite selections from earlier readings in the first column. Then have them check whether each was real or made-up. Have the group figure out if most students prefer nonfiction or fiction.

Beginning *Ask: What is fiction?* (a made-up story) *What is nonfiction?* (a true story) Tell students they will be reading one selection of each type in this chapter. Have student pairs make KWL charts for each reading and have them complete the charts when they complete the chapter.

Intermediate Have these students work in pairs to predict what text differences they expect to find in the two reading selections.

Advanced Have students list the differences between examples of fiction and nonfiction they have already read. Have them also predict what they expect to find in the two selections.

THE CALIFORNIA GOLD RUSH

an excerpt from an informational book
by Pam Zollman

DAME SHIRLEY AND THE GOLD RUSH

an excerpt from a historical novel
by Jim Rawls

207

Reading Selection Materials

Audio: *Unit 3, Chapter 5; CD 2, Tracks 5–6*
Teacher Resource Book: *Reading Summary,*
    pp. 93–94
Transparencies: #39, *Reading Summary*

Suggestions for Using Reading Summary

- Introduce new vocabulary or cognates.
- Cut the summary into strips, or jumble the sentences on an overhead transparency. Students put the sentences in order.
- Practice the reading strategy.
- Students read aloud or with a partner.
- Students paraphrase the summary.
- Students do a cloze activity.
- Students create a visual or graphic organizer, such as a timeline or storyboard, to illustrate the summary.
- Students paraphrase the summary.

Preview the Selections

1. **Interpret art** *Say: Describe the scene. What can you tell about life in California during the Gold Rush? Do you think that everyone found what they were looking for? Why or why not?*
2. **Connect** Remind students that the unit theme is *journeys*. *Ask: Why do you think people made the journey to California? Was it for political freedom? Was it for wealth or just for making a living?*

 Content Connection
Math

Tell students that during the Gold Rush in 1849, miners could make $15 a day for 10–12 hours' work. Help them use the library or the Internet to research these questions: *Was $15 a day a good salary in 1849? Why or why not? How well could someone live on $15 a day in 1849?* Have students present their findings in groups.

Learning Styles
Visual

Ask: How did people dress during the 1840s? How did they dress in the mining camps during the Gold Rush? Have students research the typical clothing of the late 1840s and that worn by people in or around the mining camps. Based on their research, have them draw and label pictures of figures from that era wearing typical clothing items. Have them write a few sentences contrasting that clothing with today's clothing.

Read the Selection

1. **Use art to understand text** Have students look at the art before answering the guide question. *Ask: What kind of houses are these? What do you think they are made of? Do you think this shelter kept out rain or wind?*

2. **Shared reading** Play the audio. Then have students take turns joining in for different parts of the text.

3. **Identify main idea and details** Have students find the main idea and details for paragraph 1. (*Example:* In 1849, so many people went to California to mine for gold that the era is called the Gold Rush and all the miners are called forty-niners.) Students can do this in small groups and then write down notes. When they have finished, have them write their notes on the board.

Sample Answer to Guide Question
Similarities: some houses are built of wood.
Differences: houses were built without a plan; some houses were made of bushes and limbs.

See Teacher Edition pp. 434–436 for a list of English-Spanish cognates in the reading selection.

Audio
CD 2. Tr. 5

The California Gold Rush
an excerpt from an informational book by Pam Zollman

1   The year 1849 changed North America's history. In that year the first of about 300,000 people from all over the world began to hurry to California to look for gold. The rush included so many people that it was called the Gold Rush. The newspapers called the Gold Rush people forty-niners because that year was so important to the growth of California. No matter whether they came in 1849 or in the following years, all the Gold Rush people were called forty-niners.

Compare and Contrast

How are the houses of the forty-niners similar to and different from houses today?

2   Most of the forty-niners were men in a hurry to get to the gold fields, the places where gold might be found. They didn't make time to plan how they'd live once they arrived. Most knew little or nothing about looking for gold. Some of the **prospectors** didn't take time to build houses or cabins. Instead they built **lean-tos** or bush houses, by piling bushes and limbs together to form a shelter. Some used tents or lived in their covered wagon. Others built **shacks** from the wood in the wagons. Some even slept in holes in the ground.

prospectors people who look for gold

lean-tos shelters with only roofs that are made of tree branches

shacks small houses that are roughly built

208 Unit 3 Journeys

MULTI-LEVEL OPTIONS *Read the Selection*

Newcomer Play the audio *Ask: Were people trying to find wood?* (no) *Did people look for gold in Georgia?* (no) *Did they look for gold in California?* (yes)

Beginning Read the Reading Summary aloud. Then do a paired reading of the selection. *Ask: What were the prospectors trying to find?* (gold) *Were they called forty-niners because they were forty-nine years old?* (no) *When did the Gold Rush begin?* (in 1849)

Intermediate Have students do a paired reading. *Ask: How many people came to California during the Gold Rush?* (300,000) *How long was the prospectors' workday?* (10 to 12 hours) *Where could prospectors sometimes find gold nuggets?* (in streams, rivers, or gullies)

Advanced Have students do a partner read aloud. *Ask: How much could a prospector earn in a day?* ($15) *Do you think the prospectors felt that the chance of earning that money was worth the hard work and risks?* (yes) *Why do you think so?* (because it was 15 times more than they could make in other places)

Compare and Contrast

How is the work of the forty-niners similar to and different from work that you do?

3   The forty-niners found that **mining** for gold was hard work. Their day began at **dawn** with a breakfast of coffee and hard biscuits. They then spent 10 to 12 hours looking for gold. The sun burned their neck and back. Once in a while, a lucky **miner** might find a gold **nugget** in a stream, river, or **gully.** Or he might find a handful of gold dust in a **crevice** between rocks. For most of the miners, though, looking for gold meant **backbreaking** work that required them to separate gold dust and flakes from **tons** of sand and gravel. In the western United States, $1 a day was good pay for a day's work. The average prospector might earn $15 per day in California, but he might earn nothing. And he might earn nothing for days.

mining looking for things found underneath the earth
dawn early in the morning
miner a person who looks for things underneath the earth
nugget a small piece of something

gully a deep, long hole made in the ground after heavy rain
crevice a small space between two things
backbreaking something that is very hard to do
tons measurement of weight; one ton = 2,000 lbs.

About the Author   Pam Zollman

Pam Zollman has been writing for children for years. Her stories have been printed in several children's magazines. Zollman teaches writing about children's stories at colleges.

➤ What question would you like to ask Pam Zollman about this selection?

Chapter 5 The California Gold Rush *and* Dame Shirley and the Gold Rush   **209**

Spelling

Silent *u*

On the board, write: *building.* Hold your hand over the *u* and *ask: Does this word sound different without the* u*?* (no) Tell students that sometimes the letter *u* is silent, especially if it is followed by an *i.*

  Apply Have students review the first reading selection and find all the words with a silent *u.* (paragraph 2: build, built; paragraph 3: biscuits)

Read the Selection

◼ Teacher Resource Book: *Venn Diagram, p. 35*

1. **Paired reading** Play the audio. Then have students practice reading aloud to each other. Have them identify the main idea and details in paragraph 3. (*Example:* Miners worked long, hard hours, but they could make a lot of money if they were lucky.)

2. **Use a graphic organizer** Draw a Venn diagram on the board, labeling one circle *forty-niners* and the other *today's workers. Ask: What kind of work do you or someone you know do? Do people sometimes work 10 to 12 hours a day? Do people make more money a day now? Do people work outside under the hot sun?*

3. **Locate derivations using dictionaries** Have students look at these glossed words and determine what words they are derived from: *prospectors, mining, miner.* Have students check the derivations in a print, online, or CD-ROM dictionary.

4. **Multi-level options** See MULTI-LEVEL OPTIONS on p. 208.

Sample Answer to Guide Question
Similarities: work begins at dawn; people work outside; some people make $15 a day for part-time work; work 10–12 hours. Differences: people don't mine gold in California anymore; people earn more than $1 or $15 for a full day's work.

About the Author

1. **Explain author's background** Pam Zollman graduated from the University of Houston and started her career as a reporter and technical writer. She began writing children's literature soon after her two sons were born. Her story, "Millie's Garden" won a fiction award from *Highlights for Children* in 1996.

2. **Discuss author's intention** Ask: *Why do you think the author chose this topic to write about? What is interesting about this topic? Do you think young children would be interested in reading about gold mining?*

Answer
Examples: How did you find your information? What sources did you use for research? Have you ever been to an old mining town?

Read the Selection

1. **Reciprocal reading** Play the audio. Have volunteers read paragraphs and ask the class questions. Then have them ask students to summarize.

2. **Make inferences about the characters** Have students look at the illustration of Dame Shirley and Fayette. *Ask: What information can we infer from this illustration? For example, how old do you think they are? What inferences can you make from the way they are dressed? Has it been a difficult journey? How do you know?*

Sample Answer to Guide Question
Similarities: making a difficult journey to gold country. Differences: Dame Shirley is with her husband, who is a doctor, not a prospector; they spent the night at a ranch, not in a tent.

See Teacher Edition pp. 434–436 for a list of English-Spanish cognates in the reading selection.

Audio
CD 2. Tr. 6

Dame Shirley and the Gold Rush
an excerpt from a historical novel by Jim Rawls

A Trip to the Mines

1   Dame Shirley rubbed the sleep from her eyes and pulled the **coarse** woolen blanket up around her shoulders. The early morning air was cool and still. She lay quietly, listening to the sounds of daybreak drifting through the cabin window. Outside, a mule **brayed,** and a screeching rooster **saluted** the rising sun.

2   It was early September 1851. Dame Shirley and her husband, Dr. Fayette Clappe, had spent the night at a ranch near Marysville, California. Today they were to begin their ride north along the Feather River to the gold mining camp of Rich Bar.

3   The couple had been **lured** to California by the Gold Rush. They were not alone. Thousands of others had come for the same reason.

4   Dame Shirley thought about how far they had come from their home in New England. At the time, no highways or railroads **linked** California with the rest of the United States. So Dame Shirley and Fayette had to sail all the way around South America to reach San Francisco—a trip of about seventeen thousand miles!

Compare and Contrast

How are the characters similar and different in the two stories?

coarse rough	**lured** attracted
brayed made a loud sound	**linked** brought together
saluted greeted	

MULTI-LEVEL OPTIONS *Read the Selection*

Newcomer Play the audio twice. The second time have students join in when they can. *Ask: Is this story about a woman during the Gold Rush?* (yes) *Is California her home?* (no) *Is her home in New England or San Francisco?* (New England)

Beginning Read the Reading Summary aloud. Then do a paired reading of the text. *Ask: Did Dame Shirley wake up in a cabin or in a hotel?* (in a cabin) *How did Dame Shirley get to Northern California?* (by stagecoach) *Who is Fayette?* (her husband)

Intermediate Have students do a partner read aloud. *Ask: What was Fayette's profession?* (He was a doctor.) *Why had they chosen the Rich Bar mining camp?* (because it had only one doctor) *What did a friend in San Francisco tell Dame Shirley?* (that she would never make it to Rich Bar alive)

Advanced Have students read silently. *Ask: Why was it hard to reach California then?* (There were no highways or railroads to California.) *How did Dame Shirley and Fayette reach San Francisco?* (by sailing around South America) *Why was the stagecoach so uncomfortable?* (It had wooden wheels.)

Compare and Contrast

How is traveling for Dame Shirley and Fayette similar to and different from the way that you travel?

5 From there, they rode a **stagecoach** north to mining country. The stage's wooden wheels had bounced and jumped over a road that was more trail than highway. It was like being trapped for several days in a small wooden box that someone was shaking. The ride was a bit longer than one hundred miles, but seemed like a thousand.

6 This morning, though, Dame Shirley and Fayette were rested and ready to continue their travels. They were going to Rich Bar to find work for Fayette. Dame Shirley and Fayette knew that Rich Bar had a population of several thousand miners. They also knew that it had just one doctor. Fayette was certain he would have plenty of opportunities to practice medicine there.

7 Friends in San Francisco had warned Dame Shirley not to go to the mines. One woman had **predicted** that she would never make it to Rich Bar alive. Another had said that Dame Shirley was crazy to think of living in a mining camp made up almost entirely of men. Even Fayette had **advised** her to remain in San Francisco. Everyone said that going to the mines was too dangerous for a woman.

---

stagecoach   a covered, four-wheel wagon   **advised**   recommended or suggested
predicted   stated something will happen in the future

Chapter 5   The California Gold Rush *and* Dame Shirley and the Gold Rush   **211**

Read the Selection

Teacher Resource Book: *Venn Diagram, p. 35; Timelines, p. 39*

1. **Paired reading**   Play the audio. Have students practice reading aloud in pairs. Then have them draw a Venn diagram to answer the guide question.

2. **Use a chronology to understand a story**   Draw a vertical timeline on the board and mark a place toward the bottom of the line; label it *September, 1851.* **Ask:** *What happened before that morning? Where were they from? How did they get to California? How far was it?* (The following information should be on the board: sailed from New England to San Francisco: 17,000 miles; rode by stagecoach to mining country: 100 miles; spent the night at a ranch in Marysville; went to Rich Bar)

3. **Multi-level options**   See MULTI-LEVEL OPTIONS on p. 210.

Sample Answer to Guide Question
Similarities: vehicles use wheels. Differences: wheels were made of wood; highway was like a trail; traveling took a long time and was uncomfortable.

A   Capitalization

Months

Have students generate all the types of words that need to begin with a capital letter. (nationalities and the names of people, cities, states, countries, planets, and stars) *Say: We also need to write the names of the months with a capital letter.*

   Apply   Have students review the paragraphs they have completed in "Dame Shirley and the Gold Rush" to find the name

of a month. (paragraph 2: September) Have students name the remaining months and write them with correct capitalization. Check for correct spelling.

Read the Selection

1. **Reciprocal reading** Play the audio. Have volunteers read paragraphs and ask the class questions. Then have them ask students to summarize.
2. **Relate to personal experience** *Ask: Have you ever ridden a horse or mule? Where were you and what happened? Do you think it would be scary to fall off a mule?*

Sample Answer to Guide Question
She was dusty and probably surprised. After she got up, she laughed and smiled.

8   But Dame Shirley would have none of it. All her life she had dreamed of travel and adventure. She once said that she was a "**thistle-seed**," ready to blow wherever the wind might take her. She felt a **restlessness** in her **soul.** She had the spirit of a **nomad.** And having come so far already, she meant to experience life in the mines, not merely to hear about it from her husband or the newspapers.

9   Dame Shirley nudged her mule again with her foot. Then she felt a strange **sensation.** Her **saddle** was slipping! Suddenly, she and the saddle were a mini-**avalanche** sliding sideways off the mule. Before she knew it, she was lying in the road, a cloud of dust mushrooming around her. Her saddle swung upside down beneath her mule. Dust filled her eyes, nose, and ears. Her fine riding outfit was coated with dust.

10   A look of horror filled Fayette's face. He quickly **dismounted** and rushed to help Dame Shirley to her feet. Shirley, though, didn't need any help. She was startled, but unhurt. Getting up, she looked at Fayette. A grin spread across her face. She began to laugh.

> **Compare and Contrast**
>
> How did Dame Shirley look before she got up from the ground? How did she look after she got up?

thistle-seed a part of a weed-like plant	**sensation** a feeling
restlessness unable to stay in one place	**saddle** a seat strapped to a horse
soul a part of a person's thoughts and feelings	**avalanche** something sliding down suddenly
nomad a person who moves from home to home	**dismounted** got off

212   Unit 3   Journeys

MULTI-LEVEL OPTIONS *Read the Selection*

Newcomer *Ask: Did Dame Shirley love travel and adventure?* (yes) *Did she fall off the mule because she was sick?* (no) *Did she fall off the mule because the saddle slipped?* (yes)

Beginning *Ask: Did Dame Shirley want to work in a mine, or did she want to read about it?* (work in a mine) *What was she riding?* (a mule) *About what time did they reach Marysville?* (midnight)

Intermediate *Ask: What made Dame Shirley love travel and adventure?* (She felt restless.) *How did she react to falling off the mule?* (She laughed.) *What did she and Fayette have for dinner in Marysville?* (hot oysters, toast, tomatoes, and coffee)

Advanced *Ask: What was the difference between Fayette's and Shirley's reactions to her falling off the mule?* (He was upset; she was amused.) *Why did the saddle slip?* (because it was too big) *Why was everyone against Dame Shirley working in the mine?* (because women didn't do that in the 1850s)

11 When he went to fix her saddle, Fayette discovered that it was far too large for her mule. He could fix it so it might hold for a bit, but he wasn't sure how **reliable** it would be. He suggested they turn back instead. At the very least, he said, she should return to the ranch and put on some clean clothes and make a fresh start.

12 Dame Shirley said no to both suggestions. She surveyed her appearance. Indeed, she was a sight. She was covered in dust, from tip to toe. But so what? This was California. This was mining country. Who on Earth was she going to run into here? Certainly not anyone who would turn up his nose at a little dust. Something about the idea of her great adventure beginning with a little **comedy** pleased her. She climbed back on her mule and rode **merrily** on.

13 Finally, at about midnight, they reached Marysville. There they spent the night after dining on a feast of hot **oysters,** toast, tomatoes, and coffee. It was their first meal since breakfast.

> **Compare and Contrast**
>
> Which events are the same in the two stories? Which are different?

---

reliable something that one can depend on	**merrily** happily
comedy something that is funny	**oysters** sea animals with a hard shell

About the Author

Jim Rawls (born 1945)

Jim Rawls lives in California. He likes to learn about the history of California. Rawls thinks many people's hopes and dreams have happened or been challenged in California. He has written many books and stories on the history of California.

➤ Why do you think Jim Rawls wrote this text? What challenges do you think he faced to write historical fiction?

Chapter 5   The California Gold Rush *and* Dame Shirley and the Gold Rush   **213**

 Spelling

Silent *gh*

On the board, write: *through*. Have students pronounce it. Cover the *gh* and **ask:** *Is there a difference without the* gh*?* (no) **Say:** *The* gh *is silent.* Have class find other *gh* words. (paragraph 8: might; paragraph 10: though; paragraph 12: sight; paragraph 13: night)

Evaluate Your Reading Strategy

Compare and Contrast *Say: You have practiced an important reading strategy. Now you can decide how well you have done. Does this statement describe how you read?*

> Comparing and contrasting stories helps me understand how the stories are the same. They also help me understand how they are different.

Read the Selection

1. **Silent reading** Give students time to read silently. Have them draw a Venn diagram to answer the guide question.
2. **Locate derivations using dictionaries** Have students look at these glossed words and determine what words they are derived from: *restlessness, sensation, dismounted, reliable, merrily.* Have students check the derivations in a print, online, or CD-ROM dictionary.
3. **Multi-level options** See MULTI-LEVEL OPTIONS on p. 212.

Sample Answer to Guide Question
Similar events: people traveled great distances to reach California; people endured hardships. Different events: Dame Shirley and her husband were not going to look for gold, but he was going to work as a doctor; they had a plan.

About the Author

Express personal opinion *Say: This author likes to learn and write about the history of his state. If you were to write an historical fiction piece about our state, what would you write about? Why do you think that would be an interesting topic?*

Answer
Example: I think he wrote this selection to inform readers about the less typical forty-niners but also to entertain. I think he faced the challenges of making the story interesting and making it sound like history at the same time. It may also have been challenging to find out what life was like during that time, such as what people ate.

Across Selections

Direct students to "The Voyage of the Lucky Dragon" (p. 166). *Say: Compare the tone and mood of these two examples of historical fiction. How are they different?* ("The Voyage of the Lucky Dragon" was more serious and scarier because the characters were running away from home out of fear, not a sense of adventure.)

Spelling, Punctuation, Capitalization

After the Reading Comprehension section, students will practice spelling, punctuation, and capitalization in the Activity Book.

Beyond the Reading

Reading Comprehension

Question-Answer Relationships

Sample Answers

1. 1849
2. Some days they earned nothing and some days up to $15.
3. 1851
4. They were traveling to Rich Bar by stagecoach.
5. Seeing the old photographs made the people and the events seem more real. They gave me a better idea of what life was like during that time.
6. Fayette was going to be a doctor in a mining town.
7. She was brave, had a sense of humor, and was willing to put up with hardships for an adventure.
8. People didn't have very good housing, the food was scarce or bad, the working conditions were poor, and the pay was unreliable.
9. Yes. It was hard moving to this city. The trip was comfortable, but I missed my family and friends.
10. I'd join the Gold Rush. It would be exciting, and I don't mind hard work.

Build Reading Fluency

Read Silently

Assessment Program: *Reading Fluency Chart, p. 116*

When students have completed the reading fluency activity, record their progress in the Reading Fluency Chart.

Reading Comprehension

Question-Answer Relationships (QAR)

"Right There" Questions

1. **Recall Facts** In "The California Gold Rush," what year changed U.S. history?
2. **Recall Facts** In "The California Gold Rush," what did the miners earn?
3. **Recall Facts** In "Dame Shirley and the Gold Rush," what year did Shirley and Fayette set out for the mining camp?
4. **Recall Facts** In "Dame Shirley and the Gold Rush," what city were they traveling to? How did they make the trip?

"Think and Search" Questions

5. **Analyze Style, Elements, and Media** View the art and photos in these readings. How do the style and elements extend (add to) the texts? What ideas do you gain?

6. **Explain** In "Dame Shirley and the Gold Rush," why was the couple traveling to the mining town?
7. **Analyze Character Traits** What kind of person was Dame Shirley?

"Author and You" Question

8. **Connect Main Ideas** Do you agree with the sentence, "Life in a mining camp was hard"? Why do you think this?

"On Your Own" Questions

9. **Compare with Your Own Experience** Have you made a difficult journey in your life?
10. **Speculate** If you lived in 1861, would you join the Gold Rush? Why or why not?

Activity Book
p. 114

Student
CD-ROM

Build Reading Fluency

Read Silently

Reading silently is good practice. It helps you learn to read faster. An effective reader reads silently for increasing lengths of time.

1. Listen to the audio recording of paragraphs 1–3 on page 210.
2. Listen to the chunks of words as you follow along.
3. Reread paragraphs 1–3 silently two times.
4. Your teacher will time your second reading.
5. Raise your hand when you are done.

MULTI-LEVEL OPTIONS *Elements of Literature*

Newcomer Replay the audio of "Dame Shirley and the Gold Rush." Direct students to the illustrations. *Ask: Are Dame Shirley and Fayette alike?* (no) Have students draw a picture of each character doing an activity he/she likes. Provide key words for picture captions.

Beginning Point out that the mule incident showed sharp character differences between Dame Shirley and Fayette. Have students draw a picture of each character doing an activity he/she enjoys. Help students find sentences in the story to use as picture captions.

Intermediate Have students make a large two-column chart with the headings *Dame Shirley* and *Fayette.* Have them find and record on the chart sentences in the text that show the traits and motivation of each of the characters.

Advanced Have students work in groups to write an essay. Ask them to compare and contrast character traits, work, and motivations of Dame Shirley and Fayette. Have them illustrate their essays and compile them into a booklet for the class library.

Listen, Speak, Interact

Present the Story of a Journey

Have you ever taken a journey? Think about your trip and tell the class about it.

1. Record notes on note cards about the details of your journey. Use these questions to help you.
   a. Where did you go?
   b. How long did it take?
   c. How did you feel before your journey? During your journey? At the end?
   d. Would you want to make this journey again? Why or why not?
2. Make visuals for your presentation.
   a. Make a map showing important places and your route.
   b. Make a timeline showing important dates.
3. Practice your presentation with a partner.
   a. Do not read your note cards. Use your visuals.
   b. Ask your partner for feedback on your presentation.
   c. Revise your presentation.
4. Give your presentation for the class.
   a. Be dramatic. Use gestures to help make your points.
   b. Pay attention to your voice. Use effective rate, volume, pitch, and tone.

Elements of Literature

Analyze Character Traits and Motivation

Authors can give the reader a lot of information about the characters in a story.

Traits are what a character is like. For example, a character can be honest.

Motivation tells us why a character does something. For example, Dame Shirley wanted adventure.

1. Work with a partner. Reread paragraphs 7–12 of "Dame Shirley and the Gold Rush," on pages 211–212.
2. Answer the following questions in your Reading Log.
   a. Why did friends warn Dame Shirley not to go to California?
   b. What words would you use to describe Dame Shirley's character traits?
   c. What is Dame Shirley's motivation for going to Rich Bar?
3. Compare and contrast your answers with other students'.

Reading Log   Activity Book   Student
                   p. 115   CD-ROM

Chapter 5 The California Gold Rush *and* Dame Shirley and the Gold Rush   **215**

Content Connection
The Arts

Help students use the Internet to research the songs that were popular during the time of the Gold Rush, such as "Oh, Susanna" and "Buffalo Gal." If possible, help students find recordings to play in class and have a class sing-along.

Learning Styles
Linguistic

Have students reread paragraph 1 of "Dame Shirley and the Gold Rush" and note the words for animal sounds: *brayed, screeching.* Have groups research and chart other onomatopoeic animal sounds (bow-wow, meow, and so on) and add appropriate illustrations. If possible, have multiple-language students add a column of equivalents in other languages (*Example:* English = *oink-oink*/Japanese = *bu-bu*).

Listen, Speak, Interact

Present the Story of a Journey

1. **Review keys to a good presentation** Remind students of other presentations they have done in class. Have them help you make a list of tips for a good presentation. Some points to include are: good eye contact and body language; clear visuals; practice beforehand; speak slowly and clearly.
2. **Newcomers** Work with these students separately. Have them make a visual to answer questions 1a–d. Help them use key phrases to accompany their visuals as they present.

Elements of Literature

Analyze Character Traits and Motivation

▌ Teacher Resource Book: *Reading Log, p. 64*

1. **Describe a character** Write on the board: *bigger than life. Say: We often say a character like Dame Shirley is "bigger than life." Think about her. What do you think the phrase means? How is Dame Shirley bigger than life?*
2. **Multi-level options** See MULTI-LEVEL OPTIONS on p. 214.

Answers
2. **a.** They were afraid it was too dangerous for a woman. **b.** brave, adventurous, funny **c.** She wants adventure.

 **ASSESS**

Have students write two sentences describing Dame Shirley.

Word Study

Learn Words from Context and Experience

Apply strategy Have students reread paragraph 8 to see how the context helps explain the word *nomad*. *Ask: Which sentences in the paragraph help you understand the word? Which phrases?* (third and fourth sentences; thistle-seed, wherever the wind might take her, restlessness)

Grammar Focus

Use Adverbs

Act out adverbs For additional practice, have students act out the following adverbs by doing something in that manner: *quietly, loudly, quickly, sadly, restlessly, softly.*

Answers
paragraph 1: quietly; paragraph 10: quickly

ASSESS

Have students answer these questions using adverbs. *Ask: How do you get up in the morning? How do you work on your homework? How do you eat breakfast?*

Word Study

Learn Words from Context and Experience

When you don't understand a word in a reading, try to understand it by using the context and your experience. Follow the steps in this example.

Word you don't know: **shelter**

1. Read the sentence that has the word in it.

   Instead they built lean-tos . . . to form a **shelter.**

2. Read the sentence that comes before this one. Look for context clues.

   Some of the prospectors didn't take time to build houses or cabins.

3. Read the sentence that follows. Look for context clues.

   Some used tents or lived in their covered wagon.

4. In the sentence that comes before, the author describes where the prospectors lived.

5. In the sentence that follows, the author gives more places where the prospectors lived.

6. From your experience, you know that houses, cabins, and tents protect people from bad weather.

7. From the context and your experience, you can guess that *shelter* means a place to live or a place that protects people.

Activity Book   Student
p. 116   CD-ROM

Grammar Focus

Use Adverbs

An **adverb** describes a verb or an adjective. It often tells how something is done. An adverb is often formed by adding *-ly* to an adjective.

She spoke soft**ly.**

"Softly" tells how she spoke.

If an adjective ends in *-y,* you change the *-y* to *-i* before adding *-ly.*

Adverbs can help make your writing more interesting and precise.

1. Reread paragraphs 1 and 10 in "Dame Shirley and the Gold Rush."
2. Identify the adverbs in each paragraph.
3. Write two sentences of your own. Use an *-ly* adverb in each one.

Activity Book   Student   Student
pp. 117–118   Handbook   CD-ROM

216   **Unit 3**   Journeys

MULTI-LEVEL OPTIONS *From Reading to Writing*

Newcomer Have students work in pairs to choose one item (food, clothing, work, housing, means of travel) to compare and contrast. Have pairs decide if their item is similar or different in the stories. Then have them draw one or two pictures of the item and place them on the Venn diagram.

Beginning Have students work in pairs to reexamine both texts. Give one student a red pen to record similarities and the other student a blue one to record differences. Have them share their findings with another pair.

Intermediate Have students work in pairs to record similarities and differences from the readings. Have them organize the items in a logical sequence within the diagram and block out the main points of their paragraph.

Advanced Have students compose the paragraph and input it on a computer and print it out. Then have pairs work together to offer ideas for revisions and proofread their work before presenting it in groups.

From Reading to Writing

Compare and Contrast Two Reading Selections

The two readings in this chapter are similar in some ways and different in others. Write three paragraphs to compare and contrast the two readings.

1. Create a Venn Diagram like this one.
   a. List the things that are different about the readings in each large circle.
   b. List the things that are the same in the space where the circles overlap.
2. Write your paragraphs using the information in the diagram.
   a. In the first paragraph, state your main idea.
   b. In the second paragraph, give reasons and examples of how the readings are the same and different.
   c. In the third paragraph, write a summary of your ideas.

The California Gold Rush — **Dame Shirley and the Gold Rush**

about the '49ers in general | about the Gold Rush | about Dame Shirley and her husband

3. Write a final draft.
   a. Use resources to check spelling.
   b. Use a variety of sentence types. Combine short sentences into compound or complex sentences.
   c. Use adverbs to make your writing interesting and more precise.
   d. If possible, prepare your final draft on a computer.

Activity Book
p. 119

Student Handbook

Across Content Areas

Learn About Natural Resources

Earth is full of natural resources. Research the natural resources that are in the area where you live.

1. Take notes from at least two resources (see page 203) to identify the natural resources in your area.

2. What other questions come to mind? Research these questions.
3. Present your research to your class.

Activity Book
p. 120

From Reading to Writing

Compare and Contrast Two Reading Selections

1. **Use a graphic organizer** Draw a large Venn diagram and discuss the similarities and differences with the class. Have volunteers fill in the organizer.
2. **Write collaboratively** Help students write the first sentence for their paragraphs. Remind them that the topic sentence should have the titles of both selections in it as well as the topic of the paragraph.
3. **Use a variety of sentences** To help students check their drafts, have them underline each compound and complex sentence, making sure that they have at least one of each.
4. **Multi-level options** See MULTI-LEVEL OPTIONS on p. 216.

Across Content Areas: Science

Learn About Natural Resources

1. **Group work** Have students discuss and research the questions in groups. Allow groups to divide the assignment into parts and assign parts to group members.
2. **Collaborate to write a news report** Have pairs of students locate two recent articles about natural resources. They should compose a brief news report about what they read. The report should be organized by the natural resources discussed (such as water, forests, air). Students should practice their report for clarity of ideas and revise as necessary.

✓ ASSESS

Have students make a list of local natural resources and a list of natural resources not found locally.

Reteach and Reassess

Text Structure Ask students to list the features of nonfiction and historical fiction. Then have them write an example of each feature from the chapter readings.

Reading Strategy Have groups compare and contrast the similarities (shopping vs. residential areas) and differences (mass transportation or lack thereof) of two cities or towns they know.

Elements of Literature Have students compare and contrast the character traits of Karana from "Island of the Blue Dolphins"

(p. 120) and Phan Thi Chi from "The Voyage of the Lucky Dragon" (p. 166).

Reassess Have students write a nonfiction or historical fiction diary entry describing a journey. Remind them to include details such as places, dates, and descriptions of people and setting.

Materials

Student Handbook
CNN Video: *Unit 3*
Teacher Resource Book: *Lesson Plan, p. 18;
Teacher Resources, pp. 35–64; Video Script,
pp. 165–166; Video Worksheet, p. 175;
School-Home Connection, pp. 133–139*
Teacher Resource CD-ROM
Assessment Program: *Unit 3 Test and Mid-Book
Exam, pp. 49–60; Teacher and Student
Resources, pp. 115–144*
Assessment CD-ROM
Transparencies
The Heinle Newbury House Dictionary/CD-ROM
Heinle Reading Library: *20,000 Leagues Under
the Sea*
Web site: http://visions.heinle.com

Listening and Speaking Workshop

Exposition: Give a Presentation About a Place

Step 1: Choose a topic.
Make a four-column chart to record the
brainstorm activity. Then have students think
about and choose their own topics.

Step 2: Research the place.
Remind students that even places in their
community may have information on the
Internet. Point out that they can research a
place by interviewing people and asking
questions.

Listening and Speaking Workshop

Exposition: Give a Presentation About a Place

> **Topic**
> In this unit, you read about
> journeys that people took. Give a
> presentation about a place that you
> would like to take a journey to.

Step 1: Choose a topic.
1. Brainstorm some places that you
   think are interesting.
2. Choose one. It can be:
   a. a city or town you know
   b. a historic site
   c. a place you have read about
   d. somewhere far away

Step 2: Research the place.
Use the resources in your school library,
or use the Internet. Use the name of your
place as a keyword for an Internet search.

Step 3: Take notes about the place.
1. Write answers to these questions on
   note cards. Use one note card for
   each idea. Add other questions you
   think of.
   a. What is the name of the place?
   b. Where is it?
   c. How do you know about it?
   d. What does it look like?
   e. Did something important happen
      there? What was it?
   f. What can you do there?

2. If something important happened
   in the place, organize your notes
   about the events in a timeline.
3. Identify any special language or
   sayings from the region or culture
   of your place. How do the language
   or the sayings reflect the region
   or culture?

Step 4: Prepare visual aids.
A visual aid is something that readers
see instead of read.
1. Use a map to show the location.
2. Show pictures of the place. Use
   pictures from the Internet or from
   a book, pictures you draw, or
   photographs and postcards.
3. Bring an item from the place if you
   have one.

Step 5: Practice your presentation.
1. Tell a partner about your place.
   Remember to clarify and support
   your ideas with evidence,
   elaborations, and examples.
2. Your partner should fill out the
   Active Listening Checklist. You
   should fill out the Speaking
   Checklist. Add an evaluation point
   based on what you want to improve.
3. Revise your presentation. Use what
   you learned from the checklists.

MULTI-LEVEL OPTIONS *Listening and Speaking Workshop*

Newcomer Have students
draw several pictures showing life
in another city or country. Then
write interview questions such as:
*Where did this happen? What
happened? Who did it happen to?
Was it fun or scary to live there?*
Newcomers interview one another
and show the drawings in
response.

Beginning Have students work
in pairs to research and draw
storyboards about a modern or
historic place. Help them include
captions. Each student should
take turns presenting their
storyboard and being interviewed
by their partner.

Intermediate Have students
research life in a historic place of
their choice and prepare a
presentation about it. Tell them to
give details of the setting, climate,
lifestyle, and important events.
Remind them to provide pictures
or maps to supplement their work.

Advanced Provide students
with a list of historic places to
choose from. Have them give
details of the setting, climate,
lifestyle, important events,
timelines, and detailed visuals for
the presentation. Tell them also to
create a brief introduction and
wrap-up.

Speaking Checklist

1. Did I speak slowly and clearly?
2. Did I explain the topic clearly?
3. Was my partner able to see my visual aid?

Active Listening Checklist

1. I liked this presentation because _____ .
2. I learned _____ .
3. I would like to know more about _____ .

Student
Handbook

Step 6: Give your presentation.

Give your presentation to the class.

1. If possible, use presentation software.
2. You may want to record your presentation on video or audio to share with your family.

Viewing Workshop

View and Think

Compare and Contrast Cultures

A culture is the way a certain group of people lives.

1. Find a video that shows life in another region or culture. Ask your librarian or teacher for help.
2. Watch the video.
   a. Where is the culture? What is the place like?
   b. How do the people live? What do the people do?
   c. What language do the people speak? How does the language reflect the region or culture?
3. Compare and contrast this culture or place to where and how you live. How is it similar? How is it different?

4. Did the video change your opinions or feelings in any way? How?
5. Think about what you learned.
   a. How did the language in the video help you learn?
   b. What did you learn from the video that you would not have learned from a book?
   c. How did the video's presentation and organization help you learn?

Further Viewing

Watch the *Visions* CNN Video for Unit 3. Do the Video Worksheet.

CNN Video

Step 3: Take notes about the place.
Write each of the questions on the board. Model noting details from "The California Gold Rush" (p. 208). Point out that the questions can form an outline. Suggest that students put notes for each item in number 1 on a separate card.

Step 4: Prepare visual aids.
Discuss with students different ideas and resources for visual aids. Point out that visuals must be large enough for the entire audience to see.

Step 5: Practice your presentation.
Tell students that one way to give feedback is to tell the presenter what you want to know more about.

Step 6: Give your presentation.
After students have presented, discuss what worked well in the presentations.

ASSESS

Have students write two sentences about how they have improved their presentation skills.

Portfolio

Students may choose to record or videotape their speeches to place in their portfolios.

Viewing Workshop

View and Think

1. **Use a map** Have students locate the place in the video on a map. Ask them how geography affects the culture portrayed.
2. **Use a graphic organizer** Draw a Venn diagram. Have volunteers fill in similarities and differences between the culture on the video and their culture.

Content Connection
Social Studies

Learning Styles
Kinesthetic

Help students find a video documentary on a historic person or place, such as those produced by educational television programs. Have groups research and create a presentation based on the video. Ask them to focus on comparing and contrasting life in that time and place with their own lives. Remind them to take the characters' frame of reference into account in their comments.

Have students create a play or mime based on their documentary presentation. Groups can write a dialogue or, for a mime, two or three narrators can provide descriptive commentary on the action. Remind students to use the facts that they found in their research.

Writer's Workshop

Exposition: Write a Research Report

Write a research report Students may want to write about an area in the United States that they have studied in history or social studies class.

Step 1: Ask questions.
Have students arrange themselves into groups according to the place they are researching. Tell groups to create additional questions.

Step 2: Research answers to your questions.
Model using an index from an academic textbook. Print out and have students examine a page of search results from a Web search.

Step 3: Record and organize information.
Practice paraphrasing information with students in preparation for this step. Have a volunteer read a paragraph from a resource. As a class, paraphrase the information.

Step 4: Write a draft.
If students do their reports collaboratively, monitor that everyone writes or illustrates a section of the report.

Writer's Workshop

Exposition: Write a Research Report

> **Writing Prompt**
>
> In this unit, you learned about a journey people made to California in the 1800s. Write a research report about a famous place people made a journey to in the history of the United States.

Step 1: Ask questions.

1. Think of a place to write about. Brainstorm with your class. Some ideas include Plymouth, Massachusetts, Texas, or Florida.
2. Think of questions you have about this place. Possible questions are:
   a. Where is the place?
   b. What time period was it in?
   c. Was it important? Why?
   d. What important things happened there during this time?
   e. How has life in this place changed?
   f. Add your own questions.

Step 2: Research answers to your questions.

1. Use multiple resources in your school library to find answers.
2. Interview an expert, such as a teacher, for more answers.
3. As you research, use tables of contents and headings. These features will help you find important information.
4. Some of your questions may change. Revise or add questions if needed.

Step 3: Record and organize information.

1. Use note cards to record information for your report.
2. Write the information in your own words. Do not copy word-for-word.
3. Use quotation marks (" . . . ") if you use someone else's words. You must copy the exact words if you do this.
   a. Write the name of the person who said the words.
   b. Write the source from which you copied the words.
4. Organize your information in an outline or a timeline. Refer to your Student Handbook.

Step 4: Write a draft.

Write five paragraphs. Use the information you organized in Step 2 to develop your paragraphs. Use a computer, if possible.

1. Your first paragraph will be the introduction.
   a. Write one sentence that is a thesis statement. This sentence tells what your report is about.
   b. Tell why your place was important.
2. Your middle paragraphs will be the body.
   a. Write information that explains what happened there.
   b. Include facts and examples.

MULTI-LEVEL OPTIONS *Writer's Workshop*

Newcomer Have students work in mixed-level groups to research and write factual reports on a historic place in the United States. Have newcomers participate in brainstorming the subject and illustrate important points.

Beginning Have beginners contribute to the list of research questions, the thesis statement, one sentence in the body, and one sentence in the conclusion. Beginners can also participate in the research, especially on the Internet, and in finding illustrations or maps.

Intermediate Have these students write the expert interview questions and work with advanced students to write a first draft of the report. Remind them to use appropriate capitalization, spelling, and punctuation—especially quotation marks.

Advanced Have students prepare the outline and conduct the expert interview. Have them also lead their group in writing the content paragraph and the conclusion. Have them edit, proofread, and revise the finished report and bibliography.

3. Your fifth paragraph will be the conclusion.
   a. Retell your thesis statement in different words.
   b. Add one or two sentences that tell what the place means to people today.
4. Include a section at the end of your report where you list the sources you used. Include books, encyclopedias, and Web sites. The title of this section is "Bibliography." Refer to your Student Handbook for correct format.

Step 5: Revise your draft.

1. Exchange reports with a partner.
2. Use the Peer Editing Checklist in your Student Handbook to tell your partner what you like about the report. Tell how to make it better.
3. Use your partner's evaluation to revise your report.
4. Add text to clarify and elaborate. Delete text if you repeat things.
5. Combine and rearrange sentences to make your writing more logical and coherent. Be sure one idea leads to the next.
6. Blend paragraphs to make the report easier to read.
7. Be sure all ideas in your report are supported with examples.

Step 6: Edit and proofread your report.

1. Proofread your revised report. Look for correct spelling, grammar, punctuation, capitalization, and paragraph indentation.
2. Use the Editor's Checklist in your Student Handbook.
3. Proofread your partner's report. Point out any errors you find.

Step 7: Publish.

1. Write the final draft of your report.
2. If you write your report by hand, use your best handwriting. If you use a computer, use the spell check and grammar check.
3. Include a picture of the place. This picture can be from the Internet or you can draw a picture.
4. Bind everyone's reports together in a book. Create a Table of Contents. Ask your teacher to help you.
5. Choose one or two students to make the cover for the book. The title of the book will be "Journeys."
6. Read your classmates' reports. Evaluate them. What are their strengths and their weaknesses?
7. Use your classmates' writing as models for your future writing.
8. Place the book in a place where a specific audience can enjoy it.

Student Handbook

Step 5: Revise your draft.
Remind students to be specific when offering suggestions or when telling what they liked about their partner's report.

Step 6: Edit and proofread your report.
If students are using a spellchecker on a computer, remind them that the computer may not always give the best suggestion.

Step 7: Publish.
After publishing the book of reports, make it available in the classroom for reading during free time.

ASSESS

Ask: What do you think was the most important step in the process of writing a research report? Why?

Portfolio

Students may choose to include their writing in their portfolios.

Cultural Connection

Tell students that food is very closely tied to a culture or region. Have students research the foods that were eaten in the culture or region during the time of their Writer's Workshop report. Have them find out about the staples, daily dishes, holiday foods, food prohibitions, if any, and eating implements.

Learning Styles
Visual

Have students create a sample menu of a meal from the time of their Writer's Workshop report, including a recipe and an illustration of the dish.

Projects

Project 1: Research an Explorer

1. **Select a person to research** If students don't have access to the Internet, provide them with a list of famous explorers. Bring in library books about explorers for them to examine.

2. **Relate information about an explorer** Model for students by giving a very brief presentation about an explorer. At the end, ask students if they have any questions about the explorer. Have students end their group presentations in the same way.

Project 2: Plan a Time Capsule

1. **Brainstorm ideas for a time capsule** Talk with students about what might be interesting for students of the future to know about. You may want to select just a few topics, such as sports, schools, and world events.

2. **Read time capsules** After students have finished their time capsules, put aside the envelopes to open on the next day.

Portfolio

Students may choose to include their projects in their portfolios.

Projects

These projects will help you expand what you learned about journeys. Work alone or with a partner. Ask your teacher or librarian if you need help.

Project 1: Research an Explorer

Explorers journey to different places. They go there to find out more about our world. Research information about a famous explorer.

1. Choose an explorer you would like to learn more about. Here are some ideas to help you brainstorm:
   a. Choose an explorer you have read about in social studies.
   b. Use the Internet. Do a keyword search for *famous explorers*.
2. Use the library to research this explorer. Take notes about important information. Be sure to cover these things:
   a. the dates the explorer lived
   b. where the explorer came from
   c. the place he or she explored
   d. why the exploration was important
3. Draw a map of where the journey took place.
4. Tell a small group what you learned. Use your map as a visual.
5. If possible, use presentation software to present your research.

Project 2: Plan a Time Capsule

A time capsule contains things from a certain time. People put things in a time capsule to show how they live. The time capsule is then saved for people to open at some time in the future.

1. Suppose that your school is making a time capsule. One hundred years from now students from your school will open the capsule.
2. What would you want students from the future to know about your life? Some ideas are: newspapers or magazines, clothes, CDs, photographs.
3. On a note card, write a description of each item.

Idea for Time Capsule
Newspaper article : July 28, 2002
Event: Lance Armstrong wins his fourth Tour de France.

---

4. Ask your teacher for an envelope. Put your note cards in the envelope.
   a. Write "Time Capsule" and your name on the envelope.
   b. Exchange envelopes with your classmates. Look inside their time capsules. What things did they write?

MULTI-LEVEL OPTIONS *Projects*

Newcomer Have students draw pictures or create collages of items they would like to include in the time capsule.

Beginning Have students draw a series of pictures that show a typical day in their lives to include in the time capsule. Help them write captions for each picture.

Intermediate After students select an item for the time capsule and complete their note cards, have them explain the importance of the item in pairs.

Advanced After students select an item for the time capsule and complete their note cards, have them write a paragraph that explains why the item will be of interest to a student 100 years from now.

Further Reading

The following books discuss the theme of journeys. Choose one or more of them. Write your thoughts and feelings about what you read in your Reading Log. Take notes about your answers to these questions:

1. How are the journeys you read about similar to experiences you have had?
2. What did the characters learn from their journeys?

The Voyage of the Lucky Dragon
by Jack Bennett, Prentice Hall, 1985. A Vietnamese boy tells the story of his family's escape from Vietnam. First they go to Indonesia, then Singapore, and finally Australia.

The Time Bike
by Jane Langton, HarperCollins, 2002. Eddy receives a gift from his uncle. At first the bike seems like an ordinary bike. But soon Eddy discovers that it can travel through time.

Dame Shirley and the Gold Rush
by Jim Rawls, Steck Vaughn, 1992. This book is based on the letters of a woman known as Dame Shirley. Her letters were published in *San Francisco Magazine* in 1854 and 1855. The letters are combined into a story about the California gold rush.

The International Space Station: A Journey into Space
by Wolfgang Engelhardt, Tessloff Publishing, 1998. This book talks about the International Space Station. Many nations, including the United States, Japan, Russia, the European Space Administration, and Canada, are working together to research life in space.

Home: A Journey Through America
by Thomas Locker, Voyager Books, 2000. This book is a collection of poems and stories written about various parts of the U.S. landscape. Included in this book are works by Carl Sandburg, Robert Frost, Henry David Thoreau, and Joseph Bruchac.

A Journey: The Autobiography of Apolo Anton Ohno
by Apolo Anton Ohno, Simon & Schuster Children's, 2002. Apolo Anton Ohno tells the story of his life as a skater and how he became a gold medalist at the 2002 Olympic Games.

Journey to the Center of the Earth
by Jules Verne, Baronet Books, 1983. A team of explorers journey into a crater in Iceland. This crater leads them to the center of the earth, where amazing and dangerous things happen to them.

Companion Web site

Reading Log

Heinle Reading Library 20,000 Leagues Under the Sea

Further Reading

1. **Read summaries to select books** Read or have volunteers read the book summaries. Ask students what they already know about any of the topics. *Ask: Have you ever seen speed-skating? Have you seen the Olympic Games?*
2. **Respond to literature** After reading a book, have students give an oral report or write a short book review. As an alternative, students can talk about their books in small groups.

Assessment Program: *Unit 3 Test, pp. 49–54; Mid-Book Exam, pp. 55–60*

Heinle Reading Library

20,000 Leagues Under the Sea by Jules Verne
In a specially adapted version
by Malvina G. Vogel

A young professor goes in search of a legendary sea monster, only to find that the sea monster is really an underwater ship invented by the mad Captain Nemo. Imprisoned on the ship, the *Nautilus,* Professor Aronnax must find a way to escape, and figure out a way to stop the mad captain from his insane attacks on innocent ships. Jules Verne's incredible tale is an amazing journey into a world of non-stop danger and adventure!

Visions Companion Site

http://visions.heinle.com
For additional student activities and teacher resources, see the Visions Companion Web site.

Unit Materials

Activity Book: *pp. 121–152*
Audio: *Unit 4; CD 2, Tracks 7–10*
Student Handbook
Student CD-ROM: *Unit 4*
CNN Video: *Unit 4*
Teacher Resource Book: *Lesson Plans, Teacher Resources, Reading Summaries, School-Home Connection, Video Script, Video Worksheet, Activity Book Answer Key*
Teacher Resource CD-ROM
Assessment Program: *Quizzes and Test, pp. 61–74; Teacher and Student Resources, pp. 115–144*
Assessment CD-ROM
Transparencies
The Heinle Newbury House Dictionary/CD-ROM
More Grammar Practice workbook
Heinle Reading Library: *Black Beauty*
Web site: http://visions.heinle.com

Visions Staff Development Handbook

Refer to the Visions Staff Development Handbook for more teacher support.

Unit Theme: Cycles

Define and discuss terms *Ask: What do you know that goes in "cycles," or goes around?* If needed, point out examples such as seasons, life, bicycles, and things that get recycled. List ideas on the board.

Unit Preview: Table of Contents

1. **Use the table of contents to locate information** *Ask: Which chapter has a poem?* (Chapter 1) *What type of reading is in Chapter 4?* (an informational book) Read the chapter titles and authors of the selections.
2. **Connect** *Ask: Which titles interest you?*

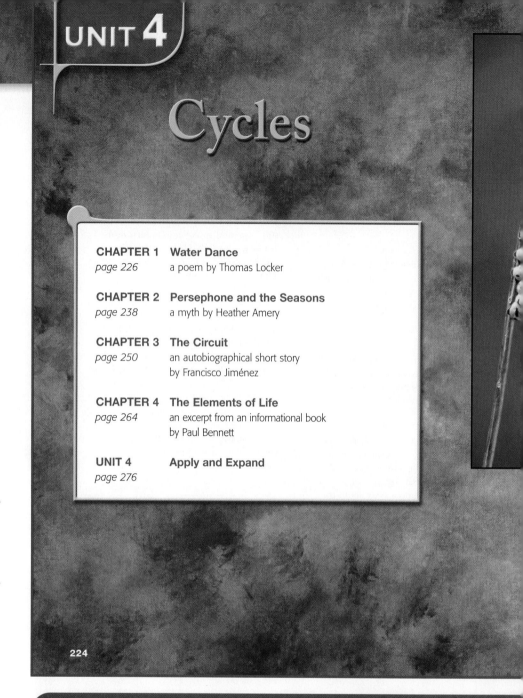

Cycles

224

UNIT OBJECTIVES

Reading
Describe mental images as you read a poem • Use chronology to locate and recall information as you read a myth • Compare text to your own knowledge and experience as you read an autobiographical short story • Find the main idea and supporting details as you read an excerpt from an informational book

Listening and Speaking
Respond to mood • Act out a story • Present an experience • Listen and take notes

Stages of Butterfly Metamorphosis, photo, Ralph A. Clevenger.

View the Picture

1. What does this picture show? How does the picture show a cycle?
2. What other cycles do you know about?

In this unit, you will read a poem, a myth, an autobiographical short story, and an excerpt from an informational book. You will also write in these forms.

225

View the Picture

1. **Art background** Ralph Clevenger has a Bachelor of Science in zoology and a Bachelor of Arts in photography. He teaches natural history photography and undersea photography at the Brooks Institute of Photography in Santa Barbara, California. Clevenger is known for his color close-ups of small animals and insects that reveal the most intimate and detailed routines of their lives.

2. **Art interpretation** Have students discuss how they think the artist captured these three "Stages of Butterfly Metamorphosis."
   a. **Interpret the photograph** *Ask: How does the photographer make you understand the development of the butterfly?*
   b. **Connect to theme** Remind students that the theme of this unit is *cycles.* Ask students to explain why this photograph is a good way to examine the theme.
   c. **Use personal experience** *Ask: Can you describe the stages of development in humans or in other animals?*

ASSESS

Have students write captions for the different stages of the cycle in the picture.

Grammar
Use comparative adjectives • Write using irregular past tense verbs • Identify dependent clauses • Recognize the active and passive voices

Writing
Write a poem • Summarize and paraphrase to inform • Write a letter to an author • Write about a process and create a diagram

Content
Math: Calculate averages • Language Arts: Distinguish the meanings of *myth* • Language Arts: Understand the influence of other languages and cultures on English • Science: Understand symbols for elements

CHAPTER 1

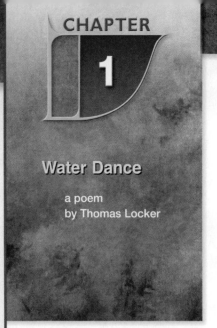

Water Dance

a poem
by Thomas Locker

Into the Reading

Objectives

Reading Describe mental images as you read a poem.

Listening and Speaking Respond to mood.

Grammar Use comparative adjectives.

Writing Write a poem.

Content Math: Calculate averages.

Chapter Materials

Activity Book: *pp. 121–128*
Audio: *Unit 4, Chapter 1; CD 2, Track 7*
Student Handbook
Student CD-ROM: *Unit 4, Chapter 1*
Teacher Resource Book: *Lesson Plan, Teacher Resources, Reading Summary, Activity Book Answer Key*
Teacher Resource CD-ROM
Assessment Program: *Quiz, pp. 61–62; Teacher and Student Resources, pp. 115–144*
Assessment CD-ROM
Transparencies
The Heinle Newbury House Dictionary/CD-ROM
Web site: http://visions.heinle.com

Objectives

Preview *Say: We will work on these objectives in Chapter 1. Can you do any of them already?*

Use Prior Knowledge

Talk About Uses of Water

Compose, organize, and revise a record
Have pairs of students record how they use water over one week's time. They should organize the information by the days of the week. Each pair then joins another pair to compare their uses of water. The group should revise their two charts to be one master list.

Use Prior Knowledge

Talk About Uses of Water

Water is part of your everyday life. How do you use water?

1. Think about all the ways that you use water. List these ways on a piece of paper.

How I Use Water
1. I brush my teeth.
2. I water my plants.

2. Share your list with a partner.
3. Based on your lists, do you think water is important? Why or why not? Talk about your answer with your partner.
4. Have a class discussion about the use of water in your community.
   a. Where does the water come from?
   b. Do you think people in your community use too much water?
   c. How can you save water?

MULTI-LEVEL OPTIONS *Build Vocabulary*

Newcomer Demonstrate different ways to tell about an action. Write on the board and *say: run.* Demonstrate running across the classroom. Show pictures of people running in a contest, jogging for exercise, hurrying to catch a bus, or running a race. With each picture say sentences such as: *He runs. She jogs. They run. He hurries.*

Beginning Have students work in small groups. Give each group an index card with an ordinary verb at the top and related vivid verbs listed below it. For example, one card may have *say* (ordinary verb) at the top and *shout, cry, whisper* listed below. Have each student rehearse reading and acting out one of the verbs. Have groups perform for the class.

Intermediate Divide the class into groups. Give each student two index cards. Have each student write an ordinary verb on one card and a related vivid verb on the other. Tell students to place all cards face down. Have students take turns looking at two cards at a time. If the cards are a pair, students may keep them.

Advanced Point out that sports writers are usually very skilled at using vivid verbs. Have pairs examine the sports section of a newspaper to identify vivid verbs. Have students record each vivid verb and write in parenthesis the related ordinary word. (*Example:* The Lions demolished (beat) the Hornets.) Provide time for sharing.

Build Background

The Water Cycle

Water moves in a cycle on Earth. First, the sun warms Earth. The water on the surface of Earth evaporates (turns to gas) as it warms. It forms clouds in the sky and falls back to Earth as rain or snow. Then the cycle begins again.

Content Connection

The amount of water on Earth never changes. The water just changes from one form to another. Earth is more than 70% water.

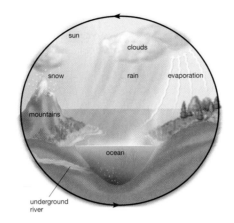

Build Vocabulary

Learn Vivid Verbs

A **verb** is a part of speech. Some other parts of speech are nouns, adjectives, and adverbs. If you choose these words carefully in your writing, you can make it vivid (interesting) and precise (exact). Compare the verbs in these sentences:

ordinary verb Kostas <u>ran</u> to school because he was late.

vivid verb Kostas <u>sprinted</u> to school because he was late.

Ran means "moved very fast." *Sprinted* means "ran very fast." *Sprinted* helps you form a clearer picture than *ran*. Kostas is sprinting because he is late.

Write the following sentences in your Personal Dictionary. The underlined words are ordinary verbs. Replace each one with a vivid verb from the box.

> trembles   leap   cascades

1. Sometimes the water <u>falls</u> down over the moss-covered rocks.
2. I <u>jump</u> from a stone cliff.
3. The earth <u>shakes</u> with my thunder.

Personal Dictionary

The Heinle Newbury House Dictionary

Activity Book *p. 121*

Student CD-ROM

Chapter 1 Water Dance   **227**

Content Connection
Science

Build Background Write on the top of a large piece of poster paper: *Water, Water Everywhere.* Challenge each student to find one interesting fact about water. (*Examples:* Tomatoes are 95% water. Three-quarters of the earth's fresh water is frozen.) Help each student add his/her fact to the poster. Keep the poster on display and invite students to add other facts they find.

Learning Styles
Musical

Build Vocabulary Tell students that they will be reading about water and the things that happen to it in nature. Ask students to work in pairs to brainstorm a list of actions related to water. (*Examples:* flow, splash, gush, drop) Tell students to rehearse using their voices to communicate the meanings of the words. For instance, they may say *flow* very slowly, stretching it out. Then have students share these expressive readings of their lists with the class.

Build Background

The Water Cycle

1. **Use a diagram** Point out stages of the water cycle. *Ask: What does the water from the ocean form in the sky?* (clouds) *What comes down from the clouds?* (rain/snow) *Where does the water in the river come from?* (rain/snow)

2. **Content Connection** Identify the forms of water: *solid—ice; liquid—water; gas—water vapor. Ask: What form do you see and use most of the time?* (liquid—water) *What form is at the North Pole?* (solid—ice)

Build Vocabulary

Learn Vivid Verbs

Teacher Resource Book: *Personal Dictionary, p. 63*

1. **Use a dictionary or thesaurus** Explain that a thesaurus lists synonyms for words. Students can find vivid words for ordinary verbs such as *run*. Point out differences in meanings for the entries.

2. **Locate pronunciation** Have students locate the pronunciation of *thesaurus* in the glossary of their Student Handbook or other sources, such as online or CD-ROM dictionaries. Ask students to record the meaning and derivation in their Reading Logs.

3. **Reading selection vocabulary** You may want to introduce the glossed words in the reading selection before students begin reading. Key words: *stream, waterfall, creeks, mist, storm front, thunderhead.* Instruct students to write the words with correct spelling and their definitions in their Personal Dictionaries. Have them pronounce each word and divide it into syllables.

4. **Multi-level options** See MULTI-LEVEL OPTIONS on p. 226.

Answers
1. cascades 2. leap 3. trembles

ASSESS

Have students write sentences using the new words.

Text Structure

Poem

1. **Examine features** Write the feature chart on the board. Direct students to "I Have No Address" (p. 156). Have them find examples of vivid language ("lines ornamented by dreams"), sense words ("beating hearts," "echo of my sound"), and the speaker in the poem (a sparrow).
2. **Multi-level options** See MULTI-LEVEL OPTIONS below.

Reading Strategy

Describe Mental Images

Model the strategy Have students close their eyes and listen as you read the example. *Ask: What did you see?* Ask them to recall words that evoked the mental images.

ASSESS

Ask students to define: *stanza, vivid language, sense words,* and *speaker.*

Text Structure

Poem

"Water Dance" is a **poem.** The writer of a poem is a poet. In a poem, the poet uses vivid language to describe an object, person, or event. Look at the chart on the right for the features of a poem.

Think about who or what the speaker is in "Water Dance."

Poem	
Stanzas	The poem has a group of lines called stanzas.
Vivid Verbs	The words help you picture exactly what is happening.
Sense Words	These words describe how things sound, smell, taste, look, or feel.
A Speaker	The speaker is the voice that is speaking in the poem. The speaker is not always the poet. Sometimes the speaker is not even a person.

Student
CD-ROM

Reading Strategy

Describe Mental Images

Many words in "Water Dance" help you form **mental images** (pictures in your mind). Describing these mental images will help you understand the poem.

> The <u>tall</u>, <u>green</u> trees <u>swayed</u> softly in the <u>gentle</u>, <u>warm</u> wind.

The underlined words help you form mental images. They help you picture how the trees look and feel.

1. Read stanzas 1 to 3 of "Water Dance."
2. Draw pictures of your mental images from stanza 3. Then list the words from the stanza that helped you draw your pictures.

3. Share your drawings with a partner. Did you form the same mental images?
4. Pause after reading each stanza of "Water Dance." In your Reading Log, describe the mental images you form.

Before you read the poem, think about your purpose in reading it. Will you read it for enjoyment or to understand something? As you read, you may want to adjust (change) your purpose so that you can appreciate the writer's craft.

Reading Log

Student
CD-ROM

MULTI-LEVEL OPTIONS *Text Structure*

Newcomer Engage students in looking at a poetry anthology with you. Point out stanzas. Have students count how many stanzas there are in different poems. Select a simple, short poem to read aloud. Use facial expressions and gestures to convey feeling words and vivid verbs.

Beginning Hand out copies of a simple poem. Have students count the stanzas. Help them identify and underline vivid verbs. Say each verb and have students act it out. Assist students in finding sensory language. Have them draw an icon, such as an eye, above the word to show the sense to which it appeals.

Intermediate Have each student select a poem from a poetry anthology or another source. Ask students to duplicate the chart on the top of p. 228 and fill it out with examples from the poems they read. Ask pairs to meet and share their poems and charts.

Advanced Have students work in pairs. Have pairs select three poems from an anthology. *Say: Compare and contrast how the poets divided the poems into stanzas. Ask: What else do you notice about how each poem is put on the page? How does the presentation help communicate the poet's message?*

Water Dance

a poem

by Thomas Locker

229

Reading Selection Materials

Audio: *Unit 4, Chapter 1; CD 2, Track 7*
Teacher Resource Book: *Reading Summary,*
  pp. 95–96
Transparencies: *#40, Reading Summary*

Suggestions for Using Reading Summary

- Introduce new vocabulary or cognates.
- Cut the summary into strips, or jumble the sentences on an overhead transparency. Students put the sentences in order.
- Practice the reading strategy.
- Students read aloud or with a partner.
- Students paraphrase the summary.
- Students do a cloze activity.
- Students create a visual or graphic organizer, such as a timeline or storyboard, to illustrate the summary.
- Students paraphrase the summary.

Preview the Selection

1. **Speculate** Tell students that the picture relates to the poem that they will read. *Ask: What is in this picture? What is the water doing? What is the title of the poem? Can water dance? Why or why not? What picture do you get when you hear the word* dance*? What do you think the poet will say about water? About dancing?*

2. **Connect** Remind students that the unit theme is *cycles.* Ask them to restate the main stages of the water cycle. Then point out that poets often try to paint a picture of something with their words. Have students guess how a poet may describe water and where it dances and how it dances.

Content Connection
The Arts

Say: The art on this page shows one way to express the idea of water dancing. Ask students to create their own artistic expressions of water dancing. Tell them to think, not only about what to draw, but about the colors and kinds of lines and shapes they choose to convey the message that water can move in a graceful or an exciting way.

Learning Styles
Natural

Say: Many writers choose to write about nature because they think that it is amazing and beautiful. Point out that the title "Water Dance" talks about an ordinary part of nature (water) doing something interesting (dancing). *Say: Brainstorm things that are beautiful or interesting in nature and think of titles that could be used for poems about them. (Example:* "Melody of the Wind"*) Use your list when you need an idea for a writing topic.*

Read the Selection

1. **Use text features** Point out the numbers and stanzas and explain their purpose. Direct students to italicized lines. Point out the pattern within the poem. Remind students to check the meanings of glossed words at the bottom of the page.

2. **Choral reading** Play the audio. Pause to check understanding and to identify features. Assign stanzas to different groups to read aloud.

3. **Describe mental images** *Ask: How does the water go down the mountains?* (It leaps, turns, and dives.) *What does the water look like in the lake?* (It's quiet and deep.)

Sample Answer to Guide Question
The water is like a person tumbling or doing somersaults, rolling downhill.

See Teacher Edition pp. 434–436 for a list of English-Spanish cognates in the reading selection.

Audio
CD 2. Tr. 7

1 SOME PEOPLE SAY that I am one thing.
Others say that I am many.
Ever since the world began
I have been moving in an endless circle.
Sometimes I fall from the sky.

2 *I am the rain.*

Describe Mental Images

What mental images do you form from this stanza?

3 Sometimes I cascade.
I tumble
down,
down,
over the **moss**-covered rocks,
through the forest shadows.

4 *I am the mountain* **stream.**

5 At the foot of the mountains,
I leap from a stone cliff.
Spiraling.
Plunging.

6 *I am the* **waterfall.**

7 In the shadows of the mountain,
I am still and deep.
I fill
and **overflow.**

8 *I am the lake.*

tumble roll	**spiraling** twisting up or down
moss a short, soft plant that grows on the ground and on trees	**plunging** diving or falling fast and far
stream a flowing body of water, smaller than a river	**waterfall** water falling from a high place
	overflow flow over the edges of something

230 Unit 4 Cycles

MULTI-LEVEL OPTIONS *Read the Selection*

Newcomer Play the audio. *Ask: Is this poem about a person?* (no) *Is it about water?* (yes) *Does the poem tell about using water in a house?* (no) *Does it tell about water in nature?* (yes)

Beginning Read aloud the poem. *Ask: What is the poem about?* (water) *What kind of water does the poet tell about first?* (rain) *Where does the poet say rainwater goes?* (streams, waterfalls, lakes, rivers, seas) *What does water turn into when the sun draws it up?* (mist)

Intermediate Have students do a paired reading. *Ask: How does the poet make the poem interesting?* (by having water, not a person, talk to the reader) *According to the poet, how does rain affect things on earth?* (The rain forms streams, waterfalls, lakes, rivers, and the sea.)

Advanced Have students do a paired reading. *Ask: How is the topic of stanza 1 similar to and different from stanza 13?* (Both talk about water in the sky; stanza 1 talks about water in a liquid form falling from the sky; stanza 13 talks about it rising into the sky in a mist form.) *What do you think the poet will talk about in the next part?* (*Example:* how the mist forms clouds and rain)

9 I wind through broad, golden valleys
joined by streams,
joined by **creeks.**
I grow ever wider,
broader and deeper.

10 *I am the river.*

Describe Mental Images

What mental images do you form when you read "Cool silver moonlight sparkles and dances"?

11 I pass through a gateway
of high stone **palisades,**
leaving the land behind.
Cool silver moonlight
sparkles and dances
on my waves.

12 *I am the sea.*

13 **Drawn** upward
by warm sunlight,
in white-silver **veils**
I rise into the air.
I disappear.

14 *I am the* **mist.**

---

creeks small streams
palisades rows of cliffs
sparkles gives off bits of light
drawn pulled toward something

veils pieces of cloth that cover the face
mist a fog, very fine drops of water forming a cloud near the ground

Chapter 1 Water Dance **231**

Read the Selection

1. **Use the illustration** Have students describe the illustration. Ask them to suggest descriptive words for *sea* and verbs to explain what it is doing.
2. **Understand terms** Have students find the meanings of the glossed words below the selection. Clarify meanings as needed.
3. **Shared reading** Play the audio. Have different groups join in for odd number stanzas. Have the entire class join in for even number stanzas.
4. **Summarize** Ask questions to help students summarize the stanzas and describe the images they see as they read the poem.
5. **Multi-level options** See MULTI-LEVEL OPTIONS on p. 230.

Sample Answer to Guide Question
I see the moonlight shining in the water. The light is like white specks that sparkle as the water moves. It's like the light is dancing on the water.

---

th **Spelling**

Vowel-consonant-*e* long vowel sounds

Have students review stanza 5. Point out the word *stone*, write it on the board, and pronounce it. ***Ask:*** *Is the sound of* o *in this word long or short?* (long) Call attention to the word *lake* in stanza 8. Write the word directly under *stone*. Pronounce it. ***Ask:*** *Is the sound of* a *in this word long or short?* (long) Follow the same procedure with the word *rise* in stanza 13. ***Ask:*** *What spelling pattern do you notice in these words?* (In words with vowel-consonant-silent *e*, the vowel has a long sound.)

 Apply *Say: Look at words on the bulletin boards, book covers, and other things around our room. Find other words that follow this spelling pattern.* (*Examples:* home, tape, time, June) List these under the words from the poem.

Read the Selection

1. **Use text features** Remind students to check the meanings of glossed words at the bottom of the page and to use the illustration to help understanding.

2. **Choral reading** Play the audio. Pause to ask comprehension questions and to describe images. Assign stanzas to different students or groups to read aloud to the class.

3. **Describe mental images** *Ask: What do the clouds look like?* (They're in many shapes and then they get dark in color and heavy like a storm is coming.) *Is the thunderhead a quiet and happy sight, or is it strong and angry?* (It's strong and angry.)

Sample Answer to Guide Question
Yes. I can see the blinding lightning and hear the noise and anger of the storm.

15 In thousands of shapes I reappear
high above the earth in the blue sky.
I float.
I drift.

16 *I am the clouds.*

17 Carried by winds
from distant seas
I move,
growing heavier,
growing darker,
returning.

18 *I am the **storm front**.*

19 At the wall of the mountains,
I rise up
as **gleaming** power-filled towers
in the darkened sky.

20 *I am the **thunderhead**.*

Describe Mental Images

Do you think the words in this stanza describe a storm well? Why or why not?

21 I blind the sky with lightning.
The earth **trembles** with my thunder.
I **rage.**
I **drench** the mountainside.

22 *I am the storm.*

---

storm front a mass of air that brings a storm
gleaming shining brightly
thunderhead a part of a large cloud; often appears before a thunderstorm

trembles shakes
rage show uncontrolled anger
drench make completely wet

MULTI-LEVEL OPTIONS *Read the Selection*

Newcomer *Ask: Are clouds made of water?* (yes) *Are clouds moved by wind?* (yes) *Do clouds turn into rain?* (yes) *Is the end of the poem about a person who dances?* (no)

Beginning *Ask: Do the clouds in the poem float away or turn into a storm?* (storm) *How does the sky look as the storm comes?* (dark) *What does the poet say makes the earth shake?* (thunder) *What does the poet say makes rainbows?* (drops of water)

Intermediate *Ask: What does the mist mentioned in stanza 14 become?* (clouds) *What vivid verb does the poet use for the action of making something wet?* (drench) *Why could you say this poem is a cycle poem?* (It starts out talking about rain and ends up talking about the same thing.)

Advanced *Ask: What do you think is the poet's attitude about water? Explain.* (He thinks it is very interesting; he shows its power and all the things it can do.) *Why does the poet describe water as dancing?* (He shows all the different and interesting ways water moves; dancers also move in many interesting ways.)

23　Storms come.
　　Storms pass.
　　I am **countless droplets** of rain
　　left floating in the silent air.
　　I reflect all the colors of sunlight.

24　*I am the rainbow.*

25　I am one thing.
　　I am many things.

26　*I am water.*

27　This is my dance through our world.

Describe Mental Images

What mental image do you form after you read the words "I am the rainbow"?

---

countless　too many to be counted

droplets　small drops

About the Author | Thomas Locker (born 1937)

Thomas Locker is both a writer and a painter. Locker's paintings make his stories and poems very special. At first, Locker only painted pictures. Then he realized that his paintings could help him tell his stories. Locker has painted pictures for about 30 books. He also wrote several of these books.

➤ The selection shows Thomas Locker's paintings. Describe how these paintings help you understand the poem better. How does Locker's choice of style and media extend the meaning of the poem?

Chapter 1　Water Dance　**233**

 Spelling

Ou/ow for /ou/ sound

Write on the board and *say: mountain.* Underline *ou*. *Ask: What other words in stanza 19 have the /ou/ sound?* (power, tower) Write these on the board. Underline *ow*. *Say: Both* ou *and* ow *can make the /ou/ sound.*

Apply　Have students find other examples. (stanza 15: thousands; stanza 16: clouds; stanza 23: countless; stanza 27: our)

Evaluate Your Reading Strategy

Describe Mental Images　*Say: You have practiced an important reading strategy. Now you can decide how well you have done. Does this statement describe how you read?*

> I use words in a text to form mental images or pictures in my mind. Describing these mental images helps me understand what I read.

Read the Selection

1. **Shared reading**　Play the audio. Have different groups join in for odd number stanzas. Have the entire class join in for even number stanzas. *Ask: After the storm passes, what happens to the water?* (The drops reflect the sunlight to make a rainbow.)
2. **Multi-level options**　See MULTI-LEVEL OPTIONS on p. 232.

Sample Answer to Guide Question
The sun is coming out with a beautiful, colorful rainbow in the sky.

About the Author

Explain author's background　Thomas Locker specializes in landscapes. His paintings have been exhibited in England and in the United States. Some of his more recent books are *In Blue Mountains* and *Cloud Dance*. *Ask: Do you think it is easier or more difficult to make illustrations for your own book? Why?*

Answer
Sample answer: These paintings help form mental images based on what I read. Locker uses painting to create a dreamy style that matches the dreamy images in the poem. This helps me better understand what the poet is trying to express.

Across Selections

▌ Teacher Resource Book: *Venn Diagram, p. 35*

Compare and contrast point of view　Have students suggest how Thomas Locker's poem about water is different from a science informational text such as "Yawning" in Unit 1. Guide students to identify similarities and differences in points of view, descriptions of the topics, use of illustrations and diagrams, and reasons for writing. Record ideas on a Venn diagram.

Spelling, Punctuation, Capitalization

After the Reading Comprehension section, students will practice spelling, punctuation, and capitalization in the Activity Book.

Beyond the Reading

Reading Comprehension

Question-Answer Relationships

Sample Answers

1. since the world began
2. The speaker is the water.
3. rain, a mountain stream, a waterfall, a lake, a river, a sea, mist, clouds, a storm front, a thunderhead, a storm, a rainbow
4. the water in nature goes through a cycle
5. because of the thunder
6. The italicized lines show when the poet is directly identifying the form of the water. The poet does this for emphasis and to make sure the reader understands his descriptions. It helps me understand the descriptions.
7. Stanza 21 is angry and scary.
8. The poet has the water describing itself in the different stages. First person makes the water seem alive and more important than third person does.
9. The poet wants us to feel that water is an important, living thing that we need to understand and appreciate.
10. The poet describes the water in each stanza and then in the italicized line gives the exact name of the water at that stage.

Build Reading Fluency

Read Aloud to Engage Listeners

Model reading aloud with expression. Remind students to keep their eyes on the words as they read. This will help them with phrasing, intonation, and pronunciation.

Reading Comprehension

Question-Answer Relationships (QAR)

"Right There" Question

1. **Recall Facts** How long has the speaker been moving in an endless circle?

"Think and Search" Questions

2. **Make Inferences** Who or what is the speaker in the poem?
3. **Identify** What different things does the speaker ("I") become? (Hint: Look at the *italic* type.)
4. **Identify Main Ideas** What main idea does this poem describe?
5. **Identify Cause and Effect** Why does Earth tremble?

"Author and You" Questions

6. **Understand Text Features** The poet uses *italic* type many times. Why do you think he does this? How does it help you understand the poem?
7. **Describe Mood** What is the mood (feeling you get) in stanza 21? Is it happy? Scary?

8. **Analyze Point of View** Why did the author write the poem in the first person ("I") instead of in the third person ("it")?

"On Your Own" Questions

9. **Speculate** How do you think the poet wants you to feel about water?
10. **Analyze Inductive Organization** In Unit 3, Chapter 4, the author used the deductive method to explain his information—he stated his main idea then supported it with details and examples. In this poem, the poet uses the inductive method. He states his details, which lead us to his main idea. Find examples of this type of organization and presentation in the poem.

Activity Book
p. 122

Student
CD-ROM

Build Reading Fluency

Read Aloud to Engage Listeners

Reading aloud helps increase your fluency and expression. Learning to read with expression makes others want to listen to you.

1. Listen to the audio recording of "Water Dance."

2. Turn to page 230 and follow along.
3. Listen to the phrasing and expression.
4. With a partner, read aloud paragraphs 1–7 three times.
5. Select your favorite two paragraphs.
6. Read them in front of the class with expression.

234 Unit 4 Cycles

MULTI-LEVEL OPTIONS *Elements of Literature*

Newcomer Draw a picture of the sun. Put a smiling face on it. Read the example sentence on the bottom of p. 235. Ask students to draw other parts of nature. Tell them to give each a human quality. (*Example:* A student might draw a cloud with a sad face with tears, or raindrops, coming down from it.)

Beginning Ask each student to draw pictures to show the meanings of the sentences in numbers 2a and 2b. Have them label the pictures with the figurative language from the sentences. Have each student create his/her own captioned picture about a part of nature with a human quality.

Intermediate Have students look at other poems about nature. Ask them to list any examples of personification they find. Provide time for students to share the results.

Advanced Assign each student an aspect of nature, such as fire, the moon, rocks, an ocean, or wind. Ask students to brainstorm a list of ways they could personify the assigned element. (*Example:* The hungry flames gobbled up the wood.) Invite students to share their ideas in groups.

Listen, Speak, Interact

Respond to Mood

"Water Dance" uses vivid words to describe how water moves around Earth. The poet uses these words to create different moods—feelings that a reader gets.

1. Work with a partner. Take turns reading aloud the stanzas. Adapt your spoken language to the audience, purpose, and occasion.

2. Read the poem to enjoy and appreciate it.

3. As your partner reads, list words that describe the different moods you feel.

4. Talk about your lists. Which stanzas made you feel a certain way?

5. Did you get any insights (new truth or knowledge) from the poem? Share your insights with your partner.

Elements of Literature

Use Figurative Language

Poets often use **figurative language.** One kind of figurative speech is **personification**—when a writer gives human characteristics to a thing. For example:

The sun <u>smiles at us</u>.

The sun is not really smiling. Personification makes the sun into a human being who is smiling. This sentence tells us that the sun is shining brightly. It also gives us the idea that the sun is a friendly thing.

1. Read the following examples of personification from "Water Dance."

   a. Cool silver moonlight sparkles and dances on my waves.

   b. I blind the sky with lightning.

2. What things are given human characteristics? What are the characteristics? How do they affect meaning?

3. Check with a partner to see if your answers are the same.

4. Write your own sentence with an example of personification.

Activity Book
p. 123

Student
CD-ROM

Chapter 1 Water Dance **235**

Content Connection
The Arts

Have students use musical instruments or other objects to make sound effects to accompany stanzas of the poem. For example, several students may gently tap out raindrops, using triangles. One may tinkle on a xylophone for the babbling of a mountain stream. Others may use drums to create sounds of thunder. Have the class perform the poem, using the instruments to set the mood of each stanza.

Learning Styles
Kinesthetic

Point out that figurative language brings to mind certain visual images, such as a sun with a smile. *Say: Figurative language can also make readers think of certain kinds of motion.* Provide an example by reading stanza 11 and wiggling your fingers loosely over the edge of imaginary waves to signify *sparkles.* Invite pairs of students to find or create examples of figurative language and show what motions these bring to their minds.

Listen, Speak, Interact

Respond to Mood

Teacher Resource Book: *Reading Log, p. 64*

1. **Reread in pairs** Pair beginning and advanced students. Have them read alternate stanzas.

2. **Newcomers** Reread with this group. Help them identify the feelings expressed in the stanzas. Write these on the board. Have students record their insights from the poem in their Reading Logs.

Elements of Literature

Use Figurative Language

1. **Explain personification** Write the example on the board. *Say: The sun can't smile. It doesn't have a mouth! People smile. When someone smiles at me, I feel happy! I think the poet is saying that you feel happy when the sun is out, just like when a person smiles at you.* Point out other examples and discuss their meanings.

2. **Multi-level options** See MULTI-LEVEL OPTIONS on p. 234.

Answers

2. **a.** the moonlight and the sea: The moonlight dances. The water possesses the waves. The light plays on the water's waves. **b.** the storm: It lights up the sky. The storm is angry and violent.

ASSESS

Have students draw a picture to illustrate one of the examples of personification from the poem.

Word Study

Distinguish Denotative and Connotative Meanings

Explain terms Have students share feelings associated with: *homework, family, kitten, shadow.* Point out the differences between the denotative meanings and connotative, or feeling, meanings. Have students find the denotative meanings in dictionaries.

Answers

2. tremble: be afraid (C), shake (D); drench: to make wet (D), to soak and make uncomfortable (C)

Grammar Focus

Use Comparative Adjectives

Make comparisons Write the adjectives and their comparative forms on the board. Have students make statements using the comparatives.

Answers

2. For adjectives ending in -e, add -r. For adjectives ending in consonant-y, change the -y to -i before adding -er. For one-syllable adjectives ending in consonant-vowel-consonant, the final consonant is doubled before adding -er.
3. heavier
4. *Examples:* Mario is nicer than Thomas. Texas is larger than Rhode Island.

ASSESS

Write: *pretty, lazy, dry.* Have students write the comparative forms. (prettier, lazier, drier)

Word Study

Distinguish Denotative and Connotative Meanings

Words can have two kinds of meanings. A **denotative meaning** is what you find in a dictionary. A **connotative meaning** is the feelings that we have about the word.

Reread these lines from the poem:

Cool silver moonlight <u>sparkles</u> and dances on my waves.

The denotative meaning of *sparkle* is "give off bits of light." But our feeling about the word is that beautiful, valuable things sparkle, like diamonds. This is the connotative meaning of *sparkle*.

1. Copy this chart in your Personal Dictionary.

Word	Meanings
tremble	_____ be afraid _____ shake
drench	_____ to make wet _____ to soak and make uncomfortable

2. Reread stanza 21. Pay close attention to the words *trembles* and *drench*. Then write D before the denotative meaning of each word, and C before the connotative meaning.

Personal Dictionary The Heinle Newbury House Dictionary Activity Book p. 124 Student CD-ROM

Grammar Focus

Use Comparative Adjectives

In Unit 3, Chapter 4, you learned to add *-er* to an adjective to make its comparative form.

Sometimes the adjective changes its spelling when you add *-er*.

1. Study this chart to see the changes.

Adjective	Comparative Form
wide	wider
blue	bluer
busy	busier
big	bigger

2. Can you make up the rules?
3. Find a comparative adjective in stanza 17 that follows one of these patterns.
4. On a piece of paper, write four sentences. Use a different comparative adjective from the chart in each sentence. Write your sentences like this:
_____ is _____er than _____ .

Activity Book pp. 125–126 Student Handbook Student CD-ROM

236   Unit 4 Cycles

MULTI-LEVEL OPTIONS *From Reading to Writing*

Newcomer Have students create poem webs. *Say: Draw something you like. Draw three branches out from it.* At the end of each branch, have students draw something they can compare their subject to. Demonstrate with the example of a dog. Draw it as a funny clown, a fluffy pillow, and a messy eater.

Beginning Ask the class to agree on a topic, such as baseball. Have them brainstorm descriptive words they may need, such as exciting, fun, lively, or surprising. List these in a column. Help students form the comparative for each descriptive word. Write these on the board. Tell students to use the list as they write.

Intermediate Suggest that students write their poems from the point of view of the object they are describing, as Thomas Locker did. Discuss how they would have to change the model to write from this perspective.

Advanced Tell students to use the model to decide on their basic ideas for a first draft. Then have them review Thomas Locker's poem as well as other examples of poetry to see how they may want to expand upon the ideas and format in their first draft.

From Reading to Writing

Write a Poem

Write a three-stanza poem about something that you like.

1. Brainstorm things you like, for example, snow, your favorite relative, a pet.
2. Use figurative language such as personification to help readers form mental images. For example, your dog might be very funny. You could write, "My dog is a clown."
3. Use comparative adjectives. Compare your favorite thing to three different things. For example, "My fish is bluer than the sky."

4. Present your poem to the class.
5. Make a class collection of the poems. As a class, evaluate the poems for their strengths and weaknesses.
6. Use your classmates' poems as models for your own writing. Determine how they can help you set your goals as a writer.

Activity Book
p. 127

Student Handbook

Across Content Areas

Calculate Averages

If a city has 8 inches of **precipitation** (rain, snow, or sleet) in one year and 10 inches the next year, then the **average precipitation** for the two years is 9 inches. Calculate an average like this:

Inches the first year	8
Inches the second year	10
Total inches for two years	18
Divide the total inches by the total number of years: 18 ÷ 2 = 9	
The average yearly precipitation is 9 inches.	

This chart shows the average amount of precipitation that falls in four cities in Arizona in a year.

City	Average Yearly Precipitation
Phoenix	7.2 inches
Tucson	12.0 inches
Winslow	8.0 inches
Yuma	3.2 inches

Copy and complete this chart to find the average yearly precipitation for the four Arizona cities together.

(A) Amount of precipitation for all cities	
(B) Number of cities	4
Average: Divide (A) by (B)	

Activity Book
p. 128

From Reading to Writing

Write a Poem

1. **Model an "I Am" poem** Model a poem similar in structure to "Water Dance" but substituting *I am* at the beginning of the sentences. *Say: I am smaller than a button. I am colder than the sea. I am whiter than the clouds. I am softer than a pillow. What am I?* (a snowflake) Have students guess what you are describing.
2. **Think-pair-share** Ask students to write their own poem following the pattern and to make an illustration for it. Then, in pairs, have students share their poems and pictures.
3. **Multi-level options** See MULTI-LEVEL OPTIONS on p. 236.

Across Content Areas: Math

Calculate Averages

Connect to personal experience *Ask: In which classes have you used or calculated averages?* (math, science) Have students calculate other averages, such as the average high and low temperatures for the week in your city.

Answers
(A) = 30.4 inches (7.2 + 12.0 + 8.0 + 3.2 = 30.4); Average: 30.4 inches ÷ 4 = 7.6 inches

ASSESS

Have students generate a list of steps for using the research resource they used.

Reteach and Reassess

Text Structure Direct students to the chart on the top of p. 228. Ask them to give examples from "Water Dance" of each element described on the chart.

Reading Strategy Read a short, descriptive poem to students. Have them draw the mental images brought to their minds by the poem. Ask students to share the results and tell what parts of the poem inspired them to draw what they did.

Elements of Literature Give each student a common classroom object, such as a ruler, pencil, or book. Ask each to draw or write a sentence that gives the item a human quality. (*Example:* The ruler stands at attention.)

Reassess Have students use the figurative language they created to describe classroom objects as the basis of a short poem or a picture.

CHAPTER 2

Persephone and the Seasons

a myth
by Heather Amery

Objectives

Reading Use chronology to locate and recall information as you read a myth.

Listening and Speaking Act out a story.

Grammar Write using irregular past tense verbs.

Writing Summarize and paraphrase to inform.

Content Language Arts: Distinguish the meanings of *myth*.

Chapter Materials

Activity Book: *pp. 129–136*
Audio: *Unit 4, Chapter 2; CD 2, Track 8*
Student Handbook
Student CD-ROM: *Unit 4, Chapter 2*
Teacher Resource Book: *Lesson Plan, Teacher Resources, Reading Summary, Activity Book Answer Key*
Teacher Resource CD-ROM
Assessment Program: *Quiz, pp. 63–64; Teacher and Student Resources, pp. 115–144*
Assessment CD-ROM
Transparencies
The Heinle Newbury House Dictionary/CD-ROM
Web site: http://visions.heinle.com

Objectives

Paired reading Have students work in pairs to read the objectives. Explain them to students. *Ask: Is there an objective that you can do already?*

Use Prior Knowledge

Share Experiences with Seasons

Use pictures Show students pictures of the four seasons from books or the Internet. Have students suggest weather, activities, and appropriate clothing from pictures.

Use Prior Knowledge

Share Experiences with Seasons

A season is a period of time that has a certain type of weather. Some parts of the world have four seasons: spring, summer, autumn (fall), and winter. Other parts of the world have two seasons: the rainy season and the dry season.

1. Make a chart like the one here.

2. Think about a place that you know about. List information about the seasons in this place.

3. Put a star (★) next to your favorite season. Put an *X* next to your least favorite season. Why did you choose these seasons? Explain your answers to a partner.

		Seasons in _____			
Season	When	Weather (rain, snow, sun)	Temperature (hot, cold, warm, cool)	Things People Do
spring	April, May, June	sunny rainy	warm	lie in the sun plant gardens

MULTI-LEVEL OPTIONS *Build Vocabulary*

Newcomer Demonstrate how to use a picture dictionary, focusing on key features (target word, syllables, simple definition, pictures). Then show a picture of a chariot and the picture of Demeter looking haggard on p. 243 to explain the vocabulary. Have students record these words in their Personal Dictionaries.

Beginning Have students add a column to their charts and head it *Picture*. Instruct them to draw or find an illustration for each word to help them recall its meaning.

Intermediate Show students how to use the dictionary function on the word-processing system they use in your class. Also, show them how to find and use dictionaries on the Internet.

Advanced Point out that there are many dictionaries for different purposes and levels. Have students visit the school media center. Ask pairs to look up the vocabulary words in three dictionaries. Have them compare and contrast the information they find in these resources.

Build Background

Hemispheres and the Seasons

Not all parts of the world have the same season at the same time. Why?

Earth is divided into two parts called hemispheres. As Earth moves around the sun, one hemisphere is turning toward it. The other hemisphere is turning away from it. The hemisphere pointing toward the sun is warmer. It is summer there. The hemisphere pointing away from the sun is cooler. It is winter there.

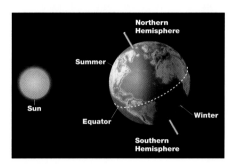

Content Connection

The **equator** is the imaginary circular line that divides Earth into the two hemispheres.

Build Vocabulary

Use a Dictionary to Find Definitions, Pronunciations, and Derivations

Read this dictionary entry.

se•ri•ous /ˈsɪriəs/ *adj.* **1** thoughtful and quiet, humorless [from Latin *sērius*]

This entry gives you the pronunciation of the word, its part of speech (*adj.* = adjective), its meaning, and its derivation (where it came from).

1. Copy this chart.
2. Look up these words in a large dictionary and fill in the chart.
3. With your teacher's help, pronounce the words.

Word	Meaning	Derivation
serious	thoughtful and quiet, humorless	Latin *sērius*
chariot		
haggard		

Personal Dictionary

The Heinle Newbury House Dictionary

Activity Book *p. 129*

Student CD-ROM

Chapter 2 Persephone and the Seasons **239**

Cultural Connection

Build Background Make a large circle on the board. Divide it into quarters. Write one of the following in each section: *spring, summer, fall, winter.* Engage students in identifying holidays and traditions from the United States and other countries that relate to the seasons. (*Examples:* Arbor Day in the United States, a time to plant trees in spring; Iriji in Nigeria, a time to celebrate the harvest in late summer)

Learning Styles
Visual

Build Vocabulary Have students create word webs for each of the vocabulary words. In addition to including the definitions they have found, have them incorporate related words, synonyms, and sentences using the words into their webs.

Build Background

Hemispheres and the Seasons

1. **Use a globe** Model the orbit of Earth and the sun. Have one student be the sun and another carry a tilted globe around the "sun." As the globe goes around, point out the hemispheres and their relationship to the sun.
2. **Identify hemispheres** Name different countries and ask students to identify which hemisphere they are in.
3. **Content Connection** Have students research the hours of daylight in their hemisphere and in the opposite hemisphere. Ask them to make a generalization about daylight in different seasons.

Build Vocabulary

Use a Dictionary to Find Definitions, Pronunciations, and Derivations

Teacher Resource Book: *Personal Dictionary, p. 63*

1. **Explain terms** Clarify key words from the example: *pronunciation, part of speech, meaning,* and *derivation.*
2. **Reading selection vocabulary** You may want to introduce the glossed words in the reading selection before students begin reading. Key words: *goddess, harvests, chariot, underworld, starving, persuade, pomegranate.* Instruct students to write the words with correct spelling and their definitions in their Personal Dictionaries. Have them pronounce each word and divide it into syllables.
3. **Multi-level options** See MULTI-LEVEL OPTIONS on p. 238.

Answers
chariot: horse-drawn two-wheeled cart; Latin *carricare;* haggard: looking worn and exhausted; Middle French *hagard*

ASSESS

Ask: If it's winter in North America, what season is it in Australia? (summer) Repeat for spring, summer, and fall.

Text Structure

Myth

1. **Recognize features** Point out the features on the chart. Direct students to Text Structure for "The Legend of Sleepy Hollow" (p. 52). Ask students to compare legends and myths. (Both are oral traditions and made-up, or partly made-up; they have amazing or powerful characters and events.)

2. **Locate pronunciation** Have students locate the pronunciation of *myth* in the glossary of their Student Handbook or other sources, such as online or CD-ROM dictionaries. Ask students to record the meaning and derivation in their Reading Logs.

Reading Strategy

Use Chronology to Locate and Recall Information

1. **Use a timeline** Point out daily schedules and calendars used to order events. Make a timeline to record similar information. Help students to record events as they read.

2. **Multi-level options** See MULTI-LEVEL OPTIONS below.

ASSESS

Ask: What do myths try to explain? (an event in nature)

Text Structure

Myth

"Persephone and the Seasons" is a **myth** from ancient Greece. A myth is a made-up story. It is an oral tradition—it was told out loud from one generation to the next for thousands of years. Look for the features of a myth as you read the selection.

As you read, notice how the myth explains an event in nature. Which event does it explain?

Myth	
Characters	Characters may have special powers that people in real life do not.
Events	Many events could never happen in real life.
Explanation	Many myths give a made-up explanation of events in nature.

Student CD-ROM

Reading Strategy

Use Chronology to Locate and Recall Information

Chronology is the order in which events happen. *Chronology* comes from the Greek root word *khronos*, which means *time*. Knowing the chronology of events can help you locate information in a text. It can also help you recall what you read.

1. Make a timeline in your Reading Log. As you read, take notes on the important events on a timeline like this.

2. After you read, use the timeline to help you locate and recall information.

Reading Log

Student CD-ROM

Persephone and the Seasons

Demeter left for the day. | Pluto took Persephone away.

MULTI-LEVEL OPTIONS *Reading Strategy*

Newcomer Review the concept of timelines by having students create sketches on timelines to show several major events in their own lives. Then explain that students may use the same type of picture timeline to show key events that happen to Persephone and Demeter in the story.

Beginning Have students create a personal timeline. Ask them to use words and short phrases to show important events in their own lives, such as their birth, starting school, moving to a new place, and so on. Then have students use words and phrases on a timeline to show key events in the story.

Intermediate *Say: Timelines often have dates on them, but some do not. The author of this myth does not give specific times, but you can use words such as* morning, midnight, *and* nine days later *to show when events happened.*

Advanced Have students write *chronology* and its definition from p. 241. Tell them to look up the word in a dictionary and add to the definition. Then have them find other words that come from *khronos*, such as chronograph. Have students record these and write paraphrased meanings in their Personal Dictionaries.

PERSEPHONE AND THE SEASONS

a myth by Heather Amery

241

Reading Selection Materials

Audio: *Unit 4, Chapter 2; CD 2, Track 8*
Teacher Resource Book: *Reading Summary, pp. 97–98*
Transparencies: #40, *Reading Summary*

Suggestions for Using Reading Summary

- Introduce new vocabulary or cognates.
- Cut the summary into strips, or jumble the sentences on an overhead transparency. Students put the sentences in order.
- Practice the reading strategy.
- Students read aloud or with a partner.
- Students paraphrase the summary.
- Students do a cloze activity.
- Students create a visual or graphic organizer, such as a timeline or storyboard, to illustrate the summary.
- Students paraphrase the summary.

Preview the Selection

Teacher Resource Book: *Web, p. 37*

1. **Create an idea web** Record words and phrases about the picture and story to create an idea web. Have students add to the idea web. Use guiding questions to have them make suggestions about who Persephone is, where she lives, and what is going to happen to her. Students can draw on information from the illustration, vocabulary, and other previous activities from this chapter.

2. **Connect** Remind students that the unit theme is *cycles*. Ask who or what will be part of a cycle.

 Content Connection
Math

Say: *In the myth that you will read, people think that spring and summer are good and that fall and winter are bad. Do you think people feel that way today?* Have each student form a hypothesis. (*Example:* Most people today like spring best.) Have students ask five family members and friends who are not in the class to identify their favorite season. Work with students to make a class graph to show the results. *Ask: Was your hypothesis correct?*

Learning Styles
Intrapersonal

Have students return to the chart they made in Use Prior Knowledge. Tell them to think about their favorite season. *Ask: What good things come to mind when you think of that season? Are there holidays in that season that you like? Have good things happened to you or your family in that season? Do you like the activities you can do?* Have students draw or write their responses.

Read the Selection

1. **Use text features** Point out paragraph numbers and remind students of their purpose. Direct students to the glossed words. Remind students to use the illustration to help understanding.

2. **Paired reading** Read the selection aloud. Pause to check understanding and to identify facts about the myth: who, where, when, and what. Have students reread the selection in pairs.

3. **Analyze events** *Ask: What are some examples of events that could not happen in real life?* (The weather is always fine. The ground doesn't open and close.)

Sample Answer to Guide Question
No, Demeter was still away.

See Teacher Edition pp. 434–436 for a list of English-Spanish cognates in the reading selection.

Use Chronology to Locate and Recall Information

Had Demeter come home when Pluto took Persephone?

Audio
CD 2, Tr. 8

1   One bright, sunny morning, the **goddess** Demeter said goodbye to her daughter Persephone. "I'll be back for supper," she called. Demeter was the goddess of all the plants in the world. She made sure the corn grew tall in the fields and fruit **ripened** on the trees. The weather was always fine and there were **harvests** all year.

2   After her mother had gone, Persephone went out to meet her friends and pick flowers with them. Searching for the very best lilies, she wandered away and was soon on her own.

3   Suddenly, she heard a noise and looked up. She saw a **chariot** pulled by four black horses, driven by Pluto, god of the **Underworld.** Pluto had fallen in love with Persephone, but knew Demeter would never allow him to marry her daughter.

4   Before Persephone could scream, Pluto dragged her into the chariot and raced away. As they **thundered** across the ground, a huge **cleft** opened. Pluto drove straight down it and the ground closed up behind them. He and Persephone had disappeared into the Underworld.

5   When Demeter came back that evening, she called to Persephone but there was no **reply.** The house was empty. When it grew dark, Demeter began to worry. Where could

goddess a female being or spirit with special powers; people in ancient Greece believed in the goddess Demeter	**Underworld** in ancient Greek myths, the place where people go when they die
ripened became ready to use or eat	**thundered** sounded like thunder
harvests times when people gather crops	**cleft** a crack or split
chariot a two-wheeled vehicle pulled by horses; used in ancient times	**reply** an answer

242   Unit 4   Cycles

MULTI-LEVEL OPTIONS *Read the Selection*

Newcomer Play the audio. *Ask: Does Persephone wander away from her friends?* (yes) *Does she want to go with Pluto?* (no) *Is Persephone's mother worried?* (yes) *Will Hermes talk to Pluto about getting Persephone back?* (yes)

Beginning Read the Reading Summary. *Ask: Is Persephone with friends or alone when Pluto comes?* (alone) *Where does Pluto take her?* (to the Underworld) *What happens to the crops while Demeter looks for Persephone?* (They die.) *Who will try to get Persephone back?* (Hermes)

Intermediate Have students do a shared reading. *Ask: Why was Persephone alone?* (She wandered away from her friends.) *How can you tell that Persephone does not want to go with Pluto?* (Pluto had to drag her off.) *How do you think Hermes will try to get Persephone back?* (*Example:* He may try to make a bargain.)

Advanced Have students read silently. *Ask: How would the story have been different if Persephone had stayed with her friends?* (*Example:* Pluto may not have grabbed her; her friends could have told her mother what happened.) *Explain Demeter's dress in paragraph 6.* (Black often means someone died.)

Persephone be? At midnight, she lit a flaming torch and set out to look for her. All night she searched, calling, "Persephone, Persephone, where are you?" But there was no answer. For nine days and nine nights, Demeter searched, not stopping to sleep or even to eat.

Use Chronology to Locate and Recall Information

What happened after Demeter stopped looking after the crops?

6 Dressed in black instead of her usual bright clothes, Demeter **wandered** all over the country as a haggard, old woman. Because she no longer looked after the crops, the corn **rotted** in the fields, no fruit ripened on the trees and the grass turned brown. There was nothing for the sheep and goats to eat and all the people grew short of food. Soon they were near to **starving.**

7 Zeus called a meeting of all the gods and goddesses. "This is very serious," he said in the voice that rolled like thunder. "Unless we can **persuade** Demeter to take care of the Earth again, all the people will die."

8 "Pluto must let Persephone leave the Underworld," said a goddess. "Only then will Demeter save the Earth."

9 Zeus called for Hermes, the messenger of the gods. "Go to Pluto and ask him, very politely, to return Persephone to her mother," he said. Hermes flew off at once. Only the gods and goddesses could go into the Underworld, the home of all the people who had died, and come out again.

---

wandered   went from place to place
rotted   became too old to eat

starving   dying from not having enough food
persuade   lead a person or group to believe or do something by arguing or reasoning with them

Chapter 2   Persephone and the Seasons   **243**

Read the Selection

1. **Use images as sources of information** Ask students to describe Demeter, the animals, and the plants in the illustration.

2. **Paired reading** Play the audio. Have students reread it aloud with partners.

3. **Summarize** *Ask: Why is Demeter wandering all over the country?* (She's looking for Persephone.) *Why isn't there any food?* (Demeter isn't taking care of the plants and weather.) *Who is Zeus?* (one of the gods) *Who goes to ask Pluto to return Persephone?* (Hermes)

4. **Use chronology to locate and recall information** Have students add events to their story timelines.

5. **Multi-level options** See MULTI-LEVEL OPTIONS on p. 242.

Sample Answer to Guide Question
The plants turned brown and died. The weather was not good for growing plants.

 Spelling

I before *e*

Say: Many people get confused about whether i *or* e *comes first in words that have those two letters together. Find the word* field *in paragraph 1. In this word,* i *comes before* e. *That is true most of the time. People use a jingle to remember how to spell these words:* "I *before* e *except after* c, *or when sounded like* ay *as in* neighbor *and* weigh." *Write the following on the board:* field, receive, reign. *Have students relate these examples to the jingle.*

Apply On the board, write: *v _ _ n, fr _ _ nd, ch _ _ f, rec_ _ pt.* Tell students that you are going to say these words as they complete them with *ie* or *ei.* **Say:** *vein, friend, chief, receipt.*

Read the Selection

1. **Use the illustration** Ask students to guess what Hermes and Pluto will say to each other.

2. **Shared reading** Continue reading the narrative aloud as students follow along. Have students join in for dialogue. *Ask: Why doesn't Pluto want to let Persephone go?* (He loves her.) *Did Persephone eat anything?* (Yes, she ate some pomegranate seeds.)

3. **Use chronology to locate and recall information** Add events to the timeline.

Sample Answer to Guide Question
She ate a few pomegranate seeds while she was in the Underworld.

10   "I will never let Persephone go," growled Pluto. "I love her and I want to marry her." "Please, Pluto," begged Hermes, "please be **reasonable.** You know Persephone doesn't love you and won't marry you."

11   "Very well," **roared** Pluto, very angry. "I'll let her go if she hasn't eaten any food while she's been here. You know the rule. If she has eaten anything in the Underworld, she must stay here forever."

12   "That's easy," said Hermes. "Let's ask her." Persephone cried, in answer to the question, "I couldn't eat anything here. I've never touched even the smallest crumb of food."

13   A **misty** ghost of a gardener was listening. "Oh yes you did," he **croaked.** "I saw you. You picked a ripe **pomegranate** and ate it."

14   "No, no," cried Persephone, "I didn't eat it all. I was so thirsty, I just swallowed a few of the seeds." "That's enough," shouted Pluto.

15   "Please, Pluto," begged Hermes, "let her go for a little while. A few seeds aren't much." "Oh, all right," growled

Use Chronology to Locate and Recall Information

When did Persephone eat something?

---

reasonable   referring to the right thing to do
roared   shouted very loudly and angrily
misty   not easy to see, as if covered by a cloud

croaked   made a deep sound like a frog
pomegranate   a fruit with many juicy red seeds

244   Unit 4   Cycles

MULTI-LEVEL OPTIONS *Read the Selection*

Newcomer *Ask: Does Pluto want to let Persephone go home?* (no) *Does Hermes make a deal with Pluto?* (yes) *Does Pluto say the girl can live with him sometimes and with her mother sometimes?* (yes) *Does spring come when Persephone goes home?* (yes) *Does fall come when she goes back to Pluto?* (yes)

Beginning *Ask: How does Pluto feel about letting Persephone go home?* (angry) *Who convinced Pluto to let her visit her mother?* (Hermes) *When will Persephone return to her mother?* (spring) *When will she go back to Pluto?* (fall)

Intermediate *Ask: How is Pluto's behavior different from Hermes's behavior?* (Hermes is calm and polite; Pluto is angry.) *Why does Persephone say she has not eaten anything?* (because she wants to get out of the Underworld) *How does Demeter show her feelings about Persephone coming home?* (She wears happy colors and takes care of Earth.)

Advanced *Ask: What do you think about Persephone saying she has not eaten?* (*Example:* She is trying to save herself, but it is still a lie. She tells the truth in the end.) *What does this myth try to explain?* (why the seasons change)

Pluto. "Persephone may go back to the Earth for half of each year but must spend the other months here with me, in the Underworld."

16   Holding Persephone's hand, Hermes flew with her out of the Underworld to Demeter. "Oh, my darling daughter," cried Demeter, hugging Persephone. "You have come back to me at last." "Yes," **sobbed** Persephone, "but I must go back to the Underworld for part of every year."

17   Demeter knew she had to accept this. At once, she looked young again. She put on her brightest clothes and began work, making new **shoots** of corn and grass grow and leaves open on the trees. It was spring all over the Earth.

18   All through the summer Demeter was happy and busy, watching the fine harvests of corn and fruit. But when Persephone had to go back to the Underworld, she was sad and it became autumn. The leaves on the trees turned brown, the grass stopped growing and the weather turned cold. It was winter until Persephone returned. Then Demeter was happy and it was spring again.

> **Use Chronology to Locate and Recall Information**
>
> What happened after Demeter began to work again?

---

sobbed cried   **shoots** small, young plant growth

About the Author | Heather Amery

Heather Amery lives in England. She has written more than 100 books for young people. Amery has many hobbies. She enjoys riding her bicycle, sailing, and swimming. She also likes to visit new places. Of course, Amery loves to read. It is a part of her everyday life.

► Heather Amery wrote her own version of this famous myth. What strategies do you think she used in researching and writing this story? What question would you ask Heather Amery about this text?

Chapter 2 Persephone and the Seasons   **245**

_th_ Spelling

Silent *b*

Ask: What is the last *consonant sound you hear in the word* crumb*? (m) Yes, but* m *is not the last letter in the word. Find the word in paragraph 12 to find out what silent letter is at the end.* (b) Tell students that *b* is usually silent after *m.*

Apply Pronounce some words that end in silent *b.* (climb, comb, lamb, thumb) Have students tell you how to spell them. Write the words on the board. Circle the silent *b.*

Evaluate Your Reading Strategy

Use Chronology to Locate and Recall Information *Say: You have practiced an important reading strategy. Now you can decide how well you have done. Does this statement describe how you read?*

> As I read, I use time words to figure out chronology. This helps me locate information and recall what I read.

Read the Selection

1. **Shared reading** Play the audio. Have groups join in for different paragraphs. *Ask: How does Demeter feel when Persephone is on Earth?* (happy) *What happens when she goes to the Underworld?* (Demeter is sad, so the plants die and it's autumn and winter.)
2. **Use a timeline** Ask students to summarize the story using their timelines.
3. **Multi-level options** See MULTI-LEVEL OPTIONS on p. 244.

Sample Answers to Guide Question
Plants started to grow. It was spring.

About the Author

Analyze author's style *Ask: How does Heather Amery make the characters seem real?* (She makes them talk, and they have feelings.)

Answer
Sample answer: Amery read different versions of this myth and other Greek myths.

Across Selections

Make comparisons *Say: This myth tries to explain why seasons change. The informational text "Why We Can't Get There from Here" (p. 196) tries to explain why space travel is impossible. Both texts try to explain real things, but they are very different. List as many differences between the two selections as you can.* (characters: gods vs. real scientists; narrative: conversations and feelings vs. facts and statistics; time: long ago vs. today; setting: country vs. space) *Say: Tell a partner which explanation was most interesting and why.*

Spelling, Punctuation, Capitalization

After the Reading Comprehension section, students will practice spelling, punctuation, and capitalization in the Activity Book.

Beyond the Reading

Reading Comprehension

Question-Answer Relationships

Sample Answers

1. picking flowers
2. the goddess of all the plants in the world
3. Hermes
4. He loves her and wants to marry her.
5. Hermes says that Persephone doesn't love Pluto, and that she won't marry him.
6. The Earth becomes brown and the plants die.
7. They decide that Persephone can spend part of the time on Earth and part of the time in the Underworld. It doesn't seem fair because Pluto didn't give Persephone a choice.
8. Demeter loves her daughter, Persephone. She's miserable when Persephone is missing and becomes happy when Persephone is there.
9. I think Persephone is sad when she returns to the Underworld every year. She doesn't want to stay in the Underworld with Pluto.
10. "The Ballad of Mulan" is a Chinese legend. It is similar to this myth because it was part of an ancient oral tradition and the hero was a woman who loved her family and returned home when she could. It is different because it has a very happy ending. The ending of "Persephone and the Seasons" is kind of sad because she still has to spend part of the year in the Underworld.

Build Reading Fluency

Read Silently and Aloud

Assessment Program: *Reading Fluency Chart, p. 116*

When students have completed the reading fluency activity, record their progress in the Reading Fluency Chart.

Reading Comprehension

Question-Answer Relationships (QAR)

"Right There" Questions

1. **Recall Facts** What is Persephone doing when Pluto takes her away?
2. **Recall Facts** What is Demeter the goddess of?
3. **Recall Facts** Who brings Persephone back to Demeter?

"Think and Search" Questions

4. **Identify Cause and Effect** Why does Pluto take Persephone?
5. **Find Supporting Arguments** Hermes and Pluto argue over letting Persephone go. What reasons does Hermes give for why Pluto should let her go?
6. **Analyze Change** How does Earth change when Persephone is in the Underworld?

"Author and You" Questions

7. **Resolve a Problem** How do the characters resolve the problem? Is it a good solution? Why?
8. **Make Inferences** How does Demeter feel about Persephone? How can you tell?
9. **Analyze Characters** How do you think Persephone feels when she must go back to the Underworld every year? Why do you think so?

"On Your Own" Question

10. **Make Connections Across Cultures** Do you know of a myth, a legend, or another oral tradition from another culture or region? Compare and contrast it to this myth.

Activity Book
p. 130

Student
CD-ROM

Build Reading Fluency

Read Silently and Aloud

Reading silently for practice then reading aloud helps you read with expression.

1. Listen to the audio recording of "Persephone and the Seasons."
2. Follow along on page 242.
3. Read silently paragraphs 1–3 three times.
4. With a partner read aloud.
5. Your partner will time you.

246 Unit 4 Cycles

MULTI-LEVEL OPTIONS *Elements of Literature*

Newcomer Have students draw two boxes on a piece of paper. Ask them to sketch the part of the story in which Persephone is picking flowers far from her friends. Tell them to draw an arrow from this box to the other. Then have them sketch Pluto stealing her away. Point to the first box. **Say:** *clue.*

Beginning Have students draw the same kind of boxed illustrations as described in the Newcomer section. Ask them to label the first box *Clue.* Have them label the other box *What happens.*

Intermediate Have students search for other examples of foreshadowing in the myth. Ask them to identify clues and tell the events to which clues are tied later in the story. (*Example:* Pluto's chariot was drawn by black horses. Black is the color of the Underworld.)

Advanced After students have identified examples of foreshadowing in the myth, point out that foreshadowing is an important technique for mystery writers also. Direct students to "The Sneak Thief" (p. 42) and have them identify one or two examples of foreshadowing.

Listen, Speak, Interact

Act Out a Story

Present a dramatic interpretation of "Persephone and the Seasons" to the class.

1. In groups, choose a character that each person will be: Persephone, Demeter, Pluto, Zeus, and the Gardener.
2. Go through the story and identify all of the dialogue (the words with "quotation marks" around them).
3. Practice the dialogue. Each person reads his or her words in the story.
4. Act out the places where there is no dialogue.

5. Evaluate yourself: Are you speaking clearly and slowly? Are you speaking loudly enough and with the right pitch and tone? Will your audience believe you?
6. Use good pronunciation and intonation.
7. After you practice, perform your story for your class or another class.
8. Ask your audience if they understood your verbal words and your nonverbal messages. Did they believe your role?

Elements of Literature

Recognize Foreshadowing

In **foreshadowing,** an author gives clues about something that will happen later in a story. Look at this example:

> It was a dark day. The clouds were heavy and black. Sam turned on the television and saw the serious face of the weather announcer.

This paragraph uses foreshadowing. It gives us the feeling that something bad will probably happen later.

Sometimes we notice foreshadowing more easily when we reread a story. That is because when we reread, we already know how the story ends.

1. Reread this sentence from paragraph 2 of "Persephone and the Seasons."

   > Searching for the very best lilies, she wandered away and was soon on her own.

2. Work with a small group. Talk about these questions:
   a. The author says that Persephone is alone. Does this tell you that something bad will happen?
   b. Why do you think so?

Activity Book
p. 131

Student
CD-ROM

Chapter 2 Persephone and the Seasons **247**

Content Connection
Language Arts

Have students work in pairs to prepare to retell an event that happened in school. After they have decided what to tell and how to tell it, ask them to figure out how to include a clue to the type of story it will be (funny, happy, surprising). Tell them to start the story with the clue. Have one student begin with the foreshadowing piece. Ask the other to tell the rest of the story.

Learning Styles
Intrapersonal

Tell students that actors prepare for their roles by trying to think and feel like the person they are pretending to be. Ask students to free-write the feelings and thoughts of a character in the story. Tell them to write about how well they feel they know the character after the writing activity.

Listen, Speak, Interact

Act Out a Story

1. **Reread in pairs** Group beginning and intermediate students. Have them choose parts and read aloud together.
2. **Newcomers** Reread with this group. Discuss the feelings of the characters. Have students choose a character and record details about his/her feelings in their Reading Logs. Assign advanced students to read the dialogue as newcomers act out the story. Have students practice and present their interpretation to the class.

Elements of Literature

Recognize Foreshadowing

1. **Personal experience** After explaining *foreshadowing,* have students suggest events in nature that foreshadow, such as animals acting tense or panicked before an earthquake.
2. **Locate derivation** Have students locate the derivation of *foreshadowing* in the glossary of their Student Handbook or other sources, such as online or CD-ROM dictionaries. Ask students to record the meaning and derivation in their Reading Logs.
3. **Multi-level options** See MULTI-LEVEL OPTIONS on p. 246.

Answers
Example: **2. a.** It's a clue that something bad will happen. **b.** People that are alone have no one to help them. In many stories, a person alone gets into trouble.

ASSESS

Have students evaluate their own performances in the enactment of "Persephone and the Seasons."

Word Study

Recognize Contractions

Make flash cards Write contracted forms on one side of flash cards and full forms on the other. Have students practice in pairs or individually.

Answers

1. couldn't, didn't, aren't
2. **a.** didn't; **b.** couldn't; **c.** wouldn't

Grammar Focus

Write Using Irregular Past Tense Verbs

1. **Apply** *Ask: What did you do after school yesterday?* List regular and irregular past tense verb forms from students' answers.
2. **Analyze** Have students identify verbs that add *-ed* to form the past tense and those verbs that are irregular.

Answers

1. heard, saw, knew
2. *Examples:* Last night I saw a great movie. We heard the school band.

ASSESS

Write on the board: *make, hear, know, see.* Have students write the irregular past tense verbs and use them in sentences.

Word Study

Recognize Contractions

Negative sentences usually use the word *not.* In speech and in informal writing, we often contract *not* with a verb. We shorten it to *n't.*

> You know Persephone does**n't** love you.

Here are some more examples:

Full Form	Contracted Form
is not	isn't
do not	don't
cannot	can't
will not	won't

1. Find three contracted forms of *not* in paragraphs 12, 14, and 15 of the reading.
2. Rewrite the following sentences, contracting *not* with its verb.
   a. Persephone did not like life in the Underworld.
   b. Demeter could not find Persephone.
   c. Pluto would not let her go.

Activity Book
p. 132

Student
CD-ROM

Grammar Focus

Write Using Irregular Past Tense Verbs

Use the past tense to talk about actions that happened in the past. The past tense form of regular verbs is the verb plus the ending *-ed* added to the verb.

> As they <u>thundered</u> across the ground, a huge cleft <u>opened</u>.

Irregular past tense verbs are formed in different ways.

> Persephone <u>went</u> out to meet her friends.

Went is the past tense form of *go.* You have to memorize the past tense forms of irregular verbs.

Simple Form	Past Tense Form
make	made
hear	heard
know	knew
see	saw

Refer to the list of irregular verbs in your Student Handbook.

1. Reread paragraph 3 of the reading. List three irregular past tense verbs.
2. Write two sentences with irregular past tense verbs.

Activity Book
pp. 133–134

Student
Handbook

Student
CD-ROM

248 Unit 4 Cycles

MULTI-LEVEL OPTIONS *From Reading to Writing*

Newcomer Work with students to create a class comic-strip version of the myth. Ask individuals or small groups to create illustrations of main events from the story. Display these in chronological order.

Beginning Have students work in pairs to create comic-strip versions of the myth. Ask them to create frames for each major event in the story. Have them use speech balloons with words or short phrases to paraphrase some of the dialogue from the story.

Intermediate Show students how to transform dialogue into indirect quotes. On the board, write: *"I will never let Persephone go," growled Pluto.* Paraphrase using an indirect quote. Write: *Pluto was angry. He told Hermes that he wouldn't let Persephone go home.* Point out that quotation marks are not needed in the paraphrase.

Advanced Ask students to focus on the friends who will receive their writing. *Ask: Why will this story interest your friend? What parts will especially appeal to him or her? Is there a book or movie you both know to which you can compare this myth?* Encourage students to keep the receivers' interests in mind as they write.

From Reading to Writing

Summarize and Paraphrase to Inform

Imagine that you have a friend who lives far away. This friend is interested in oral traditions, so you want to tell him or her about the Persephone myth. You decide to summarize the story (give its main ideas) and paraphrase some of the dialogue (restate it in your own words).

1. Review the timeline of the story that you made in the Reading Strategy section. Make sure that you included all of the main events.
2. Write a summary. It should tell the story using only the main events. Use regular and irregular past tense verbs correctly.

3. Choose some dialogue in the story that you want to include.
4. Reread the dialogue carefully. Then close your book and paraphrase it. Put this paraphrase in your summary.
5. You want your friend to have your summary right away. Should you put it in a letter or in an e-mail message?

Activity Book
p. 135

Student
Handbook

Across Content Areas

Distinguish the Meanings of *Myth*

Listed below are two definitions of the word *myth*.

> **myth** /mɪθ/ *n.* **1** stories from ancient cultures about history, gods, and heroes: *Students learn about the myths of ancient Greece and Rome.* **2** an untrue or unproved story: *His stories about his great successes in sports are myths.*

Read the following sentences. On a piece of paper, match each sentence with the correct definition. Write *Definition 1* or *Definition 2.*

1. I read a myth about the hero Hercules.
2. Monica's stories about her old school are all myths.
3. Many other cultures tell myths about why the seasons change.
4. We heard that John reads 15 books a day. But we think that this is a myth.

Activity Book
p. 136

Chapter 2 Persephone and the Seasons **249**

From Reading to Writing

Summarize and Paraphrase to Inform

1. **Review to summarize** Have students review key events to include in their summaries.
2. **Make a plan** Have students explain their summaries in pairs. Later, have students rewrite their summaries. Remind them to arrange the sequence of events in chronological order and to use past tense verb forms correctly. Students may want to prepare an illustration to accompany their summaries.
3. **Multi-level options** See MULTI-LEVEL OPTIONS on p. 248.

Across Content Areas: Language Arts

Distinguish the Meanings of *Myth*

Connect Explain different meanings of *myth*. *Ask: Which meaning is correct for the myth of "Persephone and the Seasons"?* (Definition 1) *Which meaning is correct for the myth that I am 82 years old?* (Definition 2)

Answers
1. Definition 1 2. Definition 2 3. Definition 1
4. Definition 2

 **ASSESS**

Say definitions and have students give an example of the use of *myth.*

Reteach and Reassess

Text Structure Have students review the chart on p. 240. Ask them to tell how "Persephone and the Seasons" relates to the features listed.

Reading Strategy Tell students to refer to the timeline they created for the myth (p. 240). Have them use it to answer questions such as: *Did Zeus have a meeting before or after Hermes went to see Pluto?* (before)

Elements of Literature Tell students about something that happened on the way to school. Begin with foreshadowing.

(*Example:* When I paid for my lunch yesterday, I found a lot of change in my wallet. I thought it was kind of strange since I had put money in the parking meter that morning. When I got to my car after school, I found out why I still had so much change; I forgot to put money in the parking meter, so I got a $25 ticket.)

Reassess Read a short myth or legend to students. Have them summarize it and paraphrase the dialogue.

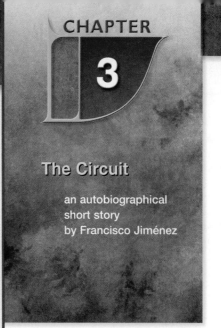

CHAPTER 3

The Circuit

an autobiographical
short story
by Francisco Jiménez

Chapter Materials

Activity Book: *pp. 137–144*
Audio: *Unit 4, Chapter 3; CD 2, Track 9*
Student Handbook
Student CD-ROM: *Unit 4, Chapter 3*
Teacher Resource Book: *Lesson Plan, Teacher
    Resources, Reading Summary, Activity Book
    Answer Key*
Teacher Resource CD-ROM
Assessment Program: *Quiz, pp. 65–66; Teacher
    and Student Resources, pp. 115–144*
Assessment CD-ROM
Transparencies
The Heinle Newbury House Dictionary/CD-ROM
Web site: http://visions.heinle.com

Objectives

Paired reading Have students take turns
reading the objectives section in pairs. *Ask: Is
there an objective from the list that you can do
already?*

Use Prior Knowledge

Talk About Moving

1. **Share personal experience** Tell students
   about a move you made. Share expectations
   and feelings you had for the new place.
2. **Use a graphic organizer** Have students
   create questions for the chart.

Objectives

Reading Compare text to your own
knowledge and experience as you read
an autobiographical short story.

Listening and Speaking Present an
experience.

Grammar Identify dependent clauses.

Writing Write a letter to an author.

Content Language Arts: Understand the
influence of other languages and cultures
on English.

Use Prior Knowledge

Talk About Moving

When people leave one home and go
to live in another, we say they have moved.
Have you ever moved? Think about
what it would feel like to move to a new
home. What questions would you have?

1. Write your questions in a chart.
2. Share your questions with a partner.
   Are any of your questions the same?
3. Which question is the most
   important one for you? Why?
   Compare with your partner.
4. State the main idea and supporting
   details of what your partner said.

5. Share your thoughts about moving
   with the class.

Questions About Moving		
The New Neighborhood	The New School	New Friends
Will the people be friendly?	Will the teachers be nice?	How will I make friends?

MULTI-LEVEL OPTIONS *Build Vocabulary*

Newcomer Ask Spanish-speaking students to serve as a panel of experts. Have them help students who don't speak Spanish to guess the meanings of the words on the chart. Ask the experts to indicate whether the guesses are right or wrong.

Beginning Have students work in small groups. If possible, assign one Spanish speaker to each group. Have students work together to do the assignment with the Spanish speaker's help.

Intermediate Suggest that when students encounter a word from a language they do not know, sometimes they may figure out what it means by comparing it to a word in a language they do know. For example, *Papá* is very similar to the English word *Papa*.

Advanced Have students work in pairs to complete the exercise. Ask them to use the help of Spanish-speaking classmates or a Spanish-English dictionary to check their answers.

Build Background

Farming in the United States

Most farms in the United States today are very large. Machines do a lot of the work, but they cannot pick some crops.

Some farmers pay migrant workers to pick crops by hand. These workers move from one farm to another.

Content Connection

California produces more food than any other state in the United States.

Build Vocabulary

Study Word Origins and Guess Meaning

There are many Spanish words in the selection you will read. You can guess the meaning of these words by using **context clues** and **language structure.** Context clues are words or sentences that are around a word. Language structure is how the word is used in the sentence.

Some English words come from Spanish, for example, *patio, plaza,* and *rodeo.* How do you think they become English words?

1. Copy this chart in your Personal Dictionary.
2. Look at the definitions at the bottom of the chart. Match the underlined words to their definitions.

Use Context Clues and Language Structure

Everything was packed. Papá said wearily, "<u>Es todo.</u>"	*that's everything*
Mamá liked the pot. "<u>Mi olla,</u>" she used to say proudly.	
"Do you like music?" he asked me. "Yes, I like <u>corridos,</u>" I answered.	

that's everything	*style of music*	*my stewpot*

Personal Dictionary   Activity Book p. 137   Student CD-ROM

Chapter 3 The Circuit **251**

Content Connection
Technology

Build Vocabulary Locate a translation dictionary by entering the words *online translation dictionary* into an Internet search engine. Show students how to use the dictionary to translate words from one language to another. Have them practice using one of these dictionaries by translating the Spanish words in Build Vocabulary into English.

Learning Styles
Intrapersonal

Build Background Ask each student to draw a vertical line three-quarters of the way down a piece of paper and label the resulting columns *Plus* and *Minus.* Ask them to label the space across the bottom of the page *Interesting.* Tell students to draw or write in the appropriate columns positive or negative feelings about being in a family that migrated. Have students record other thoughts or questions about migrant workers under *Interesting.*

Build Background

Farming in the United States

1. **Use resources** Bring in pictures of California fields. Use a map to show the large central valley in California, the San Joaquin Valley. Have students use an almanac or the Internet to find major crops of California.
2. **Content Connection** *Ask: What fruits and vegetables that are grown in California can you buy at the local grocery store?*

Build Vocabulary

Study Word Origins and Guess Meaning

Teacher Resource Book: *Personal Dictionary, p. 63*

1. **Teacher think aloud** Read the chart's first row. *Say: I know everything is ready. What might Papá say? "Everything's done. That's all. That's everything." I can use the context clues, other words in the sentences, to make guesses.*
2. **Reading selection vocabulary** You may want to introduce the glossed words in the reading selection before students begin reading. Key words: *shack, labor camp, nervous, instinct, enroll, trumpet, goose bumps.* Instruct students to write the words with correct spelling and their definitions in their Personal Dictionaries. Have them pronounce each word and divide it into syllables.
3. **Multi-level options** See MULTI-LEVEL OPTIONS on p. 250.

Answers
2. Mi olla/my stewpot; corridos/style of music

ASSESS

Have students paraphrase the information they learned in Build Background.

Text Structure

Autobiographical Short Story

1. **Understand terms** Have students use examples from other stories to clarify the features. Point out pronouns used in first-person point of view.
2. **Share background** "The Circuit" was originally published as a short story in a magazine. The author later expanded it into a book of his childhood experiences.
3. **Multi-level options** See MULTI-LEVEL OPTIONS below.

Reading Strategy

Compare Text to Your Own Knowledge and Experience

Model the strategy Read aloud the paragraph. Model comparing your own personal experience with the character's. Ask volunteers to share their experiences.

Answers

2. **a.** *Example:* I walk to the bus stop. Then I ride the bus to school. **b.** *Example:* I felt uncomfortable at a party. I tried introducing myself and telling people how I knew the host.

ASSESS

Say: Name four features of an autobiographical short story. (setting, characters, events, first-person point of view)

Text Structure

Autobiographical Short Story

"The Circuit" is an **autobiographical short story.** An autobiographical short story is a story that an author writes about his or her own life. Look for the features of an autobiographical short story as you read the selection.

Autobiographical Short Story	
Setting	The real time and place are from the author's life.
Characters	The main character is the author; other characters are people from the author's life.
Events	The action happens in a few pages.
First Person Point of View	The author tells the story—he is the narrator. He uses the pronouns *I, me, we,* and *us* to tell the story.

Student CD-ROM

Reading Strategy

Compare Text to Your Own Knowledge and Experience

When you read, what you know and some of your experiences may be similar to those in the reading selection. To understand the reading, you should compare your knowledge and experiences to characters and events in the story.

1. Read this paragraph from the selection.

   Two hours later, around eight o'clock, I stood by the side of the road waiting for school bus number twenty. When it arrived I climbed in. Everyone was busy either talking or yelling. I sat in an empty seat in the back.

2. Answer these questions to help you compare your experiences to the character's experiences.
   a. How do you get to school? Do you walk? Do you take the bus?
   b. The character doesn't know anyone on the bus. Have you ever been in a situation where you didn't know anyone? How did you feel? What did you do?

Compare your knowledge and experiences as you read "The Circuit."

Student CD-ROM

MULTI-LEVEL OPTIONS *Text Structure*

Newcomer *Say: Draw a story about your life. What would you like to talk about?* After students have chosen topics, have them make two-column charts like the one on p. 252. Ask them to list *Setting, Characters,* and *Events* in the left column. Have each place drawings on the right to show the story he/she wants to share.

Beginning Have students create a two-column chart like the one on p. 252. Have them write words and phrases in the right column to outline a story about themselves that they would like to share with the class.

Intermediate Have groups discuss these questions. *Ask: Why would a reader want to read about someone else's life? How do you think an author of an autobiography decides what events to put in his or her story? If you were going to write an autobiography, what is one event from your life you would share? Why?*

Advanced *Say: Autobiographies can be fun to read. They can also teach us about life and how people handle the events in their lives.* Ask students to tell about auto-biographies they have read. Have each student share a very brief summary of the story and tell something he/she learned about life from reading the story.

The Circuit

an autobiographical short story by Francisco Jiménez

253

Reading Selection Materials

Audio: *Unit 4, Chapter 3; CD 2, Track 9*
Teacher Resource Book: *Reading Summary,*
    pp. 99–100
Transparencies: #41, *Reading Summary*

Suggestions for Using Reading Summary

- Introduce new vocabulary or cognates.
- Cut the summary into strips, or jumble the sentences on an overhead transparency. Students put the sentences in order.
- Practice the reading strategy.
- Students read aloud or with a partner.
- Students paraphrase the summary.
- Students do a cloze activity.
- Students create a visual or graphic organizer, such as a timeline or storyboard, to illustrate the summary.
- Students paraphrase the summary.

Preview the Selection

1. **Teacher think aloud** Have students examine the illustration as you *say: The title of the story is "The Circuit." In the picture, I see a lot of people working in a large field. It's hard work. I know that many large farms use migrant workers—workers that travel from one farm to another throughout the year. They follow the work as the seasons change. That's a cycle. In the dictionary, I see that the word* circuit *is a regular route from place to place. I imagine that these workers follow a regular route throughout the year.*

2. **Connect** Remind students that the unit theme is *cycles.* Help students share their thoughts and questions about the title, the illustration, and the content of the autobiographical short story. Tell students they will read about the author's experiences and feelings during a circuit, or cycle, of a migrant family.

Community Connection

Have small groups work together. Ask students who have seen farms, home gardens, or city gardening plots in their community to describe the land, what is grown there, who cares for the land, and what types of tools or machines are used. Tell groups to compare and contrast these descriptions with the scene they see in the photo on this page.

Learning Styles
Linguistic

Have students brainstorm lists of words that come to mind as they look at the photo on p. 253. Then ask them to circle the three most descriptive words they have listed. Tell students to create a caption for the photo and include the words they have circled.

Read the Selection

1. **Use text features** Call attention to the illustration and have students make guesses about the character and setting. Point out the italics for the Spanish words. Remind students to use context clues to guess meaning.

2. **Paired reading** Play the audio. Have students read aloud with a partner.

3. **Compare text to your own experience**
   Ask: How would you feel if you had to move to a new place?

Sample Answer to Guide Question
When my family moved to a new town, I didn't want to move either. I cried and had a dreadful feeling in my stomach.

See Teacher Edition pp. 434–436 for a list of English-Spanish cognates in the reading selection.

Audio
CD 2, Tr. 9

> **Compare Text to Your Own Knowledge and Experience**
>
> Compare your experience and feelings with those of the author.

1 Yes, it was that time of year. When I opened the front door to the **shack,** I stopped. Everything we owned was neatly packed in cardboard boxes. Suddenly I felt even more the weight of hours, days, weeks, and months of work. I sat down on a box. The thought of having to move to Fresno and knowing what was in store for me there brought tears to my eyes.

2 That night I could not sleep. I lay in bed thinking about how much I hated this move.

3 A little before five o'clock in the morning, Papá woke everyone up. A few minutes later, the yelling and screaming of my little brothers and sister, for whom the move was a great adventure, broke the silence of dawn. Shortly, the barking of the dogs **accompanied** them.

4 While we packed the breakfast dishes, Papá went outside to start the *"Carcanchita."* That was the name Papá gave his old black Plymouth. . . . Papá parked the car out in front and left the motor running. . . .

---

shack a small house or shed, usually of wood and not well built

accompanied went with someone

254 Unit 4 Cycles

MULTI-LEVEL OPTIONS *Read the Selection*

Newcomer Play the audio. Reread aloud and have students join in when they can. *Ask: Is the family leaving their home?* (yes) *Is the boy happy about moving?* (no) *Is the family taking a fun trip?* (no) *Are they going to find work?* (yes)

Beginning Read the story aloud. Then do a partner read aloud. *Ask: What is the family getting ready to do?* (move) *How does the boy feel?* (sad) *What does Mamá take?* (her pot) *Where is the family going?* (to Fresno to find work)

Intermediate Have students read silently. *Ask: How does the boy feel about moving?* (sad) *What are clues to his feelings?* (tears, could not sleep, lump in throat) *What does Mamá prepare for the trip?* (a pot of beans)

Advanced Have students read silently. *Ask: Why do you think the boy is so upset about moving?* (He probably dreads going to a new school where he doesn't know the teachers or have any friends.) *How do the boy's parents probably feel about moving?* (They may not like it either, but know they have to do it to find work.)

5   Everything was packed except Mamá's pot. It was an old large **galvanized** pot she had picked up at an army **surplus** store in Santa Maria. The pot had many **dents** and **nicks,** and the more dents and nicks it **acquired** the more Mamá liked it. "*Mi olla,*" she used to say proudly.

6   I held the front door open as Mamá carefully carried out her pot by both handles, making sure not to spill the cooked beans. When she got to the car, Papá reached out to help her with it. Roberto opened the rear car door and Papá gently placed it on the floor behind the front seat. All of us then climbed in. Papá sighed, wiped the sweat from his forehead with his sleeve, and said **wearily,** "*Es todo.*"

7   As we drove away, I felt a lump in my throat. I turned around and looked at our little shack for the last time.

8   At sunset we drove into a **labor camp** near Fresno. Since Papá did not speak English, Mamá asked the camp **foreman** if he needed any more workers. "We don't need no more," said the foreman, scratching his head. "Check with Sullivan down the road. Can't miss him. He lives in a big white house with a fence around it."

> **Compare Text to Your Own Knowledge and Experience**
>
> What does it feel like to ask for help from someone you do not know?

---

galvanized   metal covered with zinc
surplus   extra, leftover
dents   holes made by a hit
nicks   small cuts or marks

acquired   got
wearily   in a tired way
labor camp   a place where many workers live
foreman   a boss of a group of workers

Chapter 3 The Circuit   **255**

Read the Selection

1. **Shared reading** Play the audio. Have students join in when they can.
2. **Analyze character relationships** Have students explain how the author feels about his parents. *Ask: Do you think the family wants to move to Fresno?* (no) *How does the author feel about his parents?* (He loves and respects them.) *How do you know?* (He helps them.)
3. **Make predictions** *Ask: Do you think the family will find a place to work at Sullivan's farm?* (yes)
4. **Multi-level options** See MULTI-LEVEL OPTIONS on p. 254.

Sample Answer to Guide Question
When I got lost on my way to school, I had to ask for help. I felt scared and embarrassed.

, Punctuation

Italics for words from other languages

Have students find the word *Carcanchita* in paragraph 4. *Say: This word is in italic print to make it stand out from English. Italics are often used for words from other languages.* Show students how to use the italic font style on a computer.

Apply *Say: Find words in paragraphs 5 and 6 that are not English words.* (mi olla, es todo)

Read the Selection

1. **Use text features** Have students guess where the boy is now, what he is doing, and what he is thinking in the illustration.
2. **Teacher read aloud** Read the selection aloud. Then have students reread the selection in pairs.

Sample Answer to Guide Question
I had to start in the middle of the year because my dad got a new job in a different state. It was scary because I didn't know anyone. I felt very lonely.

9   When we got there, Mamá walked up to the house. She went through a white gate, past a row of rose bushes, up the stairs to the house. She rang the doorbell. The porch light went on and a tall **husky** man came out. They **exchanged** a few words. After the man went in, Mamá clasped her hands and hurried back to the car. "We have work! Mr. Sullivan said we can stay there the whole season," she said, **gasping** and pointing to an old garage near the stables. . . .

10   It was Monday, the first week of November. The grape season was over and I could now go to school. I woke up early that morning and lay in bed, looking at the stars and **savoring** the thought of not going to work and of starting sixth grade for the first time that year. . . .

11   Two hours later, around eight o'clock, I stood by the side of the road waiting for school bus number twenty. When it arrived I climbed in. Everyone was busy either talking or yelling. I sat in an empty seat in the back.

> **Compare Text to Your Own Knowledge and Experience**
>
> Have you had to go to a new school in the middle of the year? How was the experience? If not, imagine what it would be like.

---

husky   strong and solid
exchanged   gave and received words and ideas

gasping   breathing in quickly, usually from surprise or shock
savoring   appreciating and enjoying an experience

256   Unit 4   Cycles

MULTI-LEVEL OPTIONS *Read the Selection*

Newcomer *Ask: Do the boy's parents find work?* (yes) *Is the boy going to a new school?* (yes) *Does the boy know a lot of English?* (no) *Does the boy want to read for his class?* (no)

Beginning *Ask: Where does the boy go in November?* (school) *What language does he speak best?* (Spanish) *What does the boy's teacher want him to do?* (read aloud) *How does the boy feel?* (scared)

Intermediate *Ask: How does the boy feel about going to school? Explain.* (He is looking forward to it because he does not have to go to work.) *Explain the boy's reaction when his teacher asks him to read.* (The boy is embarrassed because he does not know English very well.)

Advanced *Ask: Why is the boy starting school in November?* (Before that, he had to work with his parents.) *Explain the last sentence in paragraph 13.* (The teacher realizes that the boy must not know much English. He does not want the boy to feel embarrassed if he makes mistakes, so he does not make him read.)

12 When the bus stopped in front of the school, I felt very **nervous.** I looked out the bus window and saw boys and girls carrying books under their arms. I put my hands in my pant pockets and walked to the principal's office. When I entered, I heard a woman's voice say: "May I help you?" I was **startled.** I had not heard English for months. For a few seconds I remained **speechless.** I looked at the lady who waited for an answer. My first **instinct** was to answer her in Spanish, but I held back. Finally, after struggling for English words, I managed to tell her that I wanted to **enroll** in the sixth grade. After answering many questions, I was led to the classroom.

13 Mr. Lema, the sixth grade teacher, greeted me and **assigned** me a desk. He then introduced me to the class.

I was so nervous and scared at that moment when everyone's eyes were on me that I wished I were with Papá and Roberto picking cotton. After **taking roll,** Mr. Lema gave the class the assignment for the first hour. "The first thing we have to do this morning is finish reading the story we began yesterday," he said enthusiastically. He walked up to me, handed me an English book, and asked me to read. "We are on page 125," he said politely. When I heard this, I felt my blood rush to my head; I felt **dizzy.** "Would you like to read?" he asked hesitantly. I opened the book to page 125. My mouth was dry. My eyes began to water. I could not begin. "You can read later," Mr. Lema said understandingly.

nervous worried about a future event
startled surprised, sometimes enough to jump
speechless not able to speak, sometimes from surprise or sadness
instinct a natural behavior

enroll join officially
assigned gave a spot
taking roll calling out the names of students and writing down if they are present
dizzy light-headed, faint

Chapter 3 The Circuit **257**

Read the Selection

1. **Use text features** Direct attention to the illustration and have students make predictions about the conversation between the author and the principal.

2. **Shared reading** Continue the reading of the story as students follow along. Have groups join in for different parts. *Ask: Where did the author go when he first got to school? Why?* (to the office; he didn't have a class or teacher yet.) *Why didn't the author hear much English for months?* (He had been working in the fields with his family, who spoke Spanish.)

3. **Analyze character development** Have students identify how the author felt in paragraphs 12 and 13. (nervous, anxious, alone, scared) Help them explain why he felt that way and compare his feelings to what their feelings might be in those situations.

4. **Summarize** Ask students to summarize the events in the story.

5. **Multi-level options** See MULTI-LEVEL OPTIONS on p. 256.

Sample Answer to Guide Question
When my family visited France, I had trouble understanding the language. I listened very carefully and watched what others were doing to help me understand.

Punctuation

Apostrophes for time

Have students review the first sentence in paragraph 11. On the board, write: *eight o'clock.* *Say: The punctuation mark between* o *and* c *is an apostrophe.* O'clock *means "of the clock."* The apostrophe stands for f the, which is left out when we write o'clock.

Apply Write on the board:

7:00–get up

8:00–go to school

12:00–eat lunch

3:00–go home

Ask students to rewrite this information using *o'clock.*

Read the Selection

1. **Use text features** Have students guess what the boy is doing in the illustration and why he is doing it.

2. **Provide background** A *corrido* is a popular style of Mexican folk music. It is a ballad that often tells the story of a hero or great event. *Corridos* are usually set to the rhythm of a waltz or a polka.

3. **Paired reading** Read the selection aloud. Then ask students to reread aloud with a partner. *Ask: What did he do during recess?* (He practiced reading.) *Do you think the teacher is friendly or not? Why?* (Yes, he's friendly. He smiles and helps the boy every day.) *What instrument does Mr. Lema offer to teach the boy to play?* (the trumpet) *Do you think the boy wants to play?* (Yes, the sound made the boy excited.)

Sample Answer to Guide Question
I had a teacher that helped me with classwork after school.

14   During **recess** I went into the **rest room** and opened my English book to page 125. I began to read in a low voice, pretending I was in class. There were many words I did not know. I closed the book and headed back to the classroom.

15   Mr. Lema was sitting at his desk correcting papers. When I entered he looked up at me and smiled. I felt better. I walked up to him and asked if he could help me with the new words. "Gladly," he said.

16   The rest of the month I spent my lunch hours working on English with Mr. Lema, my best friend at school.

17   One Friday during lunch hour Mr. Lema asked me to take a walk with him to the music room. "Do you like music?" he asked me as we entered the building. "Yes, I like *corridos*," I answered. He then picked up a **trumpet,** blew on it, and handed it to me. The sound gave me **goose bumps.** I knew that sound. I had heard it in many *corridos*. "How would you like to learn how to play it?" he asked. He must have read my face because before I could answer, he added: "I'll teach you how to play it during our lunch hours."

> **Compare Text to Your Own Knowledge and Experience**
>
> Compare Mr. Lema to teachers you have had.

recess   a short stop or break in classes
rest room   a washroom, bathroom
trumpet   a brass musical instrument

goose bumps   small raised bumps on the skin caused by cold, fear, disgust, or excitement

258   Unit 4   Cycles

MULTI-LEVEL OPTIONS *Read the Selection*

Newcomer *Ask: Does the boy get help learning to read English?* (yes) *Does his teacher help him?* (yes) *Is the boy happy about school?* (yes) *Does the family have to move again?* (yes)

Beginning *Ask: Who helps the boy learn to read?* (Mr. Lema) *What else does Mr. Lema want to teach the boy?* (to play the trumpet) *How does the boy feel?* (excited) *When the boy gets home, what does he find out the family has to do again?* (move)

Intermediate *Ask: What kind of teacher is Mr. Lema? Explain.* (He is kind because he gives up his lunchtime to help the boy.) *How is the boy feeling about school by the end of page 258? Why?* (excited because he is learning) *What do you think the boy may have said to himself when he saw the boxes?* (*Example:* Oh, no. I want to stay. I can't believe we're moving again!)

Advanced *Ask: Why is this story in a unit about cycles?* (It begins and ends in the same way: The family's life was a cycle of moving, getting settled, and moving again.) *Why do you think the author writes stories about his life in a migrant worker family?* (*Example:* to help others who have the same problems he had)

Compare Text to Your Own Knowledge and Experience

Have you ever been in a situation like this? How did you feel? How do you think the author felt?

18   That day I could **hardly** wait to tell Papá and Mamá the great news. As I got off the bus, my little brothers and sister ran up to meet me. They were yelling and screaming. I thought they were happy to see me, but when I opened the door to our shack, I saw that everything we owned was neatly packed in cardboard boxes.

hardly   barely, almost no

About the Author

Francisco Jiménez (born 1943)

Francisco Jiménez was born in Mexico. He came to California as a young boy. "The Circuit" tells about his life as a young boy. Jiménez's family moved a lot. This made school hard for Jiménez. However, he loved to learn. Finally, Jiménez's family was able to stay in one place. Jiménez finished school. He became a teacher. Jiménez writes stories about his experiences to share with other people.

➤ What challenges did the author face in becoming a writer? What strategies do you think he used to write this story?

Chapter 3 The Circuit   **259**

A   Capitalization

Languages

Ask: What language is the boy in the story learning? (English) *Look at how that word is written in paragraph 14. What do you notice? Yes, words for languages begin with capitals. Find the word for a language in paragraph 12 and notice the capital letter.* (Spanish)

   Apply Engage students in making a list of all the languages spoken by members of your class. Use a different colored marker for the initial capital.

Evaluate Your Reading Strategy

Compare Text to Your Own Knowledge and Experience *Say: You have practiced an important reading strategy. Now you can decide how well you have done. Does this statement describe how you read?*

> As I read, I compare my own knowledge and experiences to the text. Comparing my knowledge and experiences to the text helps me understand what I am reading.

Read the Selection

1. **Use text features** Direct attention to the illustration and ask why the boxes are packed.
2. **Shared reading** Play the audio. Have students join in when they can. *Ask: Will the boy learn the trumpet?* (No, his family is moving.)
3. **Multi-level options** See MULTI-LEVEL OPTIONS on p. 258.

Sample Answer to Guide Question
I felt bad. I think the author felt sad and angry that he had to give up something he was excited about.

About the Author

1. **Explain author's background** Francisco Jiménez writes in both Spanish and English. One of his goals is to create a bridge for cultural and human understanding between the United States and Mexico.
2. **Interpret the facts** *Ask: Why do you think Francisco Jiménez wrote this story in English? What stories would you like to tell English speakers about your experiences?*

Answer
Sample answer: It's hard to be a good writer without getting an education in school. The author faced the challenge of staying in one place long enough to finish his education. He thought about how learning improved his life and limited what he included in the story from his life to events that showed this point.

Across Selections

Analyze point of view Compare and contrast the third-person point of view in "Persephone and the Seasons" (p. 248) and the first-person point of view in "The Circuit." *Ask: Which character do you know better—Persephone or Francisco Jiménez? How does the point of view make you understand the feelings and experiences of the character better?*

Spelling, Punctuation, Capitalization

After the Reading Comprehension section, students will practice spelling, punctuation, and capitalization in the Activity Book.

Beyond the Reading

Reading Comprehension

Question-Answer Relationships

Sample Answers

1. pick fruit and cotton
2. English; to play the trumpet
3. because he has to help harvest grapes before then
4. Maybe he had to stay back some years, so this was the first time he was taking sixth grade.
5. He doesn't read well; Mr. Lema thinks he is shy.
6. The family is moving again. The family follows the harvest.
7. He's used to speaking only Spanish.
8. to show the beginning of another cycle in the family's life
9. He is determined to do well in school and learn. He practiced and studied on his own and asked questions when he needed help.
10. The cycle is moving to a new place, starting in a new school, becoming comfortable there, and then moving again. I don't think it will change unless he or his parents are able to find jobs that don't require moving.

Build Reading Fluency

Rapid Word Recognition

Rapid word recognition is an excellent activity for students who struggle with irregular spelling patterns. Time students for 1 minute as they read the words in the squares aloud.

Reading Comprehension

Question-Answer Relationships (QAR)

"Right There" Questions

1. **Recall Facts** What does the author's family do to earn money?
2. **Recall Facts** What does Mr. Lema help the author learn? What does he offer to teach the author?

"Think and Search" Questions

3. **Make Inferences** Why does the author start school in November?
4. **Make Inferences** Why does he say that he is "starting sixth grade for the first time that year"? (Paragraph 10)
5. **Analyze Characters** Why does the author hesitate to read? What does Mr. Lema conclude about the author?
6. **Make Inferences** Why are there packed boxes in the shack at the end of the reading? Explain what is happening and why.

"Author and You" Questions

7. **Analyze Cause and Effect** Why was the author's first instinct to answer in Spanish when the woman at school spoke to him?
8. **Recognize Style** In paragraphs 1 and 18, the author writes, "everything we owned was neatly packed in cardboard boxes." Why does he repeat these words?

"On Your Own" Questions

9. **Evaluate** How would you describe the author? Why do you think this?
10. **Speculate** What is the cycle of the author's life? Will it change?

Activity Book
p. 138

Student
CD-ROM

Build Reading Fluency

Rapid Word Recognition

Rapidly recognizing words helps increase your reading rate. It is an important characteristic of effective readers.

1. With a partner, review the words in the box.
2. Read the words aloud for one minute. Your teacher will time you.

3. Count how many words you read in one minute.

front	whom	thought	weight	thought	front
shack	weight	whom	thought	weight	thought
weight	brought	shack	front	brought	shack
thought	shack	weight	shack	front	brought
brought	whom	front	brought	whom	weight

MULTI-LEVEL OPTIONS *Elements of Literature*

Newcomer Show students some pictures of items from your cultural background. Say simple sentences about the pictures. (*Example:* This is *sauerbraten.*) Have students repeat words from your background. Invite students to bring in pictures of things important to their cultures and share the words for these things.

Beginning Ask students to draw their families' birthday celebrations. Have students include speech balloons. Invite students to share their work. Demonstrate drawing conclusions about the people in the pictures based on their language. Get feedback on whether your ideas are correct.

Intermediate Point out that there is little dialogue spoken by the main character. Read aloud information from an encyclopedia or other source about Spanish culture. Have students write a line of dialogue that shows something about the boy's culture. (*Example:* "I love dancing to *corridos.*") (paragraph 17)

Advanced After students have read "The Circuit," ask them to review the dialogue in "Persephone and the Seasons." *Ask: What can you tell about the culture of the characters?* (*Example:* "Go to Pluto, and ask him very politely . . ." shows that Zeus believed that good manners helped people get what they needed.)

Listen, Speak, Interact

Present an Experience

Work with two classmates. Each of you will present an experience you have had. For example, you can talk about moving to a new home, changing schools, or a good experience with a teacher.

1. Tell your classmates:
   a. Who was involved?
   b. What happened?
   c. When did it happen?
   d. Where did it happen?
   e. Why did it happen?
   f. How did you feel? Why?
2. As you listen to your classmates, take notes on their main ideas and supporting evidence. Ask for clarification as needed.

3. Write summaries of your classmates' experiences on a piece of paper.
4. Let your partners read your summaries. Ask them to tell you if you understood their main ideas and supporting evidence.
5. Compare your understanding of a classmate's story with your other classmate's understanding.
6. What are your classmates' points of view (perspectives) on their experiences?
7. How are the group's experiences similar and different?
8. How are the group's experiences similar to and different from those of Francisco Jiménez?

Elements of Literature

Identify Language Use to Show Characterization

One way to understand characters is to pay attention to the kind of language they use.

1. Listen to or read paragraph 5 aloud. Mamá says "Mi olla." What does this tell you about her culture and region? What does it tell you about the author's feelings about his language and culture?

2. Listen to or read paragraph 15 aloud. Mr. Lema says "Gladly." This word is usually formal. What does this language use tell you about Mr. Lema's experience and culture?

Activity Book p. 139   Student CD-ROM

Community Connection

Help students identify words, phrases, or ways of speaking that are common in your community or school. *Ask: What could a stranger to our community or school tell about us from hearing the language we use?* (*Example:* In our school, the teachers always say, "Think about other students' feelings." That shows that respect is important in our school.)

Learning Styles
Interpersonal

Say: How we handle the events in our lives gives us a chance to show our good qualities. Ask each student to draw or write three good qualities about a partner based on the stories they shared. (*Example:* Maria's story showed me she keeps trying even during tough times. She has a good sense of humor. Maria also stands up for what she believes in.) Have them share these qualities with the class.

Listen, Speak, Interact

Present an Experience

Teacher Resource Book: *Sunshine Organizer, p. 40*

1. **Use a sunshine organizer** Have students create a sunshine organizer using the questions. Arrange students into pairs to interview and take notes on their partner's experiences.
2. **Newcomers** Have students draw a picture and tell about an experience. Help them summarize their experiences.

Elements of Literature

Identify Language Use to Show Characterization

1. **Clarify terms** On the board, write: *culture, region, language.* Explain the meanings of the terms.
2. **Model the activity** Ask a volunteer to read paragraph 5. Use guiding questions to help students answer the questions. Arrange students in pairs to read and discuss the other examples of language showing characterization.
3. **Personal experiences** Allow students to share language of characters in books, movies, or television that reflects their culture and region.
4. **Multi-level options** See MULTI-LEVEL OPTIONS on p. 260.

ASSESS

Have students write a sentence about the author's use of Spanish and what it tells you about the author.

Beyond the Reading

Word Study

Apply Letter-Sound Correspondences

Use a listening exercise On the board, write: /s/ *see, same, sun, seen;* /sh/ *she, shame, shun, sheen.* Say the sounds and words and have students repeat. Say words in random order and have students identify the sounds.

Answers
s; sh (or ʃ)

Grammar Focus

Identify Dependent Clauses

Clarify terms Review subjects and verbs. Help students identify them in simple sentences. Point out the main and dependent clauses in the example in the textbook. Have students identify subjects and verbs in each.

Answers

paragraph 4: (While) we packed the breakfast dishes . . .

paragraph 7: (As) we drove away . . .

paragraph 9: (When) we got there . . (After) the man went in . . .

paragraph 11: (When) it arrived . . .

ASSESS

Have students write two sentences using dependent clauses.

Word Study

Apply Letter-Sound Correspondences

The letter *s* in English is often pronounced like the first letter of the word *see.* However, when *s* is combined with *h*, the sound is like the first sound in the word *shoe.*

Listen as your teacher pronounces *see* and *shoe.* Can you hear the difference between the first sounds? Pronounce the two words after your teacher.

Listen as your teacher reads the following sentences from "The Circuit." Then practice reading the sentences aloud with a partner.

1. My fir**s**t in**s**tinct was to an**s**wer her in **S**pani**sh**, but I held back.
2. Finally, after **s**truggling for Engli**sh** words, I managed to tell her that I wanted to enroll in the **s**ixth grade.

In a dictionary, look at the pronunciation of the word *Spanish.* Which symbol represents the letter *s?* Which symbol represents the letters *sh?*

The Heinle
Newbury House
Dictionary

Activity Book
p. 140

Student
CD-ROM

Grammar Focus

Identify Dependent Clauses

A **dependent** clause contains a subject and a verb, but it cannot stand alone. It *depends* on the rest of the sentence.

When a dependent clause is at the beginning of a sentence, it must be followed by a comma.

Some dependent clauses tell you when something happens. They start with words like *when, as, while, before, after,* or *until.* Look at this example:

When she got to the car, Papá reached out to help her with it.

1. Find the sentences with dependent clauses in paragraphs 4, 7, 9, and 11 of the reading.
2. Underline the dependent clauses. Put an S over the subject of the sentence and a V over the verb. Circle the word at the beginning of the clause that tells when something happened.

Activity Book
pp. 141–142

Student
Handbook

Student
CD-ROM

262 Unit 4 Cycles

MULTI-LEVEL OPTIONS *From Reading to Writing*

Newcomer Use the Language Experience approach to write a class letter to Francisco Jiménez. Write on the board as students dictate the letter. Have students create illustrations of important parts of the story. Send them with the letter.

Beginning Have students work in pairs to complete the model letter on p. 263. Have both partners create illustrations of their favorite parts of the story and write short captions for their pictures. Send them with the letters.

Intermediate Tell students to use the model letter on p. 263 to get down the main ideas of their letters. Invite them to then elaborate by giving reasons and examples to support their opinions about the story.

Advanced Remind students that the reading strategy for this chapter was comparing their own experiences to ideas in the text. Suggest that students include some of this thinking in their letters to the author. Ask them to tell him what story events reminded them of events in their own lives.

From Reading to Writing

Write a Letter to an Author

Write a letter to Francisco Jiménez.

1. Work with a partner. Copy the letter parts to the right. Also refer to your Student Handbook.
2. Fill in the blanks with your own words. Tell the author what you think about the story. Ask him a question.
3. Organize and revise your letter with your partner. Use a dictionary or a thesaurus to choose vivid words.
4. Use your best handwriting or a computer. Be sure to check your spelling and punctuation.
5. Capitalize and punctuate so that your meaning is clear.

> _____ (Your Address)
>
> _____ (Date)
>
> Mr. Francisco Jiménez
> c/o Publisher
> Heinle/Thomson
> 25 Thomson Place
> Boston, MA 02210
> Dear Mr. Jiménez,
>   I read your story, "The Circuit."
> I think it is _____. I liked
> your story because _____
> I want to know _____.
> Sincerely,
>
> _____

The Heinle Newbury House Dictionary

Student Handbook

Activity Book p. 143

Across Content Areas

Understand the Influence of Other Languages and Cultures on English

English has borrowed many words from French. For example, the work *circuit* comes from old French. There are not many words in English that have the letters *u* and *i* together. We can see that French has influenced English spelling. Other examples are *gui̱de*, *flui̱d*, and *disgui̱se*.

In the year 1066, people from France invaded England and ruled it for many years. Their language and culture influenced English spellings.

1. Look up these words with *ui* in a large dictionary and check the derivations. Are they of French or English origin?

   juice/quick/nuisance/ruin/squirt

2. Can you make a generalization about English words spelled with *ui*?

Activity Book p. 144

From Reading to Writing

Write a Letter to an Author

1. **Brainstorm and list** Have students suggest words and phrases for the blanks in the letter format. List ideas on the board. Then have students create their own individual letter to the author using their own ideas or the ideas on the board.
2. **Language experience letter** For newcomers, have them dictate their letters as you write them. Tell students to practice reading the letters aloud.
3. **Multi-level options** See MULTI-LEVEL OPTIONS on p. 262.

Across Content Areas: Language Arts

Understand the Influence of Other Languages and Cultures on English

Use a dictionary Model using a dictionary to check derivations of words. Point out abbreviations for languages.

Answers
1. French; English; French; French; English
2. Words with *qui* are usually of English origin. Words with another consonant + *ui* are often of French origin.

ASSESS

Have students write sentences using the words with *ui*.

Reteach and Reassess

Text Structure Have students create a story map to show the main characters, setting, and events of the autobiography. Students may use drawings or writing to complete their organizers.

Reading Strategy Ask students to create two-column charts to show ways that the boy and the events in "The Circuit" remind them of their own experiences.

Elements of Literature Read a short story to students. Be sure it is one that includes dialogue and from which students can learn about a specific culture. *Ask: What can we tell about the culture of the main character from what he or she says?*

Reassess Have pairs of students share stories of times when their families have moved. Ask students to listen to their partners' stories and identify any similar experiences they have had.

Chapter Materials

Activity Book: *pp. 145–152*
Audio: *Unit 4, Chapter 4; CD 2, Track 10*
Student Handbook
Student CD-ROM: *Unit 4, Chapter 4*
Teacher Resource Book: *Lesson Plan, Teacher Resources, Reading Summary, Activity Book Answer Key*
Teacher Resource CD-ROM
Assessment Program: *Quiz, pp. 67–68; Teacher and Student Resources, pp. 115–144*
Assessment CD-ROM
Transparencies
The Heinle Newbury House Dictionary/CD-ROM
Web site: http://visions.heinle.com

Objectives

Teacher think aloud Read the first objective. *Say:* Main *means "something important," so the main idea is probably an important idea.* Read the other objectives. *Ask: Are there any words you know? What do you think these objectives mean?*

Use Prior Knowledge

Talk About Living and Nonliving Things

Brainstorm Have students brainstorm and list other living and nonliving things. Arrange students in pairs to complete the chart.

The Elements of Life

an excerpt from an informational book by Paul Bennett

Objectives

Reading Find the main idea and supporting details as you read an excerpt from an informational book.

Listening and Speaking Listen and take notes.

Grammar Recognize the active and passive voices.

Writing Write about a process and create a diagram.

Content Science: Understand symbols for elements.

Use Prior Knowledge

Talk About Living and Nonliving Things

Some things are living. People, cats, and bean plants are living things. Other things are nonliving, such as chairs, water, and rocks. What are the characteristics of living things and nonliving things?

1. Copy this chart on a piece of paper.
2. With a partner, discuss each of the characteristics in the chart. Does each characteristic apply to living things, nonliving things, or both? Check "Yes" or "No."
3. If you are unsure, use resources such as an expert, a science teacher, a dictionary, the Internet, or an encyclopedia to find out.

Characteristics	Living Things		Nonliving Things	
	Yes	No	Yes	No
can move around on its own	X			X
can reproduce itself	X			X
made of chemical elements	X		X	

MULTI-LEVEL OPTIONS *Build Vocabulary*

Newcomer On the board, write: *glosses* and *graphics*. Direct students to p. 30 of "Yawning." Point to the glossed words on the bottom of the page and *say: glosses.* Point to the illustration and *say: graphic.* Have volunteers point to the glosses and graphic on the facing page. Have students point out the remaining glosses and graphics in "Yawning."

Beginning Direct students to "Yawning" (p. 30). Have them copy the words *definition, gloss,* and *graphic* on stick-on notes. Ask them to work in pairs to find an example of each feature and mark it with the appropriate stick-on note.

Intermediate Write on the board: *Definition, Glosses,* and *Graphics* as column headings on the board. Direct students to "Why We Can't Get There From Here" (p. 196). Ask them to work in pairs to find examples of each feature. When they have found one, have them write it under the correct heading.

Advanced Have students brainstorm other resources that they can use to look up science terms. (*Examples:* science dictionaries, search engines, encyclopedias) Assign pairs to use one of the resources on p. 265 or on their brainstormed lists to look up *elements.* Have pairs share and compare what they find.

Build Background

Elements

Both living and nonliving things are made of elements. Elements are simple materials. Chemists are scientists who study the elements. They have so far discovered 109 different ones.

Some elements are very rare (uncommon). Others are almost everywhere. For example, the oxygen in the air is an element.

Some elements are very valuable. You may have a ring or a bracelet made of gold or silver. These are elements.

Elements combine to make other things. For example, water is made up of oxygen and hydrogen. The elements sodium and chloride combine to make ordinary table salt.

 Content Connection
Scientists have created a chart called the **Periodic Table of Elements.** It organizes all of the elements that scientists know about.

Build Vocabulary

Learn Science Terms

"The Elements of Life" has **science terms** (words related to science). You can learn new science terms in different ways.

1. **Definitions** Sometimes the author tells the meaning of a word. Check the words around it for clues.
2. **Glossaries** Often a textbook has a list of important words and their meanings. This list is a **glossary.** In this book, words are glossed at the bottom of each page.

3. **Dictionaries** If you still do not understand a word, you can find its meaning in a dictionary. A dictionary also gives the pronunciation.
4. **Graphics** Photos and drawings are used to explain scientific words and ideas. As you read, study the graphic features to locate and organize information.

The Heinle Newbury House Dictionary | Activity Book p. 145 | Student CD-ROM

Chapter 4 The Elements of Life **265**

 Content Connection
Social Studies

Build Background Have students work in three groups. Ask each group to use resources such as encyclopedias and the Internet to look up one of the following people: Antoine Lavoisier, Dmitri Mendeleyev, or Julius Lothar Meyer. Have students find out how each one helped us understand the elements. Provide time for groups to share what they discover.

Learning Styles
Linguistic

Build Vocabulary *Say: Some words have several meanings. Keep that fact in mind when you are reading a science book or article and need to look up a word in a dictionary. Read all the definitions and decide which fits the topic you are reading about.* Have students look up the word *element* in a dictionary. Based on what they read in Build Background, have them determine which meaning will apply to the informational text in this chapter.

Build Background

Elements

1. **Use common objects** Bring in examples of metals made from single elements: tin cans, an iron crow bar, aluminum foil, silver or gold jewelry. *Ask: What are these made of?* Create a list of common elements.
2. **Content Connection** Bring in copies of the Periodic Table. The Periodic Table was created in 1869 by a Russian scientist, Dmitri Mendeleyev. Point out chemical symbols for common elements, such as O (oxygen), C (carbon), and Fe (iron).

Build Vocabulary

Learn Science Terms

Teacher Resource Book: *Personal Dictionary, p. 63*

1. **Share experiences** *Say: Sometimes I see a new word when I read. I think the word is important, so I look at pictures or read the sentence again for clues.*
2. **Relate to personal experience** Have students list content area classes where they had to learn new terms. Ask them to share how they learned the terms.
3. **Locate pronunciations and derivations in a glossary** Point out that the glossary in a science textbook not only provides definitions, but sometimes also provides pronunciations and derivations. Have students try to locate the following words from the reading selection in their science textbook: *element, nuclear, cellulose, bacteria, fungi.*
4. **Reading selection vocabulary** You may want to introduce the glossed words in the reading selection before students begin reading. Key words: *categories, theory, recycled, decay, balance.* Instruct students to write the words with correct spelling and their definitions in their Personal Dictionaries. Have them pronounce each word and divide it into syllables.
5. **Multi-level options** See MULTI-LEVEL OPTIONS on p. 264.

 **ASSESS**

Ask students to list strategies for learning science words.

Text Structure

Informational Text

Recognize features Direct attention to the features chart. Clarify the meanings by giving examples from students' science lessons.

Reading Strategy

Find the Main Ideas and Supporting Details

1. **Model the strategy** *Say: Listen for the main idea and details of what I describe. I am drawing a picture of a person. I draw the head, body, arms, and legs. I color the clothes and shoes. Now, what is the main idea of my drawing? What are the details?* Guide students to notice the main idea is the person, and the parts and colors are the details.

2. **Multi-level options** See MULTI-LEVEL OPTIONS below.

Answers
1. Oxygen is a very important element.
2. It makes up about half of the earth's crust; the human body has large amounts of it; people breathe it; we need it to live.

ASSESS

Ask: What are four features of an informational text? (examples, definitions, process, and problem)

Text Structure

Informational Text

You learned that an **informational text** gives facts about a topic. "The Elements of Life" is an informational text. The chart shows some features of an informational text. Look for these features as you read the selection.

Informational Text	
Examples	gives information that supports facts
Definitions	includes meanings of special words or ideas
Process	tells how something happens and in what chronological order
Problem	tells a problem related to the topic

Student
CD-ROM

Reading Strategy

Find the Main Idea and Supporting Details

The **main idea** is the most important idea in a paragraph or larger piece of writing. **Supporting details** are facts or explanations that show how the main idea is true.

Read the following paragraph.

> Oxygen is a very important element. Almost half of the earth's crust is made up of oxygen. The human body also has a lot of oxygen. We breathe oxygen. We need oxygen to live.

1. What is the main idea in this paragraph?
2. What details support the main idea?

As you read the selection, look for the main ideas and supporting details.

Student
CD-ROM

MULTI-LEVEL OPTIONS *Reading Strategy*

Newcomer Show the ideas from the paragraph in a Main Idea Table. Draw on the board a rectangle to represent a tabletop. Write in it: *oxygen important.* Draw four legs under the table. Write one of the following on each: *Earth's crust oxygen, body oxygen, breathe oxygen, oxygen to live.* Read the notes aloud.

Beginning Read the paragraph. Use pictures and gestures to reinforce meaning. Have pairs of students use a Main Idea Table to display the ideas in the paragraph.

Intermediate Ask students to identify the main idea and supporting details in Build Background (p. 265). (Main idea: Everything is made of elements. Details: Some elements are rare; others are common; some are valuable; some can combine to make new substances.)

Advanced Ask students to note the location of the main idea in the paragraph on p. 266 and in Build Background. (the first sentence) Explain that a main idea statement is often, but not always, found at the beginning of a paragraph.

The Elements of Life

an excerpt from an informational book
by Paul Bennett

Reading Selection Materials

Audio: *Unit 4, Chapter 4; CD 2, Track 10*
Teacher Resource Book: *Reading Summary,*
  pp. 101–102
Transparencies: *#41, Reading Summary*

Suggestions for Using
Reading Summary

- Introduce new vocabulary or cognates.
- Cut the summary into strips, or jumble the sentences on an overhead transparency. Students put the sentences in order.
- Practice the reading strategy.
- Students read aloud or with a partner.
- Students paraphrase the summary.
- Students do a cloze activity.
- Students create a visual or graphic organizer, such as a timeline or storyboard, to illustrate the summary.
- Students paraphrase the summary.

Preview the Selection

Teacher Resource Book: *Know/Want to Know/Learned Chart (KWL), p. 42*

1. **Use a KWL chart** Have students describe the photo. Then ask them to complete a chart with things they know about the reading selection (title, information from the photo). Direct them to form questions for what they want to know about the elements of life. Students can use the chart to guide their reading of the informational text.

2. **Connect** Remind students that the unit theme is *cycles. Ask: What cycles are shown in the photo? Do the elements go through different cycles?*

Content Connection
Science

Ask students to make lists of living and nonliving things shown in the photograph on p. 267. Provide time for students to share their lists. If there is any disagreement about whether certain items are living or nonliving, have students refer back to the chart they created in Use Prior Knowledge.

Learning Styles
Natural

Say: We can learn many things about nature from observing the world around us. Have students discuss in small groups things they might observe and learn if they were in the place this photograph was taken.

Read the Selection

1. **Use the photos** Help students name the metals in the photos.
2. **Use text features** Have students find the meanings of glossed words at the bottom of the page.
3. **Paired reading** Play the audio or read aloud paragraphs 1–3 to students. Then have students read aloud with a partner.
4. **Find main ideas and supporting details**
   Ask: In paragraph 1, what four elements were the basic categories of all materials? (earth, air, fire, water) *In paragraph 2, what do we know about the basic substances?* (There are 109 elements that make up all things.)

Sample Answer to Guide Question
Some of the elements are metals. Gold and silver are used in jewelry. Iron is used in tools and weapons.

See Teacher Edition pp. 434–436 for a list of English-Spanish cognates in the reading selection.

---

1 In ancient times it was thought that everything could be broken down into four elements: earth, air, fire, and water. These broad **categories** seemed to account for the makeup of things until about three hundred years ago when scientists began to doubt such a simple **theory**.

2 Elements are the basic substances from which all things are made. Today we know of 109 elements. About ninety of these occur naturally on earth—the rest are made in **nuclear reactors**.

3 Some of the elements, such as gold and silver, are metals. They have been made into jewelry since early times. The element iron, too, is a metal, and has been used to make weapons and tools for over three thousand years.

> **Find the Main Idea and Supporting Details**
>
> What is the main idea of this paragraph? What are two supporting details?

Audio
CD 2. Tr. 10

Silver

Iron

Gold

categories groups or types of things
theory an idea or argument that something is true

nuclear reactors machines used to make and contain nuclear reactions

268 Unit 4 Cycles

MULTI-LEVEL OPTIONS *Read the Selection*

Newcomer Play the audio. *Ask: Are all things made from elements?* (yes) *Are there fewer than 100 elements?* (no) *Is oxygen an element?* (yes) *Can elements mix together?* (yes)

Beginning Read the Reading Summary. *Ask: What are all things made up of?* (elements) *What are examples of elements?* (gold, silver, iron, oxygen) *How many elements are there in our bodies?* (about 25) *What do we call elements that mix with other elements?* (compounds)

Intermediate Have students do a partner read aloud. *Ask: How are ideas about elements from long ago different from today's ideas?* (Long ago, people thought there were only four; today, we know there are over 100.) *How are compounds made?* (by combining two or more elements) *Why are elements important?* (They make up all things.)

Advanced Have students read silently. *Ask: Do you think scientists believe they have discovered all the elements? Explain.* (No, because paragraph 2 says "we know of . . ." and not "there are . . ." So we may still discover more.) *Why is this selection called "Elements of Life"?* (because there would be no life on Earth without elements)

4   We have many elements in our bodies—about 25 of them. Oxygen and hydrogen account for most, since these elements join together to form water, and our bodies are made up of 60 to 80 percent water.

> **Find the Main Idea and Supporting Details**
>
> What is the main idea in this paragraph? What are the supporting details?

5   Water is a compound—a combination of elements. So is the paper on which these words are printed. Paper is made of a material called **cellulose,** which comes from trees and consists of the elements carbon, hydrogen, and oxygen.

6   Elements and compounds are needed by all living things in order to stay alive. Living **organisms** obtain these **raw materials** or resources from their surroundings. But only limited amounts of these **vital** elements can be found on Earth, and so if they could be used only once, they would run out, and animals and plants would die. But in nature the elements are **recycled,** so they can be used over and over again.

The elements in these trees can still be found in a piece of paper.

cellulose   a basic substance in nearly all plant cells
organisms   living creatures
raw materials   things in a natural state, not manufactured

vital   most important, absolutely necessary
recycled   processed to be used again

Chapter 4   The Elements of Life   **269**

Read the Selection

1. **Use the photo** Direct attention to the photo and caption. Ask students to guess why the trees and paper would have the same elements.
2. **Use text features** Have students find the meanings of the glossed words. Clarify meanings as needed.
3. **Reciprocal reading** Play the audio. Divide students into small groups. Have students take turns reading a short passage, asking questions about it to group members, and asking the group to summarize.
4. **Summarize** *Ask: Which elements join to make water?* (hydrogen and oxygen) *Which elements are in trees and paper?* (carbon, hydrogen, oxygen) *Where do living things get the elements and compounds they need?* (from their surroundings)
5. **Multi-level options** See MULTI-LEVEL OPTIONS on p. 268.

Sample Answer to Guide Question
The main idea is there are many different elements in our bodies. The details are there are about 25 different elements, including oxygen and hydrogen, which make water, and are the most common elements in the body.

❯ Punctuation

Colon for lists

Write a colon on the board. *Say: This punctuation mark is a colon. One way it is used is to introduce a list. Find an example of a colon introducing a list in paragraph 1.* (. . . broken down into four elements: earth, air . . .)

Apply Ask students to rewrite the last sentence of paragraph 5 using a colon. (Cellulose is made up of several elements: carbon, hydrogen, and oxygen.)

Read the Selection

1. **Do a jigsaw reading** Have pairs of students prepare different paragraphs for reading aloud. Then have the group "put the pieces together" by reading aloud in sequence.

2. **Use the diagram** Direct students' attention to the diagram. Have them explain the steps in the process.

Sample Answer to Guide Question

The main idea is that dying is part of the cycle of life—animals and plants die and put elements back into the soil. The details are the animals and plants rot. The soil is used by new plants. Animals eat the plants. The animals and plants put substances back into the soil.

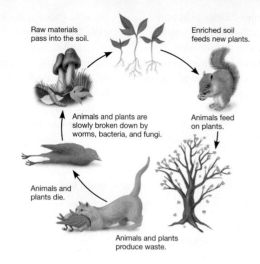

Raw materials pass into the soil.

Enriched soil feeds new plants.

Animals and plants are slowly broken down by worms, bacteria, and fungi.

Animals feed on plants.

Animals and plants die.

Animals and plants produce waste.

7   For example, when animals and plants die in a **woodland,** they are slowly broken down by worms, **bacteria,** and **fungi.** As animals and plants **rot** away, the substances from which they are made pass into the soil. The **enriched** soil feeds new plants and, in turn, animals will feed on the plants. The animals and plants produce waste, which is also broken down and taken back into the soil.

> **Find the Main Idea and Supporting Details**
>
> What is the main idea of this paragraph? What are the supporting details?

The process of death, **decay,** new life, and growth is never ending. In this way, the elements and compounds that are **essential** to life are recycled.   8

---

woodland   a forested area
bacteria   tiny living things
fungi   organisms that feed on living or dead plants or animals and cannot survive apart from them

rot   break down, usually after death
enriched   added good things to
decay   rot
essential   necessary, required

270   Unit 4   Cycles

MULTI-LEVEL OPTIONS *Read the Selection*

Newcomer *Ask: Can elements be used over and over?* (yes) *Have people caused problems by the way they use things in nature?* (yes) *Can people fix the problem?* (yes)

Beginning *Ask: Are elements used one time or over and over?* (over and over) *Where do the elements that make up living things go when plants and animals die?* (into the soil) *Who has upset the balance of nature by using elements carelessly?* (people) *Who can fix the problems?* (people)

Intermediate *Ask: How do elements get recycled?* (When plants and animals die, the elements break down into the soil. The elements in the soil are used to grow other plants and feed animals.) *How might people help to get the natural balance back?* (by reducing their use of some resources)

Advanced *Ask: Why is this selection in a unit about cycles?* (because it tells how elements are used over and over again) *How might scientists help with the goal described in paragraph 10?* (by keeping records about how we are using resources and records about what is happening with parts of nature to find ways they are related)

9 However, the activities of people have upset this **delicate natural balance.** Vital resources such as water and the elements carbon, nitrogen, sulfur, and phosphorus are no longer in balance. As a result, a large number of animal and plant **species** are in danger.

10 By understanding the earth's recycling systems and how people affect them, we can help **reduce** the **harmful** effects of human activity.

> **Find the Main Idea and Supporting Details**
>
> What is one supporting detail in this paragraph? What is the main idea?

delicate easily broken or hurt	**species** groups of living things
natural formed by nature	**reduce** make smaller in size or weight
balance in equal strength	**harmful** causing hurt or damage

About the Author

Paul Bennett

Paul Bennett likes to answer questions about science. He has written about 20 books about science. For example, he has written about why some animals hibernate (sleep for the winter), and he has written about electricity and telephones.

➤ What science question would you like to ask the author?

Chapter 4 The Elements of Life **271**

---

th Spelling

Irregular plurals

Say: For many nouns, we add -s or -es to make the word show more than one. Find an example in paragraph 6. (elements) *Some words have special spellings for the form that shows more than one, or the plural. Look at paragraph 7 to find the plural for* bacterium. (bacteria) *Find the plural for* fungus *in the same paragraph.* (fungi) *Write the singular and plural of both words on the board.*

Evaluate Your Reading Strategy

Find the Main Ideas and Supporting Details *Say: You have practiced an important reading strategy. Now you can decide how well you have done. Does this statement describe how you read?*

> As I read, I look for main ideas and supporting details that show me how the main ideas are true. Finding main ideas and supporting details helps me understand and remember the important parts of a reading.

Read the Selection

1. **Shared reading** Play the audio. Have students join in when they can. Pause to ask comprehension questions and to clarify vocabulary. *Ask: What can upset the balance of resources?* (activities of people) *What happens if the balance is upset?* (Some animals and plants may be in danger.)

2. **Find main ideas and supporting details** Use guiding questions to help students identify the main ideas and details.

3. **Locate derivations using dictionaries** Have students look at these glossed words and determine what words they are derived from: *bacteria, fungi, enriched, natural, harmful.* Have students check the derivations in a print, online, or CD-ROM dictionary.

4. **Multi-level options** See MULTI-LEVEL OPTIONS on p. 270.

Sample Answer to Guide Question
One detail is that water and some elements are not in balance. The main idea is that people have upset the natural balance.

About the Author

Interpret the facts *Ask: Why do you think Paul Bennett chose to write about the elements of life?* (He is interested in science, and he wants others to understand how people can affect the recycling of resources and materials at a more scientific level.)

Across Selections

1. **Compare and contrast text structure** Have students find similarities and differences in text structure between "Water Dance," a poem about the water cycle, and "The Elements of Life," an informational text. *Ask: Which do you think presented more information about cycles? Which did you enjoy reading more?*

2. **Compare and contrast print media with written story** Ask students to research a newspaper or magazine article about recycling. Have them compare and contrast the information presented in the article with "The Elements of Life." Which do they like better and why?

Beyond the Reading

Reading Comprehension

Question-Answer Relationships

Sample Answers

1. An element is a basic substance that things are made of. Iron is an element.
2. They know about 109 elements.
3. Oxygen and hydrogen are the most common elements in our bodies because they make up water, which is 60–80% of our bodies.
4. through the process of death, decay, new life, and growth
5. Some resources like water and some elements are out of balance.
6. I think the author feels that nature is important and that people should be careful not to upset the natural balance. In paragraph 10, the author says people can reduce the effects of their activities on nature's balance.
7. If nature's balance is not protected, there won't be enough of the elements for living creatures to survive. People will not be able to survive either.
8. I can protect the balance by making sure dangerous materials do not go into the soil or water. These materials need to be taken to hazardous waste sites.

Build Reading Fluency

Adjust Your Reading Rate to Scan

Explain that students need to adjust their reading to scan the text to locate key words. Have them read the question then scan to find the answer and identify key words.

Answers
1. silver, gold, iron 2. oxygen, hydrogen 3. elements, compounds 4. worms, bacteria, fungi

---

Reading Comprehension

Question-Answer Relationships (QAR)

"Right There" Questions

1. **Recall Facts** What is an element? Give an example.
2. **Recall Facts** How many elements do scientists know about?

"Think and Search" Questions

3. **Give Reasons** Why are oxygen and hydrogen the most common elements in our bodies?
4. **Identify Steps in a Process** How are elements recycled?
5. **Identify Cause and Effect** What has happened to nature's balance because of people?

"Author and You" Question

6. **Understand Author's Perspective** How do you think the author feels about nature? What does he think people should do for nature? Show text evidence for your answers.

"On Your Own" Questions

7. **Speculate** What could happen to Earth if nature's balance is not protected?
8. **Connect Your Experiences** What are some ways that you can protect nature's balance?

Activity Book
p. 146

Student
CD-ROM

Build Reading Fluency

Adjust Your Reading Rate to Scan

When you scan for information you adjust your reading rate to read fast. Work with a partner. Read aloud key words in the reading selection as you scan for the answers. Write your answers on a piece of paper.

1. What are the names of three metals?
2. What two elements mainly make up our bodies?
3. What are needed by all living things?
4. What three things break down dead plants and animals?

272   Unit 4 Cycles

MULTI-LEVEL OPTIONS *Elements of Literature*

Newcomer On the board, write: *diagram* and *label*. Direct students to p. 193. Ask them to point to each one. Have them find other examples in their science textbooks to share with the group.

Beginning Have students work in pairs to complete the assignment. Then direct them to p. 30. Ask them to discuss the features of the diagram on that page.

Intermediate After students have completed the exercise, ask them to draw their own version of the diagram. Have them create another format for showing a life cycle.

Advanced Have students find a diagram of a life cycle in another source. Tell them to compare and contrast how the artist has portrayed the idea. *Ask: Which is clearer? Why?*

Listen, Speak, Interact

Listen and Take Notes

Listen as your teacher reads or plays the audio recording of "The Elements of Life."

1. Before you listen, determine a purpose for your listening. Will you learn new information? Will you solve problems? Will you be entertained?
2. As you listen, take notes on the main ideas and supporting details.
3. Use the main ideas and supporting details to write an outline of the selection.
4. Use your outline to summarize the selection orally to a partner.

5. Listen to your partner's summary.
   a. Interpret your partner's verbal and nonverbal messages. Do they support your partner's purposes and perspectives?
   b. Is your partner using facts or opinions?
   c. Do you believe your partner?
   d. Do you understand the presentation? Ask questions if you do not understand something.
   e. Was your partner's information clear?
   f. What was your partner's perspective?

Elements of Literature

Use a Diagram

"The Elements of Life" includes a **diagram.** The diagram shows how elements are recycled. It has drawings and **labels** (words that explain the drawings).

1. Look at the diagram on page 270.
2. Each label explains a **step** (an action). The arrows show the **sequence** (order) in which the steps happen.

3. On a piece of paper, write the steps that the diagram shows. Number the steps in order. Start with "Animals and plants die."

Activity Book
p. 147

Student
CD-ROM

Listen, Speak, Interact

Listen and Take Notes

Teacher Resource Book: *Reading Log, p. 64*

1. **Use an outline** Before rereading the selection, create an outline format to guide students as they take notes on main ideas and supporting details. After students take notes, have pairs summarize the reading from their outlines.
2. **Newcomers** Reread with this group. Ask guiding questions to help them summarize and take notes. Write key words and phrases on the board. Students can write the expressions and outlines in their Reading Logs.

Elements of Literature

Use a Diagram

1. **Identify components of a diagram** Direct attention to the components of the diagram: pictures, labels, and arrows.
2. **Provide vocabulary** Share examples of sequence expressions for explaining a process, such as *first, next, after that, last.*
3. **Multi-level options** See MULTI-LEVEL OPTIONS on p. 272.

Answers
1. Animals and plants die.
2. Animals and plants are slowly broken down by worms, bacteria, and fungi.
3. Raw materials pass into the soil.
4. Enriched soil feeds new plants.
5. Animals feed on plants.
6. Animals and plants produce waste.

 **ASSESS**

Have students explain: *diagram, label,* and *sequence.*

Home Connection

Ask students to use their outlines to share what they have learned with someone at home. Instruct them to have the listener ask three questions he/she has about the information. Tell students to bring these questions to class. Ask them to pick one question to research. Provide time for students to find the answers to the questions and add the information to their outlines.

Learning Styles
Mathematical

Say: Diagrams can help readers understand the meaning of a selection. Mathematical tables and graphs can also help make ideas clearer. Have students look at examples. *Ask: What kind of mathematical table or graph could an author include in an article on the elements? (Example:* a pie chart showing the percent of elements occurring naturally on Earth compared to the ones made in nuclear reactors)

Word Study

Study Word Origins and Roots

Use a matching game Instruct students to write the words on a set of cards and meanings on another set. Have students play Concentration with the words in small groups.

Answers
1. bicycle 2. encyclopedia 3. cycle 4. motorcycle
5. cyclone

Grammar Focus

Recognize the Active and Passive Voices

Apply Write on the board: *We read the book. The book was read by us.* Guide students to identify verbs. Point out the helping verb in the passive voice.

Answers
2. a. P b. A c. A d. P
3. a. All living things need elements. b. New plants are fed by the enriched soil. c. Resources are obtained by living organisms from their environments. d. Worms, bacteria, and fungi break them down.

✔ ASSESS

Have students write one sentence in both the active voice and passive voice.

Word Study

Study Word Origins and Roots

Some English words have the same word origin. *Recycled* comes from the Greek root word *kyklos*. This Greek word means "wheel or circle."

The words in the box below also come from the root word *kyklos*. Match each word with the correct definition. Use a dictionary to look up any words you do not know.

cycle	motorcycle	cyclone
bicycle	encyclopedia	

Definitions
1. a vehicle with two wheels that is run by pedaling
2. a reference source
3. a process that begins and ends with the same thing
4. a vehicle with two wheels that is run by a machine
5. a violent storm in which winds move in a circle

The Heinle Newbury House Dictionary   Activity Book p. 148   Student CD-ROM

Grammar Focus

Recognize the Active and Passive Voices

Sentences in the **active voice** have subjects that do an action. Look at this example:

Nuclear reactors <u>make</u> the rest.
subject ⇒   action

Sentences in the **passive voice** have subjects that receive an action. They include the verbs *was, were, am, are, is, be,* or *been.* These verbs are added to **past participles** (a form of a verb). Look at this example:

The rest <u>are made</u> in nuclear reactors.
subject ⇐ action

1. Copy the following sentences on a piece of paper.

a. Elements are needed by all living things.
b. The enriched soil feeds new plants.
c. Living organisms obtain resources from their environments.
d. They are broken down by worms, bacteria, and fungi.
2. Write *A* for *active* and *P* for *passive* for each sentence.
3. If the sentence is active, rewrite it in the passive voice. If it is passive, rewrite it in the active voice.

Activity Book pp. 149–150   Student Handbook   Student CD-ROM

274   Unit 4 Cycles

MULTI-LEVEL OPTIONS *From Reading to Writing*

Newcomer *Say: Let's show how we check out library books.* Have students work in groups to create a detailed drawing of one of the steps. Display the steps in sequential order and help students summarize the process in a diagram. Ask the media specialist to display the finished product.

Beginning Have small groups create detailed drawings of steps in processes they use in the classroom, such as checking and turning in homework. Tell students to label objects and write short captions for the steps. Have them create a diagram to summarize the process. Display the results in the classroom.

Intermediate At the revision stage, have students review their writing to see if any of their sentences are in the passive voice. *Say: Active voice usually makes your writing clearer and less wordy. Try to change any passive sentences to active.*

Advanced Before students write, have them look through books of science experiments or other books that give directions for processes. Ask students to discuss with partners features and formats that make some directions easier to read than others. Tell students to use what they learn in their discussions as they write about processes.

From Reading to Writing

Write About a Process and Create a Diagram

Choose a process you know about. This process might be something you know how to do. Write and illustrate a paragraph that tells the steps in the process.

1. Tell what the process is about in the first sentence.
2. Write the steps that are part of the process in order.
3. Use transition words such as *first, next, then, finally*.
4. Create a diagram to show the process. If possible, create your diagram on the computer.
5. Read your paragraph to a partner. Find out if your partner understands the process. Make changes if you need to clarify your meaning.

How to Fry an Egg

Frying an egg is a little tricky, but you can do it if you practice. First, put a little oil in a non-stick pan and turn on the heat. When the oil is medium-hot, crack the egg and let the inside drop gently into the oil. Let it cook until the white part is almost set. Then use a spatula to turn the egg over. Then let the egg finish cooking. Finally, take it out and enjoy it!

Activity Book
p. 151

Student
Handbook

Across Content Areas

Understand Symbols for Elements

Chemists have given each element a name and a symbol to stand for it. The chart gives a few of them.

Element	Symbol
carbon	C
oxygen	O
hydrogen	H
sodium	Na
chlorine	Cl

Scientists use these symbols to describe chemical compounds. For example, H_2O is water. It is made of two atoms of hydrogen and one atom of oxygen. (An *atom* is the smallest possible amount of an element.) Complete these sentences.

1. NaCl is table salt. It is made up of sodium and _____ .
2. CO_2 is a gas. It has _____ atom of carbon and _____ atoms of oxygen.

Activity Book
p. 152

Chapter 4 The Elements of Life **275**

From Reading to Writing

Write About a Process and Create a Diagram

Teacher Resource Book: *Storyboard, p. 43*

1. **Compose, organize and revise a form** Ask pairs of students to research the names of five compounds. Have them create a form organized by the name of the compounds and the elements they are composed of. Pairs should exchange their forms with another pair and check each other's work. Have them revise their forms if necessary.

2. **Think-pair-share-write** Have students create storyboards to show their processes. Then arrange students in pairs to explain their processes. Model using sequence words and expressions with the different steps. Then have students use their storyboards to write as much as they can about their processes. As students share again with a different partner, they can add details and clarify steps as needed.

3. **Multi-level options** See MULTI-LEVEL OPTIONS on p. 274.

Across Content Areas: Science

Understand Symbols for Elements

Define and clarify Define *element, symbol, compound,* and *atom* for students. Direct students' attention to the chart in their textbook. Have them give the symbols for elements you name.

Answers
1. chlorine 2. one, two

ASSESS

Have students give the names of the elements as you say the symbols.

Materials

Student Handbook

CNN Video: *Unit 4*

Teacher Resource Book: *Lesson Plan, p. 23; Teacher Resources, pp. 35–64; Video Script, pp. 167–168; Video Worksheet, p. 176; School-Home Connection, pp. 140–146;*

Teacher Resource CD-ROM

Assessment Program: *Unit 4 Test, pp. 69–74; Teacher and Student Resources, pp. 115–144*

Assessment CD-ROM

Transparencies

The Heinle Newbury House Dictionary/CD-ROM

Heinle Reading Library: *Black Beauty*

Web site: http://visions.heinle.com

Listening and Speaking Workshop

Give an Oral Presentation

Review selections Have students review the selections in this unit. Divide the class into 4 groups. Assign each group one of the reading selections. Ask groups to summarize the main points and the cycle described in their selection. Then have each group share with the class.

Step 1: Identify the cycle.
Make sure students have clear steps for the cycle.

Step 2: Prepare a visual.
Remind students to use labels and arrows to show the direction of the cycle.

Listening and Speaking Workshop

Give an Oral Presentation

> **Topic**
>
> With a partner, choose a cycle from the unit. You and your partner will make a ten-minute presentation to your class about this cycle.

Step 1: Identify the cycle.

With your partner, list the steps that are part of the cycle.

Step 2: Prepare a visual.

1. Organize the steps in order in a circle form like this one.
2. Use presentation software or use a piece of posterboard.

Form for Describing a Cycle

Step 3: Make an outline.

1. On note cards, write a few sentences that summarize the steps of the cycle.

2. Support your steps with examples. Write on the note cards.

3. Put your note cards in order.

Step 4: Organize your presentation.

1. Begin your presentation by telling what the cycle is about.
2. Talk about one step at a time. Support each step with examples.
3. Summarize what the cycle is by using different words.

Step 5: Practice your presentation.

1. Practice your presentation with your partner. Take turns presenting the steps in the cycle.
2. Answer the questions on the Speaking Checklist. Your partner will do the same.
3. Make changes to your presentation if necessary.
4. Time your presentation so that you can finish in less than ten minutes.

Step 6: Give your presentation.

1. Stand in front of the room to give your presentation. Stand up straight.
2. Speak strongly to show that you understand what you are talking about.
3. Ask if there are any questions.
4. Ask your classmates to complete the Active Listening Checklist.

MULTI-LEVEL OPTIONS *Listening and Speaking Workshop*

Newcomer Ask students to focus on the water cycle as presented in "Water Dance" (p. 230). Help students work through the steps of preparing their diagrams and labeling the steps in the cycle. Have students present their diagrams in groups.

Beginning Suggest that students choose to focus on either the cycle in "Water Dance" (p. 230) or "The Elements of Life" (p. 268). Tell students to put sketches, key words, and phrases on their note cards. Have students present to small groups.

Intermediate Have students plan how they will incorporate their visuals into the presentations. *Ask: Where will you place the visual? Will you refer to it throughout your whole presentation or just at certain times? Do you need a pointer to direct attention to specific parts?* Explain that students will feel more confident if they think through these details before presenting.

Advanced If possible, videotape student presentations. Provide time for students to look at the videos privately or with a partner. Have them answer two questions. *Ask: What did I do well? What do I want to work on the next time I present?*

Speaking Checklist

1. Did you speak too slowly, too quickly, or just right?
2. Did you speak loudly enough for the audience to hear you?
3. Was your voice too high, too low, or just right?
4. Did you look at your audience?

Active Listening Checklist

1. I liked _____ because _____ .
2. I want to know more about _____ .
3. I thought the statements about the selection were interesting / not interesting.
4. The presentation did / did not stay on the topic.

Viewing Workshop

Interpret Events from Media

Use television and the Internet to learn about the cycle of weather.

1. View television and online weather reports for one week.
2. With a partner, create a form to record the information. Decide what information to record. Organize the form to make it easy to use.
3. Record the information. Include ideas and events from maps and charts.
4. Revise the form if necessary to include or delete information.
5. Interpret the information that you gathered. Answer questions such as:
   a. What weather events did you learn about?
   b. How are the weather events part of a cycle?
6. How were the television and online reports similar and different? Which do you think is better, and why?
7. How did each medium contribute to its message?
8. How did the television and online presentations influence you?
9. How did language and style of presentation help you understand?

Further Viewing

Watch the *Visions* CNN Video for Unit 4. Do the Video Worksheet.

CNN Video

Step 3: Make an outline.
Have students state clearly each of the steps in the process.

Step 4: Organize your presentation.
Remind students to introduce the topic and conclude it effectively.

Step 5: Practice your presentation.
Go over the procedure and checklists before students practice in pairs. Demonstrate effective gestures and use of visuals to clarify.

Step 6: Give your presentation to the class.
Invite another class to come hear the presentations.

ASSESS

Have students write a sentence telling the most important thing they learned in preparing their oral presentation.

Portfolio

Students may choose to record or videotape their speeches to place in their portfolios.

Viewing Workshop

View and Think

1. **View a television weather report** Help students find weather reports on television or the Internet. Call attention to maps, symbols, keys, and weather terms. Prepare a form for recording information.
2. **Take notes** Have students view and take notes daily. Then students can answer the questions as they summarize and interpret the results of their viewing.
3. **Compare and contrast** Have individuals share their findings. Then as a group, compare and contrast the different media reports.

Content Connection
Social Studies

Remind students that "Persephone and the Seasons" was a Greek myth that presented a made-up explanation for a scientific process. *Say: You have been watching scientific reports about the weather. Some myths, fables, and legends of various cultures of the past explain how certain kinds of weather came to be.* Have pairs of students look at books and Web sites to find examples.

Learning Styles
Kinesthetic

Say: Your audience will get bored if they just sit and listen to you talk for ten minutes. Think of some ways they can be involved in your presentation. For example, you could ask someone from the audience to come up and point to something on your diagram. You could ask people to raise their hands if they agree with something you say. Ask students to include at least one way to actively involve their audience in their talks.

Writer's Workshop

Compare and Contrast Ideas, Themes, and Issues

Write a report Remind students that responding to literature is a way to express your thoughts and feelings about reading selections.

Step 1: Gather information.

Point out the chart, the column headings, and row headings. Clarify terms as needed. Have students complete the chart as they reread the stories in groups.

Step 2: Write a first draft.

Model examples as needed. Review the purpose and content of each of the paragraphs.

Writer's Workshop

Compare and Contrast Ideas, Themes, and Issues

> **Writing Prompt**
>
> Compare and contrast the stories "Persephone and the Seasons" and "The Circuit."

Step 1: Gather information.

Answer these questions as you look for information from the two selections.

1. What is the theme of each story? How are they similar or different?
2. Describe the characters and their situations.
   a. Who are the main characters in each story?
   b. Who are other important characters in each story?
   c. How do the characters relate to each other?
   d. How do the characters feel about their situations? Can the characters change them?
3. What are the main ideas and events of each story? How are they the same and different?
4. What are the issues that each main character faces? Are they similar or different? How?
5. Summarize your ideas in a chart like the one shown.

Step 2: Write a first draft.

Review your notes and plan your paper. It should be five paragraphs long. Use a computer, if possible.

	"Persephone and the Seasons"	"The Circuit"
Theme	Why we have different seasons	
Main characters (who, and their traits)		
How they relate to other important characters		
Main ideas and events		
Issues		
How characters change		

1. Your first paragraph should be the introduction.
   a. Name the characters and the selections. Mention some of the other characters.
   b. Explain that you will compare the stories to show how they are similar and different.
2. The next three paragraphs of your paper should be the body.
   a. Write one paragraph about the themes and how they are the same and different.
   b. Write a paragraph describing the main events and ideas. Then tell how they are similar or different.

MULTI-LEVEL OPTIONS *Writer's Workshop*

Newcomer Have students create two-column charts headed *Persephone* and *Circuit.* Help students understand what is being asked in the questions in step 1. Have them draw responses in the respective columns. Tell students to connect similar things with lines.

Beginning Have students create two-column charts headed *Persephone* and *Circuit.* Ask them to use words and short phrases to answer the questions. Help students complete the following sentences below the chart: *One way the stories are the same is _____. One way the stories are different is _____.*

Intermediate At the revision stage, pair students who have opposing views about whether the stories are more similar or different. Suggest that these partners may be able to help them identify weak points better than students who hold the same views as they do.

Advanced After the reports are written, ask volunteers to participate in a debate. Be sure that half the volunteers think that the stories were mostly the same and half think they were mostly different. Have students use information from their reports to debate the issue. Ask the audience to decide which side has the strongest arguments.

c. Write a paragraph to describe some of the issues faced by the characters. How are they similar or different?

3. The fifth paragraph should be the conclusion.
   a. Tell if the two stories are mostly the same or different.
   b. Tell how you feel about the two stories.

4. Select and use resource and reference materials to be sure you are using standard language, varied sentence structure, and appropriate word choice.

Step 3: Revise your draft.

1. Read your draft and ask yourself these questions:
   a. Do I compare stories clearly? Will readers see how they are similar and different?
   b. Have I supported my main ideas with examples from the text?
   c. Does each body paragraph answer one question about the two stories?
   d. Does the conclusion relate back to the introduction?
   e. Are my paragraphs organized and coherent? What should I add, delete, or combine? Do I need to elaborate anything? Should I rearrange sentences?
   f. Do I use effective transition words, such as *then, next, finally?*

2. Use revising reference and resource books such as your Student Handbook or a dictionary.

3. Share your draft with a partner. Ask each other for ideas about the strong and weak points of your drafts. Use the Peer Editing Checklist in your Student Handbook.

4. Talk about the ideas you and your partner have. Make any changes you feel are necessary. Use a computer and computer software, such as a CD-ROM dictionary or thesaurus, to help you revise.

Step 4: Edit and proofread your report.

1. Proofread your revised report. Check for correct punctuation, spelling, and grammar. If you are using a computer, use the spell check and grammar check.

2. Use the Editor's Checklist in your Student Handbook and other resources and references.

3. Type your paper on a computer or use your best handwriting.

Step 5: Publish your report.

1. Make a title page for your report with your name on it.

2. Make a drawing for the cover. If you can, use computer art.

3. Reread your finished report. Evaluate how well you think your writing achieved its purpose.

The Heinle Newbury House Dictionary

Student Handbook

Step 3: Revise your draft.
Have students share their drafts and give each other feedback.

Step 4: Edit and proofread your report.
Have students work on adding and refining as needed. Point out various resources for proofreading and editing.

Step 5: Publish your report.
Allow time for students to make a title page and illustration as part of their report. Display final products for others to read and enjoy.

ASSESS

Have each student generate a checklist focusing on his/her own specific weaknesses.

Portfolio

Students may choose to include their writing in their portfolios.

Cultural Connection

Say: In Greek myths, gods and goddesses with special powers help solve problems. In stories such as "The Circuit," there are no people with special powers. Imagine that a Greek god or goddess could help the boy in "The Circuit" solve his problem. What kind of special powers might that character use? Have students draw or write how "The Circuit" could be rewritten as a Greek myth.

Learning Styles
Linguistic

Ask: How are "Water Dance" and "The Elements of Life" similar? (Both tell about a cycle in nature.) *How are they different?* (One is a poem; the other is an informational text.) Challenge students to write a poem about the cycle discussed in "The Elements of Life."

Projects

Project 1: Explore Life Cycle Events

1. **Gather and organize** Create a two-column chart for students to record findings on events and corresponding celebrations.
2. **Create a visual** Allow time for students to create visuals for the events. Help with vocabulary as needed. Students can share their projects with the class.
3. **Capitalization and punctuation** Remind students that capitalizing words brings more attention to them. They also can use exclamation points to make sentences and phrases more urgent.

Project 2: Make a Poster About a Cycle

1. **Brainstorm and list** Brainstorm as a group and list ideas for cycles. Have students choose one as the topic of their poster.
2. **Use graphic organizers** Have students decide on the best form of graphics to illustrate their cycle and its steps.

Portfolio

Students may choose to include their projects in their portfolios.

Projects

These projects will help you apply what you learned about cycles. Work alone, with a partner, or with a group of classmates. If you need help, ask a teacher, a parent, or your school librarian.

Project 1: Explore Life Cycle Events

What are the basic events in the human life cycle? How are these events different for different people? What are some ways that people celebrate these events?

1. Gather information.
   a. Create questions to ask your parents and other adults you know. Take notes on what they think the main events in a person's life are. Ask how they have celebrated these events.
   b. Revise, add, or delete questions as necessary to get complete information.
   c. Make a timeline to summarize and organize events that you learned about.
2. Create a page for each life cycle event. Use a drawing or photograph to show each event. Write a few sentences to explain the event. If possible, present your information using presentation software.
3. Use capitalization and punctuation to clarify and enhance your presentation.

Project 2: Make a Poster About a Cycle

Think of other cycles you know about that were not presented in this unit. Research information about this cycle to make a poster. Your poster will show the steps of the cycle. Or show a different cycle you know about. Use the school library or the Internet.

1. Find pictures that show the different steps of a cycle. You can print pictures out from the Internet, copy them from a book, or cut them out of old magazines. Use the name of your cycle as a keyword for an Internet search. You can also draw the pictures.
2. Explain the steps of the cycle on a piece of posterboard.
3. Glue the pictures on the posterboard. Remember to put the pictures in the correct order in which the steps happen.
4. Write one to three sentences below each picture that explain the step.
5. Present your posters to the class.

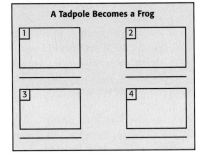

A Tadpole Becomes a Frog

MULTI-LEVEL OPTIONS *Projects*

Newcomer Have students act out how their families celebrate one of the events in their pictures. Invite students to bring in recipes, decorations, or other items to share that are related to some of the holidays.

Beginning Provide craft materials so that students can make simple reproductions of decorations, games, or costumes used in celebrating special events. Have students present these with their drawings.

Intermediate Have students from different cultural backgrounds meet to share their pictures. Ask them to find similarities in how their families celebrate major life events.

Advanced After students describe their family celebrations, have them explore how people celebrated these occasions in the past, both in this country and in other countries. *Ask: Which of your family traditions are from another country? Which are from the United States? Which are special traditions that your family created?*

Further Reading

The following is a list of books continuing the theme of cycles. Choose three of them to read. In your Reading Log, write answers to these questions.

1. What are the strengths of these books?
2. What are their weaknesses?
3. What goals can I set for myself as a writer based on my reading of these books?

The Circuit: Stories from the Life of a Migrant Child
by Francisco Jiménez, Houghton Mifflin Co., 1999. Francisco Jiménez immigrated with his family from Mexico to California as a child. He compiled many of his experiences as a migrant worker into short stories in this book.

Earth: The Incredible Recycling Machine
Paul Bennett (Contributor), Thomson Learning, 1993. This book explains how nature recycles Earth's resources through the process of the life cycle. Includes illustrations and projects about recycling.

Waste, Recycling, and Reuse: Our Impact on the Planet
by Rob Bowden, Raintree Publishers, 2002. This book examines how human development affects the planet. It discusses how pollution in one region of the world can affect a region on the other side of the world.

Life Cycles of a Dozen Diverse Creatures
by Paul Fleisher, Millbrook Press, 1998. This book compares and contrasts the lives of twelve different animals including bullfrogs, monarch butterflies, and jellyfish.

A Drop Around the World
by Barbara Shaw McKinney, Dawn Publications, 1998. This book follows the journey of a drop of rain around the world, on land, underground, in the sea, and in the sky.

El Niño and La Niña
by Sally Rose, Simon Spotlight, 1999. In 1997 and 1998, the phenomenon known as El Niño caused problems for North America's weather. This book explains how El Niño and La Niña affect weather cycles.

Yellowstone's Cycle of Fire
by Frank Staub, Carolrhoda Books, 1994. During the summer of 1988, Yellowstone National Park suffered from several forest fires. This book discusses the nature of the fires and the renewal of the land.

Companion Web site

Reading Log

Heinle Reading Library Black Beauty

Further Reading

Respond to literature Ask students to select books about cycles and prepare a composition about themes, events, main ideas, and issues faced by the main characters. Ask students to decide on the main points of their books and help them organize their information. Tell them to choose supporting details. Remind them to use an attention-grabbing introduction. Have students explain their personal reactions by telling their personal feelings about the stories.

▌ Assessment Program: *Unit 4 Test, pp. 69–74*

Heinle Reading Library

Black Beauty by Anna Sewell
In a specially adapted version
by Deidre S. Laiken

A horse's life can be filled with love and tenderness. It can also be filled with meanness and cruelty. Black Beauty learns both sides of life in this classic tale by Anna Sewell. Told from a horse's point of view, Black Beauty's own story takes you into the mind and heart of a sensitive animal searching for love and understanding. From happy times as a young foal romping with his mother, Duchess, to harsh years as a cab horse in the city and finally to a peaceful old age, Black Beauty's life shows that horses have feelings too, and sometimes even know things that people don't.

Visions Companion Site

http://visions.heinle.com
For additional student activities and teacher resources, see the Visions Companion Web site.

Unit Materials

Activity Book: *pp. 153–184*
Audio: *Unit 5; CD 3, Tracks 1–5*
Student Handbook
Student CD-ROM: *Unit 5*
CNN Video: *Unit 5*
Teacher Resource Book: *Lesson Plans, Teacher Resources, Reading Summaries, School-Home Connection, Video Script, Video Worksheet, Activity Book Answer Key*
Teacher Resource CD-ROM
Assessment Program: *Quizzes and Test, pp. 75–88; Teacher and Student Resources, pp. 115–144*
Assessment CD-ROM
Transparencies
The Heinle Newbury House Dictionary/CD-ROM
More Grammar Practice workbook
Heinle Reading Library: *Little Women*
Web site: http://visions.heinle.com

Visions Staff Development Handbook

Refer to the Visions Staff Development Handbook for more teacher support.

Unit Theme: Freedom

Create a word web Write the word *freedom* in the center of a word web on the board. Have volunteers come to the board and write words associated with *freedom.* **Say:** *The unit theme is* freedom.

Unit Preview: Table of Contents

1. **Identify genres** Read the chapter titles and authors of the reading selections. *Ask: What do you think an autobiography is? What part of Chapter 2 is based on fact?* (the speech by Lincoln) *Which selections are nonfiction?* ("Rosa Parks" and "Samantha's Story")
2. **Connect** *Ask: Do you know anything about Rosa Parks or Abraham Lincoln? Why do you think they are included in a unit on freedom?*

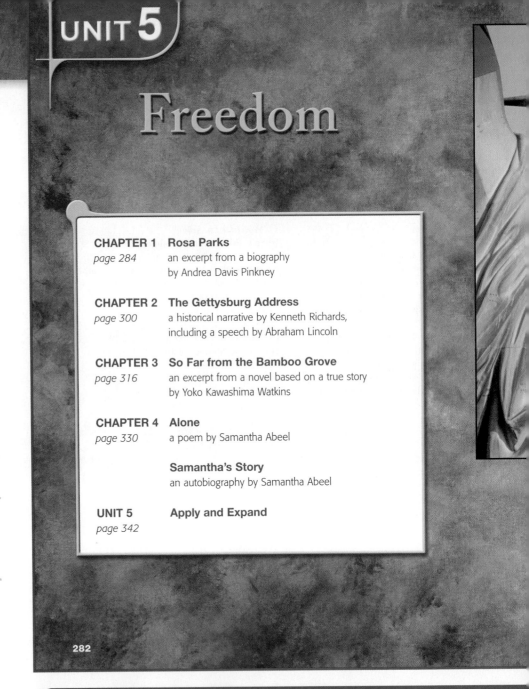

UNIT 5

Freedom

282

UNIT OBJECTIVES

Reading
Make inferences using text evidence as you read a biography • Summarize and paraphrase as you read a historical narrative and a speech • Predict as you read an excerpt from a novel • Compare and contrast as you read a poem and an autobiography

Listening and Speaking
Present reactions • Give a speech
• Present an experience with danger
• Respond to literature

The Statue of Liberty, sculpture, Frédéric Auguste Bartholdi, 1871–1886.

View the Picture

1. How does this picture show freedom?
2. What are some other ways that a picture could show freedom?

In this unit, you will read a biography, a historical narrative, a speech, a novel, a poem, and an autobiography. You will also write some of these forms.

283

View the Picture

1. **Art background** The Statue of Liberty was created by French artist and sculptor Frédéric Auguste Bartholdi (1834–1904). The people of France gave the statue to the people of the United States to commemorate the 100th anniversary of the American Declaration of Independence. This colossal gift represents freedom and democracy as well as this international friendship. Placed on Liberty Island at the entrance of New York harbor, Bartholdi believed it would be the first glimpse for many of their new country.

2. **Art interpretation** *Say: The statue is 151 feet high (46 m) and contains 31 tons of copper* (28,180 kg) *and 125 tons of steel* (113,640 kg). *The 25 windows bring the light of freedom to all who climb the 354 steps to her crown.*

3. **Connect to theme** *Say: The theme of this unit is* freedom. *How does this statue represent the ideals of freedom and democracy to you?*

ASSESS

Have students draw a symbol for freedom. Have them show and explain their symbol.

Grammar

Recognize regular and irregular simple past tense verbs • Identify clauses with subject + verb + object + infinitive • Use the conjunction *so that* to connect ideas • Use superlative adjectives

Writing

Write a biography • Write a news article • Write a historical fiction story • Write a poem

Content

Social Studies: Learn about Constitutional amendments • Math: Use vocabulary to answer math problems • Language Arts: Use punctuation and intonation • Language Arts: Identify genres

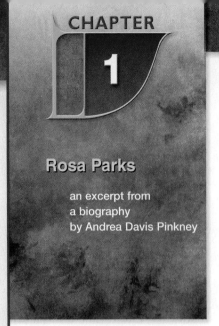

Chapter Materials

Activity Book: *pp. 153–160*
Audio: *Unit 5, Chapter 1; CD 3, Track 1*
Student Handbook
Student CD-ROM: *Unit 5, Chapter 1*
Teacher Resource Book: *Lesson Plan, Teacher
Resources, Reading Summary, Activity Book
Answer Key*
Teacher Resource CD-ROM
Assessment Program: *Quiz, pp. 75–76; Teacher
and Student Resources, pp. 115–144*
Assessment CD-ROM
Transparencies
The Heinle Newbury House Dictionary/CD-ROM
Web site: http://visions.heinle.com

Objectives

Preview Read the objectives. *Ask: Which
objectives do you already know something about?*

Use Prior Knowledge

Assess Fair and Unfair Situations

Connect to personal experience *Say: Everyone
feels that some things in their family are unfair.
Can you give an example of something that is
unfair in your family?*

Answers

2. *Sample answers:* **a.** unfair; those who are older
should be able to stay up later than those who are
younger **b.** fair; if you don't study, you deserve a
poor grade **c.** fair; everyone was treated equally
d. unfair; Tony didn't do anything wrong. He didn't
deserve to have to clean up someone else's mess.

Rosa Parks

an excerpt from
a biography
by Andrea Davis Pinkney

Objectives

Reading Make inferences using text
evidence as you read a biography.

Listening and Speaking Present
reactions.

Grammar Recognize regular and irregular
simple past tense verbs.

Writing Write a biography.

Content Social Studies: Learn about
Constitutional amendments.

Use Prior Knowledge

Assess Fair and Unfair Situations

Read these definitions of *fair* and *unfair*.

> **fair** /fɛr/ *adj.* **1** just; honest; treating all
> people or groups equally: *The judge's
> decision was fair to both sides.*
> **2** treating people in a way that they
> deserve: *It is fair that John got the lead
> in the play. He worked very hard for it.*

> **un•fair** /ʌnˈfɛr/ *adj.* not fair, treating
> one person or group better than another:
> *He was unfair in giving higher raises to
> his favorite employees.*

1. With a partner, read the following
statements.
2. Decide whether each is fair or
unfair. Why do you think as you do?
   a. Ina's younger brother can stay up
   later than she can.
   b. I got a C on the test because I did
   not study for it.
   c. His mother bought ice cream for
   the whole family.
   d. Grace made a mess, and Tony has
   to clean it up.
3. Share your answers with the class.

284 Unit 5 Freedom

MULTI-LEVEL OPTIONS *Build Vocabulary*

Newcomer Create a two-
column chart labeled
embarrassment and *promise* on a
large sheet. Have students draw
two pictures on cards of 1) an
embarrassing situation and 2) an
important promise they made.
Have students show and explain
their cards to a group. Direct the
group to attach the card under the
correct column.

Beginner Have students draw
two pictures on cards of 1) an
embarrassing situation and 2) an
important promise they made. On
the back of the cards, have
students write: *humiliation* or
commitment. Tell students to
show and describe their cards to
a partner. Have the partner guess
which word is written on the
back.

Intermediate Have groups
work to define the vocabulary
words. Ask each group to write a
situation or example for one of the
words. Tell them NOT to use the
word in the description. Have a
student read the description to the
class. Tell the class to say which
vocabulary word fits the example.

Advanced Have students work
in pairs to define and write a
sentence for each vocabulary
word. On three cards, have
students copy the sentences
leaving a blank for the word itself.
Have them exchange cards with
another pair and fill in the missing
words. Let second pairs write the
word on the back.

Build Background

Segregation in the United States

For many years, African-Americans did not have the same rights (freedoms) as other Americans. They were segregated (separated) from other Americans in some states. For example, they had to go to different schools. Usually, African-American schools were much poorer than schools for other Americans. African-Americans also had separate restaurants and stores. In many places, they were not allowed to sit in the front of public (community) buses.

Starting in the 1950s, many states changed their segregation laws. Today, segregation is illegal (against the law) in the United States.

Content Connection

Until the mid-1800s, most African-Americans in the United States were slaves. They worked for no money and had no rights.

Build Vocabulary

Use Note Cards to Remember Meaning

To help you remember the meanings of new words, make note cards of them. Review the cards by yourself or with a partner.

1. Write each of these words on a separate note card.
   a. humiliation
   b. commitment
   c. plight
2. Use a dictionary to find the meaning of each word. Write the meaning on the back of each note card.

3. Work with a partner. Take turns testing each other on the meaning of each word. Continue until both of you remember the meaning of each word.
4. As you read the selection, make new note cards for words you want to remember.

The Heinle Newbury House Dictionary   Activity Book p. 153   Student CD-ROM

Chapter 1 Rosa Parks   **285**

Content Connection
Social Studies

Build Vocabulary Provide students time to look at books and the Internet to get information about slavery in the United States in the 1800s. Have students write three or more sentences with facts that they learn about slavery, using each new vocabulary word (humiliation, commitment, plight) at least once.

Learning Styles
Intrapersonal

Build Background Ask students to list or draw the things they like most about their school, such as the playing fields, the cafeteria, or the library. *Ask: In the past, which of these things might African-American schools NOT have had?* Students should cross out those items. *Ask: How would you feel about your school if it didn't have these things? How would you feel if you knew other schools did have those things?* Have students record their thoughts in their Reading Logs.

Build Background

Segregation in the United States

1. **Use a dictionary** Have students look up *segregation* in the dictionary and read the definition.
2. **Content Connection** In 1954, the Supreme Court in *Brown vs. Board of Education* ruled that segregation in public schools was unconstitutional, but the majority of southern schools remained segregated until the 1980s.

Build Vocabulary

Use Note Cards to Remember Meaning

Teacher Resource Book: *Personal Dictionary, p. 63*

1. **Make note cards** Divide the class into groups. Assign each group two of the glossed words in the selection. Have students write words and definitions on index cards. Then have groups exchange and practice using the cards. Do this several times so that everyone has a chance to practice with the cards. Gather all the cards and store them in the classroom for students to use later.
2. **Reading selection vocabulary** You may want to introduce the glossed words in the reading selection before students begin reading. Key words: *humiliation, racism, trolleys, segregated, civil rights, activist, discrimination, boycott.* Instruct students to write the words with correct spelling and their definitions in their Personal Dictionaries. Have them pronounce each word and divide it into syllables.
3. **Multi-level options** See MULTI-LEVEL OPTIONS on p. 284.

Answers
1. a. humiliation: feeling shame; a lowering of pride or self-respect; **b.** commitment: deep loyalty; **c.** plight: an unpleasant or difficult condition

ASSESS

Have students write sentences with the three new words.

Text Structure

Biography

Review features of a biography *Say: We are going to read a biography of Rosa Parks. Is it fiction or nonfiction? (nonfiction) Was Rosa Parks a real person? (yes)*

Reading Strategy

Make Inferences Using Text Evidence

1. **Make inferences about a character's personality** *Say: We usually judge people and make inferences about what kind of person they are by what they say. How else can we make inferences about someone? (Examples: what the person does, who their friends are, where they live, what jobs they have) Say: As you read the story of Rosa Parks, look for text evidence of her actions, what she says, and the choices she makes. This evidence can help you make inferences about her character.*

2. **Locate derivation** Have students locate the derivation of *inference* in the glossary in the Student Handbook and record it in their Reading Logs.

3. **Multi-level options** See MULTI-LEVEL OPTIONS below.

✓ ASSESS

Ask: What do you expect to learn about Rosa Parks in this biography?

Text Structure

Biography

"Rosa Parks" is a **biography.** A biography tells the true story of a real person's life and experiences. Look for the features of a biography as you read the selection.

Pay attention to the important events in Rosa Parks's life. Write them in a timeline in your Reading Log.

Biography	
Events	special things the person did
Dates	when important events happened
People and Places	information about important people and places
Chronological Order	events usually written in the order that they happened

Reading Log

Student CD-ROM

Reading Strategy

Make Inferences Using Text Evidence

You can **make inferences** about people in a biography. An inference is a guess. You can use **text evidence** and your own experiences to guess what the people are like. Text evidence is information in a text. Read this text.

> Rosa Parks's mother sent her to a school in Montgomery, Alabama. During the school year, she lived with her aunt.

Text Evidence	Your Experience	Inference
Rosa lived with her aunt in Montgomery.	Children usually live with their parents.	Rosa's mother didn't live in Montgomery.

Student CD-ROM

286 Unit 5 Freedom

MULTI-LEVEL OPTIONS *Reading Strategy*

Newcomer Play the audio of the prologue. Help students to make inferences about Rosa's old school. *Ask: Did the Pine Level school have enough books? (no) Did Leona want Rosa to get a good education? (yes)* Explain that students are making an inference, or a guess.

Beginning Play the audio of the prologue. Help students make inferences about Leona. *Ask: Why did Leona work so hard? (to send Rosa to a better school) What did Leona think about education? (It was important.)* Explain that students are making an inference, or a guess, based on text evidence.

Intermediate Play the audio of the prologue. Ask students to make a guess about Leona based on the text evidence. (*Example: Leona thought a good education was very important.*) Have students compare their inferences with another pair and discuss the text evidence.

Advanced Play the audio of the prologue. *Say: What can you infer about Rosa's family?* (*Example: Rosa's mother cared about education.*) Have students defend their inferences with text evidence. (*Examples: Leona was a teacher. Leona worked hard to send Rosa to a better school.*)

ROSA PARKS

an excerpt from a biography
by Andrea Davis Pinkney

287

Reading Selection Materials

Audio: *Unit 5, Chapter 1; CD 3, Track 1*
Teacher Resource Book: *Reading Summary,
     pp. 103–104*
Transparencies: #42, *Reading Summary*

Suggestions for Using
Reading Summary

- Introduce new vocabulary or cognates.
- Cut the summary into strips, or jumble the sentences on an overhead transparency. Students put the sentences in order.
- Practice the reading strategy.
- Students read aloud or with a partner.
- Students paraphrase the summary.
- Students do a cloze activity.
- Students create a visual or graphic organizer, such as a timeline or storyboard, to illustrate the summary.
- Students paraphrase the summary.

Preview the Selection

1. **Interpret the image** Have students look at the picture of the statue of Rosa Parks. *Ask: Where is Rosa Parks? What is she doing? How would you describe her expression?*
2. **Provide background** This statue of Rosa Parks defying segregation laws by sitting in the "whites only" section of a bus is on exhibit at the Birmingham Civil Rights Institute in Birmingham, Alabama. It is one of the major exhibits in *Movement Gallery* within the institute's permanent exhibitions.
3. **Connect** Remind students that the unit theme is *freedom*. Ask them what Rosa Parks is doing that connects to the theme.

**Community
Connection**

Ask students what options they have for getting to school and around town. (the school bus, city buses, the train, the subway, car rides from a family member, and so on) Ask them which is their favorite type of transportation and why.

**Learning Styles
*Intrapersonal***

Have students examine the picture. *Ask: What do you think of when you look at this statue? How does it make you feel? How do you think Rosa Parks felt? What would you do if you were being treated unfairly? What would you do if you saw others being treated unfairly?* Have students record their thoughts in their Reading Logs.

Teacher Resource Book: *Reading Log,
     p. 64*

Read the Selection

1. **Preview using the prologue** Have a volunteer read the prologue on p. 288. *Ask: What inference can you make about schools for African-Americans? What text evidence is there?* (You can infer that the schools were very poor and in bad condition; the text says that there were few books, no windows or desks, and it was cold inside.)

2. **Identify text features** Point out to students the ellipsis used at the end of paragraph 2. *Say: This selection is an excerpt from a biography. An excerpt is part of a story, but not all of it. These three dots are called an ellipsis, and that means that something was left out.*

3. **Paired reading** Play the audio. Have students reread aloud with a partner.

Sample Answer to Guide Question
We can infer that Leona thought going to a good school was important because she saved all her money to pay for Rosa to go to a private school.

See Teacher Edition pp. 434–436 for a list of English-Spanish cognates in the reading selection.

Audio
CD 3, Tr. 1

Prologue

Rosa Parks was born in 1913. She grew up in Pine Level, Alabama. Rosa's mother, Leona, was a teacher. Rosa's grandparents had been slaves. They taught her that all people should be treated the same. But Rosa and other African-Americans were not treated the same as other Americans. Rosa had to go to an African-American school in Pine Level. This school had no desks or windows. It was cold and had very few books. Leona worked hard to send Rosa to a better school.

> **Make Inferences Using Text Evidence**
>
> Do you think Leona thought going to a good school was important? Why do you think so?

1   Leona saved every penny she could, and when Rosa was eleven years old, her mother sent her to the Montgomery Industrial School for **Black** Girls, a **private school** in Montgomery, Alabama. During the school year, Rosa lived with her aunt Fannie. At her new school Rosa learned everything, from how to read world maps to how to mix **remedies** for sick and **ailing** souls. She even took cooking lessons.

2   But a private education couldn't **shield** Rosa from the public **humiliation** of **racism** that was common in the South in the 1920s. Rosa often rode streetcar **trolleys** to school—**segregated** streetcars in which she, along with every other black rider, was forced to sit in the back. . . .

3   In 1931 a neighbor introduced Rosa to Raymond Parks. . . . He was smart, smooth talking, **forthright,** and **persistent** . . . . Raymond was a barber who worked in downtown Montgomery. He took a quick liking to Rosa. But she was not immediately **impressed** with him. He came

---

black   African-American
private school   a school run by a private group, not by the government
remedies   medicines, or things that make illnesses better
ailing   sick
shield   protect
humiliation   a feeling of shame; a lowering of pride or self-respect

racism   prejudice or unfairness against people of one race by those of another
trolleys   a kind of bus that runs on rails in the streets
segregated   separated according to race
forthright   honest
persistent   continuing to have a belief or to work for a goal
impressed   admired someone

288   Unit 5   Freedom

MULTI-LEVEL OPTIONS *Read the Selection*

Newcomer Play the audio. *Ask: Did Rosa go to a private school?* (yes) *Did Rosa get married?* (yes) *Did Rosa work?* (yes) *Did she ride to and from work on the city bus?* (yes) *Did she ride in the front of the bus?* (no) *Did this make Rosa unhappy?* (yes)

Beginning Play the audio. *Ask: Where did Rosa go to private school?* (Montgomery, Alabama) *When did she marry Raymond?* (December, 1932) *Why did she sit at the back of the bus?* (It was the law.)

Intermediate Have students do a paired reading. *Ask: What did Rosa learn at private school?* (many things: how to read maps, mix remedies, cook) *How did Rosa get to and from work?* (the city bus) *What were the rules on the bus?* (Black passengers had to pay in front, then sit in back.)

Advanced Have students read silently. Then ask students to describe Raymond. (intelligent, sincere, well-spoken, committed) *Ask: Of what group was Raymond a member?* (NAACP) *What was the group's goal?* (to help black people) *Why was Rosa tired of riding the bus?* (It was a degrading ritual.)

to Rosa's house several times to ask Rosa's mother if he could take Rosa for a drive in his car. It was clear to Leona that Raymond Parks was intelligent and **sincere.** She agreed to let him spend time with her daughter, but it was Rosa who kept turning down Raymond's offers.

4   Finally, when Rosa said yes to a short ride with Raymond, she saw that he was more than just a pretty boy with a **flashy** car. Like Rosa's grandfather, Raymond was a man of **conviction.** He was well-spoken and cared deeply about the plight of black people in the South. And he was an active member of the **National Association for the Advancement of Colored People (NAACP).**

5   The more Raymond told Rosa about his **commitment** to helping black people, the more Rosa's awareness grew. Her love for Raymond grew, too. In December 1932 Rosa McCauley and Raymond Parks were married, in Pine Level at the home of Rosa's mother. Rosa was nineteen years old. . . .

6   Rosa found work as a helper at Saint Margaret's Hospital in Montgomery. At night she worked as a **seamstress** at home, mending and tailoring clothes. Rosa was grateful for her job, but going to work drove home the sad reality of segregation. When Rosa took the city bus to work, she had to go through the same **degrading ritual** day after day. She would step on the bus at the front and buy a ticket from the driver. Then she'd have to leave the bus, walk around to the back, and enter the bus again through the rear door. All black passengers had to sit in the back. Only white people were allowed to ride at the front of the bus. This was the law. If you were black and the back of the bus was too

> **Make Inferences Using Text Evidence**
>
> Do you think Rosa enjoyed taking the bus? Use text evidence and what you know to answer.

---

sincere   honest in your thoughts and actions
flashy   showy
conviction   a strong belief
National Association for the Advancement of Colored People (NAACP)   a group that works to protect the rights of African-Americans

commitment   deep loyalty to a person or cause
seamstress   a woman whose job is sewing
degrading   causing shame
ritual   an act or actions that you repeat often

Chapter 1 Rosa Parks   **289**

Read the Selection

1. **Shared reading** Play the audio. Have students join in, with each student reading two sentences.

2. **Identify important people** Have students work in small groups. Have them list the people mentioned on p. 288 and describe their relationship to the main character, Rosa. *Ask: Which people do you think were most important to Rosa?* (her mother and Raymond) *Why?* Students can fill in this information in the biography charts of p. 286.

3. **Recall factual information** *Ask: How old was Rosa when she got married? Where did she work? Why do you think she had two jobs? Describe her daily routine riding the city bus.*

4. **Locate derivations using dictionaries** Have students look at these glossed words and determine what words they are derived from: *remedies, humiliation, trolleys, segregated, national.* Have students check the derivations in a print, online, or CD-ROM dictionary.

5. **Multi-level options** See MULTI-LEVEL OPTIONS on p. 288.

Sample Answer to Guide Question
I don't think Rosa enjoyed taking the bus at all. The text says it was a "degrading ritual" and people don't like to feel degraded.

A Capitalization

Institutions and organizations

Tell students that the first letter of each main word in the name of an institution or organization is always capitalized. *Ask: What institution is named in paragraph 1?* (the Montgomery Industrial School for Black Girls) *Ask: What letters in the name are capitalized?* (M, I, S, B, G) *Why is the* f *in* for *not capitalized?* (It's not a main word.) *Ask: What organization is named in paragraph 4?* (the National Association for the Advancement of Colored People) *Which*

letters are capitalized? (N, A, A, C, P) *Why?* (They are the first letters of the main words.)

    Apply Have students correct the capitalization errors in the following sentence. Write on the board: *Rosa worked as a helper at saint margaret's hospital.*

Read the Selection

1. **Reciprocal reading** Play the audio. Divide class into groups. Have students take turns reading sections aloud, asking the group questions and helping the group to summarize.

2. **Use a chronology to identify dates and events** Have students work in small groups to make up a chronology of Rosa's life so far. They should include dates and events. After discussing their timelines as a class, they can enter the information into their biography charts.

Sample Answer to Guide Question

I think Rosa was brave because she tried to get through the front section without the bus driver noticing. I know that bus drivers can get very upset if you don't follow the rules.

> **Make Inferences Using Text Evidence**
>
> Do you think Rosa was brave? Use text evidence and what you know to answer.

crowded, tough. You had to wait for the next bus, go through the same **drill,** and pray you would get to work on time.

7   Rosa was growing tired of this daily **disgrace.** Sometimes she would get onto the bus at the front and pay her **fare,** like always. Then before the driver had a chance to take full notice of her, Rosa would **breeze** through the front section of the bus to find her seat in the back.

8   Several drivers came to associate Rosa with her **defiance.** Once, in 1943, a driver kicked Rosa off his bus because she refused to enter the bus through the back door. . . .

9   As the wife of a **civil rights activist** (and the granddaughter of a civil rights believer), Rosa had learned three important things about changing the **unjust** treatment black people had suffered: Change takes time. Change takes strength. Change takes the help of others. Rosa Parks had all three.

10   She knew that one of the best ways to put these **advantages** to work would be to join the NAACP. But becoming an NAACP member wasn't as simple as it seemed. Rosa's husband didn't think it was a good idea. . . .

11   Raymond supported his wife's wish to stop segregation, but at the same time, he feared for her safety. . . . But . . . Rosa knew she had to join. . . . She attended the annual NAACP Montgomery meeting. This was the meeting to elect new officers. There were sixteen people at the meeting—fifteen men and Rosa Parks.

---

drill   an action or exercise that you repeat

disgrace   a cause of shame or dishonor

fare   the cost of a ride, such as on a bus, train, or boat

breeze   move quickly and easily

defiance   refusing to do something that someone in charge tells you to do

civil rights   the rights of each citizen promised by the U.S. Constitution

activist   a person who works to change things that he or she thinks are wrong

unjust   without justice, unfair

advantages   benefits, good features

290   **Unit 5**   Freedom

MULTI-LEVEL OPTIONS *Read the Selection*

Newcomer *Ask: Did Rosa always follow the rules of segregation?* (no) *Did Rosa go to an NAACP meeting?* (yes) *Did they send her home?* (no) *Did she join the NAACP?* (yes)

Beginning *Ask: What did Rosa want to change?* (segregation or unjust treatment) *What group did Rosa join?* (the NAACP) *What was her position there?* (secretary) *How long did she work for the NAACP?* (12 years)

Intermediate *Ask: Why did Rosa want to join the NAACP?* (to stop segregation) *What was the NAACP meeting for?* (to elect new officers) *Why did they elect her as secretary?* (She was a woman.) *What did she do as secretary?* (She organized meetings, kept the books, wrote letters, got new members, and answered the phone.)

Advanced *Ask: How might the bus drivers make Rosa's life difficult?* (They could prohibit her from riding the bus, which she needed to get to work.) *Why do you think Raymond was afraid for Rosa?* (Defiance and civil rights work could be dangerous.) *Do you think it was hard for Rosa to join the NAACP?* (Yes. She wasn't used to being the only woman in a group.)

12   When it came time to elect a **permanent** volunteer **secretary,** everybody looked to Rosa. They all figured secretarial work was women's work and she was the natural choice. Rosa accepted the job gladly. . . .

13   From that day on for the next twelve years, Rosa took her position as the NAACP Montgomery **chapter** secretary very seriously. . . .

14   Rosa organized branch meetings, kept the books, wrote and mailed letters and **press releases,** and at every turn, **drummed up** new members. When the office phone rang, Rosa answered it. When someone had a question about the workings of the branch, Rosa answered that, too.

> **Make Inferences Using Text Evidence**
>
> Rosa did many things as secretary of the NAACP. Make an inference about how Rosa felt about her job.

---

permanent   lasting, or meant to last, forever or for a long time

secretary   a person who works in an office and does jobs for a boss, such as writing letters and answering the phone

chapter   a local office of a large group

press releases   writings that tell the press (news) of an event that will happen

drummed up   got or increased the amount of

Chapter 1   Rosa Parks   **291**

Read the Selection

1. **Paired reading**   Read the selection aloud. Have students reread in pairs.
2. **Multi-level options**   See MULTI-LEVEL OPTIONS on p. 290.

Sample Answer to Guide Question

I can infer that Rosa was proud of her job and felt like it was important because she took her work seriously and worked hard.

---

⁹ Punctuation

Parentheses

Tell students that parentheses are used to set off additional information in a sentence. Read the first sentence of paragraph 9 aloud, omitting the information in parentheses. Now read the complete sentence aloud. *Ask: What additional information is given?* (Rosa's grandfather believed in civil rights.)

    Apply   Write the following on the board *without* the information in parentheses: *Rosa Parks (born Rosa McCauley) grew up in Pine Level, Alabama (located in the south of the United States) in the early- to mid-1900s.* Have students tell you where to add the parentheses. Then *ask: Would the sentence be complete without the information in parentheses?* (yes) *What does the information in the parentheses add to the sentence?* (extra details)

Read the Selection

1. **Silent reading** Play the audio. Then give students time to read the pages silently.
2. **Ask questions to understand text** Have students work in small groups to write questions. Then have students exchange and answer the questions.

Sample Answer to Guide Question
I can infer that the passenger didn't mind standing and didn't expect Rosa to give up her seat for him.

---

15   As branch secretary . . . she recorded all the cases of **discrimination** and **violence** against black people in the state of Alabama. The cases seemed never ending. There were hundreds of them.

16   **Documenting** these cases showed Rosa that racism in Alabama was big. It was powerful. It gathered **momentum** with each mile it covered. It would take the force of one woman's **iron will** to stop it in its tracks.

17   Turns out, Rosa Parks was that woman.

18   December 1, 1955, started out like any other Thursday for Rosa. She went to her job at the Montgomery Fair department store, where she then worked as a seamstress. When the workday ended, Rosa gathered her purse and coat and walked to the Court Square bus stop. She waited patiently for the Cleveland Avenue bus—the bus she'd taken to and from work many times. When she stepped onto the bus and paid her dime to ride, she immediately spotted an empty seat on the aisle, one row behind the whites-only section of the bus. It was **rush hour.** Any seat on any bus at this time of day was a blessing. Rosa sat back and gave a quiet sigh of relief.

19   When the bus stopped to pick up passengers at the Empire Theater stop, six white people got on. They each paid the ten-cent fare, just as Rosa had done. All but one of them easily found seats at the front of the bus. The sixth passenger, a man, didn't mind standing. He curled his fingers around a holding pole and waited for the bus to pull away.

Make Inferences Using Text Evidence

What inference can you make about the sixth passenger?

---

discrimination unfair treatment, especially because of race, gender, religion, and so forth
violence injury or damage
documenting providing written evidence
momentum the speed at which something moves

iron will strong determination (being set on doing something)
rush hour a time when people are going to and from work

292   Unit 5 Freedom

MULTI-LEVEL OPTIONS *Read the Selection*

Newcomer *Ask: Was there a lot of discrimination in Alabama?* (yes) *Did Rosa find a seat on the bus?* (yes) *Did the man at the next stop find a seat?* (no) *Did Rosa give him her seat?* (no) *Was the bus driver angry with Rosa?* (yes)

Beginning *Ask: What year was it?* (1955) *How did Rosa feel about finding a seat on the bus?* (happy, relieved) *Why did the driver tell Rosa to stand?* (so a white man could sit in her seat because that was the law) *What did Rosa do?* (She stayed in her seat.)

Intermediate *Ask: Why was Rosa happy to find a seat?* (It was rush hour.) *Why did the driver remember Rosa?* (She had broken the law on his bus in the past.) *What did the driver do to Rosa?* (He ordered her to give up her seat to a white man.) *What did Rosa do?* (She didn't move.) *How did the driver feel?* (very angry)

Advanced *Ask: Why might the driver have chosen Rosa to speak to?* (He remembered her from when she disobeyed him in the past.) *Why did Rosa refuse to move when ordered by the driver?* (She saw no reason to tolerate his demands.) *Why was the driver so angry? Explain.* (He wasn't used to being disobeyed by an African-American woman.)

20   But according to the bus segregation laws for the state of Alabama, black people were **required** to give up a bus seat if a white person was left standing. And each bus driver in the state was allowed to **lay down the letter of the law** on his bus.

Make Inferences Using Text Evidence

Do you think the bus driver liked Rosa Parks? What text evidence helps you make this inference?

21   As it turned out, Rosa was sitting on the bus that was driven by the same driver who, twelve years before, had kicked Rosa off his bus because she would not enter through the back door. The driver remembered Rosa. And Rosa sure remembered him. He glared at Rosa through his rearview mirror. He ordered her up and out of her seat. But she wouldn't move. Instead, she answered him with a question. Why, she asked, should she have to **endure** his bossing her around?

22   Well, the driver didn't **take kindly to** Rosa **challenging** him. Next thing Rosa knew, he was standing over her, **insisting** that she give up her seat to the white man who needed a seat.

---

required   had to do something
lay down the letter of the law   make sure people follow the law
endure   bear, tolerate

take kindly to   like
challenging   questioning, arguing with
insisting   demanding

Chapter 1 Rosa Parks   **293**

Read the Selection

1. **Do a jigsaw reading** Play the audio. Then have groups of students prepare different paragraphs for a choral reading. Give them time to practice. Then have the class "put the pieces together" by reading aloud in sequence.
2. **Summarize** Have students practice summarizing what has happened so far on December 1.
3. **Multi-level options** See MULTI-LEVEL OPTIONS on p. 292.

Sample Answer to Guide Question
I don't think that he liked Rosa because he had kicked her off his bus before, and this time he glared at her. People usually glare at people they don't like.

A   **Capitalization**

Street names and public places

Tell students that the first letters in the names of streets and public places are always capitalized. *Ask: In paragraph 18, what letters in the Court Square bus stop are capitalized?* (C and S) *Why?* (It's the name of a town square, which is a public place.) *How is Cleveland Avenue written?* (capital C and A) *Why?* (It's the name of a street.)

   Apply   Write on the board: *The bus went down grove street to allston avenue and stopped at coolidge corner.* Ask students to correct the capitalization errors. Explain that *Grove Street* and *Allston Avenue* should be capitalized because they are street names. *Coolidge Corner* should be capitalized because it is a public place.

Read the Selection

1. **Reciprocal reading** Play the audio. Divide the class into groups. Have students take turns reading sections aloud, asking questions of the group, and helping the group to summarize.

2. **Identify important choices** *Say: Rosa made three important choices on this page. Look at paragraphs 23–25 and identify the choices she made.* (paragraph 23: Rosa refused to move from the seat; paragraph 24: When the bus driver said he would call the police, she said to do it, and she still refused to move; paragraph 25: When Nixon proposed that she bring a case against segregation laws, she agreed.)

Sample Answer to Guide Question
Nixon felt that what she did was very important. He told Rosa that if she brought the case to court, it could help to end segregation.

Make Inferences Using Text Evidence

How do you think E. D. Nixon felt about what Rosa did? What text evidence helps you make this inference?

---

23   Rosa **clenched** her purse, which rested in her lap. When the driver asked Rosa to move a second time, Rosa put it to him plainly and firmly: No.

24   He told Rosa he would call the police if she didn't move. Rosa didn't **flinch.** Maybe she was thinking about her grandpa Sylvester's solid belief in not allowing **mistreatment** from others. Or maybe she was just fed up with giving in to segregation's iron fist. Even the **threat** of police couldn't **rouse** Rosa. Once again her answer to the bus driver was simple: Do it. And he did—**lickety-split.** The police came right away. They **arrested** Rosa and took her to the city jail. Rosa called her husband and told him the whole story. News of Rosa's arrest had already begun to spread through Montgomery's black community. . . . E. D. Nixon from the NAACP was one of the first to hear about Rosa. . . . He told Rosa and Raymond that . . . the incident . . . had the power to **pound out** segregation. If Rosa was willing—and brave enough—to bring a case against Alabama's segregation laws, she could help end segregation in the state.

25   Rosa didn't have to think long about E. D. Nixon's **proposal.** Just a short time earlier, Rosa had been staring segregation in the face and saying *no.* Now she was looking the law in the eyes, and without blinking, she said *yes.* She agreed to attack the system that kept her and every black person in the United States of America from being treated equally. Years later, in reflecting on the events that led to her decision, Rosa said, "People always say that I [didn't give] up my seat because I was tired, but that isn't true. I was not tired **physically** . . . The only tired I was, was tired of giving in."

---

clenched gripped tightly
flinch move back suddenly without thinking
mistreatment harmful behavior toward someone
threat a danger, a menace
rouse awaken and get up
lickety-split slang for "very fast, quickly"

arrested taken and held by the police, for breaking the law
pound out eliminate, get rid of
proposal something that is suggested as a possible plan
physically relating to the body

294 Unit 5 Freedom

MULTI-LEVEL OPTIONS *Read the Selection*

Newcomer *Ask: Did Rosa agree to give up her seat?* (no) *Did the driver call the police?* (yes) *Did they arrest Rosa?* (yes) *Did Rosa agree to go to court to help end segregation laws?* (yes)

Beginning *Ask: Why did the driver call the police?* (Rosa refused to move.) *What did the police do?* (They arrested Rosa.) *Did she break the law?* (yes) *What did her act help to do?* (end segregation)

Intermediate *Ask: Why did Rosa refuse to move?* (She was tired of being mistreated.) *What did Rosa agree to do after she was arrested?* (bring a court case against Alabama's segregation laws)

Advanced *Ask: Do you think Rosa was afraid of the police? Explain.* (No. She told the driver to call them.) *Rosa said she wasn't tired physically, but tired of giving in. What does that mean?* (She didn't want to give into unjust treatment anymore.)

Make Inferences Using Text Evidence

Make an inference about the effect that one person's actions can have. Use text evidence about Rosa Parks.

26 On December 5, 1955, Rosa and her attorney, Fred Gray, appeared before Judge John B. Scott in the city court of Montgomery, Alabama. Rosa was found guilty of breaking the Alabama State segregated bus law. She was fined ten dollars. Although Rosa was **convicted,** her act had **ignited** the Montgomery bus **boycott,** a civil rights movement that would change the face of segregation forever.

Epilogue

African-Americans in Montgomery showed their support for Rosa. They organized a bus boycott—they stopped riding the city's buses. The city lost a lot of money because of the boycott. In 1956, the United States Supreme Court said that segregated buses were illegal in Alabama. After this, Rosa continued to work for the rights of African-Americans.

convicted found guilty of a crime in a court of law
ignited set on fire (here, the author means "started")

boycott when people refuse to buy certain products or services for political reasons

About the Author | Andrea Davis Pinkney

Andrea Davis Pinkney grew up in a family that worked hard for civil rights. Today, she writes about important African-Americans. She wants readers to know how much these people have given to their country. Pinkney has said, "I hope their lives reflect something in each of us—the courage to fight for what we believe is right. . . ."

➤ Why do you think Andrea Davis Pinkney wrote about Rosa Parks? To inform, to entertain, or to persuade?

Chapter 1 Rosa Parks **295**

---

❾ Punctuation

Periods for initials

Tell students that sometimes people use initials instead of full names. Periods must be used after initials. Refer students to the name *E. D. Nixon* in paragraph 24. Ask for suggestions of what these initials might stand for (e.g., Edward Dean). Ask students to find another example of an initial on these pages. (Judge John B. Scott) Ask students to write their own initials. Make sure they are followed by periods.

Evaluate Your Reading Strategy

Make Inferences Using Text Evidence

Say: You have practiced an important reading strategy. Now you can decide how well you have done. Does this statement describe how you read?

When I read about a person, I use what I read and my experiences to guess what the person in the text is like. Using text evidence to make inferences helps me understand people I read about.

Read the Selection

1. **Paired reading** Read the selection aloud. Have students practice reading p. 295 in pairs.
2. **Compare and contrast print media with written story** Ask students to research a recent newspaper or magazine article about Rosa Parks. Have them write a comparison of the information presented in the article and in the reading selection. They should answer the questions: *What information is presented in the article that is not in the reading selection? What information is in the reading selection that is not in the article? Which format gave you the most complete information? Which format do you prefer?*
3. **Multi-level options** See MULTI-LEVEL OPTIONS on p. 294.

Sample Answer to Guide Question
One person's actions can have a big effect. By refusing to give up her seat, Rosa Parks helped end segregation.

About the Author

Explain author's background. *Say: This author wrote about important African-Americans because she wanted readers to know what they have given to their country. What people have been important in your life? What values, like courage or determination, have they taught you? What biographies would you write if you were an author?*

Answer
Sample answer: I think that the author wrote to inform people about Rosa Parks and to persuade people to have the courage to stand up for what is right.

Across Selections

Have students review paragraphs 6–9 of "To Risk or Not to Risk" (pp. 108–109). Have them discuss how Rosa Parks's defiance of segregation laws relate to David Ropeik's essay. (No one forced her to do it; she made her own choice; she trusted that her husband and the NAACP would support her; the risk came with a major benefit.)

Beyond the Reading

Reading Comprehension

Question-Answer Relationships

Sample Answers

1. Montgomery, Alabama
2. National Association for the Advancement of Colored People; secretary
3. Actions should include: get on, pay, get off, and enter through the back door of the bus.
4. It was caused by Rosa Parks being jailed and fined. It resulted in the desegregation of buses in Alabama.
5. She felt confident she was right. She knew what she was going to do, and she did not get upset or angry.
6. that Rosa Parks is a brave, proud, and committed person
7. Yes, many were angry. They organized a city-wide boycott.
8. Yes. She paid a fare, so she was entitled to the same service.
9. Yes. Otherwise nothing gets better.
10. In both stories, the government took away personal rights and freedom of people.

Build Reading Fluency

Read Silently and Aloud

Assessment Program: *Reading Fluency Chart, p. 116*

When students have completed the reading fluency activity, record their progress in the Reading Fluency Chart.

Reading Comprehension

Question-Answer Relationships (QAR)

"Right There" Questions

1. **Recall Facts** Where was Rosa's new school?
2. **Recall Facts** What is the NAACP? What job did Rosa Parks have in the NAACP?

"Think and Search" Questions

3. **Interpret Text Ideas** Act out the things that African-Americans in Montgomery had to do when they rode the bus.
4. **Analyze Cause and Effect** What was the cause and the effect of the Montgomery bus boycott?

"Author and You" Questions

5. **Support Your Opinion** How do you think Rosa Parks felt while she was arguing with the bus driver? Why do you think so?
6. **Understand Author's Perspective** How do you think the author wants you to feel about Rosa Parks?

7. **Speculate** Do you think that many African-Americans in Montgomery were angry about segregation? Why do you think so?

"On Your Own" Questions

8. **Evaluate** Do you think Rosa Parks was right for not giving up her seat? Why or why not?
9. **Connect Your Experiences** Do you think that people should work to change things that they think are wrong? Why or why not?
10. **Connect Issues Across Cultures** Think about "The Voyage of the Lucky Dragon" in Unit 3, Chapter 2. How do government decisions affect the people in that story and in "Rosa Parks"?

Activity Book
p. 154

Student
CD-ROM

Build Reading Fluency

Read Silently and Aloud

Reading silently for practice and reading aloud for expression are two important ways to become a fluent reader.

1. Listen to the audio recording of "Rosa Parks."

2. Follow along with the reading on page 288.
3. Read silently paragraphs 1–3 two times.
4. With a partner read aloud.
5. Your partner will time you reading aloud.

296   Unit 5   Freedom

MULTI-LEVEL OPTIONS *Elements of Literature*

Newcomer Make a two-column chart labeled *informal* and *formal*. Write *Rosa and Mrs. Parks* underneath. Replay paragraph 4 of the audio. Write the informal phrases (a pretty boy, flashy car) and formal phrases (handsome young man, expensive car) next to them. Have pairs practice reading these phrases aloud.

Beginning Write on the board: *Raymond was beyond being merely an attractive man with a nice automobile.* Direct students to paragraph 4 to find the phrase in the biography that means the same but shows a more casual tone and style. (more than just a pretty boy with a flashy car)

Intermediate Have students work independently to list some of the conversational phrases in the biography. Then have them write a more formal phrase for each. Have them share their lists in small groups.

Advanced Have students work in pairs to rewrite paragraph 21. Tell them to write it as if it were an entry in an encyclopedia. Remind them that their paragraphs should have the same basic meaning, but the style should be more formal. Have them share their paragraphs with the class.

Listen, Speak, Interact

Present Reactions

Try this activity to understand better what segregation is like.

1. Hold up a pen or a piece of paper.
2. Students holding pens will sit on the floor in a small part of the classroom. Students holding paper will stay in their seats.
3. Your class is now segregated. Present your reactions by talking about these questions as a class:
   a. How does being segregated make you feel?
   b. Do you think it would be harder to learn sitting on the floor or at your desk? Why?
   c. Do you think this segregation is fair? Explain.
   d. Are your ideas about segregation the same as your classmates' ideas?
4. Segregation was a part of the culture of the United States at the time this story took place. Based on your reading of "Rosa Parks," compare and contrast characteristics of this culture to other cultures that you know about.

Elements of Literature

Recognize Style

Listen as your teacher reads these sentences. Their meanings are similar, but their **style** is different.
   a. If . . . the bus was too crowded, that was unfortunate for you.
   b. If . . . the bus was too crowded, tough.

Which sentence sounds more conversational? Which one sounds more like something from a textbook?

1. Which of the following statements describes the author's style?
   a. It sounds like she is telling the story to us aloud.
   b. It sounds like an article from an encyclopedia.
2. The author of "Rosa Parks" uses some words from the southern region of the United States. Read these sentences. Which words do you think reflect that region and culture?
   a. Rosa learned . . . how to mix remedies for sick . . . souls.
   b. The driver didn't take kindly to Rosa challenging him.

Reading Log   Activity Book   Student
                  p. 155   CD-ROM

Chapter 1 Rosa Parks   **297**

Listen, Speak, Interact
Present Reactions

1. **React to a situation** Be sure that students holding pens sit on the floor in a small area of the room. Physically doing this will make it easier for students to express how it feels to be segregated. You may also want to do this activity over two days, so that everyone in the class experiences the same problems. Point out that segregation was a great deal more pervasive than this exercise demonstrates.
2. **Newcomers** These students can participate fully in this exercise.

Elements of Literature
Recognize Style

1. **Pair work** Have students work in pairs to explore style used in "Rosa Parks." Then discuss their answers as a class.
2. **Multi-level options** See MULTI-LEVEL OPTIONS on p. 296.

Answers
Sentence *b* is more conversational. Sentence *a* is more like a textbook. **1.** sentence *a* **2. a.** souls **b.** take kindly

ASSESS

Have students write a definition of *segregation* based on the Listen, Speak, Interact activity.

Community Connection

Write an editorial Explain to students that an editorial is an article in a newspaper or magazine that gives the opinion of the writer. Bring in editorials from newspapers and magazines to show students some examples. Use *Teacher Resource Book, pp. 52 and 53,* for models of the structure of an editorial or persuasive writing.

Community Connection

After completing the Listen, Speak, Interact activity, *ask: Now that you have experienced what segregation is like, what do you think? If you want to write to people in your community, what is the best way to share your opinions?* Have students choose the appropriate form for their purpose for writing. Guide them to choose an editorial. Instruct them to write an editorial to a community newspaper to express their opinions about segregation.

Learning Styles
Kinesthetic

Have students work in pairs. Give each pair a slip of paper with a situation from the biography to act out. (*Examples:* Rosa studying at school; Raymond taking her for a drive; the wedding; Rosa buying her ticket and riding the bus; Rosa at the NAACP; Rosa and the bus driver disagreeing; Rosa in court) Have pairs mime the situation using no verbal cues. Allow students to guess which situation each pair is acting out.

Word Study

Recognize the Suffix -ment

Expand vocabulary Have students brainstorm other words that they know ending with the suffix -ment, and write them on the board. You could provide them with the following prompts: *govern, settle, arrange, appoint.* Point out that with the verbs ending with *e*, the *e* is not dropped before adding the suffix.

Answers

1. treat (act or behave); treatment (behavior toward someone); commit (dedicate); commitment (deep loyalty or dedication)
2. a. treatment b. commitment c. agreement

Grammar Focus

Recognize Regular and Irregular Simple Past Tense Verbs

Use prior knowledge Have students form small groups and write down as many irregular past tense verbs as they can in five minutes. Compare lists, correcting any verbs that are misspelled.

Answers

1. a. sent b. took
2. *Example:* I read a science fiction book. I washed my brother's car.

ASSESS

Ask: What did you have for breakfast? How did Rosa get to work every day?

Word Study

Recognize the Suffix -ment

Remember, a suffix is a group of letters added to a root word. The suffix -*ment* changes verbs into nouns.

1. Copy and complete the chart. Use a dictionary to help you.
2. Copy and complete the following sentences with a noun from the chart.
   a. They <u>treat</u> their dogs well. The dogs receive good ____ .
   b. Elena <u>committed</u> herself to helping people read. She has a ____ to these people.
   c. Li and Ken <u>agreed</u> to stop fighting. They reached an ____ .

Verb	Meaning	+ ment ⇒ Noun	Meaning
agree	have the same idea	agreement	a decision between two or more people
treat			
commit			

The Heinle Newbury House Dictionary　　Activity Book p. 156　　Student CD-ROM

Grammar Focus

Recognize Regular and Irregular Simple Past Tense Verbs

Simple past tense verbs describe an action that already happened.

Regular simple past tense verbs end in -*ed*. **Irregular simple past tense** verbs do not end in -*ed*. They are formed in different ways. Look at the chart.

1. Complete these sentences with the past tense of the verb in parentheses.
   a. Rosa's mother ____ her to school in Montgomery. (send)
   b. She ____ the bus to work. (take)
2. Write two sentences about what you did last weekend.

Base Verb	Past Tense
Regular	
walk	walked
answer	answered
call	called
Irregular	
send	sent
take	took
have	had

Activity Book pp. 157–158　　Student Handbook　　Student CD-ROM

MULTI-LEVEL OPTIONS *From Reading to Writing*

Newcomer Have students draw a storyboard of events in their person's biography. Help them write answers to questions 1. a and b.

Beginning Have students draw a cartoon strip that shows an important event in the life of their person. Help them write captions they can add in speech bubbles.

Intermediate Have students exchange biographies with a partner. Students should say what style their partner's biography is written in (formal or informal). Working together, students should then rewrite one of the paragraphs in a different style, either more conversational or more formal.

Advanced Have students exchange biographies with a partner. Reviewers should check for an introduction, two important events, and a conclusion. They should also check that the correct forms of regular and irregular verbs are used to tell about past events.

From Reading to Writing

Write a Biography

Write a short biography of someone you know. Your biography will be three paragraphs long.

1. Interview the person and ask these questions. Summarize what the person says on note cards.
   a. What is your name?
   b. When and where were you born?
   c. What are two important events in your life? When did these events happen?
   d. What three things do you like to do?
2. Organize your note cards in chronological order.
3. Write an introduction. Tell who the person is.
4. Write the body of your biography. Describe two important events in the person's life.
5. Write a conclusion. Tell what the person likes to do.
6. Use regular and irregular simple past tense verbs to tell about past events.

Activity Book
p. 159

Student Handbook

Across Content Areas

Learn About Constitutional Amendments

The U.S. Constitution promises certain rights (freedoms) to all Americans. People can add **amendments** (changes) to the U.S. Constitution. These amendments change old laws or add new laws. The U.S. Constitution has more than 20 amendments. Here are a few:

The First Amendment gives Americans the right to say and write what they want.

The Thirteenth Amendment ended slavery in the United States.

The Nineteenth Amendment gives women the right to vote.

Match each statement with the amendment it describes.

1. I am upset about that new law. I am going to write a letter to the newspaper about it.
2. When Rosa turns 18, she will vote for the President of the United States.
3. All people must be paid for the work they do.

Activity Book
p. 160

Chapter 1 Rosa Parks **299**

From Reading to Writing

Write a Biography

1. **Small group work** Before students write, have them tell their biographies in small groups. Encourage them to ask questions and give suggestions for improvement.
2. **Multi-level options** See MULTI-LEVEL OPTIONS on p. 298.

Across Content Areas: Social Studies

Learn About Constitutional Amendments

Discuss examples of rights *Ask: What examples can you think of relating to the First Amendment? Can you think of an example of freedom of speech? Can people say what they want on the radio or in a demonstration? What about freedom of the press, which is to write what you want?*

Answers
1. First Amendment
2. Nineteenth Amendment
3. Thirteenth Amendment

 **ASSESS**

In small groups, have students list what is usually included in a biography.

Reteach and Reassess

Text Structure Draw a two-column chart with *Biography* as the heading and these four row labels: *Events, Dates, People and Places, Chronological Order.* Ask students to fill in the explanations of each item in the right-hand column.

Reading Strategy Write on the board: *It doesn't snow much here. When it does snow, school is canceled. School was canceled yesterday.* Ask students to make an inference based on text evidence. (It snowed yesterday.)

Elements of Literature *Say: I'm giving you a lot of homework.* Write on the board: *If you already have too much homework, tough. If you already have too much homework, that's unfortunate for you.* **Ask:** *Which sentence sounds more formal?*

Reassess Write on index cards: *Events, Dates, People/Places, Chronological Order, Inference, Style.* Display one card at a time, asking students to provide examples of each from "Rosa Parks."

CHAPTER 2

Into the Reading

The Gettysburg Address

a historical narrative
by Kenneth Richards,

including a speech
by Abraham Lincoln

Chapter Materials

Activity Book: *pp. 161–168*
Audio: *Unit 5, Chapter 2; CD 3, Track 2*
Student Handbook
Student CD-ROM: *Unit 5, Chapter 2*
Teacher Resource Book: *Lesson Plan, Teacher Resources, Reading Summary, Activity Book Answer Key*
Teacher Resource CD-ROM
Assessment Program: *Quiz, pp. 77–78; Teacher and Student Resources, pp. 115–144*
Assessment CD-ROM
Transparencies
The Heinle Newbury House Dictionary/CD-ROM
Web site: http://visions.heinle.com

Objectives

Preview Have a student read the objectives.
Ask: Which objectives do you already know something about?

Use Prior Knowledge

Explore Your Knowledge of Civil Wars

Recall previous reading Direct students to p. 166 to review "The Voyage of the Lucky Dragon." *Ask: Was the war in this story a civil war?* (yes) *When a civil war is over, there are usually bad feelings between the two groups. What in the story is evidence of this?* (The young man treats the family harshly and insults them.)

Answers
2. **a.** true **b.** true **c.** false **d.** true

Objectives

Reading Summarize and paraphrase as you read a historical narrative and a speech.

Listening and Speaking Give a speech.

Grammar Identify clauses with subject + verb + object + infinitive.

Writing Write a news article.

Content Math: Use vocabulary to answer math problems.

Use Prior Knowledge

Explore Your Knowledge of Civil Wars

What do you know about civil wars?

1. With a partner, copy the chart on a piece of paper.
2. Decide whether each of the following statements is true or false. Write the statement in the correct place on the chart.
   a. In a civil war, people in the same country fight against each other.
   b. The United States had a civil war in the 1800s.
   c. In a civil war, people in different countries fight against each other.
   d. After some civil wars, one country is divided into two countries.

True Statements	False Statements

300   Unit 5   Freedom

MULTI-LEVEL OPTIONS *Build Vocabulary*

Newcomer Direct students' attention to the drawing in the word square for *address* on p. 301. *Ask: Is an address given on paper? Is it spoken or read aloud?* Have students draw themselves giving an address to the class. Students may include one word in a speech bubble to tell what the address would be about.

Beginning Direct students' attention to the word square for *address* on p. 301. Ask them if they know of another meaning for the word. (location) Have students make a word square for the homonym of *address*. (*Example:* picture of an addressed envelope; sentence: My address is 12 First Street.)

Intermediate Have students work in pairs. Ask each pair to think of an orator. He/She can be someone they know or a famous person. Instruct each pair to give a brief address, naming the orator, what she/he speaks or spoke about, and what makes her/him a good orator.

Advanced Have students find synonyms for the words on p. 301. Tell students to use their prior knowledge to write one sentence about the U.S. Civil War, or civil wars in general, for each synonym. Students can read their sentences to the class.

Build Background

The U.S. Civil War

In a civil war, two or more groups from the same country fight against each other. There was a civil war in the United States from 1861 to 1865. The states were divided into two groups, the Confederacy and the Union. The Confederacy wanted to form its own country. One reason was that the Confederacy wanted to allow people to have slaves. The Union wanted all states to stay part of the United States. It also wanted to end slavery.

In July of 1863, the Union and the Confederacy fought a horrible three-day battle at Gettysburg, Pennsylvania. The Union army won. The Confederacy lost many men and supplies. This helped the Union win the war.

Content Connection

Abraham Lincoln was the president during the U.S. Civil War. He served from 1861 to 1865.

Build Vocabulary

Use Word Squares to Remember Meaning

Word squares can help you remember new words.

1. Find the definitions of these words. Use a dictionary.
   a. undivided   b. orator
2. Make a word square for each word.
3. With a partner, ask each other the meanings of the words.
4. Make more word squares as you read "The Gettysburg Address."

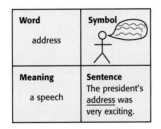

Word	Symbol
address	
Meaning	**Sentence**
a speech	The president's address was very exciting.

The Heinle Newbury House Dictionary   Activity Book p. 161   Student CD-ROM

Chapter 2 The Gettysburg Address **301**

Content Connection
Technology

Build Vocabulary Ask students to think of five words that are related to war. If they need help, start them with *battle, uniform,* and *weapon.* Have them use an electronic dictionary to find a definition for each word. Then have them make a word square for each word.

Learning Styles
Interpersonal

Build Background Have students divide into two groups: the Union and the Confederacy. Give each group three minutes to explain their position. (The Confederacy wants independence, slavery. The Union wants a united country, no slavery. Have them include any additional facts students know.) Then have the groups negotiate possible compromises and solutions. *Ask: How might the other side feel? Why? What can we do to please both sides?*

Build Background

The U.S. Civil War

1. **Analyze facts** Have each student write two questions about the paragraph. Ask and answer questions with the class.
2. **Use a map** Have students locate Gettysburg. Then ask them to identify as many individual Union and Confederate states as they can.
3. **Content Connection** Lincoln was one of the greatest American politicians and is famous for his humanitarian instincts, brilliant speeches, and unusual political skills. He was a great orator and was able to express essential concepts in simple and direct terms.

Build Vocabulary

Use Word Squares to Remember Meaning

Teacher Resource Book: *Personal Dictionary, p. 63*

1. **Brainstorm images** Have students brainstorm different images for their word squares for *undivided* and *orator.*
2. **Reading selection vocabulary** You may want to introduce the glossed words in the reading selection before students begin reading. Key words: *cemetery, dedicate, ceremony, battlefield, achievement, liberty, vain.* Instruct students to write the words with correct spelling and their definitions in their Personal Dictionaries. Have them pronounce each word and divide it into syllables.
3. **Multi-level options** See MULTI-LEVEL OPTIONS on p. 300.

Answers
1. a. united b. skilled public speaker

ASSESS

Have students write a sentence about the U.S. Civil War or Abraham Lincoln.

Text Structure

Historical Narrative and Speech

1. **Relate to personal experience** *Ask: When do we sometimes hear prepared speeches?* (elections, ceremonies, graduations) *Can you describe a speech that you have heard? Was the person a good speaker? Why?*
2. **Multi-level options** See MULTI-LEVEL OPTIONS below.

Reading Strategy

Summarize and Paraphrase

Apply strategy Have students read aloud Build Background, paragraph 2 (p. 301). Then help them find the key information to summarize and paraphrase. (For example, summary: The Union won the Battle of Gettysburg, which was the turning point of the war against the Confederacy; paraphrase: The Union won the three-day battle at Gettysburg against the Confederacy. Many Confederate soldiers died, and this gave the Union an advantage to win the war. It was in July, 1863.)

ASSESS

Have groups write a list of features of a speech.

Text Structure

Historical Narrative and Speech

"The Gettysburg Address" is a **historical narrative.** It tells about an important speech in United States history. It also contains the words of a famous **speech.** In a speech, a person presents his or her ideas to an audience (people gathered to hear someone talk). People often write speeches down so that they remember what to say and so that others can read them later. Look for the features of a historical narrative and a speech as you read the selection.

Student
CD-ROM

Historical Narrative	
Chronological Order	events usually given in the order in which they happened
Facts	true statements about people, places, and events
Primary Sources	documents, interviews, and other real information from the past
Interpretation	author's explanation of people and events

Speech	
Strong Message	tries to get readers to believe in or do something
Direct Address	uses the pronouns *we* and *us* to speak directly to the audience
Repeated Words	creates a rhythm (a beat, as in music) that may excite the audience

Reading Strategy

Summarize and Paraphrase

When you **summarize,** you tell the most important ideas of a text. You also use your own words.

When you **paraphrase,** you restate a text or a part of a text in your own words. You include all or most of the information in the text.

Summarize and paraphrase as you read "The Gettysburg Address." This will help you recall information.

Student
CD-ROM

Text	
The train arrived in the small town just as the sun was setting. A carriage drove Mr. Lincoln to the home of Mr. Wills, where he was to spend the night. . . . After dinner, the president went to his room to work on his speech.	
Summary	**Paraphrase**
Lincoln arrived and went to the house where he would sleep. He worked on his speech.	Lincoln arrived in the small town by train in the early evening. He was going to spend the night at the home of Mr. Wills. He had dinner there, and then he spent some time on his speech.

302 **Unit 5** Freedom

MULTI-LEVEL OPTIONS *Text Structure*

Newcomer Have students draw a historical narrative of a recent day in their own lives. Have them draw themselves getting up, going to school, sitting in class, and so on. Students should include drawings of the people involved in their day. Finally, have them describe what the day was like by drawing a happy face, bored face, angry face, and so on.

Beginning Write on the board: *chronological order* and *facts.* Discuss a recent event at school. Help students fill in the chart with information from the discussion. *Ask: What happened first? What happened next? Who was there? Where was it held? What did you think of the event?*

Intermediate Have students work in small groups to discuss a recent performance or sports event that took place at school. Have each group complete the *Historical Narrative* chart on p. 302 above. Then have students share their event with another group.

Advanced Have students work in pairs to write a speech to convince the class to do something, such as join a school club or recycle. Pairs should complete a *Speech* chart from p. 302 above. Have each student deliver half the speech. Ask the class to comment on the strength of the message and the rhythm of the delivery.

The Gettysburg Address

a historical narrative by Kenneth Richards,
including a speech by Abraham Lincoln

303

Reading Selection Materials

Audio: *Unit 5, Chapter 2; CD 3, Track 2*
Teacher Resource Book: *Reading Summary, pp. 105–106*
Transparencies: #42, *Reading Summary*

Suggestions for Using Reading Summary

- Introduce new vocabulary or cognates.
- Cut the summary into strips, or jumble the sentences on an overhead transparency. Students put the sentences in order.
- Practice the reading strategy.
- Students read aloud or with a partner.
- Students paraphrase the summary.
- Students do a cloze activity.
- Students create a visual or graphic organizer, such as a timeline or storyboard, to illustrate the summary.
- Students paraphrase the summary.

Preview the Selection

1. **Interpret the image** Have students look at the photo. *Ask: Who is this man? Why is he standing? Who are the people sitting in chairs? What kind of expression does the man have?*
2. **Connect to theme** *Say: The unit theme is freedom. This memorial reminds people of the human price of freedom.*

Content Connection
The Arts

Have students work in small groups. Have them research different paintings, pictures, and illustrations of Abraham Lincoln in the library or on the Internet. Instruct them to compare and contrast their findings. *Ask: Which do you like best? Why? How do they show different aspects of President Lincoln?*

Learning Styles
Intrapersonal

Direct students to the painting on this page. *Say: Imagine that you are Abraham Lincoln. You are about to give a speech about national unity and slavery.* Ask students to think about what they would see, hear, and feel in this situation. Have them record their thoughts in their Reading Logs.

Teacher Resource Book: *Reading Log, p. 64*

Read the Selection

1. **Shared reading** Play the audio. Have students join in when they can.
2. **Ask questions to understand content** On the board, write: *Who? What? Where? When? Why? How?* Have students work in two groups to write questions about the selection. Direct both groups to use each question word at least once. When they are done, have groups exchange and answer the questions.

Sample Answer to Guide Question
Mr. Wills wrote a letter to President Lincoln, asking him to come and speak at the dedication of the Soldiers' National Cemetery.

See Teacher Edition pp. 434–436 for a list of English-Spanish cognates in the reading selection.

Prologue

Many Union soldiers died in the Battle of Gettysburg. Union leaders built a **cemetery** in Gettysburg to bury these Union soldiers. This cemetery is called Soldiers' National Cemetery. This text begins right after the cemetery was built.

1   When the work was finished, the townspeople were very pleased. The brave men who had died now had an **honorable** resting place. "We must **dedicate** the cemetery," Mr. Wills said. "I will ask important people to speak at the ceremony."

2   A few days later, in Washington, D.C., President Lincoln received a letter from Mr. Wills. He asked the president to come to Gettysburg and make a few "**appropriate** remarks" at the dedication of the Soldiers' National Cemetery.

> **Summarize**
> Summarize this paragraph in one or two sentences.

Audio
CD 3. Tr. 2

3   President Lincoln was a very busy man. The war was still going on and many matters needed his close personal attention. It was very difficult for him to get away from Washington, even for a little while. But he knew, perhaps more than anyone, how important the Battle of Gettysburg had been. He wrote Mr. Wills that somehow he would find the time to come to Gettysburg.

4   The night before he was to leave Washington for the dedication, President Lincoln began working on his speech. He knew that the main speaker at the **ceremony** would be

---

cemetery   a graveyard, a place to bury the dead
honorable   respectable
dedicate   formally open in honor of someone

appropriate   correct, suitable
ceremony   a formal event usually with rituals (words and actions done many times before)

304   **Unit 5**   Freedom

MULTI-LEVEL OPTIONS *Read the Selection*

Newcomer Read the prologue aloud. Then play the audio. *Ask: Is this cemetery for soldiers from WWI?* (no) *Did President Lincoln agree to speak?* (yes) *Did Lincoln write a long speech?* (no) *Was Lincoln the only speaker at the ceremony?* (no)

Beginning Read the prologue aloud. Then play the audio. *Ask: Where was the cemetery built?* (Gettysburg, Pennsylvania) *Who did Mr. Wills ask to speak at the ceremony?* (President Lincoln) *Why did Lincoln agree to speak?* (The battle had been very important.) *Why did Lincoln write a short speech?* (He wasn't the only speaker.)

Intermediate Have students do a paired reading. *Ask: What was the ceremony for?* (to dedicate the cemetery) *Was it the end of the war?* (No, the war was still going on.) *Why did Lincoln rewrite his speech?* (He felt it didn't express the meaning of freedom or how much the country owed the soldiers.)

Advanced Have students read in pairs, alternating paragraphs. Write these events out of order, and ask students to put them in order: *Battle of Gettysburg, building of the cemetery, dedication ceremony, Lincoln travels to Gettysburg, Lincoln rewrites his speech.* Then ask students to give an oral narrative of the events.

Edward Everett of Massachusetts, the most famous **orator** in America. He realized that Mr. Everett would talk for a long time and that there would be other speakers, so Lincoln decided to make his speech very short. Because he was aware that newspapers all over the country would print his speech, he wanted it to be perfect. He worked for hours, writing and rewriting the sentences. When he had finished the first draft, he went to bed.

5 Early the next morning, the president **boarded** the special train that was to carry him and other **dignitaries** to Gettysburg. As the countryside of Maryland and Pennsylvania rolled past his window, Lincoln thought of the war. He knew that peace would eventually come to the land and that the Union would remain strong and **undivided** because

of the efforts of brave men such as those buried at Gettysburg. "My speech does not express how deeply I feel about these men," he thought. "I must rewrite it. I want people everywhere to understand what freedom means to us and how much we owe to the brave soldiers who died at Gettysburg."

Summarize
Summarize this paragraph.

The train arrived in the small town just as the sun was setting. A carriage drove Mr. Lincoln to the home of Mr. Wills, where he was to spend the night. Mr. Everett was a guest in the house also. After dinner, the president went to his room to work on his speech. 6

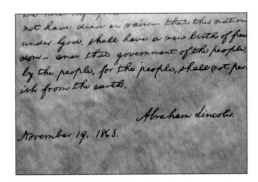

---

orator   a person who is very good at giving speeches
boarded   got on a train, ship, or other vehicle
dignitaries   important people, especially high officials
undivided   complete, whole

Chapter 2   The Gettysburg Address   **305**

---

9 Punctuation

Apostrophes for plural possession

Write on the board: *a soldier's hat/two soldiers' hats.* Explain that the plural of *soldier* is *soldiers.* Tell students that when they want to show possession with a plural noun that ends in *s,* they only need to add an apostrophe after the *s.* Direct students' attention to paragraph 2. Point out that the possessive form of the plural, *soldiers,* is *soldiers',* as in *Soldiers' National Cemetery.*

Apply Make a three-column chart on the board with these column headings: *Singular Noun, Plural Noun, Plural Possession.* In the first column, write these words: *leader, president, speaker, orator.* Have students fill in the plural forms of the nouns. Then have students write sentences, using the plural possessive form.

Read the Selection

1. **Shared reading** Play the audio. Have students join in when they can.

2. **Discuss character** *Ask: Can you think of words to describe President Lincoln?* (serious, thoughtful, firm, wise, caring) Write the words students suggest on the board, and perhaps add a few more. Then have students work in small groups and find text evidence to support two of the adjectives. When students have finished, have volunteers report to the class. (*Example: Lincoln was a thoughtful man because, even though he was very busy, he understood how important it was to give a good speech.*)

Sample Answer to Guide Question
Lincoln finished his speech after midnight. It was a very short speech—only two pages.

7 During the evening, a group of people came to sing for the president beneath his window. Lincoln opened the window to wave, and then he spoke a few words to the crowd that had gathered. When they left, he returned to his work.

8 It was past midnight before the speech was finished. Lincoln had written it on two pieces of lined paper. There were only 269 words. "It is what I would call a short, short speech," he said. Then he went to bed.

> **Paraphrase**
>
> Paraphrase this paragraph. Put it in your own words.

9 At eleven o'clock the next morning, November 19, 1863, a parade to the cemetery began. **Congressmen,** generals, and governors were in the **procession,** as well as brass bands and **military units.** Mr. Lincoln rode on a handsome horse. He wore a black suit, white gloves, and his tall, black **stovepipe hat.**

10 Nearly every citizen of Gettysburg had come to see the parade and hear the speeches. The shops and the schools in the town were closed and thousands of people lined the streets to watch the procession pass.

11 The parade **wound** slowly out of the town and up the road leading to the cemetery. Most of the people had never seen the president before. They cheered as he passed, and he waved his hand or nodded his head. The crowd followed the procession to the **ridge.**

Congressmen members of the U.S. Congress, a group that makes the nation's laws
procession a parade
military units groups of soldiers

stovepipe hat a type of tall hat
wound curved around
ridge a long, narrow, high piece of land

306 **Unit 5** Freedom

MULTI-LEVEL OPTIONS *Read the Selection*

Newcomer *Ask: Was the ceremony held in the town center?* (no) *Did Lincoln ride a horse in the parade to the cemetery?* (yes) *Was there music at the ceremony?* (yes) *Did Lincoln speak first?* (no)

Beginning *Ask: When did Lincoln finish writing his speech?* (after midnight on the night before the ceremony) *On what date was the dedication ceremony?* (November 19, 1863) *What were the colors of the decorations?* (red, white, and blue) *Who spoke before Lincoln?* (Mr. Edward Everett)

Intermediate *Ask: How long was Lincoln's speech?* (short—269 words) *How did he get to the ceremony?* (on a horse in a procession) *How did the ceremony begin?* (A band played, followed by a prayer, then another band.) *How long was Mr. Everett's speech?* (nearly two hours)

Advanced *Ask: Do you think Lincoln was popular?* (Yes. Nearly everyone in town came to greet him.) *How might the parade be different if it took place today?* (The president would be in a car; TV would be broadcasting the event.)

12 At last the parade reached the cemetery. A **platform** decorated with red, white, and blue **bunting** had been built for the speakers. President Lincoln climbed the steps to the platform and took his seat in the front row. In the distance, he could see the great **battlefield.** The sounds of fighting were gone now and autumn leaves covered the ground. There was peace at Gettysburg.

Summarize

Would you include the colors of the bunting in a summary of this paragraph? Why or why not?

---

13 A band played to open the ceremony. When the music ended, the crowd grew silent as a minister said a prayer. Following the prayer, the United States Marine Band played and then, one after another, speakers rose from their seats to **address** the crowd. They told the people that the cemetery was a grand **achievement** and that the nation was very proud of the citizens of Gettysburg. Soon it was time for Mr. Everett to speak.

14 Mr. Everett had a powerful voice and even those farthest from the platform could hear his words. He spoke for nearly two hours. When he was finished, a choir sang a **hymn** that had been written especially for the occasion. At last, the president was introduced.

Edward Everett

---

platform a flat, raised structure for making speeches
bunting decorations made of cloth or paper
battlefield a place where battles are fought

address speak to
achievement success
hymn a song of praise

Chapter 2 The Gettysburg Address **307**

Read the Selection

1. **Discuss character's motivation** *Ask: Why did Lincoln want to give a short speech?* (He knew that the main speaker would give a very long speech.) *Why did he rewrite his speech?* (He wanted it to really express how important freedom was and how deeply he felt about the soldiers who died.)
2. **Paired reading** Play the audio. Have students reread aloud with a partner.
3. **Multi-level options** See MULTI-LEVEL OPTIONS on p. 306.

Sample Answer to Guide Question
No. The colors are details and are not important to the main idea.

🔖 Punctuation

Using commas in dates

Direct students to the date in paragraph 9: *November 19, 1863.* Ask students to tell you the rule for using commas in dates. (Commas are used to separate the day from the year when dates are written out.) Write today's date on the board and ask the class to tell you where to put the comma.

Apply Have students write the dates of important events, paying attention to where they place the comma. Students can write

their birthday, relatives' birthdays, their favorite holiday, the start of vacation, and so on.

Read the Selection

1. **Listen for tone** Play the audio. *Say: Even if you don't understand all of the words, you can understand the tone of the speech by listening. What is the tone of this speech? Is it serious, sad, or hopeful? How does it make you feel?*

2. **Choral reading** Have students do a choral reading of the speech as they listen to the audio again.

Sample Answer to Guide Question
This is the right thing to do.

15   Lincoln rose slowly from his chair and put on his steel-rimmed glasses. He had a kindly, but **careworn,** face. When the crowd had grown silent, the president began to read from the two handwritten pages he held in his hand.

16   Four score and seven years ago our fathers brought forth on this continent, a new nation, **conceived** in **Liberty,** and dedicated to the **proposition** that all men are created equal.

17   Now we are **engaged** in a great civil war, testing whether that nation, or any nation so conceived and so dedicated, can long **endure.** We are met on a great battlefield of that war. We have come to dedicate a portion of that field, as a final resting place for those who here gave their lives that that nation might live. It is altogether **fitting** and proper that we should do this.

> **Paraphrase**
> Write the last sentence of this paragraph in your own words.

careworn showing signs of worry and tiredness	**engaged** involved
conceived thought of, created	**endure** survive, last
liberty freedom	**fitting** suitable, right
proposition plan, idea	

308   Unit 5   Freedom

MULTI-LEVEL OPTIONS *Read the Selection*

Newcomer *Ask: Did Lincoln speak for very long?* (no) *Did he believe in liberty?* (yes) *Did he believe that all men are created equal?* (yes) *Did he think we should forget the soldiers who died in battle?* (no)

Beginning *Ask: Who were some of the "fathers" of our country?* (Washington, Franklin, Jefferson) *When was the country born?* (1776) *Why did Lincoln say it was important to continue to fight?* (to honor the dead and to ensure freedom)

Intermediate *Ask: What are the ideas on which the country was based?* (liberty; all men are created equal; government of the people, by the people, for the people) *What document signifies the birth of the United States and when was it written?* (the Declaration of Independence, 1776) *Did Lincoln think his speech would be remembered?* (no)

Advanced *Ask: What was the Civil War testing?* (whether or not a nation based on liberty and equality could survive) *What did Lincoln say needed to be remembered?* (the efforts of the soldiers who died and what they were fighting for) *What did he ask those still alive to do?* (to be dedicated to the job the soldiers started)

18 But, in a larger sense, we can not dedicate—we can not **consecrate**—we can not **hallow**—this ground. The brave men, living and dead, who struggled here, have consecrated it, far above our poor power to add or **detract.** The world will little note, nor long remember what we say here, but it can never forget what they did here. It is for us the living, rather, to be dedicated here to the unfinished work which they who fought here have thus far so **nobly** advanced. It is rather for us to be here dedicated to the great task remaining before us—that from these honored dead we take increased **devotion** to that cause for which they gave the last full measure of devotion— that we here highly resolve that these dead shall not have died in **vain**—that this nation, under God, shall have a new birth of freedom—and that government of the people, by the people, for the people, shall not **perish** from the earth.

19 What did President Lincoln mean when he said "Four score and seven years ago"? The word *score* means twenty years, so "four score and seven years" would be eighty-seven years. In

1863, "eighty-seven years ago" would have been the year 1776. This was the year that the Declaration of Independence was written and the United States of America was born. When Lincoln spoke of "our fathers," he was referring to George Washington, Benjamin Franklin, Thomas Jefferson, and all the other political leaders who helped to **found** the new nation.

> **Paraphrase**
>
> Paraphrase the last sentence of this paragraph.

consecrate make something holy or sacred
hallow honor something as holy or sacred
detract take something good from; lower the value of something
nobly in a way that shows goodness

devotion dedication, loyalty
vain for nothing, without success
perish be killed in a sudden manner
found start and support something

Chapter 2 The Gettysburg Address **309**

A Capitalization

Historical documents

Tell students that the first letter of each main word in the name of historical documents is always capitalized. *Ask: What historical document is also the title of the reading?* (the Gettysburg Address) *What other historical document is named in paragraph 19?* (the Declaration of Independence) *What letters are capitalized?* (*D* and *I*) *Why is the* o *in* of *not capitalized?* (It's not a main word.)

Apply Have students do an Internet search using the key words *historical*

documents. Tell students to note the capitalization of the titles of these documents. Ask students to find another historical document written by Lincoln in 1864. (the Emancipation Proclamation)

Read the Selection

1. **Choral reading** Play the audio of the speech. Then have students do a choral reading. Have them read the rest of the text silently.
2. **Multi-level options** See MULTI-LEVEL OPTIONS on p. 308.

Sample Answer to Guide Question
When Lincoln said "our fathers," he meant the politicians who helped start the nation.

Read the Selection

1. **Reciprocal reading** Play the audio. Divide students into small groups. Have students take turns reading a short passage, asking questions about it to group members, and asking the group to summarize.
2. **Group work** Have students work in groups to summarize the paragraph in the Guide Question. They can write the answer collaboratively.

Sample Answer to Guide Question

Lincoln's speech emphasized that people need to remember that the soldiers died to save the democratic government, and the Union must win the war to make their deaths matter.

---

20   What did Lincoln mean when he said the war was "testing our nation"? When the United States was born, the founding fathers created a new kind of government. It was founded on the belief that all men have an equal right to liberty and freedom. As Lincoln said, the citizens of the United States have a government of the people, by the people, and for the people. In other words, they **govern** themselves by free **elections.** Many people thought that this kind of government could not last very long. Lincoln was saying that the Union had to win the war in order to prove that a nation founded on this **principle** could last.

  The president's speech **stressed** that it was not enough to just honor the soldiers who had fought at Gettysburg; but that we must not forget the reasons why they fought and died there. The soldiers gave their lives to save our government and our way of life. Lincoln was saying that Americans must work even harder now for the same cause; that unless the Union won the war and the nation was **preserved,** the soldiers would have died for nothing. 21

> **Summarize**
> Summarize this paragraph.

Plaque with Lincoln's Gettysburg Address

---

govern   rule a country, city, and so on
elections   events when people vote for or against someone or something

principle   a basic belief
stressed   emphasized, put importance on
preserved   maintained, kept in good condition

310   **Unit 5**   Freedom

MULTI-LEVEL OPTIONS *Read the Selection*

Newcomer *Ask: Did the people clap after Lincoln's speech?* (yes) *Did the Union win the Civil War?* (yes) *Did Lincoln live long after the war ended?* (no)

Beginning *Ask: How did the audience react to Lincoln's speech?* (They applauded.) *Who did Lincoln want to win the Civil War?* (the Union) *Who won?* (the Union) *In what year did the war end?* (1865) *Did Lincoln live to enjoy the peace?* (No. He was shot and killed a few days after the war ended.)

Intermediate *Ask: What was new about the U.S. government?* (the belief that all men have an equal right to freedom) *Why was it important that the Union win the war?* (to prove that a nation based on free elections could last) *What was the result of the Civil War?* (The country was reunited and slavery was ended.)

Advanced *Ask: What were the soldiers protecting by fighting?* (our government of free elections and our way of life) *Were the soldiers' sacrifices honored?* (yes, because the Union won the war) *How might the country be different today if the Confederacy had won the Civil War?* (There might still be slavery.)

22 The people **applauded** when the president's speech was finished. Then everyone joined in singing a hymn. A final prayer was said, and the ceremony ended. Mr. Lincoln **mounted** his horse, and he and the other dignitaries rode down the hill to the town.

Paraphrase

Paraphrase this paragraph.

Epilogue

The Union won the Civil War. The country was reunited, and slavery was ended. Abraham Lincoln was shot and killed in 1865, a few days after the Civil War ended.

---

applauded clapped their hands in approval

mounted climbed on

About the Author

Kenneth Richards (born 1926)

Kenneth Richards has been interested in the U.S. Civil War since he was a boy. Members of his family fought for the Union at the Battle of Gettysburg. Richards has written many books and articles about the Civil War.

➤ Why do you think Kenneth Richards wrote "The Gettysburg Address"? To inform, to entertain, or to persuade? What strategies do you think he used to gather the information to write this selection?

Chapter 2 The Gettysburg Address **311**

 Spelling

Qu for the /kw/ sound

Tell students that *qu* is pronounced like *kw*. Refer students to the word *equal* in paragraph 16 and model the pronunciation, asking students to repeat after you. Have students suggest other words that have this sound (quiz, question, equality, equator, queen, and so on).

Evaluate Your Reading Strategy

Summarize and Paraphrase *Say: You have practiced an important reading strategy. Now you can decide how well you have done. Does this statement describe how you read?*

After I read a paragraph, I summarize the most important ideas and paraphrase the text in my own words. Summarizing and paraphrasing help me remember these important ideas.

Read the Selection

1. **Reread for increased understanding** Now that students have read the explanations about the speech, have them reread the speech starting on p. 308.
2. **Read dramatically** Play the audio for the address again. Have students pay attention to the intonation and timing of the speech. Divide the speech into four sections and have pairs of students practice reading one of the sections aloud. Then have volunteers read sections aloud in front of the class, giving a "presidential" feeling to the speech.
3. **Compose, organize, and revise a letter** Have pairs of students pretend that they were in the audience as Lincoln delivered "The Gettysburg Address." They will work together to write a letter to Abraham Lincoln. They should organize the letter in three paragraphs. In the first paragraph, students should introduce themselves and give their opinion as to whether or not they liked Lincoln's speech. The second paragraph should give facts and evidence as to what was effective or not effective in the speech. The third paragraph should summarize their reactions. Students should read their letter out loud to evaluate its clarity and accuracy, and revise it if necessary.
4. **Multi-level options** See MULTI-LEVEL OPTIONS on p. 310.

Sample Answer to Guide Question
People clapped when his speech was over. After a hymn and a prayer, the ceremony was over, and Lincoln rode away on a horse with other important people.

About the Author

Explain author background *Ask: What can you tell about the author's interest in the Civil War?* (He was especially interested because his ancestors fought in the Battle of Gettysburg.)

Answer
Sample answer: I think the author wrote it to inform readers about the Civil War and Lincoln. I think he first decided which topics he wanted to include. Then he researched those topics.

Across Selections

Ask: What values did Lincoln share with Rosa Parks (p. 287)? (the value of struggling for freedom and the importance of each person's actions)

Beyond the Reading

Reading Comprehension

Question-Answer Relationships

Sample Answers

1. to give a speech at a cemetery dedication
2. November 19, 1863
3. He wrote and revised his first draft. Then he edited it and made it shorter.
4. It was a very important battle, and Lincoln wanted to express how much the nation owed to the soldiers who died.
5. to prove that a nation could be governed by the people
6. It is a famous and moving speech, so it is better to use the real words.
7. I think they felt the same way Lincoln did when he expressed how deeply he felt about the soldiers and how important the nation was.
8. People still think it is an impressive and moving speech because it was proved that a nation governed by the people can succeed.
9. I heard the President of the United States give a speech. It was about what a great nation America is and how strong it is during difficult times. The words the President used and the way he said them had a strong effect on me.
10. The speech engages the listener by using "we," "us," and "our." It also talks about things that are familiar to the listener.

Build Reading Fluency

Adjust Your Reading Rate to Memorize

Demonstrate to students that reading to memorize means adjusting your reading to be slow with stops to review your progress.

Reading Comprehension

Question-Answer Relationships (QAR)

"Right There" Questions

1. **Recall Facts** Why did President Lincoln go to Gettysburg?
2. **Recall Facts** When did the speech take place?

"Think and Search" Questions

3. **Identify Steps in a Process** What steps did President Lincoln take to write his speech?
4. **Identify Cause and Effect** Why did President Lincoln feel that his speech had to be very special?
5. **Identify Main Ideas** Based on his speech, why did Lincoln want the Union to win the war? (Hint: Look at paragraph 20.)

"Author and You" Questions

6. **Understand Genre Features** Why do you think Kenneth Richards includes the actual words of Lincoln's speech?

7. **Make Inferences** President Lincoln spoke after many other people. Even though people had been standing a long time, they cheered after Lincoln's speech. How do you think they felt about the speech?

"On Your Own" Questions

8. **Make Judgments** Why do you think people today still think Lincoln's speech was so great?
9. **Connect Your Experiences** Have you heard a speech on the radio or TV recently that had a strong effect on you? What was it about? What made it have a strong effect on you?
10. **Evaluate Oral Language** Read "The Gettysburg Address" aloud to a partner. Show that you understand. How does the speech engage the listener?

Activity Book
p. 162

Student
CD-ROM

Build Reading Fluency

Adjust Your Reading Rate to Memorize

When you memorize you must adjust your reading rate to read slowly.

1. Reread paragraph 16.

2. Read each line slowly.
3. Practice memorizing the paragraph.
4. In small groups, present the entire speech.

MULTI-LEVEL OPTIONS *Elements of Literature*

Newcomer Replay Lincoln's speech in "The Gettysburg Address." Have students raise their hands when they are made to think of the soldiers who died in the battle. Have pairs practice reading the address aloud, using their voices to show the feelings they have about the content of the address.

Beginning Replay Lincoln's speech in "The Gettysburg Address." Lincoln spoke of the soldiers who died and of the importance of freedom and equality. Have students work in pairs to listen for these references. *Ask:* What feelings do you have when he speaks of the soldiers and when he speaks of freedom and equality?

Intermediate Ask students to reread paragraph 16. Then *say:* Eighty-seven years ago this country was created based on the ideas of freedom and equality. Do these two sentences mean the same thing? How does this different choice of language change the speech? Is it as effective as Lincoln's choice of language? Why or why not?

Advanced Have students work in pairs. Tell one partner to recite the speech. Tell the other to comment on the speaker's delivery. Then have them switch roles. *Ask:* What feelings did the speaker make the listener feel? How did the listener feel about the soldiers? How did she/he feel about the Union's cause?

Listen, Speak, Interact

Give a Speech

Your school is going to dedicate the school flagpole to someone who has contributed a lot to the school. Write and give the dedication speech.

1. Decide who should be honored, for example, a teacher, the principal, or a graduate of your school who is now famous.
2. Write your speech.
   a. Start with a sentence that will get the audience's attention. Use the beginning of Lincoln's "Gettysburg Address" as a model.

   b. Tell why the person should be honored.
   c. Remember that the occasion is formal, the audience is the entire school, and your purpose is to talk about an important person.
   d. Prepare a visual that shows the person's contributions.
3. Give your speech to the class.
   a. Practice your speech before giving it. Ask a partner to evaluate your speech.
   b. Pay attention to your voice. Use the right pitch and tone to make your speech credible (believable).

Elements of Literature

Analyze and Evaluate the Delivery of a Speech

A speech is read aloud before an audience. The words and the presentation of the words—how the speaker uses his or her voice—contribute to the message.

1. Listen to the audio recording of "The Gettysburg Address."
2. Analyze the effect of the speech.
   a. What feelings do you have as you listen to the speech? Why?
   b. How does the speaker's delivery affect your feelings?
   c. What ideas do you get from the speech? How do you react to the ideas? Why?

3. Analyze the speech for the beauty of the language and the writer's skill.
   a. Why does Lincoln say "Four score and seven years ago" instead of "Eighty-seven years ago"?
   b. Why does Lincoln say ". . . we can not dedicate—we can not consecrate—we can not hallow—this ground" instead of ". . . we can not dedicate, consecrate, or hallow this ground"?

Activity Book
p. 163

Student
CD-ROM

 Content Connection
Math

Have students locate Gettysburg, PA, and Washington, D.C., on a map of the United States. Using the scale on the map, have students estimate the number of miles from Washington to Gettysburg. (approx. 70 miles) Tell students that in the mid- to late-1800s, steam trains could reach speeds of up to 60 mph. Have students estimate how long a round-trip train ride might have taken President Lincoln. (approx. 2 hours and 20 minutes)

Learning Styles
Visual

Tell students to pretend they are going to start a new country. Have students work in small groups to draw a map of this new country. Tell them to think about defending their country. Where should the mountains be in relation to the important cities? The lakes? Rivers? Suggest that they use different colors and symbols to indicate these different features. Have each group explain to the class how they decided where to locate these things.

Listen, Speak, Interact

Give a Speech

1. **Brainstorm** Help students think of people who could be honored. Write a list on the board, including one or two imaginary honorees.
2. **Newcomers** Work with these students separately and have them write the speech collaboratively. They can practice giving the speech chorally. Have volunteers lead different groups.

Elements of Literature

Analyze and Evaluate the Delivery of a Speech

1. **Analyze a speech** Play the audio for the speech as many times as students need in order to answer the questions. You may want them to discuss the questions in groups so that students can build on one another's ideas.
2. **Multi-level options** See MULTI-LEVEL OPTIONS on p. 312.

Answers

2. *Example:* **a.** I feel proud that democracy won. **b.** The speaker's tone is very serious and that made me take what he says seriously. **c.** That keeping freedom and democracy alive takes hard work and commitment. This inspired me.
3. **a.** "Four score and seven years ago" is a more imaginative, more poetic-sounding expression. **b.** The repetition adds emphasis.

 **ASSESS**

Have students tell you three strategies they can use in a speech to make it effective.

Word Study

Use the Suffix -or

Distinguish between suffixes -or and -er
Review words that take the suffix -er, such as *teacher, waiter, manager, writer.* Then say a sentence for the class to complete. For example: *A person who conducts is called a. . . .* Have students complete the sentence and spell the word. Also: *instructor, editor, machine operator, surveyor, investigator.*

Answers
2. 1st row: noun (orator); noun meaning (someone who orates) 2nd row: verb (govern); noun meaning (someone who governs)

Grammar Focus

Identify Clauses with Subject + Verb + Object + Infinitive

Identify parts of speech Give students other sentences to identify phrases in. Write: *She wanted her son to stay home. The student asked the librarian to help her. The team wanted the coach to end practice early.*

Answers
1. a. He asked the president to come.
   b. He wanted it to be perfect.

ASSESS

In pairs, have students write three sentences with a subject + verb + object + infinitive construction.

Word Study

Use the Suffix -or

The suffix -or can change verbs into nouns. The suffix means "someone who does something."

Verb		Noun
act	+ -or →	act**or** (someone who acts)

For Verbs Ending in e

Drop the final e before adding the suffix -or.

create + -or → creat**or** (someone who creates)

Verb +	Suffix ⇒	Noun	Noun Meaning
orate +	-or ⇒		
+	-or ⇒	governor	

1. Copy this chart in your Personal Dictionary.
2. Fill in the correct verb and noun. Then write the meanings of each noun. Use a dictionary if needed.

Personal Dictionary   The Heinle Newbury House Dictionary   Activity Book p. 164   Student CD-ROM

Grammar Focus

Identify Clauses with Subject + Verb + Object + Infinitive

A **clause** is a group of words that contains a subject and a verb. Some clauses contain a verb, a subject, an object, and an infinitive.

A **subject** is a noun that does the action. A **verb** is a word that describes an action. An **object** is a word that takes the action of the verb. An **infinitive** contains the word *to* plus a simple verb.

I want you to go home.

I is the subject. *Want* is the verb. *You* is the object. *To go* is the infinitive.

1. Write the following sentences on a piece of paper. Underline the subject once. Underline the verb twice. Circle the object. Draw a box around the infinitive.
   a. He asked the president to come.
   b. He wanted it to be perfect.
2. Write two of your own sentences using these parts of speech.

Activity Book pp. 165–166   Student Handbook   Student CD-ROM

314   Unit 5   Freedom

MULTI-LEVEL OPTIONS *From Reading to Writing*

Newcomer Have students draw the events that occurred in "The Gettysburg Address" to go with the newspaper articles. Remind them to follow chronological order. (battle, building of the cemetery, Mr. Wills writes to Lincoln, Lincoln travels to Gettysburg, the parade, the music, the speeches)

Beginning Have students work in pairs to brainstorm newspaper headlines for the reading. Students may want to look at newspapers or magazines for ideas. *Ask: What headline would make people want to read your articles?*

Intermediate Have students work in pairs to edit the articles. Have pairs check for correct chronological order and accurate facts. Remind students that news articles are different from speeches. Editors should comment on the writers' word choice and ask if the facts are accurate and objective.

Advanced Have students exchange articles with a partner. Editors should check for chronological order and factual accuracy. If writers have not included an example of the subject + verb + object + infinitive form, editors should suggest where one might be used.

From Reading to Writing

Write a News Article

Imagine that you and a partner are newspaper reporters in Gettysburg in 1863. Write a news article about Lincoln's visit and the speech.

1. Organize your ideas.
   a. Review the summaries and paraphrases that you wrote about Lincoln's visit. Review your analyses of the Gettysburg Address on page 313.
   b. Put your ideas in the order in which you want to present them.
2. Compose your news article. Use a computer.
   a. Tell who, what, when, and where it happened. Tell why it was important.

b. Tell about the speech and its effect on the audience.
3. Use the computer to revise, edit, and publish your article.
4. Evaluate how well your news article informs and influences the reader.
5. How does the purpose of your news article compare with Kenneth Richards's historical narrative of the event? Evaluate how the two forms of writing influence and inform.

Activity Book
p. 167

Student Handbook

Across Content Areas

Use Vocabulary to Answer Math Problems

In "The Gettysburg Address," you learned that **score** can mean "20 years." Look at these other words for numbers of years. Use the words to figure out the math problems below.

decade 10 years

century 100 years

millennium 1,000 years

1. Two decades is ____ years.
2. Two score and one century is ____ years.
3. Half a millennium is ____ years.
4. One score minus one decade is ____ years.
5. Which is larger, eight centuries or one millennium?

Activity Book
p. 168

From Reading to Writing

Write a News Article

1. **Collaborative writing** Have students work in pairs or small groups to write their stories. When they are finished, they should proofread their stories and compile them into a classroom newspaper.
2. **Multi-level options** See MULTI-LEVEL OPTIONS on p. 314.

Across Content Areas: Math

Use Vocabulary to Answer Math Problems

Write math word problems Have students make up math problems using the new terms. Students can write the problems in groups and then exchange and answer them.

Answers
1. 20 **2.** 140 **3.** 500 **4.** 10 **5.** one millennium

 **ASSESS**

Ask students to list two differences between writing a newspaper article and writing a research report.

Reteach and Reassess

Text Structure Assign one feature of a historical narrative (chronological order, facts, primary sources, and interpretation) to four groups. Have each group write a definition of their assigned feature. Have volunteers write their group's definition on the board.

Reading Strategy Provide students with a short article, or have them find one in a newspaper or magazine. Have students summarize and paraphrase the article.

Elements of Literature Share the first paragraph of M. L. King Jr.'s "I Have a Dream" speech with the class. Ask students to comment on the beauty and rhythm of the language.

Reassess Create a two-column chart titled *The Gettysburg Address*. Label the columns *Order* and *Facts*. Have students fill in the chart.

So Far from the Bamboo Grove

an excerpt from a novel based on a true story by Yoko Kawashima Watkins

Chapter Materials

Activity Book: *pp. 169–176*
Audio: *Unit 5, Chapter 3; CD 3, Track 3*
Student Handbook
Student CD-ROM: *Unit 5, Chapter 3*
Teacher Resource Book: *Lesson Plan, Teacher Resources, Reading Summary, Activity Book Answer Key*
Teacher Resource CD-ROM
Assessment Program: *Quiz, pp. 79–80; Teacher and Student Resources, pp. 115–144*
Assessment CD-ROM
Transparencies
The Heinle Newbury House Dictionary/CD-ROM
Web site: http://visions.heinle.com

Objectives

Preview Read the objectives. *Ask: What excerpts from novels have we already read?* (*Example:* "How I Survived My Summer Vacation")

Use Prior Knowledge

Describe Getting Help

Teacher think aloud *Say: Many people help me in big and small ways. My neighbor helps when I need a ride somewhere. The school secretary helps me by taking my phone messages.* Have students give other examples.

Objectives

Reading Predict as you read an excerpt from a novel.

Listening and Speaking Present an experience with danger.

Grammar Use the conjunction *so that* to connect ideas.

Writing Write a historical fiction story.

Content Language Arts: Use punctuation and intonation.

Use Prior Knowledge

Describe Getting Help

People help each other all the time. Describe a time when someone helped you do something.

1. Think of how someone has helped you. Did someone help you with your homework? Help you clean the house? Help you carry something heavy?
2. Draw a picture of this person helping you.
3. Label the people and things in the picture.
4. Describe your picture to a partner.
5. Listen carefully as your partner describes his or her picture.

MULTI-LEVEL OPTIONS *Build Vocabulary*

Newcomer If possible, have students work with a partner who speaks a different language. Have them share the drawings they made of getting help. Tell students to write or say the labels for items in their language. Ask for volunteers to teach the group some words from their language using their drawing as a visual.

Beginning Direct students to the Korean and English words on p. 317. Ask them to write those words in other languages they know. Students should work with a partner to understand and pronounce all three versions of the vocabulary.

Intermediate Have students work in two groups. One group takes a class survey and writes down how to say *Thank you* in different languages. The other group writes ways of saying *Go now!* Ask each group to share the survey results with the class. Students who know other languages can assist with correct pronunciation.

Advanced Have students work in pairs to read the Korean sentences on p. 317. Have them decide which word in Korean means "go." (kaseyo) Have them survey the class and record the phrases in other languages.

Build Background

World War II in Korea

World War II was mostly fought in Europe and Asia. It started in 1939 and ended in 1945. Before World War II, Japan took over Korea. Most Koreans did not like this. In 1945, Japan seemed to be losing the war. Many Japanese people living in Korea tried to return to Japan. This was difficult and dangerous because some Koreans felt that the Japanese were enemies.

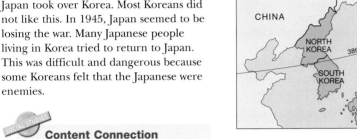

Content Connection
In 1948, Korea was divided into two countries, North Korea and South Korea.

Build Vocabulary

Use Text Features to Understand

The selection you will read includes Korean words. The Korean words are in *italic* type. The English meanings of the Korean words are in **parentheses** (. . .). You can use these text features to learn new words.

Korean word   **English word**
"*Komapsŭmnida* (Thank you)," whispered Hideyo.

Read these sentences. Use the text features to help you understand.

1. The woman said, "*Ŭnhe rŭl ichi an gesŭmnida* (I will not forget your kindness)."
2. He whispered, "*Chosim haesŏ kaseyo* (Go carefully)."
3. "*Chigŭm kaseyo* (Go now)!"

Activity Book
p. 169

Student
CD-ROM

Chapter 3 So Far from the Bamboo Grove **317**

Cultural Connection

Learning Styles
Natural

Build Vocabulary Have students write three sentences with words and phrases from another language. The sentences can be on the theme of getting or giving help. Have students write the non-English words in darker print, or in all capital letters, followed by their meanings in English in parentheses. Provide time for students to share their sentences and teach their classmates some of the words.

Build Background Have students work in small groups. Direct them to the map on this page. Using this map, and others as needed, ask students to imagine they are in North Korea. They must plan their route to Japan. *Ask: What route would you take? What would you pack to make such a trip? What bodies of water would you have to cross? What might the terrain be like? What animals might you run into? How long might it take you?*

Build Background

World War II in Korea

1. **Use prior knowledge** *Ask: What do you know about World War II? What countries were involved? What words or people do you associate with World War II?* Write students' comments on the board.
2. **Use a map** Have students locate Korea, Japan, and China on the map.
3. **Content Connection** Toward the end of the war in the Pacific, the former Soviet Union and the United States agreed to divide Korea at the 38th parallel. North Korea was communist, and South Korea was democratic.

Build Vocabulary

Use Text Features to Understand

Teacher Resource Book: *Personal Dictionary, p. 63*

1. **Understand phonetic symbols** *Say: The mark over certain vowels in the Korean words means that the vowel is short or unstressed.*
2. **Reading selection vocabulary** You may want to introduce the glossed words in the reading selection before students begin reading. Key words: *bamboo, gratitude, thirty-eighth parallel, boundary, farewell, watchtower, searchlight, escapees.* Instruct students to write the words with correct spelling and their definitions in their Personal Dictionaries. Have them pronounce each word and divide it into syllables.
3. **Multi-level options** See MULTI-LEVEL OPTIONS on p. 316.

ASSESS

Have students write two sentences about what they learned about Korea.

Text Structure

Fiction Based on a True Story

1. **Clarify features** Explain to students that although the people and settings are real, what the characters say or do is often the fictional part of the story.
2. **Multi-level options** See MULTI-LEVEL OPTIONS below.

Reading Strategy

Predict

Using prediction *Say: You probably use prediction without even thinking about it. When you watch a TV show, you can often predict what is going to happen, and it can make you laugh, or it can make you afraid. When we can't predict what will happen, the story may be more interesting but also more confusing.*

ASSESS

Have students give an example of using prediction outside of the classroom.

Text Structure

Fiction Based on a True Story

The selection "So Far from the Bamboo Grove" is from a novel. A novel is fiction. It is a story that fills a book. Most novels are made up, but this novel is based on a true story. The story takes place in Korea near the end of World War II. Look for the features of fiction based on a true story as you read the selection.

Fiction Based on a True Story	
Setting	a real time and place in history
Characters	real people
Plot	the main events
Problems	events that happen because of the setting of the story
Problem Resolution	how problems are solved

Student CD-ROM

Reading Strategy

Predict

When you **predict** you guess what will happen next. You use text clues and your experience to predict what will happen in a story. Read this paragraph:

> Sue yawns and looks at her watch. She says, "It's late and I'm tired." Then she stands up.

Look at the chart. Using the clues and your experience, you can predict that Sue will go to sleep.

As you read the selection, predict what will happen next. Share your ideas with the class.

Text Clues	Your Experience	You Predict
Sue yawns. Sue is tired. It is late.	People go to sleep when they are tired.	Sue will go to sleep.

Student CD-ROM

318 Unit 5 Freedom

MULTI-LEVEL OPTIONS *Text Structure*

Newcomer Have students choose an event in their lives that could be made into a novel. It could be as minor as getting up and out of the house in the morning or as significant as a move from one country to another. Help students make charts like the one on p. 318. Students can use words and/or pictures to tell their stories.

Beginning Have students choose an event in their lives that could be made into a novel. It could be as minor as getting up and out of the house in the morning or as significant as a move from one country to another. Help students make charts like the one on p. 318. Then have students use the chart to tell their stories to a partner.

Intermediate Have students think of a novel they have read. Ask them to fill out a chart like the one on p. 318 for the novel. Have students tell a partner about the novel, using the chart as a guide.

Advanced Have students choose a novel they have read and fill out a chart like the one on p. 318. Have them report on the novel to a partner, using the chart as a guide. Partners should write three questions to ask, such as: *Is it based on a true story? Who was your favorite character and why? Would you recommend the novel?*

So Far from the Bamboo Grove

an excerpt from a novel based on a true story

by Yoko Kawashima Watkins

319

Reading Selection Materials

Audio: *Unit 5, Chapter 3; CD 3, Track 3*
Teacher Resource Book: *Reading Summary,*
    pp. 107–108
Transparencies: #43, *Reading Summary*

Suggestions for Using Reading Summary

- Introduce new vocabulary or cognates.
- Cut the summary into strips, or jumble the sentences on an overhead transparency. Students put the sentences in order.
- Practice the reading strategy.
- Students read aloud or with a partner.
- Students paraphrase the summary.
- Students do a cloze activity.
- Students create a visual or graphic organizer, such as a timeline or storyboard, to illustrate the summary.
- Students paraphrase the summary.

Preview the Selection

1. **Interpret the image** Have students look at the illustration. *Ask: What medium is this? Is this a realistic painting? Why? What are the main colors the artist used? What mood or feeling do they create?*
2. **Make an inference from an illustration** *Ask: What can we infer about this boy? How old do you think he is? Do you think he is from a poor family? Why? What do you think his mood is? Why?*
3. **Connect to theme** *Say: The theme of this unit is freedom. In this story, we will read about the danger a boy experiences for freedom.*

Content Connection
Science

Have students work in small groups to do research on bamboo. *Ask: What does it look like? Where does it grow? What is it used for? What is a bamboo grove?* A volunteer from each group should report the findings to the class.

Learning Styles
Intrapersonal

Direct students to the picture on this page. *Say: Imagine that you must leave home and you must carry your belongings. What would you take with you, and why? Would you bring items to help you survive? Would you bring items of sentimental value to help you remember home? What would you miss most about your home? How would you feel as you were leaving?* Have students make a list of the contents of their bags.

Read the Selection

1. **Shared reading** Play the audio. Have students join in when they can.

2. **Identify characters** *Ask: Who are the characters so far?* (Hideyo, Mr. and Mrs. Kim) *Do you think the boy and the adults are related? Why or why not?* (No. They are called "the generous Korean family," not "the boy's family.")

3. **Check comprehension** *Ask: Why do you think he is leaving at night? What did he pack with him? What did Mr. and Mrs. Kim give him to take?*

Sample Answer to Guide Question
He is going on a secret trip. I don't think he will be coming back.

See Teacher Edition pp. 434–436 for a list of English-Spanish cognates in the reading selection.

Audio
CD 3, Tr. 3

Predict

What kind of trip do you think Hideyo is taking? Do you think he will be coming back?

1 But he must go, Hideyo said. As soon as the spring work was finished and when the moon was dark, so that he would not be **spotted.**

2 When the last supper with the **generous** Korean family was finished, he gathered his few belongings. His student's **uniform,** underwear, pants, and socks were washed and folded by Mrs. Kim. Hideyo put the fur coat in the bottom of the **rucksack,** then the family **album** and savings book, then his clothes.

3 Mrs. Kim packed large rice balls in a **bamboo** box and Mr. Kim handed Hideyo a little money. Hideyo tried to refuse the money, for Mr. Kim was a poor farmer who had to give almost all his earnings to the **government,** but Mr. Kim insisted that he carry some Korean money.

spotted seen
generous very giving
uniform a special kind of clothing worn by people belonging to certain groups
rucksack a bag carried on the back

album a book with blank pages for saving photographs and other things
bamboo tall plant of the grass family, used in houses and furniture
government the people who rule a place or country

320 **Unit 5** Freedom

MULTI-LEVEL OPTIONS *Read the Selection*

Newcomer Play the audio. *Ask: Is Mrs. Kim leaving?* (no) *Is Hideyo leaving?* (yes) *Did Mrs. Kim give Hideyo food?* (yes) *Did Mr. Kim give him money?* (yes) *Are they sad?* (yes)

Beginning Read the Reading Summary aloud. Then do a paired reading. *Ask: Were the Kims generous?* (yes) *Were they rich?* (no) *Where did they live?* (on a farm in Korea) *What happened when Hideyo tried to thank them?* (He began to cry.)

Intermediate Have students do a paired reading. *Ask: What is Hideyo taking with him?* (a fur coat, family album, savings book, clothes, food, and some Korean money) *Where did he get the food and money?* (from Mrs. and Mr. Kim) *Why did Mrs. Kim put his things in a burlap bag?* (so he would look like an ordinary Korean, not Japanese)

Advanced Have students read silently. *Ask: What are some examples of the Kims' generosity?* (They feed Hideyo, wash his clothes, pack him food, and give him money.) *What kind of a man do you think Mr. Kim is?* (hard worker, kind, gentle) *Why is it important that Hideyo not look Japanese?* (He's leaving Korea during a war involving Japan.)

4   He wanted to tell Mrs. Kim many things to express his **gratitude,** but the tears came and his chest tightened. Mrs. Kim held his hands and cried, *"Aigo!"* an **expression** of sadness. He shook hands with Mr. Kim, and the hand, rough from years of hard work in the fields, seemed gentle and soft. Mr. Kim, in tears, bit his **chapped** lips and nodded his wrinkled face, as if to say, "Don't say anything. I understand."

5   Then, because a rucksack would give away the fact that he was Japanese, Mrs. Kim put the rucksack in a **burlap** bag tied with a long rope and told him to carry it around his hips like a Korean.

Predict

What might happen to Hideyo if he looks Japanese?

---

gratitude   thankfulness, appreciation
expression   a word or group of words
chapped   dried, cracking

burlap   a rough cloth used to make bags for holding coffee beans, onions, and so on

Chapter 3   So Far from the Bamboo Grove   **321**

Read the Selection

1. **Paired reading** Have students read aloud to each other. Then have them discuss the Guide Question in groups.
2. **Imagine a character's thoughts** *Ask: What do you think Hideyo would like to write to Mr. and Mrs. Kim if he could send them a letter?* (He would thank them for their care and protection.)
3. **Locate derivations using dictionaries** Have students look at these glossed words and determine what words they are derived from: *spotted, chapped.* Have students check the derivations in a print, online, or CD-ROM dictionary.
4. **Multi-level options** See MULTI-LEVEL OPTIONS on p. 320.

Sample Answer to Guide Question
If he looks Japanese, he might be taken as a spy by the police or the authorities.

A Capitalization

Titles before names

Tell students that titles before names are always capitalized. Direct the students to paragraph 3. The title *Mrs.* before *Kim* tells us that she is a married woman. Note that the first letter in the title is capitalized. *Ask: What other title is in this paragraph?* (Mr.) *How is it written?* (capital M) Say that titles that are not followed by a name are *not* capitalized.

Apply Ask students for examples of other titles. (Dr., Ms.) For each example, ask

how the title should be written before a name, and ask what the title means. For example, *Dr. Gonzalez* should be written with a capital *D.* It means that Gonzalez has completed the necessary schooling to be a doctor.

Read the Selection

1. **Reciprocal reading** Play the audio. Divide students into small groups. Have students take turns reading a short passage, asking questions about it to group members, and asking the group to summarize.

2. **Paraphrase** Have students close their books and listen as you read paragraph 7 aloud. Then have students paraphrase the paragraph in their own words.

Sample Answer to Guide Question
I think he will be caught by the Communists *or* I think he will escape.

Predict

What do you think will happen to Hideyo when he tries to cross the river?

6 Hee Cho went with Hideyo as far as the river. Imjŏon, the fourth-largest river in Korea, crosses the **thirty-eighth parallel.** American soldiers controlled southern Korea, and Hideyo knew he would be safer once he crossed this **boundary.** The river was four miles from the Kims' house. As they left the house the sun was about to set. Hideyo kept looking back, waving to Mr. and Mrs. Kim and Hee Wang. Just before they **vanished** into the deep forest he waved a towel three times for a final **farewell.** At their doorway the Kims waved back.

7 The river was well guarded by the **Communists.** From a **watchtower** nearby, a **searchlight** swept over the area, throwing its strong **beam** on the river surface. Hideyo untied his burlap bag and took off all his clothes, even his rubber-soled tabi. He shoved them all into the bag, put the bag on his head, and fastened it to him with the rope. That way, if the bag fell off his head it would still be tied to him.

---

thirty-eighth parallel a line that marks the border between North and South Korea

boundary a line dividing two places

vanished disappeared

farewell good-bye for a long time or forever

Communists people who are part of a group in which all businesses and land are owned by the government

watchtower a tower from which something is guarded

searchlight a strong, movable lamp used for seeing at a distance in the dark

beam a ray of light

322 **Unit 5** Freedom

MULTI-LEVEL OPTIONS *Read the Selection*

Newcomer *Ask: Did Hideyo run to the mountains?* (no) *Did he run to the river?* (yes) *Was it daytime?* (no) *Was it dangerous?* (yes) *Did Hee Cho cross the river?* (no)

Beginning *Ask: Did Hideyo go to the river alone?* (No, Hee Cho went with him.) *How far away was the river?* (four miles) *What was the light on the river?* (a searchlight) *Did Hee Cho continue with him?* (No, they said goodbye at the river.)

Intermediate *Ask: Why was the river an important boundary?* (It separated the Communists in the north from the Americans in the south.) *Was it safe to cross the river?* (No, there was a searchlight and Communist soldiers.) *Was Hee Cho going to cross the river with Hideyo?* (No, they said goodbye at the edge of the river.)

Advanced *Ask: Who do you think Hee Cho and Hee Wang are?* (Hideyo's Korean friends; Mr. and Mrs. Kim's children) *Why did Hideyo think he'd be safer if he crossed the river?* (Americans controlled southern Korea across the river; Communists controlled the side he was on.)

8 He **cast his eyes** onto the dark, wide river and wondered if he could swim across. The thought flashed through his mind that if he was spotted and killed, this running water would be **crimsoned** by his blood.

9 The boys looked at each other. They shook hands.

10 Hee Cho whispered, "*Chosim haesŏ kaseyo* (Go carefully)."

11 "*Komapsŭmnida* (Thank you)," whispered Hideyo.

12 "*Chaphi jianko kaseyo* (Travel so that you do not get caught)."

13 "*Ŭnhe rŭ ichi an gesŭmnida* (I will not forget your kindness)."

14 "*Chigŭm kaseyo* (Go now)!"

Predict

Do you think that Hideyo will try to swim across the water?

cast his eyes looked	**crimsoned** made red in color

Chapter 3 So Far from the Bamboo Grove **323**

Read the Selection

1. **Silent reading** Play the audio. Then give students time to read silently.
2. **Speculate** *Ask: Do you think the boys are about the same age?* (yes) *Do you think they are good friends?* (yes) *Hideyo says "I will not forget your kindness." What kind things do you think Hee Cho might have done for him?* (Perhaps he shared a room with him, was generous to him, and helped him feel at home.)
3. **Multi-level options** See MULTI-LEVEL OPTIONS on p. 322.

Sample Answer to Guide Question
Yes, that is how he has to cross the river.

 Spelling

Two-syllable words with -*ed* ending

Tell students that we double the final consonant when we add -*ed* to a two-syllable word that has the stress on the final syllable. Draw students' attention to the example in paragraph 6: *American soldiers controlled southern Korea.* Break down *controlled.* **Ask:** *How many syllables does* control *have?* (two) *Where is the stress in* control*?* (on the final syllable) *So what do we do when we add* -ed*?* (We double the final consonant, the *l*, giving us *controlled*.)

Apply Have students look at paragraph 7. **Ask:** *Why doesn't this rule apply to* fasten/fastened*?* (The stress is not on the final syllable.) Write on the board: *occur, wonder, refer, permit, exhaust.* Have students decide which words should have a doubled final consonant before -*ed.* (occurred, referred, permitted)

Read the Selection

1. **Listen for the main idea** Play the audio while students listen with their books closed. Then have students tell you what they understood from the story. Write questions they have on the board. Then have them read silently and answer the questions after they have read the end of the story.

2. **Paired reading** Have students practice reading aloud with a partner.

3. **Imagine the character's situation** *Say: Do you think you could swim across a river in the middle of the night? How would you feel? Would you do something dangerous like this if it were the only way to escape to freedom?*

Sample Answer to Guide Question
Yes, I think he will be seen because the light sweeps over him many times, and he is getting tired of diving under.

15   When the searchlight had passed over them, Hideyo slipped into the river. It was much colder than he had expected and the **current** was very strong. He swam. Each time a light came toward him he dove under, so that only his bag showed, half **submerged** and looking, he hoped, like a floating log. Again and again he had to dive.

16   Gunfire burst in the air, **echoing** in a thousand directions. Hideyo did not know whether it was aimed at him, at some other **escapees,** or at wild animals. The light swept over him again and he submerged deeper. He could see the shore not far from him, but the current kept pushing him downstream and so many **submergings** slowed him.

> **Predict**
> Now do you think Hideyo will be seen? What clues from the story make you think this?

---

current   a flow of water
submerged   under the surface of the water
echoing   repeating of a sound caused by bouncing off a hard surface

escapees   people who try to get away
submergings   times gone under the surface of the water

324   Unit 5   Freedom

MULTI-LEVEL OPTIONS *Read the Selection*

Newcomer *Ask: Did Hideyo go in the river?* (yes) *Was the water warm?* (no) *Did he hear gunfire?* (yes) *Did he make it to the other side?* (yes)

Beginning *Ask: Was it easy to swim?* (no) *Why not?* (The water was cold and the current was strong; it was night; there was gunfire.) *What did Hideyo do each time the light came near him?* (He went underwater.) *Who did he think of when he got to the other side?* (the Kim family)

Intermediate *Ask: Was it an easy trip across the river? Explain.* (No. The water was cold; the current was strong; and he was being shot at.) *How did Hideyo feel when he made it to the other side?* (exhausted, relieved) *What did the air on the other side "smell" like to him?* (freedom) *What did he hope?* (that the Kim family would know somehow that he was safe)

Advanced *Ask: How do you think Hideyo felt as he was crossing the river?* (cold, afraid, determined) *What does it mean when it says, "He took a deep breath of freedom"?* (He was safe from arrest.) *Do you think Hideyo's journey is over now? Why or why not?* (No, he still has to get to Japan.)

17 Again gunfire. A bullet hit the bag on Hideyo's head and dropped to the surface. He could hear the bullets piercing the waters all around him. He dove deeper and let the current carry him. Then he swam again. When he finally reached the south side he lay as dead when the light shone his way, then crawled toward the bushes, **exhausted.**

18 He had escaped across the dangerous thirty-eighth parallel. He took a deep breath of freedom. He thanked God for the Kim family and hoped that they would see in a dream that he had made it to the other side.

Predict

What do you think will happen to Hideyo now? Will his life get better? Why?

exhausted   extremely tired

About the Author

Yoko Kawashima Watkins (born 1933)

"So Far from the Bamboo Grove" is about Yoko Kawashima Watkins's childhood. Watkins is Japanese. She spent her early years in North Korea. Near the end of World War II, her family escaped from North Korea. Her family had many problems on their way back to Japan. Later, Watkins married an American soldier and moved to the United States.

➤What strategies do you think Yoko Kawashima Watkins used to write her novel? What challenges did she face?

Chapter 3   So Far from the Bamboo Grove   **325**

 Spelling

Silent *l*

Direct students' attention to the word *half* in paragraph 15. Model the pronunciation. Ask students what letters they hear. (h-a-f) Explain that *l* is sometimes silent before the letter *f*.

Apply Write on the board and *say: wolf* and *calf.* Ask students to decide which word has the silent *l.* (calf)

Evaluate Your Reading Strategy

Predict *Say: You have practiced an important reading strategy. Now you can decide how well you have done. Does this statement describe how you read?*

When I read, I use clues in the text to predict what will happen next. When I predict, I understand the reading better.

Read the Selection

1. **Paired reading** Have students read aloud to each other. Then have them discuss the Guide Question in groups.

2. **State the problem resolution** Remind students that in fiction based on a true story, there is a problem and then a resolution. *Ask: What was the problem at the beginning of the story?* (Hideyo needed to escape to South Korea without being caught.) *What was the resolution?* (He left at night and swam across the river to safety.)

3. **Locate derivations using dictionaries** Have students look at these glossed words and determine what words they are derived from: *submerged, echoing, escapees, submergings.* Have students check the derivations in a print, online, or CD-ROM dictionary.

4. **Multi-level options** See MULTI-LEVEL OPTIONS on p. 324.

Sample Answer to Guide Question
He will find his way back to Japan safely. His life will get better because he has freedom now.

About the Author

Analyze facts Have students work in small groups to read the author information aloud and come up with two questions to ask. They can also write an answer to the question about the author. Then have groups exchange questions and compare answers.

Answer
Sample answer: The author probably used her memories and also her imagination. She visualized the scenes and situations. She faced the challenge of keeping the story realistic and interesting at the same time.

Across Selections

Ask: What other selection have we read in this unit about a brave person? ("Rosa Parks," p. 287) *What did Rosa Parks have in common with Hideyo?* (They both took risks to improve their lives; they got help from others; they were part of a minority.)

Beyond the Reading

Reading Comprehension

Question-Answer Relationships

Sample Answers

1. a Japanese boy in Korea
2. He is trying to escape to southern Korea, across the thirty-eighth parallel.
3. Hideyo packs his belongings, says goodbye, walks to the river, and swims across to safety.
4. Koreans don't carry rucksacks; Japanese do.
5. South of that parallel, Korea is protected by Americans against the Communists.
6. He swims underwater so that he can't be seen; on the surface of the water, his bag looks like a log.
7. He feels sad and afraid he won't see them again. I feel sad, too, but I usually see people again.
8. Hideyo escapes successfully.
9. Koreans use burlap bags, but Japanese use rucksacks. Freedom is valued by both cultures. Rice is eaten in both cultures. My family values freedom and we eat rice, too.
10. He wants to keep some of his belongings, including his family album and savings book.
11. He feels relieved and exhausted.
12. I think his escape across the river was very exciting because I wasn't sure if he would be caught or escape successfully.

Build Reading Fluency

Repeated Reading

Assessment Program: *Reading Fluency Chart,* p. 116

As students read aloud, time the reading and count the number of incorrectly pronounced words. Record results in the Reading Fluency Chart.

Reading Comprehension

Question-Answer Relationships (QAR)

"Right There" Questions

1. **Recall Facts** Who is Hideyo?
2. **Recall Facts** What is Hideyo trying to do in the story?

"Think and Search" Questions

3. **Recognize Plot** What is the plot of this story?
4. **Make Inferences** Why would carrying a rucksack tell others that Hideyo is Japanese?
5. **Identify Cause and Effect** Why does Hideyo want to cross the thirty-eighth parallel?
6. **Give Reasons** Why does Hideyo swim underwater? Why does he leave his bag on the surface?

"Author and You" Questions

7. **Connect Your Experiences** How do you think Hideyo feels when he says good-bye to the Kims? How do you feel when saying good-bye to people you care about?

8. **Analyze Problem Resolution** What is the resolution of the story?
9. **Analyze Characteristics of Cultures** What differences between Korean and Japanese culture did you notice in the story? What are the common characteristics? How does your family's culture compare or contrast?

"On Your Own" Questions

10. **Speculate** Hideyo would probably travel more quickly if he carried nothing. Why do you think Hideyo brings his things with him?
11. **Identify Themes** How does Hideyo feel when he gets across the river?
12. **Analyze Plot** Is the plot exciting to you? Why or why not?

Activity Book
p. 170

Student
CD-ROM

Build Reading Fluency

Repeated Reading

Repeated reading helps increase your reading rate and builds confidence. Each time you reread, you improve your reading fluency.

1. Turn to page 320.
2. Your teacher or partner will time you for six minutes.
3. With a partner, take turns reading each paragraph aloud.
4. Stop after six minutes.

326   Unit 5   Freedom

MULTI-LEVEL OPTIONS *Elements of Literature*

Newcomer Explain to students that the Kims help Hideyo because they care about him. Play the audio of paragraphs 1–6 again, pausing at the end of each. Have students raise their hands when they hear an example of the Kims' caring for Hideyo and his caring for them.

Beginning Play the audio again, stopping at the end of each paragraph. Have students work in pairs to identify what the characters do in each paragraph and to speculate about why they do it.

Intermediate Have students work in pairs to reread the story. Have them take notes listing the paragraph number, the action that occurs, and their guess at the motivation for these actions.

Advanced Have students work in pairs. Have them reread the information about the author and discuss her motivation for writing "So Far from the Bamboo Grove." Did she write to inform, persuade, get famous, or make money? Have students explain what they think motivated her.

Listen, Speak, Interact

Present an Experience with Danger

Think about a time when you or someone you know has been in danger. Write notes on a piece of paper.

1. Interview your partner about his or her dangerous experience.
   a. Ask questions with who, what, when, where, why, and how.
   b. Add and revise questions.
   c. Take notes on note cards.
2. Tell your partner's story to the class.
   a. Use your voice and gestures to make the story interesting.
   b. Use your voice to make people believe you.

3. After presenting the story, ask your classmates if they believed you.
4. Listen to another classmate's presentation. Did you understand your classmate's verbal and nonverbal messages? If not, ask for clarification.

Elements of Literature

Analyze Character Motivation

Motivation is the reason why someone does something. For example, you may work after school to earn money for college. Your motivation is to go to college. "So Far from the Bamboo Grove" describes people who do dangerous things. What is their motivation for doing these things?

1. Work with a small group. Answer these questions.
   a. Why does Hideyo swim through the cold river at night? What is his motivation?

   b. Why do you think the Kims help Hideyo? What is their motivation?
2. Identify other things that the characters do. What is the motivation for each one?
3. Present one of your ideas to the class.

Activity Book
p. 171

Student
CD-ROM

Chapter 3 So Far from the Bamboo Grove **327**

Home Connection

Have students ask family members about World War II or another war. What was it like to be a child in those times? Did any relatives fight? Have students take notes about their relatives' personal memories of living during a war or information that was passed down in the family. Remind students to record information that answers *who, what, when, where,* and *why* questions.

Learning Styles
Musical

Countries usually have a national anthem, or theme song, based on the principles of the country. They also often have other songs that are written during times of war to encourage feelings of patriotism. Have students share national anthems and other patriotic songs. Ask students to explain what principles they represent and when they are sung. (celebrations, holidays) Volunteers can sing for the class.

Listen, Speak, Interact

Present an Experience With Danger

1. **Share personal experiences** To help students think of dangerous situations, have volunteers briefly explain a situation they were in, such as crossing a dangerous street, getting lost, or getting into an accident while riding a bike without a helmet. *Say: If you don't have a dangerous story, you can tell about what happened to someone you know. Remember, after your partner tells your story to the class, students will say if the story was believable or not. Don't exaggerate too much!*

2. **Newcomers** Pair these students with more fluent students. Students can help newcomers by asking additional questions to clarify and expand their stories.

3. **Compose, organize, and revise a news report** Extend the activity by having pairs of students compose a news report about one of their experiences with danger. The report should be organized by the *wh-* questions; *who, what, when, where, why* and *how*. Have students present their news report to the class. The class should evaluate the clarity and effectiveness of the report and whether it answered all of the questions. Students should revise their reports according to class feedback.

Elements of Literature

Analyze Character Motivation

1. **Discuss personal motivation** Ask students questions to help them express their own motivations. *Ask: Do you have a job? What motivates you to work? Do you play on a sports team? What motivates your team to play hard?*

2. **Multi-level options** See MULTI-LEVEL OPTIONS on p. 326.

Answers
Examples: **1. a.** He is motivated to cross the river without being seen so that he can escape to freedom. **b.** The Kims love him like a son. Perhaps he has lived with them for a long time. **2.** Mrs. Kim packed him some food because she didn't want him to be hungry.

✓ ASSESS

Have students write about what motivates them to study English or do well in school.

Word Study

Identify the Latin Root Word *Grat*

1. **Use a dictionary** Tell students to use the dictionary to look up *gratuity.* Ask them to make up sentences using the word.

2. **Locate derivations of unfamiliar words** For additional practice locating derivations, have students use a dictionary, a CD-ROM dictionary, or an online dictionary to locate the derivations of the following words from the reading selection: *expression, vanished, parallel, submerged, exhausted.*

Grammar Focus

Use the Conjunction *So That* to Connect Ideas

Express ideas with *so that* Write on the board: *I study English so that _____. I try to go to bed early so that _____.* Have students complete the sentences and make up other sentences with *so that.*

Answers

paragraph 1: As soon as the spring work was finished and when the moon was dark, so that he would not be spotted. paragraph 12: Travel so that you do not get caught. paragraph 15: Each time a light came toward him he dove under, so that only his bag showed . . .

ASSESS

Have students write sentences using *grateful* and *congratulate.*

Word Study

Identify the Latin Root Word *Grat*

Root words are words from which other words are made. The root word *grat* comes from the Latin word *gratus.* It means "pleasing." You can use *grat* with several suffixes to make new words.

In "So Far from the Bamboo Grove," Hideyo feels *gratitude* (thankfulness) toward Mrs. Kim. *Gratitude* has the root *grat.*

1. Copy the chart in your Personal Dictionary.
2. Look at the words and their definitions. Read the sentences.
3. Write your own sentences using words with *grat.*

Notice that you add an *e* to *grat* before adding *ful.*

Use the Root Word *Grat*

gratify give satisfaction or pleasure: It will <u>gratify</u> me to see you learn English.

My Sentence It will gratify me to show you around my classroom.

grateful thankful, appreciative: I am <u>grateful</u> for all your help.

My Sentence

congratulate praise for something well done or important: I <u>congratulate</u> you for winning the prize.

My Sentence

Personal Dictionary

The Heinle Newbury House Dictionary

Activity Book p. 172

Student CD-ROM

Grammar Focus

Use the Conjunction *So That* to Connect Ideas

A **conjunction** is a word that joins two clauses. A clause is a part of a sentence that has a subject and a verb. *So that* is a conjunction. The clause with *so that* usually gives a reason.

I put on my swimsuit <u>so that</u> I could swim.

1. Copy the chart on a piece of paper.
2. Read paragraphs 1, 12, and 15 from the selection.
3. In your chart write the sentence from each paragraph that uses the conjunction *so that.*

Use the Conjunction *So That*

Paragraph	Sentence
1	
12	
15	

4. On a piece of paper, write two sentences with *so that.*

Activity Book pp. 173–174

Student Handbook

Student CD-ROM

MULTI-LEVEL OPTIONS *From Reading to Writing*

Newcomer Have students draw a cartoon strip of an animal escaping from somewhere. The story should have at least three drawings: one showing where the animal is (e.g., behind a fence), one showing why it wants to escape (e.g., to get a treat), and one showing how it escapes (e.g., digs under the fence). Have students add a title.

Beginning Have students work in pairs to write their stories. For every action they write, students should use the conjunction *so that* to give the reason for the action.

Intermediate Have students work in pairs to choose a time, place, and main character for their stories. Tell pairs to write the first paragraph together. Then have one partner write the second paragraph with the plot while the other writes the final paragraph with the resolution. Have pairs reunite to read the full story.

Advanced Remind students to use the conjunction *so that* in their stories to connect ideas. Have partners exchange just the first two paragraphs of their stories. Ask students to predict what they think will happen. Then have them check their predictions by reading the ending.

From Reading to Writing

Write a Historical Fiction Story

Hideyo faces many problems while trying to escape from northern Korea. Write your own story about someone trying to escape from a place. Your story will be five paragraphs long. Use the Narrative Draft form in your Student Handbook as a guide.

1. Choose a real time and place in history for your story. Use textbooks or library resources to help you.
2. Write what happens as your character tries to escape. Remember to answer: Who? What? When? Where? Why? How?
3. Tell your character's motivation.
4. Think of a title for your story.
5. Revise and edit your writing using the Editor's Checklist in your Student Handbook. Use a computer, if possible.
6. When you are finished, exchange papers with a partner. Peer edit each other's work.
7. How well did you and your partner achieve your purpose for writing?

Activity Book
p. 175

Student
Handbook

Across Content Areas

Use Punctuation and Intonation

In "So Far from the Bamboo Grove," Mrs. Kim says, "Aigo!" Notice the **exclamation point (!)** after *aigo*. An exclamation point shows forceful speech, as when you are angry, surprised, or frustrated.

A **question mark (?)** comes at the end of a question. You can make informal questions with just a single word. You do this by raising your voice at the end of the word.

Listen as your teacher pronounces this exclamation and question. Can you hear the difference in intonation?

No! No?

1. Read the following sentences and respond in writing with *no*. To clarify your answer, punctuate *no* with an exclamation point or a question mark.
   a. I can't come now.
   b. Would you write my science report for me?
2. Read the sentences and the "no" responses with a partner. Use the correct intonation.

Activity Book
p. 176

Reteach and Reassess

Text Structure Make a blank chart with two columns and five rows and headed *Fiction Based on a True Story* (see p. 318). Without looking back at their books, have students fill in the five features and then the corresponding information from the story.

Reading Strategy Write on the board: *Joe rubs his stomach and looks at the clock. He says, "It's noon, and I'm hungry." Then he gets up.* Ask students to predict what will happen next. (Joe will get something to eat.)

Elements of Literature Provide students with a short newspaper or magazine article. Have them identify the motivation of the people in the article.

Reassess Have students think about a time when they faced danger. Have them write or draw how they escaped the danger and what they are grateful for (who or what helped them escape).

From Reading to Writing

Write a Historical Fiction Story

1. **Brainstorm** Brainstorm with students different historical situations when people had to escape from a place. Situations may include: escaping from an enemy in a war, escaping slavery through the Underground Railroad, escaping from a political situation, escaping from a natural disaster.
2. **Write collaboratively** Some students may want to write with a partner. Have students group themselves according to the situation they want to write about.
3. **Compose, organize, and revise a letter** A variation of this activity is to have pairs of students write a letter to a friend describing their joint escape from a place. The letter should have three paragraphs. Paragraph 1 gives a general description. Paragraph 2 answers the *wh-* questions. Paragraph 3 summarizes the escape and tells what will happen next. Students should exchange papers with another pair of students, peer edit each other's work, and revise as necessary.
4. **Multi-level options** See MULTI-LEVEL OPTIONS on p. 328.

Across Content Areas:
Language Arts

Use Punctuation and Intonation

Use intonation to express doubt Have students make surprising statements about things they don't do, and have students express doubt or surprise by replying *No?* For example: *I never eat candy. No? I never play video games. No?*

Answers
1. No? 2. No!

 **ASSESS**

Write the following dialogue:
A: My favorite dessert is raw vegetables.
B: What That's so strange
Have students punctuate the dialogue and read it according to the punctuation. (What? That's so strange!)

CHAPTER

4

Into the Reading

Chapter Materials

Activity Book: *pp. 177–184*
Audio: *Unit 5, Chapter 4; CD 3, Tracks 4–5*
Student Handbook
Student CD-ROM: *Unit 5, Chapter 4*
Teacher Resource Book: *Lesson Plan, Teacher Resources, Reading Summary, Activity Book Answer Key*
Teacher Resource CD-ROM
Assessment Program: *Quiz, pp. 81–82; Teacher and Student Resources, pp. 115–144*
Assessment CD-ROM
Transparencies
The Heinle Newbury House Dictionary/CD-ROM
Web site: http://visions.heinle.com

Objectives

Preview Have a student read the objectives.
Ask: What do you think an autobiography is? Have you ever read one? Who wrote it?

Use Prior Knowledge

Talk About Strengths and Weaknesses

Generalize about strengths and weaknesses
After students have shared their lists, ask what the most common strengths and weaknesses are. *Ask: Can you make a general statement about students in this class?*

Alone

a poem
by Samantha Abeel

Samantha's Story

an autobiography
by Samantha Abeel

Objectives

Reading Compare and contrast as you read a poem and an autobiography.

Listening and Speaking Respond to literature.

Grammar Use superlative adjectives.

Writing Write a poem.

Content Language Arts: Identify genres.

Use Prior Knowledge

Talk About Strengths and Weaknesses

Everybody has strengths—things they are good at. Everybody has weaknesses—things they are not good at. Your strengths are part of who you are. An example might be that you can make people laugh. An example of a weakness might be that you can't run really fast.

1. Copy the chart shown on a piece of paper.
2. Write a few of your strengths and weaknesses.
3. Talk about your list with a partner. How are your lists the same and different?

4. Summarize each other's strengths and weaknesses.

Strengths	Weaknesses
can make people laugh	can't run very fast

330   Unit 5 Freedom

MULTI-LEVEL OPTIONS *Build Vocabulary*

Newcomer Have students write on slips of paper: *to, two, too.* Ask them to hold up the correct form as you say sentences. *Say: I had two slices of pizza for lunch. I have too much homework. I go to the mall after school.*

Beginning Have students work in pairs to write sentences using *to, two,* and *too* but leaving a blank line for these words. Have them copy the sentences on the board. Then have other students read and fill in the sentences.

Intermediate Have students work in pairs to find examples of words that sound the same but have different spellings and meanings. (*Examples:* hear/here, pair/pear, your/you're, right/write) Ask each pair to use these words to write an exercise for the class to do. Use Build Vocabulary on p. 331 as a model.

Advanced Have students work in small groups to list words that sound the same but have different spellings and meanings. Instruct each group to write a creative paragraph or a poem using as many of the words as possible. Ask a volunteer from each group to read the work to the class.

Build Background

Learning Disabilities

Some people have trouble learning. Their trouble can be caused by a learning disability—something that gets in the way of learning. People with learning disabilities can be very smart. With the help of technology, medicine, and other people, people with disabilities can do many great things.

Content Connection

About 10 to 15 percent of children in the United States have learning disabilities. Many receive special teaching in school to help them succeed.

Build Vocabulary

Spell Frequently Misspelled Words

Some words sound the same but have different spellings and meanings. One example is *to*, *two*, and *too*. When you write, be sure you choose the correct spelling.

Read the following sentences. Look at the definitions for each pair of words. Choose the correct word to complete each sentence. Write the words and their definitions in your Personal Dictionary.

1. There is a place where the (sun / son) and its flowers bow in shadow.
   a. **son** a male child
   b. **sun** the star that gives heat and light to the earth

2. Yet one (hour / our) of my day was a refuge.
   a. **hour** a time period of 60 minutes
   b. **our** belonging to us

3. I could (rays / raise) my hand in class.
   a. **rays** thin lines of light or energy
   b. **raise** lift up

Personal Dictionary

Activity Book
p. 177

Student CD-ROM

Chapter 4 Alone *and* Samantha's Story **331**

Cultural Connection

Build Vocabulary Ask students to think of two words from another language that sound the same but have different spellings and meanings. Have students make a sentence in English for each word (with the words in their language). Engage the class in figuring out the meaning of the words from context.

Learning Styles
Linguistic

Build Background Have students work in small groups to do research on learning disabilities. They may want to focus on different types of learning disabilities, on statistics, on resources available to help, or on successful people who overcame learning disabilities. Each group should present their findings orally or in a written report.

Build Background

Learning Disabilities

> Teacher Resource Book: *Web, p. 37*

1. **Use prior knowledge** Draw a web on the board and have students tell you what they know about learning disabilities. *Ask: Do you know what might be difficult if you have a learning disability?*

2. **Content Connection** Advances in neurology and psychology have helped us better understand how the brain receives, interprets, stores, and retrieves information. This has resulted in better ways to assist children with learning disabilities.

Build Vocabulary

Spell Frequently Misspelled Words

> Teacher Resource Book: *Personal Dictionary, p. 63*

1. **Use prior knowledge** *Ask: What words do you sometimes misspell? Do you ever confuse* there, they're, *and* their*?* List students' words on the board, and suggest other frequently misspelled words. Create a class display of these words and attach definitions, drawings, and examples to help them remember the differences.

2. **Reading selection vocabulary** You may want to introduce the glossed words in the reading selections before students begin reading. Key words: *veil, disabilities, refuge, learning disabled, coping, compensating, excel.* Instruct students to write the words with correct spelling and their definitions in their Personal Dictionaries. Have them pronounce each word and divide it into syllables.

3. **Multi-level options** See MULTI-LEVEL OPTIONS on p. 330.

Answers
1. **b.** sun **2. a.** hour **3. b.** raise

ASSESS

Dictate these sentences: *Our clock is broken. Rays of sun came through the window.*

Text Structure

Poem and Autobiography

1. **Recall genre features** Before students look at the text, write two idea webs on the board, labeled *poem* and *biography*. Brainstorm and record the features of these genres. (stanza, repetition, rhymes; events/settings in a person's life/dates/chronological order) *Say: We are going to read an autobiography. How do you think it might be different from a biography? Who is the main character? What person do you think it is written in?*

2. **Multi-level options** See MULTI-LEVEL OPTIONS below.

Reading Strategy

Compare and Contrast Texts

Use a graphic organizer Help students visualize the difference between *compare* and *contrast*. Point to the Venn diagram and the middle overlapping area. *Say: This is what is similar. This shows the meaning of* compare. *These other areas show the meaning of* contrast. *They show what is different.*

ASSESS

Have students compare and contrast a biography and an autobiography.

Text Structure

Poem and Autobiography

In this chapter you will read a poem and an autobiography. Look at the charts. They show features of some poems and autobiographies. Look for these features as you read.

Poem	
Images	The poem includes descriptions that help readers create mental images (pictures in their minds).
Repetition	The poem repeats some words and phrases.

Autobiography	
First Person Narration	The author tells the story using the pronouns *I, me, we, us.*
Main Character	The main character is the author.
Events	The autobiography tells the story of the author's life.
Setting	The autobiography is set in a real time and place.

Student CD-ROM

Reading Strategy

Compare and Contrast Texts

When you **compare,** you see how things are similar. When you **contrast,** you see how things are different. Look at the example. It shows how you can compare and contrast a lemon and a banana.

Compare Both are yellow and are fruit.

Contrast A banana is sweet. A lemon is not.

1. Compare and contrast "Alone" and "Samantha's Story" as you read.
2. Think about how the descriptions in each selection are similar and different.

3. Copy a diagram like this in your Reading Log. As you read, write your comparisons and contrasts on it.

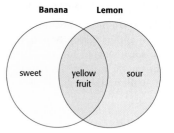

Reading Log

Student CD-ROM

MULTI-LEVEL OPTIONS *Text Structure*

Newcomer Help students understand images using pictures from magazines. On the board, write: *"Blue Sky."* Tell students this is the title of a poem. Tape pictures around the title. Have students choose the images that fit the title. (Pictures should include outdoor as well as unrelated indoor scenes, cars, and so on.)

Beginning Write the text to a familiar song, such as "Row, Row, Row Your Boat," on the board. Ask students to point out examples of the features of a poem listed in the chart on p. 332.

Intermediate Pair Intermediate and Advanced students. Give them the following image frames: *Pretty as a _____. Light as a _____. Smart as a _____. Tired as a _____. Hungry as a _____.* Have students create new images of their own and share their images with another pair.

Advanced Pair Advanced and Intermediate students. Give them the following image frames: *Pretty as a _____. Light as a _____. Smart as a _____. Tired as a _____. Hungry as a _____.* Have students create new images of their own and share their images with another pair.

Alone

a poem by Samantha Abeel

Samantha's Story

an autobiography by Samantha Abeel

333

Reading Selection Materials

Audio: *Unit 5, Chapter 4; CD 3, Tracks 4–5*
Teacher Resource Book: *Reading Summary,*
    pp. 109–110
Transparencies: #43, *Reading Summary*

Suggestions for Using Reading Summary

- Introduce new vocabulary or cognates.
- Cut the summary into strips, or jumble the sentences on an overhead transparency. Students put the sentences in order.
- Practice the reading strategy.
- Students read aloud or with a partner.
- Students paraphrase the summary.
- Students do a cloze activity.
- Students create a visual or graphic organizer, such as a timeline or storyboard, to illustrate the summary.
- Students paraphrase the summary.

Preview the Selections

1. **Interpret the image** Have students look at the illustration. *Ask: How old do you think Samantha is? What's she doing?* (looking out the window, thinking) *What do you think she might be thinking about?*
2. **Connect to theme** *Say: The theme of this unit is* freedom. *We have read selections about freedom from discrimination, slavery, and government. This story is about a personal freedom from an inner struggle or conflict. Samantha is troubled about something.*

 Cultural Connection

Learning Styles
Interpersonal

Share a Dr. Seuss rhyme with the class as an example of poetry written for young children. Divide the class into small groups. Have students share any children's poem they know in another language. Have them compare and contrast the various poems. Some questions to consider are: *Do they all rhyme? Do they have similar themes? Are they all happy?* Each group can vote on their favorite poem and recite it to the rest of the class.

Direct students to the picture on this page. *Ask: How do you think this girl feels? Does she seem happy? Sad? Lonely?* Ask students to describe the girl's mood. Remind students that setting and body language can give important insights. *Ask: Why might she be looking out the window? Does her posture offer any clues?* Have students discuss in small groups.

Reading Selection

Read the Selection

1. **Choral reading** Play the audio. Then lead the class in a choral reading of the poem.
2. **Identify text features** *Ask: How many verses are there?* (one) *Are there any rhyming words?* (no) *What words or phrases are repeated?* (a place where)
3. **Read poetry aloud** Have students practice reading the poem aloud to each other in pairs. Then ask volunteers to read the poem to the class.
4. **Relate to personal experience** *Ask: Where do you like to go when you need to be alone? Is there any place in nature where you like to sit? Is there a place in your neighborhood or home where you like to go and think?*

Sample Answer to Guide Question
The poem will be shorter, use more images, and use repetition.

See Teacher Edition pp. 434–436 for a list of English-Spanish cognates in the reading selection.

Audio
CD 3. Tr. 4

Compare and Contrast

Look at the poem. How do you think it will be different from Samantha's autobiography?

Alone
a poem by Samantha Abeel

There is a place where we all go
when we must sit alone:
A place where the birds are free to fly,
A place where the sun and its flowers bow in shadow,
A place where the fog is like a **veil**
and everything is protected,
A place where our souls are set free
and we are allowed to play our own song.

veil   a light cloth worn over the face

MULTI-LEVEL OPTIONS *Read the Selection*

Newcomer Play the audio. *Ask: In Samantha's poem, are birds free to fly?* (yes) *Did Samantha like the seventh grade?* (no) *Did she like numbers?* (no) *Did she like to write?* (yes)

Beginning Play the audio. *Ask: Does Samantha feel free when she's alone?* (yes) *Was Samantha good at math in school?* (no) *What subject did she like?* (writing)

Intermediate Have students do a paired reading. *Ask: Does Samantha like to be alone? What language in the poem makes you think so?* (birds are free; everything is protected; souls are free; allowed to play our own song) *What does Samantha compare to a tree?* (people) *Why?* (Both are bright and dark, and both are full of shine and shadow.)

Advanced Have students do a paired reading. *Say: Give examples of language from the poem that show what Samantha thinks about being alone.* (birds are free; everything is protected; souls are free; allowed to play our own song) *What is Samantha's main strength?* (writing) *What is her main weakness?* (math)

Samantha's Story
an autobiography by Samantha Abeel

Compare and Contrast

What is the first difference you see between this selection and "Alone"?

1   A TREE that stands in the moonlight reflects the light, yet also casts a shadow. People are the same. They have gifts that let them shine, yet they also have **disabilities,** shadows that **obscure** the light. When I started this project in seventh grade, I had trouble telling time, counting money, remembering even the simplest of addition and subtraction problems. Yet no matter how hard it was to stay **afloat** in this ocean of troubles, there was something inside of me, something that became my **life preserver**—and that was writing.

2   SEVENTH GRADE was a horrible year. I hated school. . . . Yet one hour of my day was a **refuge.** Here, there weren't any concepts with numbers, measurements, algebra, or failure. It was my seventh-grade writing class. I had begun to **experiment** with creative writing in sixth grade, but in seventh grade I discovered how much writing was a part of me and I was a part of it.

3   TO BUILD on this, my mother asked Mrs. Williams, who was my English teacher, if she would work with me by giving me writing assignments and **critiquing** them as a way of focusing on what was right with me and not on what was wrong. . . . I discovered that by crawling inside and becoming what I wrote, it made my writing and ideas more powerful.

---

disabilities   things that take away a normal ability
obscure   hard to see or understand
afloat   on or above the water; not in bad trouble, surviving
life preserver   equipment used to keep a person above water

refuge   a place of safety
experiment   test, try something
critiquing   evaluating, especially someone's written work

Chapter 4   Alone *and* Samantha's Story   **335**

Read the Selection

1. **Use art to preview** Have students look at the illustration. Ask students to describe the scene and say what the girl is doing.
2. **Shared reading** Play the audio. Have students join in when they can.
3. **Summarize** Have students work in pairs to answer these questions. *Ask: How does she say that people are like trees in the moonlight?* (Like a tree in the moonlight, people have a dark side—a disability—as well as a bright side—their gifts.) *What is the main idea of paragraph 2?* (Even though she hated seventh grade, her writing class was her refuge.)
4. **Locate derivations using dictionaries** Have students look at these glossed words and determine what words they are derived from: *disabilities, critiquing.* Have students check the derivations in a print, online, or CD-ROM dictionary.
5. **Multi-level options** See MULTI-LEVEL OPTIONS on p. 334.

Sample Answer to Guide Question
This selection is written in narrative form and it is longer.

See Teacher Edition pp. 434–436 for a list of English-Spanish cognates in the reading selection.

---

th **Spelling**

Silent *w*

Write on the board and *say: write.* Ask students what sounds they hear. (/r/, long /i/, /t/) Explain that when a word begins with *wr,* the *w* is silent. Brainstorm and record other examples of the silent *w.* (wrap, wreath, wreck, wrestle, wriggle, wrinkle, wrist, wrong, and so on)

    Apply In groups, have students write a poem or a paragraph using as many of the *wr-* words as they can. Have the groups do choral readings of their work. Let each group select a leader.

Reading Selection

Read the Selection

1. **Reciprocal reading** Play the audio. Divide students into small groups. Have students take turns reading a short passage, asking questions about it to group members, and asking the group to summarize.

2. **Check comprehension** *Ask: How was her English teacher able to help her?* (by focusing on what was right, rather than what was wrong) *Why was it better for Samantha in the special education class?* (She could ask questions without feeling stupid.) *What do some people think about students in special education?* (They think that they have no abilities.) *How does she describe special education?* (It means that you learn differently.)

Sample Answer to Guide Question
In the poem, she is very isolated and says there is a place where we all must go to sit alone. In the story, she feels good as part of her special education class.

Compare and Contrast

How do Samantha's feelings in this paragraph compare to her feelings in the poem?

---

4   IN EIGHTH GRADE I was finally recognized as **learning disabled.** I was taken from my seventh grade algebra class, where I was totally lost, and placed in a **special education resource** classroom. Special education changed my life. It was the best thing that ever happened to me. I could raise my hand in that class, even when being taught the most **elementary concepts,** and say, "I don't get it." It was the most wonderful feeling in the world. Eighth grade was my best year at the junior high. It is an **illusion** that students in special education have no abilities. Special education just means that you learn differently. I am so thankful for **specially** trained teachers who have been able to help me and many other kids like me.

5   IF YOU STRUGGLE with a disability, the first thing you need to do is find something that you are good at, whether it's singing or skate boarding, an interest in science or acting, even just being good with people. Then do something with that. If you are good with people, then **volunteer** at a nursing home or at a day care center; if you love skate boarding, work toward a **competition.** If it's singing, join a school choir. Even if you can't read music (like me) or read a script, you can find ways of **coping** and **compensating.** . . .

---

learning disabled   someone who has problems learning things
special education resource   materials for teaching students who need extra help
elementary concepts   simple ideas
illusion   a mistaken idea

specially   carefully, with more attention than usual
volunteer   do something without being forced or paid
competition   an organized event in which people try to do something better than everyone else
coping   facing problems and trying to overcome them
compensating   fighting against a weakness with a strength

336   Unit 5   Freedom

MULTI-LEVEL OPTIONS *Read the Selection*

Newcomer *Ask: Did Mrs. Williams help Samantha?* (yes) *Was Samantha put in a special education class?* (yes) *Did she like this?* (yes) *If you have a disability, does Samantha think you should give up?* (no)

Beginning *Ask: Who was Mrs. Williams?* (Samantha's English teacher) *When did Samantha's teachers realize she had a learning disorder?* (in eighth grade) *What did they do?* (They put her in a special education class.) *Did this help?* (yes) *What's the first thing you should do if you have a disability?* (find something you're good at and do it)

Intermediate *Ask: How did Mrs. Williams help Samantha?* (She gave her writing assignments and critiqued them, focusing on her strengths, not her weaknesses.) *What important thing happened in the eighth grade?* (The school realized she was learning disabled.) *What's her advice to others?* (Do what you like; keep trying; don't give up.)

Advanced *Ask: How does Samantha see students in special education?* (They have abilities; they just learn differently.) *What do you think Samantha would say to students struggling in English class?* (You can find ways to compensate. Keep trying. You can excel.)

Compare and Contrast

Think about what Samantha says in her poem and autobiography. How is what she says the same? How is it different?

6   REMEMBER that if you have trouble in school, it might not be because you don't fit the school, it might be because the school doesn't fit you. Be an **advocate** for yourself. Keep trying. You may not fit in now, but whether you're seven or seventy, one day you will find a place where you **excel.**

---

advocate   a worker for a cause; a supporter   **excel**   do very well

About the Author | Samantha Abeel (born 1978)

Samantha Abeel grew up and went to school in Traverse City, Michigan. She got help with her learning disabilities from special education teachers in her school. She then went to college. She studied English and art history. Samantha Abeel likes to write. She is working on her second book.

➤ What question would you like to ask Samantha Abeel? What challenges did she overcome?

Chapter 4 Alone *and* Samantha's Story   **337**

 Spelling

Evaluate Your Reading Strategy

Ch for /k/ sound

Tell students that many words related to sounds and music start with the /k/ sound but are spelled with *ch.* One example they know is *choral* reading. Have students find a word in paragraph 6 that starts with the sound of /k/ but is spelled with *ch.* (choir)

   Apply Have pairs look up additional sound and music words that start with *ch* and sound like /k/. (chord, chorus)

Compare and Contrast Texts *Say: You have practiced an important reading strategy. Now you can decide how well you have done. Does this statement describe how you read?*

When I read two texts by the same author, I look for ways they are the same. I also look for ways they are different. Comparing and contrasting helps me see the connections between ideas.

Read the Selection

1. **Silent reading** Have students read the entire autobiography silently and write the answer to the Guide Question.
2. **Relate to personal experience** *Ask: Have you ever felt lost or stupid in a class? How did you deal with the problem? Which subject area would you like special assistance with? Do you think you would feel relief like Samantha did?*
3. **Multi-level options** See MULTI-LEVEL OPTIONS on p. 336.

Sample Answer to Guide Question
Similarities: She says that you feel better when you can do what you are good at; everyone has strengths. Differences: In the poem, she uses the image of going to a place to be alone; in the autobiography, she writes about interacting with other people (in school or in volunteering).

About the Author

Make inferences *Ask: What can we infer about the author's personality from her writing and this text? What characteristics does she seem to have?* (*Example:* Samantha is positive, creative, hard-working, sensitive, and thoughtful.)

Answer
Sample answer: I would like to ask Samantha if she was still friends with her classmates from eighth-grade special education. She overcame a learning disability to become a writer.

Across Selections

Say: Samantha wrote, "Be an advocate for yourself." Did Rosa Parks follow advice like this? Explain your answer. (Yes. She stopped "giving in" by challenging segregation laws that treated her unfairly; she worked for the NAACP to improve conditions for herself and all African-Americans.)

Spelling, Punctuation, Capitalization

After the Reading Comprehension section, students will practice spelling, punctuation, and capitalization in the Activity Book.

Beyond the Reading

Reading Comprehension

Question-Answer Relationships

Sample Answers

1. fly
2. She is put in a special education class.
3. a lonely place, a place to be yourself
4. She was bad at math and felt like a failure.
5. In "Alone" I get a lonely feeling. The place isn't warm, but it seems to be safe.
6. She is thankful because her teachers helped her see the positive things about herself. I'm thankful for my teachers, too, because they praise me when I do well and encourage me.
7. There is a very positive tone in the story, which makes her message stronger.
8. Abeel's writing shows that we can have inner freedom when we learn to use our strengths and abilities. In the other readings, the freedom that characters strove to attain was external, not internal.
9. She might have dropped out of school.
10. They both experienced difficulty because of limitations (learning disability and limited knowledge of English). They also had good teachers who helped them work around their limitations. Their experiences were different because Samantha was placed in a special class, but the author of "The Circuit" was in a regular class.

Build Reading Fluency

Read Aloud to Engage Listeners

Model reading aloud with expression. Remind students to keep their eyes on the words as they read. This will help them with phrasing, intonation, and pronunciation.

Reading Comprehension

Question-Answer Relationships (QAR)

"Right There" Questions

1. **Recall Facts** In "Alone," what are birds free to do?
2. **Recall Facts** In "Samantha's Story," what help does Samantha get to make schoolwork easier?

"Think and Search" Questions

3. **Describe Setting** In "Alone," how is the place described?
4. **Recognize Cause and Effect** In "Samantha's Story," why did Samantha hate school in the seventh grade?

"Author and You" Questions

5. **Recognize Mood** In "Alone," what feelings do you get about the place in the poem? A warm feeling? A cold feeling?
6. **Connect Your Experiences** Why is Samantha thankful for her teachers? How does her school experience compare with yours?

7. **Recognize Tone** What tone does Samantha Abeel use in the autobiography? How does it add to the effect of the text?

"On Your Own" Questions

8. **Compare and Contrast Themes Across Texts** How do the poem and the autobiography connect with the theme of freedom? Compare and contrast them with other readings in the unit.
9. **Speculate** What might have happened to Samantha without special education?
10. **Connect Issues Across Texts** What connections do you see between Samantha's school experiences and those of the boy in "The Circuit" (Unit 4, Chapter 3)? Compare and contrast.

Activity Book
p. 178

Student
CD-ROM

Build Reading Fluency

Read Aloud to Engage Listeners

Reading aloud helps increase your fluency and expression. Learning to read with expression makes others want to listen to you.

1. Listen to the audio recording of "Alone."

2. Turn to page 334 and follow along.
3. Listen to the phrasing and expression.
4. With a partner, practice reading aloud.
5. Read the poem aloud with expression in front of the class.

MULTI-LEVEL OPTIONS *Elements of Literature*

Newcomer Play paragraph 1 of "Samantha's Story" again. Help students understand the metaphor. Draw the tree a) reflecting the moonlight with a plus (+) sign and b) casting a shadow with a minus (−) sign. Ask students to draw their own metaphor of a person with strengths (+) and weaknesses (−).

Beginning Ask students to close their eyes while you play the audio of paragraph 1 of "Samantha's Story." Then have students draw the images that formed in their minds as they listened. Have students discuss how the images help them see things in different ways.

Intermediate Play paragraph 1 of "Samantha's Story." Tell students to visualize the images the author is trying to convey. *Say: Visualize yourself in a wild ocean. You can't swim anymore. Now see a life preserver appear and float toward you. How does the preserver change the scene? What else could this metaphor represent?*

Advanced Have students work in pairs to reread paragraph 1 of "Samantha's Story." Have them think of another metaphor to represent light and dark, and strength and weakness. Have pairs share their metaphors with the class.

Listen, Speak, Interact

Respond to Literature

How did you respond to "Alone" and to "Samantha's Story"?

1. Work with a small group to review "Alone" and "Samantha's Story."

2. Talk about what you liked and did not like about the selections.

3. Write what you liked on one note card. Write what you did not like on another note card.

4. Choose one person in the group to present the review to the class.

5. Practice reading the poem "Alone" aloud. Memorize it if you can. Present it to your group. Use correct pronunciation and intonation.

Elements of Literature

Recognize Figurative Language

Figurative language helps readers see mental images—pictures in their minds. A **metaphor** is a type of figurative language. It describes something by presenting it as something else.

Anna's beautiful blue eyes were two sparkling jewels.

This metaphor describes Anna's eyes as jewels. We know that her eyes are not really jewels, but the metaphor helps us picture her eyes.

1. Find the metaphors in the following sentences from "Samantha's Story." In your Reading Log, write the real things and the things that are presented as real.

a. A tree that stands in the moonlight reflects the light, yet also casts a shadow. People are the same. They have gifts that let them shine, yet they also have disabilities, shadows that obscure the light.

b. Yet no matter how hard it was to stay afloat in this ocean of troubles, there was something inside of me, something that became my life preserver—and that was writing.

2. Write two sentences of your own containing metaphors.

Reading Log   Activity Book   Student
p. 179   CD-ROM

Listen, Speak, Interact

Respond to Literature

1. Discuss criteria for evaluating a selection Discuss with students what makes us like a piece of literature. Here are some examples of criteria you could suggest: images, interesting plot, characters we can relate to, easy to understand.

2. Newcomers Work with these students, having each student tell you one thing they like and dislike about the selection.

Elements of Literature

Recognize Figurative Language

1. Teacher think aloud *Say: My best friend is a life preserver in my life. I can always count on her to see things clearly when I can't and to give me caring advice when I need it.* **Ask:** *What or who in your life is a life preserver for you? What is a shadow in your life?* Then encourage students to come up with other images before writing their sentences.

2. Multi-level options See MULTI-LEVEL OPTIONS on p. 338.

Answers

1. a. real: people, gifts, disabilities; presented as real: tree, light, shadow; **b.** real: troubles, writing; presented as real: ocean, life preserver

 **ASSESS**

Have groups of students write some metaphors having to do with English or with learning English.

Community Connection

Have students research opportunities to hear poetry being read in their communities. Students can check local papers and magazines as well as flyers around school for listings of "poetry slams" or more traditional poetry readings. Have each student bring information to share with the class about one upcoming scheduled event or on a venue that often hosts poetry readings.

| Learning Styles
Mathematical |
|---|

Tell students that there are many different types of poetry. One type, called *haiku,* is a traditional Japanese poetry form composed of three lines of five, seven, and five syllables, respectively. Haiku poems are usually about nature. Have students work in pairs to write haiku poetry, paying careful attention to the numerical pattern of syllables. Students should share their poems with the class. The class should keep count of the syllables as they listen.

Word Study

Learn Related Words

Expand vocabulary Have students make new words with the suffix *-able* by completing these sentences. *Say: If you can understand something, it is . . .* (understandable). *If you can solve a math problem, it is . . .* (solvable). Point out that students should drop the final *-e* before adding *-able*.

Answers
2. **a.** abilities **b.** disabilities **c.** capable

Grammar Focus

Use Superlative Adjectives

Identify superlative adjectives Write on the board: *interesting, exciting, strong, unusual, short.* Have students give the superlative form for each of the adjectives.

Answers
2. Paragraph 1: When I started this project . . . remembering even the <u>simplest</u> of . . . subtraction problems. Paragraph 4: I could raise . . . being taught the <u>most elementary</u> concepts, and say, "I don't get it." It was the <u>most wonderful</u> feeling in the world. *Students may also identify:* It was the <u>best</u> thing that ever happened to me. Eighth grade was my <u>best</u> year at the junior high.

✔ ASSESS

Ask: What are you capable of doing? What are some of your natural abilities?

Word Study

Learn Related Words

Some English words have the Latin form **able** or **ible**. *Able* and *ible* mean having the skill and power to do something.

1. Copy the chart in your Personal Dictionary.
2. From the list below, write the correct definitions of the underlined words.
   a. things that people can do
   b. things that people cannot do
   c. having the power to do something well
3. Use a dictionary to help you.

Sentence	Meaning
She was a talented and <u>capable</u> person.	
They have <u>disabilities</u>, shadows that obscure the light.	
People in special education still have <u>abilities</u>.	

Personal Dictionary   The Heinle Newbury House Dictionary   Activity Book p. 180   Student CD-ROM

Grammar Focus

Use Superlative Adjectives

Adjectives are words that describe nouns (people, places, or things). **Superlative adjectives** compare three or more nouns. They make writing more vivid or precise.

> Juan is the tall**est** person in the class.

This sentence compares Juan to all the other students in the class.

Superlative adjectives are formed by adding *-est* to short adjectives. They can also be formed by putting the word *most* or *least* in front of long adjectives.

Superlative adjectives usually have the article *the* in front of them: *the* tallest person.

1. Find superlative adjectives in paragraphs 1 and 4 of "Samantha's Story."
2. Write the sentences on a piece of paper. Underline the superlative adjectives.
3. Write two sentences of your own.

Activity Book pp. 181–182   Student Handbook   Student CD-ROM

MULTI-LEVEL OPTIONS *From Reading to Writing*

Newcomer Have students draw themselves in the place where they are free to be themselves. Help them write key words that explain how the place sounds and feels.

Beginning Have students close their eyes and visualize their special place. Ask them to dictate to you the mental images that come to mind when they think of this place. *Ask: What things do you see? What colors? How do they make you feel?* Students can use the notes to start their poems.

Intermediate Have students close their eyes and visualize their special place. *Say: Think of a metaphor to describe this place. Use that metaphor as the central image in your poem.* Have students exchange poems. Ask reviewers: *Did the author's use of figurative language help you visualize the special place?*

Advanced Have students exchange poems with a partner. Reviewers should check for use of figurative language and superlative adjectives. Reviewers should comment on the imagery. How does the poem make them feel? Can they visualize the place from the writer's descriptions?

From Reading to Writing

Write a Poem

Samantha Abeel writes a poem to tell about a place where she is free to be herself. Write a poem about a place where you are free to be yourself. As you plan your writing, and as you write, think about what you discover about yourself in your place.

1. Describe the place in your poem. Use figurative language, such as metaphors, to tell how this place looks, sounds, smells, and feels.
2. Use superlative adjectives in your description.
3. Draw a picture of your place.

4. Choose print or cursive handwriting, and copy your poem onto your picture.
5. Read your poem and share your picture with the class.
6. Make a collection of your class's poems. Create a cover and table of contents. Share the collection with another class or place it in the library.

Activity Book
p. 183

Student
Handbook

Across Content Areas

Identify Genres

When authors write, they choose the **genre**—a type of literature—that helps them express their message best.

1. Look at page 282 of this book.
   a. The first selection, "Rosa Parks," has the words *a biography* under the title. The genre is biography.
   b. What is the genre of "So Far from the Bamboo Grove"?
2. With a partner, identify the genres of "Alone" and "Samantha's Story." Why do you think Abeel chose to write about her special place in a poem?

3. Discuss the following writing topics. Which genre would you choose? Both answers are possible, but you have to explain your choice.
   a. Why the Seasons Change (Informational text or poem?)
   b. A Trip in Time (Myth or science fiction?)

Activity Book
p. 184

Chapter 4 Alone *and* Samantha's Story   **341**

Reteach and Reassess

Text Structure Read a short poem to the class (it could be the same Dr. Seuss poem you read earlier in the chapter). Have students use a chart such as the one on p. 332 to identify the features of the poem.

Reading Strategy Have students compare and contrast "Alone" and the poem you chose on a Venn diagram.

Elements of Literature Ask students to find examples of figurative language in newspaper or magazine articles, print

advertisements, TV commercials, menus, and so on. Discuss these examples as a class.

Reassess Have students compare and contrast the two readings in the chapter, saying which one they preferred and why.

From Reading to Writing

Write a Poem

1. **Compose orally** Before students write their poems, have volunteers compose poems orally to help generate ideas.
2. **Multi-level options** See MULTI-LEVEL OPTIONS on p. 340.

Across Content Areas: Language Arts

Identify Genres

1. **State personal preferences** *Ask: What is your favorite genre to read? What is your least favorite genre? Why? Can you name a favorite book and tell what genre it is?*
2. **Locate derivation and pronunciation** Have students locate the derivation and pronunciation of *genre* in the glossary in their Student Handbook or other sources, such as online or CD-ROM dictionaries.

Answers
1. **b.** a novel based on a true story
2. "Alone" is a poem and "Samantha's Story" is an autobiography. *Example:* Her special place was imaginary, so it worked well with poetry.
3. *Example:* **a.** informational text; I know many facts about this subject and would like to learn more. **b.** science fiction; I have a lot of good ideas using science facts for imaginary time travel.

ASSESS

Have students list four different genres they have read.

Materials

Student Handbook
CNN Video: *Unit 5*
Teacher Resource Book: *Lesson Plan, p. 28;*
  Teacher Resources, pp. 35–64; Video Script,
  pp. 169–170; Video Worksheet, p. 177;
  School-Home Connection, pp. 147–153
Teacher Resource CD-ROM
Assessment Program: *Unit 5 Test, pp. 83–88;*
  Teacher and Student Resources,
  pp. 115–144
Assessment CD-ROM
Transparencies
The Heinle Newbury House Dictionary/CD-ROM
Heinle Reading Library: *Little Women*
Web site: http://visions.heinle.com

Listening and Speaking Workshop

Present an Autobiographical Narrative

Present the topic Give examples of times in your life when something happy, sad, or exciting happened. Tell students to choose any topic they feel comfortable discussing.

Step 1: Use a Sunshine Organizer to organize your narrative.
Have students brainstorm topics in groups before they complete their organizers.

Step 2: Plan your narrative.
Have students add more ovals to their organizers for sense descriptions. Ask volunteers to offer examples of descriptions. Provide examples of similes and metaphors.

Listening and Speaking Workshop

Present an Autobiographical Narrative

> **Topic**
>
> Think of an important time in your life. An example might be when something exciting happened. Another example might be a time when a big event occurred and changed your life. Tell what happened. Tell how you felt during this time.

Step 1: Use a Sunshine Organizer to organize your narrative.

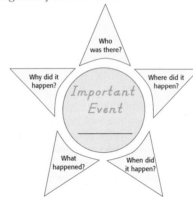

Step 2: Plan your narrative.

1. Use your organizer to think about the details of this important time in your life.
2. Decide which senses—sight, sound, smell, touch, taste—you will use to describe this time. Use figurative language.

3. Think of things you can compare with the event. Create similes or metaphors to make your story interesting.

Step 3: Prepare your narrative.

1. Write each main idea of your narrative on a note card.
2. Present the details in chronological order.
3. Think of a way to get your audience's attention. For example, you can ask them to think about an important time in their lives.
4. Include music to help set the mood for your audience.
5. Prepare visuals to give information and make your presentation interesting.

Step 4: Practice your narrative with a partner.

1. Use your note cards. Make sure they are in order.
2. Practice speaking slowly and clearly.
3. Listen to your partner's narrative.
4. Complete the checklists. Exchange checklists with your partner.
5. Revise your narrative using the checklists.

Step 5: Present your narrative.

Present your revised narrative to a friend, family member, or your class. Record your presentation if possible.

342 **Unit 5** Freedom

MULTI-LEVEL OPTIONS *Listening and Speaking Workshop*

Newcomer Help students think about an important time or event in their lives. Then suggest subjects related to the event: people, places, objects, and so on. Have students create visuals with drawings, cut outs from magazines, clip-art, or photos. Help students to add labels to their visuals.

Beginning Have students create one visual for each part of their web and write a note card for each visual. Then have them work in pairs to share their visuals, using their note cards to help them explain each visual to their partners.

Intermediate Have students share their completed note cards with their partners. Tell partners to brainstorm an attention-getting opening. Have them ask information questions to help their partners add details to their cards. Instruct students to refine their cards and then practice their narratives in small groups.

Advanced Have students exchange note cards for peer review. Tell reviewers to check for chronological order, descriptions using senses, details of the events, and high interest level. Ask students to revise their narratives based on the reviews. Then have them practice their narratives in small groups.

Active Listening Checklist

1. I liked ____ because ____ .
2. I want to know more about ____ .
3. I thought your narrative was interesting / not interesting.
4. Your presentation did / did not stay on the topic.

Speaking Checklist

1. Did you speak too slowly, too quickly, or just right?
2. Did you speak loudly enough for the audience to hear you?
3. Did you include descriptions using senses?

Step 6: Listen actively and purposely.

1. Listen to your classmates' presentations. Listen for main ideas and details.

2. Determine ways to evaluate your presentation and those of your classmates.
3. Create your own evaluation form.

Student
Handbook

Viewing Workshop

View and Think

Compare and Contrast Visual Media with a Written Story

1. View pictures and videos about Korea during World War II. Use the Internet and library resources.
2. Find and interview someone who participated in World War II or who has studied it extensively.
3. Compare and contrast the pictures and videos you find to "So Far from the Bamboo Grove."
4. Answer the following questions:
   a. What new information did you learn?

   b. What information is the same or different from the selection?
   c. Which purposes and effects are the same or different? Do the pictures and videos explain, persuade, or inform? Are the purposes and effects the same in "So Far from the Bamboo Grove"?

Further Viewing

Watch the *Visions* CNN Video for Unit 5. Do the Video Worksheet.

CNN Video

Content Connection
Technology

Tell students that during wars, reporters go to the battle areas and send back information and photos to TV stations and newspapers. Have students work in small groups to do an Internet search using the keywords *wartime correspondents, journalists,* and *reporters.* Have students discuss the technology reporters use to relay information. *Ask: How do they get photos to the media? How do they send video footage of the events?*

Learning Styles
Kinesthetic

Have students work in groups. Ask them to use the pictures, videos, and information they researched about Korea during WWII to write short skits. The skits should include reporters in the field relaying information to TV news anchors. Have them present their skits to the class. Groups can also make a background "anchor desk" with maps and pictures.

Step 3: Prepare your narrative.
Discuss with students different possibilities for music or visuals. Ideas for visuals could include: a title page, a drawing of the scene, a person with a thought bubble.

Step 4: Practice your narrative with a partner.
Remind students to complete their checklists after presentations.

Step 5: Present your narrative.
Have students adjust their presentations based on feedback from the checklists.

Step 6: Listen actively and purposely.
Point out the difference between listening passively and listening actively with a purpose. Remind students that they should listen for main ideas and details.

ASSESS

Have students write two sentences about how they have improved in their presentation skills.

Portfolio

Students may choose to record or videotape their speeches to place in their portfolios.

Viewing Workshop

View and Think

Teacher Resource Book: *Venn Diagram, p. 35*

1. **Locate resources** Assist students in locating library books and videos to watch. You may want to show a segment of a movie in class.
2. **Use a graphic organizer** Draw a Venn diagram. Fill in similarities and differences as the class compares the visual media with the written story.
3. **Respond to media presentations** Have students explain their likes and dislikes about the print and visual/film presentations of Korea during WW II. Instruct students to support their opinions with examples.

Writer's Workshop

Response to Literature: Write a Biographical Narrative

Step 1: Research the person.
Have students think of people they might write about, including sports stars, politicians, singers, world leaders, and historical figures.

Step 2: Write a first draft.
Remind students of their audience and purpose for writing. Then instruct students to select a voice and a style appropriate to their audience and purpose. If necessary, review voice and style with students. **Say:** *Voice is how the writer shows his or her own personal feelings to the reader. The writer does this through sentence structure, style, and tone. The reader feels like the writer is speaking directly to him or her.*
Also say: *Style is how writers use language to express their thoughts and feelings. It includes word choice, mood, and tone.* Have students use the selected voice and style as they write their drafts. Tell students to produce coherent written text by organizing their ideas using headings and the five-paragraph essay structure. Instruct students to use effective transitions to make their writing coherent. When students have completed their drafts, have them underline details that help the reader picture the person and events.

Writer's Workshop

Response to Literature: Write a Biographical Narrative

> **Writing Prompt**
> Research a person that you respect. Write a biography of a part of that person's life.

Step 1: Research the person.

1. Ask yourself questions about what you want to know about the person.
2. Gather facts from library reference and resource books and the Internet. Use the person's name as the keyword for an Internet search. If the person is someone you know, interview the person and people who know the person to get facts.
3. Use tables of contents and text headings to locate and organize your information. Also use information in photos, illustrations, and charts.
4. Organize the events in a timeline. Write the dates the events happened in time order.

(Name of Person I Respect)

Dates:

Events:

5. Evaluate your research. Is it accurate? Is it complete? Did you overlook any important sources of information? Do you need to revise your questions? Are there any new questions that you need to ask yourself?

Step 2: Write a first draft.

1. Use a computer, if possible, to create your draft.
2. Outline your narrative. It should be five paragraphs long.
3. Use chronology to tell the events. Use transition words like *first, next, then,* and *finally.*
4. Cite the sources of your information using the format in your Student Handbook.
5. Use headings to organize your biography. Also use graphic features such as boldface and italics for important words or information.

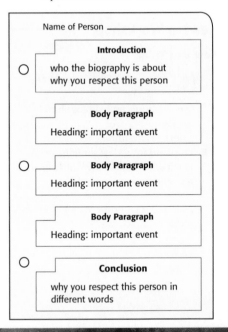

MULTI-LEVEL OPTIONS *Writer's Workshop*

Newcomer Have students create an illustrated biography of Rosa Parks, using the information in Chapter 1 as a reference (pp. 288–295). Copy the timeline from p. 344. Help students to scan the reading for dates to add to the timeline. Then have them arrange their illustrations on it.

Beginning Tell students to choose a person and complete this sentence frame: *I respect _____ because _____.* Then have students work in pairs to discuss their *why* statements. Instruct them to work together to write questions they want to ask about both subjects.

Intermediate Have students work in pairs to compare timelines. Partners should look for organization (whether the events in are order), interest (if this narrative seems interesting), and a list of three important events. Students should revise based on feedback, doing more research if necessary before writing.

Advanced Have students read their narratives aloud in small groups for feedback. Instruct the groups to give each writer a list of additional questions they would like to ask about the subject. Then have students revise their biographies and share them with the class.

Step 3: Revise.

1. Reread your draft. Answer the following questions:
   a. Do readers know why I chose to write about this person?
   b. Did I describe the person and events clearly?
   c. Did I put the events in chronological order?
   d. Did I use reference materials and other resources, such as computer software, to revise my writing?
   e. Did I use chronological time words like *first, next,* and *then* to blend paragraphs together?
   f. Do I need to add or delete text to make my meaning clearer?
   g. How well does my writing achieve its purpose of informing the reader?
2. Share your narrative with a partner.
3. Listen to your partner's comments. Revise your narrative. Use a computer, if possible.
4. Review your partner's narrative. Give comments that will help your partner revise his or her narrative.

Step 4: Edit and proofread.

1. Proofread your revised narrative. Make sure you used standard punctuation, spelling, and grammar. Choose references and resources such as computer software, your Student Handbook, a dictionary, or an expert such as your teacher.
2. Make sure you vary your sentence structure using simple, compound, and complex sentences.

3. Proofread a classmate's writing and give helpful suggestions.

Step 5: Publish.

Prepare a class biography collection for your school library.

1. Collect everyone's work in a binder.
2. If the narratives were prepared electronically, use the software's spell check and grammar check.
3. Make a table of contents to organize the biographies.
4. Choose a title for the binder. Write your teacher's name and the school year. Draw a picture for the cover of the binder.
5. If possible put your collection of biographies on a web site.

Step 6: Evaluate.

1. Review the collection of biographies. Write answers to these questions.
   a. What are the strengths of this collection?
   b. What are its weaknesses?
   c. How can I use this collection to become a better writer?
2. Discuss your answers with your class.

The Heinle Newbury House Dictionary

Student Handbook

Step 3: Revise.
Have students write the letter of each question next to the corresponding text in their drafts. Monitor for completeness.

Step 4: Edit and proofread.
Remind students to complete the Editor's Checklist.

Step 5: Publish.
After students have finished compiling the biographies, have them think of another class in the school that might like to read the collection. Share the collection with that class.

Step 6: Evaluate.
Some criteria students can use to evaluate the collection could include: variety of types of people, visuals, neatness, and correctness of grammar and spelling.

ASSESS

Ask: Which assignment was more difficult, the autobiography or the biography? Why do you think so?

Portfolio

Students may choose to include their writing in their portfolios.

Content Connection
Math

Learning Styles
Linguistic

Have students review the collection of biographies and chart the subjects by *People We Know* and *Famous People.* Ask them to use the totals to create word problems. Provide this example as a model: *Out of 15 students, 5 wrote about someone they know. How many wrote about a famous person?* Have students make subcategories (parents, friends, athletes, and so on) and chart those statistics.

Have students list the best qualities from all the people in the biographical narratives. Have them work in small groups to combine these qualities into one "superperson." *Ask: What does this person do? How does this person behave towards others? What has she/he accomplished?* Have each group write a description of their superperson. Have volunteers from each group describe the person to the class.

Projects

Project 1: Investigate Service Learning

1. **Discuss personal experience** Have students describe volunteer experience they already have to give other students ideas and confidence to get involved.
2. **Plan a class project** Do a simple class service project for the school or the community. It may be easier for students to participate in a group service activity.
3. **Do a presentation about service learning** Volunteers can give their presentation to another class or to younger students.

Project 2: Start a Freedom Magazine

1. **Organize material logically** Have students discuss what would go on each page and why some things should go together.
2. **Utilize computer skills** This project offers an opportunity for students who are skilled at formatting on computers.

Portfolio

Students may choose to include their projects in their portfolios.

Projects

These projects will help you expand your ideas about freedom. Work with a partner or a small group.

Project 1: Investigate Service Learning

Reread "Samantha's Story" on page 335 with the purpose of taking action.

Abeel tells us to do something with our strengths. What action could you take to improve the lives of other people?

One way to take action is to volunteer your time to help others. This is often called service learning.

1. Brainstorm some places where you could serve and list them in a chart.

Place	Service
Senior Citizen Center	Play cards or board games
	Entertain with music
Library	Organize magazines

2. With the help of your teacher, guidance counselor, or parents, choose a place where you can help others.
3. Find out when and how you can volunteer.
4. After you finish your service, write a summary of your experience.
   a. Tell where you worked.
   b. Tell what you did.
   c. What did you learn about your strengths and weaknesses? What other things did you learn?

5. Give a presentation about your experience. Use visuals and presentation software.

Project 2: Start a Freedom Magazine

Think about the different kinds of freedom discussed in this unit. Use that information to create a freedom magazine.

1. Work with a small group.
2. Use multiple sources to find pictures that show freedom. Look in books for words people have used to describe freedom.
3. Search the Internet for times in history when people struggled for freedom. Use the keywords "freedom" and "history."
4. Ask your social studies teacher about famous people who have fought for freedom.
5. Use magazines and newspapers to locate information about people seeking freedom today.
6. Summarize your information in an outline. Use your outline to write short news articles about people seeking freedom.
7. Organize your articles and pictures in the form of a magazine. Create a table of contents. Look at published magazines as models.
8. Use a computer to publish your magazine.

MULTI-LEVEL OPTIONS *Projects*

Newcomer Pair newcomers with advanced students for project 2. Have newcomers research and organize pictures that show freedom. Have advanced students write page introductions and the captions for the pictures.

Beginning Work with students to review the unit and make a list of the different kinds of freedom discussed. Suggest that students find a picture to represent each kind of freedom. Help students write captions for their pictures.

Intermediate Have students ask friends and family what freedom means to them. Tell students to include these responses in their newspapers. Remind them to use quotation marks. They may also want to include photos of the people they interview, placing them next to their quotes.

Advanced Pair advanced students with newcomers. Have advanced students write the captions for the pictures that newcomers find.

Further Reading

The following books discuss the theme of freedom. Choose one or more of them. Write your thoughts and feelings about what you read in your Reading Log. Take notes about your answers to these questions:

1. What is your definition of freedom?
2. How have the characters you read about changed the world around them?

The Gettysburg Address
by Kenneth Richards, Children's Press, 1994. This book discusses the Battle of Gettysburg and President Lincoln's famous speech.

So Far from the Bamboo Grove
by Yoko Kawashima Watkins, Beech Tree Books, 1994. This is a novel based on a true story of a boy who escapes from Korea after World War II.

Reach for the Moon
by Samantha Abeel, Scholastic, Inc., 2001. Samantha Abeel has overcome her learning disorder to create this book of poetry and prose.

Amistad Rising: The Story of Freedom
by Veronica Chambers, Harcourt, 1998. This is a work of historical fiction about a revolt aboard a ship, the *Amistad*, in 1839.

Walking the Road to Freedom: A Story About Sojourner Truth
by Jeri Ferris, Carolrhoda Books, 1989. This biography is about the life of the African-American speaker who spoke out against slavery.

Let It Shine: Stories of Black Women Freedom Fighters
by Andrea Davis Pinkney, Gulliver Books, 2000. This book is a collection of biographies about women who fought against racism. Included are stories about Rosa Parks, Biddy Mason, and Harriet Tubman.

Riding Freedom
by Pam Muñoz Ryan, Scholastic, Inc., 1999. This book is based on the true story of Charlotte "Charley" Darkey Parkhurst. At the age of 12, Charlotte realizes that she does not have the same opportunities as boys. She cuts her hair and disguises herself as a boy.

Companion Web site

Reading Log

Heinle Reading Library Little Women

Further Reading

1. **Read summaries to select books** Read or have volunteers read the book summaries. Have students identify the books that they would like to read. Instruct students to make comments about the books, using superlative adjectives. (*Example:* "Amistad Rising" sounds like the most exciting book.)

2. **Choose appropriate form for purpose** After students have read at least one book, *say: Now that you have read a book, you want to let others know about it. What's the best form of writing to use for this purpose?* Have students choose the appropriate form for their purpose for writing. Guide them to choose a review. Instruct students to write a short book review. Create a class collection of book reviews. Tell students to use the reviews to help them decide which books to read. Have them continue to add reviews to the collection as they read more books.

Assessment Program: *Unit 5 Test, pp. 83–88*

Heinle Reading Library

Little Women by Louisa May Alcott
In a specially adapted version by Lucia Monfried

The warmhearted story of the four March sisters . . . Meg, Jo, Beth, and Amy growing up in 19th century America. Their happy family life is disturbed when their father leaves for the Civil War and is shaken further when their mother must leave to nurse their wounded father back to health. But family love and loyalty keeps them together. As the years pass, the girls become women and learn more about life and love. Louisa May Alcott's timeless classic shows the joys of growing up in a warm and loving family.

Visions Companion Site

http://visions.heinle.com
For additional student activities and teacher resources, see the Visions Companion Web site.

Unit Materials

Activity Book: *pp. 185–216*
Audio: *Unit 6; CD 3, Tracks 6–9*
Student Handbook
Student CD-ROM: *Unit 6*
CNN Video: *Unit 6*
Teacher Resource Book: *Lesson Plans, Teacher Resources, Reading Summaries, School-Home Connection, Video Script, Video Worksheet, Activity Book Answer Key*
Teacher Resource CD-ROM
Assessment Program: *Quizzes, Test, and End-of-Book Exam, pp. 89–108; Teacher and Student Resources, pp. 115–144*
Assessment CD-ROM
Transparencies
The Heinle Newbury House Dictionary/CD-ROM
More Grammar Practice workbook
Heinle Reading Library: *A Christmas Carol*
Web site: http://visions.heinle.com

Visions Staff Development Handbook

Refer to the Visions Staff Development Handbook for more teacher support.

Unit Theme: Visions

Describe visions *Say: A vision is a mental image or a dream of the future.* **Ask:** *Did you ever have a vision or dream? What was it?* Have students describe their visions.

Unit Preview: Table of Contents

1. **Use text features** *Ask: Which chapters have readings about houses and towns?* (Chapters 2, 4) *Which chapter has a play?* (Chapter 1)
2. **Connect** *Ask: Which chapters seem interesting to you?*

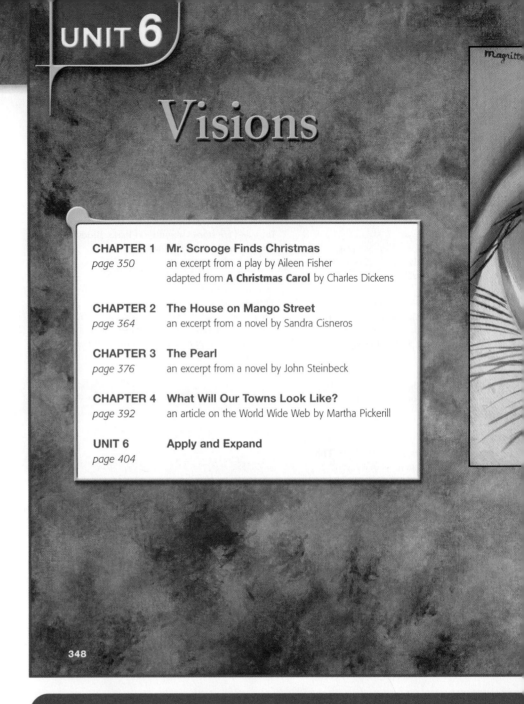

UNIT 6

Visions

348

UNIT OBJECTIVES

Reading
Use chronology to locate and recall information as you read an excerpt from a play • Paraphrase to recall information as you read an excerpt from a novel • Make inferences using text evidence as you read an excerpt from a novel • Summarize text to recall ideas as you read an article on the World Wide Web

Listening and Speaking
Present a scene from the play • Talk about mental images • Listen to and present the story • Give a persuasive speech

Le Faux Miroir (The False Mirror), René Magritte, oil on canvas,1928.

View the Picture

1. What is the artist trying to show by choosing this medium, this style, and these elements?
2. How do color, shape, and line influence the artist's message?
3. How does the art represent the meaning of "visions"? Did the artist do a good job?

In this unit, you will read a play, excerpts from two novels, and an article from the World Wide Web. You will practice writing these forms.

349

Grammar

Use the present perfect tense • Spell frequently misspelled words • Use conjunctions to form compound sentences • Use *will* to predict future events

Writing

Write a persuasive letter • Write a description • Write a fiction story • Create a form, interview, and summarize

Content

Math: Answer math questions about currency • Science: Learn about animal habitats • Social Studies: Learn about bodies of water • Science: Learn about acid rain

View the Picture

1. **Art background** Rene Magritte (1898–1967), a Belgian surrealist painter, was known for a precise, almost photographic technique that contrasted with and highlighted an unexpected visual imagery. Surrealism, a primarily European movement, was influenced by the psychoanalytic work of Sigmund Freud and Carl Jung. In this painting, Magritte surprises us by turning the notion that the eye is the mirror of the soul on its head; he calls it "The False Mirror," and its vision reflects the sky, not the person.

2. **Art interpretation** *Ask:* Have students describe the painting and their reaction to it.
   a. **Interpret the painting** *Ask: What does the artist's close-up of an eye reflecting sky and clouds make you think about?*
   b. **Connect to theme** Tell students that the theme of this unit is *visions.* *Ask: Do you think Magritte's vision might have more than one meaning in this painting?*

ASSESS

Have students draw a picture of a vision they had.

Chapter Materials

Activity Book: *pp. 185–192*
Audio: *Unit 6, Chapter 1; CD 3, Track 6*
Student Handbook
Student CD-ROM: *Unit 6, Chapter 1*
Teacher Resource Book: *Lesson Plan, Teacher Resources, Reading Summary, Activity Book Answer Key*
Teacher Resource CD-ROM
Assessment Program: *Quiz, pp. 89–90; Teacher and Student Resources, pp. 115–144*
Assessment CD-ROM
Transparencies
The Heinle Newbury House Dictionary/CD-ROM
Web site: http://visions.heinle.com

Objectives

Paired reading Have students work in pairs and take turns reading the objectives. Explain the objectives to students.

Use Prior Knowledge

Talk About the Past, Present, and Future
Gather and organize Review the chart and its headings. Add specific years or other time expressions, such as *four months ago, right now,* and *someday soon,* to clarify the meanings of past, present, and future. Model examples of appropriate verb tenses.

Mr. Scrooge Finds Christmas

an excerpt from a play
by Aileen Fisher

adapted from
A Christmas Carol
by Charles Dickens

Objectives

Reading Use chronology to locate and recall information as you read an excerpt from a play.

Listening and Speaking Present a scene from the play.

Grammar Use the present perfect tense.

Writing Write a persuasive letter.

Content Math: Answer math questions about currency.

Use Prior Knowledge

Talk About the Past, Present, and Future

Time is divided into three parts: past, present, and future. The past has already happened. The present is happening right now. The future will happen later.

1. Make a chart like the one below on a piece of paper.
2. List something you did in the past. Use the past tense or the past perfect tense.
3. List something you are doing in the present. Use the present tense or the present progressive tense.
4. List something you will do in the future. Use the future tense.
5. Share your answers with a small group. Listen carefully as your classmates share their answers.

Past	Present	Future
Last year I learned to swim.	Now I live in Newtown.	Next year, I will study biology.

350 Unit 6 Visions

MULTI-LEVEL OPTIONS *Build Vocabulary*

Newcomer Have students fold a piece of paper in half. Help them write *Meaning* on the left side. Have them draw a calendar and show a holiday they celebrate. On the right side, help them write *Feelings.* On this side, have them draw pictures to express feelings they have about the holiday.

Beginning Have students fold sheets of paper to form two columns. Under the heading *Meaning,* have them write the name of a holiday and a few words to tell what the holiday celebrates. (*Example:* Año Viejo, Ecuador's New Year) Under the heading *Feelings,* have them write words for feelings they have about the holiday.

Intermediate Have students make word webs for the three words/phrases in Build Vocabulary. Ask them to include on the webs the definitions, synonyms, related words, and the associations they make with the words.

Advanced Have students write the vocabulary words across the top of a piece of paper. Ask them to list any words or ideas they associate with each term under that word. Then have them look up the definitions. Have them discuss how their associations with the words do or do not reflect the words' actual meanings.

Build Background

Scrooge

"Mr. Scrooge Finds Christmas" is based on the novel "A Christmas Carol" by Charles Dickens. The setting of the story is London, England, in the mid-1800s. At that time, many people in England did not have jobs, and most people had very little money. Some of the people who did have money were greedy. They wanted more money than they already had.

The main character in the story is named Ebenezer Scrooge. Scrooge is a rich, greedy man. He is also a selfish man who does not care about helping others.

Many English words have their origins in fiction. "A Christmas Carol" is a very popular story. Mr. Scrooge and his traits are so well known that his name has become a noun in the English language. Someone who is a *scrooge* is a person who has money but is very selfish.

Content Connection

Charles Dickens (1812–1870) is considered to be one of the greatest British authors. He wrote 16 novels including *David Copperfield* and *A Tale of Two Cities*.

Build Vocabulary

Distinguish Denotative and Connotative Meanings

Denotative meanings of words are the definitions you find in a dictionary. Connotative meanings refer to the feelings that we attach to the word.

The denotative definition of *Christmas* is "the Christian holiday celebrating the birth of Jesus Christ." But for many people, *Christmas* suggests many other things, such as gift-giving and special food. These are some of the connotative meanings of *Christmas*.

As you read the selection, look for these other words and phrases that have connotative meanings. Check the dictionary for the denotative meanings. Ask your teacher about their connotations. Remember that connotative meanings can be negative or positive.

a. idiot   **b.** idle people   **c.** charity

The Heinle Newbury House Dictionary

Activity Book p. 185

Student CD-ROM

Chapter 1   Mr. Scrooge Finds Christmas   **351**

Community Connection

Build Background Tell students that there are many organizations that help the poor and others in need. Divide students into small groups. Have groups research organizations in your community, such as local charities, food pantries, and so on. Tell them to list different ways they can help the needy in the community using what they learned about these organizations. (*Examples:* donate clothes, donate food, volunteer time at a food pantry, give money to a charity)

Learning Styles
Visual

Build Vocabulary Have each student select a glossed word from the selection. Ask them to read the definitions as well as think about associations with and connotations of their words. Tell each student to use art to write the word in a manner that shows its connotative meaning. (*Example: Extravagant* might be written with lots of flourishes and curlicues in yellow, gold, and glitter markers.)

Build Background

Scrooge

▌ Teacher Resource Book: *Word Wheel, p. 36*

1. **Use a Word Wheel** Have students create a Word Wheel for *scrooge*.
2. **Content Connection** Dickens pointed out problems in society during the 1800s. *Ask: What problems did Dickens see?*

Build Vocabulary

Distinguish Denotative and Connotative Meanings

▌ Teacher Resource Book: *Personal Dictionary, p. 63*

1. **Clarify meaning and usage** Remind students that they can use a dictionary, thesaurus, or software (such as a CD-ROM dictionary) to clarify meaning and usage. These sources sometimes provide usage notes that often help distinguish denotative and connotative meanings. For example, have students look up *peanut butter* in The Heinle Newbury House Dictionary. The denotative meaning is "a soft, creamy food made from crushed peanuts." The usage note says that "peanut butter and jelly sandwiches are a favorite food of American children." The connotative meaning might be "a familiar food that reminds me of my childhood."
2. **Reading selection vocabulary** You may want to introduce the glossed words in the reading selection before students begin reading. Key words: *ghost, clerk, humbug, fate, shock, charity, benevolence, haunted.* Instruct students to write the words with correct spelling and their definitions in their Personal Dictionaries. Have them pronounce each word and divide it into syllables.
3. **Multi-level options** See MULTI-LEVEL OPTIONS on p. 350.

Answers
1. an unintelligent person/very foolish or stupid person
2. people who are not busy/lazy or bad people
3. giving to others/kind feelings and helpfulness

ASSESS

Ask: What is an antonym for scrooge?

Text Structure

Play

1. **Use a graphic organizer to define and explain features** Write the features chart on the board. Have students give examples of the features from other selections or plays they have seen.
2. **Multi-level options** See MULTI-LEVEL OPTIONS below.

Reading Strategy

Use Chronology to Locate and Recall Information

Use personal experiences Ask students to recall yesterday's events using chronology and time words.

Answers
a. 2 b. 4 c. 1 d. 6 e. 5 f. 3

ASSESS

Ask for definitions of: *scenes, names of characters, setting, stage directions,* and *dialogue.*

Text Structure

Play

"Mr. Scrooge Finds Christmas" is a **play.** In a play, actors act out a story. The actors speak lines in front of an audience. They pretend to be characters in the play. Look for the features of a play as you read the selection.

Usually, actors act on a **stage**—a raised floor. This stage is usually decorated to show the setting.

As you read, think about the play's setting. What do you think the stage looks like?

Play	
Scenes	different parts of the story
Names of Characters	names before each line of dialogue to tell you which character is speaking
Setting	where and when the story happens
Stage Directions	actions that the characters do
Dialogue	what the characters say to each other

Student CD-ROM

Reading Strategy

Use Chronology to Locate and Recall Information

Chronology is the order in which events happen. You can use chronology to **locate** information in a text. Chronology can also help you **recall** (remember) what you read.

Copy the following sentences on a piece of paper. In what order do you think the events happen? Number the events in chronological order. Use *1* for the first event, *2* for the second event, and so on.

_____ **a.** He went to work.
_____ **b.** He went home.
___/___ **c.** Bob got up early.
_____ **d.** He went to bed.
_____ **e.** He had dinner with his family.
_____ **f.** He worked all day.

Student CD-ROM

MULTI-LEVEL OPTIONS *Text Structure*

Newcomer Show students a picture of actors on stage. Point to the stage. *Say: stage.* Point to an actor. *Say: actor.* Point to the actor's mouth. *Say: dialogue.* Point to the scenery. *Say: scenery.* Then repeat the words one by one and invite volunteers to point to each feature.

Beginning Show students several pictures of actors performing on stage. Point out the features described in Text Structure. Ask students to draw a stage and actors for a story they know. Have them label the features.

Intermediate Have pairs of students look at play scripts in a book or from another resource. Ask them to identify the features discussed on p. 352.

Advanced Have students work in groups. Ask them to select a story they read in a previous unit, such as "Island of the Blue Dolphins." Tell them to discuss how the story could be transformed into a play. Ask them to talk about how each of the features described on p. 352 could be handled.

MR. SCROOGE FINDS CHRISTMAS

an excerpt from a play by Aileen Fisher

adapted from *A Christmas Carol* by Charles Dickens

353

Reading Selection Materials

Audio: *Unit 6, Chapter 1; CD 3, Track 6*
Teacher Resource Book: *Reading Summary,*
    pp. 111–112
Transparencies: *#44, Reading Summary*

Suggestions for Using Reading Summary

- Introduce new vocabulary or cognates.
- Cut the summary into strips, or jumble the sentences on an overhead transparency. Students put the sentences in order.
- Practice the reading strategy.
- Students read aloud or with a partner.
- Students paraphrase the summary.
- Students do a cloze activity.
- Students create a visual or graphic organizer, such as a timeline or storyboard, to illustrate the summary.
- Students paraphrase the summary.

Preview the Selection

▌ Teacher Resource Book: *Sunshine Organizer, p. 40*

1. **Use a graphic organizer** Have students study the picture and the title. Help them make predictions about the play. Have students fill in their predictions on a sunshine organizer. *Ask: Who are these people? Where do you think they are? What are they doing? What do they look like? How do they make you feel? What do you think they will say and do?*

2. **Connect** Remind students that the unit theme is *visions*. *Ask: Do you think these people are visions or are they real?*

Content Connection
The Arts

Learning Styles
Interpersonal

Say: This is a photograph of an actor portraying a character in a stage play. Ask: What is the mood of the character in the photograph? (sour, mean, unhappy) *How do the costume, hair, makeup, and body language contribute to that mood?* (the person seems shriveled up, has messy hair, wearing many layers of mismatched clothes, body is hunched over, hands are curled up)

Have students meet in small groups to discuss the photograph on p. 353. *Ask: What kind of person do you think he is? What do you think he would say to you? What can you tell from the look on his face? What can you tell from his body language? What can you tell from his clothes? How do you think the photograph fits in with the title of the play?*

Read the Selection

1. **Use text features** Point out the list of characters, dialogue, and stage directions. Ask students to describe the characters in the illustration. Remind students to use the illustration and glossed words to help understanding.

2. **Read dramatically** Play the audio. Pause to check understanding and to identify setting and events. Have students reread and act out parts.

3. **Use chronology to locate and recall information** Guide students to identify the key events in the selection and arrange in chronological order on a timeline.

Sample Answer to Guide Question
He shivered and rubbed his hands together; he looks "furtively" at Scrooge.

See Teacher Edition pp. 434–436 for a list of English-Spanish cognates in the reading selection.

Audio
CD 3. Tr. 6

Characters	
EBENEZER SCROOGE	BOB CRATCHIT, *his* **clerk**
FRED, *Scrooge's nephew*	MARLEY'S **GHOST**
A **SOLICITOR**	BOY **CAROLERS**
GHOST OF CHRISTMAS PAST	}
GHOST OF CHRISTMAS PRESENT	} *three spirits*
GHOST OF CHRISTMAS YET TO COME }	

Scene 2

1 **Setting:** *The office of Scrooge and Marley.*

Use Chronology to Locate and Recall Information

What did Bob Cratchit do before he got up to put more coal in the fire?

At Rise: *On a stool, hunched over a high bookkeeper's desk, sits* BOB CRATCHIT. *He has a long white muffler around his neck.* SCROOGE *sits at his desk at the other side of the room. There is a meager fire in the grate on each side of the room. BOB shivers, rubs his hands. Then, with a* **furtive** *glance at* SCROOGE, *gets off his stool, takes the* **coal** *shovel and carefully approaches the coal-box.*

2 **Scrooge** (*Looking up, angrily*): At three o'clock in the afternoon, Cratchit? Wasting coal, so close to closing time?

3 **Bob:** It's cold and foggy, sir. Penetrating . . .

4 **Scrooge:** Cold, nonsense! Haven't you a candle there on your desk?

5 **Bob:** Yes, sir. But the figures suffer when my hand shakes.

6 **Scrooge:** Warm your hands over the candle, then. How many times do I have to tell you? If you persist in being so **extravagant** with the coal, we shall have to part company, you and I. I can get another clerk, you know. More easily than you can get another position, I **warrant.**

---

solicitor   a salesperson
clerk   a person who keeps records in an office
ghost   the spirit of a dead person
carolers   people who sing Christmas songs

furtive   sneaky
coal   a mineral that people burn for heat
extravagant   using too much
warrant   guarantee

354   Unit 6   Visions

MULTI-LEVEL OPTIONS *Read the Selection*

Newcomer Play the audio. Then do a choral reading with students joining in when they can. *Ask: Does Bob work for Mr. Scrooge?* (yes) *Is Mr. Scrooge a caring boss?* (no) *Does Mr. Scrooge like Christmas?* (no)

Beginning Read aloud the story. Then have volunteers read parts aloud. *Ask: Where are Mr. Scrooge and Bob?* (at work) *Who is the boss?* (Mr. Scrooge) *Who is cold?* (Bob Cratchit) *Who likes Christmas?* (Fred) *Who does not like Christmas?* (Mr. Scrooge)

Intermediate Read aloud the story. Then have volunteers read parts aloud. *Ask: How does Mr. Scrooge treat Bob?* (He is mean and stingy with him.) *How does Mr. Scrooge show his feelings about holidays?* (He says mean things like, "Bah! Humbug!" He doesn't see why others celebrate.)

Advanced Have students read silently. Then have volunteers read parts aloud. *Ask: What does Mr. Scrooge mean when he says that he wants to keep Christmas in his own way?* (He doesn't want to celebrate.) *Why do you think Mr. Scrooge feels that way?* (Maybe he is mean; he had a sad life and doesn't feel like celebrating.)

7   **Bob** *(Going back to stool):* Yes, sir. *(Rubs hands over candle. Huddles in muffler. After a moment of silence, FRED bursts into the room.)*

8   **Fred** *(Cheerfully):* A Merry Christmas, uncle! God save you!

9   **Scrooge** *(Without looking up):* Bah! **Humbug!**

10 **Fred:** Christmas is a humbug, uncle? You don't mean that, I am sure!

Use Chronology to Locate and Recall Information

What does Scrooge say after Fred wishes him Merry Christmas?

11 **Scrooge:** I do. Merry Christmas! What reason have you to be merry? You're poor enough.

12 **Fred:** Come, then, what reason have you to be dismal? You're rich enough.

13 **Scrooge** *(Banging down ruler):* Bah! Humbug!

14 **Fred:** Don't be **cross**, uncle.

15 **Scrooge:** What else can I be when I live in such a world of fools as this? What's a Christmas-time to you but a time for

paying bills without money; a time for finding yourself a year older, and not an hour richer? If I could work my will, every idiot who goes about with "Merry Christmas" on his lips should be boiled with his own **pudding,** and buried with a **stake** of holly through his heart.

16 **Fred:** Uncle!

17 **Scrooge:** Keep Christmas in your own way, and let me keep it in mine. Much good it has ever done you.

18 **Fred:** I have always thought of Christmas-time as a good time . . . a kind, forgiving, **charitable,** pleasant time; the only time I know of when men and women seem by one consent to open their shut-up hearts freely . . . I say, God bless it! *(BOB claps his hands, then, embarrassed at his impulse, huddles over his work.)*

---

humbug an expression meaning "nonsense!"
cross angry
pudding a smooth, sweet dessert made with eggs and milk

stake a narrow, pointed piece of wood
charitable giving help or money to those who need it

Chapter 1   Mr. Scrooge Finds Christmas   **355**

Read the Selection

1. **Understand terms** Have students find the meanings of the italicized phrases in the selection. Clarify meanings as needed.

2. **Use the illustration** Ask students to describe the picture and suggest the conversation and feelings of the characters.

3. **Group reading** After students listen to the audio or to your reading of the selection, have them reread it in groups of three. *Ask: Does Scrooge like Christmas? What does he think of it?* (No. He thinks there is no reason to celebrate or be happy because everyone is so poor.)

4. **Use chronology to locate and recall information** *Ask: When does Fred enter—before or after Bob Cratchit goes back to work?* (after) Ask other questions to help students summarize important events of the selection and add them to the timeline.

5. **Multi-level options** See MULTI-LEVEL OPTIONS on p. 354.

Sample Answer to Guide Question
He says, "Bah! Humbug!"

❜ Punctuation

Colon to introduce dialogue

Have students return to line 3. *Say: Look at the punctuation mark after the word name Bob. It is a colon. In a play, a colon is used to separate the character's name from the dialogue, which is what the character says. Look at line 4 to see another example.* (Scrooge: Cold, nonsense!)

Apply Have pairs work together. *Say: Write a dialogue you and your partner might say when you see each other first thing in the morning. Remember to use colons.* If necessary, write an example on the board:

Kim: Hi, how are you?
Leah: Fine. What did you do last night?
Kim: I listened to music.

Read the Selection

1. **Use the illustration** Ask students to describe the characters and suggest what they are talking about.

2. **Dramatic reading** Read the selection. Then have some students read the parts aloud as others act them out. *Ask: Who enters the office after Fred leaves?* (a solicitor) *What is he collecting?* (money for a fund) *Why does he want to buy with the fund?* (some food and something to keep the poor people warm) Then have students reread the selection in small groups and add events to the timeline.

Sample Answer to Guide Question
"Well, Merry Christmas, uncle! And a happy New Year!"

---

19 **Scrooge** *(To BOB):* Let me hear another sound from *you,* and you'll keep your Christmas by losing your position.

20 **Fred:** Don't be angry, uncle. Come, **dine** with us tomorrow.

21 **Scrooge:** Good afternoon!

22 **Fred:** I want nothing from you. I ask nothing of you. Why cannot we be friends?

23 **Scrooge:** Good afternoon!

24 **Fred** *(Shrugging, cheerfully):* Well, Merry Christmas, uncle! And a happy New Year!

25 **Scrooge:** Good *afternoon!* (FRED *stops at* BOB'S *desk, and they exchange smiles and greetings.* BOB *goes with him to the door. As* FRED *exits, a* SOLICITOR *comes in with books and papers.* BOB **gestures** *him toward* SCROOGE *then goes back to his work.)*

> **Use Chronology to Locate and Recall Information**
>
> What is the last thing that Fred says to Scrooge?

26 **Solicitor:** Scrooge and Marley's, I believe? Have I the pleasure of addressing Mr. Scrooge or Mr. Marley?

27 **Scrooge:** Mr. Marley has been dead these seven years.

28 **Solicitor** *(Presenting credentials):* At this **festive** season of the year, Mr. Scrooge, it is more than usually desirable that we should make some slight **provision** for the poor and **destitute** . . .

29 **Scrooge:** Are there no prisons? No workhouses?

30 **Solicitor:** There are. But, under the impression that they scarcely **furnish** Christian cheer, a few of us are **endeavoring** to raise a fund to buy the poor some meat and drink, and means of warmth. What shall I put you down for?

31 **Scrooge:** Nothing!

---

dine   eat a meal
gestures   makes a movement with the head or hand to show something
festive   joyful

provision   preparation
destitute   without any money or hope of having any
furnish   provide, give something
endeavoring   trying

MULTI-LEVEL OPTIONS *Read the Selection*

Newcomer *Ask: Does Mr. Scrooge want to go to Fred's house for Christmas?* (no) *Will Mr. Scrooge give money for the poor?* (no) *Does Mr. Scrooge want to give Bob the day off for Christmas?* (no) *Will spirits try to help Mr. Scrooge?* (yes)

Beginning *Ask: Who wants Mr. Scrooge to come to Christmas dinner?* (Fred) *What does the solicitor want Mr. Scrooge to give for poor people?* (money) *What does Mr. Scrooge want Bob to do on Christmas?* (work) *Who is going to try to help Mr. Scrooge?* (spirits)

Intermediate *Ask: How do you think Bob feels about his boss?* (unhappy with his mean treatment but dependent on him for a job) *Why doesn't Mr. Scrooge want to give money for poor people?* (He thinks they are poor because they don't want to work.) *What do you think the spirits want to do?* (change Mr. Scrooge into a kind man)

Advanced *Ask: What do you think Fred and Bob may have said to each other as Fred left?* (that it is a shame that Mr. Scrooge is so unhappy) *Do you think Marley liked to help others when he was alive?* (no) *What is the chain around Marley?* (all the objects from his old business)

32 **Solicitor:** You wish to be anonymous—is that it?

33 **Scrooge:** I wish to be left alone. I don't make merry myself at Christmas, and I can't afford to make idle people merry. Good afternoon, sir.

34 **Solicitor:** *Good afternoon!* (SOLICITOR *goes out, shaking his head.* BOB *opens door for him, then hurries back to his stool.*)

35 **Scrooge** (*Glaring at* BOB): You'll want all day tomorrow, I suppose?

36 **Bob:** If quite **convenient,** sir.

37 **Scrooge:** It's not convenient, and it's not fair.

38 **Bob:** It's only once a year, sir.

39 **Scrooge** (*Bangs down ruler*): A poor excuse for picking a man's pocket every twenty-fifth of December!

Curtain

Scene 3

40 **Before Rise:** MARLEY'S GHOST *and* THREE SPIRITS *appear in spotlight on darkened stage (or enter before curtain).*

41 **Marley:** There!

42 **1st Spirit:** I see what you mean, Mr. Marley. Ebenezer Scrooge is a bad case.

43 **2nd Spirit:** No wonder you need help, if you want to try to **reform** *him.*

44 **3rd Spirit:** He's been this way so long, I'm afraid it's a bad habit.

45 **Marley:** Surely we must try to save him, my friends. We can at least warn him, at least give him a chance to escape my **fate.** (*Clanks chain*) Poor man, he has no idea what lies ahead of him if he doesn't change his ways.

46 **1st Spirit:** What is your plan? How can we warn him? When?

convenient acceptable and suitable to one's time or needs

reform improve

fate the force that is thought to determine events

Chapter 1 Mr. Scrooge Finds Christmas **357**

Read the Selection

1. **Use text features** Point out the end of scene 2 and the beginning of scene 3. Have students describe the illustration and make predictions about Scrooge's vision. Review meanings of glossed words.

2. **Shared reading** Play the audio. Have students join in when they can.

3. **Make predictions** *Ask: How do you think the spirits will try to help Scrooge?*

4. **Use a timeline** Ask questions to help students summarize key events to include on their timelines.

5. **Describe the stage** Have students use the stage directions to compare and contrast the settings of scenes 2 and 3.

6. **Multi-level options** See MULTI-LEVEL OPTIONS on p. 356.

Sample Answer to Guide Question
Tomorrow is Christmas. Bob Cratchit wants the day off as a holiday.

A Capitalization

Holidays

Say: Look at how Christmas *is written in line 19. What do you notice? Yes, the names for holidays start with a capital letter. Look at line 24 to find another example.* (New Year)

Apply Have each student complete the following on a strip of paper: *My favorite holiday is ___.* Remind them to use capital letters at the beginnings of words for holidays. Have students share their sentences and tell why the holiday is their favorite. Hang all the completed sentences on a bulletin board or wall with the heading *Our Favorite Holidays.*

Read the Selection

1. **Use the illustrations** Have students suggest the conversation and feelings of the characters.
2. **Dramatic reading** Read aloud and have students act out the selection. Have students reread and act out the selection in small groups and add events to the timeline.

Sample Answer to Guide Question
He will talk to Scrooge first and warn him. He will clank his chain.

Use Chronology to Locate and Recall Information

What is Mr. Marley going to do before he calls the spirits?

47 **Marley:** This very night of **Christmas Eve!** After closing the office, he will take his dinner in the usual tavern, read the papers, go over his accounts, and then home to bed. I know his lodgings well. Fact is, they used to belong to me. He will be quite alone in the house. I will appear before him as he gets drowsy.

48 **2nd Spirit:** Won't it be rather a **shock** to him—to see you?

49 **Marley:** He needs a shock to open his eyes, poor fellow.

50 **3rd Spirit:** And what about us? Where do we come in?

51 **Marley:** You wait in the shadows until I call you. First I must lay the groundwork. When I stand before Ebenezer in my usual waistcoat, tights, and boots, I will clank this **infernal** chain about my middle—this chain made of cash-boxes, keys, padlocks, **ledgers,** deeds, and heavy purses wrought in steel!

52 **1st Spirit:** He will be scared out of his wits!

53 **Marley:** He needs to be. I will tell him that he is forging a chain just like mine, that I have no rest, no peace, because in life my spirit never roved beyond the narrow limits of our **countinghouse.** It is no way to live.

54 **2nd Spirit:** Can a man of business understand such talk, Mr. Marley?

55 **Marley:** We must make him understand, my friends. We must get him to see that **mankind,** not money, is his business. That common welfare is his business. **Charity,** mercy, forbearance, and **benevolence** are all his business! And you are to impress it upon him.

56 **Spirits:** How?

Christmas Eve the night before Christmas, December 24
shock surprise in a bad way
infernal terrible
ledgers journals in which numbers are recorded, especially for businesses

countinghouse a business office
mankind people
charity giving to the needy
benevolence kindness

358 Unit 6 Visions

MULTI-LEVEL OPTIONS *Read the Selection*

Newcomer *Ask: Do the spirits plan to visit Mr. Scrooge?* (yes) *Do they want to scare him?* (yes) *Do they want to show him how to make more money?* (no) *Do they want to teach him to be kind?* (yes)

Beginning *Ask: Who will visit Mr. Scrooge?* (Marley and three spirits) *When will they visit?* (Christmas Eve) *How do they think their visit will make him feel?* (scared) *What do they hope their visit will do for Mr. Scrooge?* (help him learn what is important in life)

Intermediate *Ask: How do the spirits plan for their visit to Mr. Scrooge?* (They talk about what they will do, who will do what, and what they hope to accomplish.) *How do they expect to affect Mr. Scrooge?* (They hope to show him that money isn't as important as being happy and making others happy.)

Advanced *Ask: Why is it helpful that Marley is part of the plan?* (He knows Mr. Scrooge and his habits, so he might know how to convince him.) *What is one hint that the spirits may be able to convince Mr. Scrooge to change his ways?* (Example: Mr. Scrooge was not always mean and bitter about Christmas.)

Use Chronology to Locate and Recall Information

List in chronological order the events that the spirits will show Mr. Scrooge.

57 **Marley:** I will warn Ebenezer that he will be **haunted** by three Spirits in his sleep tonight. *(Points to* 1ST SPIRIT*)* As Ghost of Christmas Past, you will take him back to his life as a schoolboy and as an **apprentice,** and show him that Christmas meant something to him then. That he shouted "Merry Christmas" with the rest of them, in good spirit. *(Points to* 2ND SPIRIT*)* As Ghost of Christmas Present, you will show him how joyously his clerk Bob Cratchit will celebrate Christmas with his family tomorrow, for all Bob's **meager salary.** *(Points to* 3RD SPIRIT*)* And you, as Ghost of Christmas Yet to Come, will show him what will happen if he dies as he is—if he does not change.

58 **1st Spirit:** And all this to be done tonight?

59 **Marley:** Tonight, while Ebenezer Scrooge lies **abed.** Otherwise, we shall be too late for Christmas tomorrow.

60 **Spirits:** Lead on! We're with you! *(In a moment* BOY CAROLERS *come singing "God Rest You Merry, Gentlemen." After a stanza or two, they move on. A brief pause . . . then* SCROOGE *and* GHOST OF CHRISTMAS PAST *enter before curtain.)*

haunted   visited by ghosts
apprentice   a person who is learning a skill from an expert

meager   very little
salary   payment received for work
abed   an old way of saying "in bed"

About the Author | Charles Dickens (1812–1870)

Charles Dickens grew up in London, England. At the age of 12, Dickens worked in a factory to help his family. Later, he wrote for a newspaper. In 1836, Dickens published his first book. Shortly after, he became very famous as a writer.

➤ Why do you think Charles Dickens wrote "A Christmas Carol"? To entertain or to give his opinion about greed?

Chapter 1   Mr. Scrooge Finds Christmas   **359**

Read the Selection

1. **Shared reading**   Play the audio. Have students join in when they can.
2. **Multi-level options**   See MULTI-LEVEL OPTIONS on p. 358.

Sample Answer to Guide Question
They will show Scrooge as a boy, Christmas at Bob Cratchit's house, and Christmas after he dies.

About the Author

1. **Explain author background**   Charles Dickens often read aloud his stories for the public—sometimes for charity, sometimes for pay. He also made sure that working people could come to his performances.
2. **Interpret the facts**   *Ask: Why do you think Charles Dickens wanted to share his stories with working people?* (He wanted to help them have happier lives.)

Answer
I think Dickens wrote "A Christmas Carol" to both entertain and to give his opinion about greed.

Across Selections

Teacher Resource Book: *Venn Diagram, p. 35*

Compare and contrast   Have students work in pairs. Direct them to the text structure chart for "The Legend of Sleepy Hollow" (p. 52). Have students compare and contrast it with the text structure of this play. Have them record information on a Venn diagram. (similarities: made-up or exaggerated characters, events, and settings; differences: oral tradition/written dialogue, legends are narratives/plays have scenes and stage directions)

Spelling, Punctuation, Capitalization

After the Reading Comprehension section, students will practice spelling, punctuation, and capitalization in the Activity Book.

 Spelling

Lie or *lay*

Write on the board: *lie, lay.* Direct students to line 51. Copy on the board: *First, I must lay the groundwork.* **Say:** Lay *means "to put something down or in place."* What is the spirit putting in place? (groundwork, a plan) Then have students read line 59. Copy on the board: *Tonight, while Ebenezer Scrooge lies abed.* **Say:** Lie *means "to rest in a horizontal position."* Where is he resting? (in bed) Point out that the simple past of *lay* is *laid* and of *lie* is *lay.*

Evaluate Your Reading Strategy

Use Chronology to Locate and Recall Information   *Say: You have practiced an important reading strategy. Now you can decide how well you have done. Does this statement describe how you read?*

As I read, I look for words that help me figure out when events happened. Using chronology helps me find and remember information in the text.

Beyond the Reading

Reading Comprehension

Question-Answer Relationships

Sample Answers

1. a bookkeeper
2. Mr. Scrooge
3. Ebenezer
4. keys, cash boxes, ledgers, and other bookkeeping objects
5. that people are more important than money
6. that Scrooge will end up in chains just like he did
7. Marley wasn't a nice person; otherwise, he wouldn't be in chains now.
8. because coal costs money and Scrooge hates to spend money
9. He needs the money to support his family and it is difficult to find jobs.
10. Scrooge thinks work is more important than people, family, or holidays. Fred thinks people should celebrate holidays and enjoy friends and family.
11. I think Scrooge will change because I think Charles Dickens wants people to change and help others.
12. It is a time when people spend time with friends and family instead of working.
13. The plot is similar, but the spirits looked different from the mental image the text gave me.

Build Reading Fluency

Audio CD Reading Practice

Explain that reading silently while listening to the audio recording helps improve reading fluency. Remind them to keep their eyes on the words. Repeat the audio recording as needed.

Reading Comprehension

Question-Answer Relationships (QAR)

"Right There" Questions

1. **Recall Facts** What is Bob Cratchit's job?
2. **Recall Facts** Who is Fred's uncle?
3. **Recall Facts** What is Mr. Scrooge's first name?

"Think and Search" Questions

4. **Identify** What is Marley's chain made of?
5. **Paraphrase** What does Marley want Mr. Scrooge to understand?
6. **Make Inferences** What does Marley think will happen to Mr. Scrooge if Scrooge does not change?

"Author and You" Questions

7. **Make Inferences** Do you think Marley was a nice person while he was alive? Why or why not?
8. **Analyze Characters** Why doesn't Mr. Scrooge want Bob Cratchit to use coal in the office?

9. **Analyze Characters** Why do you think Bob Cratchit continues to work for Mr. Scrooge?
10. **Analyze Conflict** What is the conflict between Scrooge and his nephew, Fred?

"On Your Own" Questions

11. **Predict** Do you think Mr. Scrooge will change after the three spirits visit him? Why or why not?
12. **Understand Setting** Why do you think this play is set during Christmas?
13. **Compare Communication** Read the same passage in Dickens's novel or view these scenes in the film version. How are these versions the same or different? What did you learn from the other version?

Activity Book
p. 186

Student
CD-ROM

Build Reading Fluency

Audio CD Reading Practice

Listening to the Audio CD of "Mr. Scrooge Finds Christmas" is good reading practice. It helps you to learn to read with expression.

1. Listen to Scene 2 on the Audio CD.
2. Follow along in your student book on page 354.
3. Listen to the phrases, pauses, and expression of the reader.

MULTI-LEVEL OPTIONS *Elements of Literature*

Newcomer Demonstrate acting out the parts of Scrooge and the solicitor. (Change your position and change your voice to indicate that you are acting out two different people.) Work with students to understand the dialogue. Then have pairs imitate what you have demonstrated.

Beginning Point to the dialogue and read it without expression or body language. Have students repeat after you. Then point to the stage directions and read them. Reread the dialogue using the stage directions. Have students repeat what you have demonstrated.

Intermediate Discuss with students the role of a director for a play. *Say: A director is like a peer editor. He or she tells actors what is good about their performances and gives ideas for improving.* Divide the class into groups of three. Have two students play the part of the actors. Have one be the director and give feedback.

Advanced Explain how directors work with actors. Divide the class into small groups. Ask each group to select a short play from a book or drama magazine. Have group members decide who will play each role and who will direct. Provide time for students to rehearse and then perform their plays for the class.

Listen, Speak, Interact

Present a Scene from the Play

Work with a group to present a scene from "Mr. Scrooge Finds Christmas."

1. Meet with three other students. You will present Scene 2 or Scene 3 of the selection.
2. Each student should play a character.
3. With your group, read the scene aloud. Practice it a few times. Use gestures, tone of voice, and pitch to show what your character is feeling and to engage your listeners.
4. Present your scene to your class. If you can, memorize your part.
5. Evaluate each other's presentations for content, credibility, and delivery.

Elements of Literature

Recognize Dialogue and Stage Directions

In a play, **stage directions** tell what the characters are supposed to do. Stage directions are often in parentheses (. . .). Sometimes, they are also in *italic* type.

> **Scrooge:** *(Banging down ruler)* Bah! Humbug!

1. With a partner, read these lines from the selection.

> **Solicitor:** Good afternoon! *(SOLICITOR goes out, shaking his head. BOB opens door for him, then hurries back to his stool.)*
>
> **Scrooge** *(Glaring at BOB):* You'll want all day tomorrow, I suppose?

2. Use the stage directions and act out these lines. Speak slowly, clearly, and loudly. Use a tone that helps the listener understand your mood. Use nonverbal language such as gestures.
3. Listen to your partner's interpretation of these lines. Interpret the use of verbal and nonverbal language. Is your partner credible (believable)? Are you persuaded that your partner is expressing true feelings?

Activity Book
p. 187

Student
CD-ROM

Chapter 1 Mr. Scrooge Finds Christmas **361**

Listen, Speak, Interact

Present a Scene from the Play

1. **Reread in groups** Play the audio again as students follow along. Then have groups practice and present their interpretations of one of the scenes. Remind students to use the stage directions for information about the roles and appropriate actions. Have them use the pictures for body language and facial expressions.
2. **Newcomers** Reread one scene with this group. Then as you read, have students act out different roles. Help them add gestures and expressions as they listen to the script.

Elements of Literature

Recognize Dialogue and Stage Directions

1. **Clarify terms** Read and clarify the explanation. Model speaking clearly and slowly. Explain *tone, mood,* and *nonverbal language.* Ask students to practice and critique their own interpretations of the lines from the play.
2. **Multi-level options** See MULTI-LEVEL OPTIONS on p. 360.

✔ ASSESS

Have students choose an example of stage directions from the reading and demonstrate appropriate actions or expressions.

🏳 Cultural Connection

Have students who are from similar backgrounds work in groups. Ask them to find a short story from another culture. Have them summarize the story and then use the Readers Theater approach to turn it into a skit or simple play. Help them write dialogue and give them time to practice and perform for their classmates.

Learning Styles
Musical

Tell students that, in addition to dialogue and stage directions, some plays use music to set the mood and tell the story. Have students watch a scene from a film version of Dickens's novel. Engage students in a discussion of the music and how it fits what is happening in the story.

Word Study

Analyze Contractions

Teacher Resource Book: *Web, p. 37*

Make word webs Write on the board: *don't = do + not*. Review the meaning of *contraction*. Point out the apostrophe for the missing letter(s). Have students list other contractions they know and create word webs for them.

Answers
2. You'll; It's
3. You will; It is

Grammar Focus

Use the Present Perfect Tense

Use a timeline Make a timeline to show how actions started in the past and continue up to the present as you model sentences in the present perfect. *Ask: Have you ever visited Washington? Have you ever had a scary dream?*

Answers
1. have lived
2. has worked
3. have played

 **ASSESS**

Have students write two sentences about things they have done in the past, using the present perfect.

Word Study

Analyze Contractions

You form **contractions** by joining two words together. You also drop some letters from the second word. In their place, put an apostrophe (').

do + not ➔ don't

1. Copy this chart.
2. In the chart, list the contractions.
3. Write the two words that form each contraction.

Sentences	Contractions	Words in Contractions
You're rich enough!	you're	you are
You'll be happy.		
It's not convenient.		

Note: Don't confuse *it's* (it is) with *its* (the possessive): The dog wagged its tail.

Activity Book p. 188   Student CD-ROM

Grammar Focus

Use the Present Perfect Tense

The **present perfect tense** is used to show that something started in the past and continues up to the present.

Mr. Marley has been dead these seven years.

Study the chart to learn how to form the present perfect tense.

Copy and complete these sentences. Use the present perfect tense of the verbs in parentheses.

1. We ____ in Houston for two years. (live)
2. My mother ____ at the bank for a long time. (work)
3. I ____ soccer for six years. (play)

Present Perfect Tense			
Subject	**Auxiliary Verb**	**Past Participle**	**Rest of Sentence**
I You We They	have	lived	here for one year.
He She It	has		

Activity Book pp. 189–190   Student Handbook   Student CD-ROM

MULTI-LEVEL OPTIONS *From Reading to Writing*

Newcomer Help students create a group picture letter. On big sheets, write: *Dear Scrooge.* Under that draw a horizontal rectangle and three squares, side by side, under the rectangle. Ask students to draw what Scrooge should do in the rectangle and draw three reasons he should take this action in the squares.

Beginning Use a Language Experience Approach. Work with students to write a class letter. Leave enough space between the sentences to allow students to illustrate the meaning of what they have written.

Intermediate Have students use the model to create a first draft. *Say: The first and last parts of a persuasive letter are very important. The opening should get Mr. Scrooge's attention and give him a reason to read on. The ending should leave him with something to think about. Add these parts to your letter.*

Advanced *Say: You don't want your letter to sound like everyone else's. You want your personality to come through. What are some of your qualities? Can you use your logic, kindness, or humor to get through to Mr. Scrooge? Add your own voice to the letter.*

From Reading to Writing

Write a Persuasive Letter

When you persuade, you cause a person to believe or do something.

With a partner, write a persuasive letter to Mr. Scrooge. Try to persuade him to give money to needy people.

1. Organize your letter.
   a. List two reasons why he should give money to needy people.
   b. List one reason why he might not want to give money to needy people. Give your opinion of this reason.
2. Compose your persuasive letter.
3. Reread your letter to evaluate if it achieves its purpose.

(Date)

Dear Mr. Scrooge,

I think that you should give money to needy people. One reason is that _____ .

Another reason is that _____ _____ . I know that you do not want to do this. You think that _____ . But I think that _____

I hope this letter has persuaded you.

Yours truly,

_____

Activity Book
p. 191

Student
Handbook

Across Content Areas

Answer Math Questions About Currency

Currency is money. In the United States, the currency is made up of **coins** and paper **dollars.**

1. Look at the chart. It tells you how much the currency is worth.
2. Work with a partner to solve this math problem.

   Nick has 5 quarters, 3 dimes, and 2 nickels. Dean has 4 quarters, 5 dimes, 3 nickels, and 6 pennies. How much money does each boy have? Who has more money?

Currency	Worth	
penny	1 cent	$ .01
nickel	5 cents	$ .05
dime	10 cents	$ .10
quarter	25 cents	$ .25
dollar	100 cents	$1.00

Activity Book
p. 192

From Reading to Writing

Write a Persuasive Letter

1. **Brainstorm and list** Have students suggest reasons for and against giving money to needy people. List ideas on the board.
2. **Think-quickwrite-pair-share** Have students write their persuasive ideas and explanations. Arrange students in pairs to share ideas. Remind them that the point is to convince someone to do something.
3. **Write a draft** As students write, remind them to follow the letter format.
4. **Choose appropriate form for purpose** *Ask: If you want to let students in our school know what you think about rich people giving money to needy people, what's the best form of writing to use for this purpose?* Have students choose the appropriate form for their purpose for writing. Guide them to choose an editorial. Instruct students to write an editorial that expresses their opinions on this topic to the school newspaper.
5. **Multi-level options** See MULTI-LEVEL OPTIONS on p. 362.

Across Content Areas: Math

Answer Math Questions About Currency

Use examples Bring in examples of real or play coins and bills. Have students find combinations of coins as you say money amounts and determine amounts from coin combinations. *Say: I need 85 cents.* (3 quarters, 1 dime) *I have one quarter and two dimes. How much is it?* (45 cents)

Answers
2. Nick has $1.65; Dean has $1.71; Dean has more money.

 ASSESS

Have students write math problems using the facts on the chart. Instruct students to exchange and solve one another's problems.

Reteach and Reassess

Text Structure Have students sketch a stage on which actors are performing a scene from the play they read. Ask them to label the features described on p. 352.

Reading Strategy Tell students to create a sequence chain outlining the events of the play they read. Students may use drawings, phrases, or sentences to tell about key parts of the play.

Elements of Literature Divide the class into pairs. Give each a copy of a few lines of dialogue between two people from a simple play. Have students identify the dialogue and stage directions. Have them read aloud the dialogue using the stage directions.

Reassess Have students write a persuasive letter telling why they do or do not think "Mr. Scrooge Finds Christmas" is a good play to share during the holidays.

The House on Mango Street

an excerpt from a novel
by Sandra Cisneros

Chapter Materials

Activity Book: *pp. 193–200*
Audio: *Unit 6, Chapter 2; CD 3, Track 7*
Student Handbook
Student CD-ROM: *Unit 6, Chapter 2*
Teacher Resource Book: *Lesson Plan, Teacher Resources, Reading Summary, Activity Book Answer Key*
Teacher Resource CD-ROM
Assessment Program: *Quiz, pp. 91–92; Teacher and Student Resources, pp. 115–144*
Assessment CD-ROM
Transparencies
The Heinle Newbury House Dictionary/CD-ROM
Web site: http://visions.heinle.com

Objectives

Prereading for vocabulary Read aloud the objectives. *Ask: Is fiction a real or make-believe story? What is a habitat? Say: The title is "The House on Mango Street." What words can you use to describe a house?*

Use Prior Knowledge

Talk About the Meanings of *Home*

■ Teacher Resource Book: *Cluster Map, p. 38*

Gather and organize Have students create a cluster map about *home*.

Use Prior Knowledge

Talk About the Meanings of *Home*

The place where you live is your home. This is the **denotative** definition of *home*—the definition that you find in a dictionary. *Home* also has many **connotative** meanings—feelings and attitudes that the word *home* makes you think of. For example, when you hear the word *home*, you may think of a warm, safe place.

1. Work with a partner. Talk about the denotative and connotative meanings of the word *home*.
2. Write your ideas in a Cluster Map like this one.

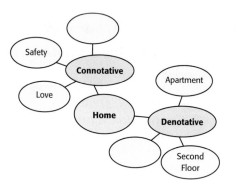

3. With your classmates, talk about the connotative meanings that are most important to you.

MULTI-LEVEL OPTIONS *Build Vocabulary*

Newcomer Draw a bird's eye view of a house. Point to the area in front. *Say: front yard.* Point to the area in back. *Say: backyard.* Have pairs of students draw or act out other opposites. (*Example:* One might hold up a big book; the other might hold up a small book.)

Beginning Draw a two-column chart labeled: *Opposites.* Then draw a long line. *Say: long.* Draw a short line. *Say: short.* Have students volunteer other opposite pairs they know and record them on the chart.

Intermediate Ask students to use a thesaurus to find synonyms for the words they have selected as answers.

Advanced *Say: Sometimes authors use opposites to help readers understand vocabulary they use.* Write the following example on the board: *The family lived in a humble, not a fancy, house.* Have students write sentences using this model.

Build Background

Chicago

The selection you will read takes place in Chicago, Illinois. Chicago is the third largest city in the United States, with a population of about three million. It is located on Lake Michigan. People from many different cultures live in Chicago. The city has many different ethnic neighborhoods—areas where people of the same culture live.

Content Connection
Chicago became a city in 1837. Chicago is a major center for business and industry.

Build Vocabulary

Identify Antonyms

Antonyms are words that have opposite meanings. For example, the antonym of *large* is *small*. Using antonyms can help you make your writing more precise.

1. Read each of the following sentences. Choose the correct antonym for each underlined word. Use a dictionary or ask your teacher.
2. Choose two antonyms. Use them in a sentence. Write the sentences in your Personal Dictionary.

a. There is no <u>front</u> yard, only four little elms by the curb.
(back/side)

b. There are stairs in our house, but they are <u>straight</u> hallway stairs.
(plain/crooked)

c. "For the time being," says Mama. "<u>Temporary</u>," says Papa.
(permanent/changing)

Personal Dictionary | The Heinle Newbury House Dictionary | Activity Book p. 193 | Student CD-ROM

Chapter 2 The House on Mango Street **365**

Content Connection
Math

Build Background Draw a large three-column chart on the board or on chart paper. Head the columns: *Chicago, Our City, Comparison.* (If you live in Chicago, write a different city name.) Break the class into groups. Assign each to find one statistic, such as population or area, for Chicago and the comparison city. Have students compute a percentage to compare the two statistics. (*Example:* Chicago, 228 square miles; Houston, 598 square miles; Chicago is 38% as big as Houston.)

Learning Styles
Kinesthetic

Build Vocabulary Review with students how the game Charades is played. Then have students pick slips of paper on which you have written opposite pairs, such as *awake/asleep* and *heavy/light.* Have students act out the words. Ask the class to identify the opposite pairs.

Build Background

Chicago

1. **Use a map** Have students find Chicago on a U.S. map. *Ask: What lake is near Chicago? What state is it in? What states are near Chicago? Is Chicago a large or small city?*

2. **Relate to personal experience** Ask students to discuss what they know about Chicago. If possible, ask a student who has lived or visited there to describe it.

3. **Content Connection** One-third of Chicago was destroyed in a fire in 1871, but by 1889, it had the first skyscraper. *Ask: What large cities do you know? What's good about living in a city? What's not so good?*

Build Vocabulary

Identify Antonyms

Teacher Resource Book: *Personal Dictionary, p. 63*

1. **Use a chart** Write on the board: *hot, tall, ugly, heavy, old.* Have students say opposites, or antonyms. (cold, short, beautiful, light, young)

2. **Reading selection vocabulary** You may want to introduce the glossed words in the reading selection before students begin reading. Key words: *rent, landlord, lottery, temporary.* Instruct students to write the words with correct spelling and their definitions in their Personal Dictionaries. Have them pronounce each word and divide it into syllables.

3. **Multi-level options** See MULTI-LEVEL OPTIONS on p. 364.

Answers
1. **a.** back **b.** crooked **c.** permanent

 **ASSESS**

Say: back, permanent, large. Have students give the antonym for these words.

Text Structure

Fiction

Define and explain features Have students work in groups. Assign different groups "The Sneak Thief" (p. 42) or "How I Survived My Summer Vacation" (p. 76). Have them expand their charts with examples of these text features from those stories.

Reading Strategy

Paraphrase to Recall Information

1. **Teacher think aloud** *Say: "The house on Mango Street is ours, . . ." I know the narrator has a house, and it's on Mango Street. So, I can paraphrase it as "We have a house on Mango Street."*
2. **Multi-level options** See MULTI-LEVEL OPTIONS below.

Answer

Example: We have a house on Mango Street. We don't rent it. We own it.

ASSESS

Have students define: *characters, events,* and *setting.*

Text Structure

Fiction

Fiction is a type of story that includes characters and events imagined by the author. Look for the features of fiction as you read "The House on Mango Street."

The events that happen in the story make up the **plot.** When you read fiction, the author wants you to follow the plot to find out how the story ends.

Fiction	
Characters	The people in the story are made up.
Events	The things that happen in the story are made up.
Setting	The events happen in a certain time and place.

Student
CD-ROM

Reading Strategy

Paraphrase to Recall Information

When you **paraphrase,** you state what the author says, but you use your own words. Paraphrasing can help you remember information that you read.

1. To paraphrase, follow these steps.
   a. Read the part of the text that you are going to paraphrase several times, until you are sure you know what it means.
   b. Close your book. Write or say the meaning of the text in your own words.
   c. Open your book and check your paraphrase against the text. Did you include all or most of the information? Did you use your own words?

2. Paraphrase this part of the text.

   The house on Mango Street is ours, we don't have to pay rent to anybody. . .

3. As you read the selection, paraphrase parts of it that you want to remember.

Student
CD-ROM

MULTI-LEVEL OPTIONS *Reading Strategy*

Newcomer Tell students about what you like to do at home. Act out what you are saying. (*Example:* I like to cook. My favorite food to make is pasta. I also like to exercise.) Have students paraphrase your ideas by drawing what you have told them.

Beginning Mime the actions as you tell students about what you like to do at home. Have them use a few words to paraphrase what you have said. (*Example:* cook and exercise)

Intermediate After students have responded to number 2, ask them to meet in small groups. Have them compare and contrast the way they paraphrased the sentence.

Advanced Suggest that students use their paraphrases as part of a double-entry journal. Have them create two columns on a page. Tell them to head the columns *Paraphrases* and *Reactions.* As they paraphrase important parts of the story, also have them record feelings or experiences those portions of the story bring to mind.

The House on Mango Street

an excerpt from a novel
by Sandra Cisneros

367

Reading Selection Materials

Audio: *Unit 6, Chapter 2; CD 3, Track 7*
Teacher Resource Book: *Reading Summary,*
pp. 113–114
Transparencies: #44, *Reading Summary*

Suggestions for Using Reading Summary

- Introduce new vocabulary or cognates.
- Cut the summary into strips, or jumble the sentences on an overhead transparency. Students put the sentences in order.
- Practice the reading strategy.
- Students read aloud or with a partner.
- Students paraphrase the summary.
- Students do a cloze activity.
- Students create a visual or graphic organizer, such as a timeline or storyboard, to illustrate the summary.
- Students paraphrase the summary.

Preview the Selection

1. **Use the illustration** Have students describe the scene. Ask questions to help students make predictions about the picture and the people who live there. *Ask: What does the house look like? Where is it? Who do you think lives there? What is the neighborhood like? What other places do you think are near this house? Would you like to live in this house or in this neighborhood? Why or why not?*

2. **Connect** Remind students that the unit theme is *visions*. *Ask: Do you think the people have a vision or dream? What kind of a vision or dream might they have?*

Content Connection
Technology

Bookmark a real estate web site on the Internet. Have students find small, urban homes that are for sale. Ask them to read the descriptions of the homes. Have students compare the descriptions to the illustration on p. 367.

Learning Styles
Intrapersonal

Have students draw or write a reflective journal entry. *Ask: How would you feel about living in the home shown on page 367? How would you describe the house if someone asked you where you lived? What is the best thing about this house? What is the worst thing?*

Reading Selection

Read the Selection

1. **Use text features** Ask students to describe the houses in the picture. Remind students to use the glossed words to help understanding.
2. **Teacher read aloud** Read the selection aloud. Pause to check understanding and to identify characters, setting, and events.
3. **Analyze point of view** Ask volunteers to identify who is writing the story. Point out *I, we,* and *our ,* which indicate the first-person point of view.

Sample Answer to Guide Question
We moved away fast from the apartment on Loomis Street.

> See Teacher Edition pp. 434–436 for a list of English-Spanish cognates in the reading selection.

Audio
CD 3, Tr. 7

1   We didn't always live on Mango Street. Before that we lived on Loomis on the third floor, and before that we lived on Keeler. Before Keeler it was Paulina, and before that I can't remember. But what I remember most is moving a lot. Each time it seemed there'd be one more of us. By the time we got to Mango Street we were six— Mama, Papa, Carlos, Kiki, my sister Nenny and me.

2   The house on Mango Street is ours, we don't have to pay **rent** to anybody, or share the yard with the people downstairs, or be careful not to make too much noise, and there isn't a **landlord** banging on the ceiling with a broom. But even so, it's not the house we'd thought we'd get.

3   We had to leave the **flat** on Loomis quick. The water pipes broke and the landlord wouldn't fix them because the house was too old. We had to leave fast. We were using the **washroom** next door and carrying water over in empty milk gallons. That's why Mama and Papa looked for a house, and that's why we moved into the house on Mango Street, far away, on the other side of town.

> **Paraphrase to Recall Information**
> Paraphrase the first sentence of this paragraph.

rent the amount of money paid to live somewhere	**flat** an apartment
landlord a person who owns land that he or she rents to others	**washroom** a bathroom

368   Unit 6 Visions

MULTI-LEVEL OPTIONS *Read the Selection*

Newcomer Play the audio. Then read aloud and have students join in when they can. *Ask: Has the narrator's family always lived in the house on Mango Street?* (no) *Has the family moved many times?* (yes) *Did the narrator's parents hope to move into a nice house?* (yes) *Does the narrator think the house on Mango Street is nice?* (no)

Beginning Read aloud the story. Have volunteers read different paragraphs. *Ask: How many houses does the narrator remember living in?* (four) *Why did the family leave the house before Mango Street?* (no water) *What kind of house does the family want?* (a nice, big one) *Does the narrator like the house on Mango Street?* (no)

Intermediate Have students read the story silently. *Ask: What may have been one reason the family moved often?* (They needed more room for more people.) *What does the narrator see as the good and bad things about the house on Mango Street?* (good: It's theirs; bad: It's small.)

Advanced Have students read silently. *Ask: What do the narrator's parents mean by "a real house"?* (one that they own, where they have enough room and everything works) *How do you predict the narrator would feel about inviting classmates to the house? Why?* (uncomfortable because it is old and not pretty)

4   They always told us that one day we would move into a house, a real house that would be ours for always so we wouldn't have to move each year. And our house would have running water and **pipes** that worked. And inside it would have real stairs, not hallway stairs, but stairs inside like the houses on T.V. And we'd have a basement and at least three washrooms so when we took a bath we wouldn't have to tell everybody. Our house would be white with trees around it, a great big yard and grass growing without a fence. This was the house Papa talked about when he held a **lottery** ticket and this was the house Mama dreamed up in the stories she told us before we went to bed.

5   But the house on Mango Street is not the way they told it at all. It's small and red with tight steps in front and windows so small you'd think they were holding their breath. Bricks are **crumbling** in places, and the front door is so **swollen** you have to push hard to get in. There is no front yard, only four little elms the city planted by the curb. Out back is a small garage for the car we don't own yet and a small yard that looks smaller between the two buildings on either side. There are stairs in our house, but they're **ordinary** hallway stairs, and the house has only one washroom. Everybody has to share a bedroom—Mama and Papa, Carlos and Kiki, me and Nenny.

> **Paraphrase to Recall Information**
>
> Paraphrase the first two sentences in this paragraph.

---

pipes   tubes through which liquids pass
lottery   a game in which people buy tickets
    with numbers

crumbling   falling into pieces
swollen   increased in size
ordinary   normal, regular

Chapter 2   The House on Mango Street   **369**

Read the Selection

1. **Understand terms** Have students find the meaning of the boldfaced words in the selection. Clarify meanings as needed.
2. **Use the illustration** Remind students that the illustration can help understanding.
3. **Paired reading** Ask volunteers to read the selection aloud. Then, have students reread it in pairs. *Ask: How often did the family move?* (every year) *What was inside the dream house?* (running water, real stairs, a basement, three bathrooms) *What was outside the dream house?* (trees, a big yard, grass, a fence)
4. **Compare and contrast** Guide students to point out similarities and differences between the dream house and the real house on Mango Street. Have students suggest why the family did not get the dream house.
5. **Multi-level options** See MULTI-LEVEL OPTIONS on p. 368.

Sample Answer to Guide Question
The house on Mango Street is different from the dream house my parents had described. Everything about the house was too small, or tiny.

 Spelling

Their/there/they're

On the board, write: *their.* Have students find it in paragraph 5. Have students say and spell it aloud with you. *Say:* Their*, spelled this way, means "belonging to a group of people or things." The sentence is about the steps. The narrator is imagining that the steps are holding* their *breath.* Have students find *there* and *they're* in sentence 6 of paragraph 5. *Say: These two words are pronounced the same way as* their (point to the word on the board) *but are spelled differently and have different meanings. You will learn more about them later in the chapter.*

    Apply On the board, write: *The family was crowded in the family's house. The students finished the students' work.* Have students rewrite the sentences to include the word *their.* (the family's house = their house; the students' work = their work)

Read the Selection

1. **Shared reading** Read the selection aloud to students or have volunteers read aloud portions. *Ask: What was the building on Loomis Street like?* (old, run-down, in a dangerous neighborhood) *What did the sign at the Laundromat say?* (that it was open) *Why did the owner put up the sign?* (so people would still use it)

2. **Analyze character development** *Ask: Why did the narrator feel "like nothing" when the nun said, "You live* there*?"* (The narrator realized it was not a nice place to live.)

Sample Answer to Guide Question
I was playing in front of my old house on Loomis and a nun who I knew from school walked by.

> **Paraphrase to Recall Information**
>
> Paraphrase the first sentence of this paragraph.

6   Once when we were living on Loomis, a **nun** from my school passed by and saw me playing out front. The **laundromat** downstairs had been boarded up because it had been **robbed** two days before and the owner had painted on the wood YES WE'RE OPEN so as not to lose business.

7   Where do you live? she asked.

8   There, I said pointing up to the third floor.

9   You live *there*?

10   *There*. I had to look to where she pointed—the third floor, the paint peeling, wooden bars Papa had nailed on the windows so we wouldn't fall out. You live *there*? The way she said it made me feel like nothing. *There*. I lived *there*. I nodded.

---

nun a woman in a religious group   **robbed** stole something from someone
laundromat a place to clean clothes

370   Unit 6 Visions

MULTI-LEVEL OPTIONS *Read the Selection*

Newcomer *Ask: Was the family's old house over a laundromat?* (yes) *Was the narrator proud of that house?* (no) *Is the narrator proud of the house on Mango Street?* (no) *Do the parents say the family will live on Mango Street forever?* (no)

Beginning *What was below their house on Loomis Street?* (a laundromat) *How did the narrator feel about the house?* (ashamed) *What about the house on Mango Street?* (ashamed) *How long do the parents say the family will live on Mango Street?* (for a while)

Intermediate *What can you conclude about the Loomis Street neighborhood from paragraph 6?* (that it may not have been a safe place) *What does the narrator mean by "it made me feel like nothing"?* (the question about the house was embarrassing)

Advanced *How do you think the parents would feel if they knew the narrator's feelings about the house? Why?* (sad because they are doing the best they can) *What goal might the narrator set based on feelings about the neighborhood?* (*Example:* to get a job when possible and help the family move)

> **Paraphrase to Recall Information**
>
> Paraphrase this paragraph.

11 I knew then I had to have a house. A real house. One I could point to. But this isn't it. The house on Mango Street isn't it. **For the time being,** Mama says. **Temporary,** says Papa. But I know how those things go.

for the time being for a brief time   **temporary** for the time being

About the Author

Sandra Cisneros (born 1954)

Sandra Cisneros was born in Chicago, Illinois. As a child, Cisneros lived in a Spanish-speaking neighborhood like the one in "The House on Mango Street." After college, she worked as a teacher. In 1984, she published "The House on Mango Street." Cisneros has also written many novels, several books of poetry, and a book of short stories. She writes in English and in Spanish.

➤ Why do you think Cisneros wrote about the neighborhood she chose? What challenges do you think she faced in becoming a successful writer?

Chapter 2 The House on Mango Street **371**

---

❾ Punctuation

Italics for emphasis

Read aloud paragraph 9, emphasizing *there*. Ask students what they noticed about your reading of the word. (It is emphasized more than the rest of the words.) *Say: The special print,* italics, *lets me know I should emphasize that word. Why did the author want this word emphasized?* (to show the nun was surprised)

Apply Have students read paragraph 10 chorally, emphasizing the italicized words.

Evaluate Your Reading Strategy

Paraphrase to Recall Information *Say: You have practiced an important reading strategy. Now you can decide how well you have done. Does this statement describe how you read?*

> As I read, I state what the author says in my own words. Paraphrasing helps me recall information I read.

Read the Selection

1. **Use the illustration** Have students describe the narrator and guess what she is thinking about.
2. **Shared reading** Play the audio. Have students join in when they can. *Ask: What did the narrator want?* (a real house) *How does she feel about the house?* (disappointed)
3. **Summarize** Ask questions to help students summarize the differences between the dream and reality of life in the city.
4. **Multi-level options** See MULTI-LEVEL OPTIONS on p. 370.

Sample Answer to Guide Question
Someday I have to have a house I can be proud of. My parents say we will get a better house, but I think we're staying in this one on Mango Street.

About the Author

Explain author's background Similar to the narrator of the story, Sandra Cisneros moved yearly during her childhood between Mexico City and Chicago. It was difficult to have friends. *Ask: How do you think Sandra Cisneros used her own experiences in the writing of this story?* (She described her own feelings about moving and about the dream house and "real houses.")

Across Selections

Compare and contrast Have students contrast the house on Mango Street to the house that Karana built in "Island of the Blue Dolphins" (p. 120). (*Examples:* crowded/isolated; in a city/on an island; bought/made by user)

Spelling, Punctuation, Capitalization

After the Reading Comprehension section, students will practice spelling, punctuation, and capitalization in the Activity Book.

Beyond the Reading

Reading Comprehension

Question-Answer Relationships

Sample Answers

1. six people
2. four times
3. The landlord refused to fix the pipes.
4. It has water and pipes that work, real stairs, a basement, and several bathrooms. It has a large yard with trees, grass, and a fence.
5. It is small and falling apart. It has one bathroom, three bedrooms, no front yard, a garage, and a small yard.
6. The author is telling this story. The narrator seems about 15 years old; she looks about this age in the illustrations.
7. I don't think the author is happy with the house on Mango Street. The house is not like the dream house.
8. I think the writer can describe places and people's feelings very well.
9. I reread the section I didn't understand well. Then I looked for context clues. I also read more slowly and carefully than the first time.
10. Students' answers may include information about describing people and places clearly.

Build Reading Fluency

Read Aloud to Engage Listeners

Model reading aloud with expression. Remind students to keep their eyes on the words as they read. This will help them with phrasing, intonation, and pronunciation.

Reading Comprehension

Question-Answer Relationships (QAR)

"Right There" Questions

1. **Recall Facts** How many people are in the family?
2. **Recall Facts** How many times can the author remember moving?

"Think and Search" Questions

3. **Explain** Why did the family move out of the apartment on Loomis?
4. **Describe** Describe the house that Papa talked about and Mama dreamed up in stories.
5. **Describe** Describe the house on Mango Street.

"Author and You" Question

6. **Identify the Narrator** Who do you think is telling the story? How old do you think the narrator is? What makes you think this?

"On Your Own" Questions

7. **Analyze Characters** Do you think the narrator is happy with the house on Mango Street? Why do you think this?
8. **Appreciate Writer's Craft** Why do you think the author is famous for her writing?
9. **Monitor Comprehension** When you had difficulty understanding the reading, what did you do? Did you reread the sentences? Did you look for clues? Did you read more slowly?
10. **Discover Models** How can you use this selection as a model for your writing?

Activity Book p. 194   Student CD-ROM

Build Reading Fluency

Read Aloud to Engage Listeners

Reading aloud helps increase your fluency and expression. Learning to read with expression makes others want to listen to you.

1. Listen to the audio recording of "The House on Mango Street."
2. Turn to page 368 and follow along.
3. Pay attention to phrasing and expression.
4. With a partner, read aloud paragraphs 1–2 three times.
5. Select your favorite paragraph.
6. Read in front of the class with expression.

372 Unit 6 Visions

MULTI-LEVEL OPTIONS *Elements of Literature*

Newcomer Read aloud paragraph 10, using gestures, body language, and the illustration on p. 370 to clarify meaning. Ask students to raise their hands when they hear *I, we,* and *me.*

Beginning Divide the class into pairs. Give each pair a copy of paragraph 10. Have students circle *I, me,* and *we.* Have them read the paragraph chorally with you and point to themselves when they say the first-person pronouns.

Intermediate After students have discussed first person in relation to this chapter, have them review previous chapters to find additional selections written as first-person narratives. ("How I Survived My Summer Vacation, " "The Circuit," and "Samantha's Story")

Advanced Have students discuss the author's purpose in using first person for this story. *Ask: How would the story have been different if it had been written in third person?* (It would not have been as personal. The reader would not have been as likely to feel the main character's feelings.)

Listen, Speak, Interact

Talk About Mental Images

With your classmates, talk about your mental images of the house on Mango Street. Images are the pictures you make in your mind.

1. Listen to the audio recording of paragraphs 4 and 5 of the selection.
2. Close your eyes as you listen. Pay attention to the pictures you make in your mind.

3. Draw pictures of your images of how the real house and the imaginary house look.
4. Describe your pictures to a small group.
5. Listen to the entire recording. What effect does the author's choice of language have on you? What is the author's perspective?

Elements of Literature

Recognize First-Person Narratives

A narrative is often the telling of a story. Sometimes a character in the narrative tells the story. The character uses the pronouns *I, me, we,* and *us* to tell the story. This is called a **first-person narrative.**

1. Using the chart, find three sentences in "The House on Mango Street" that show first-person narrative. Look in paragraphs 4, 10, and 11.
2. Write the sentences in your Reading Log. Underline the pronouns *I, we, me,* and *us.*
3. Write a first-person narrative that is one paragraph long.
4. Share your narrative with a partner.

First-Person Narrative		
Who?	**How?**	**Example**
A character in the narrative tells the story.	The character uses the pronouns *I, me, we,* and *us.*	We didn't always live on Mango Street.

Reading Log   Activity Book p. 195   Student CD-ROM

Home Connection

Have students write a first-person narrative telling some of the things that they like about their home. As an alternative, have students complete the sentence frame *I like* _____ with illustrations showing things that each likes about his/her home.

Learning Styles
Mathematical

Show students some house floor plans from real estate brochures, home design magazines, or real estate ads in a newspaper. Point out that the plans show the shapes and sizes of rooms. To further develop an image of the house on Mango Street, have students draw floor plans of how they imagine the inside of the house looks, including dimensions for each room. Then have students figure out the overall square footage of the house they drew.

Listen, Speak, Interact

Talk About Mental Images

1. **Reread in small groups** After listening to the audio recording, have students reread, pointing out words and expressions that help visualize the houses. Encourage students to get a mental image in their minds before drawing.
2. **Newcomers** Reread with this group. Brainstorm a list of descriptive words and phrases about the two houses. Allow time for students to draw and list descriptive phrases about their drawings.

Answers
5. *Sample answer:* The author's choice of language makes me feel like she's a good friend. She also describes the places well, which helps me feel like I have been to those places. The author compares the houses she's lived in with the "dream house" her parents talk about.

Elements of Literature

Recognize First-Person Narratives

1. **Clarify terms** Explain *first-person narrative.* Guide students to point out words and phrases from the story that indicate *first person* and *narrative.*
2. **Multi-level options** See MULTI-LEVEL OPTIONS on p. 372.

Answers
1. They always told us . . . ; And our house . . . ; And we'd have . . . ; Our house . . . ; I had to look . . . ; I knew then I had to. . . .

ASSESS

Have students define *first-person narrative.*

Word Study

Learn English Words from Other Languages

Identify cognates with languages in the classroom Brainstorm and list English words that have been borrowed from other languages that students know.

Answers
1. kindergarten 2. magazine 3. mango 4. ranch

Grammar Focus

Spell Frequently Misspelled Words

Recognize *there, they're, their* Write the words on the board and number them *1, 2, 3.* Have students say the number of the correct word as you *say: Paul and Mike read their books.* (3) *They're feeling fine.* (2) *Put the papers over there.* (1)

Answers
paragraph 2: . . . there isn't a landlord . . .
paragraph 5: There is no . . . ; There are . . . ; but they're . . . paragraph 9: You live *there?*

 **ASSESS**

On the board, write: *apartamento, famille, Telefon.* Have students guess the English cognates. (apartment, family, telephone)

Word Study

Learn English Words from Other Languages

Many words in English come from other languages. Knowing about word origins helps you understand historical influences of other languages and cultures on English. People from many countries live in English-speaking countries. They bring their languages and cultures with them. English speakers borrow or adapt some of their words. Here are some examples.

mango (Tamil)   *lottery* (Dutch)

magazine (Arabic)   *kindergarten* (German)

ranch (Spanish)

Complete these sentences with one of the examples. Use a dictionary for words you don't know.

1. My sister is not in first grade yet. She is still in _____ .
2. I had nothing to do, so I decided to read a _____ .
3. This _____ is delicious!
4. We keep sheep on our _____ .

Personal Dictionary   The Heinle Newbury House Dictionary   Activity Book p. 196   Student CD-ROM

Grammar Focus

Spell Frequently Misspelled Words

Some words are pronounced the same, but they have different spellings and meanings.

The words *their, there,* and *they're* all sound the same. However, they are different parts of speech and have different meanings.

1. Read paragraphs 2, 5, and 9 of "The House on Mango Street."
2. Find sentences with *there* and *they're.*
3. Write three sentences of your own using each of these words. Be sure to use the correct part of speech in your sentence.

There, They're, and Their		
Word	**Meaning**	**Sentence**
there	Meaning 1: at or to a specific place	The play starts at seven, and I must be *there* by six.
	Meaning 2: to indicate a place	That chair over *there* is broken.
	Meaning 3: to begin a statement	*There* is still time before school starts.
they're	the contraction of *they are*	*They're* going to the movies.
their	possessive form of *they*	*Their* house was on Mango Street.

Activity Book pp. 197–198   Student Handbook   Student CD-ROM

374 Unit 6   Visions

MULTI-LEVEL OPTIONS *From Reading to Writing*

Newcomer Show students model floor plans from real estate ads. Have students use them as models to create their own dream houses. Help students label the rooms and yards. Provide time for students to show their sketches to classmates.

Beginning Have students list rooms and outdoor spaces of a house where they have lived or would like to live. Tell them to include one or two describing words for each. (*Example:* yellow kitchen, grassy yard) Have them draw a sketch beside each word to show the details.

Intermediate Suggest that students write in first person. *Say: It is easy to get mixed up and write part of a piece in first person and then switch to second or third person by mistake. When you have a first draft, meet with a partner. Read each other's work to be sure you used first person throughout.*

Advanced *Say: You may wish to describe a house located far from here. If so, do some research on the Internet to find out what kinds of houses are in that location. Also, think about special features of the area. For example, a seaside house might need to be built on stilts. Include realistic details in your writing.*

From Reading to Writing

Write a Description

Write a five-paragraph description of a place where you have lived or want to live.

1. Choose a genre such as a letter, science fiction, or realistic fiction.
2. Decide on your purpose. For example, do you want to entertain the reader or to discover your own thoughts and feelings?
3. Use technology to create, revise, and edit your work.
4. As you write, answer these questions:
   a. Where is the place?
   b. How do you know about it?
   c. What is it like?
   d. Why do you want to live there?

5. Revise your draft.
   a. Blend your paragraphs by using transitional words.
   b. Use conjunctions and dependent clauses to combine some of your short sentences into longer ones.
   c. Rearrange some of your sentences if necessary.
   d. Use vivid adjectives and adverbs and prepositional phrases to describe the place.
6. Write a final draft. Include a visual. Present your work to the class.

Activity Book
p. 199

Student
Handbook

Across Content Areas

Learn About Animal Habitats

Habitats are places where animals live. There are different habitats for different animals.

cave a hole in the ground, usually with an opening in the side of a hill

desert a place with little or no rain and large areas of sand and rock

jungle a hot, rainy place with many trees and plants

tundra a very cold area with no trees near the Arctic

What do you think is the habitat of each of these animals? Use references and resources to help you.

monitor lizard	cave
bat	desert
chimpanzee	jungle
polar bear	tundra

Activity Book
p. 200

From Reading to Writing

Write a Description

Teacher Resource Book: *Cluster Map, p. 38*

1. **Use a cluster map** Have students brainstorm and list descriptive words and phrases about a place. Then, direct them to organize their ideas on a cluster map. They can use the questions in the model to help create their charts. Have students follow the model as they write their drafts.
2. **Newcomers** First, have students draw a picture of the place. Then help them describe the place. Write key words and phrases on the board. Have them use these ideas and their own ideas to make their draft of the description.
3. **Multi-level options** See MULTI-LEVEL OPTIONS on p. 374.

Across Content Areas: Science

Learn About Animal Habitats

Explain terms Use pictures to clarify the habits described. Have students suggest other habitats, such as the ocean and forest, and animals that live there.

Answers
monitor lizard: desert
bat: cave
chimpanzee: jungle
polar bear: tundra

 **ASSESS**

Have students identify one additional animal for each of the habitats.

Reteach and Reassess

Text Structure Remind students that features of fiction include characters, events, and settings. *Say: In some stories, one feature stands out more than others. Which feature stood out most in this story?* (setting) *Give examples.*

Reading Strategy *Say: You can use paraphrasing to write a summary. Read the important story events you have written in your own words. Summarize the story by writing the main idea and the most important supporting details from your notes.*

Elements of Literature Read aloud a short selection that is written in first person. Then ask students to identify first-person pronouns the writer used.

Reassess Read a description of a setting from a short story. Ask students to paraphrase the description in writing or by drawing a sketch.

Chapter Materials

Activity Book: *pp. 201–208*
Audio: *Unit 6, Chapter 3; CD 3, Track 8*
Student Handbook
Student CD-ROM: *Unit 6, Chapter 3*
Teacher Resource Book: *Lesson Plan, Teacher Resources, Reading Summary, Activity Book Answer Key*
Teacher Resource CD-ROM
Assessment Program: *Quiz, pp. 93–94; Teacher and Student Resources, pp. 115–144*
Assessment CD-ROM
Transparencies
The Heinle Newbury House Dictionary/CD-ROM
Web site: http://visions.heinle.com

Objectives

Paired reading Have students work in pairs and take turns reading the objectives. *Ask: What other excerpts from novels have we read?* ("How I Survived My Summer Vacation," "The Voyage of the *Frog*," "Island of the Blue Dolphins," "The Voyage of the Lucky Dragon," "Dame Shirley and the Gold Rush," "So Far from the Bamboo Grove," "The House on Mango Street")

Use Prior Knowledge

Talk About the Ocean

Use a map Ask students to point out and name oceans on a map or globe.

CHAPTER 3

Into the Reading

The Pearl

an excerpt from a novel
by John Steinbeck

Into the Reading

Objectives

Reading Make inferences using text evidence as you read an excerpt from a novel.

Listening and Speaking Listen to and present the story.

Grammar Use conjunctions to form compound sentences.

Writing Write a fiction story.

Content Social Studies: Learn about bodies of water.

Use Prior Knowledge

Talk About the Ocean

The ocean is very important to people. We get food from it, we travel on it, and we have fun in it.

1. Copy the Cluster Map on a piece of paper.
2. With a partner, add your ideas to the Cluster Map.
3. Discuss the ideas with your partner.
4. Choose one idea cluster. Present your ideas to the class.

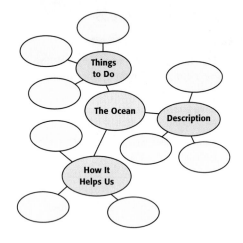

MULTI-LEVEL OPTIONS *Build Vocabulary*

Newcomer Draw or show a picture of a canoe with a paddle. Label both and label the back of the canoe, *stern.* Have students draw all three on separate cards. Pronounce each word. Have students pronounce the words after you and hold up the correct card.

Beginning Draw or show a picture of a canoe with a paddle. Label the items, and label the back of the canoe, *stern.* Have students draw the pictures and write the words on three cards. Pronounce each word. Have students pronounce it after you and hold up the appropriate card. Then have them practice in pairs.

Intermediate Assign pairs of students to choose two glossed words from the selection to look up in a dictionary. Have them work out the pronunciations of the words and find their origins. Provide time for pairs to share their words with the class.

Advanced Have groups work together. Ask students to write the vocabulary words across the top of a page. Tell them to list words that they know from other languages that have the same meanings. Ask students to note whether any of the words appear to have the same derivation as the English word. (*Example: decorate* /Spanish *decorar*)

Build Background

Oysters

Oysters are types of shellfish (water animals with outer shells). They mainly live in large bodies of water along the coast (the part of water near land). Many people like to eat oysters. Some oysters have pearls in their shells. Pearls are white, round jewels. People have used pearls to make jewelry for thousands of years.

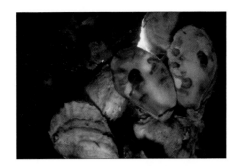

 Content Connection

The largest pearl ever discovered was found in the Philippines in 1934. It weighed more than 14 pounds.

Build Vocabulary

Locate Pronunciations and Derivations

When you look up the meaning of a new word in a dictionary, you can also find its pronunciation and its derivation (origin).

1. Read these dictionary entries for words from "The Pearl."
   a. What is the definition?
   b. Find the pronunciation. Your teacher will show you how to use the symbols.
   c. What is the derivation of the word? Which language does it come from originally?
2. For each word, write a sentence in your Personal Dictionary.

> **stern** /stɜrn/ *n* the rear section of a ship [Middle English *sterne*]
>
> **coordination** /koʊˌɔrdn'eɪʃən/ *n* the act of making arrangements for a purpose [Latin *ōrdinā tiō,* arrangement]
>
> **decorate** /'dɛkəˌreɪt/ *v* to beautify, make festive [Latin *decorāre,* to beautify]

Personal Dictionary | The Heinle Newbury House Dictionary | Activity Book *p. 201* | Student CD-ROM

Chapter 3 The Pearl **377**

Content Connection
Science

Build Background Have the class create a KWL chart. Under the *K(now)* column, have students list information about oysters, based on students' prior knowledge and their discussion of Build Background. Have them list questions they want to answer under *W(ant to Know)*. Break the class into small groups and assign each a question to research. Record what students learn through their research under *L(earned)*.

| Teacher Resource Book: *Know/Want to Know/Learned Chart (KWL), p. 42*

Learning Styles
Linguistic

Build Vocabulary Have groups of students brainstorm a list of words related to the ocean and also to related jobs. Have each group cut out six circles about six inches in diameter. Tell students to select six of their words and write one on each circle. Have them include the definition, pronunciation, and derivation of each word on its circle. Form a class collage of the words. Display it for students to refer to as they work on this chapter.

Build Background

Oysters

1. **Use illustrations** Bring in photos of and resources on oysters and pearls. Explain that oysters have hard outer shells that protect the soft muscle inside. They attach themselves to rocks or the ocean floor. *Ask: Have you ever seen or eaten oysters? Do you like them?*

2. **Content Connection** The over 14-pound pearl was the size of a football. Only one oyster in a thousand produces a pearl naturally. Pearls are cultivated, or made, by putting a tiny bit of sand in an oyster and harvesting it six years later.

Build Vocabulary

Locate Pronunciations and Derivations

1. **Use a dictionary** Have students locate the key for pronunciation in a dictionary. Help them find symbols and key words for the pronunciation of the sounds.

2. **Locate pronunciations and derivations** Remind students that they can locate pronunciations and derivations of unfamiliar words in dictionaries, glossaries, and other sources such as online dictionaries and CD-ROM dictionaries. Have them locate the words in this activity in each of these sources. Also have them locate the following words from the reading selection: *irritating, oxygen.*

3. **Reading selection vocabulary** You may want to introduce the glossed words in the reading selection before students begin reading. Key words: *pearlers, grain, irritate, melody, gleam, illusion.* Instruct students to write the words with correct spelling and their definitions in their Personal Dictionaries. Have them pronounce each word and divide it into syllables.

4. **Multi-level options** See MULTI-LEVEL OPTIONS on p. 376.

Answers
1. c. Middle English; Latin; Latin

 **ASSESS**

Have students list three facts about oysters.

Text Structure

Realistic Fiction

1. **Recognize features** Point out the features chart. Give examples using other realistic fiction, such as "The Voyage of the *Frog* " (p. 89).
2. **Multi-level options** See MULTI-LEVEL OPTIONS below.

Reading Strategy

Make Inferences Using Text Evidence

Teacher think aloud *Say: If I see smoke, I think there may be a fire. I know that something burning makes smoke. So, I make a guess or inference based on what I know.*

ASSESS

Ask: What are three features of realistic fiction? (characters like real people, setting in a real place, plot events that could happen)

Text Structure

Realistic Fiction

"The Pearl" is **realistic fiction.** This type of story includes made-up characters and events that could be real. Take notes in your Reading Log as you read the selection. Think about the following points.

1. Analyze the characters' traits, motivations, and relationships.
2. What problems do the characters have? How do the characters change?
3. What is the story setting? Analyze it. How does it contribute to the effect of the story?
4. Summarize the story plot. How do you think the characters' problems will be resolved?

Realistic Fiction	
Characters	The people in the story act like real people. They have traits, motivations, problems, and relationships.
Setting	The story happens in a real place.
Plot	The story has a beginning, a middle, and an end. The events of the story could happen in real life.

Reading Log

Student CD-ROM

Reading Strategy

Make Inferences Using Text Evidence

You learned that you can **make inferences** as you read. When you make inferences, you use **text evidence.** Remember that text evidence is the information in a selection. You also use your knowledge and experience.

Read these sentences. What inference can you make?

> John got off his bike. Sweat was dripping from his brow and he was breathing heavily.

You may know that you sweat and breathe heavily after a long bike ride. You can make an inference that John just finished a bike ride.

Make inferences based on text evidence, your knowledge, and experiences as you read "The Pearl."

Student CD-ROM

MULTI-LEVEL OPTIONS *Text Structure*

Newcomer Help students differentiate between realistic and nonrealistic fiction. Show pictures from both realistic and fanciful books. Have students determine whether each is realistic or not. *Ask: Could this happen?*

Beginning Ask students to look at illustrations from books in your classroom library. Tell each student to pick an example of a book that appears to be realistic based on the art in it and one that does not appear to be realistic.

Intermediate Ask students to work in pairs. Have them review the stories they have read in previous units. Tell them to make a list of selections that are realistic and ones that are not. (realistic: "The Circuit"; not realistic: "Persephone and the Seasons")

Advanced Have students look at young-adult book reviews in a library journal or other source. Ask them to predict, based on the titles, which books are realistic fiction and which are fantasy. Have them skim the reviews to check their predictions.

The Pearl

an excerpt from a novel
by John Steinbeck

379

Reading Selection Materials

Audio: *Unit 6, Chapter 3; CD 3, Track 8*
Teacher Resource Book: *Reading Summary,*
pp. 115–116
Transparencies: #45, *Reading Summary*

Suggestions for Using Reading Summary

- Introduce new vocabulary or cognates.
- Cut the summary into strips, or jumble the sentences on an overhead transparency. Students put the sentences in order.
- Practice the reading strategy.
- Students read aloud or with a partner.
- Students paraphrase the summary.
- Students do a cloze activity.
- Students create a visual or graphic organizer, such as a timeline or storyboard, to illustrate the summary.
- Students paraphrase the summary.

Preview the Selection

1. **Brainstorm** Have students suggest questions they have about the pearl in the photo and in the title of the reading selection. List questions on the board.
2. **Make color associations** Have students work in groups. Tell students that people usually connect pearls to the color white. They also connect colors to other jewels. Have students brainstorm and record a list of other jewels they know and group them by color.
3. **Connect** Remind students that the unit theme is *visions. **Ask:** If you found a pearl like this, what would you do with it? What kind of vision or dream would you have for your future?*

Home Connection

Remind students that they learned in Build Background that pearls have been valuable for thousands of years. Have students ask family members if they have anything made of pearls. Tell students to make sketches of these pearl items. Provide time for students to share and tell about their sketches.

Learning Styles
Natural

Tell students that the main character in the story is Kino, who dives into the ocean to look for oysters. Show students a diagram of the zones of the ocean. Help them locate where oysters live. Point out other sea animals that live in this zone. Keep the diagram on display as students read about Kino's dive.

Read the Selection

1. **Use text features** Call attention to the prologue and illustration. Direct students to glossed words and their meanings at the bottom of the page. Remind students to use these features to guide their reading.

2. **Teacher read aloud** Read the selection as students follow along. Then ask volunteers to read aloud portions of the selection.

3. **Identify characters and setting** *Ask: Who are Kino and Juana? Where do they live? What do they do for a living?*

Sample Answer to Guide Question
People have been collecting oysters for the pearls for many years. The pearls are worth a lot of money because the King of Spain was rich from them.

See Teacher Edition pp. 434–436 for a list of English-Spanish cognates in the reading selection.

Audio
CD 3, Tr. 8

Prologue

The main character of this story is Kino, a poor Native American man living in Mexico. Kino is a pearl diver (a person who looks for pearls in the sea). He lives in a small Indian village in Mexico with his wife, Juana, and his baby son, Coyotito. Coyotito becomes sick after he is stung by a scorpion. (A scorpion is a type of spider with poison in its long, pointed tail.) Kino and Juana do not have money to pay a doctor to take care of Coyotito. When the reading begins, the family goes out to sea in their small boat. Kino hopes that he will find a pearl that he can sell for money.

1   Now Kino and Juana slid the canoe down the beach to the water, and when the bow floated, Juana climbed in, while Kino pushed the stern in and waded beside it until it floated lightly and trembled on the little breaking waves. Then in coordination Juana and Kino drove their double-bladed paddles into the sea, and the canoe creased the water and hissed with speed. The other **pearlers** were gone out long since. In a few moments Kino could see them clustered in the **haze,** riding over the oyster bed.

2   Light **filtered** down through the water to the bed where the **frilly** pearl oysters lay fastened to the rubbly bottom, a bottom **strewn** with shells of broken, opened oysters. This was the bed that had raised the King of Spain to be a great power in Europe in past years, had helped to pay for his wars, and had decorated the churches for his soul's sake. The gray oysters with ruffles like skirts on the shells, the **barnacle**-crusted oysters with little bits of weed **clinging** to

Make Inferences Using Text Evidence

What inference can you make about oysters in this paragraph? What text evidence tells you this?

---

pearlers people who look for pearls
haze a condition in the air similar to light fog
filtered passed through
frilly decorated like a lace border

strewn scattered
barnacle a small shellfish that grows on rocks and the bottoms of ships
clinging holding closely or tightly

380   Unit 6 Visions

MULTI-LEVEL OPTIONS *Read the Selection*

Newcomer Play the audio. *Ask: Is Kino's job to look for pearls?* (yes) *Does Kino need money to take his son to a doctor?* (yes) *Is it easy to find pearls?* (no) *Does Kino carry a basket in his hand?* (yes)

Beginning Read aloud the Reading Summary. *Ask: Is Kino poor or rich?* (poor) *Who needs a doctor?* (Kino's son, Coyotito) *What does Kino hope to find?* (pearls) *What does a person need to find a pearl?* (luck)

Intermediate Have students do a paired reading. *Ask: How does Kino hope to get money to take his son to a doctor?* (by finding a pearl he can sell) *How do people find pearls?* (by diving into the sea, finding oysters, and opening them to see if there are pearls inside)

Advanced Have students read silently. *Ask: What are some of Kino's traits?* (He cares about his family. He is positive and hopeful.) *How likely is it that a diver will find a pearl?* (It is rare.) *What clues support your answer?* (The author says pearls are accidents and that finding one requires luck.)

the skirts and small crabs climbing over them. An accident could happen to these oysters, a **grain** of sand could lie in the folds of muscle and **irritate** the flesh until in self-protection the flesh coated the grain with a layer of smooth **cement.** But once started, the flesh continued to coat the foreign body until it fell free in some **tidal flurry** or until the oyster was destroyed. For centuries men had dived down and torn the oysters from the beds and ripped them open, looking for the coated grains of sand. **Swarms** of fish lived near the bed to live near the oysters thrown back by the searching men and to **nibble** at the shining inner shells. But the pearls were accidents, and the finding of one was luck, a little pat on the back by God or the gods or both.

3 Kino had two ropes, one tied to a heavy stone and one to a basket. He stripped off his shirt and trousers and laid his hat in the bottom of the canoe. The water was oily smooth. He took his rock in one hand and his basket in the other, and he slipped feet first over the side and the rock carried him to the bottom. The bubbles rose behind him until the water cleared and he could see. Above, the surface of the water was an **undulating** mirror of brightness, and he could see the bottoms of the canoes sticking through it.

> **Make Inferences Using Text Evidence**
>
> Why does Kino have one rope tied to a heavy stone? What experience tells you this?

grain a very small, hard piece of something	**flurry** a rush of activity
irritate annoy, bother	**swarms** large groups of people or animals
cement a substance that holds things together	**nibble** take small bites
tidal referring to the rise and fall of the ocean's surface	**undulating** moving in a waving motion

Chapter 3 The Pearl **381**

Read the Selection

1. **Use the illustration** Have students point out the oysters and guess how Kino looks for pearls.
2. **Paired reading** Play the audio. Have students read it in pairs. *Ask: Why do oysters make pearls?* (to protect themselves from something inside their shells) *What starts the process?* (a grain of sand)
3. **Sequence events** Have students describe the process of making a pearl and Kino's preparations before diving.
4. **Locate derivations using dictionaries** Have students look at these glossed words and determine what words they are derived from: *frilly, tidal, undulating.* Have students check the derivations in a print, online, or CD-ROM dictionary.
5. **Relate to personal experience** Have students guess how long Kino will be able to stay under the water looking for oysters. Students may want to time how long they can hold their breath and then discuss the difficulties of Kino's job.
6. **Multi-level options** See MULTI-LEVEL OPTIONS on p. 380.

Sample Answer to Guide Question
He's tied to a heavy stone so he can get down to the bottom of the ocean where the oysters are. I know that stones are heavy and when I throw a stone into the water, it always sinks.

---

th Spelling

/Oy/ vowel sound

Say: What sound do you hear at the beginning of the word oysters*?* (/oy/) *Find the word in paragraph 2 to see what letters spell that sound.* (o-y) Point out that many words students know have the /oy/ sound spelled with *o-y.* Ask students to brainstorm a list. (*Examples:* boy, joyful, loyal, annoy, toy)

    Apply Ask students to find a name in the prologue with the /oy/ sound (Coyotito) and a word in paragraph 2 (destroyed).

Read the Selection

1. **Use the text features** Have students describe what Kino is doing in the illustration.

2. **Jigsaw reading** Read the selection aloud. Then divide students into small groups. Have students prepare different sections to teach to their group. *Ask: Why does Kino hook his foot in the loop on the rock?* (so he can stay underwater) *Who is singing?* (Kino) *Do you think he is singing out loud?* (no)

3. **Relate to personal experience** *Ask: Do you sing as you work? What songs do you sing?*

Sample Answer to Guide Question
Kino is a careful worker because he moves cautiously. He remembers and keeps traditions of his culture, and he sings old songs as he works.

Make Inferences Using Text Evidence

What inference can you make about Kino? What text evidence tells you this?

4   Kino moved **cautiously** so that the water would not be **obscured** with mud or sand. He hooked his foot in the loop on his rock and his hands worked quickly, tearing the oysters loose, some singly, others in clusters. He laid them in his basket. In some places the oysters clung to one another so that they came free in lumps.

5   Now, Kino's people had sung of everything that happened or existed. They had made songs to the fishes, to the sea in anger and to the sea in calm, to the light and the dark and the sun and the moon, and the songs were all in Kino and in his people—every song that had ever been made, even the ones forgotten. And as he filled his basket the song was in Kino, and the beat of the song was his pounding heart as it ate the **oxygen** from his held breath, and the **melody** of the song was the gray-green water and the little **scuttling** animals and the clouds of fish that flitted by and were gone. But in the song there was a secret little inner song, hardly **perceptible,** but always there, sweet and

cautiously carefully	**melody** a song
obscured hidden from view	**scuttling** moving quickly
oxygen a gas in the air that living things need	**perceptible** capable of being seen

382   **Unit 6**   Visions

MULTI-LEVEL OPTIONS *Read the Selection*

Newcomer *Ask: Does Kino move fast in the water?* (no) *Do Kino's people have songs for everything?* (yes) *Do Kino and Juana want to find a pearl?* (yes) *Can Kino stay underwater for a long time?* (yes)

Beginning *Ask: How does Kino move in the water?* (slowly, carefully) *What do Kino's people have for everything that happens?* (a song) *How long can Kino stay underwater?* (two minutes) *What do oyster shells do when they are touched?* (close up)

Intermediate *Ask: What would happen if Kino moved through the water quickly?* (He wouldn't be able to see the oysters because he would kick up mud.) *What kinds of songs do Kino's people sing?* (songs about the events in their lives) *What does the phrase* chance was against it *mean?* (Not many oysters have pearls in them.)

Advanced *Ask: What are some examples of descriptions that appeal to the senses?* (bubbles rose behind him, pounding heart, gray-green water) *How likely does Kino think it is that he will find a pearl? Explain.* (He thinks it is unlikely, but he still has high hopes because he wants to find a pearl so desperately.)

secret and clinging, almost hiding in the counter-melody, and this was the Song of the Pearl That Might Be, for every shell thrown in the basket might contain a pearl. Chance was against it, but luck and the gods might be for it. And in the canoe above him Kino knew that Juana was making the magic of prayer, her face set **rigid** and her muscles hard to force the luck, to tear the luck out of the gods' hands, for she needed the luck for the **swollen** shoulder of Coyotito. And because the need was great and the desire was great, the little secret melody of the pearl that might be was stronger this morning. Whole phrases of it came clearly and softly into the Song of the Undersea.

6   Kino, in his pride and youth and strength, could remain down over two minutes without strain, so that he worked **deliberately,** selecting the largest shells. Because they were disturbed, the oyster shells were tightly closed. A little to his right a **hummock** of rubbly rock stuck up, covered with young oysters not ready to take. Kino moved next to the hummock, and then, beside it, under a little overhang, he saw a very large oyster lying by itself, not covered with its clinging brothers. The shell was partly open, for the overhang protected this ancient oyster, and in the lip-like muscle Kino saw a ghostly **gleam,** and then the shell closed down. His heart beat out a heavy rhythm and the melody of the maybe pearl **shrilled** in his ears.

> **Make Inferences Using Text Evidence**
>
> Why does Kino work "deliberately"? What text evidence tells you this?

---

rigid stiff
swollen enlarged in size
deliberately slowly, carefully

hummock a small mound or hill
gleam a bright light
shrilled made a high-pitched sound

Chapter 3 The Pearl   **383**

Read the Selection

1. **Use the illustration** Have students identify the characters in the picture and guess what they are doing and why.
2. **Use text features** Have students find the meanings of the boldfaced words at the bottom of the page.
3. **Jigsaw reading** Continue the reading of the story as students follow along. Then form new groups. Have students prepare different sections to teach to their group. *Ask: Who is praying?* (Juana) *What is she praying for?* (good luck and for a pearl) *Why does the family need the luck?* (The baby, Coyotito, is sick.)
4. **Locate derivations using dictionaries** Have students look at these glossed words and determine what words they are derived from: *cautiously, obscured, scuttling, swollen, deliberately.* Have students check the derivations in a print, online, or CD-ROM dictionary.
5. **Summarize** Have students restate the key events of the plot so far. Use guiding questions as needed.
6. **Make predictions** Have students guess if the family will have luck in finding a pearl.
7. **Multi-level options** See MULTI-LEVEL OPTIONS on p. 382.

Sample Answer to Guide Question
He wanted to make sure he picked good oysters, so he took his time. The text says that he picked the largest shells.

Ph for /f/ sound

Ask: What sound do you hear at the beginning of the word phrases? (/f/) *Find the word in paragraph 5 to see what letters make that sound.* (p-h) *The letters* p-h usually *make the sound /f/.*

   Apply Tell students that you are going to dictate a sentence for them to write. Point out that some of the words will have the /f/ sound spelled with p-h. *Say: Phil took a photo of Dad talking on the phone.*

Read the Selection

1. **Use the illustration** Have students discuss what Kino is doing in the illustration.
2. **Shared reading** Listen to the audio. Have students join in when they can.

Sample Answer to Guide Question

She doesn't want the boat to turn over as Kino gets in. I know that when you get into a small boat from the water, one side of the boat goes down as you pull yourself up.

Slowly he forced the oyster loose and held it tightly against his breast. He kicked his foot free from the rock loop, and his body rose to the surface and his black hair gleamed in the sunlight. He reached over the side of the canoe and laid the oyster in the bottom.

Make Inferences Using Text Evidence

Why does Juana steady the boat? What experience or knowledge tells you?

7   Then Juana **steadied** the boat while he climbed in. His eyes were shining with excitement, but in **decency** he pulled up his rock, and then he pulled up his basket of oysters and lifted them in. Juana sensed his excitement, and she pretended to look away. It is not good to want a thing too much. It sometimes drives the luck away. You must want it just enough, and you must be very **tactful** with God or the gods. But Juana stopped breathing.

---

steadied   made firm   **tactful**   careful in dealing with
decency   respectful concern for doing the right thing

384   **Unit 6**   Visions

MULTI-LEVEL OPTIONS *Read the Selection*

Newcomer *Ask: Does Kino find a special oyster?* (yes) *Does he think it has a pearl in it?* (yes) *Does he take the oyster to the boat?* (yes) *Is he afraid it does not have a pearl in it?* (yes)

Beginning *Ask: What does Kino find?* (a big oyster) *What does he think he sees in it?* (a pearl) *Where does he take it?* (to the boat) *What does Juana want Kino to do?* (open it)

Intermediate *Ask: How does Kino feel when he finds the big oyster?* (very excited but afraid to believe in his good fortune) *Why do you think Kino wanted to open the big oyster last?* (to delay being disappointed if the oyster did not have a pearl in it)

Advanced *Ask: In paragraph 6, what does* the maybe pearl *mean?* (Kino hoped he saw a pearl, but he was afraid to believe it was true.) *Do you agree with Juana's feeling in paragraph 7 that it is not good to want something too much?* (Example: No, because if you don't want something very much, you won't work hard to make it happen.)

Very deliberately Kino opened his short strong knife. He looked **speculatively** at the basket. Perhaps it would be better to open *the* oyster last. He took a small oyster from the basket, cut the muscle, searched the folds of flesh, and threw it in the water. Then he seemed to see the great oyster for the first time. He squatted in the bottom of the canoe, picked up the shell and examined it. The **flutes** were shining black to brown, and only a few small barnacles **adhered** to the shell. Now Kino was **reluctant** to open it. What he had seen, he knew, might be a reflection, a piece of flat shell accidentally drifted in or a complete **illusion.** In this Gulf of uncertain light there were more illusions than realities.

8   But Juana's eyes were on him and she could not wait. She put her hand on Coyotito's covered head. "Open it," she said softly.

> **Make Inferences Using Text Evidence**
>
> How do you think Juana is feeling as Kino looks at the oysters? What experience tells you this?

speculatively in an uncertain way	**reluctant** not wanting to do something
flutes long, round holes	**illusion** an idea that is not real
adhered attached to	

UNIT 6 • CHAPTER 3
Reading Selection

Read the Selection

1. **Use the illustration** Have students tell what the characters in the picture are doing.
2. **Paired reading** Play the audio. Have students reread aloud in pairs. *Ask: Does Kino open the large oyster first?* (no) *Why not?* (He doesn't want to make God or the gods unhappy.) *What does Kino use to open the oysters?* (a short, strong knife) *Is Juana patient or impatient?* (impatient) *How do you know?* (She tells Kino to open the oyster.)
3. **Locate derivations using dictionaries** Have students look at these glossed words and determine what words they are derived from: *steadied, tactful, adhered.* Have students check the derivations in a print, online, or CD-ROM dictionary.
4. **Make predictions** Have students restate the key events of the plot and predict what is inside the oyster.
5. **Multi-level options** See MULTI-LEVEL OPTIONS on p. 384.

Sample Answer to Guide Question
Juana is feeling very excited, hopeful, and impatient. She stopped breathing as she was watching Kino. When I am excited about what someone is doing, I watch them closely and I breathe differently, too.

---

th **Spelling**

Gh for /f/ sound

Write on the board and *say: laugh, rough, cough. Ask: What is the last sound you hear in each word?* (/f/) *That's right. The letters* gh *can sometimes sound like an* f.

Apply *Say: Find an example of the /f/ sound with* gh *in paragraph 7.* (enough)

Read the Selection

1. **Use the illustration** Ask students to guess what Kino is thinking about in the illustration.
2. **Shared reading** Play the audio. Then ask volunteers to join in for different sections. *Ask: Why does Juana moan?* (She's surprised at how large the pearl is.) *How did Kino hurt his hand?* (He smashed it at the doctor's.) *Why?* (Maybe he was angry because the doctor wouldn't help Coyotito.)

Sample Answer to Guide Question
Maybe Kino was thinking how lucky he was to find the pearl and how it may help them and their sick baby.

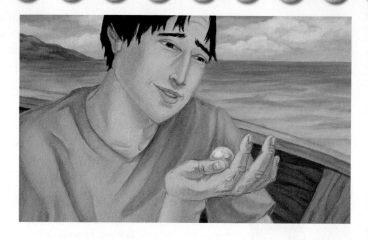

9   Kino **deftly** slipped his knife into the edge of the shell. Through the knife he could feel the muscle tighten hard. He worked the blade lever-wise and the closing muscle parted and the shell fell apart. The lip-like flesh **writhed** up and then **subsided.** Kino lifted the flesh, and there it lay, the great pearl, perfect as the moon. It captured the light and **refined** it and gave it back in silver **incandescence.** It was as large as a sea-gull's egg. It was the greatest pearl in the world.

10   Juana caught her breath and moaned a little. And to Kino the secret melody of the maybe pearl broke clear and beautiful, rich and warm and lovely, glowing and **gloating** and **triumphant.** In the surface of the great pearl he could see dream forms. He picked the pearl from the dying flesh and held it in his palm, and he turned it over and saw that its curve was perfect. Juana came near to stare at it in his hand, and it was the hand he had smashed against the doctor's gate, and the torn flesh of the knuckles was turned grayish white by the sea water.

> **Make Inferences Using Text Evidence**
>
> What do you think Kino was thinking as he looked at the pearl? What experience tells you this?

---

deftly   skillfully
writhed   twisted and turned in pain
subsided   became less strong
refined   made finer; improved

incandescence   a bright shining light
gloating   showing great pleasure, bragging
triumphant   successful

386   **Unit 6**   Visions

MULTI-LEVEL OPTIONS *Read the Selection*

Newcomer *Ask: Is there a pearl in the oyster?* (yes) *Is it a big one?* (yes) *Are Kino and Juana excited?* (yes) *Is the baby getting better?* (yes)

Beginning *Ask: What was in the big oyster?* (pearl) *What size was it?* (big) *How did Kino and Juana feel?* (excited) *How is the baby feeling at the end of the story?* (better)

Intermediate *Ask: How does the author let readers know that the pearl is large?* (by comparing it to a sea-gull's egg) *Why did Juana call for Kino when she looked at the baby's arm?* (She was excited that the baby was getting better.) *What do you think will happen next?* (Kino will sell the pearl and use the money for his family.)

Advanced *Ask: What does the sentence "... he could see dream forms" mean?* (that this pearl could make Kino's dreams come true) *How do you think the pearl will affect the family's life?* (The man and woman will have money to take care of their baby; the man may not have to dive for oysters anymore.)

11   **Instinctively** Juana went to Coyotito where he lay on his father's blanket. She lifted the **poultice** of seaweed and looked at the shoulder. "Kino," she cried shrilly.

12   He looked past his pearl, and he saw that the swelling was going out of the baby's shoulder, the **poison** was **receding** from its body. Then Kino's fist closed over the pearl and his emotion broke over him. He put back his head and **howled.** His eyes rolled up and he screamed and his body was rigid. The men in the other canoes looked up, startled, and then they dug their paddles into the sea and raced toward Kino's canoe.

> **Make Inferences Using Text Evidence**
>
> Why do you think emotion broke over Kino? What text evidence tells you this?

instinctively   in a way that is done from feeling instead of knowledge

poultice   a mixture of herbs placed on the body as medicine

poison   a substance that may hurt or kill people, animals, and plants

receding   lessening

howled   cried loudly

About the Author

John Steinbeck (1902–1968)

John Steinbeck was born in Salinas, California. By the age of 15, he was writing short stories and sending them to publishing companies. He went to Stanford University. He then worked as a writer. John Steinbeck wrote many books and became famous. Some of his best known works are *Of Mice and Men, The Grapes of Wrath,* and *East of Eden.* Steinbeck received awards for his writing, including the Pulitzer Prize and the Nobel Prize. He also spent time studying sea life. John Steinbeck is remembered as one of the greatest writers of the 20th century.

➤ How do you think John Steinbeck got the information and background knowledge he needed to write *The Pearl*? What strategies did he use? What questions would you ask him?

Chapter 3 The Pearl   **387**

 Spelling

Silent *k*

Ask: What consonant sound do you hear at the beginning of knife*? Yes, the first sound in the word is /n/. There is a silent letter before the* n. *Look at paragraph 9 to find out what it is.* (k) *Find another word that begins with silent* k *in paragraph 10.* (knuckles)

   Apply *Write on the board:* Karl knows how to make knots in knit kites. *Have students identify the words that start with silent* k.

Evaluate Your Reading Strategy

Make Inferences Using Text Evidence

Say: You have practiced an important reading strategy. Now you can decide how well you have done. Does this statement describe how you read?

> As I read, I look for clues about characters and events. I apply these clues to my own experience and knowledge. This helps me make inferences to understand the story better.

Read the Selection

1. **Shared reading** Play the audio. Have students join in when they can.
2. **Locate derivations using dictionaries** Have students look at these glossed words and determine what words they are derived from: *deftly, writhed, subsided, refined, incandescence, gloating, triumphant, receding.* Have students check the derivations in a print, online, or CD-ROM dictionary.
3. **Multi-level options** See MULTI-LEVEL OPTIONS on p. 386.

Sample Answer to Guide Question
Kino realized he was lucky. He howled because he was so happy.

About the Author

1. **Analyze facts** John Steinbeck studied marine biology at Stanford, although he never finished his degree. He traveled widely and spent time in Mexico. *Ask: How do you know Steinbeck loved the ocean?* (He studied and wrote about it.)
2. **Provide background** The Pulitzer Prize refers to one of various literary or journalistic prizes awarded by the will of the distinguished American newspaper journalist Joseph Pulitzer. Hungarian-born, Pulitzer held high standards for American journalism and decided to award excellence in the field in an effort to preserve these standards. The Prizes were first awarded in 1917 and have continued annually to today.

Answers
Examples: He studied about the ocean, so he wrote about things he knew. I would ask if he had ever found a pearl.

Across Selections

Connect to theme Discuss the narrator's vision in "The House on Mango Street" and Kino's vision in "The Pearl." (a perfect house like ones on television; enough money to raise his son well) *Ask: Were the visions realistic?* (Yes. Their visions were possible, so they were realistic.) *What is needed to make a dream a reality?* (The characters show that it takes a lot of hard work and a belief that their visions can happen.)

Beyond the Reading

Reading Comprehension

Question-Answer Relationships

Sample Answers

1. The baby's name is Coyotito.
2. The ropes are tied to a large rock and to a basket. The rock helps Kino stay underwater; the basket is used to collect oysters.
3. Pearlers dive to the bottom of the sea and pick oysters. Then they open them and look inside for pearls.
4. I think Kino dives for oysters because that is probably the job his father had.
5. The pearl symbolizes hope for a better life for the family.
6. As the author tells the story, he sometimes explains why an event is happening by telling what happened in the past.
7. I think Kino feels as if it were not true, but then he is very happy. When Kino sees the swelling go down in his son's shoulder, he is very relieved and happy.
8. I think Kino will sell the pearl and use the money to help his family have a better life.
9. What would've happened if Kino had not found the pearl? What else could he have done to help Coyotito?

Build Reading Fluency

Repeated Reading

Assessment Program: *Reading Fluency Chart, p. 116*

As students read aloud, time the reading and count the number of incorrectly pronounced words. Record results in the Reading Fluency Chart.

Reading Comprehension

Question-Answer Relationships (QAR)

"Right There" Questions

1. **Recall Facts** What is the name of Kino and Juana's baby?
2. **Recall Facts** Kino uses two ropes when he dives. What are they tied to? Why?

"Think and Search" Question

3. **Explain** How do the pearlers find pearls?

"Author and You" Questions

4. **Analyze Characters** Why do you think Kino dives for oysters?
5. **Recognize Symbolism** What does the pearl symbolize (represent) to Kino and Juana?
6. **Analyze Organization** How does the author organize and present the story? Is it chronological? How does he tell the reader about past events?

"On Your Own" Questions

7. **Recognize Character Traits** How do you think Kino feels after finding the pearl? How do you think Kino feels after seeing the swelling go down in Coyotito's shoulder?
8. **Predict** What do you think Kino will do with the pearl?
9. **Raise Questions** Based on what you read and on your own knowledge, what additional questions would you ask about this story?

Activity Book
p. 202

Student
CD-ROM

Build Reading Fluency

Repeated Reading

Repeated reading helps increase your reading rate and builds confidence. Each time you reread, you improve your reading fluency.

1. Turn to page 380.
2. Your teacher or partner will time you for six minutes.
3. With a partner, take turns reading each paragraph aloud.
4. Stop after six minutes.

MULTI-LEVEL OPTIONS *Elements of Literature*

Newcomer Have students draw the events described in sentences 1–3 on separate slips of paper. Have them put the slips in order and copy the words *Beginning, Middle,* and *End* on the appropriate slips.

Beginning Write sentences 1–3 on the board. Have volunteers draw quick sketches next to each sentence to remind the class of its meaning. Engage the class in using the sentences and sketches to indicate when the events occurred.

Intermediate Have students duplicate the story map on their papers. Ask them to place the events described in 1–3 on their maps. Then have them return to the story to find additional important events that happened and add those to their story maps.

Advanced Have students create a detailed story map showing the events from 1–3 along with other key parts of the story. Remind students that they learned about the climax of a story in Unit 2, Chapter 1 (p. 83). Have them mark the climax of "The Pearl" on the story map. (when Kino opened the oyster and saw the pearl)

Listen, Speak, Interact

Listen to and Present the Story

Understand and enjoy the story by listening to it and then acting it out.

1. With your class, listen to the audio recording of the story.
   a. What effect does the telling of the story have on you?
   b. Take notes on the main ideas.
   c. Monitor your understanding and ask for clarification if you don't understand something.

2. With a partner, act out a part of the story for your classmates.
   a. Write out dialogue and stage directions.
   b. Use gestures and nonverbal language.
3. Watch and listen to your classmates' presentations. Evaluate their performances. Were they believable? Did they tell the story accurately?

Elements of Literature

Analyze Plot and Problem Resolution

The **plot** is the main events that make up a story. A story's plot usually has a beginning, a middle, and an end. The chart shows what happens in each part.

Decide if each sentence below: (a) introduces the problem; (b) shows how the character tries to solve the problem; or (c) shows how the problem is resolved.

1. Then Kino's fist closed over the pearl and his emotion broke over him.
2. But the pearls were accidents, and the finding of one was luck.
3. Slowly he forced the oyster loose and held it tightly against his breast.

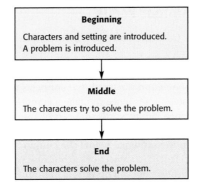

The Plot of a Story

Beginning
Characters and setting are introduced. A problem is introduced.

Middle
The characters try to solve the problem.

End
The characters solve the problem.

 Activity Book p. 203

 Student CD-ROM

Chapter 3 The Pearl **389**

Listen, Speak, Interact

Listen to and Present the Story

Teacher Resource Book: *Reading Log, p. 64*

1. **Reread in pairs** Arrange students into pairs for rereading. Pair beginning and advanced. Have them choose a portion to act out.
2. **Newcomers** Reread with this group. Have students suggest dialogue lines. Make a list on the board. Help students with pronunciation and intonation. After students practice, have them give their presentation to the class.
3. **Evaluate** Have students write an evaluation of their own presentations in their Reading Logs.

Elements of Literature

Analyze Plot and Problem Resolution

1. **Use a chart** Copy the chart and explain the main parts of a plot line.
2. **Multi-level options** See MULTI-LEVEL OPTIONS on p. 388.

Answers
1. c 2. a 3. b

 **ASSESS**

Have students describe what happens in the beginning, middle, and end of the plot of a story.

Cultural Connection

Say: Many writers use what they know to create settings, characters, and plots. John Steinbeck's family took vacation trips to the seashore. He studied marine biology in college. He traveled to Mexico later in his life. He also liked to observe how the people in his community who did not have a lot of money lived. Engage students in a discussion of how the author's experiences relate to the characters, setting, and plot of "The Pearl."

Learning Styles
Intrapersonal

Direct students to question 1a. in Listen, Speak, Interact. *Say: Even though Kino and Juana's life may be different from yours, you feel some of the same feelings they felt as you read the story.* Ask students to draw or write a journal entry. *Say: Think about a time you wanted something very badly and got it. What or who helped you to get what you wanted? How did you feel when you got it?*

Word Study

Learn Words from Latin

Use flash cards Have students make flash cards with words on one side and meanings on the other to practice learning the new vocabulary.

Answers
1. extend 2. attend 3. intense 4. intend

Grammar Focus

Use Conjunctions to Form Compound Sentences

Write on the board: *Kino was happy, and he shouted loudly.* Point out the two clauses and the conjunction. Have students identify subjects and verbs.

Answers
2. a. (Because) they <u>were disturbed</u> , the oyster shells <u>were</u> tightly <u>closed</u> . b. He never <u>found</u> a pearl before, (but) today he <u>was</u> lucky. c. Juana <u>sensed</u> his excitement, (and) she <u>pretended to look</u> away.

ASSESS

Have students write two sentences using conjunctions.

Word Study

Learn Words from Latin

The spelling of many English words has been influenced by other languages and cultures. The word *pretended* is used in "The Pearl." This word comes from the Latin word *tendere* meaning *to stretch*.

The words listed in the box also come from *tendere*.

> **attend** be present at
>
> **extend** make longer in space and time; stretch out
>
> **intend** plan to do something
>
> **intense** strong in feeling or emotion; concentrated

Complete each sentence with the correct word from the box.

1. The store is going to _____ its business hours.
2. Will you _____ the party?
3. She showed _____ happiness at her wedding.
4. I _____ to finish my homework.

Personal Dictionary   The Heinle Newbury House Dictionary   Activity Book p. 204   Student CD-ROM

Grammar Focus

Use Conjunctions to Form Compound Sentences

You have learned that a clause is a part of a sentence. It has a subject and a verb. A **conjunction** is a word that connects two clauses in a sentence to make a compound sentence. Some words that can be used as conjunctions are *and, but, or,* and *because.*

In the sentence below, the conjunction is circled. The subject of each clause is underlined once. The verb is underlined twice.

> Then Kino's <u>fist</u> <u>closed</u> over the pearl (and) his <u>emotion</u> <u>broke</u> over him.

1. Copy these sentences on a piece of paper.
   a. Because they were disturbed, the oyster shells were tightly closed.
   b. He never found a pearl before, but today he was lucky.
   c. Juana sensed his excitement, and she pretended to look away.
2. Circle the conjunction in each sentence. Underline the subject of each clause once and the verb twice.

Activity Book pp. 205–206   Student Handbook   Student CD-ROM

390   Unit 6   Visions

MULTI-LEVEL OPTIONS *From Reading to Writing*

Newcomer Have students create a story map like the one on p. 389. Tell them to draw the setting in the first box and show the problem that the characters are having. In the second box, tell them to show how the characters are trying to solve the problem. In the third box, ask them to draw how the problem is solved.

Beginning Have students use drawings and short captions to tell their story on a story map like the one on p. 389. Provide time for students to share their stories in small groups.

Intermediate Remind students that they are writing *realistic* fiction. Point out that one of the reasons John Steinbeck was such a talented writer was because he used things he had observed to make his stories seem real. Suggest that students base the stories they are writing on familiar people, places, and problems.

Advanced *Say: John Steinbeck did not just tell readers that Kino found a pearl and that it solved his problems. Reread paragraphs 7–9. Notice how the author built suspense into the plot by stretching out the resolution of the problem. You may want to follow this model in telling how the problem in your story is solved.*

From Reading to Writing

Write a Fiction Story

Make up a story about someone who solves a problem.

1. Your story should have a beginning, a middle, and an end.
2. Use conjunctions to make compound sentences in your story.
3. Combine other sentences into complex sentences using words like *when, while, if,* and *that.*
4. Be sure your clauses have a subject and a verb, and that the subjects and verbs agree.
5. Select reference materials, such as your Student Handbook, for revising and for editing final drafts.
6. As you revise and edit, decide if you need to elaborate—say more about—any of your ideas.

Title of Story _____

Beginning

Who are the characters?
What is the main character's problem?

Middle

What happens as the main character tries to solve the problem?

End

What happens when the main character solves the problem?

Student Handbook   The Heinle Newbury House Dictionary   Activity Book *p. 207*   Student CD-ROM

Across Content Areas

Learn About Bodies of Water

More than 70% of the earth's surface is covered with water. Water is found in oceans, seas, lakes, rivers, and waterfalls. Look at the chart. It shows information about some bodies of water. Use a globe or world map to locate each place.

Activity Book *p. 208*

Largest Ocean	Pacific Ocean	area: 64,186,000 square miles (166,241,000 sq. km.)
Largest Sea	South China Sea	area: 1,149,000 square miles (2,974,600 sq. km.)
Largest Lake	Caspian Sea, Europe-Asia	area: 143,245 square miles (371,000 sq. km.)
Largest River	Nile River, Africa	length: 4,241 miles (6,825 km.)
Largest Waterfall	Angel Falls, Venezuela	height: 3,281 feet (979 meters)

Chapter 3 The Pearl   **391**

From Reading to Writing

Write a Fiction Story

1. **Make a storyboard** After students choose characters and a problem, have them create a storyboard to show the events leading to the resolution of the problem.
2. **Think-quickwrite-pair-share** Ask students to write as much as they can about their storyboards. Remind them to check verb forms. Have students share their ideas with a partner before making a final copy.
3. **Multi-level options** See MULTI-LEVEL OPTIONS on p. 390.

Across Content Areas: Social Studies

Learn About Bodies of Water

Use a map Bring in globes, atlases, or world maps. Have students identify the different oceans and continents. Point out the compass rose and review directions. Allow students to locate and identify countries that they know.

 **ASSESS**

Have students name the largest bodies of water.

Reteach and Reassess

Text Structure Have students review the features of realistic fiction on p. 378. Then ask them to defend the following statement: *The characters in "The Pearl" are realistic.* Ask them to use story examples.

Reading Strategy Ask students to share some of the inferences they made about characters in "The Pearl." Have them identify story details and personal experiences that support their inferences.

Elements of Literature Read aloud a short story. *Say: Use a story map to tell the beginning, middle, and end of the story. Draw or write the main events in each part of the story.*

Reassess Have pairs of students share the stories they wrote for From Reading to Writing. Ask listeners to make three inferences about story characters based on what their partners wrote or drew.

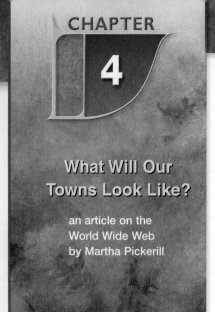

CHAPTER 4

What Will Our Towns Look Like?

an article on the
World Wide Web
by Martha Pickerill

Into the Reading

Chapter Materials

Activity Book: *pp. 209–216*
Audio: *Unit 6, Chapter 4; CD 3, Track 9*
Student Handbook
Student CD-ROM: *Unit 6, Chapter 4*
Teacher Resource Book: *Lesson Plan, Teacher Resources, Reading Summary, Activity Book Answer Key*
Teacher Resource CD-ROM
Assessment Program: *Quiz, pp. 95–96; Teacher and Student Resources, pp. 115–144*
Assessment CD-ROM
Transparencies
The Heinle Newbury House Dictionary/CD-ROM
Web site: http://visions.heinle.com

Objectives

Use personal knowledge Read the objectives aloud. Explain key words. *Ask: Are there any objectives that you can already do?*

Use Prior Knowledge

Test Your Knowledge of Natural Resources

Use photos Have students identify resources they use from pictures of water, trees, fuels, minerals, animals, and so on.

Answers
1. **a.** false **b.** true **c.** false **d.** false

Objectives

Reading Summarize text to recall ideas as you read an article on the World Wide Web.

Listening and Speaking Give a persuasive speech.

Grammar Use *will* to predict future events.

Writing Create a form, interview, and summarize.

Content Science: Learn about acid rain.

Use Prior Knowledge

Test Your Knowledge of Natural Resources

In this chapter, you will read about natural resources. Natural resources are things from nature that people use.

1. Test what you already know about natural resources. Decide if each of these statements is true or false.
   a. We can use as many natural resources as we want. The earth will make more.
   b. We can help conserve natural resources by recycling things.
   c. It is better to travel by car than by bicycle.
   d. There is very little we can do to save natural resources.

2. Now make a **Know/Want to Know/Learned** Chart. Complete the first two columns now. Complete the third column at the end of the chapter.

Topic: *Natural Resources*

Know	Want to Know	Learned
What do I already know about the topic?	What do I want to know about the topic?	What did I learn about the topic?

MULTI-LEVEL OPTIONS *Build Vocabulary*

Newcomer Draw a leaf on one stick-on note and a building on another. Show one. *Say: nature.* Show the other. *Say: made by people.* Show pictures of a marsh and a factory. Pronounce the vocabulary word for each picture. Have volunteers place the appropriate stick-on note on each picture.

Beginning Draw a leaf on one stick-on note and a building on another. Show one. *Say: nature.* Show the other. *Say: made by people.* Show pictures a marsh and a factory. Pronounce the vocabulary word for each picture and stick on the label. Have volunteers find additional examples in the classroom and make their own stick-on notes.

Intermediate After students have sorted the vocabulary, ask them to look around the classroom and identify three other items that fit each category. (*Examples:* nature—plants, tree outside window, fish in aquarium; made by people—plastic ruler, desk, carpet)

Advanced After students complete the task, ask each to write a sentence stating a relationship between the categories. Then ask each to write a sentence giving an example of that relationship. (*Example:* People use things from nature to make useful items. For example, they use lead and wood to make pencils.)

Build Background

Fossil Fuels

Fossil fuels are natural resources that are used to make energy. We get them from the earth's crust (outside layer of the earth). Some fossil fuels are oil, gas, and coal.

Fossil fuels took thousands of years to form. They come from plants and animals that lived many years ago. The amount of fossil fuels we have is limited. We cannot replace them.

Oil well

Content Connection

Fossil fuels make energy when they are burned. They can be used to heat homes and to make gas for cars.

Build Vocabulary

Put Words into Groups

The reading selection includes words that relate to nature. It also includes words that relate to things made by people.

1. Read the list of words and their definitions.
2. Write the words in the correct columns of a chart.

Nature	Made by People

innovation a new thing made with creativity

organic without chemicals

factory a place where things are manufactured

marsh a wet area of land with many plants and birds

grain a single seed of a plant

The Heinle Newbury House Dictionary

Activity Book p. 209

Student CD-ROM

Chapter 4 What Will Our Towns Look Like? **393**

Build Background

Fossil Fuels

1. **Use pictures in books** Bring in books with pictures of the different fossil fuels. Point out that *gas* can be gasoline or gases such as propane and butane.
2. **Relate to personal experience** Have students talk about fuels they use. Ask students where or how these fuels can be bought.
3. **Content Connection** Have students research fossil fuel production and consumption statistics on the Internet. *Ask: Which countries consume the most? Which countries produce the most?*

Build Vocabulary

Put Words into Groups

Teacher Resource Book: *Personal Dictionary, p. 63*

1. **List-group-label** Have students brainstorm and list things they see around the school. On the board, write: *Nature, Made by People.* Have students sort the items on the list by the categories.
2. **Reading selection vocabulary** You may want to introduce the glossed words in the reading selection before students begin reading. Key words: *inventions, polluted, revolutionized, innovations, preserve, environment.* Instruct students to write the words with correct spelling and their definitions in their Personal Dictionaries. Have them pronounce each word and divide it into syllables.
3. **Multi-level options** See MULTI-LEVEL OPTIONS on p. 392.

Answers
Nature: organic, marsh, grain; Made by People: innovation, factory, industrial

ASSESS

Ask: What are three types of fossil fuels? (oil, gas, coal)

Text Structure

Informational Text

1. **Recognize features** Copy the features chart and clarify items. *Ask: What other readings have been informational texts?* ("Yawning," "Why We Can't Get There from Here," "The California Gold Rush," "To Risk or Not to Risk")
2. **Multi-level options** See MULTI-LEVEL OPTIONS below.

Reading Strategy

Summarize Text to Recall Ideas

Apply Ask students to give examples of other times they summarize things, such as reporting about a sports match or a good movie. Have volunteers give a summary about a sports match or a movie. Explain that only the important points are used in a summary.

ASSESS

Have students identify the four features of an informational text.

Text Structure

Informational Text

You have learned that an **informational text** explains facts about a topic. In this selection, the author explains how people can take care of things in nature.

The chart lists some features of an informational text. Look for these features in "What Will Our Towns Look Like?"

As you read, identify the author's purpose. Is it just to inform, or does the author have another purpose as well?

Informational Text	
Problem	The author explains a problem.
Examples	Examples are details that show how something is true.
Solutions	The author explains ways to solve the problem.
Headings	Headings are titles used within a text to organize it. They help the reader locate information.

Student CD-ROM

Reading Strategy

Summarize Text to Recall Ideas

When you **summarize** part of a reading, you say or write the most important information in the reading. Summarizing helps you remember what you read. How would you summarize this paragraph?

> Casey and her family care about protecting natural resources. They always turn the lights out when they leave a room. They recycle newspapers, bottles, cardboard boxes, and soda cans. They never leave the water running. They even pick up garbage in the neighborhood park.

You can summarize the paragraph in one sentence:

> Casey and her family do many things to protect natural resources.

As you read the selection, stop to summarize parts of it that you want to recall.

Reading Log

Student CD-ROM

MULTI-LEVEL OPTIONS *Text Structure*

Newcomer Present a science library book on a topic related to the environment. Point out the headings. Have students look at the "The Gettysburg Address" (p. 304) and point to the heading there (Prologue). Ask them to find another heading on p. 311 (Epilogue).

Beginning Divide the class into pairs. Give each a science book on an environmental topic. Ask students to look through the book, paying special attention to the headings. Have them fold a piece of paper in half. *Say: Draw a problem you think the book tells about on one side. Draw a solution to it on the other.*

Intermediate Have small groups of students skim science books on environmental problems. *Say: Based on the headings and other features, what problem do you think the book discusses? What solution do you think the author suggests?* Have students read the information on the cover to check their predictions.

Advanced *Say: Based on what you have learned so far by doing the activities in this chapter, what problems and solutions do you think the author of "What Will Our Towns Look Like?" discusses? What headings do you predict might be found in this selection?* Tell students to check their predictions as they read.

What Will Our Towns Look Like?

an article on the World Wide Web
by Martha Pickerill

395

Reading Selection Materials
Audio: *Unit 6, Chapter 4; CD 3, Track 9*
Teacher Resource Book: *Reading Summary,*
pp. 117–118
Transparencies: #45, *Reading Summary*

Suggestions for Using Reading Summary

- Introduce new vocabulary or cognates.
- Cut the summary into strips, or jumble the sentences on an overhead transparency. Students put the sentences in order.
- Practice the reading strategy.
- Students read aloud or with a partner.
- Students paraphrase the summary.
- Students do a cloze activity.
- Students create a visual or graphic organizer, such as a timeline or storyboard, to illustrate the summary.
- Students paraphrase the summary.

Preview the Selection

Teacher Resource Book: *Venn Diagram, p. 35*

1. **Use the illustration** Have students describe the city. *Ask: Where do you think this city is? What year do you think it is? Why?* Read the title of the selection and have students discuss if towns in the future will look like the one in the illustration.

2. **Use a Venn diagram** *Ask: How is the city in the picture different from our city or town?* As students brainstorm ideas, make a list on the board. Then have students compare and contrast the futuristic city with their own city or town on a Venn diagram. Refer back to the diagram after students complete the reading selection.

3. **Connect** Remind students that the unit theme is *visions. Ask: What vision does the artist have of the future? Is it going to be better or worse than now? Do you think the author of this article has the same vision of the future as this artist?*

 Cultural Connection

Remind students that a people's culture is made up of what they believe, what they think about things, and how they behave. *Say: Look at the picture of a city of the future on page 395. What can you tell about the culture of the people who built it?* Students may discuss or draw their responses.

Learning Styles
Natural

Tell students to list or draw natural resources that they think would be used to build and run the city they see on p. 395. *Ask: Do you think this city is more helpful or harmful to the environment than ours? Why?*

Read the Selection

1. **Use text features** Direct attention to the art, labels, and headings. Remind students to use these features to help their understanding of the text.
2. **Paired reading** Read the selection to the students. Have students reread aloud in pairs.

Sample Answer to Guide Question
Inventions make life easier and more comfortable, but they also use resources and harm the environment.

See Teacher Edition pp. 434–436 for a list of English-Spanish cognates in the reading selection.

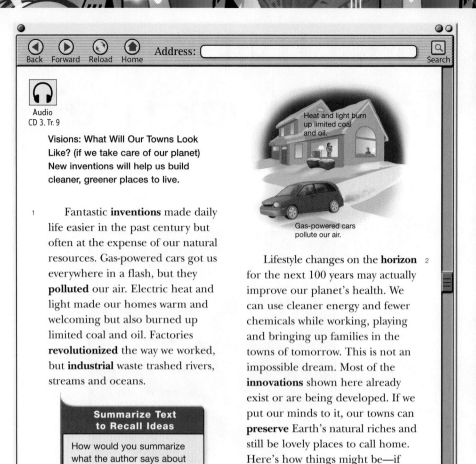

Address:

Audio
CD 3. Tr. 9

Visions: What Will Our Towns Look Like? (if we take care of our planet) New inventions will help us build cleaner, greener places to live.

Heat and light burn up limited coal and oil.

Gas-powered cars pollute our air.

1 Fantastic **inventions** made daily life easier in the past century but often at the expense of our natural resources. Gas-powered cars got us everywhere in a flash, but they **polluted** our air. Electric heat and light made our homes warm and welcoming but also burned up limited coal and oil. Factories **revolutionized** the way we worked, but **industrial** waste trashed rivers, streams and oceans.

> **Summarize Text to Recall Ideas**
>
> How would you summarize what the author says about inventions?

Lifestyle changes on the **horizon** 2 for the next 100 years may actually improve our planet's health. We can use cleaner energy and fewer chemicals while working, playing and bringing up families in the towns of tomorrow. This is not an impossible dream. Most of the **innovations** shown here already exist or are being developed. If we put our minds to it, our towns can **preserve** Earth's natural riches and still be lovely places to call home. Here's how things might be—if we make the **environment** a top concern.

inventions new things created from an idea
polluted made dirty
revolutionized caused a new way of doing something
industrial related to making and selling products
horizon the place in one's view where Earth and sky meet; the near future

innovations new things made with creativity
preserve protect from harm or change
environment the air, land, water, and surroundings that people, plants, and animals live in

396 Unit 6 Visions

MULTI-LEVEL OPTIONS *Read the Selection*

Newcomer Play the audio. *Ask: Do we use too many natural resources?* (yes) *Are our air and water dirty?* (yes) *Can we fix these problems in the future?* (yes) *Can clean fuel help to fix the problem?* (yes)

Beginning Read aloud the Reading Summary. *Ask: What uses up a lot of resources and pollutes the world?* (some inventions) *Where could people work so they don't use so much fuel?* (at home) *What can we use less of to grow foods?* (chemicals)

Intermediate Have students do a paired reading. *Ask: How are modern inventions related to problems in the environment?* (They use up natural resources; they release pollution into the air and water.) *How can we save the environment in the future?* (by finding ways of doing things that don't harm the environment)

Advanced Have students read silently. *Ask: Why do people use inventions that harm the environment?* (They want easy ways to do things; they may not know that they are harming the planet.) *Why are we thinking of new ways to use resources and protect Earth now?* (We don't want to run out of resources later.)

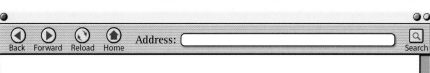

3 **Work/Transportation**

More grownups will work in their homes and keep in touch with **co-workers** through computers. Others will make a short trip to a nearby office park. A few will ride swift electric trains to the nearest city. Cars and trucks will run on clean, hydrogen-powered fuel cells. Most entertainment and stores will be close by, so we'll often travel on old-fashioned, earth-friendly bicycles.

> **Summarize Text to Recall Ideas**
>
> Summarize how changes in transportation will affect the environment.

Food 4

We'll grow fruits, **grains** and vegetables close to home, either in our gardens or on nearby **organic farms.** Since the farms will use natural forms of pest control, such as **predatory insects,** there will be far fewer chemicals in the food supply.

co-workers people with whom one works
grains single seeds of plants

organic farms farms that do not use chemicals to grow food
predatory insects insects that eat other insects

Read the Selection

1. **Use text features** Direct attention to the headings for the paragraphs and explain their purpose. Ask students to describe the photo and decide which heading it is related to.
2. **Paired reading** Read the selection aloud. Then have students read it again in pairs. *Ask: Does the author say more people will work in offices or work at home in the future?* (at home) *Will cars and trucks use gas(oline) in the future?* (no) *What type of fuel will they use?* (hydrogen-powered fuel cells) *Will farms use more chemicals or natural forms for controlling insects?* (natural forms)
3. **Locate derivations using dictionaries** Have students look at these glossed words and determine what words they are derived from: *polluted, revolutionized, industrial, predatory.* Have students check the derivations in a print, online, or CD-ROM dictionary.
4. **Multi-level options** See MULTI-LEVEL OPTIONS on p. 396.

Sample Answer to Guide Question
Trains will be electric, so there won't be pollution. Cars and trucks will use hydrogen-powered fuel cells, so it will be better for the air.

A Capitalization

Headings

Say: The author of this selection used headings to help you find information. Look at page 397. What do you notice about the headings for paragraphs 3 and 4? Yes, we start the important words in a heading with capital letters. What does that remind you of? (titles) *That's right. Headings are like titles for parts of a reading.*

Apply Write on the board: *fuel for homes, clean water, you can help.* Ask students to capitalize these as headings. (Fuel for Homes, Clean Water, You Can Help)

Read the Selection

1. **Use text features** Ask students to point out headings and explain their importance. Have them discuss the photo.
2. **Jigsaw reading** Play the audio or read the selection aloud. Then have groups of students prepare different sections of the reading selection to teach to the whole class.
3. **Analyze words** Call attention to glossed words. Guide students to connect the words (appliances, recycling, mall) to their own lives.

Sample Answer to Guide Question
Houses will use mainly solar energy and won't have to depend on outside sources or power.

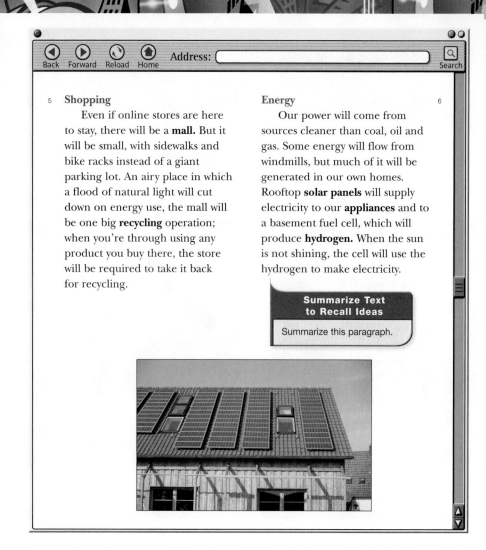

5 **Shopping**

Even if online stores are here to stay, there will be a **mall.** But it will be small, with sidewalks and bike racks instead of a giant parking lot. An airy place in which a flood of natural light will cut down on energy use, the mall will be one big **recycling** operation; when you're through using any product you buy there, the store will be required to take it back for recycling.

Energy 6

Our power will come from sources cleaner than coal, oil and gas. Some energy will flow from windmills, but much of it will be generated in our own homes. Rooftop **solar panels** will supply electricity to our **appliances** and to a basement fuel cell, which will produce **hydrogen.** When the sun is not shining, the cell will use the hydrogen to make electricity.

> **Summarize Text to Recall Ideas**
> Summarize this paragraph.

mall a building or group of buildings with shops, theaters, restaurants, and so on

recycling related to the collection, processing, and reuse of waste materials, such as used bottles and newspapers

solar panels panels that take in sunlight to make energy

appliances machines used for a certain purpose

hydrogen the lightest element that is a gas

398 Unit 6 Visions

MULTI-LEVEL OPTIONS *Read the Selection*

Newcomer *Ask: Will malls be bigger in the future?* (no) *Will all our fuel come from coal, gas, and oil?* (no) *Could the sun help heat our homes?* (yes) *Will we find new ways to make our water clean?* (yes)

Beginning *Ask: What size will malls of the future be?* (small) *What will stores do with used products?* (recycle, use them again) *Where may we get power to heat our houses?* (wind, sun) *What will help to make dirty water clean again?* (special plants and animals)

Intermediate *Ask: How will small neighborhood malls help the environment?* (People will need less fuel to get to them; less fuel will be needed to heat and light the malls.) *What is an advantage of the way water may be cleaned up in the future?* (It uses things in nature, not fuel-using machines.)

Advanced *Ask: Besides helping the environment, why might people like the fuel solutions described in paragraph 6?* (These types of energy may cost less.) *How fast do you think these changes will take place? Why?* (It will take time to figure out how to do these things and to convince people to try new ways.)

7 **Waste**

Plumbing lines will empty into enclosed **marshes,** where special plants, fish, snails and **bacteria** will naturally **purify** wastewater. Clean water will flow back into streams and **reservoirs.**

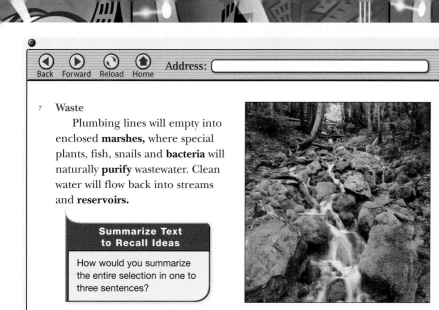

Summarize Text to Recall Ideas

How would you summarize the entire selection in one to three sentences?

marshes   wet areas of land with many plants
bacteria   tiny living things

purify   make clean
reservoirs   bodies of water saved for use

About the Author

Martha Pickerill (born 1964)

Martha Pickerill was born in Ames, Iowa. She knew she wanted to be a writer when she was in sixth grade. She studied journalism in college. After college she worked as a newspaper reporter in Ames. Her job helped her become a better writer. She says, "To be a reporter in Ames, Iowa, you REALLY have to be able to dig. It's not like there's a million fascinating stories just waiting to be told."

➤ What type of research do you think Martha Pickerill had to do to write this article?

Chapter 4   What Will Our Towns Look Like?   **399**

Read the Selection

1. **Use text features** Direct attention to headings, glossed words, and the photo.
2. **Jigsaw reading** Read the selection aloud. Have students continue to work in their groups to prepare a jigsaw reading.
3. **Multi-level options** See MULTI-LEVEL OPTIONS on p. 398.

Sample Answer to Guide Question
Future life will be better because of quicker, more efficient transportation, fewer chemicals in foods, cleaner energy sources, more recycling, and better waste handling.

About the Author

Evaluate information about the author Read the author biography to students. *Ask: How do you know Martha Pickerill enjoys writing?* (She studied journalism and worked as a newspaper reporter.)

Answer
Example: Martha Pickerill had to research science inventions and ideas.

Across Selections

Compare and contrast visions Compare and contrast Martha Pickerill's vision of future life with Sandra Cisneros's vision of a real house in "The House on Mango Street." Help students decide whose vision is more optimistic and explain why.

Spelling, Punctuation, Capitalization

After the Reading Comprehension section, students will practice spelling, punctuation, and capitalization in the Activity Book.

---

th **Spelling**

Y for long /i/ sound

Have students find the word *recycling* in paragraph 5. Write the word on the board. Circle the *y.* **Say:** *The letter* y *can make the long /i/ sound.* Write *hydrogen* on the board. Circle the *y.* Have students say the word with you and note the sound *y* makes.

Apply **Say:** *Write these words in which* y *sounds like long /i/:* cry, type, myself.

Evaluate Your Reading Strategy

Summarize Text To Recall Ideas *Say: You have practiced an important reading strategy. Now you can decide how well you have done. Does this statement describe how you read?*

When I read, I summarize the most important information in a text. Summarizing helps me understand and remember a reading.

Beyond the Reading

Reading Comprehension

Question-Answer Relationships

Sample Answers

1. Cars will not use gas but hydrogen-powered fuel cells.
2. coal and oil
3. solutions to environmental problems that will make life better in the future
4. No, cleaner energy and fewer chemicals are already being used or tested.
5. They have polluted the air.
6. The author believes that most people like going to the mall to shop and to see other people.
7. The author's vision is a clean, safe, and comfortable future without hurting or destroying resources and the environment.
8. The headings help me find the part of the article where I can find specific information.
9. I think I can help the environment by recycling materials, saving water, and turning off lights when they're not being used.
10. How much will it cost to make new electric trains and to change all the cars to hydrogen-powered fuel cells?

Build Reading Fluency

Adjust Your Reading Rate to Scan

Explain that students need to adjust their reading to scan the text to locate key words. Have them read the question then scan to find the answer and identify key words.

Answers
1. at home 2. on hydrogen-powered fuel 3. fewer
4. yes 5. energy from windmills and solar panels

Reading Comprehension

Question-Answer Relationships (QAR)

"Right There" Questions

1. **Recall Facts** What prediction does the author make about cars?
2. **Recall Facts** What two resources are electric heat and light burning up?

"Think and Search" Questions

3. **Identify Theme** What is the theme of the selection?
4. **Identify Supporting Details** Does the author think that using cleaner energy and fewer chemicals is an "impossible dream"? Why not?

"Author and You" Questions

5. **Analyze Cause and Effect** What have gas-powered cars done to the environment?

6. **Make Inferences** Why does the author write that there will always be malls?
7. **Connect to Theme** What is the author's vision of the future?
8. **Use Text Features** How do the headings help you locate information?

"On Your Own" Questions

9. **Compare Your Experiences** What can you do to help the environment?
10. **Ask Questions** What questions did you think of after reading the selection?

Activity Book
p. 210

Student
CD-ROM

Build Reading Fluency

Adjust Your Reading Rate to Scan

Remember that when you scan for information you need to adjust your reading rate to read quickly. Work with a partner. Read aloud key words in the reading selection as you scan for the answers. Write your answers on a piece of paper.

1. Where will people work from in the future?
2. How will trucks and cars run?
3. Will we use more or fewer chemicals to grow food?
4. Will we still have malls?
5. What types of energy will we use?

MULTI-LEVEL OPTIONS *Elements of Literature*

Newcomer Divide the class into groups of three. Give each a set of three cards. Have students draw a symbol on each card that will help them remember the purposes for writing explained on p. 401. Have students use these "bookmarks" to indicate three selections in Units 1–6 that are examples of each type of writing.

Beginning Have students copy onto slips of paper: *inform, persuade,* and *entertain.* Have them look at illustrations and titles of books and magazines in your classroom library to find an example of each.

Intermediate Have each student find another Web site, book, or article about protecting the environment. Ask students to compare and contrast those authors' purposes with the purposes identified for "What Will Our Towns Look Like?"

Advanced *Say: Authors communicate their purposes through the information they include in their writing and how they organize it. Their tone, or attitude, also supports their purpose. What is the tone of this piece? How does it support the purpose?* (a positive tone to convince us that we can make changes)

Listen, Speak, Interact

Give a Persuasive Speech

Give a speech to persuade people to take care of the environment.

1. Use multiple sources to research environmental issues.
   a. Use the headings in the selection to locate and organize your information.
   b. Use the Table of Contents of this book to find other selections about the environment.
   c. Use other library resources such as newspapers, magazines, or the Internet.
2. Summarize and organize your information from these resources by outlining your ideas.
3. Look at your research and choose a topic you want to make a speech about.

Ways to Persuade	
Appeal to Logic	Give facts to support your opinion. Tell about real problems.
Appeal to Emotion	Say things so that listeners respond with their feelings.
Appeal to Ethics	Explain why taking care of the environment is the right thing to do.

4. Use different ways to persuade. Look at the chart for ideas.
5. Put some of your research findings in a chart. Use this visual with your audience.
6. Present your persuasive speech to a small group.
7. Listen to your classmates' speeches. What is each person's purpose?
8. Analyze your classmates' speeches. Who gave the most persuasive speech?

Elements of Literature

Identify Author's Purpose

The **author's purpose** is the reason why the author writes a text.

Purposes for Writing	
to inform	to give information about a topic
to persuade	to try to get the reader to agree with an opinion
to entertain	to give the reader enjoyment

1. When Martha Pickerill wrote "What Will Our Towns Look Like?" what was her purpose? Note that an author may have more than one purpose for writing.
2. What features of the text support your ideas of the author's purpose?
3. Did she succeed in her purpose?

Activity Book
p. 211

Student
CD-ROM

Chapter 4   What Will Our Towns Look Like?   **401**

Listen, Speak, Interact

Give a Persuasive Speech

1. **Use a chart** Help students clearly identify their issues and positions. Have them list arguments for and against their positions. Tell students to use their strongest arguments in a persuasive speech.
2. **Newcomers** Have students suggest possible topics for their environmental speeches. List them on the board and have students choose one to develop. Help them express clearly their positions. Model appropriate tone for persuasive speaking.

Elements of Literature

Identify Author's Purpose

1. **Explain terms** Read the explanation and have students think of examples of reading selections that inform, persuade, and entertain. (*Examples:* inform: "Elements of Life," persuade: "Samantha's Story," entertain: "How I Survived My Summer Vacation")
2. **Use personal experiences** Have students share times when they wrote something to inform, persuade, and entertain.
3. **Multi-level options** See MULTI-LEVEL OPTIONS on p. 400.

Answers
1. to inform and persuade
2. The headings help give information. The introduction helps persuade.
3. yes

 **ASSESS**

Have students state the three purposes for writing.

Content Connection
The Arts

Have students listen to one or more folk songs about the environment. *Ask: What part of nature is the song about? What was the songwriter's purpose in creating this song? What details from the song lyrics support that purpose?*

Learning Styles
Musical

Suggest that students find or create tapes of mood music or sound effects to introduce or provide background for their speeches. (*Example:* A student could play a relaxing piece of music with woodland sounds and then play sounds of city traffic if his/her speech is about noise pollution.)

Word Study

Study the Latin Prefix co-

Use a word map Write on the board: *co-* + *workers = co-workers*. Explain the meaning of *co-* and how it affects the meaning of a root word.

Answers

2. coexist: be present or live under the same circumstances together; coauthor: a person who writes a book with another person; costar: an actor with just as important a part as another actor.

Grammar Focus

Use *Will* to Predict Future Events

Apply *Ask: Will it be sunny or rainy tomorrow? Will our team win the game tomorrow?* Write the predictions on the board. Point out *will* + verb for future predictions.

Answers

2. More grownups will <u>work</u> . . . ; Others will <u>make</u> a . . . ; A few will <u>ride</u> swift . . . 3. Example: I will go to college. I will live in a large house. I will be happy.

ASSESS

Have students write sentences using *coexist, co-worker, coauthor, costar.*

Word Study

Study the Latin Prefix co-

You have learned that a prefix is a group of letters added to the beginning of a word. A prefix may change the meaning of a word.

The word *co-workers* is used in the selection. This word has the prefix *co-*. This prefix is from Latin and means "together or with." *Co-workers* means "people who work together."

Root Word	Word	Meaning
exist (to be present)	coexist	
author (a person who writes a work)	coauthor	
star (an actor with an important part)	costar	

Personal Dictionary   The Heinle Newbury House Dictionary   Activity Book p. 212   Student CD-ROM

1. Copy and complete the chart in your Personal Dictionary.
2. Guess the meaning of each word that has the prefix *co-*. Use the meaning of each root word to help you.
3. Write a sentence for each word.

Grammar Focus

Use *Will* to Predict Future Events

When you predict, you tell what is going to happen in the future. The word *will* + a simple verb is often used to predict a future event. A simple verb is a verb form with no endings or other changes. *Climb* is a simple verb. *Climbed* is not a simple verb.

Tony <u>will win</u> the race.

It <u>will rain</u> tomorrow.

1. Look at paragraphs 3 through 7 of the Web article. Find three sentences that use *will*.
2. Write the sentences on a piece of paper. Underline the simple verb.
3. Write three sentences with *will* to predict what will happen to you in the future.

Activity Book pp. 213–214   Student Handbook   Student CD-ROM

402 Unit 6 Visions

MULTI-LEVEL OPTIONS *From Reading to Writing*

Newcomer Break the class into groups. Have each draw an idea from the selection. Ask a parent, community worker, or other teacher to read the selection and visit your class. Have a student from each group point to their drawing and ask *Will this work?* Help students summarize the results in a short sentence or two.

Beginning Help the class form a basic question about each part of the selection. Have students rehearse reading the resulting list of questions. Have them work in small groups to interview one another using the questions. Have each group summarize the responses. (*Example:* Shopping idea: will work)

Intermediate After students plan their questions, discuss follow-up questions. *Say: Sometimes, the interviewee may give you a short answer or an answer you don't fully understand. Be ready to ask follow-up questions. Good follow-up questions often start with* How *or* Why. *Give ideas, such as* Why do you think so? How would that work?

Advanced Call special attention to step 5. Suggest that students' summaries of results will be more interesting and convincing if they include examples and quotes. For example, *say: Four out of five people said that they would be willing to take public transportation. Our principal said, "I would use the time on a bus to read."*

From Reading to Writing

Create a Form, Interview, and Summarize

Work with a partner to find out what other people think about the ideas in "What Will Our Towns Look Like?" Interview people and create a chart to record your findings.

1. Reread the selection. Develop some questions you want to ask.
2. Go over your questions carefully to revise them. Are your questions clear? Are they too long?
3. Create, organize, and revise a form that you will use to conduct your interviews. Make a place for the following information.

   a. The interviewer's name
   b. The interviewee's name
   c. The questions
   d. The answers

4. Conduct your interviews. You and your partner should interview at least five people each.
5. Evaluate your interview forms. Make a chart to record what people think about the ideas. Organize and revise the chart as necessary.
6. Share your summaries in class.
7. Send a summary of your findings to your town government. Use a letter or an e-mail.

Activity Book
p. 215

Student
Handbook

Across Content Areas

Learn About Acid Rain

When fossil fuels burn, they create harmful chemicals. For example, an automobile creates gases when it burns gasoline. These gases can make the air dirty. We call this **pollution.** Pollution may come back to the ground as **precipitation**—rain, sleet, and snow.

Some scientists say that this precipitation, which is called acid rain, can hurt farm crops, forests, and water. They also think that acid rain can **damage** the **surfaces** of some buildings.

Match each word with its definition:

1. pollution
2. precipitation
3. damage
4. surfaces

   a. hurt
   b. outside layer of things
   c. the dirtying of air, water, and earth
   d. the release of moisture in the air

Activity Book
p. 216

Chapter 4 What Will Our Towns Look Like? **403**

From Reading to Writing

Create a Form, Interview, and Summarize

1. **Prepare questions** Review question words and question formation. Have students prepare their own questions to ask.
2. **Newcomers** Have students suggest possible questions. List them on the board and have students practice asking them. Tell them to choose five of the questions for their interviews.
3. **Multi-level options** See MULTI-LEVEL OPTIONS on p. 402.

Across Content Areas: Science

Learn About Acid Rain

1. **Define key vocabulary** Ask students if they have ever eaten a lemon and how it tasted. Explain that an acid is something sour or burning, just like the acid in a lemon.
2. **Use context clues** Remind students to guess the meaning of new words using clues in the reading.

Answers
1. c 2. d 3. a 4. b

 **ASSESS**

Give a definition of: *pollution, precipitation, damage,* and *surfaces.* Have students identify the word you are defining.

Reteach and Reassess

Text Structure Have students use a Venn diagram to compare and contrast the text structure of "What Will Our Towns Look Like?" with an informational text from another source, such as a magazine.

Reading Strategy Read aloud a short magazine or Web site article about an environmental issue. Have students write a brief summary or create a drawing summarizing the ideas.

Elements of Literature Bookmark Web sites such as an online encyclopedia, a folktale site, and a site by an environmental group trying to persuade people to take action. Have students identify the purpose of each site.

Reassess Have students use a search engine to find a Web site they think does a good job of telling about the environment. Ask students to show the sites they found and give short persuasive speeches to convince the class that the site is worth visiting.

Materials

Student Handbook
CNN Video: *Unit 6*
Teacher Resource Book: *Lesson Plan, p. 33;*
Teacher Resources, pp. 35–64; Video Script,
pp. 171–172; Video Worksheet, p. 178;
School-Home Connection, pp. 154–160
Teacher Resource CD-ROM
Assessment Program: *Unit 6 Test and*
End-of-Book Exam, pp. 97–108; Teacher
and Student Resources, pp. 115–144
Assessment CD-ROM
Transparencies
The Heinle Newbury House Dictionary/CD-ROM
Heinle Reading Library: *A Christmas Carol*
Web site: http://visions.heinle.com

Listening and Speaking Workshop

Write and Present a Persuasive Role Play

Speak persuasively Review appeal to logic, emotion, or ethics for persuasive speeches.

Step 1: Analyze the characters.
Arrange students in pairs to talk about the characters.

Step 2: Identify reasons.
List all possible reasons for and against giving money. Choose the two strongest for each position to write on note cards.

Listening and Speaking Workshop

Write and Present a Persuasive Role Play

Topic

In "Mr. Scrooge Finds Christmas," you met Mr. Scrooge and the Solicitor. These men have different ideas about helping others. Present a role play. The Solicitor will try to persuade Mr. Scrooge to give money to the needy.

Step 1: Analyze the characters.

1. Work with a partner. One of you will be Mr. Scrooge. The other will be the Solicitor.
2. Answer the following questions. Use information from the selection and your own experiences.
   a. What does each man care about?
   b. Why do you think each man thinks this way?
   c. Who is a happier person?
3. Write your answers and other ideas in a Cluster Map.

Step 2: Identify reasons.

1. On a note card, list two reasons why the Solicitor thinks Mr. Scrooge should give money to the needy.
2. List two reasons why Mr. Scrooge does not want to give money to the needy. Write these reasons on a note card.

Step 3: Write dialogue.

1. Write what the characters will say. The dialogue should be a conversation. Use quotation marks around the words people say.
2. How will you start the dialogue? Will it begin when the Solicitor enters Mr. Scrooge's office?
3. Use the reasons you listed in Step 2.
4. How will your dialogue end? Will the Solicitor persuade Mr. Scrooge to give money to the needy?

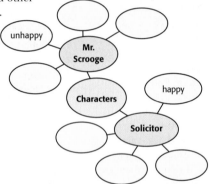

MULTI-LEVEL OPTIONS *Listening and Speaking Workshop*

Newcomer Work with the class to write a short dialogue such as:

Solicitor: Please help.
Mr. Scrooge: Why should I?

Help two students rehearse these lines. Have other students act out vignettes, such as hungry people getting food and cold people getting coats, in response to the dialogue.

Beginning Use a Language Experience Approach to write a simple dialogue with the class. Duplicate the results. Have pairs act out the dialogue using the Language Experience script. Tell students to use their voices, faces, and gestures to make their performances interesting.

Intermediate *Say: Words are only part of our message. Body language is important, too. What actions and facial expressions do people use when they are asking a favor? What actions and expressions show that a person doesn't want to do something?* Tell students to include these ideas in their stage directions.

Advanced Have students create several awards for performances, such as the *Most Convincing Award* or *Most Expressive Award*. After all the performances, have a secret ballot and an awards "ceremony."

Step 4: Organize your role play.

1. Add stage directions. How do the characters move?
2. Write the stage directions next to the dialogue on each note card.

Step 5: Practice.

1. Practice your role play in front of another pair of students.
2. Ask them to complete the Active Listening Checklist.
3. Use the checklist to revise your role play.
4. Listen carefully to your classmates' role play.

Active Listening Checklist

1. Did each character give reasons for his opinion?
2. Did they speak slowly and clearly?
3. Were they believable?

Step 6: Present your role play.

1. Use tone of voice to show how your character feels.
2. If possible, videotape your role play.
3. Review what you liked about your role play. Talk about how you could improve.

Student Handbook

Viewing Workshop

View and Think

Compare and Contrast a Play and a Movie

1. Ask your librarian or an adult to help you find a movie version of "A Christmas Carol."
2. Compare and contrast "Mr. Scrooge Finds Christmas" with the movie. Do the characters in the movie look as you imagined them? Does the setting?
3. You read only part of "Mr. Scrooge Finds Christmas." The movie shows the rest of the story. Were you surprised by what happened in the movie? Explain.

4. What is the purpose of the movie? Does it entertain, inform, or persuade? Is the purpose of the play the same or different?
5. Does the filmmaker do a good job of presenting the story? Why or why not?
6. How does using film help present Dickens's message?

Further Viewing

Watch the *Visions* CNN Video for Unit 6. Do the Video Worksheet.

CNN Video

Content Connection
The Arts

Have students research typical dress in London during the mid-1800s. Instruct students to use art and craft materials to make simple hats, vests, or other costume pieces to wear during their role plays.

Learning Styles
Linguistic

Read aloud a few paragraphs of *A Christmas Carol* by Charles Dickens. Ask students to comment on how hearing the story differs from experiencing the play and the movie.

Step 3: Write dialogue.
Brainstorm and record other settings for the dialogue. Help students make a choice. Help with appropriate beginnings and conclusions.

Step 4: Organize your role play.
Add gestures and action to the characters to make them persuasive. Remind students to place stage directions in parentheses.

Step 5: Practice.
Help students with intonation and pronunciation as needed. Direct attention to the checklist and have students give each other suggestions.

Step 6: Present your role play.
If possible, invite another class or parents to attend the presentations.

ASSESS

Have students write two sentences telling what they liked the best about their own presentation and what they would like to do better next time.

Portfolio

Students may choose to record or videotape their oral presentations to place in their portfolios.

Viewing Workshop

View and Think
Read the instructions aloud.

1. **Use graphic organizers** Create a two-column chart to help students as they record similarities and differences they notice between the play and video versions of *A Christmas Carol.*
2. **Analyze purpose** Have students work in groups. Tell them to discuss whether or not the movie accomplished its purpose.
3. **Respond to media presentations** Have students explain their likes and dislikes about the print and film presentations of the story. Instruct students to support their opinions with examples.

Writer's Workshop

Response to Literature: Collaborate to Write a Persuasive Letter

Brainstorm ideas. Have students suggest possible changes for the city or town.

Step 1: Brainstorm.
Have students list reasons they think the change will be an improvement.

Step 2: Find facts to support your solutions.
After students have done some research, have them summarize the main ideas and details that support their reasons.

Step 3: Write a draft of your letter.
Remind students of their audience and purpose for writing. Call attention to the model. Point out that the form and style of writing a business letter differs from that of a personal letter. Instruct students to select a voice and a style appropriate to their audience and purpose. If necessary, review voice and style with students. Have students use the selected voice and style as they write their drafts.

Writer's Workshop

Response to Literature: Collaborate to Write a Persuasive Letter

Writing Prompt
With a partner, think about the city or town where you live. Is there a problem to be solved? Does the city need to recycle more? Does it need more public transportation?

Write a five-paragraph letter to the mayor (or person in charge) of your city or town. Try to persuade the mayor to solve the problem.

Step 1: Brainstorm.
1. Think of solutions for the mayor to consider.
2. Choose two of these solutions.
3. Write each solution on a separate note card.

Step 2: Find facts to support your solutions.
1. Use note cards to summarize information you find.
   a. Use the name of the problem as the keyword for an Internet search.
   b. Talk to adults who know about the topic.
   c. Use and interpret maps, graphs, or tables you find to help support your position.
2. Organize your information, outlining the main idea and supporting details.

Step 3: Write a draft of your letter.
1. Use business letter format.
2. Organize your ideas in coherent paragraphs. Follow the model.
3. Remember to indent each paragraph.
4. Be sure to use capital letters for the names of people, places, and organizations.

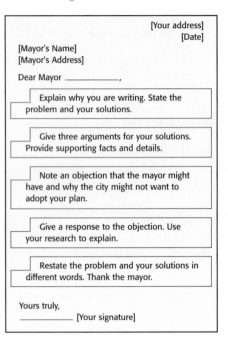

MULTI-LEVEL OPTIONS *Writer's Workshop*

Newcomer Have partners write at the top of a page: *Dear Mayor*. Ask one partner to draw on the left something in the community. Have the other partner show on the right how a change could improve that part of the community. Ask students to sign their names at the bottom of the message.

Beginning Have partners draw something in the community as it is now, and then show a change they suggest. Help them write a caption to tell how the change would make the community better. Ask them to add a greeting and their signatures.

Intermediate Tell students that there are several kinds of details they can include to support their ideas. Suggest that they incorporate some of the following: statistics, quotes from citizens, and examples of how the idea has worked in other places.

Advanced In small groups, have students read at least three persuasive letters to the editor from a newspaper. Have them rank the letters from most persuasive to least persuasive. Ask students to list qualities that make the highest ranked letter the most convincing. Tell students to use what they learned to draft their letters.

Step 4: Revise, edit, and proofread.

1. Exchange letters with another pair of students. Ask them to answer the questions in the Writing Checklist.

2. As you revise, check your facts. Do you need more facts to support your argument? If so, use resource materials such as reading selections in this book or experts to revise your letter.

3. As you edit, make sure that your facts are accurate. Check resource materials such as Internet sites or primary sources.

4. Talk about your classmates' answers. Make any necessary changes.

5. Proofread your revised letter. Look for punctuation, spelling, and grammar mistakes.

6. Use the Editor's Checklist in your Student Handbook.

Step 5: Write your final draft.

If you are writing your letter by hand, use your best handwriting. Use manuscript or cursive. If you are using a computer, check for typing mistakes.

✓ **Writing Checklist**

1. Is my reason for writing this letter clear?

2. Do I say what problem needs to be resolved?

3. Do I say why a change is needed?

4. Do I give possible solutions?

Step 6: Mail or e-mail your letter.

Send your letter to the mayor. Ask your teacher for the address.

Step 7: Post copies of your letters.

Post copies of all the letters on a bulletin board. Review the letters and ask yourself these questions.

1. What are the strengths of these letters?

2. What are their weaknesses?

3. How can these letters help me set goals to become a better writer?

The Heinle
Newbury House
Dictionary

Student
Handbook

Step 4: Revise, edit, and proofread.
Review editing and proofreading points. Give clarification and explanation as needed. Then in small groups, have two pairs share their letters and give each other feedback on their drafts.

Step 5: Write your final draft.
Have students make adjustments and corrections.

Step 6: Mail or e-mail your letter.
If possible, have students send their letters by postal mail or e-mail.

Step 7: Post copies of your letters.
Display copies on a bulletin board or your school Web site. Allow time for students to read one another's letters. Post any responses to the letters.

 ASSESS

Have students make a checklist for writing persuasive letters.

Portfolio

Students may choose to include their writing in their portfolios.

 Home Connection

Say: *Family members don't usually like it when children beg for things. But you can use what you learned to persuade someone in your family to do something that you think would be good for you or the family. For example, you might try to convince an older brother to lend you his CDs sometimes. Write reasons that will convince your family member. Support your reasons with facts and examples.*

Learning Styles
Intrapersonal

Remind students that they used a formal tone and language to write to the mayor. Point out that they would use a less formal tone if they were writing to someone near their age. They would also use examples that relate to a young person's life. Ask students to write a letter to the girl in "The House on Mango Street" trying to persuade her to feel more positive about her home.

Projects

Project 1: Interpret Text Ideas in a Video

1. **Gather and organize** Have students choose a selection and list ideas about it.
2. **Represent your ideas** Help students plan their presentation effectively using visuals, script, and actions.

Project 2: Present "Vision for My Future"

1. **Gather and organize** Have students list possible goals. Tell them to consider steps that would lead to one of the goals.
2. **Represent your ideas** Remind students to use drawings, labels, and symbols on the poster.

Portfolio

Students may choose to include their projects in their portfolios.

Projects

These projects will help you develop your ideas about visions.

Project 1: Interpret Text Ideas in a Video

Think about the visions that are expressed in this unit. With a small group, choose one reading selection and create a video presentation about the visions in it.

1. Decide which selection to use.
2. List two or three ideas about visions from the text that you want to interpret (express in your own way).
3. Write the script—the words—for your video. It can be a drama (a play) or a documentary (informational). Remember: You are writing your interpretation of the ideas.
4. Write the stage directions and plan the visuals for your video.
5. Practice your script several times. Then record it on videotape.
6. Show your video to your class. Take it home to share with your family. If you can't make a video recording, perform your work for your class.

Project 2: Present "Vision for My Future"

Think about your visions for your life.

1. Think about where you would like to be and what you would like to be doing 10 years from now.
2. What steps do you need to take to make these goals happen?
3. Create a storyboard on poster board to describe the steps. Use words and illustrations to show what will happen.
4. Use capitalization and punctuation to enhance meaning.
5. Present your "Vision for My Future" to your class. Display your poster.

MULTI-LEVEL OPTIONS *Projects*

Newcomer Have students write the phrase *I will* at the top of each panel of the storyboard. During their presentation, have them say these words and then show their pictures.

Beginning Help students complete the sentence *I will* with a word or short phrase as the text for each panel of their storyboard. Have students read their statements as they present their work.

Intermediate After students have completed their storyboards, ask each to find at least one library book that relates to their goals. Have students read their books and then meet with other students who have similar visions. Invite them to share what they learned about reaching their goals.

Advanced After students have written about their visions, introduce the concept of *action plans. Say: To make an action plan, you list the little steps you need to take to reach each goal. You tell what the step is, when you hope to achieve it, and who might help you.* Ask each student to create an action plan for one of the goals in his/her vision.

Further Reading

These books explore the theme of visions. Read one or more of them. Write your thoughts about what you read in your Reading Log. Then answer these questions:

1. Compare and contrast an artist's vision of the future with a scientist's.
2. What are your visions for the future?
3. As you review your readings, set goals for yourself as a writer. Who do you want to write like?

A Christmas Carol
by Charles Dickens, Bantam Classics, 1999. This is the famous story of Ebenezer Scrooge. Scrooge, a man who loves money more than people, has strange visitors on Christmas Eve.

The House on Mango Street
by Sandra Cisneros, Vintage Books, 1991. This is the story of a Hispanic girl growing up in Chicago, Illinois, in the 1980s.

The Pearl
by John Steinbeck, Penguin USA, 2000. This is a classic story about Kino, a poor Mexican pearl diver who finds a very valuable pearl. Kino thinks that finding the pearl will solve most of his problems. However, owning the pearl changes the life of Kino and his family in ways that he never imagined.

Future World: A Beginner's Guide to Life on Earth in the 21st Century
by Sarah Angliss and Colin Uttley, Copper Beech Books, 1998. This book predicts what the future will be like. It talks about possible sources of power and future jobs. It also discusses the effects of population growth on the planet.

Eye on the Wild: A Story About Ansel Adams
by Julie Dunlap, Carolrhoda Books, 1995. Ansel Adams saw beauty in the landscape of the American West. This biography tells about his life as a photographer.

Visions: Stories About Women Artists
by Leslie Sills, Albert Whitman, 1993. This book discusses the lives and works of famous women artists such as Mary Cassatt and Leonora Carrington.

How the Future Began: Communications
by Anthony Wilson, Kingfisher Publications, 1999. This book talks about communications with a focus on telecommunications and computers. It also considers communications in the future.

Companion
Web site

Reading Log

Heinle
Reading Library
A Christmas Carol

Further Reading

1. **Respond to literature** Have students select one or more books about visions and prepare a written report. Tell them to describe the visions of the authors. Ask them to compare and contrast visions of scientists and artists. Instruct students to give their own personal response by pointing out characteristics and qualities of the authors that they would like to set as goals for their own writing.

2. **Choose appropriate form for purpose** After students have read at least one book, *say: Now that you have read a book, you want to let others know about it. What's the best form of writing to use for this purpose?* Have students choose the appropriate form for their purpose for writing. Guide them to choose a review. Instruct students to write a short book review. Create a class collection of book reviews. Tell students to use the reviews to help them decide which books to read. Have them continue to add reviews to the collection as they read more books.

Assessment Program: *Unit 6 Test, pp. 97–102; End-of-Book Exam, pp. 103–108*

Heinle Reading Library

A Christmas Carol by Charles Dickens
In a specially adapted version
by Malvina G. Vogel

"Bless Us, Everyone!" That's not the way old Ebenezer Scrooge starts out thinking about Christmas. To the miserly merchant, Christmas is just an excuse for people to have a day off from work. He has no use for traditional joys. But a series of encounters—both warmly human and otherworldly—change Scrooge's mind and spirit forever, in this, the most beloved of all Christmas stories.

Visions Companion Site

http://visions.heinle.com
For additional student activities and teacher resources, see the *Visions Companion* Web site.

Skills Index

Reading

prologue, 164
purpose of text, 343
  entertain, 9, 82, 97, 139, 187, 295, 311, 359, 401
  express, 97, 139, 175
  influence/persuade, 9, 82, 97, 139, 187, 295, 311, 315, 343, 401
  inform, 9, 82, 97, 111, 139, 187, 295, 311, 315, 343, 359, 394, 401
scientific process, 132
simile, 342
thesis statement, 67, 220, 221
topic of informational text, 132
topic sentence, 67

Literary Response
compare and contrast ideas, themes, issues, 22, 46, 60, 66, 98, 127, 140, 201, 217, 223, 252, 254–259, 278–279, 297, 326, 330, 332, 334–337, 338, 343, 400, 409
connect ideas, themes, issues, 10, 15, 22, 27, 39, 51, 73, 87, 103, 112, 117, 126, 127, 131, 140, 153, 161, 163, 179, 191, 192, 205, 214, 217, 227, 239, 246, 251, 265, 275, 285, 296, 297, 299, 301, 312, 315, 317, 326, 331, 338, 347, 363, 365, 375, 377, 392, 393, 400, 403
interpret
  through discussion, 61, 339
  through enactment, 47, 68, 247, 297, 389, 404–405, 408
  through journal writing, 4, 16, 25, 35, 47, 52, 69, 74, 113, 132, 149, 154, 159, 180, 189, 191, 201, 206, 215, 223, 240, 252, 281, 286, 332, 339, 347, 373, 378, 409
  through media, 277, 408
make connections, 10, 15, 22, 27, 39, 51, 73, 87, 103, 117, 126, 131, 140, 153, 161, 163, 179, 191, 192, 205, 214, 217, 227, 239, 246, 251, 265, 272, 275, 285, 296, 297, 299, 301, 312, 315, 317, 326, 331, 338, 363, 365, 375, 377, 392, 393, 400, 403
offer observations, 10, 22, 34, 46, 60, 69, 82, 98, 112, 126, 140, 149, 158, 174, 188, 200, 214, 223, 234, 246, 260, 272, 281, 296, 297, 312, 326, 338, 347, 409
raise questions, 10, 59, 66, 112,

140, 209, 217, 245, 263, 271, 344, 388, 400
react, 297
speculate, 10, 82, 98, 214, 234, 260, 272, 296, 326, 338
support responses
  own experiences, 34, 74, 112, 113, 201, 214, 272, 296, 312, 326, 338
  relevant aspects of text, 16, 60, 83, 112, 140, 157, 199, 246, 266, 272, 296, 326, 401

Literary Terms
adaptation, 348, 353
analogy, 154, 339, 341, 342
bibliography, 221
character, 52, 74, 118, 164, 180, 206, 240, 252, 318, 332, 352, 366, 378, 405
characterization, 52, 158, 261
  changes, 246, 260, 278
  conflict, 278–279, 360
  motivation, 215, 327, 329, 378
  point of view, 234, 252, 373
  relationship, 278, 378
  traits, 60, 126, 174, 214, 215, 278, 378, 388
climax, 83
deductive/inductive organization, 141, 143, 199, 201, 234
dialogue, 47, 85, 247, 249, 352, 361, 389, 404–405
direct address, 35, 302
elements of literature, 11
excerpt, 2, 14, 72, 86, 116, 130, 162, 178, 204, 264, 284, 316, 350, 364, 376
fiction, 74, 118, 164, 180, 206, 318, 366, 378
figurative language, 154, 158, 191, 235, 237, 339, 341, 342
first-person point of view, 234, 252, 332, 373
foreshadowing, 189, 247
free verse, 154, 161
key words, 200, 272, 400
labels, 273, 316
metaphor, 154, 339, 341, 342
mood, 88, 148, 159, 175, 234, 235, 338, 342
narrator, 47, 372
nonfiction, 206
novel, 318
personification, 235, 237
playwright, 404–405
plot, 40, 83, 118, 164, 174, 180, 318, 326, 366, 378, 389
point of view, 81, 234, 252, 261, 332, 373
problem resolution, 40, 47, 65,

88, 99, 127, 164, 174, 177, 246, 318, 326, 363, 378, 389, 394
prologue, 164
quotation, 16, 23, 46, 98, 220, 247, 404
rhyme, 154, 161
rhythm, 302
scene, 352, 361
scientific process, 132
script, 408
setting, 52, 60, 61, 74, 118, 164, 206, 252, 318, 332, 338, 352, 360, 366, 378, 405
simile, 342
speaker, 228
stage directions, 352, 361, 389, 405, 408
stanza, 154, 161, 228, 234, 235, 236
storyboard, 408
style, 159, 214, 260, 297
symbolism, 388
theater, 47
theme, 112, 127, 158, 326, 347, 400
thesis statement, 67, 220, 221
third-person point of view, 234, 261
tone, 61, 88, 159
topic of informational text, 132
topic sentence, 67

Purposes
adjust purpose, 46, 61, 83, 98, 99, 103, 140, 194, 196–199, 200, 202, 228, 247, 249, 272, 312, 388, 400
appreciate writer's craft, 158, 228, 372
complete forms, 12, 27, 38, 39, 50, 61, 64, 66, 86, 100, 102, 104, 113, 114, 116, 130, 132, 144, 146, 160, 176, 192, 205, 237, 238, 250, 251, 264, 277, 278, 298, 300, 314, 328, 330, 392, 393
entertain, 9, 82, 97, 139, 187, 295, 311, 359, 401
establish purpose, 228
inform, 9, 28, 82, 97, 111, 139, 187, 295, 311, 315, 343, 359, 394, 401
models for writing, 13, 37, 49, 63, 64, 68, 85, 129, 147, 161, 221, 237, 263, 275, 313, 344, 346, 363, 372, 391, 406
write a response, 217, 339

Reading Strategies
cause and effect, 22, 34, 98, 112, 126, 132, 134–139, 199, 234,

■ Writing

■ Viewing and Representing

Credits

Steinbeck and John Steinbeck IV. Used by permission of Viking Penguin, a division of Penguin Putnam Inc.

Pp. 395–399, WHAT WILL OUR TOWNS LOOK LIKE?, by Martha Pickerill. Used with permission from *TIME for Kids* magazine, © 2002.

Illustrators

Barry Ablett: pp. 155–157 (© Barry Ablett/Irmeli Holmberg); **Matthew Archambault:** pp. 54–58 (© Matthew Archambault/Scott Hull Associates); **Shelly Bartek:** pp. 254–259 (© Shelly Bartek/Munro Campagna); **Ralph Canaday:** pp. 75–80 (© Ralph Canaday/Wilkinson Studios, LLC); **Viviana Diaz:** pp. 380–386 (© Viviana Diaz/Irmeli Holmberg); **James Edwards:** pp. 90–91, 93–96 (© James Edwards/The Beranbaum Group); **Bill Ersland:** pp. 181–186 (© Bill Ersland/Irmeli Holmberg); **Tom Foty:** pp. 41–45 (© Tom Foty/Munro Campagna); **Gershom Griffith:** pp. 18, 20 (© Gershom Griffith/Craven Design Studios, Inc.); **Clint Hansen:** pp. 354–358 (© Clint Hansen/Scott Hull Associates); **Greg Harris:** p. 134 (© Greg Harris/Cornell and McCarthy, LLC); **Kveta Jelinek:** p. 395 (© Kveta Jelinek/Three In a Box, Inc.); **Rosanne Kaloustian:** pp. 120–124 (© Rosanne Kaloustian/Irmeli Holmberg); **Cheryl Kirk Noll:** pp. 319–325 (© Cheryl Kirk Noll/Christina A. Tugeau); **Mapping Specialists, Ltd.:** pp. 7, 15, 25, 51, 68, 73, 92, 117, 163, 177, 191, 205, 301, 317, 365; **Julie Perterson:** pp. 367–371 (© Julie Peterson/Square Moon); **Andy Powell:** pp. 333, 335–337 (© Andy Powell/Scott Hull Associates); **Precision Graphics:** pp. 3, 30, 32, 193, 198, 227, 239, 270, 396; **Rex Schneider:** p. 153 (© Rex Schneider/Blue Mouse Studios); **Richard Stergulz:** p. 308 (© Richard Stergulz/Wilkinson Studios, LLC); **Carol Stutz:** pp. 275, 316, 408 (© Carol Stutz); **Carlotta Tormey:** pp. 210–212 (© Carlotta Tormey/Wilkinson Studios, LLC); **Raoul Vitale:** pp. 242–244 (© Raoul Vitale/Scott Hull Associates); **Suling Wang:** pp. 166–172 (© Suling Wang/Kolea Baker)

Author Photos

p. 33 (Haleh V. Samiei); p. 45 (Falcon Travis); p. 59 (Washington Irving, © Bettmann/CORBIS); p. 81 (Robin Friedman); p. 97 (Gary Paulsen); p. 111 (David Ropeik); p. 125 (Scott O'Dell, reprinted by permission of Houghton Mifflin Children's Books); p. 139 (Karin Vergoth); p. 157 (Hamza El Din, © Kim Harwood); p. 187 (Jane Langton, © Janet Boynton); p. 199 (Neil de Grasse Tyson, © Jared Pava); p. 209 (Pam Zollman, © Sue Erb); p. 213 (Jim Rawls); p. 233 (Thomas Locker); p. 259 (Francisco Jiménez); p. 295 (Andrea Davis Pinkney); p. 337 (Samantha Abeel); p. 359 (Charles Dickens, © Bettmann/CORBIS); p. 371 (Sandra Cisneros, © 2002, all rights reserved Armando Rascón); p. 387 (John Steinbeck, © Hulton Archive/Getty Images); p. 399 (Martha Pickerill)

Photos

American Museum of Natural History: p. 12 (© Negative no. 35604, courtesy of the Library, American Museum of Natural History)

Art Resource: (All © Art Resource, NY) p. 53 (*The Headless Horseman Pursuing Ichabod Crane, 1858* by John Quidor © Smithsonian American Art Museum, Washington, D.C./Art Resource, NY); p. 89 (*Sea-piece by Moonlight,* oil on canvas by Erich Lessing © Erich Lessing/Art Resource, NY); p. 241 (*Proserpine, 1874* by Dante Gabriel Rossetti, oil on canvas © Tate Gallery, London/Art Resource, NY); p. 251 (© Morton Beebe/CORBIS); p. 253 (© Joseph Sohm; ChromoSohm Inc./CORBIS); pp. 348–349 (*Le Faux Miroir (The False Mirror), 1935,* by Rene Magritte © Phototheque R. Magritte—ADAGP/Art Resource, NY)

CORBIS: (All © Corbis) pp. xii–1 (© Stapleton Collection/CORBIS); pp. 5–6 (© Vo Trung Dung/CORBIS); p. 21 (© Jan Butchofsky-Houser/CORBIS); p. 26 (© Chuck Savage/CORBIS); p. 29 (© Royalty-Free/CORBIS); pp. 70–71 (© Sanford/Agliolo/CORBIS); p. 87 (© Randy Lincks/CORBIS); p. 105 (© Duomo/CORBIS); p. 106 (© Joe McDonald/CORBIS); p. 107

(© Japack Company/CORBIS); p. 119 (© Nik Wheeler/CORBIS); p. 131 (© Tom Brakefield/CORBIS); p. 135 (© Wolfgang Kaehler/CORBIS); p. 136 (© Michael DeYoung/CORBIS); p. 137 (© Ed Kashi/CORBIS); p. 138 (© Chris Hellier/CORBIS); p. 138 (© Academy of Natural Sciences of Philadelphia/CORBIS); p. 138 (© Bettmann/CORBIS); pp. 150–151 (© Franklin McMahon/CORBIS); p. 165 (© Nik Wheeler/CORBIS); p. 179 (© Carl & Ann Purcell/CORBIS); p. 195 (© Roger Ressmeyer/CORBIS); p. 196 (© AFP/CORBIS); p. 207 (© Bettmann/CORBIS); p. 208 (© CORBIS); p. 209 (© Steve Starr/CORBIS); pp. 224–225 (© Ralph A. Clevenger/CORBIS); p. 265 (© Chris Collins/CORBIS); p. 267 (© Richard Hamilton Smith/CORBIS); p. 268 (© David Lees/CORBIS); p. 268 (© CORBIS); p. 269 (© Peter Johnson/CORBIS); pp. 282–283 (© Kevin Fleming/CORBIS); p. 287 (© Raymond Gehman/CORBIS); p. 303 (© Bettmann/CORBIS); p. 304 (© CORBIS); p. 305 (© Todd Gipstein/CORBIS); p. 306 (© Medford Historical Society Collection/CORBIS); p. 307 (© Bettmann/CORBIS); p. 309 (© CORBIS); p. 311 (© Lester Lefkowitz/CORBIS); p. 353 (© Robbie Jack/CORBIS); p. 377 (© Stephen Frink/CORBIS); p. 397 (© Jon Feingersh/CORBIS); p. 398 (© Chinch Gryniewicz; Ecoscene/CORBIS); p. 399 (© Michael T. Sedam/CORBIS)

Fortean Picture Library: p. 9 (© Fortean Picture Library)

Getty Images: (All © Getty Images) p. 17 (© C. McIntyre/PhotoLink/Getty Images); p. 19 (© Getty Images); p. 108 (© Joe McBride/Getty Images); p. 109 (© Paul Chesley/National Geographic/Getty Images); p. 133 (© Stephen Wilkes/Getty Images); p. 268 (© Marco Prozzo/Getty Images); p. 334 (© Darrell Gulin/Getty Images); p. 393 (© Getty Images)

Index Stock Imagery: (All © Index Stock Imagery) p. 31 (© Omni Photo Communications, Inc./Index Stock Imagery); p. 310 (© Jeff Greenberg/Index Stock Imagery); p. 379 (© Eric Kamp/Index Stock Imagery)

Photo Edit: (All © Photo Edit) p. 110 (© Michael Newman/Photo Edit)

Robert Rines/Academy of Applied Science: p. 11 (© Robert Rines/Academy of Applied Science)

Texas Parks & Wildlife: p. 133 (Photo courtesy of Texas Parks & Wildlife © 2002, Phil A. Dotson)

Author and Reading Selection Index

Skills Index

■ Grammar, Usage, and Mechanics

■ Listening and Speaking

Teacher Edition Index

Presentations

autobiography, 342–343

biography, 148

body/movements/gesturing, 215, 327, 361, 389

connections

community, TE/39, 153, 253, 339

home, TE/181, 273

debate, 175

descriptions, 64–65, 72, 189, 218–219, 316

dialogue, 47, 247, 361, 389, 404–405; TE/360, 363

discussion, 61, 226

enactment, 35, 47, 68, 144–145, 247, 297, 361, 389, 404–405, 408; TE/216

evaluate, 65, 215

others' presentations, 35, 47, 65, 99, 113, 141, 145, 175, 215, 218, 219, 237, 273, 276, 277, 313, 327, 342, 343, 361, 401, 405

own presentations, 65, 215, 218, 219, 247, 276, 277, 342, 343, 405

experience, 261, 327, 346; TE/401

ideas, 141, 327

informational, 35, 201, 217, 408

interview, 11, 85, 99, 144–145

literature review, 339; TE/223, 347, 409

multi-level options, TE/64, 144, 218, 222, 276, 312, 342, 404

narrative, 342–343

news report, TE/217, 327

opinion, 112, 126, 140, 200

oral summary, 148, 273, 276–277, 346; TE/223, 347

poem, 237, 338, 339

reaction, 297, 313

record, 148, 342

rehearse, 65, 144, 215, 218, 247, 276, 313, 342, 361, 405, 408; TE/360

report, 67

review, 339; TE/223, 347, 409

role-play, 47, 144–145, 361, 389, 404–405

scene, 361

speech, 312, 313, 401

story, 215, 247, 327, 389

technology, use of, 148, 218, 219, 222, 280, 346, 405, 408

Purpose

determine purpose, 68, 141, 201, 273, 313, 343, 401

distinguish intonation patterns, 88, 158, 201, 234, 329, 360

distinguish sounds, 48, 201, 262

engage listeners, 46, 47, 65, 68, 126, 145, 158, 219, 234, 276, 313, 327, 338, 342, 361, 372, 405

interact, 11

organize, 144, 162, 192, 218, 276, 280, 299, 342, 403, 405

produce intonation patterns, 46, 47, 68, 98, 126, 158, 234, 329, 338, 339, 361, 372, 405

produce sounds, 48, 68, 262

solve problem, 203; TE/315

summarize, 34, 65, 148, 192, 200, 201, 273, 276, 280, 299, 330, 346, 378, 403; TE/7, 33, 56, 79, 81, 91, 110, 111, 231, 243, 257, 269, 293, 311, 335, 371, 383

take notes, 11, 35, 64–65, 72, 141, 144, 162, 175, 189, 201, 215, 218, 261, 273, 276, 280, 285, 299, 327, 339, 342, 389

understand major idea, 68, 99, 141, 201, 250, 261, 273, 275, 312, 343, 389; TE/169

understand supporting evidence, 141, 157, 261, 273, 296, 343

▣ Reading

Comprehension

analyze characters, 60, 61, 99, 126, 164, 188, 246, 260, 278, 327, 360, 372, 388; TE/43, 55, 77, 79, 95, 120, 121, 122, 124, 137, 171, 184, 186, 254, 255, 257, 289, 306, 307, 321, 324, 370, 404

author perspective, 10, 81, 98, 140, 157, 158, 261, 272, 296, 373; TE/9, 389

author purpose, 9, 33, 35, 45, 59, 82, 97, 111, 125, 139, 173, 187, 213, 295, 311, 359, 371, 394, 401; TE/400

author strategy, 3, 11, 23, 33, 35, 61, 73, 81, 132, 141, 159, 173, 175, 227, 245, 259, 311, 387, 399; TE/185

build background, 3, 15, 27, 39, 51, 73, 87, 103, 117, 131, 153, 163, 179, 193, 205, 227, 239, 251, 265, 285, 301, 317, 331, 351, 365, 377, 393; TE/198, 252, 258, 287

community connection, TE/51, 351

cause and effect, 22, 34, 98, 112, 126, 132, 134–139, 199, 234, 246, 260, 272, 296, 312, 326, 338, 400

chronology, 37, 40, 42–45, 46, 63, 129, 143, 146, 240, 242–245, 266, 286, 299, 302, 342, 345, 352, 354–359, 388; TE/157, 211, 290

compare and contrast, 22, 28, 46, 60, 66, 127, 140, 201, 206, 208–213, 215, 217, 223, 246, 252, 254–259, 261, 297, 332, 334–337, 338, 343, 360; TE/33, 45, 97, 125, 138, 233, 245, 271, 295, 369, 371

connect, 3, 10, 15, 22, 27, 39, 51, 73, 87, 103, 112, 117, 126, 131, 140, 153, 161, 163, 179, 191, 192, 205, 214, 217, 227, 239, 246, 265, 272, 275, 285, 296, 299, 301, 312, 315, 317, 326, 331, 338, 363, 365, 375, 377, 392, 393, 400, 403

details, 4, 16, 34, 126, 174, 400; TE/197

dialogue, 47, 247, 249, 352, 361, 389; TE/354, 360

draw conclusions, 10, 188; TE/187, 199

draw inferences, 4, 6–9, 46, 60, 74, 76–81, 82, 83, 99, 126, 234, 246, 260, 286, 288–295, 312, 326, 360, 378, 380–387, 400; TE/75, 168, 210, 319, 321, 337

evaluate, 34, 46, 82, 140, 200, 260, 284, 296, 312; TE/58, 166, 320, 336

experience for comprehension, use of, 28, 30–33, 74, 82, 113, 201, 216, 238, 252, 254–259, 272, 296, 297, 312, 318, 326, 338, 378, 380–387; TE/xii, 47, 51, 52, 87, 99, 131, 141, 183, 198, 212, 317, 334, 337

explain, 10, 34, 127, 139, 174, 188, 214, 277, 280, 297, 343, 372, 388

fact and opinion, 16, 23, 28, 104, 106–111; TE/19

graphic organizers, 265

bar graphs, 37

charts, 4, 12, 13, 16, 24, 27, 28, 38, 39, 40, 50, 51, 52, 61, 64, 66, 73, 74, 86, 88, 100, 102, 104, 114, 116, 118, 130, 132, 144, 146, 154, 159, 160, 164, 176, 180, 190, 194, 201, 202, 203, 205, 206, 228, 237, 238, 240, 250, 251, 252, 264, 266, 275, 278, 286, 298, 300, 302, 314, 318, 328, 330, 332, 340, 346, 350, 362, 363, 373, 374, 389, 391, 392, 393, 401, 402; TE/17, 35, 53, 89, 133, 148, 163, 267, 352, 389

Cluster Web, 2, 14, 162, 178, 204, 364, 376, 404; TE/143, 282, 375

diagrams, 30, 32, 101, 127, 145, 152, 192, 206, 217, 227, 239, 270, 273, 275, 332, 342; TE/21, 97, 126, 209, 233, 272, 395

graphs, 37, 406

maps, 7, 15, 25, 51, 68, 73, 92, 117, 163, 177, 191, 205, 215, 301, 317, 365, 391, 406; TE/7, 63, 305

multi-level options, TE/126

tables, 406

timelines, 40, 63, 143, 218, 240, 249, 286, 344; TE/83, 157, 245, 357, 362

Venn Diagram, 127, 192, 206, 217, 332; TE/21, 97, 126, 209, 233, 395

word squares, 301

identify, 16, 18–21, 22, 27, 34, 48, 52, 54–59, 60, 62, 84, 88, 90–97, 104, 106–111, 112, 114, 126, 132, 134–139, 140, 142, 154, 156–157, 158, 188, 200, 216, 228, 230–233, 234, 246, 262, 266, 268–271, 272, 312, 314, 326, 327, 328, 341, 360, 372, 400, 404; TE/19, 44, 172, 196, 282, 289, 290, 294, 320, 380

images, 52, 54–59, 61, 88, 154, 156–157, 158, 159, 228, 230–233, 332, 339, 373; TE/338

interpret, 4, 16, 25, 35, 47, 52, 61, 68, 69, 74, 113, 132, 149, 154, 159, 180, 189, 200, 201, 206, 215, 223, 240, 247, 252, 277, 281, 286, 296, 347, 409

knowledge for comprehension, use of, 2, 14, 26, 28, 30–33, 38, 50, 72, 74, 83, 86, 99, 102, 116, 130, 152, 162, 178, 192, 201, 204, 226, 238, 250, 252, 254–259, 264, 284, 300, 316, 330, 350, 364, 376, 378, 380–387, 392; TE/161, 179, 193, 205, 317

main idea and details, 16, 18–21, 28, 200, 214, 234, 266, 268–271, 273, 278, 312; TE/110, 136, 196, 208, 324

make judgments, 46, 82, 98, 112, 141, 312

make modifications

asking questions, 10, 66, 112, 344, 388, 400, 404; TE/292, 301, 304

break-in reading, TE/95, 96, 124

guided reading, TE/57, 137

jigsaw reading, TE/134, 270, 293, 382, 383, 398, 399

Teacher Edition Index

Reading Strategies

cause and effect, 22, 34, 98, 112, 126, 132, 134–139, 199, 234, 246, 260, 272, 296, 312, 326, 338, 400

choral reading, TE/156, 157, 186, 187, 197, 230, 232, 308, 309, 334

chronology, 37, 40, 42–45, 46, 63, 129, 143, 240, 242–245, 266, 286, 299, 302, 342, 345, 352, 354–359, 388; TE/157, 211, 290

compare and contrast, 22, 28, 46, 60, 66, 127, 140, 201, 206, 208–213, 215, 217, 223, 246, 252, 254–259, 261, 297, 332, 334–337, 338, 343, 360; TE/21, 33, 45, 59, 97, 125, 138, 139, 233, 245, 271, 295, 369, 371

compare with own experience, 22, 28, 30–33, 60, 74, 82, 98, 112, 113, 127, 201, 214, 223, 252, 254–259, 297, 312, 326, 338, 400; TE/99, 107, 109, 131, 141, 183, 198, 212, 295, 334, 337, 381

conclusions, 10, 188; TE/187, 199

distinguish fact from opinion, 23, 104, 106–111

evaluate, 34, 46, 82, 140, 200, 260, 284, 296, 312; TE/9, 21, 33, 45, 59, 81, 97, 111, 125, 139, 157, 173, 187, 199, 213, 233, 245, 259, 271, 295, 311, 325, 337, 339, 359, 371, 387, 399

experts, 146, 147, 148, 203, 205, 220, 222, 239, 280, 346, 377, 405

home connection, TE/147

imagery, 52, 54–59, 61, 88, 154, 156–157, 158, 159, 228, 230–233, 332, 339, 373; TE/338

inferences, 4, 6–9, 46, 60, 74, 76–81, 82, 83, 99, 126, 234, 246, 260, 286, 288–295, 312, 326, 360, 378, 380–387, 400; TE/75, 168, 210, 319, 321, 337

main idea and details, 16, 18–21, 28, 200, 214, 234, 266, 268–271, 273, 278, 312; TE/110, 136, 196, 208, 324

make judgments, 46, 82, 98, 112, 141, 312

mental images, 52, 54–59, 61, 88, 154, 156–157, 158, 159, 228, 230–233, 332, 339, 373; TE/338

multi-level options, TE/16, 28, 82, 104, 118, 132, 154, 174, 180, 240, 266, 286, 388

paraphrase to read, 68, 118, 120–125, 164, 166–173, 249, 302, 306, 308–309, 311, 360, 366, 368–371; TE/322

predict, 83, 98, 174, 180, 182–187, 188, 318, 320–325, 360, 388; TE/43, 45, 57, 77, 79, 95, 121, 123, 137, 166, 255, 257, 357, 367, 383, 385

read aloud, TE/6, 18, 21, 33, 43, 90, 139, 166, 256, 334, 368, 380

recognize tone and mood, 61, 88, 90–97, 159, 175, 234, 235, 338; TE/156, 158, 174, 177, 308

reteach and reassess, TE/13, 25, 37, 49, 63, 85, 101, 115, 129, 143, 161, 177, 191, 203, 217, 237, 249, 263, 275, 299, 315, 329, 341, 363, 375, 391, 403

selection preview, TE/5, 17, 29, 41, 53, 75, 89, 105, 119, 133, 155, 165, 181, 195, 207, 229, 241, 253, 267, 287, 303, 319, 333, 353, 367, 379, 395

sequence of events, 126, 164, 240, 242–245, 273, 275, 280, 342, 344; TE/129, 381, 388, 391

summarize, 34, 148, 200, 201, 249, 302, 304–305, 307, 310, 378, 394, 396–399; TE/7, 33, 56, 79, 81, 91, 110, 111, 231, 243, 257, 269, 293, 311, 335, 371, 383

text evidence, 4, 6–9, 74, 76–81, 99, 140, 200, 286, 288–295, 318, 378, 380–387

unit preview/theme, TE/xii, 70, 150, 224, 282, 348

References, 68, 87, 103, 203, 218, 220, 221, 279, 329, 343, 344, 345, 346, 375, 401

atlas, 203

dictionary, 15, 27, 62, 63, 87, 103, 117, 131, 160, 179, 190, 203, 205, 239, 262, 263, 264, 265, 274, 279, 285, 298, 301, 314, 340, 351, 374, 377; TE/227, 321, 325, 328, 335, 341, 381, 383, 385, 387, 397

encyclopedia, 203, 221, 264

experts, 27, 65, 146, 147, 148, 203, 205, 219, 220, 222, 239, 264, 280, 345, 346, 377, 405, 406, 407

glossary/glosses, 103, 265; TE/103, 117

primary sources, 302

software, 87, 103, 117, 147, 279, 345

synonym finder, 87, 103; TE/227

thesaurus, 87, 103, 203, 263, 279; TE/227

Text Sources

anthology, 221, 237, 341, 345

classic work, 53, 119, 207, 241, 308, 353, 379

contemporary work, 5, 17, 29, 41, 75, 89, 105, 133, 155, 165, 181, 195, 208, 210, 229, 253, 267, 319, 334, 335, 367, 395

electronic text, 68, 144, 148, 191, 203, 218, 220, 221, 222, 264, 277, 280, 343, 344, 345, 346, 401; TE/87

home connection, TE/147

informational text, 4, 16, 28, 68, 104, 132, 144, 148, 194, 218, 266, 394

Internet, 68, 144, 148, 191, 203, 218, 221, 222, 264, 277, 280, 343, 344, 345, 346, 401; TE/87, 393

magazine, 203, 205, 346, 401

manual, 67, 146, 147, 220, 221, 279, 344, 345, 391, 407

newspaper, 203, 205, 346, 401

novel, 318

play, 352

poetry, 161, 228, 237, 341

textbook, 68, 148, 218, 278, 280, 329

Vocabulary Development, 103

affixes, 24, 62, 100, 114, 142, 160, 176, 190, 193, 202, 298, 314, 402

analogies, 154, 156–157, 339, 341, 342; TE/196

antonyms, 27, 365

compound words, 12

connections
community, TE/27, 179
cultural, TE/193, 317, 331

connotative meaning, 236, 351, 364; TE/167

content area words, 3, 13, 15, 25, 27, 37, 39, 49, 51, 63, 73, 85, 87, 101, 103, 115, 117, 129, 131, 143, 153, 161, 163, 177, 179, 191, 193, 203, 205, 217, 227, 237, 239, 249, 251, 263, 265, 275, 285, 299, 301, 315, 317, 329, 331, 341, 351, 363, 365, 375, 377, 391, 393, 403; TE/3, 5, 11, 15, 17, 23, 41, 47, 61, 65, 67, 75, 83, 87, 99, 103, 105, 117, 127, 131, 133, 145, 155, 159, 163, 175, 189, 195, 201, 205, 207, 215, 219, 227, 229, 235, 241, 247, 251, 265, 267, 277, 285, 301, 303, 313, 319, 343, 345, 353, 365, 367, 377, 393, 401, 405

context clues, 3, 103, 153, 179, 216, 251, 265, 318; TE/254

contractions, 36, 100, 190, 248, 362; TE/31, 55

denotative meaning, 3, 15, 27, 39, 51, 62, 73, 84, 128, 131, 153, 160, 163, 176, 179, 190, 193, 205, 236, 249, 251, 265, 274, 284, 285, 301, 314, 328, 331, 340, 351, 364, 365, 374, 393, 403; TE/18, 20, 30, 32, 42, 43, 56, 57, 76, 90, 93, 106, 107, 108, 109, 110, 120, 121, 123, 124, 135, 137, 198, 230, 231, 232, 242, 265, 269, 355, 368, 380, 398

derivatives, 24, 62, 84, 100, 239, 240, 251, 263, 274, 328, 351, 374, 377, 390, 402; TE/21, 103, 135, 137, 163, 189, 209, 247, 265, 271, 286, 289, 321, 325, 328, 335, 341, 381, 383, 385, 387, 397

figurative language, 154, 156–157, 158, 191, 235, 237, 339, 341; TE/157

frequently misspelled words, 51, 128, 331, 374

homophones, 128, 331; TE/31, 51, 121, 369

italicized words, 234, 317, 344, 352, 361; TE/95, 230, 254, 255, 371

listening to selections, 39, 103, 193

multi-level options, TE/2, 14, 26, 38, 50, 72, 86, 102, 116, 130, 152, 162, 178, 192, 204, 226, 238, 250, 264, 284, 300, 316, 330, 350, 364, 376, 392

multiple-meaning words, 153; TE/156

personal dictionary, 12, 15, 24, 27, 39, 51, 62, 73, 84, 87, 100, 103, 114, 128, 131, 142, 160, 163, 176, 179, 193, 205, 227, 236, 251, 314, 328, 331, 340, 365, 377, 402

phonetic symbols, TE/317

reference aids, 15, 62, 63, 103, 117, 131, 160, 179, 190, 205, 239, 262, 274, 279, 298, 301, 314, 340, 375, 377

related words, 3, 15, 39, 40, 49, 73, 85, 101, 103, 113, 115, 131, 163, 177, 228, 262, 265, 340, 390, 393; TE/273, 351

repetition, 154, 161, 302

root words, 24, 62, 84, 100, 114, 160, 176, 190, 193, 216, 274, 328, 390, 402

synonym finder, 87, 103; TE/227

synonyms, 87

thesaurus, 87, 103, 203, 263, 279; TE/227

word list, 205

word origins, 24, 62, 84, 100, 239, 240, 251, 263, 274, 328, 351, 374, 377, 390, 402

word square, 301

Word Wheel, 131; TE/351

Word Identification, 317

  context, 3, 103, 153, 179, 216, 251, 265, 318; TE/254

  cultural connection, TE/331

  derivations, 24, 62, 84, 100, 239, 240, 251, 263, 274, 328, 351, 374, 377, 390, 402; TE/21, 103, 135, 137, 163, 189, 209, 247, 265, 271, 286, 289, 321, 325, 328, 335, 341, 381, 383, 385, 387, 397

  dictionary, 15, 27, 62, 63, 87, 103, 117, 131, 160, 179, 190, 203, 205, 239, 262, 263, 264, 265, 274, 279, 285, 298, 301, 314, 340, 351, 374, 377; TE/227, 321, 325, 328, 335, 341, 381, 383, 385, 387, 397

  glossary, 265; TE/103, 117, 205

  language structure, 3, 202, 251

  letter-sound correspondences, 48, 262

  meanings/glosses, 3, 15, 27, 39, 51, 62, 73, 84, 128, 131, 153, 160, 163, 176, 179, 190, 193, 205, 236, 249, 251, 265, 274, 284, 285, 301, 314, 328, 331, 340, 351, 364, 365, 374, 393, 403; TE/18, 20, 30, 32, 42, 43, 56, 57, 76, 90, 93, 106, 107, 108, 109, 110, 120, 121, 123, 124, 135, 137, 198, 230, 231, 232, 242, 265, 269, 355, 368, 380, 398

  prefixes, 114, 176, 190, 193, 402

  pronunciation, 48, 51, 117, 128, 154, 239, 262, 265, 338, 339, 377; TE/103, 205, 227, 341

  root words, 24, 62, 100, 114, 160, 176, 190, 193, 216

    Greek, 24, 240, 274

    Latin, 239, 328, 340, 390, 402

  suffixes, 24, 62, 100, 142, 160, 202, 298, 314

  word map/web, TE/362, 402

■ Writing

Connections

  authors

    challenges, 125, 200, 213, 259, 371

    perspective, 10, 81, 98, 140, 157, 158, 261, 272, 296, 373; TE/9, 389

    purpose, 9, 33, 35, 45, 59, 82, 97, 111, 125, 139, 173, 187, 213, 295, 311, 359, 371, 394, 401; TE/347, 363, 400, 409

    strategies used, 3, 11, 23, 33, 35, 61, 73, 81, 132, 141, 159, 173, 175, 227, 245, 259, 311, 387, 399; TE/185

  collaboration with other writers, 67, 68, 85, 116, 162, 177, 201, 263, 364, 403, 404–405, 406–407; TE/161, 203, 217, 310, 315, 329

  correspondence

    e-mail, 249, 403, 407

    mail, 249, 403, 407

Forms

  biography, 148, 299, 344–345

  composition, TE/281

  connections

    cultural, TE/279, 317

    home, TE/147, 327, 373

  description, 13, 63, 64, 191, 375

  dialogue, 49, 85, 249, 389, 404–405; TE/91, 355

  editorial, TE/297

  e-mail, 249, 403, 407

  fiction, 85, 329, 375, 378, 391

  form, TE/275

  historical fiction, 329

  informational text, 25, 115, 143, 408

  instructions, 129, 146–147

  interview form, 403

  journal, 4, 16, 25, 35, 47, 52, 69, 74, 113, 132, 149, 154, 159, 180, 189, 191, 201, 206, 215, 223, 240, 252, 281, 286, 332, 339, 347, 373, 378, 409; TE/191

  letter, 191, 249, 263, 363, 375, 403, 406–407; TE/311, 329

  magazine article, 203, 205

  manual, 146–147

  memoir, 191; TE/191

  mystery, 49

  narrative, 191, 342–343, 344–345; TE/373

  news report, 315, 346; TE/217, 327

  paragraph, 13, 25, 37, 63

  persuasive letter, 363, 406–407

  phrases, TE/296

  play, 404–405, 408

  poem, 161, 237, 341

  poster, 68, 148, 280, 408

  problem solution, 47, 101, 177, 391, 406–407; TE/325

  process, 275

  realistic fiction, 85, 375, 378

  report, 66–67, 203, 278–279, 315; TE/409

  research report, 66–67, 203, 220–221

  review, 217, 278–279, 339; TE/149, 223

  science fiction, 375

  speech, 313

  story, 101, 329, 391

  summary, 201, 217, 249, 261, 346, 403

Inquiry and Research

  concept map, 2, 14, 162, 178, 204, 342, 364, 376, 404; TE/63, 143, 241

  evaluation, 278–279, 344

  guest speakers, TE/39, 153

  learning log, 4, 16, 25, 35, 47, 52, 69, 74, 113, 132, 149, 154, 159, 180, 189, 191, 201, 206, 215, 223, 240, 252, 281, 286, 332, 339, 347, 373, 378, 409

  multiple resources, 203, 220, 279, 329, 344, 345, 346, 401, 407; TE/69

  on-line searches, 63, 144, 148, 191, 218

  organize ideas, 2, 14, 74, 115, 141, 144, 146, 162, 178, 192, 204, 218, 220, 263, 277, 280, 299, 315, 342, 344, 346, 363, 364, 376, 401, 404–405, 406; TE/275, 281, 311, 327, 329

  outline, 115, 220, 273, 276, 344, 406

  periodicals, 203, 205, 346

  presentations, 64–65, 144–145, 218–219, 276

  prior knowledge, 14, 129, 143, 275, 299, 316, 375, 404

  questions, 10, 11, 66, 115, 146, 218, 220, 250, 263, 280, 327, 329, 344, 345, 403; TE/301

  sources, citation of, 191, 203, 220, 221, 344

  summarize ideas, 65, 66, 148, 249, 276, 278, 280, 299, 346, 403, 406

  take notes, 11, 35, 127, 144, 162, 203, 217, 218, 220, 222, 276, 280, 285, 299, 327, 339, 342, 378, 404, 405, 406

  technology presentations, 67, 146, 147, 148, 161, 219, 222, 275, 276, 277, 280, 315, 346, 408

  timelines, 40, 63, 143, 218, 220, 240, 249, 280, 286, 344; TE/83, 357, 362

Purpose

  appropriate form, 12, 13, 23, 24, 25, 36, 37, 48, 49, 62, 63, 84, 85, 100, 101, 114, 115, 128, 129, 142, 143, 160, 161, 176, 177, 190, 191, 202, 203, 216, 217, 235, 236, 237, 248, 249, 262, 263, 274, 275, 298, 299, 314, 315, 328, 329, 339, 340, 341, 344–345, 362, 363, 365, 366, 374, 375, 390, 391, 402, 403

  appropriate literary devices, 23, 37, 49, 129, 161, 339, 342, 344–345, 346

  audience and purpose, 345

    appropriate style, 159, 297

    appropriate voice, 274

  establish purpose, 375

  home connection, TE/407

  ideas, 74, 162

  multi-level options, TE/112, 158, 296

  precise wording, 37, 49, 67, 73, 203, 216, 227, 263, 340, 365

  purposes, 407

    compare across selections, TE/295, 409

    describe, 13, 63, 64, 191, 342, 375

    develop, 37

    discover, 372

    entertain, 9, 82, 85, 97, 139, 187, 295, 311, 359, 375, 401

    express, 49, 97, 139, 161, 235, 237, 263, 278–279, 342–343, 375

    influence/persuade, 9, 82, 97, 139, 187, 295, 311, 315, 363, 401; TE/406, 407

    inform, 9, 13, 25, 28, 63, 82, 97, 111, 115, 129, 139, 143, 146–147, 187, 191, 249, 275, 295, 311, 315, 342–343, 346, 359, 394, 401, 408

    paraphrase, 164, 220, 249

    problem solve, 13, 37, 47, 85, 88, 99, 101, 127, 177, 203, 237, 315, 363, 406–407

    record, 38, 194, 196–199, 220, 277

    reflect on ideas, 65, 162, 203, 217

    summarize, 65, 148, 201, 249, 276, 278, 280, 299, 346, 403, 406

  reteach and reassess, TE/115

  transitions, 67, 113, 115, 275, 345, 375

Writing Process

  analyze writing

    criteria, 279

    others' writing, 61, 147, 221, 279, 345

    own writing, 64, 147, 217, 221, 263, 275, 279, 315, 329, 342, 345, 403

  develop drafts, 13, 25, 37, 49, 63, 64, 67, 85, 101, 115, 129, 143, 146–147, 161, 177, 191, 203, 217, 220–221, 237, 249, 263, 275, 278–279, 299, 315, 329, 341, 342, 344, 363, 375, 391, 403, 404, 406; TE/311, 327

  edit drafts, 67, 147, 221, 279, 315, 329, 345, 375, 391, 403, 407

  evaluate writing, 64, 147, 221, 237, 279, 315, 329, 345, 363, 403, 407

  multi-level options, TE/12, 24, 36, 48, 62, 66, 84, 100, 114, 128, 142, 146, 160,

Teacher Edition Index

Viewing and Representing

Analysis

Interpretation

Production

Assessment

Learning Styles

Activity Book Contents

Activity Book Contents

Student CD-ROM Contents

Unit 1: Mysteries

Chapter 1: The Loch Ness Monster

Build Vocabulary: Use Language Structure to Find Meaning
Capitalization: Titles
Text Structure: Informational Text
Reading Strategy: Making Inferences Using Text Evidence
Elements of Literature: Use Visuals
Word Study: Analyze Compound Words
Grammar Focus: Understand the Conjunction *but*

Chapter 2: Mystery of the Cliff Dwellers

Build Vocabulary: Learn Context Words by Grouping
Spelling: Irregular Plurals
Text Structure: Informational Text
Reading Strategy: Find the Main Idea and Supporting Details
Elements of Literature: Write Quotes
Word Study: Root Words and Suffixes
Grammar Focus: Use Prepositional Phrases

Chapter 3: Yawning

Build Vocabulary: Identify Antonyms
Spelling: *Your* and *You're*
Text Structure: Informational Text
Reading Strategy: Compare the Text to Your Own Experiences
Elements of Literature: Recognize Direct Address
Word Study: Write Using Contractions
Grammar Focus: Write Dependent Clauses

Chapter 4: The Sneak Thief

Build Vocabulary: Learn Words Related to Train Travel
Punctuation: Possessives
Text Structure: Mystery
Reading Strategy: Use Chronology to Locate and Recall Information
Elements of Literature: Recognize Problem and Resolution
Word Study: Apply Knowledge of Letter-Sound Correspondences
Grammar Focus: Identify Simple, Compound, and Complex Sentences

Chapter 5: The Legend of Sleepy Hollow

Build Vocabulary: Spell Frequently Misspelled Words
Punctuation: Apostrophes for Contractions
Text Structure: Legend
Reading Strategy: Identify Imagery
Elements of Literature: Analyze Setting and Tone
Word Study: Identify Root Words and the Suffix *-less*
Grammar Focus: Use Pronoun Referents

Unit 2: Survival

Chapter 1: How I Survived My Summer Vacation

Build Vocabulary: Use Precise Wording
Punctuation: Hyphens for Compound Adjectives
Text Structure: Realistic Fiction
Reading Strategy: Make Inferences Using Text Evidence and Experience
Elements of Literature: Analyze Plot
Word Study: Identify Words with Latin Roots
Grammar Focus: Use Progressive Tenses

Chapter 2: The Voyage of the *Frog*

Build Vocabulary: Use Reference Sources
Capitalization and Punctuation: Dialogue
Text Structure: Adventure Story
Reading Strategy: Recognize Tone and Mood
Elements of Literature: Recognize and Analyze Problem Resolution
Word Study: Understand the Suffix *-ly*
Grammar Focus: Use the Future Tense

Chapter 3: To Risk or Not to Risk

Build Vocabulary: Learn Vocabulary through Reading
Spelling: Plurals with *-es* and *-ies*
Text Structure: Informational Text
Reading Strategy: Distinguish Fact from Opinion
Elements of Literature: Identify Transition Words
Word Study: Identify the Prefixes *over-* and *under-*
Grammar Focus: Use Present Tense and Subject-Verb Agreement

Chapter 4: Island of the Blue Dolphins

Build Vocabulary: Locate Pronunciations of Unfamiliar Words
Spelling: /oo/ and /e/ Sounds
Text Structure: Fiction Based on a True Story
Reading Strategy: Paraphrase to Recall Information
Elements of Literature: Compare and Contrast Themes and Ideas
  across Texts
Word Study: Spell Frequently Misspelled Words
Grammar Focus: Identify the Past and the Past Perfect Tense

Chapter 5: The Next Great Dying

Build Vocabulary: Use a Word Wheel
Punctuation: Commas in Series and Numbers
Text Structure: Informational Text
Reading Strategy: Identify Cause and Effect
Elements of Literature: Analyze Deductive and Inductive Organization
  and Presentation
Word Study: Identify the Suffix *-ion*
Grammar Focus: Recognize Dependent Clauses

Unit 3: Journeys

Chapter 1: I Have No Address

Build Vocabulary: Identify Multiple Meaning Words
Spelling: Long /a/ Sound with *ai* or *ay*
Text Structure: Poem
Reading Strategy: Recognize Figurative Language
Elements of Literature: Recognize Style, Tone, and Mood
Word Study: Recognize the Suffix *-ity*
Grammar Focus: Use Apostrophes with Possessive Nouns

Chapter 2: The Voyage of the Lucky Dragon

Build Vocabulary: Learn Words Related to Emotions
Spelling: *-tion* and *-ly* Endings
Text Structure: Historical Fiction
Reading Strategy: Paraphrase to Recall Information
Elements of Literature: Recognize Mood
Word Study: Analyze the Prefix *un-*
Grammar Focus: Identify Subject and Object Pronouns

Chapter 3: The Time Bike

Build Vocabulary: Use Context to Understand New Words
Capitalization and Punctuation: Cities and States
Text Structure: Science Fiction
Reading Strategy: Predict
Elements of Literature: Recognize Foreshadowing
Word Study: Study the Prefix *bi-*
Grammar Focus: Write Using Contractions

Chapter 4: Why We Can't Get There From Here

Build Vocabulary: Apply Knowledge of Root Words
Capitalization: Stars and Planets
Text Structure: Informational Text
Reading Strategy: Use Preview Questions, Reread, and Record
Elements of Literature: Analyze Organization and Presentation of Ideas
Word Study: Identify the Suffix *-est*
Grammar Focus: Use Superlative Adjectives

Student CD-ROM Contents

Chapter 5: The California Gold Rush _and_ Dame Shirley and the Gold Rush

Build Vocabulary: Study Words Systematically
Spelling: Silent _u_ and _gh_
Text Structure: Nonfiction and Historical Fiction
Reading Strategy: Compare and Contrast
Elements of Literature: Analyze Character Traits and Motivation
Word Study: Learn Words from Context and Experience
Grammar Focus: Use Adverbs

Unit 4: Cycles

Chapter 1: Water Dance

Build Vocabulary: Learn Vivid Verbs
Spelling: /ou/ and Silent _e_ Sounds
Text Structure: Poem
Reading Strategy: Describe Mental Images
Elements of Literature: Use Figurative Language
Word Study: Distinguish Connotative Meanings
Grammar Focus: Use Comparative Adjectives

Chapter 2: Persephone and the Seasons

Build Vocabulary: Use a Dictionary to Find Definitions
Spelling: _i_ Before _e_ and Silent _b_
Text Structure: Myth
Reading Strategy: Use Chronology to Locate and Recall Information
Elements of Literature: Recognize Foreshadowing
Word Study: Recognize Contractions
Grammar Focus: Write Using Irregular Past Tense Verbs

Chapter 3: The Circuit

Build Vocabulary: Study Word Origins and Guess Meaning
Capitalization: Languages
Text Structure: Autobiographical Short Story
Reading Strategy: Compare Text to Your Own Knowledge and Experience
Elements of Literature: Identify Language Use to Show Characterization
Word Study: Apply Letter-Sound Correspondence
Grammar Focus: Identify Dependent Clauses

Chapter 4: The Elements of Life

Build Vocabulary: Learn Science Terms
Punctuation: Colons for Lists
Text Structure: Informational Text
Reading Strategy: Find the Main Idea and Supporting Details
Elements of Literature: Use a Diagram
Word Study: Study Word Origins and Roots
Grammar Focus: Recognize the Active and Passive Voices

Unit 5: Freedom

Chapter 1: Rosa Parks

Build Vocabulary: Use Note Cards to Remember Meaning
Capitalization: Organizations, Public Places, and Street Names
Text Structure: Biography
Reading Strategy: Make Inferences Using Text Evidence
Elements of Literature: Recognize Style
Word Study: Identify the Suffix -_ment_
Grammar Focus: Recognize Regular and Irregular Simple Past Tense Verbs

Chapter 2: The Gettysburg Address

Build Vocabulary: Use Word Squares to Remember Meaning
Punctuation: Apostrophes and Commas
Text Structure: Historical Narrative and Speech
Reading Strategy: Summarize and Paraphrase
Elements of Literature: Analyze the Delivery of a Speech

Word Study: Use the Suffix -_or_
Grammar Focus: Identify Phrases with Verb + Object + Infinitive

Chapter 3: So Far from the Bamboo Grove

Build Vocabulary: Use Text Features
Capitalization: Titles
Text Structure: Fiction Based on a True Story
Reading Strategy: Predict
Elements of Literature: Analyze Character Motivation
Word Study: Identify the Latin Root Word _Grat_
Grammar Focus: Use the Conjunction _so that_ to Connect Ideas

Chapter 4: Alone _and_ Samantha's Story

Build Vocabulary: Spell Frequently Misspelled Words
Spelling: Silent _w_ Spelling and _ch_ for the /k/ Sound
Text Structure: Poem and Autobiography
Reading Strategy: Compare and Contrast Variant Texts
Elements of Literature: Recognize Figurative Language
Word Study: Learn Related Words
Grammar Focus: Use Superlative Adjectives

Unit 6: Visions

Chapter 1: Mr. Scrooge Finds Christmas

Build Vocabulary: Distinguish Connotative Meanings
Capitalization: Holidays
Text Structure: Play
Reading Strategy: Use Chronology to Locate and Recall Information
Elements of Literature: Recognize Dialogue and Stage Directions
Word Study: Analyze Contractions
Grammar Focus: Use the Present Perfect Tense

Chapter 2: The House on Mango Street

Build Vocabulary: Identify Antonyms
Punctuation: Italics for Emphasis
Text Structure: Fiction
Reading Strategy: Paraphrase to Recall Information
Elements of Literature: Recognize First-Person Narratives
Word Study: Learn English Words from Other Languages
Grammar Focus: Spell Frequently Misspelled Words

Chapter 3: The Pearl

Build Vocabulary: Locate Derivations
Spelling: _Oy_ Sound Spelling, _ph_ and _gh_ for the /f/ Sound, Silent _k_
Text Structure: Realistic Fiction
Reading Strategy: Make Inferences Using Text Evidence
Elements of Literature: Analyze Plot and Problem Resolution
Word Study: Learn Words from Latin
Grammar Focus: Study Conjunctions

Chapter 4: What Will Our Towns Look Like?

Build Vocabulary: Put Words into Groups
Spelling: _Y_ for Long /i/ Sound
Text Structure: Informational Text
Reading Strategy: Summarize Text to Recall Ideas
Elements of Literature: Identify Author's Purpose
Word Study: Study the Latin Prefix _co-_
Grammar Focus: Use _will_ to Predict the Future

English-Spanish Cognates

Unit 1: Mysteries

Unit 1, Chapter 1
The Loch Ness Monster, *page 5*

animal	animal
attack	atacar
computer	computadora
creature	criatura
description	descripción
dinosaur	dinosaurio
discover	descubrir
enormous	enorme
explore	explorar
family	familia
famous	famoso
fortune	fortuna
group	grupo
image	imagen
immediately	inmediatamente
material	material
meter	metros
million	millón
modern	moderno
monster	monstruo
mysterious	misterioso
object	objeto
operation	operación
photograph	fotógrafo
prehistoric	prehistórico
produce	producir
scientist	cientista
seconds	segundos
sonar	sonar
special	especial
tourist	turista

Unit 1, Chapter 2
Mystery of the Cliff Dwellers, *page 17*

abandon	abandonar
ancient	anciano
archeologist	arqueólogo
ceremony	ceremonia
climate	clima
conserve	conservar
cultivate	cultivar
descendant	descendiente
disappear	desaparecer
enemies	enemigos
group	grupo
Indians	indios
mystery	misterio
observe	observar
palace	palacio
physical	físico
probably	probablemente
protection	protección
region	región
religious	religioso
ruins	ruinas
symbolize	simbolizar
visit	visitar

Unit 1, Chapter 3
Yawning, *page 29*

air	aire
alert	alerta
article	artículo
athletes	atletas
attention	atención
concert	concierto
diary	diario
difficult	difícil
example	ejemplo
extra	extra
group	grupo
habit	hábito
idea	idea
machine	máquina
muscle	músculo
music	música
nervous	nervioso
oxygen	oxígeno
paralyze	paralizar
position	posición
possible	posible
problem	problema
scientist	cientista
seconds	segundos
simple	simple
video	vídeo
violinist	violinista

Unit 1, Chapter 4
The Sneak Thief, *page 41*

attention	atención
conclusion	conclusión
contents	contenido
continue	continuar
definitely	definitivamente
exactly	exactamente
inspector	inspector
minutes	minutos
taxi	taxi
terminal	terminal
visit	visitar

Unit 1, Chapter 5
The Legend of Sleepy Hollow, *page 53*

anaconda	anaconda
appetite	apetito
chimney	chiminea
commander	comandante
completely	completamente
convince	convencer
direction	dirección
distant	distante
enormous	enorme
exclaim	exclamar
expert	experto
fable	fábula
families	familias
figure	figura
hours	horas
mysterious	misterioso
parts	partes
Revolutionary	revolucionario
salary	salario
terrible	terrible
terror	terror
timid	tímido
valley	valle

Unit 2: Survival

Unit 2, Chapter 1
How I Survived My Summer Vacation, *page 75*

absolutely	absolutamente
American	americano
calm	calma
camp	campamento
computer	computadora
different	diferente
direction	dirección
diversion	diversión
editor	editor
family	familia
herb	hierba
idea	idea
idiot	idiota
inspiration	inspiración
interrupt	interrumpir
letter	letra
line	linea
minutes	minutos
muscle	músculo
nerves	nervios
novel	novela
paper	papel
plate	plato
problem	problema
promise	prometer
respond	responder
rich	rico
routine	rutina
seriously	seriamente
silence	silencio
strange	extraño
tea	té

Unit 2, Chapter 2
The Voyage of the *Frog*, *page 89*

American	americano
apart	aparte
captain	capitán
coast	costa
current	corriente
different	diferente
direction	dirección
distance	distancia
dolphin	delfín
explain	explicar
extra	extra
gallons	galones
interrupt	interrumpir
introduce	introducir
memories	memorias
miles	millas
moment	momento
ocean	océano
pass	pasar
pause	pausa
plastic	plástico
radio	radio
silence	silencio

Unit 2, Chapter 3
To Risk or Not to Risk, *page 105*

accident	accidente
active	activo
actual	actual
artificial	artificial
benefits	beneficios
continue	continuar
control	control
correctly	correctamente
decide	decidir
decisions	decisiones
estimate	estimar
familiarity	familiaridad
final	final
important	importante
interesting	interesante

Unit 2, Chapter 4
Island of the Blue Dolphins, *page 119*

animals	animales
center	centro
comfortable	confortable
curved	curvado
difficulty	dificultad
direction	dirección
equal	igual
except	excepto
legend	leyenda
move	mover
protect	proteger
utensils	utensilios

Unit 2, Chapter 5
The Next Great Dying, *page 133*

animal	animal
catastrophe	catástrofe
comet	cometa
complete	completo
creatures	criaturas
destruction	destrucción
different	diferente
dinosaur	dinosaurio
disaster	desastre
dozen	dozena
eliminate	eliminar
estimate	estimar
event	evento
exist	existir
extinct	extinto
extinction	extinción
form	forma
history	historia
humans	humanos
identify	identificar
individual	individual
insect	insecto
medicines	medicinas
million	millón
museum	museo
native	nativo
natural	natural
organism	organismos
period	periódo
planet	planeta
plant	planta
present	presentar
probably	probablemente
progress	progresar
represent	representar
science	ciencia
scientists	cientistas
skeleton	esqueleto
space	espacio
species	especies
theories	teorías

(Unit 1, Chapter 1 continued)

millions	millones
modern	moderno
modified	modificado
natural	natural
opinion	opinión
pass	pasar
psychologist	psícólogo
psychology	psicología
reactions	reacciones
respond	responder
risks	riesgos
scientists	cientistas
tendency	tendencia

English-Spanish Cognates

Unit 3: Journeys

Unit 3, Chapter 1
I Have No Address, *page 155*

east	este
globe	globo
humanity	humanidad
lines	líneas
rose	rosa
tranquil	tranquilo
tranquility	tranquilidad
united	unido
universe	universo
west	oeste

Unit 3, Chapter 2
The Voyage of the Lucky Dragon, *page 165*

abolish	abolir
announce	anunciar
anxiously	ansiosamente
assembly	asamblea
authority	autoridad
balance	balancear
camp	campamento
centre	centro
Chinese	chino
communists	comunistas
consult	consultar
control	control
cruelly	cruelmente
declare	declarar
depend	depender
direction	dirección
economic	económico
family	familia
government	gobierno
ideas	ideas
instant	instante
instructions	instrucciones
marine	marino
national	nacional
nervously	nerviosamente
official	oficial
operations	operaciones
pirate	pirata
population	población
progress	progreso
prologue	prólogo
promise	prometer
province	provincia
public	público
rest	resto
second	segundo
serious	serio
serve	servir
silence	silencio
state	estado
traitors	traidores
Vietnamese	vietnamita
visit	visitar
zone	zona

Unit 3, Chapter 3
The Time Bike, *page 181*

attic	ático
battery	batería
bicycle	bicicleta
character	carácter
circle	círculo
curtain	cortina
December	diciembre
decide	decidir
diamond	diamante
different	diferente
elephant	elefante
front	frente
idea	idea
interest	interés
invitation	invitación
majestic	majestuoso
marks	marcas
minus	menus
minute	minuto
model	modelo
moment	momento
move	mover
mysterious	misterioso
perfect	perfecto
phosphorescent	fosforescente
plastic	plástico
ruby	rubí
surprise	sorpresa
triangular	triangular

Unit 3, Chapter 4
Why We Can't Get There from Here, *page 195*

accelerate	acelerar
assume	asumir
astronauts	astronautas
basketball	básquetbol
calculation	calculación
compared	comparado
connect	conectar
correctly	correctamente
cosmos	cosmos
distance	distancia
energy	energía
escape	escapar
fiction	ficción
galaxy	galaxia
million	millón
planets	planetas
problem	problema
reality	realidad
scientific	científico
second	segundo
solar	solar
space	espacio
structure	estructura
universe	universo

Unit 3, Chapter 5
The California Gold Rush, *page 208*

history	historia
important	importante
miner	minero
plan	planear

Dame Shirley and the Gold Rush, *page 210*

adventure	aventura
cabin	cabina
coffee	café
comedy	comedia
continue	continuar
doctor	doctor
historical	histórico
horror	horror
miner	minero
mines	minas
mule	mulo
nomad	nómada
north	norte
novel	novela
opportunities	oportunidades
population	población
practice	practicar
rancho	rancho
saluted	saludó
sensation	sensación
tomatoes	tomates

Unit 4: Cycles

Unit 4, Chapter 1
Water Dance, *page 229*

air	aire
circle	círculo
colors	colores
distant	distante
float	flotar
move	mover
pass	pasar
reflect	reflejar
silent	silencioso
valleys	valles

Unit 4, Chapter 2
Persephone and the Seasons, *page 241*

accept	aceptar
disappear	desaparecer
fine	fino
fruit	fruta
persuade	persuadir
part	parte
plants	plantas
reasonable	razonable
serious	serio

Unit 4, Chapter 3
The Circuit, *page 253*

accompany	acompañar
adventure	aventura
camp	campamento
car	carro
enter	entrar
front	frente
garage	garage
moment	momento
motor	motor
move	mover
music	música
nervous	nervioso
office	oficina
principal	principal
rose	rosa
seconds	segundos
silence	silencio

Unit 4, Chapter 4
The Elements of Life, *page 267*

activities	actividades
affect	afectar
air	aire
animals	animales
balance	balance
carbon	carbón
categories	categorías
combination	combinación
consist	consistir
delicate	delicado
elements	elementos
essential	esencial
material	material
nature	naturaleza
naturally	naturalmente
nuclear	nuclear
occur	ocurrir
organism	organismo
oxygen	oxígeno
phosphorus	fósforo
plants	plantas
resources	recursos
recycle	reciclar
reduce	reducir
scientist	cientista
simple	simple
theory	teoría

Unit 5: Freedom

Unit 5, Chapter 1
Rosa Parks, *page 287*

accept	aceptar
active	activo
association	associación
attack	atacar
avenue	avenida
cases	casos
community	comunidad
conviction	convicción
decision	decisión
discrimination	discriminación
disgrace	desgracia
document	documentar
enter	entrar
finally	finalmente
illegal	ilegal
important	importante
incident	incidente
insist	insistir
intelligent	inteligente
member	miembro
movement	movimiento
national	nacional
patient	paciente
permanent	permanente
police	policia
position	posición
proposal	propuesta
ritual	ritual
secretary	secretaria
section	sección
segregation	segregación
sincere	sincero
system	sistema
unjust	injusto
violence	violencia
volunteer	voluntario

Unit 5, Chapter 2
The Gettysburg Address,
page 303

attention	atención
battle	batalla
cause	causa
cemetery	cementerio
civil	civil
continent	continente
dedicate	dedicar
declaration	declaración
dedicated	dedicado
devotion	devoción
dignitaries	dignatarios
distance	distancia
election	elección
eventually	eventualmente
famous	famoso
final	final
honor	honor
important	importante
independence	independencia
liberty	libertad
music	música
nation	nación
national	nacional
November	noviembre
occasion	ocasión
perfect	perfecto
personal	personal
platform	plataforma
political	político
portion	porción
preserved	preservado
president	presidente
procession	procesión
proposition	proposición
silent	silencioso
soldiers	soldados
union	unión

Unit 5, Chapter 3
So Far from the Bamboo Grove,
page 319

album	álbum
animals	animales
Communists	comunistas
current	corriente
direction	dirección
expression	expresión
generous	generoso
final	final
gratitude	gratitud
Japanese	japonés
Korean	coreano
miles	millas
parallel	paralelo
passed	pasó
uniform	uniforme

Unit 5, Chapter 4
Alone, *page 334*

protect	proteger
veil	velo

Samantha's Story, *page 335*

abilities	abilidades
autobiography	autobiografía
center	centro
competition	competición
concept	concepto
critique	criticar
education	educación
elementary	elementaria
experiment	experimentar
horrible	horrible
illusion	ilusión
music	música
ocean	océano
part	parte
poem	poema
resources	recursos
refuge	refugio

Unit 6: Visions

Unit 6, Chapter 1
Mr. Scrooge Finds Christmas,
page 353

celebrate	celebrar
convenient	conveniente
escape	escapar
excuse	excusa
extravagant	extravagante
family	familia
habit	hábito
idiot	idiota
impulse	impulso
moment	momento
move	mover
position	posición
present	presente
salary	salario
silence	silencio

Unit 6, Chapter 2
The House on Mango Street,
page 367

garage	garage
lottery	lotería
mango	mango
move	mover
ordinary	ordinario

Unit 6, Chapter 3
The Pearl, page 379

accident	accidente
ancient	anciano
animals	animales
calm	calma
canoe	canoa
capture	capturar
cement	cemento
coordination	coordinación
curve	curva
decorate	decorar
doctor	doctor
emotion	emoción
exist	existir
illusion	ilusión
magic	mágica
melody	melodía
minute	minuto
muscle	músculo
oxygen	oxígeno
oyster	ostra
palm	palma

part	parte
pearl	perla
perfect	perfecto
realities	realidades
reflection	reflección
rock	roca
scorpion	escorpión
secret	secreto
triumphant	triunfante

Unit 6, Chapter 4
What Will Our Towns Look Like?,
page 395

actually	actualmente
cars	carros
computers	computadoras
electric	eléctrico
electricity	electricidad
energy	energía
families	familias
fantastic	fantástico
fruit	fruta
garden	jardín
horizon	horizonte
impossible	imposible
industrial	industrial
innovations	inovaciones
limited	limitado
natural	natural
oceans	océanos
office	oficina
operation	operación
preserve	preservar
product	producto
resources	recursos
transportation	transportación